THE JOSSEY-BASS READER ON SCHOOL REFORM

Introduction by
Lesley Iura

JOSSEY-BASS
A Wiley Company
San Francisco

Jossey-Bass books and products are available through most bookstores. To contact Jossey-Bass directly, call (888) 378-2537, fax to (800) 605-2665, or visit our website at www.josseybass.com.

Substantial discounts on bulk quantities of Jossey-Bass books are available to corporations, professional associations, and other organizations. For details and discount information, contact the special sales department at Jossey-Bass.

Printed in the United States of America.

Credits are on pp. 523–524.

Library of Congress Cataloging-in-Publication Data

The Jossey-Bass reader on school reform.
      p.   cm.—(The Jossey-Bass education series)
Includes bibliographical references.
   ISBN 0-7879-5524-8 (alk. paper)
   1. Educational change—United States—History—20th century.
  2. Education—Aims and objectives—United States—History—20th century. I. Jossey-Bass Inc. II. Series.
   LA216 .J67 2001
   370'.973-dc21

                          00-011528

FIRST EDITION

PB Printing 10 9 8 7 6 5 4 3 2 1

The Jossey-Bass
Education Series

CONTENTS

PART THREE
Reform as Response to Social Diversity and Student Needs

PART FOUR
Reform as Restructuring the Governance and
Organization of Schooling

PART FIVE
Reform Through Standards, Curriculum, Pedagogy, and Assessment

SOURCES

CHAPTER ONE
John Dewey. *The Educational Situation.* Chicago: University of Chicago Press, 1902.

CHAPTER TWO
David Tyack and Larry Cuban. *Tinkering Toward Utopia: A Century of Public School Reform.* Cambridge, Mass.: Harvard University Press, 1995.

CHAPTER THREE
Diane Ravitch. *The Troubled Crusade: American Education 1945–1980.* New York: Basic Books, 1983.

CHAPTER FIVE
Benjamin Fine. "Soviet Education Far Ahead of U.S. in Science Stress." *New York Times,* Nov. 11, 1957, pp. 1, 11.

CHAPTER NINE
National Center on Education and the Economy. *America's Choice: High Skills or Low Wages!* Washington, D.C.: NCEE, 1990.

CHAPTER THIRTEEN
National Commission on Teaching and America's Future. *What Matters Most: Teaching for America's Future.* Washington, D.C.: NCTAF, Sept. 1996.

CHAPTER FOURTEEN
Jonathan Kozol. *Savage Inequalities: Children in America's Schools.* New York: Random House, 1991.

CHAPTER FIFTEEN
Richard Rothstein. "Bilingual Education: The Controversy." *Phi Delta Kappan.* May 1998, Vol. 79.

CHAPTER SIXTEEN
Joy G. Dryfoos. *Full-Service Schools; A Revolution in Health and So-cial Services for Children, Youth, and Families.* San Francisco: Jossey-Bass, 1994.

CHAPTER SEVENTEEN
John E Chubb and Terry M. Moe. *Politics, Markets and America's Schools.* Washington, D.C.: The Brookings Institution, 1990.

CHAPTER EIGHTEEN
Eric A. Hanushek and others. *Making Schools Work: Improving Perfor-mance and Controlling Costs.* Washington, D.C.: The Brookings Institu-tion, 1994.

CHAPTER NINETEEN
Joe Nathan. *Charter Schools: Creating Hope and Opportunity for Amer-ican Education.* San Francisco: Jossey-Bass, 1996.

CHAPTER TWENTY
Lynn Olson. "Following the Plan." *Education Week,* Apr. 14, 1999, 19(31).

CHAPTER TWENTY-ONE
Philip C. Schlechty. *Inventing Better Schools.* San Francisco: Jossey-Bass, 1997.

CHAPTER TWENTY-TWO
Caroline Hendrie. "A Mixed Record for Reconstitution Flashes a Yellow Light for Districts." *Education Week,* July 7, 1998, 17(42).

CHAPTER TWENTY-THREE
Nancy L. Ames and Edward Miller. *Changing Middle Schools: How to Make Schools Work for Your Adolescents.* San Francisco: Jossey-Bass, 1994.

CHAPTER TWENTY-FOUR
David C. Berliner and Bruce J. Biddle. *The Manufactured Crisis: Myths, Fraud, and the Attack on America's Public Schools.* New York: Perseus Books, 1995.

CHAPTER TWENTY-FIVE
Robert Rothman. *Measuring Up: Standards, Assessment and School Reform.* San Francisco: Jossey-Bass, 1995.

CHAPTER TWENTY-SIX
David J. Hoff. "With 2000 Looming, Chances of Meeting National Goals Iffy." *Education Week,* Jan. 13, 1999, 18(18).

CHAPTER TWENTY-SEVEN
David K. Cohen. "A Revolution in One Classroom: The Case of Mrs. Oublier." *Educational Evaluation and Policy Analysis,* Fall 1990, 12(3).

CHAPTER TWENTY-EIGHT
Marc S. Tucker and Judy B. Codding. *Standards for Our Schools: How to Set Them, Measure Them, and Reach Them.* San Francisco: Jossey-Bass, 1988.

CHAPTER TWENTY-NINE
Robert M. Hauser. "What If We Ended Social Promotion?" *Education Week,* Apr. 7, 1999, 18(30).

CHAPTER THIRTY
John L. Goodlad. *Teachers for Our Nation's Schools.* San Francisco: Jossey-Bass, 1990.

CHAPTER THIRTY-ONE
Theodore R. Sizer. *Horace's Compromise: The Dilemma of the American High School.* Boston: Houghton Mifflin, 1984.

ABOUT THE AUTHORS

Nancy L. Ames is director of Family, School, and Community Programs at the Education Development Center.

David C. Berliner is dean of the College of Education at Arizona State University.

Bruce J. Biddle is professor of psychology at the University of Missouri at Columbia.

John E. Chubb is a nonresident fellow at the Brookings Institution, Washington, D.C.

Judy B. Codding, a former teacher and administrator, is vice president of the National Center on Education and the Economy.

David K. Cohen is currently John Dewey Collegiate Professor of Education and professor of public policy at the University of Michigan

Larry Cuban is professor of education at Stanford University.

John Dewey (1859–1952) was an American philosopher and educator. His noted works include *The School and Society* (1899) and *Democracy and Education* (1910).

Joy G. Dryfoos, an independent researcher and author, is also adjunct professor at the Columbia University School of Public Health.

Robert Evans is a clinical and organizational psychologist and director of the Human Relations Service in Wellesley, Massachusetts.

Benjamin Fine (1905–1975) was education editor of the *New York Times* from 1941 to 1958.

John I. Goodlad is professor emeritus of education at the University of Washington, where he is president of the Institute for Educational Inquiry and codirector of the Center for Educational Renewal.

Eric A. Hanushek is professor of economics and public policy and director of the W. Allen Wallis Institute of Political Economy at the University of Rochester.

Robert M. Hauser is Vilas Research Professor of Sociology at the Center for Demography at the University of Wisconsin–Madison.

Caroline Hendrie is an assistant managing editor for *Education Week*. She covers urban education and desegregation, as well as the states of New Jersey and New York.

David J. Hoff is an assistant editor for *Education Week*. He covers assessment, math, and science curriculum, and the states of Arkansas and Maine.

Jonathan Kozol is an American educator and author. His works include *Death at an Early Age* and *Savage Inequalities*.

Edward Miller has served as editor of the *Harvard Education Letter*.

Terry M. Moe is professor of political science at Stanford University and a senior fellow at the Hoover Institution.

Joe Nathan is senior fellow of the Hubert Humphrey Institute of Public Affairs at the University of Minnesota, where he directs the Center for School Change.

Lynn Olson is a senior editor for *Education Week*. Her beat includes national policy and the state of Oregon.

Diane Ravitch is a senior fellow at the Brookings Institution and Manhattan Institute and a research professor at New York University. She served as Assistant Secretary of Education in the Bush administration.

Robert Rothman, formerly a writer and editor at *Education Week,* is a senior associate at the National Alliance for Restructuring Education.

Richard Rothstein is a research associate of the Economic Policy Institute in Washington, D.C.

Phillip C. Schlechty is president and CEO of the Center for Leadership in Education Reform in Louisville, Kentucky.

Theodore R. Sizer, educator and author, has served as dean of the Harvard Graduate School of Education, headmaster at Phillips Academy, and chairman of the Coalition of Essential Schools.

Mark S. Tucker is president of the National Center on Education and the Economy.

David Tyack is Vida Jacks Professor of Education and Professor of History at Stanford University.

INTRODUCTION

How to educate our children is a subject of consuming interest to our nation. Who should run the schools? What should be taught—and how? And what skills will students need to learn for adulthood? The answers to these questions come in opinions that are innumerable and strongly held. From desegregation to school choice, panaceas for real and perceived problems in our schools have been offered up by policymakers, assorted blue-ribbon panels, think tanks, and political candidates eager to assume the mantle of "Education President." But the work of reform has also taken place quietly—through the good work of teachers, principals, and other reformers who are making changes at the grassroots level.

This anthology is intended to serve as an introduction to some of the big issues that have shaped and continue to shape policy, practice, and debate over public schooling. It was a difficult volume to put together, because—like reform itself—there were many directions it could have taken. We considered covering all of the major grassroots reform models, such as Success for All, the Coalition of Essential Schools, and the Edison Project, but we discovered that this was ground well trod by others. We contemplated presenting both pro and con positions on a long list of controversial issues, like standards and inclusion, but practical concerns of space and reprint rights kept these efforts in check. Ultimately we decided to focus on the larger school reform landscape—to provide a general history and context for current reforms.

The book is divided into five parts. Part One offers historical overviews of education reform from David Tyack, Larry Cuban, and Diane Ravitch. A brief excerpt from John Dewey serves as a wry reminder that reform bandwagons are nothing new. In Part Two, we present the public documents that have served as catalyst or foundation for reforms. Many key commission reports are here—from "A Nation at Risk" to "Goals 2000." This section also includes the most important court opinions and legislation—notably *Brown* v. *Board of Education* and *Lau* v. *Nichols* (bilingual education). Part Three provides a sampling of proposals for balancing social inequalities, such as using funding, instructional language, or access to social services as levers for improvement.

Part Four looks at governance and organizational structure as levers for reform. Included in this section are an excerpt from John E. Chubb and Terry M. Moe's *Politics, Markets, and America's Schools,* Eric A. Hanushek's perspective on performance incentives, and Phillip C. Schlechty's argument for the school district's role in reform. Finally, Part Five is concerned with matters closer to the classroom, such as teaching, testing, standards, and the problems of translating policy into practice.

From the industrial revolution to the information age our expectations of schools have changed dramatically. We want them to develop students' intellect, character, and citizenship. We want them to cultivate compassion and build community. We want them to help maintain our global economic prosperity. And we disagree vehemently about whether, why, and how this is to be accomplished. However, of one thing we can be certain: the debate will continue, reforms will come and go, and education will move slowly, inexorably toward a brighter future.

WELCOME to *The Jossey-Bass Reader on School Reform.* With the Jossey-Bass education readers we hope to provide a clear, concise overview of important topics in education and to give our audience a useful knowledge of the theory and practice of key educational issues. Each reader in this series is designed to be informative, comprehensive, and portable.

Your feedback is important. If you are familiar with articles, books, or reports that have a national sustained audience and that address the topic of this reader, please send us an e-mail at readers@jbp.com.

In the interest of readability, the editors have slightly adapted the following selections for this volume. For the complete text, please refer to the original source.

PART ONE

PERSPECTIVES ON REFORM

THE EDUCATIONAL SITUATION

John Dewey

The more things change, the more they stay the same. Anyone who has worked to reform schools becomes aware of the Sisyphean cycle Dewey talks about in this short passage. Written nearly one hundred years ago, it predicts the failure of the many attempts at school reform that followed in the twentieth century.

Dewey was arguably the largest single influence on American education in the twentieth century. While Dewey is deserving of an entire volume himself, this brief excerpt gives the reader a taste of his experience with and understanding of schools. His work, despite its age, is still applicable to school reform today.

○

CONSIDER THE WAVE by which a new study is introduced into the curriculum. Someone feels that the school system of his (or quite frequently nowadays her) town is falling behind the times. There are rumors of great progress in education making elsewhere. Something new and important has been introduced; education is being revolutionized by it; the school superintendent, or members of the board of education, become somewhat uneasy; the matter is taken up by individuals and clubs; pressure is brought to bear on the managers of the school system; letters are written to the newspapers; the editor himself is appealed to to use his great power to advance the cause of progress; editorials appear; finally the school board ordains that on and after a certain date the particular new branch—be it nature study, industrial drawing, cooking, manual training, or whatever—

shall be taught in the public schools. The victory is won, and everybody—unless it be some already overburdened and distracted teacher—congratulates everybody else that such advanced steps are taking.

The next year, or possibly the next month, there comes an outcry that children do not write or spell or figure as well as they used to; that they cannot do the necessary work in the upper grades, or in the high school, because of lack of ready command of the necessary tools of study. We are told that they are not prepared for business, because their spelling is so poor, their work in addition and multiplication so slow and inaccurate, their handwriting so fearfully and wonderfully made. Some zealous soul on the school board takes up *this* matter; the newspapers are again heard from; investigations are set on foot; and the edict goes forth that there must be more drill in the fundamentals of writing, spelling, and number.

PROGRESS OR REGRESS?

David Tyack, Larry Cuban

Tyack and Cuban provide a great historical review of American school reform efforts and ideology. A wise educator often looks at the change process as "one step forward, two steps back," a slow dance toward improved student outcomes. Although educators, policymakers, and parents fervently hope that we are making progress with reforms, the value of these reforms continues to be in the eye of the beholder.

○

"IS THE EDUCATIONAL UTOPIA IN SIGHT?" W. W. Carpenter, an educator in Missouri, the show-me state, asked that question in 1931 amid the joblessness and suffering caused by the Great Depression. He was not being sarcastic or rhetorical. His answer was "yes," for he believed Americans were "approaching with steady progress" the goal of giving every child an appropriate education. In pursuing this goal, he said, "we are carrying on the most important experiment in democracy the world has ever seen, the results of which may determine educational procedures for centuries to come."[1]

Carpenter was not an idiosyncratic optimist. He expressed two opinions common among Americans and nearly axiomatic among educational leaders: that progress was the rule in public education and that better schooling would guarantee a better society. Progress was an animating ideal that gave direction and coherence to reforms. It was also, educators believed, a plain fact documented by trends in educational practice: Americans were gaining not only more schooling but also a better education.[2]

To be sure, America had its share of school haters who believed that the best education was extramural. Also, from time to time some citizens have longed for a return to what they saw as a golden age in the past. But typically when people have proclaimed public education a "failure," as an author did in *Look* magazine in 1946, the chief criticism was that the schools did not match the modern template of progress. When *Life* magazine printed the questionnaire "How Good Is Your School?" in 1950, the items on the checklist of excellence were precisely those sought by up-to-date professional leaders whose program of progress seemed the public's.[3]

Until recently, citizens thought that public schools were good and getting better. Consider the results of public opinion surveys. In 1940 Gallup interviewers asked a large sample of adults their views about public education. Eighty-five percent agreed "that young people today are getting a better education in school than their parents got." At about the same time Swedes were asked a similar question; only 38 percent of fathers in Sweden thought their sons had been better educated than they had. In another Gallup poll in 1946, 87 percent of parents said that they were satisfied with the schools their children attended, up seven points from a similar survey in 1943.[4]

Teachers fared well in early public opinion surveys. In a poll in 1946, 60 percent won top ratings, 29 percent middling, and only 8 percent poor. Recognizing that teachers generally had low salaries and overcrowded classrooms in the mid-1950s, two-thirds of citizens polled said that they would be willing to pay more taxes if the extra money went to higher pay for teachers. In 1957 three-quarters of parents said that they would like to have a daughter become a teacher.[5]

When asked for criticisms of the schools, 40 percent of citizens in 1946 could think of nothing wrong. Nothing. This echoed the results of a poll in 1938 in which citizens were asked, "If you were running the school in this community, what changes would you make?" "None" was the answer of 24 percent, 29 percent did not answer, and from the rest emerged a scatter of minor complaints (only 1 percent called for stricter discipline).[6]

Opinion has changed. Now regress in public schools seems as axiomatic to many people as progress did during the previous hundred years. After 1969—the year when the Gallup organization began systematic yearly surveys of public opinion about public education—it became clear that the doctrine of steady educational progress no longer made sense to most people. As criticisms of education mushroomed, polls revealed lower rankings of the schools and of teachers year by year. On average, citizens rated schools as B– institutions in 1974 and C– institutions in 1981. In 1978, 41 percent of Americans declared that schools were worse than they used to be, and only 35 percent thought they were better; a *New York Times* study five years later found the two opinions evenly balanced at 36 percent.[7]

The most influential school reform report of the 1980s, *A Nation at Risk,* quotes, as if it is obviously true, Paul Copperman's assertion that "for the first time in the history of our country, the educational skills of one generation will not surpass, will not equal, will not even approach, those of their parents." A litany of dismal statistics in the report purports to show that regress, not progress, is the trend in public education.[8]

But the belief that better schools make a better society—the deeply ingrained utopian conviction about the importance of schooling—is alive and well.

Schools can easily shift from panacea to scapegoat. If the schools are supposed to solve social problems, and do not, then they present a ready target. In recent years, allegedly worse schools have been blamed for lack of economic competitiveness and other societal problems. Some observers have interpreted the supposed decline of education as a trumpet call to reform public schools. Others, believing that public education is mostly beyond repair, have argued that the way to regenerate schooling is to create a market system of education in which parents can choose their children's schools, either public or private, and pay the tuition through vouchers funded by taxes.[9]

Notions of progress or regress in education and society are, of course, highly debatable, though at any one time they may seem self-evidently true or false. In an epoch of history as tortured as the twentieth century, the very idea of human progress strikes many people as absurd. A sense of progress is always relative—now compared with then, one group compared with others. Since the expectations and experiences of people differ, so do their appraisals of whether things are getting better or worse. If one group advances, its progress may undermine the comparative advantage of another group, so that gain for one can seem loss for another. Thus success in keeping youths from impoverished families in high schools can erode the privilege of prosperous families who once regarded secondary education as their own middle-class preserve.[10]

Beliefs in progress or regress always convey a political message. Opinions about advance or decline in education reflect general confidence in American institutions. Faith in the nation and its institutions was far higher in the aftermath of success in World War II than in the skeptical era of the Vietnam War and Watergate. Expectations about education change, as do media representations of what is happening in schools. And the broader goals that education serves—the visions of possibility that animate the society—also shift in different periods, making it necessary to ask how people have judged progress, from what viewpoints, over what spans of time.[11]

When the issues are framed in this way, it becomes obvious that there is no simple answer to the question whether schooling or the society has gotten better or worse. The notions of progress or regress—the concepts of a golden age in the future or in the past—raise complex puzzles in American educational history. Why did progress once seem plausible, indeed indisputable, to educational leaders and to most of the public? How did policy elites translate the concept of progress into a systematic program of reform? Progress for whom—who was left out of this forward march? How did dispossessed groups create their own politics of progress or challenge the dominant faith in improvement? How and why did public opinion about the quality of schooling shift even as the general faith in its importance to society persisted? And finally, how has the debate over progress and regress framed political choices and policy talk about public education in recent years?

Progress as Ideology and "Fact"

We see two interwoven strands in the belief system that decreed that schools were improving and through them the nation. The first, well represented by Horace Mann, was the religious and political faith of the common school reformers of the mid-nineteenth century. They drew on and appealed to a pervasive Protestant-republican ideology that held that proper education could bring about a secular millennium, could make the United States quite literally God's country. In the Progressive era of the early twentieth century this evangelical enthusiasm became merged with a second faith that animated educational reformers: that a newly discovered "science" of education provided the precise tools needed to guide the course of social evolution.[12]

The rhetoric of Carpenter, the Missourian educator, echoed that of Mann. No educational task was menial if seen as part of the brightly lit path of progress. A school planner, absorbed in the details of improving ventilation and plumbing, found transcendent importance in his work. The schoolhouse was to America in the 1920s what the cathedral was to the Middle Ages, he believed: "something of the same spirit . . . is seeking expression in furnishing to the youth of our land nobler temples in which their hearts, minds, and bodies may better adjust themselves to the demands of a practical civic brotherhood." In America even blackboards "are essentially democratic" tools.[13]

"Dull and phlegmatic indeed" must be the person who is not "thrilled by the progress made in seventy-five years," wrote two prominent educators in 1925, "and by what that progress means to the age-long, world-wide struggle for the betterment of human living." The modern public school of Detroit, they believed, "has ceased to be a prison and is becoming a childish utopia." Schools that ministered "to the whole nature of the pupil, not simply to his intellect," were producing "a social revolution as complete and as far-reaching as the progress of democracy itself." Children were also learning academic subjects better, they said, despite complaints by some parents that "in the good old days of drill and discipline, the children really learned something."[14]

During the first half of the twentieth century, the chief American architects of reform and arbiters of educational "progress" constituted a policy elite we call the administrative progressives. These reformers were a group unified by similar training, interests, and values. They were the first generation of professional leaders educated in the new schools of education. These white men—few women and almost no people of color were admitted to the inner circle of movers and shakers—carved out lifelong careers in education as city superintendents, education professors, state or federal officers, leaders in professional organizations such as the National Education Association (NEA), and foundation officials. They shared a common faith in "educational science" and in lifting education "above politics" so that experts could make the crucial decisions. Occupying key positions and sharing definitions of problems and solutions, they shaped the agenda and implementation of school reform more powerfully from 1900 to 1950 than any other group has done before or since.[15]

With the confidence of Teddy Roosevelt creating the Panama Canal, these reformers developed a blueprint for educational progress. Though sometimes nostalgic about the values and experiences common in the rural and small town America of their youth, they still located an educational golden age in the future rather than in the past. The pathway to that golden future was punctuated with orderly bumps called "problems" to be smoothed out by experts. The evidence that they were making progress came in equally orderly statistics of success. Those who lived to mid-century had good reason to believe that they had achieved most of their goals, for graphs of institutional trends—the "facts" they enshrined at the center of their faith in educational science—showed steady upward movement.[16]

Their program for progress stemmed from a shared conviction that education was the prime means of directing the course of social evolution. They sought to expand access to education so that more young people could attend schools for longer periods of time. They thought that schooling should be both more differentiated and more standardized: differentiated in curriculum to fit the backgrounds and future destinies of students; and standardized with respect to buildings and equipment, professional qualifications of staff, administrative procedures, social and health services and regulations, and other educational practices. Year by year, decade by decade, they moved confidently forward. In their view, progress was a fact: the schools in 1950 were far superior to those in 1900.[17]

The administrative progressives worked for change at the local, state, and federal levels, collaborating with foundations that shared their blueprints for change. Confronting this "educational trust," the American Federation of Labor complained that education was becoming "Rockefellerized" (John D. Rockefeller's General Education Board had subsidized agents hired by the U.S. Bureau of Education at a dollar a year). The federal government and foundations conducted state and local surveys of schools that were highly prescriptive in character and issued monographs on reforms favored by the administrative progressives. Critics complained of groupthink and suppression of dissenting views.[18]

The new educational ideology of progress through science, efficient management, and professionalism gave the appearance of turning educational policy into a process of rational planning, surely not political bargaining. Take the long view, said an official of the NEA, whose state affiliates were the most powerful lobbyists for school legislation in the state capitols: "An efficient state school system cannot be created overnight, nor does it spring up as the result of incantations and the waving of a magic wand. It is the result always of persistence during a long period of steady effort." An ever present danger was that "the educational forces may be prevailed upon to accept weakening compromises with the opponents of good school conditions. . . . 'Be sure that you are right, then go ahead' is a good motto for a program of school legislation." Creating a sound structure of reformed schools demanded long-range planning based on research, "continuous and effective publicity," and "organized unity of purpose in the entire educational profession."[19]

The administrative progressives believed that school governance would be more efficient and expert if it were more buffered from lay control. There *was* something they wanted less of—the influence of school boards, whose members they sometimes accused of being corrupt or ignorant meddlers. In fact, one of the mandarins of the movement, Charles H. Judd of the University of Chicago, argued that local school boards should be abolished. Education should be controlled as much as possible by specially trained professionals certified by the state.[20]

At the beginning of the twentieth century, educational leaders collaborated with business and professional elites to transform the character of urban school politics. They wanted to eliminate ward school committees and to cut the size of central school boards. From 1890 to 1920 the average number of central board members in cities of more than 100,000 inhabitants dropped from twenty-one to seven, and most cities eliminated ward boards. But it was not only the size of the central boards that was a problem; the reformers also wanted to increase the number of prosperous and well-educated members and to adopt a model of policy making patterned on that of business corporations. The board, they believed, should delegate decisions to the superintendent and central staff, experts assumed to serve the interests of all the children. This form of governance increasingly became the expressed norm in city school systems, if not always the actuality.[21]

In the countryside, the consolidation of school districts decimated the number of lay school trustees. Local school districts declined from 127,531 in 1932 to 16,960 in 1973. Between 1930 and 1980 the number of one-room schools nose-dived from 130,000 to less than 1,000. As the number of small town superintendents and rural supervisors of teachers rose steadily, these administrators took over some of the functions formerly performed by lay trustees.[22]

The administrative progressives believed that the U.S. Bureau of Education should take the lead in informing state legislators about what a modern school should be (they lobbied Congress in the early 1920s to make the bureau a *department* of education with expanded powers). In 1919 the Bureau issued *A Manual of Educational Legislation,* addressed to state legislators who served on education committees. It laid out a whole program of state legislation designed to standardize schooling to match the program of "reorganization" (their version of systemic reform) favored by the administrative progressives, treating such topics as school consolidation, increased state financing, physical education, improved school construction, state certification for teachers, and standard textbooks and curriculum. A comparison of that plan with a summary of "state legal standards for the provision of public education" in 1978 shows that most of the recommendations of 1919 were put into practice in the following six decades.[23]

Prodded by professional organizations like the NEA, state legislatures increasingly standardized schools across the nation according to the model of a modern school proposed by the policy elite. To carry out their new regulatory roles, state departments of education increased enormously during the twentieth century. In 1890 there was, on average, one staff member in

state departments of education for every 100,000 pupils; in 1974 there was one for about every 2,000. Regulations ballooned: in California the state education code took about two hundred pages in 1900, in 1985 more than twenty-six hundred.[24]

Educators lobbied state governments to require local schools to meet minimum requirements in order to receive state aid. These included the quality and safety of buildings, the qualifications of teachers, the length of the school term, congruence with the state course of study, and even the size of flags and pictures on the walls. University professors developed "score cards"—appealing to a sense of competition—to evaluate schools. These featured precise specifications about playground space and apparatus, pupils' desks, globes and musical equipment, hygiene and sanitation, and even "community spirit." Thirty-four state departments of education managed to "standardize" more than 40,000 schools by 1925 in accord with legislation, regulations of the state board, or rulings of the state superintendents. Private accreditation agencies also insisted on greater institutional uniformity, especially at the secondary level, all in the name of progress.[25]

In elaborate surveys of urban schools, the administrative progressives placed their template of a modern school system on city after city to see how well the existing schools measured up to their ideal of educational "progress." In addition to upgrading the quality of the school plant and the qualifications of teachers, they wanted the standard city system to have a large staff of certified specialists and administrators; elaborate fiscal accounting; uniform student record cards and guidance procedures; standardized intelligence and achievement tests; a diversified curriculum that included vocational training, physical education, and a host of elective courses at the secondary level; and a policy of grouping children by ability.[26]

Basic to their conception of educational science was a conviction that children had different abilities, interests, and destinies in life. Hence schools should treat them differently; this was their concept of equality of educational opportunity. They gave different labels to students who did not fit their definition of "normal," and they created tracks and niches for them. Progress to these experts meant a place for every child and every child in his or her place.[27]

Prodded by a variety of lay reformers to expand social and health services, educational administrators added programs of physical education and recreation and gave instruction in health. Hundreds of cities added vacation schools (later called summer schools), school lunch programs, and medical and dental care, especially for the children of working-class immigrant families. States and urban districts began creating special schools or classes for physically and mentally handicapped students—the number of separate state or district schools for such children increased from 180 in 1900 to 551 in 1930. Cities also created new categories of classes for "misfits"—children who were too "backward" to proceed at the normal rate in graded classrooms or too unruly for the teachers to handle.[28]

To achieve reforms such as these, the administrative progressives believed, schools should become larger. They did. The number of students per school has jumped more than sixfold in the last half-century. The one-room school became a vanishing breed. Early in the twentieth century the modal high school had perhaps 100 students, but by 1986 over half enrolled more than 1,000 students. The total number of high schools remained fairly constant at about 24,000 between 1930 and 1980, but the number of high school graduates jumped in these years from 592,000 to 2,748,000.[29]

A major proof of progress, educational leaders believed, was increased access to schooling for young people for ever longer periods of time. In 1900 only half the population five to nineteen years old were enrolled in school; by 1950, this proportion had increased to nearly eight in ten (and by 1990 to more than nine in ten). The average number of days these students spent in school grew steadily from 99 in 1900 to 158 in 1950, increasingly only marginally from then on. Another sign of progress was a tripling of per-pupil expenditures (in constant dollars) from 1920 to 1950; in the following three decades the average sum per student tripled again. Yet another indication of progress was the steady rise in rates of literacy, from 89 percent in 1900 to 97 percent in 1950.[30]

Supremely confident, the administrative progressives all along proclaimed their reforms as being in the national interest and in the interest of the schoolchildren—hence as obvious progress. This progress, they believed, required ever higher costs per pupil. Many school districts and professional associations added publicity departments to persuade citizens that the reforms were worth the money.[31]

In the firm belief that they were the trustees of the public interest, superintendents and other policy elites of the first half of the century tended to dismiss their opponents as ignorant or self-interested. They portrayed the decentralized urban ward boards of education as corrupt and accused them of meddling in professional matters. They regarded the rural foes of school consolidation as backward yokels who did not know what was good for their children. The big school was better because it permitted more differentiation of curriculum, and school boards and parents who did not recognize this fact were behind the times. Teachers who opposed guidance by expert administrators were unprofessional trouble-makers. Such foot-draggers might slow reforms, but the trends were going in the right direction. History was progressive.[32]

Progress for Whom?

Although most groups made some advances in the quality of their schooling—even those who were most subordinated, southern rural blacks—the apparent march of progress to mid-century left many people behind. A probe behind aggregated national statistics and the upbeat rhetoric of the administrative progressives reveals major disparities in educational opportunities. These inequalities stemmed from differences in place of residence, family occupation and income, race, and gender, and from physical and mental handicaps. At mid-century American public education was not a seamless system of roughly similar common schools but instead a diverse and unequal set of institutions that reflected deeply embedded economic and social inequalities. Americans from all walks of life may have shared a common faith in individual and societal progress through education, but they hardly participated equally in its benefits.[33]

The people who suffered most from inequalities—the poor blacks, working-class immigrants, the disabled, females—had little influence over educational policy. A system of governance and finance rooted in local school boards and state legislatures and professionally guided by the administrative progressives placed most power in the hands of prosperous, white, male leaders born in the United States who tended to assume the correctness of their own culture and policies. In the South, school systems were part of a caste system that legally assigned blacks to a separate and distinctly unequal education; relatively few white educators challenged these inequities. Most educational policymakers did not notice, much less seek to correct, gender inequalities. Although educators did try to create special, usually segregated, niches in the system for children with special needs, hundreds of thousands of physically handicapped and other impaired children were excluded from school as "uneducable." Because New Deal reformers regarded public schools as unresponsive to poor youth, they chose to create their own programs, such as the National Youth Administration, to assist the impoverished. A number of educational leaders were concerned about the highly unequal funding of rural schools and tried to give them more state aid, but such efforts fell far short of their goal of equalizing school finance. Many people remained outside the magic circle of the politics of progress, excluded, segregated, or given an inferior education despite the rhetoric of democracy and equality of educational opportunity.[34]

In 1940 where children lived largely determined the resources available for their schooling. The biggest fiscal dividing line was between urban and rural schools, and this was in turn magnified by gross regional differences in school funding. The young people who needed schooling the most generally received the least. At that time the poorest rural families tended to have the most children. Typically, the communities in which they lived had meager resources to devote to building schools and paying teachers. In 1930 families in the southeastern region of the United States had to nurture and educate one-quarter of the children of the nation on one-tenth of the income. Farmers raised 31 percent of the country's children but received only 9 percent of the national income. By contrast, the urban Northeast commanded 43 percent of the nation's income but had only 30 percent of the children, while the figures for the West were 9 and 5 percent, respectively. The median years of schooling for urban whites aged twenty-five years and over in 1940 were 9.6 but only 8.0 for those in farming communities; among blacks the comparable figures were 6.8 (urban) and 4.1 (rural).[35]

In much of America, rural schools were well supported and effective, but in impoverished regions—much of the South, the Dust Bowl, Appalachia, and the cut-over forest lands of the upper Midwest—families had to struggle hard to provide even the most rudimentary education for their children. Cities spent twice as much per pupil on teacher salaries and school buildings as did rural districts. In 1940 30 percent of city dwellers had completed high school compared with only 12 percent of farmers.[36]

In 1940 about two out of three blacks lived in rural areas, overwhelmingly in the South. Racial oppression compounded inequalities created by the poverty of the region. Disenfranchised, blacks had to make do with the starvation diet of school funds that white officials allocated to the segregated "colored" schools. Blacks constituted over a quarter of the public school students but received only 12 percent of revenues. Half of the black teachers had gone no further than high school, compared with 7 percent of white teachers. They often lacked the most basic aids to learning—textbooks, slates and chalk, or desks—and frequently had very large classes when the children were not needed for farm labor. A visitor to East Texas described a typical black school:

> The building was a crude box shack built by the Negroes out of old scraps and scrap lumber. Windows and doors were badly broken. The

floor was in such condition that one had to walk carefully to keep from going through cracks and weak boards. Daylight was easily visible through walls, floors, and roof. The building was used for both church and school. Its only equipment consisted of a few rough hewn seats, an old stove brought from a junk pile, a crude homemade pulpit, a very small table, and a large water barrel. . . . Fifty-two children were enrolled. . . . No supplies, except a broom, were furnished the district during the year.[37]

Among whites who lived in cities—generally considered to be the most favored group educationally—class background strongly shaped educational opportunity. In northeastern cities, only 56 percent of youth coming from low-income families entered high school in 1935–36, compared with almost nine in ten who came from prosperous homes. In Maryland in 1938 students' chances of going beyond eighth grade neatly matched the prestige of their fathers' occupations.[38]

Once inside the high school, despite an official ideology that public education should be class-blind, working-class and upper-strata students typically had quite different experiences. In the 1940s Elmtown High School in Illinois, even the hooks for coats were segregated by social class, not by official school policy but by the mores of the students. Within the classroom pupils received an unequal education in college and general tracks. Grades and vocational guidance tended to reflect family status. Forty percent of Americans polled by Gallup in 1940—most of this 40 percent being from low-income groups—agreed with the statement that "teachers favor the children of parents who have the most money or the best position in the community."[39]

Inequality of educational opportunity based on gender was less obvious to most people in 1940 than racial or class disparities, in part because girls and boys had roughly equal access to instruction and performed at roughly similar levels. To the degree that educators paid attention to sex differences among pupils at all, they tended to worry about boys because they seemed to have more trouble learning to read, outnumbered girls in remedial classes, created more discipline problems, and dropped out of high school in somewhat greater numbers. One response was to try to make the schools more attractive to boys by creating sex-segregated vocational courses and tracks, by adopting textbooks attuned to the interests of boys, and by stressing competitive, male-only athletic teams.[40]

At mid-century most people regarded such differentiation by gender and other forms of sex-stereotyped activities as "natural," not as a form of institutional sexism, as reformers twenty years later would claim. Two kinds of gender discrimination did attract some attention, however: the common practice of firing women—but not men—when they married; and the predominance of men in the higher administrative ranks in a profession in which females outnumbered males as teachers by about five to one. The shortage of teachers during World War II undermined the policy of firing married women teachers, but the practice of hiring men for administrative jobs continued unabated in the postwar years.[41]

Programs for handicapped children and those with special needs were pretty much a patchwork in the first half of the twentieth century. In 1938 they served less than 1 percent of all pupils, up substantially from a decade earlier but far short of the 10 percent of children covered by federally funded programs for children with special needs in the 1970s. State legislatures and large urban districts sometimes provided separate schools for pupils who were blind, deaf, or physically or mentally handicapped, but millions of impaired children never saw the inside of a public school. Compulsory attendance laws frequently exempted disabled children, for whom an appropriate education was often regarded more as a charity than as a right. Much of the time the initiative to provide for sick and "crippled" children came not from within the educational system but from women's groups and from parents of affected children.[42]

The largest proportion of "special" students in city schools were placed in upgraded classes for "backward" children and "disciplinary" classes for unruly pupils (almost all students in both of these were boys). Indeed, much of special education was deliberately designed to meet the needs of the organization quite as much as the interests of the "special" children. Such differentiated classes buffered students and teachers in the graded-school mainstream from "misfits," children who did not advance at the expected rate or who caused discipline problems. In such cul-de-sac classes they were kept from receiving a standard education, not excluded from school but segregated.[43]

Progress for whom?—the answers to that question suggest the unevenness of the "progress" achieved by top-down planning by the administrative progressives, however impressive were aggregate trends such as the increasing rate of retention of students or the growing expenditures per student. At mid-century the subordinated or underserved families of the nation probably considered the utopia of equal education to be not just around the corner but at best on a far-distant horizon. Yet soon some groups barred from equal opportunities joined their activist allies to create a new politics of schooling. They challenged society to distribute educational opportunities more fairly and to realize what Gunnar Myrdal called "the American Creed": a commitment to "liberty, equality, justice, and fair opportunity for everybody." Could this rhetoric of hope, the doctrine of progress, really apply to everyone?[44]

A New Politics of Progress

In recent decades social protest groups have called attention to discrimination and deprivation and declared injustice mutable, not just the way things are. African Americans, feminists, Hispanics, Native Americans, and parents of handicapped children all entered the arena of educational politics and broke open the "closed system" of governance. In the process they created new goals and strategies of school reform. These groups joined forces in large-scale social protest movements and moved issues of equity to the forefront of the newspapers, the television news, and the agendas of the courts, legislatures, and school boards. People who had been ignored or subordinated demanded to participate in "progress." They developed a new style of activist reform and could take much of the credit for desegregation in the South, new attention to the children of immigrants, attacks on discriminatory gender practices, and better education of children with special needs.[45]

A major catalyst for this campaign for "simple justice" was the Supreme Court's decision in *Brown v. Board of Education* in 1954. Its immediate target was the racial segregation of students, but its language of justification and its force as a legal and moral precedent encouraged not only blacks but other groups as well to demand educational equity as a right. The Justices maintained that "it is doubtful that any child may reasonably be expected to succeed in life if he is denied the opportunity of an education." That gave protest groups a broad mandate. Activists working for women's rights, for the handicapped, for immigrant students, and for the poor were able to draw on this doctrine that individual and societal progress demanded progress in schooling.[46]

The administrative progressives had envisioned progress at the result of a gradual and expertly designed institutional evolution. There was little legitimate place for social conflict in this model of reform planned and executed largely from the top down. Protest and advocacy groups pushing for equity for outsiders, by contrast, often regarded social conflict as essential to educational advance. When they found, as they often did, that local school boards were unresponsive or unsympathetic to their demands, they organized demonstrations and boycotts to publicize and advance their groups' demands. They also pushed class action suits in the courts and lobbied for legislation and administrative regulations at the state and national levels.[47]

At first, many of the groups seeking greater educational opportunity worked to achieve greater access to the mainstream, to share the same resources, to enjoy the equality of opportunity envisaged by the American creed, and to participate in the forms of "progress" already enjoyed by more favored parts of the society. Blacks pressed to desegregate public schools so that they could share the same educational advantages as whites. In part this campaign reflected a desire to erase the stigma of racial oppression and to realize the universalistic goal of equality so eloquently stated by Martin Luther King, Jr., in his famous speech in 1963, "I Have a Dream." Advocates for handicapped pupils argued that an appropriate education for the disabled was a *right*, not a gift. They sought to mainstream those with special needs in regular classrooms in the "least restrictive environment" that was possible for them. No longer should children with special needs be ignored or labeled and warehoused. Feminists sought to abolish all gender distinctions in school policies and practices so that both girls and boys would have the same opportunities and not be restricted by segregation in vocational classes or physical education, by sex-stereotyping by counselors and teachers, and by unequal treatment in competitive athletics. Through Title I of the Elementary and Secondary Education Act of 1965 reformers targeted funds to students from low-income families to prevent poverty from restricting school opportunities and academic achievement. President Lyndon Johnson declared that proper schooling could prevent poverty, not merely ameliorate the lives of the poor, echoing a claim made by Horace Mann more than a century before. A faith in the possibility of progress fueled both protest and federal policymaking in the 1960s.[48]

This attention to equality in the two decades following the *Brown* decision produced progress that looked rapid and impressive if compared with the glacial pace of equalization in previous decades. Consider the experience of blacks, for example. By the end of the 1960s, segregation of the races had been challenged as legal policy across the South, and mostly because of reassignment of students there, the proportion of African Americans in nearly *all-black* schools decreased from two-thirds to one-third from 1968 to 1980 (though most African Americans were still in *majority-black* schools because of residential segregation). In 1967 almost one-third of black high school students across the country dropped out before graduation, but by 1989 this rate had been cut in half and approximated the proportion of whites who quit school. In 1976, after a decade in which the proportion of blacks attending college had more than doubled, almost one-third of black high school graduates enrolled in some form of higher education, about the same rate as for whites. During the 1980s the gap between whites and blacks on achievement tests in the National Assessment of Educational Progress declined significantly.[49]

Equalization of opportunity proceeded slowly, however, if compared not with the pace of change prior to *Brown* but with expectations aroused by campaigns for social justice in education. Although Johnson's War on Poverty relied heavily on schools as an agent of reform, actual redistribution of educational resources lagged far behind need, for "savage inequalities" persisted, particularly in urban and rural schools that enrolled the poor and people of color. Leaders of protest groups began to question how much progress in fact had occurred. Did the poor and people of color really have access to good schools? A spate of depressing books with titles like *Our Children Are Dying* and *Death at an Early Age* said no.[50]

Leaders of protest groups also began to redefine what they meant by progress. Was open access to the mainstream really the solution? Black activists argued that the schools that their children attended were permeated with institutional racism. Hispanics said that immigrant children encountered cultural imperialism that denied their language and heritage. Feminists complained that girls had to struggle against a male-dominated and sexist institution. Perhaps some form of separatism and a pluralistic definition of progress was needed to replace the older notion of equality as sameness. Many blacks, dismayed by continuing resistance to desegregation and seeing that demographic changes in cities were making "minorities" into majorities as white families migrated to the suburbs, began to think that control of schools in their own communities offered a more potent lever of advancement than desegregation. Some advocated all-black and all-male Afrocentric schools. Although Title IX of the 1972 Education Amendments provided activists with legal mandates to secure identical coeducation, they found it an uphill battle to counter institutional sexism. Instead of trying to equalize coeducational schools, a few feminists argued for single-sex schools for girls. Some Hispanic leaders thought that bilingual-bicultural education should aim at preserving immigrant languages and heritages, not simply serve as a transition to the English language and an Anglo-dominated curriculum.[51]

Questioning Progress

The pace of social and educational change after *Brown* was entirely too rapid for many who had benefited most from the older educational order. Many conservatives opposed busing to relieve racial isolation, affirmative action, bilingual classes for the children of immigrants, the banning of prayer and Bible reading, the mainstreaming of children with special needs (especially those with emotional problems and learning disabilities), and the feminist agenda for gender equality.

The politics of education, once so predictable that political scientists called school districts "closed systems," erupted in conflicts between contending groups. As the media played up student unrest, violence, drugs, and overcrowded schools, images of blackboard jungles became etched in the public's consciousness. Controversies within the educational profession—strikes, collective bargaining, racial disputes—altered the stereotype of teachers as disinterested public servants. Formerly favored by the top-down governance of the administrative progressives, prosperous whites asked: Was all this turmoil *progress?*[52]

In the abstract, people may favor giving all children a fair chance, but at the same time they want *their* children to succeed in the competition for economic and social advantage. As David K. Cohen and Barbara Neufeld observe, "public schools are one of the few American institutions that try to take equality seriously. Yet their service in this cause has been ambiguous and frequently compromised, for the schools are a public institution oriented to equality in a society dominated by private institutions oriented to the market." When secondary schools succeed in retaining and graduating minorities and the poor, for example, they appear to lessen the advantage once enjoyed by middle-class whites. In an age when "accountability" is measured more and more by scores on standardized tests, "progress" in enrolling previously excluded youth in high schools and colleges seems to lead to "regress" in academic achievement.[53]

At the very time when the poor and people of color were beginning to gain access to more equal schooling, social scientists were starting to question the value of education. Would equality of resources produce equality of results? Was schooling a route out of poverty, a means of redistributing opportunity? While some wondered, "Does schooling make a difference?" others wrote that Americans were becoming "overeducated" for their prospects in the job market. It is perhaps no coincidence that such issues arose just when "nontraditional" students were gaining entry into colleges. Conflicts about the question "progress for whom?" helped to set the stage for public doubts about whether schooling was progressing or regressing. As policy talk about decline shaped the politics of school reform beginning in the mid-1970s, the equity gains of the previous generation were increasingly downplayed or identified as the source of problems.[54]

Public perceptions and expectations of schools, well charted by Gallup polls, have so changed in recent decades that an institution once secure in the public confidence has regressed in public esteem to a point where the 1930s, 1940s, or 1950s seem another world, to some even a golden age, despite the obvious gross inequities of those decades. Opinions about schools reflect a more general enchantment or disenchantment about institutions, both public and private. In 1946 the nine in ten who expressed satisfaction with public schools probably indicated the pride that attended victory in World War II. Just as schools then enjoyed the benefit of patriotic glory, they have suffered, along with most other institutions, a sharp decline of confidence in an era that has produced the Vietnam War, Watergate, Irangate, the ballooning deficit, the S&L scandal, and other debacles. In 1958, 58 percent of Americans said they trusted the government; by 1978, this figure had dropped to 19 percent. The decline of confidence in public schools needs to be juxtaposed to that larger growing cynicism about institutions in general and to a widespread worry of parents that their children's economic future is clouded.[55]

Today the notion of steady improvement of schools is widely rejected, people have no trouble identifying defects, and citizens lack trust in those who would lead in education. Yet all this needs to be seen in context: citizens have not lost their faith in the importance of schooling both for the individual and for society; the nearer the observer is to the schools, the better they look; and confidence in schools is higher than trust in most other institutions. In one poll people placed schools second only to churches as institutions serving the public interest, ahead (in descending order) of local government, state government, the courts, and the federal government. It appears that people trust most the institutions that are closest to hand.[56]

The Gallup polls provide many ways to assess whether people thought the schools were progressing or regressing. When asked whether "children today get a better—or worse—education than you did?" 61 percent of respondents said *better* in 1973 but only 41 percent said so in 1979. In 1969, 75 percent of respondents said they would like a child of theirs to "take up teaching in the public schools as a career" but only 45 percent wanted that in 1983. And in 1974, 48 percent of people polled gave an A or B grade to the schools, but in 1983 (shortly after *A Nation at Risk*) only 31 percent gave A or B grades.[57]

Overall, the polls indicate a fairly consistent and dramatic drop in public confidence in the schools in the 1970s and early 1980s—suggesting a deep-seated questioning of the traditional view of educational progress—and then a slight recovery of esteem for public education later in the 1980s. Public opinion, however, has been somewhat volatile, as indicated in an 11 percent rise from 1988 to 1990 in people who thought that the schools had gotten worse in the previous five years and a 13 percent rise from 1983 to 1988 in respondents who thought teaching a good career for their children.

Important differences appear when responses to the polls are broken down by group. The most disaffected people have been blacks and inner-city dwellers (the two categories overlap considerably, of course). In 1991, 42 percent of the national sample gave A or B ratings to the local public schools but only 28 percent of blacks and 27 percent of inner-city residents did so. In view of the high drop-out rates, violence, inadequate financing, discrimination, and high turnover of teachers and students in urban schools, such low ratings are hardly surprising. These schools *do* desperately need improvement, and local citizens know it.[58]

In general, however, familiarity with local schools seems to breed not contempt but respect. Parents who have children in public schools tend to rate public education much more highly than the average respondent, and those polled have a higher opinion of local schools than they do of schools in general. Parents give high ratings to the particular schools their children attend. Here are the percentages of different groups who gave the schools an A or B in 1985, for example:

Rating of nation's schools by all respondents	27
Rating of local schools by all respondents	43
Rating of local school district by parents	52
Parents' rating of school attended by oldest child	71

A more detailed picture of parents' opinions about the schools emerges when parents say whether the school their oldest child attended matches the definition of "an effective school" developed by educators. These are the percentages of people who said that the description fit the school very or fairly accurately:

Safe, orderly school environment	84
Student progress measured, reported	80
Staff has high expectations, demands achievement	74
Staff, parents agree on school goals	70
Principal helps teachers	54[59]

Although breakdowns of the polls show that the schools looked better up close and that parents (who presumably knew the most about public education) had fairly favorable views of their own children's education, the overall decline in confidence is nonetheless striking. Why did this occur? Because nonparents rate schools significantly lower than parents do, changing demographics help to explain why the public ratings of schools dropped so precipitously between 1974 and 1983. The proportion of adults who had children in school fell from 39 percent to 27 percent in those years. In addition, as we have said, the media often presented very negative images and accounts of schools, and there was a general decline in confidence in institutions of all kinds.[60]

The slide in the ratings also resulted, of course, from perceived faults in the schools. From 1969 onward parents had no trouble identifying defects (perhaps in part because they were themselves notably better educated than adults in the 1940s). Each year the pollsters asked people this open-ended question: "What do you think are the biggest problems with which the public schools of this community must deal?" There was remarkable consistency in the answers during the twenty years from 1969 to 1988. If one looks at the top five or six problems, "discipline" was first for sixteen of the twenty years and always included. About 25 percent listed it each year. Next in frequency and intensity, starting in 1976, was drugs. Integration/busing was always in the top five or six "problems" until 1982, when it disappeared from that select circle. Finding and keeping good teachers was almost always on the short list, as was finance. Curriculum/standards appeared in the top five each year beginning with 1976, when "back to basics" became a common plea in policy talk, and persisted in the 1980s as federal officials and commentators in the media reported declines in test scores.[61]

Parents shared the blame with teachers for what the public saw as a pervasive lack of respect for authority among the students. In 1984, 50 percent of the respondents gave teachers an A or B grade, but only 33 percent rated parents A or B for the way they raised their children (in another poll, 60 percent of teachers rated parents as fair or poor for the way they were "performing their roles" in the family, and in 1993 teachers said more help from parents was their number-one priority in improving education).[62]

Although citizens recognize that problems in schools resulted in large part from outside pathologies—violence, drugs, fragile families, poverty —the incessant din of criticism of schools profoundly discouraged educators. When teachers were asked why they became dissatisfied and left the profession, their top two grievances were "public attitudes toward schools" and "treatment of education by the media." In 1961 about

80 percent of public school teachers said that they "certainly" or "probably" would teach again. In 1981 teachers had more years of experience and substantially more professional preparation (half of them had masters' degrees) than their predecessors of twenty years before, but less than half indicated that they would have chosen to teach if they were starting over again.[63]

The public does not blame only educators or parents for the defects of public schools. Consider the percent of A and B ratings given in 1992 to national and state officials for their leadership in education:

President Bush:	15
Congress:	7
Governors:	19
State legislators:	14[64]

One reason people are cynical about national and state leaders is that they suspect that the goals these leaders have set are unrealistic, the sort of hyperbole they have come to expect from politicians.[65]

The public trusts local institutions the most: 57 percent want district school boards to have more control of education (compared with 26 percent who want more federal control). One lesson for reformers is that decentralized approaches to change, drawing on local knowledge of problems and potential solutions, will be likely to capture public support. But this does not mean that citizens are interested only in their own backyard. In 1989, 57 percent of Gallup respondents said that they thought that inner-city schools had deteriorated, and 93 percent believed it important to improve them. That same year 83 percent said that extra funds should be allotted to schools in poorer communities.[66]

The Politics of Progress and Regress

In recent years, and particularly during the Reagan and Bush administrations, the older assumption that schools were growing better, generation by generation, has been replaced by a common assertion that public education is in decline. Indeed, the most influential call for school reform during the 1980s declared that the whole *nation* was "at risk" in international economic competition because of educational regress. "We have, in effect, been committing an act of unthinking, unilateral educational disarmament," the report declared. Many policymakers have narrowed the currency of educational success to one main measure—test scores—and reduced schooling to a means of economic competitiveness, both personal and national. *A Nation at Risk* was only one of many elite policy commissions of the 1980s that declared that faulty schooling was eroding the economy and that the remedy for both educational and economic decline was improving academic achievement.[67]

The historian Lawrence A. Cremin questions the assertion that bad schools are responsible for a deteriorating economy: "to contend that problems of international competitiveness can be solved by educational reform . . . is not merely utopian and millennialist, it is at best foolish and at worst a crass effort to direct attention away from those truly responsible for doing something about competitiveness and to lay the burden instead on the schools." We agree with his critique of this ideological smokescreen and think that much of the recent policy talk about schools has restricted discussion of educational purposes and obscured rather than clarified the most pressing problems, especially those of the schools that educate the quarter of American students who live in poverty. These children are indeed, in the phrase of the Carnegie Foundation for the Advancement of Teaching, "an imperiled generation."[68]

We believe that much of the evidence for alleged decline in public education is faulty. We raise doubts about the assertion that test scores have substantially declined, and that this, along with increasing "functional illiteracy" and "cultural illiteracy," proves that students are not learning as much as previous generations did. We think some uses of international test score comparisons are dubious. In questioning the validity of evidence and in denying the notion of a golden age in the past, we do not mean to urge complacency about the present state of academic achievement. Schools need thorough improvement, including better teaching of complex intellectual skills.

While federal officials were demonstrating on wall charts that test scores have been declining—a message that the media amplified and retailed to a public enamored of batting averages and statistical comparisons—a number of scholars questioned both the quality and the meaning of the evidence. Test results have varied, and some did indicate decline, especially during the late 1960s and early 1970s, but across the board they did not prove regress in academic achievement. Rather, the most valid measures for the purpose—the scores from the National Assessment of Educational Progress (NAEP)—attest to fairly level performance from 1970 to 1990.[69]

The most common and dramatic index of decline, and the one prominently featured on the wall charts comparing the academic performance of states, was the average score on the Scholastic Aptitude Test (SAT) of the College Entrance Examination Board. The problems with using this statistic are substantial: the SAT was designed to measure aptitude for college, not achievement in general; it was not intended to be used to compare states (the proportion of high school seniors sitting for the voluntary test varied greatly by state, and the states having the largest proportion of test takers not surprisingly scored the worst); and the number of students taking the test has expanded greatly over the years in question, especially among lower socioeconomic groups and minorities, whereas it had once been taken by small numbers of prosperous students who ranked high academically. IQ scores, a more representative measure of how "smart" students were than the voluntary SAT, rose in the 1970s. On several of the College Board achievement tests, scores rose between 1967 and 1976, the years of the largest reputed declines.[70]

Standardized achievement tests used by the schools are another kind of evidence sometimes used to demonstrate decline. Carl F. Kaestle, an expert on the history of literacy, estimates, however, that students performed about the same in reading in 1940 as in 1970 or 1983. To the degree that there were test declines in the 1970s, they had bottomed out, and test scores were on the rise in the early 1980s. Thus, Kaestle quips, "instead of a 'rising tide of mediocrity,' [the National Commission on Excellence in Education] should have proclaimed a rising tide of test scores."[71]

In recent years critics have argued that the schools are turning out illiterates in growing numbers. In 1982 Secretary of Education Terrell Bell claimed that half the population was functionally illiterate. In 1993 a newspaper headline on a new report issued by the Department of Education proclaimed, "Study Says Half of Adults in U.S. Can't Read or Handle Arithmetic." On the tests used in this study, the prosperous did far better than the poor, whites better than blacks, and those born in the United States better than immigrants (the tests were in English). Clearly, many people today lack the intellectual skills they need to cope with the complex demands of modern economic and political life. Does this mean that the long march to eradicate illiteracy has come to a standstill?[72]

The answer to that question depends on what is meant by literacy. In 1979 the Census reported that less than 1 percent of Americans regarded themselves as illiterate. Such self-reports have been the traditional basis of statistics on literacy, and these have indeed indicated steady progress. When people speak of "functional literacy," however, they mean the ability to meet educational requirements in adult life, and this definition is continually being ratcheted upward. Over time a literate person has been defined as a graduate of the third grade, or fifth grade, or even high school.[73]

In 1987 a best-selling author, E. D. Hirsch, Jr., popularized an even stricter version of literacy, the "cultural literacy" that specified what an educated person should know. Hirsch complained that "we cannot assume that young people today know things that were known in the past by almost every literate person in the culture."[74]

The idea of a decline from a golden age of common cultural knowledge appeals to many people, but when scholars summarize evidence on what students actually knew in the past—by trying to match test results in similar subjects across time and place—they typically discover little difference in students' knowledge—or "cultural literacy"—then and now. A *New York Times* quiz in American history given in the 1940s and repeated in 1976 found roughly the same (meager) results in both times.[75]

If studies of test scores and literacy over time cast doubt on the notions of a golden age and subsequent regress in the last generation, what about international comparisons of academic achievement? Doesn't everyone know that American students end up near the bottom on this score card? Not necessarily—American students scored second, after Finland, on a recent international reading test. It is true that American students have done worse than students of most other industrialized nations on many of the examinations, and that is a warning signal, but there are important defects in the score cards when they are used to compare nations.[76]

The most important problem is that the samples of people taking the tests have often been incomparable. In the early mathematics and science evaluations, notes analyst Iris C. Rotberg, the "assessments compared the average score of more than three-fourths of the age-group in the U.S. with the average of the top 9% of the students in West Germany, the top 13% in the Netherlands, and the top 45% in Sweden. It is not surprising that U.S. students did not do well in these comparisons." Another distortion comes from different patterns of curriculum in different countries; only a fifth of American students in twelfth-grade mathematics study calculus—which is on the examination—whereas in other nations almost all students do so. And finally, the motivation of the students taking the tests complicates comparisons; in some nations—Korea, for example—pupils are expected to uphold the national honor, whereas many U.S. youths regard the test as yet another boring set of blanks to pencil in on answer sheets.[77]

Most experts believe that the NAEP assessments provide the best current measures of stability or change over time in the academic achievement of pupils in American schools. These indicators offer a far more representative sampling than the SAT or international appraisals and test similar content over time. From 1970 to 1990 the NAEP tests showed some variation by age and subject, but overall the trend lines were fairly flat. Both minorities and children from impoverished families, however, improved their performance on the tests, significantly narrowing the gap between them and Caucasian and middle-class children and youth.[78]

Relatively stable results during those years can be interpreted in various ways, depending on the economic, political, or social context within which they are explained. One approach—favored by the Reagan and Bush administrations—juxtaposes rising per-pupil costs and "stagnant" NAEP achievement results (or worse, the dropping SAT scores) and concludes that Americans are not getting their money's worth from the public schools (especially in comparison with other nations). The logic of this contention can easily lead to the conclusion that public educators are lazy or incompetent, or both.[79]

Suppose, instead, that one juxtaposes relatively stable achievement, together with improving test scores among minorities and the poor, with changes from 1950 to the late 1980s in social conditions that could be expected to lower the academic performance of pupils: a tripling of the percentage of children living in single-parent families (which often means poverty for mothers and their children); an increase in teenage pregnancy; catastrophic rates of unemployment for young adult blacks; soaring arrest rates for youths under eighteen; and high rates of drug abuse and violence. We could go on to list many other challenges to educators: heavy TV watching, a sharp rise in the number of students with low proficiency in English, rising teenage part-time employment, the growing poverty of children, and gang activity in the schools.[80]

Would it not be reasonable to applaud the success of educators in holding learning steady in the face of so many impediments? David C. Berliner, an educational psychologist, argues that "the public school system of the United States has actually done remarkably well as it receives, instructs, and nurtures children who are poor, without health care, and from families and neighborhoods that barely function." For all their defects, schools may still be the most positive influence many children encounter, given the turbulence and dysfunction in many impoverished neighborhoods.[81]

Reflections

The ideologies of progress or regress in schooling are political constructs. Leaders have used them to mobilize and direct reform, persuading followers that they were joining a triumphal upward march to a utopian future or arresting a devastating backward slide. In both cases, people have held that their beliefs were supported by facts, but "progress" or "regress" in education lay much in the eye of the beholder. In periods both of supposed progress and supposed regress, the most severe problems were those in the bottom tier of schools that served the poor and people of color, yet these groups were all too often ignored.

The doctrines of progress and regress gave coherence and force to educational reform, though each imposed blinders on policymakers. The common school crusaders of the nineteenth century employed millennial rhetoric to persuade citizens to create a public system of schools. The administrative progressives were certain that their "scientific" plan for progress met the needs of all people. In both cases there were many people left behind by the apparent march of progress. When these outsiders mobilized in social movements to secure educational equality, they sometimes used a similar rhetoric of hope.

The prophets of regress, like the prophets of progress, have used hyperbole to motivate the public. Only if a complacent citizenry was aroused to danger would it act to rescue the schools and the economy. Those who were insistent about the regress of schooling often neglected the effect of talk of gloom and doom on the morale of teachers and on the commitment of parents to public education. The hyperbole of progress and decline more often obscured than illuminated the task of reform.

When critics say that schools have never been worse, advocates may be tempted to try to prove that they have never been better. We make neither claim. The public schools, for all their faults, remain one of our most stable and effective public institutions—indeed, given the increase in social pathologies in the society, educators have done far better in the last generation than might have been expected. At the same time, it is clear that the public schools need to do a better job of teaching students to think, not just in order to (supposedly) rescue an ailing economy but to serve broad civic purposes as well.[82]

As Cremin noted, the attempt in recent years to blame alleged educational decline for the nation's woes is irresponsible. The argument that poor schools produce poor workers and that improved schools would solve economic ills has two major defects: it scapegoats educators; and it blurs understanding of a labor market in which the largest proportion of new jobs are relatively unskilled and millions of skilled workers are jobless.[83]

Robert Kuttner, a columnist for *Business Week,* observes that "improving the schools and reforming job training are . . . relatively easy. The hard part is improving the kinds of jobs that the economy offers." While business executives "bemoan the poor quality of applicants" for low-paying jobs, when they offer jobs at a decent wage, "qualified applicants line up at dawn. In circles where experts earnestly call for additional highly skilled workers, the dirty little secret is the scarcity of jobs that require more advanced skills." While "millions of college graduates are working at jobs that require only a high school diploma," he notes, the biggest demand for new workers arises in dead-end jobs like janitor, nurse's aide, and fast-food worker. The federal government has estimated that about half of the new jobs workers found in 1992 were part-time, temporary, and typically without good benefits. "The entire system has fragmented," observes Labor Secretary Robert B. Reich.[84]

It would take no great effort of the imagination to attribute U.S. economic ills to worldwide recession and to mismanagement on the part of business and government. Witness, for example, the effects of burgeoning deficits, deregulation of S&Ls that permitted a few knaves to squander billions of dollars of other people's savings, slowness to upgrade factories or to adopt new strategies of management, or undue attention to the short-term bottom line of profits. It may be convenient to blame the schools for lack of economic competitiveness, but this strategy distorts both educational and economic analysis. Good schools can play an important role in creating a just, prosperous, and democratic society, but they should not be scapegoats and are not panaceas.

The intensity of both optimism and pessimism about the state of schooling reflects a continuing conviction that good education is critical both for the individual and for the society. In recent years about four in five Americans have told pollsters that they think that schools are "extremely important" in shaping "one's future success." Likewise, almost nine in ten said that "developing the best educational system in the world" is "extremely important" to America's future. The issue at hand, then, is not to convince citizens that schooling is important; there is still a deep faith that better education is linked to societal progress. The key problem is to devise plausible policies for improvement of schooling that can command the support of a worried public and the commitment of the educators upon whom reform must rely.[85]

NOTES

1. W. W. Carpenter, "Is the Educational Utopia in Sight?" *The Nation's Schools* 8 (September 1931): 71, 72, 71–73.

2. Henry Perkinson, *The Imperfect Panacea: American Faith in Education, 1865–1965* (New York: Random House, 1968); the notion of progress was, and is, so pervasive in educational writing that it has appeared in book titles as if axiomatic—see, for example, Ellwood P. Cubberley, *Readings in Public*

Education in the United States: A Collection of Sources and Readings to Illustrate the History of Educational Practice and Progress in the United States (Boston: Houghton Mifflin, 1934), or U.S. Department of Education, *Progress of Education in the United States of America, 1980–81 through 1982–83: Report for the Thirty-Ninth International Conference of Education, Sponsored by UNESCO* (Washington, D.C.: U.S. Department of Education, 1983); the recent program to assess academic achievement sponsored by the federal government since the late 1970s is called the National Assessment of Educational Progress.

3. Harlan Logan, "The Failure of American Education," *Look,* May 28, 1946, pp. 28–32, 34; "How Good Is Your School? 'Life' Test Will Tell You," *Life,* October 16, 1950, pp. 54–55; David K. Cohen, "Willard Waller: on Hating School and Loving Education," in Donald J. Willower and William Lowe Boyd, eds., *Willard Waller on Education and Schools: A Critical Appraisal* (Berkeley: McCutchan, 1989), ch. 5. For a penetrating critique of the notion of a golden educational age in the past, see Patricia Albjerg Graham, *S.O.S.: Sustain Our Schools* (New York: Hill and Wang, 1992).

4. *What People Think about Youth and Education,* National Education Association (NEA) Research Bulletin no. 5, November 1940 (Washington, D.C.: NEA, 1940), pp. 195–196; George H. Gallup, *The Gallup Poll: Public Opinion, 1935–1971* (New York: Random House, 1972), vol. 1, p. 597; Hadley Cantril and Mildred Strunk, *Public Opinion, 1935–46* (Princeton: Princeton University Press, 1951), p. 178.

5. Gallup, *Gallup Poll,* vol. 1, p. 598; vol. 2, pp. 1366, 1513.

6. Ibid., vol. 1, p. 597; Cantril and Strunk, *Public Opinion,* p. 178.

7. Stanley M. Elam, ed., *A Decade of Gallup Polls of Attitudes toward Education, 1969–1978* (Bloomington, Ind.: Phi Delta Kappa, 1978); Stanley Elam, ed., *The Gallup/Phi Delta Kappa Polls of Attitudes toward Public Schools, 1969–88: A Twenty-Year Compilation and Educational History* (Bloomington, Ind.: Phi Delta Kappa Educational Foundation, 1989), p. 5; Hans N. Weiler, "Education, Public Confidence, and the Legitimacy of the Modern State: Do We Have a Crisis?" *Phi Delta Kappan* 64 (September 1982): 9; *New York Times,* April 11, 1983, p. A18.

8. National Commission on Excellence in Education, *A Nation at Risk: The Imperative for Educational Reform* (Washington, D.C.: GPO, 1983), p. 11, passim.

9. Ibid.; John Chubb and Terry Moe, *Politics, Markets and America's Schools* (Washington, D.C.: Brookings Institution, 1990).

10. David K. Cohen and Barbara Neufeld, "The Failure of High Schools and the Progress of Education," *Daedalus* 110 (Summer 1981): 69–90; for a broad

analysis of the idea of progress in America, see Rush Welter, "The Idea of Progress in America," *Journal of the History of Ideas* 16 (June 1955): 401–415; for a critique of liberal notions of progress, see Christopher Lasch, *The True and Only Heaven: Progress and Its Critics* (New York: W. W. Norton, 1991).

11. Weiler, "Public Confidence"; Arthur Alphonse Ekirch, Jr., *The Idea of Progress in America, 1815–1860* (New York: Columbia University Press, 1944).

12. Ernest Tuveson, *Redeemer Nation: The Idea of America's Millennial Role* (Chicago: University of Chicago Press, 1968).

13. Fletcher B. Dresslar, *American School Buildings,* U.S. Bureau of Education Bulletin no. 17, 1924 (Washington, D.C.: GPO, 1924), pp. 11–14, 66–67, 89–90, 32; for a summary of progress made during the nineteenth century, see William T. Harris's report to the Paris Exposition of 1900—*Elementary Education* (Albany: J. B. Lyon Co., 1900); on the congruence between the Protestant-republican notion of millennial progress and faith in educational "science," see David Tyack and Elisabeth Hansot, *Managers of Virtue: Public School Leadership in America, 1820–1980* (New York: Basic Books, 1982), pts. 1 and 2.

14. Otis W. Caldwell and Stuart A. Courtis, *Then and Now in Education, 1845–1923: A Message of Encouragement from the Past to the Present* (Yonkers-on-Hudson: World Book Co., 1925), pp. vi, 118, 147.

15. For one leader's view of progress, see David Snedden, "The High School of Tomorrow," *The School Review* 25 (January 1917): 1–15; on declining public participation in school decision making, see Ronald E. Butchart, "The Growth of an American School System: The Coconino County, Arizona, Experience" (M.A. thesis, Northern Arizona University, 1973); for a study of innovations regarded as necessary for progress and their gradual implementation, see Paul R. Mort and Francis G. Cornell, *American Schools in Transition: How Our Schools Adapt Their Practices to Changing Needs* (New York: Teachers College Press, 1941), chs. 1–3.

16. William Bullough, " 'It Is Better to Be a Country Boy': The Lure of the Country in Urban Education in the Gilded Age," *The Historian* 35 (February 1973): 183–195; when a leading architect of reform, Charles H. Judd of the University of Chicago, wrote a book on educational trends in the first third of the twentieth century, he organized his chapters into what he called "problems," but it was obvious that progress was on the way: *Problems of Education in the United States* (New York: McGraw-Hill, 1933).

17. Ellwood P. Cubberley, *Changing Conceptions of Education* (Boston: Houghton Mifflin, 1909); James Russell, *Founding Teachers College: Reminiscences of the Dean Emeritus* (New York: Teachers College Press, 1937);

George D. Strayer, "Progress in City School Administration during the Past Twenty-Five Years," *School and Society* 32 (September 1930): 375–378.

18. "Shall Education Be Rockefellerized?" *American Federationist* 24 (March 1917): 206–209; Institute for Public Service, *Rainbow Promises of Progress in Education* (New York: Institute for Public Service, 1917); Robert Rose, "Career Sponsorship in the School Superintendency" (Ph.D. diss., University of Oregon, 1969); Henry Pritchett, "Educational Surveys," in Carnegie Foundation for the Advancement of Teaching, *Ninth Annual Report of the President and Treasurer* (New York: Merrymount Press, 1914), pp. 118–123; Hollis L. Caswell, *City School Surveys: An Interpretation and Appraisal* (New York: Teachers College Press, 1929).

19. William G. Carr, "Legislation as a Factor in Producing Good Schools," *American School Board Journal* 81 (December 1930): 37–38.

20. Charles H. Judd, "School Boards as an Obstruction to Good Administration," *The Nation's Schools* 13 (February 1934): 13–15.

21. Ellwood P. Cubberley, *Public School Administration: A Statement of the Fundamental Principles Underlying the Organization and Administration of Public Education* (Boston: Houghton Mifflin, 1916); David B. Tyack, *The One Best System: A History of American Urban Education* (Cambridge: Harvard University Press, 1974), pt. 4.

22. National Center for Educational Statistics (NCES), *Digest of Educational Statistics, 1974* (Washington, D.C.: GPO, 1975), p. 53 (hereafter cited as NCES, *Digest,* by date); NCES, *Digest, 1988,* table 67; for a discussion of the rationale for consolidation of rural schools and the demand for professional supervision of them, see Ellwood P. Cubberley, *Rural Life and Education: A Study of the Rural-School Problem* (Boston: Houghton Mifflin, 1914); William B. McElhenny, "Where Do We Stand on School District Reorganization?" *Journal of the Kansas Law Association* 16 (November 1947): 245–251.

23. Lynn Dumenil, "The Insatiable Maw of Bureaucracy: Antistatism and Education Reform in the 1920s," *The Journal of American History* 77 (September 1990): 499–524; U.S. Bureau of Education, *A Manual of Educational Legislation for the Guidance of Committees on Education in the State Legislatures,* Bulletin no. 4, 1919 (Washington, D.C.: GPO, 1919); The National Institute of Education, *State Legal Standards for the Provision of Public Education: An Overview* (Washington, D.C.: GPO, 1978); Judd, *Problems,* p. 116.

24. NCES, *Digest, 1988,* table 61; John W. Meyer et al., *Bureaucratization without Centralization: Changes in the Organizational System of American Pub-*

lic Education, 1940–1980, Project Report no. 85-A11, Institute for Research on Educational Finance and Governance, Stanford University, 1985, table 1; we are indebted to Jane Hannaway for information on the California code.

25. Edith A. Lathrop, *The Improvement of Rural Schools by State Standardization* (Washington, D.C.: GPO, 1925), pp. 10–13, 34; George J. Collins, *The Constitutional and Legal Bases for State Action in Education, 1900–1968* (Boston: Massachusetts Department of Education, 1968); on the needs of rural schools, see Newton Edwards and Herman G. Richey, *The School in the American Social Order: The Dynamics of American Education* (Boston: Houghton Mifflin, 1947), p. 689; for differences between urban and rural schools, see Harlan Updegraff and William R. Hood, *A Comparison of Urban and Rural Common-School Statistics*, U.S. Bureau of Education Bulletin no. 21, 1912 (Washington, D.C.: GPO, 1912); for samples of school laws, see National Education Association, Educational Research Service, *State School Legislation, 1934*, Circular no. 3, March 1935 (Washington, D.C.: 1935).

26. Caswell, *Surveys*.

27. Larry Cuban and David Tyack, "Match and Mismatch—Schools and Children Who Don't Fit Them," in Henry M. Levin, ed., *Accelerated Schools*, forthcoming; Strayer, "Progress"; Lewis M. Terman, ed., *Intelligence Tests and School Reorganization* (Yonkers-on-Hudson: World Book, Co., 1922); Charles H. Judd, "Education," in *Recent Social Trends in the United States: Report of the President's Research Committee on Social Trends* (New York: McGraw-Hill, 1933), pp. 330, 338.

28. Judd, "Education," pp. 345–346; Lewis Terman, *The Hygiene of the School Child* (Boston: Houghton Mifflin, 1929); Robert W. Kunzig, *Public School Education of Atypical Children*, U.S. Bureau of Education Bulletin no. 10, 1931 (Washington, D.C.: GPO, 1931), p. 74; NCES, *Digest, 1990*, p. 63.

29. NCES, *Digest, 1988*, table 67.

30. National Center for Educational Statistics, *120 Years of American Education: A Statistical Portrait* (Washington, D.C.: GPO, 1993), pp. 14, 21, 34–35 (hereafter cited as NCES, *120 Years*); NCES, *Digest, 1990*, p. 66.

31. American Association of School Administrators, *The American School Superintendency* (Washington, D.C.: American Association of School Administrators, 1952), p. 444; NCES, *Digest, 1990*, p. 48.

32. For the opinion of one fascinating "trouble-maker" on the regime of the administrative progressives, see Margaret Haley, "Why Teachers Should Organize," NEA, *Addresses and Proceedings, 1904* (Washington, D.C.: NEA,

1905), pp. 145–152 (hereafter cited as NEA, *Addresses and Proceedings*, by date); of course, the administrative progressives were not the only interest group influencing legislation and educational philosophy—see Jesse H. Newlon, *Educational Administration as Social Policy* (New York: Charles Scribner's Sons, 1934).

33. On blacks' self-help in education, see James D. Anderson, *The Education of Blacks in the South, 1860–1935* (Chapel Hill: University of North Carolina Press, 1988); Michael B. Katz, *Reconstructing American Education* (Cambridge: Harvard University Press, 1987); W. Lloyd Warner, Robert J. Havighurst, and Martin B. Loeb, *Who Shall Be Educated? The Challenge of Unequal Opportunities* (New York: Harper and Brothers, 1944).

34. George S. Counts, *The Social Composition of Boards of Education* (Chicago: University of Chicago Press, 1927); David Tyack, Robert Lowe, and Elisabeth Hansot, *Public Schools in Hard Times: The Great Depression and Recent Years* (Cambridge: Harvard University Press, 1984), chs. 3–4; for an outstanding example of an educator who did attend to inequalities, see Leonard Covello, *The Heart Is the Teacher* (New York: McGraw-Hill, 1958).

35. Edwards and Ritchey, *Social Order,* pp. 635, 688–699; disparities of local wealth still frustrate meaningful equality in education, as Jonathan Kozol has documented in *Savage Inequalities: Children in America's Schools* (New York: Crown, 1991).

36. Henry S. Shryock, Jr., "1940 Census Data on Numbers of Years of School Completed," *Milbank Memorial Fund Quarterly* 20 (October 1942): 372; Paul R. Mort, *Federal Support for Public Education: A Report of an Investigation of Educational Need and Relative Ability of States to Support Education as They Bear on Federal Aid to Education* (New York: Teachers College, Bureau of Publications, 1936); for an account of the virtues of rural schools, often downplayed by educators, see Wayne E. Fuller, *The Old Country School: The Story of Rural Education in the Middle West* (Chicago: University of Chicago Press, 1982).

37. The visitor to the Texas school is quoted in Doxey Wilkerson, *Special Problems of Negro Education* (Washington, D.C.: GPO, 1939), p. 99—see also pp. 15–49; Horace Mann Bond, *The Education of the Negro in the American Social Order* (New York: Prentice Hall, 1934); Charles S. Johnson, *Shadow of the Plantation* (Chicago: University of Chicago Press, 1934); Harvey Kantor and Barbara Brenzel, "Urban Education and the 'Truly Disadvantaged': The Historical Roots of the Contemporary Crisis, 1945–1990," in Michael B. Katz, ed., *The "Underclass" Debate: Views from History* (Princeton: Princeton University Press, 1993), pp. 366–402.

38. Edwards and Ritchey, *Social Order,* p. 703; Howard M. Bell, *Youth Tell Their Story: A Study of the Conditions and Attitudes of Young People in Maryland between the Ages of Sixteen and Twenty-Four* (Washington, D.C.: American Council on Education, 1938), pp. 59–60.

39. August Hollingshead, *Elmtown's Youth: The Impact of Social Classes on Adolescents* (New York: John Wiley, 1949), chs. 6, 8; "What People Think about Youth and Education," *NEA Research Bulletin* 18 (November 1940): 215; Bernard D. Karpinos and Herbert J. Sommers, "Educational Attainment of Urban Youth in Various Income Classes," *Elementary School Journal* 42 (May 1942): 677–687; Jeannie Oakes, *Keeping Track* (New Haven: Yale University Press, 1985).

40. David Tyack and Elisabeth Hansot, *Learning Together: A History of Coeducation in American Public Schools* (New Haven: Yale University Press and the Russell Sage Foundation, 1990), ch. 7.

41. Naomi J. White, "Let Them Eat Cake! A Plea for Married Teachers," *Clearing House* 13 (September 1938): 135–139; there was a conscious program to recruit more men into teaching—see "Teaching: A Man's Job," *Phi Delta Kappan* 20 (March 1938): 215; Elisabeth Hansot and David Tyack, "The Dream Deferred: A Golden Age for Women Administrators?" (Stanford, Calif.: Institute for Research on Educational Finance and Governance, 1981); Tyack and Hansot, *Learning Together,* chs. 7–9.

42. John G. Richardson, "Historical Expansion of Special Education," in Bruce Fuller and Richard Rubinson, eds., *The Political Construction of Education: The State, School Expansion, and Economic Change* (Westport, Conn.: Praeger, 1992), pp. 207–221; Kunzig, "Atypical Children"; Frank M. Phillips, *Schools and Classes for Feeble-Minded and Subnormal Children, 1926–1927,* U.S. Bureau of Education Bulletin no. 5, 1928 (Washington, D.C.: GPO, 1928); James H. Van Sickle, James H. Witmer, and Leonard P. Ayres, *Provision for Exceptional Children in Public Schools,* U.S. Bureau of Education Bulletin no. 14, 1911 (Washington, D.C.: GPO, 1911); NCES, *120 Years,* p. 44.

43. Joseph L. Tropea, "Bureaucratic Order and Special Children: Urban Schools, 1890s–1940s," *History of Education Quarterly* 27 (Spring 1987): 29–53; Barry M. Franklin, "Progressivism and Curriculum Differentiation: Special Classes in the Atlanta Public Schools, 1898–1923," *History of Education Quarterly* 29 (Winter 1989): 571–593.

44. Gunnar Myrdal, *An American Dilemma: The Negro Problem and American Democracy* (New York: Harper and Brothers, 1944), pp. xlvi–xlviii.

45. Frances Piven and Richard Cloward, *Poor Peoples' Movements: Why They Succeed, How They Fail* (New York: Pantheon, 1977).

46. *Brown v. Board of Education,* 347 U.S. 493 (1954); Richard Kluger, *Simple Justice: The History of Brown v. Board of Education and Black America's Struggle for Equality* (New York: Vintage Books, 1977); Kantor and Brenzel, "Urban Education"; David Neal and David L. Kirp, *The Allure of Legalization Reconsidered: The Case of Special Education* (Stanford, Calif.: Institute for Research on Educational Finance and Governance, 1983).

47. Joseph Gusfield, ed., *Protest, Reform, and Revolt: A Reader in Social Movements* (New York: John Wiley, 1970); Anthony Obershall, *Social Conflict and Social Movements* (Englewood Cliffs, N.J.: Prentice Hall, 1973).

48. Robert Newby and David Tyack, "Victims without 'Crimes': Some Historical Perspectives on Black Education," *Journal of Negro Education* 40 (Summer 1971): 192–206; Lawrence A. Cremin, *Popular Education and Its Discontents* (New York: Harper & Row, 1990), ch. 3; Nancy Frazier and Myra Sadker, *Sexism in School and Society* (New York: Harper & Row, 1973); Susan S. Klein, ed., *Handbook for Achieving Sex Equity through Education* (Baltimore: Johns Hopkins University Press, 1985).

49. Gary Orfield, *Public School Desegregation in the United States, 1968–1980* (Washington, D.C.: Joint Center for Policy Studies, 1983), pp. 12, 15–19; NCES, *Digest, 1991,* pp. 110, 181; Harold Hodgkinson, "What's Right with Education," *Phi Delta Kappan* 61 (November 1979): 160–162; Jennifer O'Day and Marshall S. Smith, "Systemic School Reform and Educational Opportunity," in Susan Fuhrman, ed., *Designing Coherent Education Policy: Improving the System* (San Francisco: Jossey-Bass, 1993), pp. 233–267.

50. Jonathan Kozol, *Savage Inequalities: Children in America's Schools* (New York: Crown, 1991); Nat Hentoff, *Our Children Are Dying* (New York: Viking, 1966); Jonathan Kozol, *Death at an Early Age: The Destruction of the Hearts and Minds of Negro Children in the Boston Public Schools* (Boston: Houghton Mifflin, 1972).

51. Henry M. Levin, ed., *Community Control of Schools* (Washington, D.C.: Brookings Institution, 1970); Madeline Arnot, "A Cloud over Coeducation: An Analysis of the Forms of Transmission of Class and Gender Relations," in Stephen Walker and Len Barton, eds., *Gender, Class, and Education* (New York: Falmer Press, 1983), pp. 69–92.

52. On public concerns about the schools, see Elam, *Gallup Polls, 1969–88;* George R. Kaplan, *Images of Education: The Mass Media's Version of America's Schools* (Washington, D.C.: National School Public Relations Association and the Institute for Educational Leadership, 1992).

53. Cohen and Neufeld, "Failure," p. 70.

54. James S. Coleman et al., *Equality of Educational Opportunity* (Washington, D.C.: GPO, 1966); Christopher Jencks et al., *Inequality: A Reassessment of the Effect of Family and Schooling in America* (New York: Basic Books, 1972); Donald M. Levine and Mary Jo Bane, eds., *The "Inequality Controversy": Schooling and Distributive Justice* (New York: Basic Books, 1975).

55. Elam, *Gallup Polls, 1969–88*, p. 9; Weiler, "Public Confidence"; Daniel E. Griffiths, "The Crisis in American Education," *New York University Education Quarterly* 14 (Fall 1982): 1–10.

56. Weiler, "Public Confidence"; Elam, *Gallup Polls, 1969–88*, p. 9; Griffiths, "Crisis."

57. Elam, *Gallup Polls, 1969–88*, pp. 220, 221, 225; Stanley M. Elam, Lowell C. Rose, and Alex M. Gallup, "The Twenty-Fourth Gallup/Phi Delta Kappa Poll of the Public's Attitudes toward the Public Schools," *Phi Delta Kappan* 74 (September 1992): 45.

58. Stanley M. Elam, Lowell C. Rose, and Alec C. Gallup, "The Twenty-Third Annual Gallup Poll of the Public's Attitudes toward the Public Schools," *Phi Delta Kappan* 73 (September 1991): 55; Stanley M. Elam and Alec M. Gallup, "The Twenty-First Annual Gallup Poll of the Public's Attitudes toward the Public Schools," *Phi Delta Kappan* 71 (September 1989): 49.

59. Elam, *Gallup Polls, 1969–88*, pp. 172–173, 186.

60. Ibid., p. 5.

61. Ibid., pp. 3–5.

62. Ibid., p. 3; Gene Maeroff, "Reform Comes Home: Policies to Encourage Parental Involvement in Children's Education," in Chester E. Finn and Theodor Rebarber, eds., *Education Reform in the Nineties* (New York: Macmillan, 1992), pp. 158–159; Susan Chira, "What Do Teachers Want Most? Help from Parents," *New York Times*, June 23, 1993, p. B6.

63. "Teachers Are Better Educated, More Experienced, But Less Satisfied than in the Past: NEA Survey," *Phi Delta Kappan* 62 (May 1982): 579; National Center for Educational Statistics, *Condition of Education, 1982* (Washington, D.C.: GPO, 1983), pp. 104–105.

64. Elam, Rose, and Gallup, "Twenty-Fourth Gallup Poll," p. 46.

65. Elam, Rose, and Gallup, "Twenty-Third Gallup Poll," pp. 43–44.

66. Elam, *Gallup Polls, 1969–88*, pp. 187–188; Elam and Gallup, "Twenty-First Gallup Poll," pp. 45, 49.

67. National Commission on Excellence in Education, *A Nation at Risk,* p. 5; for a critique of conventional interpretations of school achievement data and the reforms based on them, see Daniel Koretz, "Educational Practices, Trends in Achievement, and the Potential of the Reform Movement," *Educational Administration Quarterly* 24 (August 1988): 350–359.

68. Cremin, *Popular Education,* p. 103; The Carnegie Foundation for the Advancement of Teaching, *An Imperiled Generation: Saving Urban Schools* (Princeton: Carnegie Foundation for the Advancement of Teaching, 1988).

69. Lawrence C. Stedman and Marshall S. Smith, "Recent Reform Proposals for American Education," *Contemporary Education Review* 2 (Fall 1983): 85–104; Lawrence C. Stedman and Carl F. Kaestle, "Literacy and Reading Performance in the United States, from 1880 to the Present," *Reading Research Quarterly* 27 (Winter 1987): 8–46; Carl F. Kaestle, "The Decline of American Education: Myth or Reality?" (Ms., University of Wisconsin, November 1992); Gerald W. Bracey, "Why Can't They Be like We Were?" *Phi Delta Kappan* 73 (October 1991): 104–117.

70. David C. Berliner, "Educational Reform in an Era of Disinformation," paper presented at the meeting of the American Association of Colleges of Teacher Education, San Antonio, Texas, February 1992, pp. 7–15; Bracey, "Why?" pp. 108–110.

71. Carl F. Kaestle et al., *Literacy in the United States: Readers and Reading since 1880* (New Haven: Yale University Press, 1991), p. 130, chs. 3–4.

72. Kaestle, *Literacy,* 75–76; William Celis III, "Study Says Half of Adults in U.S. Can't Read or Handle Arithmetic," *New York Times,* September 9, 1993, pp. A1, A16; Paul Copperman, *The Literacy Hoax: The Decline of Reading, Writing, and Learning in the Public Schools and What We Can Do about It* (New York: William Morrow, 1978); Frank E. Armbruster, *Our Children's Crippled Future: How American Education Has Failed* (New York: Quadrangle Books, 1977).

73. Daniel P. Resnick and Lauren B. Resnick, "The Nature of Literacy: An Historical Exploration," *Harvard Educational Review* 47 (August 1977): 370–385.

74. E. D. Hirsch, Jr., *Cultural Literacy: What Every American Needs to Know* (Boston: Houghton Mifflin, 1987), p. 8; see also Allan Bloom, *The Closing of the American Mind: How Higher Education Has Failed Democracy and Impoverished the Souls of Today's Students* (New York: Simon and Schuster, 1987).

75. *New York Times,* June 21, 1942, p. 1; *New York Times,* May 2, 3, 4, 1976; Allan Nevins, "American History for Americans," *New York Times Maga-*

zine, May 3, 1942, pp. 6, 28; Dale Whittington, "What Have Seventeen-Year-Olds Known in the Past?" *American Educational Research Journal* 28 (Winter 1992): 759–783; Chester E. Finn, Jr., and Diane Ravitch, "Survey Results: U.S. Seventeen-Year-Olds Know Shockingly Little About History and Literature," *American School Board Journal* 174 (October 1987): 31–33. In Kaestle, *Literacy,* pp. 80–89, Lawrence C. Stedman and Carl F. Kaestle discuss the conceptual and technical problems with then-and-now studies and conclude that "our educated guess is that schoolchildren of the same age and socioeconomic status have been performing at similar levels throughout most of the twentieth century" (p. 89).

76. Berliner, "Disinformation," pp. 37–43.

77. Iris C. Rotberg, "I Never Promised You First Place," *Phi Delta Kappan* 72 (December 1990): 297, 296–303; Ian Westbury, "Comparing American and Japanese Achievement: Is the United States Really a Low Achiever?" *Educational Researcher* (June/July 1992): 18–24; Gerald W. Bracey, "The Second Bracey Report on the Condition of Public Education," *Phi Delta Kappan* 74 (October 1992): 108.

78. National Assessment of Educational Progress, *Accelerating Academic Achievement* (Princeton: Educational Testing Service, 1990); Bracey, "Condition"; Stedman and Smith, "Proposals"; O'Day and Smith, "Systemic Reform."

79. Bracey, "Why Can't They Be Like We Were?" p. 112; Berliner, "Disinformation," p. 28. Bracey and Berliner question the meaning of rising per-pupil costs. They point out that public schools are legally and morally bound to provide an appropriate education for all children who come to their doors, and that the computation of educational costs typically includes sharply rising expenditures for special education. When U.S. expenditures for K–12 schooling were expressed as a percent of per capita income in 1985, the United States came fourteenth in a list of sixteen industrialized nations.

80. Office of Educational Research and Improvement, *Youth Indicators, 1988: Trends in the Well-Being of Youth* (Washington, D.C.: GPO, 1988); "Social Well-Being," *Education Week,* October 21, 1992, p. 3.

81. Berliner, "Disinformation," p. 21; Bracey, "Second Bracey Report," pp. 112–113.

82. Robert Rothman, "Revisionists Take Aim at Gloomy View of Schools," *Education Week,* November 13, 1991, pp. 1, 12–13.

83. Cremin, *Popular Education,* p. 103; Clark Kerr, "Is Education Really All That Guilty?" *Education Week,* February 27, 1991, p. 30; Henry M. Levin and Russell W. Rumberger, "The Low Skill Future in High Tech," *Stanford*

Educator, Summer 1983, pp. 2–3; Peter T. Kilborn, "Job Security Hinges on Skills, Not on an Employer for Life," *New York Times,* March 12, 1994, pp. A1, A7.

84. Robert Kuttner, "Training Programs Alone Can't Produce $20-an-Hour Workers," *Business Week,* March 8, 1993, p. 16; Reich is quoted in Peter T. Kilborn, "New Jobs Lack the Old Security in Time of 'Disposable Workers,'" *New York Times,* March 3, 1993, pp. A1, A6.

85. Elam, *Gallup Polls, 1969–88,* pp. 9, 222.

3

REFORMERS, RADICALS, AND ROMANTICS

Diane Ravitch

Ravitch gives historical perspective on major movements in school reform, from Sputnik to *A Nation at Risk*. Some movements have died quiet deaths, some have incorporated bits of themselves into the fabric of contemporary schooling, and some, renamed and superficially refashioned, are being resurrected as current reform efforts. The many "new" ideas in school reform that you will find in the pages of this book are reforms that have come and gone. For every generation, what's old can become new again.

⸻ ○ ⸻

UNLIKE HIGHER EDUCATION, where the mood was one of confidence and optimism as the 1960s began, America's elementary and secondary schools were struggling to readjust to the new demands of the post-Sputnik era. The Soviet launch of the world's first artificial satellite on October 4, 1957, promptly ended the debate that had raged for several years about the quality of American education. Those who had argued since the late 1940s that American schools were not rigorous enough and that life adjustment education had cheapened intellectual values felt vindicated, and, as one historian later wrote, "a shocked and humbled nation embarked on a bitter orgy of pedagogical soul-searching." National magazines discovered a new crisis in education, and critics like Admiral Hyman Rickover—known as the father of the nuclear submarine—vociferously blamed the schools for endangering the nation's security by falling behind the Russians in science, mathematics, and engineering. Regardless of what was said, there was Sputnik itself, orbiting the earth as a constant reminder that political supremacy was tied to technological prowess. For the first time since the end of World War II, people of all political backgrounds agreed that the national interest depended on improving the quality of America's schools.[1]

Out of the new mood arose a clamor for the federal government to do something, and do it quickly. President Eisenhower had staunchly opposed any general federal aid to schools, on the grounds that federal aid would inevitably lead to federal control. Yet, aware that the baby boom had strained the finances of many school districts, Eisenhower repeatedly tried to gain congressional approval for a federal school construction program. Even so limited a purpose as school construction was stymied by the same political factors—race, religion, and fear of federal control—that had blocked previous federal aid bills. After Sputnik, however, the broad popular demand for a federal response to meet the Russian challenge prompted Congress to pass the National Defense Education Act in 1958 (NDEA). This act provided fellowships, grants, and loans to encourage the study of science, mathematics, and foreign languages and funded school construction and equipment. The active federal aid lobby, defeated so many times in the past, was happy to latch onto national security as a vehicle to establish the legitimacy of the federal role in supporting education.[2]

Well before Sputnik, there were clear signs of discontent with the quality of American schools. Government officials repeatedly expressed concern about the shortage of graduates in scientific and technological fields. Additionally, the critics of progressivism complained about the neglect of the basic academic disciplines—English, history, science, mathematics, and foreign languages. The historian Arthur Bestor insisted that scholars had a responsibility for the way their disciplines were presented in the public schools. Nor was Bestor alone in his belief that what was taught in the schools was obsolescent, trivial, or insufficiently challenging. Many others, in the academic world and the government, criticized the quality of secondary school teaching, especially in the fields of science and mathematics. In 1952, mathematicians at the University of Illinois organized a project to develop new materials for high school teachers, with the intention of introducing adolescents to the way that mathematicians think. In the spring of 1956, under the leadership of physicist Jerrold Zacharias, a group of scientists at MIT formed the Physical Science Study Committee, which aimed to revise the content and methods of physics teaching in secondary schools, in part to correct what was taught but also to attract more students into careers in science.[3]

Sputnik came to be a symbol of the consequences of indifference to high standards. In popular parlance, Sputnik had happened not because of what the Russians had done but because of what American schools had failed to do. The prototypical response to Sputnik was the Rockefeller Brothers Fund's report *The Pursuit of Excellence,* which appeared in 1958. While the NEA's *Education for All American Youth,* published in 1944, epitomized the progressive educators' expansive vision of the school as a grand social service center meeting the needs of the individual and the community, *The Pursuit of Excellence* presented a contrasting vision of the proper relation between school and society. It advocated the development of human potential as a national goal and insisted that the nation could encourage both excellence and equality without compromising either. It spoke of challenges and greatness, of high performance, of moral and intellectual excellence. Like most reports, it made nothing happen, but it accurately reflected hopes for the renewal of American society through the infusion of higher educational aspirations.[4]

During the late 1950s, the much-discussed "crisis in the schools" attracted the attention of the major foundations, which had previously focused their resources on higher education. In late 1956, almost a year before the orbiting of Sputnik, the Carnegie Corporation agreed to support a series of studies of public education by James B. Conant, former president of Harvard University and ambassador to West Germany. When Conant's first report, *The American High School Today,* was published in 1959, beleaguered school officials seized upon it as a set of practical recommendations to translate the exhortations of *The Pursuit of Excellence* into reality. Conant urged the spread of the comprehensive high school, which he defined (in progressive terminology) as one "whose programs correspond to the educational needs of *all* the youth in the community." To be comprehensive, a high school had to fulfill three tasks: first, to provide "a good general education for *all* the pupils" (which meant that all students were required to take courses in English and American literature and composition, as well as in social studies); second, to offer the noncollege-bound majority good elective nonacademic courses (such as vocational, commercial, and work-study); and third, to provide the academically talented students with advanced courses in fields such as mathematics, science, and foreign languages. He urged the elimination of high schools too small to be "comprehensive," that is, with a senior class smaller than one hundred. Conant opposed tracking of students into separate curricula (for

example, "college prep" versus vocational), but he endorsed ability grouping, so that fast and slow students would get the appropriate level of academic challenge. A skillful blend of dedication to both academic excellence
and democratic values, Conant's high school study became a surprise
bestseller. Though some professional educators complained that Conant's
recommendations were too conservative, John Gardner, president of the
Carnegie Corporation (and, coincidentally, author of *The Pursuit of Excellence*) noted approvingly that Conant "became overnight the most
quoted authority on American education," and his celebrated report "was
debated in PTA's, school boards, superintendents' offices, and educational
conferences throughout the nation."[5]

During the same period, the Ford Foundation addressed the "crisis in
the schools" with two major efforts: a "Comprehensive School Improvement Program" (CSIP), which funded leading communities to serve as
model districts for educational reform, and a "Great Cities–Gray Areas
Program," to help big-city school systems create compensatory and remedial programs for their increasing numbers of low-income pupils. Unlike the Conant report, which sought to strengthen traditional secondary education, Ford's CSIP encouraged the implementation of innovative
practices in curriculum, staffing, technology, and facilities, such as team
teaching, nonprofessional personnel, flexible scheduling, programmed instruction, federally sponsored science curricula, teacher-devised curricula, independent study, language laboratories, open-space classrooms,
nongraded programs, and school-university cooperation. Both programs
were bellwethers of a sort, one by stressing innovation as the key to school
improvement, the other by confronting the issues of educating poor
children.[6]

The great flurry of public interest that followed the orbiting of Sputnik
was invaluable for those who wanted the schools to pay more attention to
gifted students and to raise academic standards. The Conant report provided parents and citizens' groups with a handy check-list to use in gaug-
ing the quality of their high schools. The definition of the "crisis" riveted
the attention of school officials on such matters as enrollments in science,
mathematics, and foreign languages. Able students were encouraged to
enroll in advanced courses and to work hard to get into elite colleges.
Standardized achievement scores rose steadily, as did high school enrollments in advanced academic courses. For the first time in the twentieth century, foreign language enrollments grew: in 1955, only 20 percent of high
school students were studying any foreign language, a figure that rose to
24 percent by 1965.[7]

At the National Science Foundation (NSF), the furor over Sputnik significantly increased the agency's role in secondary school curriculum reform. Established by Congress in 1950 to promote basic research and education in the sciences, NSF initially had little to do with precollege programs. Soon, however, it began to sponsor science fairs and summer institutes for high school teachers of mathematics and science. In 1956, responding to governmental concern about manpower shortages in scientific and technical fields, NSF funded the MIT Physical Science Study Committee's revision of the secondary school physics curriculum. In the wake of Sputnik, NSF expanded its high school curriculum revision projects to include the fields of mathematics, biology, chemistry, and social science. From these efforts eventually came a number of innovative curricula, including "the new math," "the new social studies," and substantial revisions in the natural sciences.

Convinced that the right combination of talent and funding would correct the flaws of the schools, the curriculum reformers took up their task with missionary zeal. The flurry of activity by university scholars and high school teachers offered promise of transforming American education: "Action sprung up at schools and colleges across the land. Hundreds of talented persons—scientists, science teachers, psychologists, film makers, writers, apparatus designers, artists, etc.—formed themselves into groups according to shared notions of what high school science might become. At first this meant high school mathematics and the natural sciences, but then it became extended to high school social sciences, and then to elementary and junior high science." Each new curriculum package was tested, retested, and revised. Thousands of teachers attended summer institutes and inservice programs to learn how to use the new materials and methods.[8]

The curriculum reformers shared a common outlook. They hoped to replace current methods—characterized by teacher-led "telling" and student recitation—with curriculum packages that used "discovery," "inquiry," and inductive reasoning as methods of learning; the rationale was that students would find the field more interesting and would retain longer what they learned if they "figured out," through carefully designed exercises or experiments, the basic principles of the field. They hoped to end the traditional reliance on a single textbook by creating attractive multimedia packages that included films, "hands-on" activities, and readings. They emphasized the importance of understanding a few central concepts in a discipline, rather than trying to "cover" an entire field, the way current courses in science or history did. Where present curricula stressed the informational, descriptive, and applied aspects of a subject (the discipline's "product"), the new curricula would teach the structure of the academic discipline; students would learn how a scientist or mathematician or social scientist thinks (the discipline's "processes"). Put another way, instead of learning "about" science, students would "do" science. The reformers agreed on the importance of cognitive growth, in keeping with the principle enunciated by one of the moving forces of the curriculum reform movement, Harvard psychologist Jerome Bruner, that "any subject can be taught effectively in some intellectually honest form to any child at any stage of development."[9]

As the new curricula were devised and revised in the early years of the 1960s, the climate for educational change was unusually receptive. The political and social context seemed charged by the energy, youth, and dynamism of the Kennedy administration, and the status quo in every area of endeavor was under reexamination. For the first time, the problem of educational change was jointly attacked by federal agencies, university scholars, major philanthropic foundations, big-city school systems, and almost everyone else in the field. On all educational fronts, innovation was the watchword, and some observers confidently spoke of "the revolution in the schools." In 1963, Francis Keppel, U.S. commissioner of education, observed that in the past decade, "more time, talent, and money than ever before in history have been invested in pushing outward the frontiers of educational knowledge, and in the next decade or two we may expect even more significant developments."[10]

With funds from foundations and government, school systems experimented with the new (supposedly "teacher-proof") curricula, new patterns of staffing and scheduling, new ways of training teachers, and new technology. Admirers of behaviorist B. F. Skinner claimed that the teaching machine and programmed instruction would revolutionize the classroom. Others, touting the virtues of television teaching, talking typewriters, computers, and multimedia equipment, envisioned the advent of "the automated classroom." The new technology, it was believed, had made the traditional, egg-crate school obsolete; in a school where students sometimes worked individually, sometimes joined in large groups for television instruction, and sometimes worked in team-taught situations, it would no longer make sense to have equal-sized classrooms with fixed walls. "The new schoolhouse" would have flexible furnishings, movable walls, and open spaces, and indeed such schoolhouses already existed in places such as San Mateo, California; Wayland, Massachusetts; Boulder City, Nevada; and Newton, Massachusetts.[11]

The expected pedagogical revolution in the schools was not to be, however. It was swept aside by the onrush of the racial revolution, which presented a forceful challenge to the political, social, and economic basis of American schools. Between 1963 and 1965, the nation's social fabric sustained a series of jolts: violence against blacks and civil rights workers in the South; the assassination of President Kennedy; the rediscovery of poverty; the beginning of American involvement in Vietnam. Meanwhile, the movement of blacks to northern cities brought the problems of racial segregation and slums to urban schools. Civil rights leaders in North and South brought their demands for integration, equality, and justice to the doors of the public schools; in the context of such transcending demands, the pedagogical revolution was no revolution at all.

Before long, the pursuit of excellence was overshadowed by concern about the needs of the disadvantaged. As the racial crisis and the urban crisis became the nation's most pressing problems, the Cold War competition with the Soviets moved to the back burner and lost its motivating power. Identifying the gifted and stimulating high achievement paled as a national goal in comparison to the urgency of redressing racial injustice. Government agencies and foundations redirected their agendas to search for mechanisms to meet the needs of disadvantaged minority children, and scores of compensatory programs were created throughout the country. Such efforts were multiplied by congressional passage of the Elementary and Secondary Education Act in 1965, with its focus on educating poor children.

The many remedial and compensatory programs initiated by local school systems, state education departments, and federal agencies were born in crisis, and there was neither time enough nor knowledge enough to satisfy the rising expectations of long-denied and angry minorities. Programs were tried, hastily evaluated, declared a failure. In some cities civil rights groups conducted demonstrations to demand integration and to protest inferior schooling. In others, black community groups demanded control of the public schools by the black community. Critics charged that the curriculum, the professionals, the tests, the bureaucratic organization, and the methods of the conventional school were inherently biased against blacks.

Since none of these demands for change was ever fully satisfied, and, more importantly, since none—even if fully satisfied—had the power to produce in immediate and tangible form the desired goal of full racial equality, the schools bore the brunt of black anger. No matter how well or how badly the schools taught reading or writing or history, poor black children still lived in slums, black unemployment was still double the white rate, and black poverty remained high. Even what the schools could do well, if they were good schools, was not equal to the burden placed on them. And so, because they could not solve the problem of racial inequality and did not have within their power the means to redress demands for justice, the schools became the targets of intense criticism.

Amid the extreme social dissension of the late 1960s, the schools—because of their role in generating values and teaching ways of knowing—were directly affected by antiwar protests, the splintering of the liberal center, the rise of the counterculture, the growth of racial separatism, and demands for "relevant" curricula by everyone who wished to change society. When the decade of the 1960s opened, the problems of the schools seemed solvable, if only enough talent, commitment, and money could be mobilized; by the late 1960s, the waning of national self-esteem was evident in the schools. Where once there had been a clear sense of purpose about educational goals, now there was uncertainty. The educational pendulum began to swing back toward a revival of progressivism. When the new progressivism burst forth in the mid-1960s, it sought to combine a critique of schools and a critique of society. It grew out of a bitter reaction against the inadequacies of American public schools in educating minority children and a profound hostility to the typical public school's commitment to such values as competition and order. It blamed American society for the persistence of racism and inequality; it blamed the bureaucratic nature of the educational system for failing to respond to children as individuals; it blamed the teaching profession for serving its own interests instead of the interests of children.

The rise of the new progressivism mirrored the social and political trends of the time and grew in response to racial unrest, antiwar sentiment, and student activism. While the new progressivism was eventually well supported by government and foundations, and its influence affected many public and private schools, its chief product was a substantial body of educational protest literature. The forerunner of the new movement was A. S. Neill's *Summerhill,* which appeared in 1960, the very time when post-Sputnik pressures to raise academic standards were widespread, an unfortuitous moment for a book celebrating the virtues of permissiveness. One of the book's few reviews came from Margaret Mead, who called it "a ghost of the 1920s" and worried that it might "set off a wave of uncritical behavior among a new class of parents just emerging into a literate interest in pedagogy."[12]

Despite Mead's dismissal, *Summerhill*—an autobiographical, anecdotal account of Neill's libertarian boarding school in England—was destined to become a classic of educational radicalism. Directly challenging the discipline that characterized traditional schools, Neill held that the child "is innately wise and realistic. If left to himself without adult suggestion of any kind, he will develop as far as he is capable of developing." At Summerhill, children did not have to attend classes unless they wanted to, and Neill was quite willing to wait until they wanted to; one of his students, he proudly noted, lived at Summerhill for thirteen years without ever going to a single lesson. "Parents are slow in realizing how unimportant the learning side of school is," wrote Neill. "Children, like adults, learn what they want to learn. All prize-giving and marks and exams sidetrack proper personality development. . . . All that any child needs is the three R's; the rest should be tools and clay and sports and theater and paint and freedom." These echoes from an earlier strain of American progressivism had scant resonance in 1960, at a time when American educators were striving to meet the public's demands for excellence. But by 1969, in a changed atmosphere, *Summerhill* was selling at the rate of more than two hundred thousand copies a year.[13]

Summerhill was soon followed by a plethora of scathing critiques of the American school. In *Compulsory Mis-Education,* Paul Goodman (an admirer of Neill's) attacked compulsory education and argued that the prolongation of schooling for adolescents "is psychologically, politically, and professionally damaging." Adolescents are "herded into" schools, where they are "brainwashed," bribed, and pressured, subdued, policed, and regimented. In place of this destructive, standardized system, Goodman suggested several alternatives: attendance should be voluntary, as at Summerhill; some children should have no school at all; some classes should use the city's resources as a school; unlicensed adults in the community should be engaged as educators; big urban schools should be decentralized into small units of twenty to fifty children and housed in storefronts or clubhouses. He believed that schools should be "havens for those scholarly by disposition" and that the nonscholarly majority should get job training and learn about life outside the school, in real-life situations.[14]

In 1967, criticism of the schools—and in particular, urban schools in black neighborhoods—reached a crescendo with the publication of Jonathan Kozol's *Death at an Early Age* and Herbert Kohl's *36 Children.* The two young men, former classmates at Harvard, became elementary school teachers, Kozol in Boston, Kohl in New York City. Kozol, whose book won the National Book Award, recounted a year in a school where the teachers were racist, cruel, and contemptuous of the children. Kohl described a year of teaching in which he set aside the sterile prescribed curriculum and encouraged the children to express themselves through creative writing.[15]

In the dozens of critical books published about the schools during the late 1960s, several types emerged: the account of the public school principal struggling against an uncaring society and bureaucratic system to educate black children (Nat Hentoff, *Our Children Are Dying*); the memoirs of the articulate young teacher who triumphs over his principal, the other teachers, and the system by treating his pupils as human beings (James Herndon, *The Way It Spozed to Be* and *How to Survive in Your Native Land*); the experiences of the dedicated radical who defies the public schools and social convention by creating an experimental private school, which is impecunious but educationally exciting (George Dennison, *The Lives of Children;* Steve Bhaerman and Joel Denker, *No Particular Place to Go*); the reflections of the teacher who has realized that the curriculum and the methods of the school actually crush the joy of learning (John Holt, *Why Children Fail*); the polemic by the journalist who discovers that education must be an extension of the human potential movement, a means to achieve moments of ecstasy (George Leonard, *Education and Ecstasy*), or by the educator who declares that intellectual goals must make way for "affective education," directed to students' feelings and attitudes (Terry Borton, *Reach, Touch and Teach: Student Concerns and Process Education*).[16]

The indictment of the school was overwhelming. In the eyes of the critics, the school destroyed the souls of children, whether black or white, middle-class or poor. It coerced unwilling youths to sit through hours of stultifying classes, breaking their spirits before turning them out as either rebellious misfits or conforming cogs in the great industrial machine. It neglected the needs of individuals while slighting the history and culture of diverse minorities. It clung to a boring, irrelevant curriculum and to methods that obliterated whatever curiosity children brought with them. It drove away creative teachers and gave tenure to petty martinets. For those who agreed with the critics, there was no alternative other than to change the schools or to abandon them.

As the school became the focus of criticism for everyone who found fault with American society or the American character, a consensus developed among education policy makers in government and foundations. The schools, went the new consensus, needed to be changed radically. The long-heralded "revolution in the schools," prophesied only a few years earlier, had not come to pass; teaching machines, team teaching, nongraded classrooms, and even the curriculum reforms supported by the National Science

Foundation had not brought about the dramatic improvement that was anticipated. The new curricula, like the "new math" and the "new science," were conceived when the nation demanded excellence and were designed to stimulate the interest of college-bound youth; only a half dozen years later, the new curricula were seen as solving yesterday's problem. In terms of the current crisis, they were no longer relevant. They offered little promise of erasing racial inequality and none at all of radically transforming the school and the society. Thus the new consensus was founded on belief in the failure of the schools, the uselessness of piecemeal reforms like curriculum change, and the necessity for sweeping change. Every new idea had a constituency, whether it was racial balancing of schools, parent participation, black community control, or anything else that promised to break the grip of traditional practice. The courts began to order busing, the Ford Foundation supported demonstrations of community control in minority neighborhoods in New York City, the federal government funded scores of experimental programs. The underlying assumptions in the various approaches were, first, that there was little in the schools worth preserving; second, that anything innovative was bound to be better than whatever it replaced; third, that the pathology of the schools was so grave that the only change worth attempting must be of a fundamental, institutional, systemic kind; and fourth, that the way to change society and to turn it against war and racism was to change (or abandon) the schools.

It was in this atmosphere that a variety of new movements for educational change developed, distinguished from one another largely by the extent to which they assumed that the public schools could be "saved" or were even worth saving. The "open education movement," which achieved national prominence in the late 1960s and early 1970s, aimed to reform public schools by changing the methods and goals of schooling. The "free school movement," which emerged during the same period, consisted of a loose network of private schools animated by Summerhillian principles, aware of each other, hostile to traditional methods, and committed to radical politics. The "alternative schools movement" was an effort to bring some of the principles of the free schools into the public schools, in order to reduce student discontent. The "deschooling movement," which was stimulated by Ivan Illich's book *Deschooling Society,* was not so much an educational movement as it was a literary sensation. Its practical effect was to lend support to the fast-growing assumption that out-of-school activities were equal in educational value, and perhaps actually superior, to in-school activities. None of these movements was isolated from the others;

they shared certain assumptions about the failure of the existing public schools, the corruptness of American society, and the need to adopt radical changes in school and society.

These movements and ideologies gained their greatest success at the same time that belief in the egalitarian potential of compensatory education faltered. Quickly developed in response to the racial turmoil of the mid-1960s, the Great Society educational reforms were oversold; extravagant claims were made—in part to pass legislation and in part to gain political credit for the new programs—that federal intervention in education would eliminate the achievement gap between white and black children and that poor children who participated in preschool Head Start programs would enter regular school on a par with middle-class children. That neither the knowledge nor the experience existed to fulfill such promises did not become apparent until 1969, when two critiques dashed hopes that education alone could end inequality and end it quickly. One was the Westinghouse assessment of Head Start, which concluded that the initial gains made by poor children in preschool programs were washed out in subsequent years; the other was a controversial article by educational psychologist Arthur Jensen, who argued that the genetic limitations of blacks explained why "compensatory education has been tried and it apparently has failed." While both Jensen and the Westinghouse study were vigorously rebutted, their effect nonetheless was to dampen the enthusiasm of those who believed that more money and more schooling would produce a leveling-up of society.[17]

Yet for most radical critics of American schools, especially those who agreed with writers like A. S. Neill and Paul Goodman, the outcome of compensatory education was never a live issue, for it promised only to place minority students into a soul-deadening mainstream. What mattered to the radical critics was that even in supposedly successful schools with high test scores and good college admission records, students were expected to produce "right" answers, to compete against each other, to conform, and to acquiesce to the demands of the school system, in preparation for similar demands from the larger social system. The problem with the schools, the critics believed, was not just their curricula or their textbooks or their methods—none of which the critics liked—but their repressive nature, their demands for conformity. These critics were indifferent to reforms that attempted to raise test scores because such reforms did nothing to change the essential character of American education or American society.

In this climate of scorn, disappointment, and despair about American schools, Joseph Featherstone's articles in the *New Republic* about the

British infant schools caused a minor sensation. In three articles in August and September, 1967, Featherstone reported "a profound and sweeping revolution in English primary education, involving new ways of thinking about how young children learn, classroom organization, the curriculum, and the role of the teacher." His straightforward, graphic, and admiring account of classrooms where children were busily and happily learning presented a sharp contrast to the current reputation of American schools. Featherstone's articles publicized the findings of Britain's Plowden Commission, which ringingly endorsed the activity-centered infant school. Within a year after Featherstone's articles appeared, the magazine sold one hundred thousand offprints, and the British model (which Featherstone referred to offhandedly as "the free day," the "integrated curriculum," or the "integrated day") became the talk of American education.[18]

Featherstone described a typical day at the Westfield Infant School in Leicestershire County. Early in the day, even before the teachers arrive, the children (ages five to seven) are "reading, writing, painting, playing music, tending to pets." Children work (and play) individually or in small groups, rarely as an entire class. The classroom is noisy, because the children move about and talk freely. Children learning and playing flow back and forth among the classroom, hallway, and playground. There are no assigned places, rather there are well-equipped tables and activity areas for art, number work, sand and water play, quiet reading, a play corner with dolls and furniture. The routine of the day "is left completely up to the teacher, and the teacher, in turn, leaves options open to the children. . . . [T]here is no real difference between one subject in the curriculum and another, or even between work and play." Not only is the children's writing profuse and fluent, but the older children teach the younger ones how to read. The teacher who oversees all of this purposeful activity "sometimes sits at her desk, and the children flock to her for consultations, but more often she moves about the room advising on projects, listening to children read, asking questions, giving words, talking, sometimes prodding." The essential ingredient in the success of the British infant school, Featherstone concluded, was the teacher's belief "that in a rich environment young children can learn a great deal by themselves and that most often their own choices reflect their needs."

The impetus for the new methods, Featherstone believed, came about in part because the children involved were very young, and the infant schools were separate institutions; infant school teachers were trained together with nursery school teachers, and their "subject matter," in effect, was the development of the individual child, how he learns and grows. The best practice, he held, reflected developmental psychologist Jean Piaget's influence, particularly his belief that "children learn to think in stages, and that in the early stages they learn mainly from the testimony of their senses, and not so much through words." Thus, the emphasis in the infant school on concrete experience and activity. Another important element in the shift to individual learning was the influence of the government inspectors, who in many English counties had functioned as educational advisory agents, disseminating new ideas and training new teachers in progressive practices.

Before the publication of Featherstone's articles, there was a handful of Americans trying to adapt the methods of the British infant school to American schools. As news of the "revolution" in the British primary schools got out, more and more educators saw the British model as a potential answer to the urgent need for a reliable-but-revolutionary innovation. The British model offered everything: learning activities were individualized and based on play and experience; teaching was informal and responded to children's needs and interests; the children were learning, and they enjoyed school. British practices struck a responsive chord in part because they encompassed the tenets of America's own educational progressivism: that children learn at different rates; that children want to learn; that the best way to motivate learning is through projects, experiences, and activities; that, for children, the distinction between "work" and "play" is false; that division of knowledge into subjects is artificial; and that such external stimuli as grades and tests cannot compare to the power of the child's own interest. For American educators who had been brought up on the progressive creed of Dewey, Kilpatrick, and Rugg, the British "integrated day" sounded a familiar melody which had been drowned out by the attacks of academic critics and the hysteria of the post-Sputnik era. Young teachers who abhorred the "authoritarianism" of the traditional school saw in the British concept the possibility of infusing the classroom with a humane and democratic spirit. Part of its instant mass appeal was the fact that it offered so much to so many different audiences.

At some point, the approach that Featherstone described was christened "open education," and its fortunes soared as faith in the promise of compensatory education plummeted. Little more than three years after his articles appeared, open education experienced a meteoric success. State education departments, federal agencies, teacher-training institutions, magazines, network commentators, foundations, and individual educators flocked to its banner. In cities and towns across the nation, school officials knocked down the walls between classrooms or designed their new buildings without walls. In 1970, when the New York State Department of Education held a one-day conference on open education, more than two thousand teachers attended. In 1968, only about thirty articles mentioning the British primary reforms were published in the United States, but by 1971, the number had grown to over three hundred. The near-evangelistic appeal of open education created a boom in transatlantic travel; by 1969, study teams from twenty American cities made the pilgrimage to England to learn first-hand about informal education.[19]

Because the principles of open education attracted support across a wide spectrum, efforts to disseminate it were diverse. In the highly compressed history of open education, one of the pioneer practitioners was Lillian Weber, a professor at the City College of New York. Weber spent eighteen months observing British infant schools in 1965/66; she began the Open Corridor Program in the fall of 1967 in a Harlem public school. Working with teachers who volunteered, she brought together four or five classrooms, linked by a common corridor, as a school-within-a-school; she showed teachers how to encourage interaction among different age levels and to replace whole-group instruction with individual and small-group lessons. Weber sought "a minimum of changes, taking hints from the scale and intimacy in English schools." Word of her understated approach and good working relationships with teachers spread, and the program was requested by several other public schools. In 1969, Weber established an advisory service to help teachers implement open education methods. Within a few years, the advisory center was conducting summer institutes, publishing a journal, and receiving funding from the federal government and the Ford Foundation. Its major purpose was to provide support and reinforcement for teachers interested in open education.[20]

Significant efforts to teach open education were made by such colleges and universities as the Bank Street College of Education, Wheelock College, Newton College, the University of Connecticut, the University of Illinois, and the University of Colorado. By far the most effective university-based program for disseminating open education was developed at the University of North Dakota. A statewide study had found that 59 percent of all elementary school teachers lacked a college degree and that the state ranked fiftieth in the nation in the educational level of its elementary teachers. A member of the state study committee had read Featherstone's articles on the British primary school, and the committee agreed that upgrading the credentials of so many teachers offered the opportunity to train a new kind of teacher with a new outlook and new methods. To pursue that goal, the University of North Dakota created the New School of Behavioral Studies in Education in 1968. Headed by Vito Perrone, an advocate of open education, the New School set up a teacher-swap, sending graduate students to district schools as interns while the regular teachers attended the

New School. Both teachers and interns were trained in the theory and practice of open education. Because of its experimentation with new methods of training teachers, the New School received substantial federal funding.[21]

Probably the most influential source of thinking and practice on the subject of open education emanated from an unusual network of individuals and institutions clustered about the Shady Hill School in Cambridge, Massachusetts, and the Education Development Center (EDC) in Newton, Massachusetts. Shady Hill was a private progressive school, founded in 1915, and EDC was a major, federally funded regional laboratory for the improvement of education. As ideas and individuals flowed from one institution to the other, a link was forged between the old progressivism and the new progressivism, and between the post-Sputnik curriculum reformers and the advocates of open education.

Teachers at Shady Hill included William Hull, who had become enthusiastic about the practices of British infant schools after a visit to Leicestershire County in 1961; Hull's teaching assistant, John Holt; and David Armington, who visited Leicestershire with Hull in 1962. Subsequently, Armington worked at EDC (as did his wife, a former headmistress of a British infant school), and Holt left teaching to devote full time to writing critically about American schools. In the early 1960s, Hull, Holt, and Armington met frequently to discuss education and children's thinking. Their discussions were joined for a time by Anthony Kallet, a Shady Hill teacher who visited Leicestershire schools in 1963 and stayed on for ten years, maintaining a lively correspondence with his friends at Shady Hill about informal practices in British schools. It was Hull who suggested to Joseph Featherstone in 1966 that he travel to Leicestershire, where he visited Kallet and observed infant schools.[22]

EDC grew out of an organization called Educational Services Incorporated (ESI), which had been created in 1958 as a vehicle for disseminating and testing the PSSC secondary school physics course, the first NSF-funded new curriculum. In the early 1960s, ESI received additional support from NSF to develop a new elementary science curriculum called the Elementary Science Study (ESS). Like other scientists engaged in curriculum reform, David Hawkins, the director of ESS, believed that children should learn science by doing science, not by being told about science. Hawkins was responsive to progressive methods, in part because his wife had been a teacher in a progressive school in California in the 1930s. Hawkins's writings became classics among supporters of open education.[23]

One of the schools selected to try out ESS materials was Shady Hill. By the mid-1960s, the connections between Shady Hill and ESS were many. William Hull circulated Anthony Kallet's letters from Leicestershire to ESS staff, keeping them informed about the new methods in Britain, and ESS produced mathematical materials designed by Hull. ESS staff, including Hawkins, exchanged visits with educators from Leicestershire. Years later, Hawkins recalled that his trip to England came at a time when he felt disillusioned about the minimal effect of the NSF-funded curricula in high school science. In England, he and his wife, Frances, saw schools where teachers "were really doing the kind of thing that Frances had been trying to do in the thirties. That had great influence on us. In particular, I don't think that we saw anything that we couldn't have seen in San Francisco in a few classrooms in the thirties, but here it was widely practiced with lots of perceptive professional support. And that was something that hadn't existed in San Francisco."[24]

The curriculum developed at ESS consisted of a series of units which used concrete materials—both everyday objects and special equipment—to demonstrate the process of scientific thinking rather than "right answers." The curricula prepared previously for high school science students were tightly organized, logically sequenced, and supposedly "teacher-proof." The ESS units were intended to be used by individual students, in no special order, and to encourage what British infant school proponents called "messing about." Ironically, while NSF curriculum development had begun in the strongly cognitive, antiprogressive spirit of the late 1950s, the curriculum developers at ESS followed the concepts of "inquiry" and "discovery" full circle back to the progressive tradition. And the more they expected to revolutionize the classroom by introducing their new curricula, the more frustrated they were by the structure and values of the typical classroom. When they saw how teachers converted their carefully conceived experiments into verbalized, abstract lessons in skills instead of letting students use them to explore freely, the ESS scientists despaired of their ability to transport the culture of science into the school as it existed.[25]

By the mid-1960s, the ESS staff had become convinced that the production of new curricula was too limited a goal. Their hothouse discussions with innovative educators, their trips abroad, their exchanges with British practitioners, their grounding in progressive educational philosophy (both British and American) made them impatient with what now seemed to be merely piecemeal reform. In an internal memorandum at ESS, Hull noted that some staff had come to realize that a new science curriculum would change little unless there was "a revolution in the underlying assumptions which would permit basic changes in classroom organization. . . . It is now clearer than ever that there cannot be good science, or good anything else, in classrooms without basic changes in attitudes and expectations."[26]

Believing that its mission should be to act as a catalyst for large-scale institutional change, ESS asked NSF in 1964 to fund a teacher-training project whose object would be to spread innovative practices and break the school's reliance on the textbook and rote learning. NSF, which was authorized by Congress to underwrite scientific research and development, not organizational reform, turned down the request. A similar proposal by ESS to the U.S. Office of Education was also turned down. When federal funds became available in 1965, ESS and its parent organization became part of EDC, a new federal regional laboratory. Headed by a British educator from Leicestershire, EDC took a leading role in promoting open education, by sponsoring workshops, providing an advisory service for teachers, and preparing instructional materials for open classrooms. EDC received a major contract to administer a Follow Through program for post–Head Start children, based on the principles of open education. EDC ran British Infant School Model projects in Laurel, Delaware; Chicago; Washington, D.C.; Paterson, New Jersey; Philadelphia; Rosebud, Texas; Lackawanna County, Pennsylvania; Johnston County, North Carolina; and Burlington, Vermont. The projects stressed informal methods, physical reorganization of the classroom, provisioning of the classroom with manipulative materials, and other features of the British model. Over time, however, the emphasis faded as the original directors departed, teachers came and went, and the federal government began to demand evaluations based on standardized tests.[27]

Clearly, the movement toward open education was fueled by enthusiastic advocates who believed that it could transform American education. Yet, while there was vigorous activity in many cities and towns across the nation, the number of teachers trained to run an open classroom or of school board members who had heard of the British model was relatively small. Some leaders of the movement, like Lillian Weber, thought that it was best to grow slowly and to build understanding from the ground up. But in the nature of things, at least in American education, a new and exciting trend is rarely allowed to go unheralded for long, and such was the case with open education. In 1970, open education received the kind of publicity that turned it into a Movement with a capital M.

In May, 1970, Beatrice and Ronald Gross introduced readers of the *Saturday Review* to open education. In their account, they went further than Featherstone on some crucial matters. Where Featherstone had specified that British infant schools were for children ages five to seven, the Grosses stated that the new practices were appropriate for children between the ages of five and twelve. Where Featherstone pointed out that

Piaget's views about how children learn were theories, the Grosses asserted that Piaget "proved that it is a waste of time to tell a child things that the child cannot experience through his senses." Where Featherstone had cited Piaget's belief that learning moves in stages from concrete experiences to abstract thinking, the Grosses wrote, "Piaget is critical of classrooms where the teacher is the dominant figure, where books and the teacher's talking are basic instructional media, and where large group instruction is the rule, and oral or written tests are used to validate the whole process." When children in need of stimulation are subjected to such an environment, they held, their minds may be damaged or "actually atrophy." These embellishments and simplifications of complicated pedagogical issues were symptomatic: open education was being turned into a crusade, an object of faith for true believers, capable of "saving" American education.[28]

A few months later, Charles Silberman's best-selling *Crisis in the Classroom* projected open education into the public limelight as nothing previously had done. An accomplished journalist, Silberman had been invited by the Carnegie Corporation of New York to prepare a study of teacher education. But Silberman saw another story breaking and, with his keen intuition, captured the zeitgeist of the late 1960s. He sought out the people who were in the forefront of innovative pedagogical activity, and he found that their thinking converged on the British model. His book brought open education to a vast public, in part because he had the imprimatur of the prestigious Carnegie Corporation behind his recommendations, but more because he was able to write, as few in the education profession could, in a powerful, vivid, and graceful style.[29]

Others had lauded the British model because, compared to traditional didactic methods, it seemed to be more enjoyable for students and teachers, better suited to the learning styles of different children, and more attuned to the way children think: in short, a better way of learning and teaching. Silberman put the case for informal education in a far broader context. It was not just the schools that were in a state of crisis, he noted; American society as a whole was gripped by a sense of disaster and an "apocalyptic vision. . . . [A] new consensus of anxiety seems to have taken hold of the nation." Much of this anxiety stemmed from the realization that many of the young did not accept the authority of the older generation, nor care much for its accumulated knowledge. Citing a recent poll of young people, Silberman warned that as many as 40 percent of college students sympathized with radicalism (a figure far higher than the findings of other polls), and that "dissent and alienation [were] moving rapidly into the high school and even the junior high." He pointed to the large rock festivals in the summer of 1969 as evidence of "the reservoir of alienation that may lie beneath the surface."[30]

Silberman argued that the national crisis "may well be a religious or spiritual crisis of a depth and magnitude that has no parallel since the Reformation." Yet in the face of this profound upheaval shaking American society, the nation's educating institutions—its schools and colleges, churches, newspapers, magazines, television stations, and networks—had all failed. None was adequate to the needs of the present or the future. What was to be done? The problem of the collapse of "meaning and purpose in our lives, in our society, and in our world" was to be addressed by a "transformation of the schools." Like that of many a reformer in the past, Silberman's diagnosis of the ills of society turned quickly into a treatise on the ills of the public schools and how to cure them.[31]

Silberman's opinion of the public schools concurred with the most extreme views of the radical critics of the late 1960s. American schools, he complained, were "grim, joyless places . . . oppressive and petty . . . intellectually sterile and esthetically barren," preoccupied above all with "order and control," demanding "docility and conformity." The curriculum was characterized by "banality and triviality": "Much of what is taught is not worth knowing as a child, let alone as an adult, and little will be remembered." The blame for this terrible, repressive institution lay not with the teachers, who were on the whole rather decent, well-meaning people; no, the "central problem" of American schools was "mindlessness," the fact that so few people in the schools took time "to think seriously or deeply about the purposes or consequences of education." "Mindlessness" accounted for

> the preoccupation with order and control, the slavish adherence to the timetable and lesson plan, the obsession with routine qua routine, the absence of noise and movement, the joylessness and repression, the universality of the formal lecture or teacher-dominated "discussion" in which the teacher instructs an entire class as a unit, the emphasis of the verbal and de-emphasis of the concrete, the inability of students to work on their own, the dichotomy between work and play. . . .[32]

The antidote to the crisis in the classroom was "the new English primary schools." Like so many others, Silberman had gone to England and come back a missionary for informal education. In a chapter of his book titled "It Can Happen Here," he detailed the activities of such American practitioners as Lillian Weber of New York and Vito Perrone of North Dakota. But, while other champions of informal education limited their proposed reforms to the early years, Silberman extended the same principles to the high school years, which were also afflicted by "mindlessness." Like the elementary school, the high school needed a complete revamping and an infusion of student freedom. In the high school programs he admiringly described, students had a large measure of freedom in deciding which courses to take, which courses would be offered, whether to receive grades or some other kind of evaluation, how to spend large blocks of unscheduled time, how to dress and groom themselves, and whether to leave the school building for lunch.[33]

Crisis in the Classroom had a dramatic effect on the fortunes of informal education. Silberman did what none of the previous advocates of the British model had attempted: he universalized open education. It was not just that Silberman brought the story of open education to a large popular audience. Silberman transformed the British model from a teaching method appropriate for young children into a philosophy directed to all educational institutions and all age groups; he elevated it from a pedagogical approach into an ideology about children, learning, and schooling that was intended to revive society and the quality of life in America. Though Silberman warned that informal education was not a panacea for all educational ills, it was difficult to read his enthusiastic promotion of the British model without seeing it as the answer to the alienation, anomie, and other social ills that Silberman so eloquently described. Similarly, while he warned that it would be wrong for Americans to make the mistake of swinging too far in the direction of child-centered schools, his strictures on the need for balance were outweighed by his fervent endorsement of child-centered methods and child-centered ideas.

Silberman both reported the growing groundswell of interest in open education and added to it. By the time his book appeared, open education had already found a committed following; it was perceived as a pedagogical innovation well suited to the age of student disaffection and protest because it stressed participation, freedom, and feelings, while downplaying tradition, authority, and structured teaching. The New York State commissioner of education, Ewald B. Nyquist, publicly endorsed open education, saying that it offered "unique opportunities for humanizing and individualizing learning, making it relevant, meaningful, and personally satisfying." He described it as "person-centered, idea-centered, experience-centered, problem-oriented, and interdisciplinary," in contrast to traditional education with its "information-gathering, fact-centered, course-centered, subject-centered, grade-getting, and bell-interrupted activity." Under Nyquist's leadership, the state education department sponsored teacher workshops in open education and convened statewide conferences of teachers and principals to promote its implementation. Beginning in the late 1960s, the Ford Foundation actively promoted open education by subsidizing publications, teacher training projects, and experiments in elementary schools, high schools, and universities. Open education in the elementary school meant that children exercised a large degree of choice in selecting activities and materials; in the high school, like the Parkway School in Philadelphia (a "school-without-walls"), it meant that students used the city and its institutions as their classrooms and were freed from the usual subject-matter requirements; at the university level, it meant a significant increase in off-campus learning, independent study, student-designed courses, and unstructured programs.[34]

Open education was an idea whose time had come, and there was no shortage of enthusiasm for it. The problem, which became more acute as enthusiasm grew, was defining it. After Silberman, books and articles about open education proliferated, and each one seemed to define the theory and practice of open education somewhat differently. Some advocates refused to define it, since to practice open education meant, they said, to be flexible, open to new ideas, ready to respond to children's interests, and free from predetermined lesson plans. But other advocates believed that it would be impossible to disseminate open educational practice without giving teachers some reliable examples of what to do and how to teach. So, one focus of proponents of open education was simply to try to explain what it was, how to do it, and how to evaluate it.

Its advocates tended to define it in terms of what it was not, which accounted for much of its appeal to those seeking to disassociate themselves from the old, discredited ways of teaching: it was not traditional; it was not achieved by merely removing walls; it was not the same as team teaching, individualized instruction (which relied on preprogrammed materials), or nongraded classes. One researcher, after trying to explain why open education seemed so vague and formless, concluded that the best way to define it was to observe an open classroom.[35]

Others, however, did try to rationalize it and showed, despite disclaimers to the contrary, that open education was not "open" to every educational strategy, or at least not to methods associated with traditional practice. One advocate, Charles H. Rathbone, explained the open classroom in terms of *how* children learn (through their own experience) and *what* they learn (only what they themselves experience). To Rathbone, the fundamental concepts of open education were, first, that every child is "a self-activated maker of meaning, an active agent in his own learning process . . . a self-reliant, independent, self-actualizing individual"; and, second, that there is no "inherently indispensable body of knowledge that every single child should know." Knowledge, in his view, comes only from personal experience, and no two people have the same experience: "Thus, what two children carry in their heads as 'chair' or 'aunt' or 'black' will never be absolutely identical."[36]

Proponents of open education envisaged a new role for the teacher in the open classroom as a "facilitator" of the child's experiences rather than as a transmitter of knowledge. The role of the teacher in such a classroom, wrote Rathbone, was not to provide either answers or questions but to observe the child, to anticipate his needs, and to provide opportunities for the child to find his own questions and answers. "This means that in open education the teacher is mainly *assistant to* not *director of* the child's activity." Both Rathbone and John Holt endorsed the idea that the teacher was like a travel agent, helping the child go where the child wants to go.[37]

Another prolific proponent of open education was Roland S. Barth, who published several articles in 1969 and 1970 describing British informal practices as grounds for "a revolution" in American education. In his book *Open Education and the American School,* Barth compiled a list of twenty-nine assumptions shared by open educators about children and learning. For example, open educators assume that: "children are innately curious and will explore without adult intervention"; "if a child is fully involved in and having fun with an activity, learning is taking place"; "objective measures of performance may have a negative effect on learning"; "there is no minimum body of knowledge which is essential for everyone to know." From these assumptions, Barth concluded that

> open education has no curriculum. . . . In a real sense, children's own experiences are the subject matter—the content—of their learning. These experiences are good and bad, productive and nonproductive, pleasant and unpleasant. Open educators worry less about whether a child has had a particular experience than about the quality and meaning for him of the experiences he has had. It is for time and future experience to assess the significance of a student's experience, not for the adult to judge.[38]

However, Barth's own experience tempered his initial zeal. He participated in a disastrous effort to introduce open education in a small, almost all black, urban school. Supported as a demonstration by the school system, a university, and foundation funds, the project was riddled with problems: the staff was overloaded with specialists; the old and new teachers regarded each other with suspicion; the school had unstable leadership. Meanwhile, the open educators were astonished to discover that the children did not welcome the opportunity to explore freely and make their own decisions; instead, they became disruptive and "ganged up by tens and twenties outside the bathrooms and at the water fountains." Fearful of choices, they became "merciless in their demands for teacher-imposed order." Before long, the new teachers began clutching at traditional practices; "they set up reading groups and introduced basal texts, required seats, and homework." Especially disheartening to the experimental teachers was the negative attitude of parents, who complained about the permissiveness of the teachers and the noisiness of the classrooms. As one parent explained to a teacher, "You have had a certain kind of educational experience . . . teacher as source of knowledge and control, child as respectful and obedient responder, and you made it. If our children have the same kind of educational experience, *they too* will make it." By the end of the school year, all of the open educators had quit or were dismissed.[39]

Open classrooms ran into difficulty, but nonetheless the spirit of innovation spread rapidly. Nearly three years after the publication of his book, Charles Silberman wrote that "hardly a day has gone by . . . and certainly not a week, in which I have not heard of another teacher, or group of teachers, or school, or school system that is moving (or thinking about moving) in the directions I proposed and described." Indeed, it was not only the open classroom, however it was defined, that was gaining in influence in the early 1970s; schools large and small, in big cities and small towns, were adopting educational innovations advocated by school reformers. Typically, such innovations emphasized the students' role in selecting their own activities; the introduction of student-designed and student-taught courses; the elimination of traditional high school graduation requirements; the replacement of traditional subject-matter courses with courses and mini-courses organized around student interests; expansion of the number of courses and activities available to the student; flexible scheduling; de-emphasis or elimination of letter grades; random or mixed-ability grouping of children, instead of grouping by age or ability; academic credit for off-campus programs, community involvement, and nontraditional study.[40]

That there was a pragmatic basis to such changes was apparent. The extraordinary stress in the society outside the schools had created nearly intolerable strains within many schools in terms of student resistance to traditional authority. As authority in the larger society eroded, authority in the schools also came under attack; discipline problems increased, as did truancy and vandalism. When the Gallup organization began its annual opinion poll about public education in 1969, lack of discipline was identified as the leading problem of the schools. Many schools adopted innovative programs with the hope that a loosening of academic demands, a more relaxed relationship with teachers, and a curriculum more relevant to contemporary social issues would pacify student discontent, improve student behavior, and reduce truancy. Such changes were also attractive to many of the younger teachers, who had been college students in the mid-1960s and shared their generation's ambivalence about the exercise of adult authority. However, the loosening of adult authority only exacerbated the public's perception that lack of discipline was the most important problem in the schools and contributed to the steady decline of public confidence in the schools during the 1970s.[41]

School critics disagreed on whether the public school was salvageable. Those who thought there was still hope embraced open education, while those who thought the public schools were beyond salvation set out to create the "free school movement," entirely outside the reach of the public schools. Beginning in the mid-1960s, these parent-controlled, privately financed "free schools" were developed by people who had participated in the civil rights movement, the New Left, and the counterculture. There was a fringe even beyond the "free school movement" which opposed the institution of the school altogether as an oppressive social device that unjustly monopolized the power to assign people to social roles, to discriminate against those who do not hold its credentials, and to make them dependent on its degrees for future advancement. The idea of "deschooling," put forth by the radical priest Ivan Illich, was widely discussed when it first appeared in 1970, but it had little practical effect other than to give momentary impetus to interest in lowering the compulsory schooling age. Since Illich attacked even the free school movement, because it shared the conventional assumption "that social man needs a school if he is to be born" while reinforcing "the dominant system of compulsory knowledge," he found few allies to support his proposal for disestablishing schools and permitting people to devise their own "learning webs."[42]

While "deschooling" proved to be a rhetorical phenomenon rather than an educational movement, the free school movement grew out of the dissident political and social activism of the 1960s. As Ann Swidler points out in her study *Organization Without Authority: Dilemmas of Social Control in Free Schools,* the free schools were "only the most visible of a whole collection of alternative organizations," such as free clinics and legal collectives and communes, created by countercultural groups. "What united these diverse organizations was their rejection of authority as a valid principle for regulating group life." The free schools shared an information network called the New Schools Exchange, which published a newsletter, a directory of innovative schools, books, and position papers. Far more than the open education movement, which adapted to the bureaucratic, institutional requirements of the public schools, the free schools were the inheritors of the libertarian Summerhillian spirit. What this meant in practice, in the words of free school advocate Allen Graubard, was "doing away with all of the public school apparatus of imposed disciplines and punishments, lock-step age gradings and time-period divisions, homework, frequent tests and grades and report cards, rigid graded curriculum, standardized classrooms, dominated and commanded by one teacher with 25 to 35 students under his or her power." According to Graubard, the number of free schools grew rapidly during the late 1960s and early 1970s, reaching perhaps five hundred by 1972. The average free school had an enrollment of about thirty-three students, which meant that less than twenty thousand children attended a free school during this period.[43]

Free schools were an expression of both political and cultural radicalism. One free school guidebook was dedicated to "the millions of children still in prison in the United States and to the handful of adults trying to spring them." The authors observed that "it is a revolutionary act to be involved in a free school. Saying 'no' to the heart of a culture—their schools—and establishing an alternative system for learning is an explicit rejection of a *set* of beliefs, and the web of premises, myths, rituals —the underlying faith—that goes with a *set* of beliefs." In free schools, Swidler writes, "Adults allow children to explore their environment, to discover what they themselves want to learn, to play, make noise, move around, or even do nothing. But what is really distinctive about these schools is not so much their pedagogy or educational philosophy as their purpose: they are designed as models of a new kind of society. They abolish authority relations between teachers and students—not simply to educate children better but to create a new sort of human being and a new model of cooperative social life."[44]

The quest for ideological solidarity drew adherents to the free schools, but ideological conflicts split and destroyed the parent-run free schools at a dizzying rate. One researcher estimated that the average life span of a free school was eighteen months. This high mortality rate was due not so much to the difficulty of financing a complex undertaking as to the nature of free school ideology, which was vulnerable to schisms: it promised divergent ends (freedom and learning) to parents seeking ideological purity and then, because it eschewed leadership and representative democracy as means of governance, lacked mechanisms for resolving conflicts. Sometimes a free school divided between those who were "traditional" libertarians and those who wanted to impose their political radicalism. Sometimes it split between parents who wanted a completely unstructured environment and those who wanted teachers to place some limits on children and to instruct them in reading and writing.[45]

Despite the fact that so few students attended free schools, the existence of the free school movement was treated by the mass media as a major phenomenon, threatening the very survival of the public schools. Public secondary schools felt some of the same demands for change and for student participation that animated the free schools, and many responded by creating alternative schools. Sometimes this was accomplished by splitting up a large high school into "mini-schools," or schools-within-schools, in order to overcome the anonymity of the bureaucratic institution and to bring about closer contact between teachers and students. Typically, however, alternative schools borrowed countercultural mechanisms to achieve traditional goals. They were usually organized as separate institutions for problem students who were likely to drop out of school, including students "who have emotional problems that cause difficulty in a conventional school, students who have high academic ability and who want to learn in a place where they can be creative," and low-achieving students with poorly developed skills. Compared to the traditional high school, the usual secondary alternative school was small in size, its rules were fewer, and students had greater freedom in such matters as selecting courses and teachers, leaving campus, and smoking cigarettes. Close relationships with teachers and counselors were substituted for the customary rules and regulations. Academic credit was available for classroom studies, but also for work-study, participation in community agencies, and independent study. Although traditional subject matter was sometimes offered, classroom studies tended to reflect student interests, such as arts, crafts, political activism, environmentalism, transcendental meditation, and the occult. Instead of letter-grades, students often received written evaluations or pass-fail or credit-no credit assessments.[46]

Still, while alternative schools traced their roots to the countercultural influence of the free school movement, they proved to have staying power because they served a variety of purposes. Some districts saw in the alternative school a rationale for creating a special school for gifted students; others satisfied the complaints of conservative parents by establishing "fundamental" alternative schools that stressed basic skills, dress codes, and patriotism; some called the traditional high school or elementary school an alternative; still others designed interest-centered alternative schools around fine arts, science, physical education, the humanities, or the performing arts. In some districts, like Ann Arbor, Michigan, the alternative high school was an attractively packaged vocational program that placed students in paid and unpaid jobs in the community. In Houston, Texas, district officials replaced their technical and vocational high schools with alternative schools, established an alternative high school to train personnel to meet the needs of the local health-care industry, and set up special alternative schools for those interested in the arts and for the gifted. Despite their origin in the counterculture, the alternative schools became domesticated: successful ones reduced the dropout rate, removed troublesome or unhappy students from traditional schools, and provided programs tailored for the special needs of different groups of students.[47]

The alternative school idea survived because, lacking a definition, it became whatever school boards and principals chose to make of it. The open education movement, however, did not survive *as a movement* because, lacking a definition, it became identified with the ideas and practices of its extremely child-centered advocates, those who zealously opposed whatever was traditional in the structure, content, or methods of the classroom. Their ideological tenets stressed the freedom of the child, the passivity of the teacher, equality between teacher and child, the virtues of play and unstructured activity, and distrust of extrinsic motivation. Open classroom teachers who expected their methods to work as the ideology said it would were in for a rude awakening. Nothing prepared them for criticism from parents and other teachers about the noisiness of their classrooms and the neglect of "basics." They were taken aback when children demanded that teachers take a more active role or asked to learn from a textbook; they did not know how to deal with discipline problems because they were not supposed to have any. Advocates of open education saw the teachers' problems not as a failing of the theory but as a result of the teachers' incomplete commitment to a new way of life.[48]

As early as 1971, some proponents of open education began to warn that it was turning into a fad. Joseph Featherstone reported that of the American informal classrooms he had visited, "the best are as good as anything I've seen in England; the worst are a shambles." Alarmed by the camp followers who belittled skills and discipline, Featherstone wrote, "I'm growing wary of slogans like open education.... Currently I'm seeking to enlist everybody in favor of open, informal schooling into a movement whose one slogan will be a demand for decent schools." Shortly after Roland Barth's book about open education appeared, Barth wrote an article titled, "Should We Forget about Open Education?" in which he complained that open education had become a new orthodoxy and the source of futile ideological battles among teachers. By 1974, Donald A. Myers, who had studied open classrooms in New York State, speculated on "Why Open Education Died." Myers asserted that it was not "a discrete concept but rather a collection of best existing practices." American observers, he complained, failed to see that good teachers in informal British classrooms provided more structure, not less; emphasized the three Rs; and provided a sensible balance between intrinsic and extrinsic motivation. "What is our attraction to play," he wondered, "especially when it is advocated as a vehicle through which students learn cognitive concepts and skills? Why is it difficult for so many American educators to acknowledge that writing a sentence, speaking clearly, playing the piano, or learning inferential statistics, is simply difficult work?"[49]

As disillusionment grew among proponents and laymen, the movement dissipated. The number of articles about open education in professional education journals peaked between 1972 and 1974 and then dwindled rapidly. By the latter date, demands that schools go "back to the basics" had begun to be expressed in school districts across the country. In many districts, the "back to basics" forces blamed programs like open education for lowering academic standards and undermining discipline. By 1975, when the College Entrance Examination Board announced that scores on its Scholastic Aptitude Test had fallen steadily for a decade, experimental programs were on the defensive. Though many open classrooms in elementary schools survived the "back to basics" movement and budget cuts, they did so usually as alternatives available for parents and teachers who chose them rather than as the wave of the future for all American education.[50]

Very likely, the cause of informal education was harmed rather than advanced by its propagandists, who blew it up out of all proportion to the reality of either British or American schools. Some teachers found it a valuable technique, which they used well; others did not. Some children responded well to informal methods; others needed a more structured environment. British teachers understood this far better than did their American admirers. Smitten by British informal methods, American writers portrayed their advance in British schools as though it were a revolutionary contest between the forces of light and the forces of darkness. The reality was different. A 1976 study in Britain concluded that about 17 percent of teachers used informal methods, another 25 percent used formal methods, and the majority used "what have been termed mixed styles, incorporating elements of both formal and informal practice." Contrary to American belief, "a high degree of permissiveness does not appear to be the norm. . . . Teacher control of physical movement and talk is generally high. . . . [E]ight out of ten teachers require their pupils to know their multiplication tables by heart." Similarly, a national survey conducted in 1978 by the British Inspectorate concluded that while most teachers varied their teaching method according to the circumstances, about three-quarters of the primary teachers "employed a mainly didactic approach, while less than one in twenty relied mainly on an exploratory approach."[51]

British scholars have challenged the simplistic notion that teachers can be easily divided between progressives and traditionalists; most, it turns out, use a variety of teaching styles. Nor is it at all obvious that individualization necessarily promotes student-directed "discovery" learning. Brian Simon, codirector of a major research study of primary schools in England, observed that while there was a "fundamental change" in primary schools, it is "extremely doubtful" that "it ever amounted to anything which might be called a revolution." Simon reported that a large-scale observation study of over one hundred primary school classrooms showed that most work was individualized, but most teaching was "didactic in character": "The promotion of enquiry or discovery learning appeared almost nonexistent. . . . Collaborative group work or enquiry was also found to be seldom realized. . . . Further, as regards the content of education, a major emphasis on 'the basics' was also found. . . . Certainly there was little evidence there of any fundamental shift either in the content of education or in the procedures of teaching and learning, in the sense that didacticism still largely prevails."[52]

As the federal government's role in financing public education grew larger, it became a major promoter of innovative practices. To some extent, almost every federal program encouraged local education agencies to do something that they might not otherwise do: to devote increased resources to the special needs of poor children, to monitor and correct racial segregation, to provide career education, to make special provision for non–English-speaking children, to offer free medical services and free lunches to poor children, and so on. Beyond its commitment to equity in the provision of educational services for all children, the federal government actively intervened to prod school districts to move away from traditional methods of teaching and learning. By the early 1970s, about 10 percent of all federal funds for public schools was allocated specifically to promote educational innovations; in 1974, this amounted to about $350 million annually, spent through a wide variety of programs.[53]

Federal policy makers believed that a major cause of the schools' troubles was their rigidity and traditionalism, and that federal dollars should be used to free the schools from existing practices. The lure of federal funds prompted a number of school districts to try innovative practices; the largest single federal "change-agent" program, Title III of the Elementary and Secondary Education Act of 1965, allocated money to states and local districts for "innovative projects" (its annual budget by

1974 was $150 million). Local school districts used Title III funds to initiate open classrooms, team teaching, multi-age grouping, and alternative schools, as well as for inservice training to prepare the staff to implement innovative practices. Federal funds also spurred experiments in teacher education, through such ambitious programs as the Teacher Corps (established in 1965 to recruit idealistic young people into teaching careers) and the Trainers of Teacher Trainers program (which from 1969 to 1974 expended about $40 million on a multitude of innovative activities, such as North Dakota's New School for Behavioral Studies and model open classrooms in Harlem).[54]

In 1970, the Nixon administration launched one of the most ambitious federal efforts to reform the schools. Educational policy makers in the new administration decided that the time had come to "pause and reflect" on the disappointing results of previous reform efforts. They concluded that federal reform programs had thus far failed to produce lasting improvement because: they had fostered piecemeal change with little overall coherence; education reform had been inadequately related to social science research; too much direction had come from the federal and state bureaucracies and not enough initiative from the local school officials; and there had not been enough involvement by the local community. In the end, the Nixon policy makers' conclusions dovetailed with the consensus shared by reform-minded analysts in the foundations and universities. What was needed, they decided, was *comprehensive* change. Toward this end, President Nixon announced the Experimental Schools Program (ESP), which he described, in his March, 1970, message to Congress, as a strategy for building "a bridge between educational research and actual practice." At the same time, the president proposed the creation of the research-oriented National Institute of Education, which later administered ESP.[55]

In order to win funding, local districts had to propose programs of comprehensive change. Although "comprehensive" was never defined, applicants were told that the plan must involve students at all twelve grade levels; must include curriculum, staff development, community involvement, administration, and organization; and must be organized around "a central theme or educational concept that reflects change from what exists at present to what education ought to be in terms of the needs and aspirations of the learners." Because ESP was supposed to use research to identify effective practices, between 25 and 30 percent of program funds were earmarked for research and evaluation. ESP officials planned three different evaluations: an in-house study by the local project staff; a second evaluation by outside social scientists; and a third to synthesize the findings of all the others.[56]

Eventually eighteen districts, both urban and rural, won substantial federal funding. Their proposals reflected the reform ideas and language that were currently in the air. They promised to individualize, to humanize, to stress process instead of product, to retrain teachers to use diagnostic approaches, and to provide learning environments in which every child would experience success. The Minneapolis district won its grant by describing a subsystem of alternative elementary schools that was already either underway or in the planning stages: a traditional school, a "continuous progress" (nongraded) school, an open school, and a free school. The Franklin Pierce district in Pierce County, Washington, pledged to individualize the learning experience of each student by introducing a dozen new curricula and by breaking free of "lock-step" programs, "and the typical regimentation of rigid course offerings, and rigid class schedules." Berkeley, California, won a five-year grant for $7 million by proposing to establish twenty-four alternative schools around the central theme of decreasing institutional racism. Whatever was avant-garde found a place in one of Berkeley's alternative schools. In addition to such standard innovations as nongraded classrooms and peer teaching, Berkeley ESP stressed ethnicity. One program, Black House, was for blacks only; another, Casa de la Raza, was for Chicanos only. Both were subsequently closed by the U.S. Office for Civil Rights for operating as segregated schools. There was a counterculture elementary school and high school, and a multicultural school whose students and faculty were balanced equally among whites, blacks, Chicanos, and Asians.[57]

In terms of the ambitious goals that it set for itself, ESP failed. For the $55 million that was expended over a five-year period, the results were meager. Districts that already intended to innovate, like Minneapolis, continued to do so. Some districts used the funds to help get through a fiscal crisis or to buy needed equipment but showed little evidence of lasting, "comprehensive" change. Of Berkeley's twenty-four alternative schools, only one survived; additionally, the Berkeley ESP diverted attention from the district's previous commitment to total, voluntary desegregation, and layoffs of controversial ESP staff after the program ended plunged the district into bitter wrangling.

The ten rural sites that received ESP money had other kinds of problems, due in part to the unreceptivity of rural districts to rapid change. Teachers resented programs they felt were imposed on them, and internal conflicts undermined many of the projects. In South Umpqua, Oregon, considered one of the most successful projects, the end of the project was followed by a conservative backlash: "many of the ES programs have been discontinued, library books and curriculum materials are now scrutinized by a watchdog committee, a new board has been elected, the superintendent and associate superintendent have left, and the new administration has a mandate to get things back to normal." While some of this backlash was attributable to the times, a federal evaluator concluded that "the swing of the pendulum is greater in South Umpqua because of ESP."[58]

In many districts, the in-house evaluation was useless as an evaluation because of the close association between its authors and local school officials. Several of the professional evaluations commissioned by the National Institute of Education were rejected by the agency as deficient; even the social scientists stumbled on the difficulty of assessing a concept as broad and vague as "comprehensive" change: what could not be defined could not be evaluated. The final, synthesizing evaluation of the entire program was never carried out.

The program failed not because of the backwardness or insincerity of local school officials but because it laid bare the contradictions and vacuousness inherent in much of the contemporary rhetoric of educational reform. Like the policy makers at foundations and universities and many popular critics, the staff at ESP assumed that previous reform efforts had failed because they were too piecemeal; ESP intended to demonstrate that comprehensive, holistic change of an entire district or subdistrict was possible and that extensive community involvement would strengthen the process of comprehensive change. These goals were not attained because they were inherently unattainable.

First of all, neither federal nor local officials knew what "comprehensive" change meant, and yet federal officials insisted that each proposal had to claim that it would be "comprehensive." Saying that a project would be comprehensive did not make it so. Many local officials rewrote their proposals at the direction of federal monitors and used whatever words would satisfy the demands of ESP officials. Yet, the more they wrote to please the federal officials, the less the proposals reflected local interests. "Comprehensive" was a buzz-word, a word that local officials learned to invoke at the right time if they wanted federal funds. In the same way, school officials somewhat ritualistically described what they were doing as "humanistic," "affective," "individualized," and so forth, as though it were possible to change the reality of an activity by renaming it in warm, reformist terminology.

Nor did the federal insistence on the importance of community involvement contribute to meeting reform objectives. Instead, the inclusion of community participation multiplied the number of interests and demands to be included in the project and further frustrated the possibility of coherent, comprehensive educational change. When federal officials pressed

local officials both for comprehensive change and for community participation, they made unwarranted assumptions about the unity of interests
among administrators, teachers, parents, and community members. Federal reformers did not realize, a district superintendent later complained,
that "the community represents such a diverse population that its involvement only created different factions of interest who wanted different things
to happen in school."[59]

Perhaps a more important problem was that federal officials never understood that their priorities were not the same as the priorities of local
school officials. The federal officials, like their predecessors in Democratic
administrations, came to the project believing that the federal government
had a responsibility to reform local schools and that their research-based
ideas about educational theory and practice were superior to those held by
people working in the schools. They further imagined that they could
direct change by winning a written commitment from the local superintendent, who, with adequate federal monitoring, would see to it that
the reform process was securely implemented. An insightful study of ESP
by Peter Cowden and David K. Cohen concluded that the federal officials'
hopes for comprehensive change "never approached fulfillment. What
change occurred . . . did so in fragmented ways, and was typically modest and piecemeal." Federal officials imagined that the right mechanisms
or processes could bring about sweeping change in an entire school district. "But a school district is not a single, centrally directed, coherent system that can, upon a decision, change direction. It consists of many units
and individuals with different needs, interests, and opinions. And the work
of central administrators, principals, and teachers is only weakly interde-
pendent—they by no means all pull together."[60]

Local officials applied for ESP funds with the expectation that they
would enhance the prestige of their district or get more money to hire specialists, buy new materials, or plan a program for a special group like potential dropouts. They did not usually see their schools as negatively as
federal officials did. Furthermore, while they might promise comprehensive change, they knew that a school system is not a tightly organized,
hierarchical chain of command. They could ask (or tell) teachers to participate in inservice training programs, and they could buy new curricula,
but they could not force teachers to do what they did not want to do. Ironically, what ESP may have demonstrated is the impossibility of "holistic"
change, and the likelihood that piecemeal, incremental change may be appropriate to the highly decentralized nature of school systems, which are
made up of semiautonomous schools and staffed by relatively autonomous
teachers.

How, then, did "piecemeal change" get such a bad reputation? In large measure, the assumption that piecemeal change had been tried and failed stemmed from the troubled history of the curriculum revisions sponsored by the NSF in the aftermath of Sputnik. What was thought of at the time as the single greatest venture in recasting American education had not transformed the schools. Seen from the perspective of the early 1970s, the NSF-funded programs had assembled the nation's best scholars, who had revised the curricula to reflect the latest knowledge and the best methodology, yet still the schools remained essentially untouched. This led reformers to conclude that tinkering with the parts of the system was insufficient and that some kind of sweeping, comprehensive change was necessary to change the system itself.

But this version of what happened to the NSF curriculum revisions was not the whole story, and the actual NSF experience sheds light on the politics of school reform. Between 1956 and 1975, NSF funded fifty-three projects, forty-three in mathematics and the natural sciences and ten in the social sciences. By the end of this period, when NSF conducted a review of its curriculum development activities, it was clear that the new science curricula had been far more successful than the others. In the 1976/77 school year, almost 60 percent of all school districts were using one or more of the federally funded science programs in grades seven through twelve; 40 percent were using more than one, and even in the elementary grades about 30 percent of the districts reported using at least one of the NSF science curricula. In addition, the NSF science programs had substantial secondary effects in that they prompted substantial revisions in the content and methods of the most popular commercial textbooks. Since it was not necessarily the purpose of NSF to put commercial textbook publishers out of business, but rather to improve the content and approach of science teaching, it can be judged to have achieved a significant influence through its relatively small investment in reforming the science curricula.[61]

Mathematics and the social sciences presented very different problems. The revisions in mathematics, like those in science, were begun before Sputnik, gathered considerable NSF funding after Sputnik, and were intended to improve the mathematical preparation of the college-bound. "The new math," as the revisions were called, was not a single program but rather the product or approach that evolved from several mathematics reform groups. Students and teachers knew it as a collection of new concepts like "sets," "numeration in bases other than 10," and "prime numbers." One mathematics scholar, Bruce R. Vogeli, defined it as the premise that "mathematical learning is more effective and efficient if the fundamental unifying ideas of mathematics are stressed—if the internal structure of the discipline is emphasized." The major NSF program was developed by the School Mathematics Study Group (SMSG), which wrote a new secondary curriculum and then a new elementary curriculum between 1958 and 1962. By 1967, according to Vogeli, not only were SMSG texts widely used and widely emulated by commercial publishers, but "no series was marketable that was not identified as 'modern.'"[62]

The initial victory of the "new math" was illusory, however. It was severely criticized by mathematicians who complained that it was too abstract and that it neglected significant applications of mathematics; it encountered unanticipated resistance from teachers, particularly at the elementary level, who found it difficult to teach; and it was strongly disliked by parents, who resented the mystification of the third R and worried about their children's lack of computation skills. By the end of the 1960s, the combination of criticism and resistance routed "new math" from most elementary schools and fed the emergence of a "back to basics" movement. By the late 1970s, when NSF surveyed the status of precollege mathematics, its reviewers found that such topics as sets and nondecimal numeration systems were "practically non-existent in newer elementary-school curriculum materials." The proportion of school districts using NSF mathematics curricula dropped from 30 percent in the early 1970s to only 9 percent by 1976/77. And while mathematics professors predicted that hand-held computers eventually would restore a reformulated version of modern mathematics to the classroom, mathematics teachers expressed satisfaction with the return to the methods and concepts they were comfortable with; they told NSF observers "with near perfect regularity . . . that they applaud the return to traditional content, [traditional] instructional methods, and higher standards of student performance."[63]

The new social science courses underwritten by NSF encountered other obstacles. Like NSF-funded courses in science, the new social studies encouraged the use of discovery methods and student inquiry and introduced multimedia materials to supplement written texts. By 1976/77, when the NSF survey was completed, about 25 percent of school districts were using NSF social science materials. However, the surveyors found that most social studies teachers continued to use the textbook as the most important source of knowledge and to be most concerned that students learn the content, the subject matter of the field. For the most part, the social studies curriculum had changed little; it was still devoted largely to history and government, and it followed the textbook, with little reference to the social sciences. At first glance, it appeared that nothing had changed, but in fact the survey caught a snapshot of a field rapidly retreating from an era of curricular fragmentation, characterized by mini-courses and electives devoted to social activism, ethnicity, valuing, and self-realization.[64]

Why did teachers continue to hold a transmission-of-knowledge view of education when it was held in so little regard by university professors? In the view of spokesmen for the National Council for the Social Studies, the curriculum reformers had misunderstood the needs of classroom teachers. Teachers, they said, are primarily concerned with managing their classroom and teaching students good citizenship. Their failure to use new materials and new methods came not from any obstructionist motive. "Instead, it is simply more appropriate to them to continue doing what they have done before—practices consistent with their own values and beliefs and those they perceive, probably accurately, to be those of their communities. The new materials just don't fit." Teachers who were familiar with the new curricula thought they were best for elite groups of students "who had attained the basics and perhaps more important, proper self-discipline." Used with other students, the new materials threatened the teachers' ability to control the classroom. "Some of the support by teachers for the 'back to basics' movement," the authors believed, "may even be interpreted as reaction to the demands of the curriculum reform attempts of the 1960s—the new topics and content organizations, and unusual teaching roles not only seemed difficult to carry out but flew in the face of the teachers' view of the needs of students and the school."[65]

Controversy over "Man: A Course of Study" (MACOS), an NSF-funded anthropology course used in the upper elementary grades, brought the entire NSF curriculum-development effort under congressional scrutiny in 1976. Like other new curricula, MACOS was innovative in its content, its methodology, and its pedagogy. Its units included the life cycle and behavior patterns of salmon, herring gulls, baboons, and Netsilik Eskimos. Its developers at ESI (the same organization that was also instrumental in the dissemination of British informal methods) expected that the course would encourage children to speculate on "What is human about human beings? How did they get that way? How can they be made more so?" The course "touched on such inflammatory subjects as evolution, infanticide, wife sharing, senilicide, and 'communal living,'" which made commercial publishers reluctant to sponsor it. As the course began to be broadly disseminated, it came under attack in widely scattered communities by conservative critics who objected to its subject matter and its cultural relativism. When an Arizona congressman challenged the appropriateness of federal subsidy for a curriculum that was so offensive to local communities, a House subcommittee held hearings, NSF conducted an internal review of MACOS, and the General Accounting Office investigated the financial relationship between NSF and MACOS' developers. MACOS survived the criticisms and challenges, but its notoriety "brought about a precipitous drop in sales from which the course . . . never recovered."[66]

The era of curriculum reform, which began with great expectations, ended quietly. There had been substantial gains, especially in the physical sciences, and there had been losses. Even the losses could be turned into gains, however, if they advanced understanding of the conditions that impede educational change. There was much to be learned from the NSF efforts to revise precollege curricula. Both the way the new materials were prepared and the methods they incorporated later created problems for the new curricula that could not have been foreseen in the years of heady optimism. When the curriculum reform movement began in the 1950s, school critics persistently complained that existing curricula were mediocre and lacked rigor, and that the educational system was controlled by an "interlocking directorate" of professional educators. These assumptions shaped certain of the movement's characteristics.

• First, despite repeated references to curriculum "revisions," the reformers aimed to replace the existing curriculum, not just to improve it. This guaranteed not only substantial institutional resistance, but also the necessity of massive teacher retraining.

• Second, the reformers sorely underestimated the reluctance of teachers to discard their knowledge, their methods, and their beliefs about teaching. They did not anticipate the number of teachers who had difficulty utilizing inquiry and discovery methods, who believed in the value of "covering the field," who relied on the textbook to organize their courses, and who were unable to manage a classroom of individualized learners.

• Third, many of the materials were prepared for college-bound students; average and below-average students had difficulty dealing with the conceptual approach of the new courses.

• Fourth, the new curricula were prepared by prominent university scholars and teachers from leading secondary schools, with little participation by professors of education and teachers from typical secondary schools. The lack of involvement of teacher educators undoubtedly slowed the absorption of the new materials by those who trained new teachers, and the paucity of representative teachers probably deprived the projects of persons familiar with the wide range of abilities represented in the average public school classrooms.

• Fifth, the new curricula were funded by foundations and federal agencies, which freed them of the political constraints of state and local education agencies and the marketplace constraints on textbook publishers. This freedom was a mixed blessing, however, because the "constraints" of politics and the marketplace tend to determine whether a new curriculum will be adopted.[67]

Like ESP, with its hopes for "comprehensive" change, the curriculum reform movement exemplified the pitfalls of trying to impose sweeping change on an institution as multidimensional as the American school. Regardless of what the state superintendent or the school superintendent or the principal may recommend, classroom teachers have a considerable degree of control over what and how they teach; even when a new curriculum is put in their hands, the way they use it may alter it beyond recognition. Recognizing the diversity of interests and individuals in the nation's thousands of school districts and hundreds of thousands of schools does not argue against the value of curriculum reform. It does suggest, though, that any planned reform is filtered through the experiences, intentions, and purposes of those who implement it. In view of the number of actors involved, and the degree of their autonomy, lasting change in an institution as various as the school is invariably incremental and piecemeal.

Although for nearly twenty years alternating waves of reforms and crusades had swept through the schools, they seemed to be in some ways unchanged. But every effort to make the school better had left its mark. The more limited and specific the goal, the more likely was the reform to endure. More children were in school for more years than at any time in the past. School buildings were better equipped and more commodious. More teachers had college degrees. Classes were smaller. There were more curricula to choose from, more methods in use, and a greater variety of materials. The schools may not have been saved, but they had survived nonetheless.

NOTES

1. Lawrence A. Cremin, *The Transformation of the School: Progressivism in American Education, 1876–1957* (New York: Alfred A. Knopf, 1961), p. 347; Hyman Rickover, *Education and Freedom* (New York: E. P. Dutton, 1959). See also, for reactions to Sputnik, Kermit Lansner, ed., *Second-Rate Brains* (New York: Doubleday, 1958).

2. Barbara Barksdale Clowse, "Education as an Instrument of National Security: The Cold War Campaign to 'Beat the Russians' from Sputnik to the National Defense Education Act of 1958" (Diss., University of North Carolina at Chapel Hill, 1977), pp. 99–102 (published as *Brainpower for the Cold*

War: The Sputnik Crisis and the National Defense Education Act of 1958 [Westport, Conn.: Greenwood Press, 1981]).

3. Max Beberman, *An Emerging Program of Secondary School Mathematics* (Cambridge, Mass.: Harvard University Press, 1958). See chapter 2, pp. 72–79.

4. Rockefeller Brothers Fund, *The Pursuit of Excellence* (New York: Doubleday, 1958).

5. James B. Conant, *The American High School Today* (New York: McGraw-Hill, 1959), pp. 15, 37–38; Carnegie Corporation of New York, *Fiftieth Annual Report and Annual Report for the Fiscal Year Ended September 30th, 1961* (New York: Carnegie Corporation, 1961), p. 24; see also, A. Harry Passow, *American Secondary Education: The Conant Influence* (Reston, Va.: National Association of Secondary School Principals, 1977); *New York Times,* February 13, 1978.

6. Paul M. Nachtigal, *A Foundation Goes to School: The Ford Foundation Comprehensive School Improvement Program, 1960–1970* (New York: Ford Foundation, 1972).

7. Edward A. Krug, *The Secondary School Curriculum* (New York: Harper & Bros., 1960), pp. 258–59; President's Commission on Foreign Language and International Studies, *Strength Through Wisdom: A Critique of U.S. Capability* (Washington, D.C.: Government Printing Office, 1979).

8. National Science Foundation, *What Are the Needs in Precollege Science, Mathematics, and Social Science Education? Views from the Field* (Washington, D.C.: Government Printing Office, 1980), p. v.

9. Jerome Bruner, *The Process of Education* (Cambridge, Mass.: Harvard University Press, 1960), p. 33.

10. Ronald Gross and Judith Murphy, eds., *The Revolution in the Schools* (New York: Harcourt, Brace & World, 1964), p. 1.

11. Don D. Bushnell, "Computers in Education," in Gross and Murphy, *Revolution in the Schools,* pp. 68–69; Jonathan King, "The New Schoolhouse," in Gross and Murphy, *Revolution in the Schools,* pp. 128–36.

12. Margaret Mead, *American Sociological Review* 26 (June 1961): 504.

13. A. S. Neill, *Summerhill: A Radical Approach to Child Rearing* (New York: Hart, 1960), pp. 4, 25, 29; "Introduction," *Summerhill: For and Against* (New York: Hart, 1970). For a critical assessment of Neill's thought, see Robin Barrow, *Radical Education: A Critique of Freeschooling and Deschooling* (New York: John Wiley, 1978).

14. Paul Goodman, *Compulsory Mis-Education* (New York: Vintage, 1964), pp. 22, 32–33, 55–57, 67, 126, 141.

15. Jonathan Kozol, *Death at an Early Age: The Destruction of the Hearts and Minds of Negro Children in the Boston Public Schools* (New York: Houghton Mifflin, 1967); Herbert Kohl, *36 Children* (New York: New American Library, 1967).

16. Nat Hentoff, *Our Children Are Dying* (New York: Viking Press, 1966); James Herndon, *The Way It Spozed to Be* (New York: Simon and Schuster, 1968); James Herndon, *How to Survive in Your Native Land* (New York: Simon and Schuster, 1971); George Dennison, *The Lives of Children: The Story of the First Street School* (New York: Random House, 1969); Steve Bhaerman and Joel Denker, *No Particular Place to Go: The Making of a Free High School* (Carbondale: Southern Illinois University Press, 1972, rev. ed., 1982); John Holt, *How Children Fail* (New York: Pitman, 1964); George B. Leonard, *Education and Ecstasy* (New York: Delta, 1968); Terry Borton, *Reach, Touch and Teach: Student Concerns and Process Education* (New York: McGraw-Hill, 1970).

17. See Arthur R. Jensen, "How Much Can We Boost IQ and Scholastic Achievement?" *Harvard Educational Review* 39 (1969): 1–123. The article and responses to it were printed in *Environment, Heredity, and Intelligence* (Cambridge, Mass.: Harvard Educational Review, 1969). Westinghouse Learning Corporation, *The Impact of Head Start: An Evaluation of the Effects of Head Start on Children's Cognitive and Affective Development* (Washington, D.C.: Clearinghouse for Federal Scientific and Technical Information, June 1969).

18. Joseph Featherstone, "Schools for Children," *New Republic,* August 19, 1967, pp. 17–21; idem, "How Children Learn," *New Republic,* September 2, 1967, pp. 17–21; idem, "Teaching Children to Think," *New Republic,* September 9, 1967, pp. 15–25.

19. Diane-Marie Hargrove Blinn, "Open Education: An Analysis of the Practical Purport, Historical Context, and Parent Doctrine of an Educational Slogan" (Diss., University of Chicago, 1981), p. 3; Ewald B. Nyquist and Gene R. Hawes, eds., *Open Education: A Sourcebook for Parents and Teachers* (New York: Bantam, 1972), p. 82; Beatrice and Ronald Gross, "A Little Bit of Chaos," *Saturday Review,* May 16, 1970, pp. 71–73, 84–85.

20. Blinn, "Open Education," pp. 258–60; also Harold Howe, "Openness— the New Kick in Education" (New York: The Ford Foundation, 1972).

21. Note: In 1972, as federal funds diminished, the New School was absorbed by the University's College of Education and became the Center for Teaching and Learning; its activities were cut back, but its commitment to open education remained undiminished. Blinn, "Open Education," pp. 266–70; Vito Perrone and Warren Strandberg, "The New School," in Nyquist and

Hawes, *Open Education: A Sourcebook,* pp. 275–91; Vito Perrone, *Open Education: Promise and Problems* (Bloomington, Ind.: Phi Delta Kappa, 1972); Paul M. Nachtigal, *Improving Rural Schools* (Washington, D.C.: Government Printing Office, 1980), pp. 7–8.

22. Blinn, "Open Education," p. 165.

23. See David Hawkins, *The Informed Vision* (New York: Agathon Press, 1974).

24. Blinn, "Open Education," interview with Hawkins, p. 242.

25. Blinn, "Open Education," pp. 333–34.

26. William Hull, "Elementary Science," internal memorandum, ESS, Newton, Massachusetts, September 1968, p. 1 (cited in Blinn, "Open Education," p. 243).

27. Nyquist and Hawes, *Open Education: A Sourcebook,* p. 392; Blinn, "Open Education," pp. 245–49.

28. Beatrice and Ronald Gross, "A Little Bit of Chaos," p. 84.

29. Charles Silberman, *Crisis in the Classroom* (New York: Random House, 1970).

30. Ibid., pp. 13, 21, 28.

31. Ibid., pp. 28–29.

32. Ibid., pp. 10, 11, 122, 152, 173, 207–8.

33. Ibid., pp. 324, 340–48.

34. Ewald B. Nyquist, "Open Education: Its Philosophy, Historical Perspectives, and Implications," in Nyquist and Hawes, *Open Education: A Sourcebook,* p. 83; Howe, "Openness—the New Kick in Education."

35. Bernard Spodek, "Open Education: Romance or Liberation?" in *Studies in Open Education,* ed. Bernard Spodek and Herbert J. Walberg (New York: Agathon Press, 1975), pp. 3–8.

36. Charles H. Rathbone, "The Implicit Rationale of the Open Education Classroom," in *Open Education: The Informal Classroom,* ed. Charles H. Rathbone (New York: Citation Press, 1971), pp. 100, 104.

37. Ibid., pp. 106–7.

38. Roland S. Barth, "Teaching: The Way It Is/The Way It Could Be," *Grade Teacher,* January 1970, p. 101; idem, "When Children Enjoy School," *Childhood Education,* January 1970, pp. 195–200; idem, *Open Education and the American School* (New York: Agathon Press, 1972), pp. 7–48, 50.

39. Ibid., pp. 138, 139, 142, 156.

40. Charles Silberman, ed., *The Open Classroom Reader* (New York: Vintage Books, 1973), p. xvi.

41. The Gallup poll of public attitudes toward education was published each September in *Phi Delta Kappan,* beginning in 1969.

42. Ivan Illich, *Deschooling Society* (New York: Harper & Row, 1970), p. 72; Illich's critique of the free school movement is quoted in Allen Graubard, *Free the Children: Radical Reform and the Free School Movement* (New York: Pantheon Books, 1972), pp. 297–98.

43. Ann Swidler, *Organization Without Authority: Dilemmas of Social Control in Free Schools* (Cambridge, Mass.: Harvard University Press, 1979), pp. 2–3; Graubard, *Free the Children,* p. 40.

44. Salli Rasberry and Robert Greenway, *Rasberry Exercises: How To Start Your Own School . . . and Make a Book* (Freestone, Calif.: Freestone, 1970), p. 37; Swidler, *Organization Without Authority,* pp. 2–3.

45. William A. Firestone, "Ideology and Conflict in Parent-Run Free Schools," *Sociology of Education* 49 (1976): 169–75.

46. Robert R. Sutcliffe, "Hard Science in a Soft School," *Science Teacher,* September 1973, pp. 30–32; Philip DeTurk and Robert Mackin, "Lions in the Park: An Alternative Meaning and Setting for Learning," *Phi Delta Kappan,* March 1973, pp. 458–60; R. Bruce McPherson, Steven Daniels, and William P. Stewart, "Options for Students in Ann Arbor," *Phi Delta Kappan,* March 1973, pp. 469–70; Richard St. Germain, Roger D. Carten, and James Meland, "Roseville Faces Disaffection with Alternative High Schools," *Phi Delta Kappan,* May 1975, p. 637.

47. Rita M. Hymes and Franklin O. Bullock, "Alternative Schools: Answer to the Gifted Child's Boredom," *The Gifted Child Quarterly* 19 (1974): 340–45; Gene I. Maeroff, "The Traditional School: Keep It Among the Alternatives," *Phi Delta Kappan,* March 1973, pp. 473–75; Frederick S. Bock and Wanda Gomula, "A Conservative Community Forms an Alternative High School," *Phi Delta Kappan,* March 1973, pp. 471–72; Philip G. Jones, "All About Those New 'Fundamental' Public Schools, What They're Promising, and Why They're Catching On," *American School Board Journal,* February 1976, pp. 24–31; Shirley Boes Neill, "Pasadena's Approach to the Classic School Debate," *American Education,* April 1976, pp. 6–10; Community High School, "Course Guide: Community Resource Program" (Ann Arbor, Mich.: Ann Arbor Public Schools, September 1982); Hunter O. Brooks and Paula R. Barker, "Alternative Schools in a Traditional Setting," *Social Education,* November 1973, pp. 650–51; Fred M. Hechinger, "The All-New 'Law and Order' Classroom," *Saturday Review,* May 3, 1975,

pp. 40–41; see also, *Phi Delta Kappan* special issue on alternative schools, April 1981.

48. Jerome De Bruin, "A Descriptive Analysis of Experiences of Five First-Year Teachers Attempting Open Education," in Spodek and Walberg, *Studies in Open Education*, p. 214.

49. Joseph Featherstone, "Tempering a Fad," *New Republic*, September 25, 1971, pp. 17–21; Joseph Featherstone, foreword to Roland S. Barth, *Open Education and the American School*, p. x; Roland S. Barth, "Should We Forget about Open Education?" *Saturday Review World*, November 6, 1973, pp. 58–59; idem, "Beyond Open Education," *Phi Delta Kappan*, February 1977, pp. 489ff.; Donald A. Myers, "Why Open Education Died," *Journal of Research and Development in Education* 8 (1974): 62–63; see also, Donald A. Myers and Daniel L. Duke, "Open Education as an Ideology," *Educational Research* 19 (June 1977): 227–35.

50. Blinn, "Open Education," pp. 444–46; "Back to Basics in the Schools," *Newsweek*, October 21, 1974, pp. 87–95.

51. Neville Bennett, *Teaching Styles and Pupil Progress* (London: Open Books, 1976), pp. 43, 149; British Department of Education and Science, *Primary Education in England: A Survey by HM Inspectors of Schools* (London: Her Majesty's Stationery Office, 1978), pp. 26–27; British Department of Education and Science, *Education 5 to 9: An Illustrative Survey of 80 First Schools in England* (London: Her Majesty's Stationery Office, 1982), pp. 48–49.

52. Brian Simon, "The Primary School Revolution: Myth or Reality?" in *Research and Practice in the Primary Classroom*, ed. Brian Simon and John Willcocks (London: Routledge & Kegan Paul, 1981), pp. 23–24; see also, Maurice Galton and Brian Simon, eds., *Progress and Performance in the Primary Classroom* (London: Routledge & Kegan Paul, 1980), pp. 33–35, and Neville Bennett et al., *Open Plan Schools* (London: NFER Publishing, 1980).

53. Peter W. Greenwood, Dale Mann, and Milbrey Wallin McLaughlin, *Federal Programs Supporting Educational Change, III: "The Process of Change"* (Santa Monica, Calif.: Rand Corporation, 1975), p. 1.

54. Greenwood, Mann, and McLaughlin, *Federal Programs Supporting Educational Change*, pp. 1, 13–14; Malcolm M. Provus, *The Grand Experiment: The Life and Death of the TTT Program as Seen Through the Eyes of Its Evaluators* (Berkeley, Calif.: McCutchan, 1975), p. 146. For a study of the Teacher Corps, see Ronald G. Corwin, *Reform and Organizational Survival: The Teacher Corps as an Instrument of Educational Change* (New York: John Wiley, 1973). For analyses of the Trainers of Teacher Trainers program,

see Donald N. Vigelow, ed., *Schoolworlds '76: New Directions for Educational Policy* (Berkeley, Calif.: McCutchan, 1976), pp. xii–xviii, 287–303.

55. *New York Times,* March 4, 1970; Robert E. Herriott and Neal Gross, eds., *The Dynamics of Planned Educational Change: Case Studies and Analyses* (Berkeley, Calif.: McCutchan, 1979), p. 51.

56. U.S. Office of Education, *Experimental Schools Program, 1971. Experimental Schools Projects: Three Educational Plans* (Washington, D.C.: Government Printing Office, 1972), pp. 149–50.

57. For the plans of these three funded districts, see ibid.; for descriptions of the Berkeley program, see Diane Divoky, "Berkeley's Experimental Schools," *Saturday Review,* September 16, 1972, pp. 44–50; Francisco Hernandez, "Casa de la Raza—An Alternative School for Chicano Students," in *Alternative Schools: Ideologies, Realities, Guidelines,* ed. Terrence E. Deal and Robert R. Nolan (Chicago: Nelson Hall, 1978), pp. 191–8; for the outside evaluation of the Berkeley schools, see Institute for Scientific Analysis, "Educational R&D and the Case of Berkeley's Experimental Schools," a report submitted to the National Institute of Education, November 1976; for an in-depth analysis of the projects in Berkeley, Franklin Pierce, and Minneapolis, see Louise Frankel Stoll, "The Price of a Gift: The Impact of Federal Funds on the Political and Economic Life of School Districts" (Diss., University of California at Berkeley, 1978).

58. Nachtigal, *Improving Rural Schools,* p. 11; see also, Paul M. Nachtigal, ed., *Rural Education: In Search of a Better Way* (Boulder, Colo.: Westview Press, 1982); for an overview of ESP and evaluations of other rural sites, see Herriott and Gross, *Dynamics of Planned Educational Change.*

59. Peter Cowden and David K. Cohen, "Divergent Worlds of Practice: The Federal Reform of Local Schools in the Experimental Schools Program," unpublished study prepared for the National Institute of Education, 1979, pp. 16, 29.

60. Ibid., p. 21.

61. Suzanne Kay Quick, "Secondary Impacts of the Curriculum Reform Movement: A Longitudinal Study of the Incorporation of Innovations of the Curriculum Reform Movement into Commercially Developed Curriculum Programs" (Diss., Stanford University, 1977).

62. Bruce R. Vogeli, "The Rise and Fall of the 'New Math'" (Address delivered at Teachers College, Columbia University, February 5, 1976), pp. 4, 17.

63. Morris Kline, *Why Johnny Can't Add: The Failure of the New Math* (New York: St. Martin's Press, 1973); see also, Seymour B. Sarason, *The Culture of the School and the Problem of Change,* 2nd ed. (Boston: Allyn & Bacon,

1982), chap. 4; Marilyn N. Suydam and Alan Osborne, *The Status of Precollege Science, Mathematics, and Social Science Education: 1955–1975,* vol. 2, *Mathematics Education* (Washington, D.C.: Government Printing Office, 1978), p. 32; Iris Weiss, *Report of the 1977 National Survey of Science, Mathematics, and Social Studies Education* (Research Triangle Park, N.C.: Research Triangle Institute, 1978), p. 79; James T. Fey, "Mathematics Teaching Today: Perspectives from Three National Surveys," in *What Are the Needs in Precollege Science, Mathematics, and Social Science Education?* p. 25.

64. *The Status of Precollege Science, Mathematics, and Social Science Education: 1955–1975: An Overview and Summary of Three Studies* (Washington, D.C.: Government Printing Office, 1978), p. 8; Hazel Whitman Hertzberg, *Social Studies Reform, 1880–1980* (Boulder, Colo.: Social Science Education Consortium, 1981), pp. 155–57.

65. James P. Shaver, O. L. Davis, and Suzanne M. Helburn, "An Interpretive Report on the Status of Precollege Social Studies Education Based on Three NSF-Funded Studies," in *What Are the Needs in Precollege Science, Mathematics, and Social Science Education?* pp. 6–12.

66. Peter B. Dow, "Innovation's Perils: An Account of the Origins, Development, Implementation, and Public Reaction to *Man: A Course of Study*" (Diss., Harvard University, 1979), pp. 181, 374, 464; see also, Karen B. Wiley, "The NSF Science Education Controversy: Issues, Events, Decisions" (Boulder, Colo.: Social Science Education Consortium, 1976).

67. See, Karen B. Wiley and Jeanne Race, *The Status of Precollege Science, Mathematics, and Social Science Education: 1955–1975,* vol. 3, *Social Science Education* (Boulder, Colo.: Social Science Education Consortium, 1977), pp. 299–312; see also, Christopher Dede and Joy Hardin, "Reforms, Revisions, Reexaminations: Secondary Science Education Since World War II," *Science Education* 57 (1973): 485–91.

PART TWO

MILESTONES

4

Opinion of the Court,
Brown v. Board of Education

U.S. SUPREME COURT

Brown v. *Board of Education* was supposed to be the beginning of the end of racial segregation. Starting what was arguably to become the largest school reform effort in the country, the U.S. Supreme Court's 1954 decision was one of the cornerstones of the civil rights movement. More than forty years later, most people would agree that desegregation efforts have largely failed. The gap between the test scores of white and black students, while not as pronounced as before, remains. Black students, along with other ethnic minorities from low-income families, often attend schools that have unpardonable amounts of deferred maintenance and a shortage of both educational materials and teaching staff. Although different camps of educators argue about whether we have failed desegregation or desegregation has failed us, most agree that the United States has not achieved the desired results outlined in the opinion of the Court, delivered by Chief Justice Earl Warren.

○

THESE CASES COME TO US from the States of Kansas, South Carolina, Virginia, and Delaware. They are premised on different facts and different local conditions, but a common legal question justifies their consideration together in this consolidated opinion.[1] [347 U.S. 483, 487]

In each of the cases, minors of the Negro race, through their legal representatives, seek the aid of the courts in obtaining admission to the public schools of their community on a nonsegregated basis. In each instance,

[347 U.S. 483, 488] they had been denied admission to schools attended by white children under laws requiring or permitting segregation according to race. This segregation was alleged to deprive the plaintiffs of the equal protection of the laws under the Fourteenth Amendment. In each of the cases other than the Delaware case, a three-judge federal district court denied relief to the plaintiffs on the so-called "separate but equal" doctrine announced by this Court in *Plessy* v. *Ferguson,* 163 U.S. 537. Under that doctrine, equality of treatment is accorded when the races are provided substantially equal facilities, even though these facilities be separate. In the Delaware case, the Supreme Court of Delaware adhered to that doctrine, but ordered that the plaintiffs be admitted to the white schools because of their superiority to the Negro schools.

The plaintiffs contend that segregated public schools are not "equal" and cannot be made "equal," and that hence they are deprived of the equal protection of the laws. Because of the obvious importance of the question presented, the Court took jurisdiction.[2] Argument was heard in the 1952 Term, and reargument was heard this Term on certain questions propounded by the Court.[3] [347 U.S. 483, 489]

Reargument was largely devoted to the circumstances surrounding the adoption of the Fourteenth Amendment in 1868. It covered exhaustively consideration of the Amendment in Congress, ratification by the states, then existing practices in racial segregation, and the views of proponents and opponents of the Amendment. This discussion and our own investigation convince us that, although these sources cast some light, it is not enough to resolve the problem with which we are faced. At best, they are inconclusive. The most avid proponents of the post-War Amendments undoubtedly intended them to remove all legal distinctions among "all persons born or naturalized in the United States." Their opponents, just as certainly, were antagonistic to both the letter and the spirit of the Amendments and wished them to have the most limited effect. What others in Congress and the state legislatures had in mind cannot be determined with any degree of certainty.

An additional reason for the inconclusive nature of the Amendment's history, with respect to segregated schools, is the status of public education at that time.[4] In the South, the movement toward free common schools, supported [347 U.S. 483, 490] by general taxation, had not yet taken hold. Education of white children was largely in the hands of private groups. Education of Negroes was almost nonexistent, and practically all of the race were illiterate. In fact, any education of Negroes was forbidden by law in some states. Today, in contrast, many Negroes have achieved outstanding success in the arts and sciences as well as in the business and professional world. It is true that public school education at the time of the Amendment had advanced further in the North, but the effect of the Amendment on Northern States was generally ignored in the congressional debates. Even in the North, the conditions of public education did not approximate those existing today. The curriculum was usually rudimentary; ungraded schools were common in rural areas; the school term was but three months a year in many states; and compulsory school attendance was virtually unknown. As a consequence, it is not surprising that there should be so little in the history of the Fourteenth Amendment relating to its intended effect on public education.

In the first cases in this Court construing the Fourteenth Amendment, decided shortly after its adoption, the Court interpreted it as proscribing all state-imposed discriminations against the Negro race.[5] The doctrine of [347 U.S. 483, 491] "separate but equal" did not make its appearance in this Court until 1896 in the case of *Plessy* v. *Ferguson,* involving not education but transportation.[6] American courts have since labored with the doctrine for over half a century. In this Court, there have been six cases involving the "separate but equal" doctrine in the field of public education.[7] In *Cumming* v. *County Board of Education,* 175 U.S. 528, and *Gong Lum* v. *Rice,* 275 U.S. 78, the validity of the doctrine itself was not challenged.[8] In more recent cases, all on the graduate school [347 U.S. 483, 492] level, inequality was found in that specific benefits enjoyed by white students were denied to Negro students of the same educational qualifications. *Missouri ex rel. Gaines* v. *Canada,* 305 U.S. 337; *Sipuel* v. *Oklahoma,* 332 U.S. 631; *Sweatt* v. *Painter,* 339 U.S. 629; *McLaurin* v. *Oklahoma State Regents,* 339 U.S. 637. In none of these cases was it necessary to re-examine the doctrine to grant relief to the Negro plaintiff. And in *Sweatt* v. *Painter, supra,* the Court expressly reserved decision on the question whether *Plessy* v. *Ferguson* should be held inapplicable to public education.

In the instant cases, that question is directly presented. Here, unlike *Sweatt* v. *Painter,* there are findings below that the Negro and white schools involved have been equalized, or are being equalized, with respect to buildings, curricula, qualifications and salaries of teachers, and other "tangible" factors.[9] Our decision, therefore, cannot turn on merely a comparison of these tangible factors in the Negro and white schools involved in each of the cases. We must look instead to the effect of segregation itself on public education.

In approaching this problem, we cannot turn the clock back to 1868 when the Amendment was adopted, or even to 1896 when *Plessy* v. *Ferguson* was written. We must consider public education in the light of its full development and its present place in American life throughout [347 U.S. 483, 493] the Nation. Only in this way can it be determined if segregation in public schools deprives these plaintiffs of the equal protection of the laws.

Today, education is perhaps the most important function of state and local governments. Compulsory school attendance laws and the great expenditures for education both demonstrate our recognition of the importance of education to our democratic society. It is required in the performance of our most basic public responsibilities, even service in the armed forces. It is the very foundation of good citizenship. Today it is a principal instrument in awakening the child to cultural values, in preparing him for later professional training, and in helping him to adjust normally to his environment. In these days, it is doubtful that any child may reasonably be expected to succeed in life if he is denied the opportunity of an education. Such an opportunity, where the state has undertaken to provide it, is a right which must be made available to all on equal terms.

We come then to the question presented: Does segregation of children in public schools solely on the basis of race, even though the physical facilities and other "tangible" factors may be equal, deprive the children of the minority group of equal educational opportunities? We believe that it does.

In *Sweatt* v. *Painter, supra,* in finding that a segregated law school for Negroes could not provide them equal educational opportunities, this Court relied in large part on "those qualities which are incapable of objective measurement but which make for greatness in a law school." In *McLaurin* v. *Oklahoma State Regents, supra,* the Court, in requiring that a Negro admitted to a white graduate school be treated like all other students, again resorted to intangible considerations: ". . . his ability to study, to engage in discussions and exchange views with other students, and, in general, to learn his profession." [347 U.S. 483, 494] Such considerations apply with added force to children in grade and high schools. To separate them from others of similar age and qualifications solely because of their race generates a feeling of inferiority as to their status in the community that may affect their hearts and minds in a way unlikely ever to be undone. The effect of this separation on their educational opportunities was well stated by a finding in the Kansas case by a court which nevertheless felt compelled to rule against the Negro plaintiffs:

> Segregation of white and colored children in public schools has a detrimental effect upon the colored children. The impact is greater when it has the sanction of the law; for the policy of separating the races is usually interpreted as denoting the inferiority of the negro group. A sense

of inferiority affects the motivation of a child to learn. Segregation with the sanction of law, therefore, has a tendency to [retard] the educational and mental development of negro children and to deprive them of some of the benefits they would receive in a racial[ly] integrated school system.[10]

Whatever may have been the extent of psychological knowledge at the time of *Plessy* v. *Ferguson,* this finding is amply supported by modern authority.[11] Any language [347 U.S. 483, 495] in *Plessy* v. *Ferguson* contrary to this finding is rejected.

We conclude that in the field of public education the doctrine of "separate but equal" has no place. Separate educational facilities are inherently unequal. Therefore, we hold that the plaintiffs and others similarly situated for whom the actions have been brought are, by reason of the segregation complained of, deprived of the equal protection of the laws guaranteed by the Fourteenth Amendment. This disposition makes unnecessary any discussion whether such segregation also violates the Due Process Clause of the Fourteenth Amendment.[12]

Because these are class actions, because of the wide applicability of this decision, and because of the great variety of local conditions, the formulation of decrees in these cases presents problems of considerable complexity. On reargument, the consideration of appropriate relief was necessarily subordinated to the primary question—the constitutionality of segregation in public education. We have now announced that such segregation is a denial of the equal protection of the laws. In order that we may have the full assistance of the parties in formulating decrees, the cases will be restored to the docket, and the parties are requested to present further argument on Questions 4 and 5 previously propounded by the Court for the reargument this Term.[13] The Attorney General [347 U.S. 483, 496] of the United States is again invited to participate. The Attorneys General of the states requiring or permitting segregation in public education will also be permitted to appear as amici curiae upon request to do so by September 15, 1954, and submission of briefs by October 1, 1954.[14]

It is so ordered.

NOTES

1. In the Kansas case, *Brown* v. *Board of Education,* the plaintiffs are Negro children of elementary school age residing in Topeka. They brought this action in the United States District Court for the District of Kansas to enjoin enforcement of a Kansas statute which permits, but does not require, cities

of more than 15,000 population to maintain separate school facilities for Negro and white students. Kan. Gen. Stat. 72-1724 (1949). Pursuant to that authority, the Topeka Board of Education elected to establish segregated elementary schools. Other public schools in the community, however, are operated on a nonsegregated basis. The three-judge District Court, convened under 28 U.S.C. 2281 and 2284, found that segregation in public education has a detrimental effect upon Negro children, but denied relief on the ground that the Negro and white schools were substantially equal with respect to buildings, transportation, curricula, and educational qualifications of teachers. 98 F. Supp. 797. The case is here on direct appeal under 28 U.S.C. 1253. In the South Carolina case, *Briggs* v. *Elliott,* the plaintiffs are Negro children of both elementary and high school age residing in Clarendon County. They brought this action in the United States District Court for the Eastern District of South Carolina to enjoin enforcement of provisions in the state constitution and statutory code which require the segregation of Negroes and whites in public schools. S. C. Const., Art. XI, 7; S. C. Code 5377 (1942). The three-judge District Court, convened under 28 U.S.C. 2281 and 2284, denied the requested relief. The court found that the Negro schools were inferior to the white schools and ordered the defendants to begin immediately to equalize the facilities. But the court sustained the validity of the contested provisions and denied the plaintiffs admission [347 U.S. 483, 487] to the white schools during the equalization program. 98 F. Supp. 529. This Court vacated the District Court's judgment and remanded the case for the purpose of obtaining the court's views on a report filed by the defendants concerning the progress made in the equalization program. 342 U.S. 350. On remand, the District Court found that substantial equality had been achieved except for buildings and that the defendants were proceeding to rectify this inequality as well. 103 F. Supp. 920. The case is again here on direct appeal under 28 U.S.C. 1253. In the Virginia case, *Davis* v. *County School Board,* the plaintiffs are Negro children of high school age residing in Prince Edward county. They brought this action in the United States District Court for the Eastern District of Virginia to enjoin enforcement of provisions in the state constitution and statutory code which require the segregation of Negroes and whites in public schools. Va. Const., 140; Va. Code 22-221 (1950). The three-judge District Court, convened under 28 U.S.C. 2281 and 2284, denied the requested relief. The court found the Negro school inferior in physical plant, curricula, and transportation, and ordered the defendants forthwith to provide substantially equal curricula and transportation and to "proceed with all reasonable diligence and dispatch to remove" the inequality in physical plant. But, as in the South Carolina case, the court sustained the validity of the contested provisions and denied the plaintiffs admission to the white schools during the equalization program. 103 F. Supp. 337. The case is here on direct appeal under 28 U.S.C. 1253. In the Delaware case, *Gebhart v. Belton,* the plaintiffs are Negro children of both elementary and high school age residing in New Castle County. They brought this action in the Delaware Court of Chancery to enjoin enforcement of provisions in the state constitution and statutory code which require the segregation of Negroes and whites in public schools. Del. Const., Art. X, 2; Del. Rev. Code 2631 (1935). The Chancellor gave judgment for the plaintiffs and ordered their immediate admission to schools previously attended only by white children, on the ground that the Negro schools were inferior with respect to teacher training, pupil-teacher ratio, extracurricular activities, physical plant, and time and distance involved [347 U.S. 483, 488] in travel. 87 A. 2d 862. The Chancellor also found that segregation itself results in an inferior education for Negro children (see note 10, *infra*), but did not rest his decision on that ground. Id., at 865. The Chancellor's decree was affirmed by the Supreme Court of Delaware, which intimated, however, that the defendants might be able to obtain a modification of the decree after equalization of the Negro and white schools had been accomplished. 91 A. 2d 137, 152. The defendants, contending only that the Delaware courts had erred in ordering the immediate admission of the Negro plaintiffs to the white schools, applied to this Court for certiorari. The writ was granted, 344 U.S. 891. The plaintiffs, who were successful below, did not submit a cross-petition.

2. 344 U.S. 1, 141, 891.

3. 345 U.S. 972. The Attorney General of the United States participated both Terms as amicus curiae.

4. For a general study of the development of public education prior to the Amendment, see Butts and Cremin, *A History of Education in American Culture* (1953), Pts. I, II; Cubberley, *Public Education in the United States* (1934 ed.), cc. II-XII. School practices current at the time of the adoption of the Fourteenth Amendment are described in Butts and Cremin, *supra,* at 269–275; *Cubberley, supra,* at 288–339, 408–431; Knight, *Public Education in the South* (1922), cc. VIII, IX. See also H. Ex. Doc. No. 315, 41st Cong., 2d Sess. (1871). Although the demand for free public schools followed substantially the same pattern in both the North and the South, the development in the South did not begin to gain momentum until about 1850, some twenty years after that in the North. The reasons for the somewhat slower development in the South (e.g., the rural character of the South and the different regional attitudes toward state assistance) are well explained in Cubberley, *supra,* at 408–423. In the country as a whole, but particularly in the South, the War [347 U.S. 483, 490] virtually stopped all progress in

public education. Id., at 427–428. The low status of Negro education in all sections of the country, both before and immediately after the War, is described in Beale, *A History of Freedom of Teaching in American Schools* (1941), 112–132, 175–195. Compulsory school attendance laws were not generally adopted until after the ratification of the Fourteenth Amendment, and it was not until 1918 that such laws were in force in all the states. Cubberley, *supra,* at 563–565.

5. Slaughter-House Cases, 16 Wall. 36, 67–72 (1873); *Strauder* v. *West Virginia,* 100 U.S. 303, 307–308 (1880): "It ordains that no State shall deprive any person of life, liberty, or property, without due process of law, or deny to any person within its jurisdiction the equal protection of the laws. What is this but [347 U.S. 483, 491] declaring that the law in the States shall be the same for the black as for the white; that all persons, whether colored or white, shall stand equal before the laws of the States, and, in regard to the colored race, for whose protection the amendment was primarily designed, that no discrimination shall be made against them by law because of their color? The words of the amendment, it is true, are prohibitory, but they contain a necessary implication of a positive immunity, or right, most valuable to the colored race—the right to exemption from unfriendly legislation against them distinctively as colored—exemption from legal discriminations, implying inferiority in civil society, lessening the security of their enjoyment of the rights which others enjoy, and discriminations which are steps towards reducing them to the condition of a subject race." See also *Virginia* v. *Rives,* 100 U.S. 313, 318 (1880); *Ex parte Virginia,* 100 U.S. 339, 344–345 (1880).

6. The doctrine apparently originated in *Roberts* v. *City of Boston,* 59 Mass. 198, 206 (1850), upholding school segregation against attack as being violative of a state constitutional guarantee of equality. Segregation in Boston public schools was eliminated in 1855. Mass. Acts 1855, c. 256. But elsewhere in the North segregation in public education has persisted in some communities until recent years. It is apparent that such segregation has long been a nationwide problem, not merely one of sectional concern.

7. See also *Berea College* v. *Kentucky,* 211 U.S. 45 (1908).

8. In the *Cumming* case, Negro taxpayers sought an injunction requiring the defendant school board to discontinue the operation of a high school for white children until the board resumed operation of a high school for Negro children. Similarly, in the *Gong Lum* case, the plaintiff, a child of Chinese descent, contended only that state authorities had misapplied the doctrine by classifying him with Negro children and requiring him to attend a Negro school.

9. In the Kansas case, the court below found substantial equality as to all such factors. 98 F. Supp. 797, 798. In the South Carolina case, the court below found that the defendants were proceeding "promptly and in good faith to comply with the court's decree." 103 F. Supp. 920, 921. In the Virginia case, the court below noted that the equalization program was already "afoot and progressing" (103 F. Supp. 337, 341); since then, we have been advised, in the Virginia Attorney General's brief on reargument, that the program has now been completed. In the Delaware case, the court below similarly noted that the state's equalization program was well under way. 91 A. 2d 137, 149.

10. A similar finding was made in the Delaware case: "I conclude from the testimony that in our Delaware society, State-imposed segregation in education itself results in the Negro children, as a class, receiving educational opportunities which are substantially inferior to those available to white children otherwise similarly situated." 87 A. 2d 862, 865.

11. K. B. Clark, *Effect of Prejudice and Discrimination on Personality Development* (Midcentury White House Conference on Children and Youth, 1950); Witmer and Kotinsky, *Personality in the Making* (1952), c. VI; Deutscher and Chein, "The Psychological Effects of Enforced Segregation: A Survey of Social Science Opinion," 26 *J. Psychol.* 259 (1948); Chein, "What are the Psychological Effects of [347 U.S. 483, 495] Segregation Under Conditions of Equal Facilities?" 3 *Int. J. Opinion and Attitude Res.* 229 (1949); Brameld, *Educational Costs, in Discrimination and National Welfare* (MacIver, ed., (1949), 44–48; Frazier, *The Negro in the United States* (1949), 674–681. And see generally Myrdal, *An American Dilemma* (1944).

12. See Bolling v. Sharpe, post, p. 497, concerning the Due Process Clause of the Fifth Amendment.

13. Assuming it is decided that segregation in public schools violates the Fourteenth Amendment (a) would a decree necessarily follow providing that, within the [347 U.S. 483, 496] limits set by normal geographic school districting, Negro children should forthwith be admitted to schools of their choice, or (b) may this Court, in the exercise of its equity powers, permit an effective gradual adjustment to be brought about from existing segregated systems to a system not based on color distinctions? 5. On the assumption on which questions 4(a) and (b) are based, and assuming further that this Court will exercise its equity powers to the end described in question 4(b), (a) should this Court formulate detailed decrees in these cases; (b) if so, what specific issues should the decrees reach; (c) should this Court appoint a special master to hear evidence with a view to recommending specific terms for such decrees; (d) should this Court remand to the courts of first instance with directions to frame decrees in these cases, and if so what general directions

should the decrees of this Court include and what procedures should the courts of first instance follow in arriving at the specific terms of more detailed decrees?

14. See Rule 42, Revised Rules of this Court (effective July 1, 1954). [347 U.S. 483, 497]

5

SOVIET EDUCATION FAR AHEAD OF U.S.

Benjamin Fine

Predating our fear of Japanese educational superiority, the launch of Sputnik in 1957 engaged the United States in unprecedented scrutiny of and increased funding for education, mainly in mathematics and science. During the Cold War, and later in our economic competition with Japan, the United States saw education as a tool for national security.

○

THE SOVIET UNION is far outstripping the United States in its emphasis on technical and scientific education, it was reported yesterday.

A two-year study made by the United States Office of Education shows that the Soviet Union is making almost frantic efforts to gain over-all supremacy in the field of education. High priority is given to schools and colleges, both in financial support and in the social status accorded to teachers.

The 226-page report on Soviet education notes that the Moscow Government has challenged its schools to serve the Communists' political, military and economic objectives at home and abroad.

Since 1927 the Soviet Union has shown almost fantastic gains in every level of education. Thirty years ago the country's ten-year primary-secondary school system had 11,000,000 students. Today it has more than 30,000,000.

College Enrollment Soars

Enrollment in semi-professional schools for technicians has jumped from 180,000 to 1,961,000 since 1927. In higher educational institutions it skyrocketed from 169,000 to 1,867,000. During the same period in the United States, college enrollment has increased from 1,114,000 to 2,996,000.

Numbers alone are quite meaningless. The report, unfortunately for the United States, indicates that the Russians have attained quality in education, as well as quantity. The Soviet high school graduate, at the end of ten years, is better educated in academic subjects than the American graduate after twelve years.

Secondary school graduates in the Soviet Union have taken courses in physics and biology for five years, chemistry for four years, astronomy for one year and mathematics for ten years.

Few in U.S. Take Sciences

In the United States fewer than one-third of the high school graduates have taken a year of chemistry. One-fourth have studied physics, while a seventh have taken advanced mathematics.

The primary-secondary education program in the Soviet Union is a tenyear schedule, compared with twelve years in the United States. In the Soviet Union algebra and geometry begin in the sixth grade. Trigonometry and an introduction to calculus start in the ninth and tenth grades. Natural science begins in the fourth grade.

A typical program for the seventh-grade pupil includes a study of zoology, the anatomy and physiology of man, mathematics, history, geography, biology, a study of the Russian language and literacy reading, physics, chemistry, a foreign language, physical education, technical drawing, practical shop work and agriculture and sex hygiene.

The greatest emphasis is given to science and foreign languages, both obviously necessary as instruments of state policy. Forty percent of the secondary-school pupils during the 1955–56 school year in the Soviet Union studied German, 40 percent English and 20 percent French, Spanish or Latin.

English is stressed in Soviet schools and colleges. Sixty-five percent of the students in the Soviet institutions of higher learning study English. By contrast, a negligible number of American students, either in high school or college, take courses in the Russian language.

Although all phases of education receive support in the Soviet Union, the lion's share is reserved for the sciences. The scientists, engineers and technicians are the elite of the land. Boys and girls are encouraged, through subsistence grants and subsidies, to go into the "technical field."

The results have been publicized on various occasions. The Soviet Union graduates 80,000 engineers a year, compared with fewer than 30,000 in the United States.

The Soviet Union now is taking the lead on the secondary level, long the domain of the United States. Last year 1,500,000 students were graduated from Soviet secondary schools, compared with 1,300,000 in the United States.

American Concepts Cited

In making public the report, Dr. Lawrence G. Derthick, United States Commissioner of Education, said that, even though the Soviet Union apparently was outpacing the United States in the field of education, the American concepts of freedom and liberty must not be abandoned. He cited the well-known fact that the Soviet students, as well as teachers, were regimented, and had to follow a rigid party line.

"I believe the American concept of education, and the resources available in American young people for the pursuit of learning, are unsurpassed," Dr. Derthick declared. "We in America know that freedom is indispensable to good education, that liberty of the mind accomplishes more than regimentation.

"It would be tragic, therefore, if the evolution of education in the U.S.S.R. should be considered as any cause to question our basic concepts of freedom in education. Rather, it should challenge every American to reexamine the extent to which we as a people support our democratic system of education.

"It should, in fact, challenge Americans to take new interest in meeting the needs of our schools, colleges and universities as they serve the purposes of our society: freedom, peace and the fullest development of the individual."

Soviet Fills Specific Needs

Because it is a dictatorship, the Soviet Union is able to decide the number of skilled personnel needed in various fields for the most effective development of Soviet power. This ranges from the number of ballet stars or athletes to be trained to the quantity of science and engineering graduates that will be needed.

Throughout the education system runs the Communist party shadow. The secret police maintain surveillance on the political reliability of all school personnel, from teachers, students and administrators to the lowliest member of the system. The secret police, through their "spetsotdel" or special department, are an integral part of every administrative unit to education.

The surveillance is carried on with almost fantastic energy, the report found. Inspectors, culled from the ranks of politically reliable teachers, visit schools. They sit in on lessons and examinations. They study the Communist party youth organizations. They check on school discipline and even review the teaching problems with staff members.

Instead of visiting the schools to see whether the educational programs are satisfactory, as is done by supervisors in the United States, the Communist teacher-inspectors make certain that the official policy of the party is carried out in the Soviet schools.

Report's Major Findings

Among the major findings in the United States Office of Education report are these:

- Science and all technical subjects have become the primary concern of the Soviet school system. In a sense, the two Soviet space satellites symbolize the supreme interest of the Russians in anything relating to science or engineering. Seventy percent of the advanced degrees conferred by Soviet high educational institutions are in scientific and technological fields.

- The Soviet school child gets a much heavier program than his counterpart in the United States. He goes to school six days a week, has a rigid course of studies and is under constant pressure to excel. Instead of the "leisurely" pace of American schools, there is a continuous drive for top performance.

- More attention is paid to the gifted child. He is singled out at an early age and given special instruction. Though many American schools have classes for superior children, in the Soviet Union there is a definite attempt to find gifted children, especially those with a scientific bent, and encourage them to work at full capacity.

- School teachers and college professors are the elite of Soviet society. They are encouraged to improve their professional status by attending conferences, reading academic journals and continuing with their studies. There is no teacher shortage in the Soviet Union. In the United States the shortage is serious.

o The Soviet school system is rigid and inflexible. All children take similar courses through high school, get frequent examinations and are assigned a tremendous amount of homework. Students must conform to the Communist Party line. They are not encouraged to question the issues raised by their teachers.

o All education in the Soviet Union is under the domination of the Communist party. Much of the curriculum of the persons preparing to be teachers consists of studies in Communist political principles.

o The outstanding characteristic of the Soviet educational system is its authoritarian policy. The party determines the number of persons needed in any field; the Government fixes quotas for enrollments and assigns graduates to jobs in industry.

Science Gets 53 Percent of Time

Up to 1955, 40 percent of the total primary-secondary school program was devoted to the sciences.

Two years ago Moscow announced that "more time will be devoted to teaching physics, chemistry and biology by reducing the study of humanities to secondary importance." As a result, the sciences now get 53 percent of the students' time, the humanities and social studies 47 percent.

In the United States educators have begged students, without much success, to take more of the physical sciences. Soviet students are graduated from secondary schools with years of instruction in physics, chemistry, biology and mathematics.

Not many American students get that kind of academic diet. Few United States college students take as much science as the Soviet secondary graduates have had.

Only the Soviet state has the power to open, direct or operate a school or university. Government control of educational facilities, teaching staff and instructional methods is complete.

The United States Office of Education has no control over local or state schools. It can give direction and guidance through studies, reports or experiments that it may undertake. In a sense, the Office of Education is a "clearing house" for educational matters.

The citizens control the American public school system, as Dr. James B. Conant, president-emeritus of Harvard University, said last Friday evening. Grassroots support and advice are constantly sought. Dr. Conant spoke at a meeting of the New York State Citizens Committee for the Public Schools.

A Difference Is Freedom

Probably the most striking difference between the Soviet and the American school systems lies in the freedom that teachers have here. The Soviet teacher never knows when he or she is being watched or spied upon.

In another respect the Soviet school system is ahead of the American. The size of the average class is down to seventeen, compared with twenty-seven in the United States. Because there is no shortage of teachers, class size can be kept low. But there is a lack of classroom space. Most Soviet schools operate on a double-shift basis. Most schools are in use from 8 A.M. to 8 P.M.

The Soviet Union has gone far in making education an instrument of the state. The report indicates that Soviet education, while far ahead of what it was a generation ago, is still beset by inconsistencies and contradictions. Since the schools must follow Communist line, educational practices change with the zigzag policies enunciated in the Kremlin.

6

ELEMENTARY AND SECONDARY EDUCATION ACT, TITLE I: HELPING DISADVANTAGED CHILDREN MEET HIGH STANDARDS

PART A: IMPROVING BASIC GRANTS OPERATED BY SCHOOL DISTRICTS

Established in 1965 as a part of President Johnson's War on Poverty, Title I of the Elementary and Secondary Education Act (ESEA) became important to reform because it addressed financial inequities among students and districts. Title I began a new and unprecedented federal involvement with public schools, particularly for children from low-income communities. That ESEA has survived through several administrations and for more than three decades points to its popularity and importance. Schools in low-income areas have depended on federal funds to do everything from maintaining facilities to purchasing technology. Although some of the wording has changed from the original legislation, the intent of ESEA remains stable.

○

What's New
The Educational Excellence for All Children Act of 1999:

○ Supports the next stage of standards-based reform—implementing challenging standards and aligned assessments in every state—by retaining the current Title I requirement that states establish content standards, student performance standards, and assessments aligned to the standards by the 2000–01 school year;

○ Holds districts and schools accountable for increases in performance of all students—including the lowest-performing students—by encouraging states to implement one rigorous accountability system for all schools and requiring them to at least develop one such system for their Title I schools;

○ Authorizes additional funding for states and school districts to implement immediate, intensive intervention in low-performing schools and districts to improve their performance;

○ Supports high-quality instruction by having Title I districts (1) set aside funds for high-quality professional development activities, (2) ensure that new Title I teachers are certified in the field in which they are teaching, and (3) raise the minimum qualifications for paraprofessionals working in Title I programs;

○ Retains schoolwide provision that gives high-poverty schools—those schools with a poverty-level of 50 percent or higher—the flexibility to use Title I funds to improve the instructional program of the entire school;

○ Strengthens schoolwide efforts to improve high-poverty schools by encouraging the use of coherent research-based strategies for reforming the entire school;

○ Incorporates key research findings on improving the teaching and learning of reading, including encouraging districts to provide early identification and intervention for children who have trouble learning to read;

○ Helps districts and schools develop high-quality instructional programs through peer review of schoolwide plans, school improvement plans, district Title I plans, and district improvement plans;

○ Strengthens provisions to help limited English proficient (LEP) students learn English and meet their state's challenging content and performance standards, including requiring states to give state reading and language arts assessments in English to LEP students who have been in the United States for three consecutive years or longer;

○ Ensures equitable learning opportunities for Title I students who attend private schools by clarifying the issues on which public and private school officials are to consult, and by specifying that the equitable participation requirements apply to professional development and parental involvement;

○ Encourages school districts to provide extended learning in Title I schools and to use extended learning time as a specific intervention to be provided to students in Title I schoolwide programs who are having difficulty in meeting high academic standards;

○ Strengthens equal treatment for Title I schools by ensuring that they receive resources comparable to those received by other schools within a district, focusing on such factors as staff quality, curriculum and course offerings, and safe school facilities; and

○ Supports the improvement of Title I by reserving 0.3 percent of Title I funds for national evaluation, state partnerships to gather information necessary to improve program management, applied research, technical assistance, and information dissemination.

○

ENACTED IN 1965 AS PART OF THE WAR ON POVERTY to help our most disadvantaged students, Title I now provides more than $8 billion each year on behalf of over 11 million children in 45,000 schools and is the largest federal investment in elementary and secondary education.

Title I funding helps improve teaching and learning in schools with concentrations of low-achieving and poor children to help them meet challenging state academic standards. By targeting federal resources to school districts and schools with the highest concentrations of poverty—where academic performance tends to be low and the obstacles to raising performance are the greatest—Title I helps address the severe educational problems facing high-poverty communities.

Of the 11 million Title I students, about two-thirds are enrolled in grades 1–6.[1] Minority students participate at rates higher than their proportion of the student population: non-Hispanic whites make up 36 percent of Title I participants, Hispanic students make up 30 percent, and African-American students 28 percent.[2] In comparison, non-Hispanic whites are 64 percent of nationwide public school students, while Hispanics are 14 percent and African Americans are 17 percent of all students.[3]

The Title I grants to school districts serve about 260,000 preschool children, 167,000 private school children, close to 300,000 migrant children, and some 200,000 children identified as homeless. Title I services are provided to about 2 million students with limited English proficiency—almost one-fifth of all students served by the program and growing—and to 1 million students with disabilities.[4]

During the 1970s and most of the 1980s, Title I contributed to closing the achievement gap between students in urban disadvantaged communities and their peers in low-poverty areas[5] and between minority and non-minority students.[6] However, during the late 1980s and early 1990s, the achievement gap widened again.

Prior to 1994, program evaluations indicated that fundamental change was needed in Title I to help at-risk students achieve to the same high standards expected of other children.[7] As a result, the Congress and the Administration restructured Title I in 1994 to focus on helping low-performing students master challenging curriculum and meet high standards.

What We've Learned

The 1994 reauthorization of Title I focused on supporting schools, districts, and states to ensure that all children meet the same challenging standards. The reforms were designed to link the program to standards-based state and local reform efforts across the nation. Though there has been progress in establishing state standards across the country, states and school districts have not fully implemented them in their classrooms.

High-poverty schools are beginning to show gains in student performance.

It has been just five years since Congress enacted the Improving America's Schools Act of 1994 and, under the schedule mandated by that law, many states are still phasing in the 1994 provisions. Nonetheless, there is growing evidence that standards-based reforms supported by Title I are having a positive effect on teaching and learning. With federal support and encouragement, all 50 states, the District of Columbia, and Puerto Rico have made great progress in establishing high academic standards in reading and mathematics.

Most important, the effect of standards-based reform is beginning to be seen. Reading and math performance among nine-year-olds in high-poverty public schools and among the lowest-achieving fourth-graders has improved significantly on the National Assessment of Educational Progress.[8] Similarly, three-year trends reported by states and districts show progress in the percentage of students in the highest-poverty schools who meet state standards for proficiency in mathematics and reading.[9]

Nonetheless, despite the progress that states and districts have made, a substantial achievement gap remains between students in the highest-poverty schools and their peers in low-poverty schools.[10]

Title I concentrates resources on
communities with the greatest needs.

Title I is intended to help address the greater educational challenges facing high-poverty communities by concentrating extra resources on school districts and schools with the highest concentrations of poverty, low academic performance, and great obstacles to raising performance. The record shows that the 1994 reforms heightened the concentration of resources where the need is the greatest:

○ While the highest-poverty schools make up only about 15 percent of schools nationwide, they receive 46 percent of Title I funds. About three-fourths (73 percent) of the funds go to schools with 50 percent or more students who are eligible for free or reduced-price lunch.[11]

○ In 1997–98, Title I helped 95 percent of the nation's highest-poverty schools (where three out of every four students are from low-income families), up from 79 percent in 1993–94. The proportion of the highest-poverty secondary schools receiving Title I funds also increased as a result of the 1994 amendment, from 61 percent to 93 percent.[12]

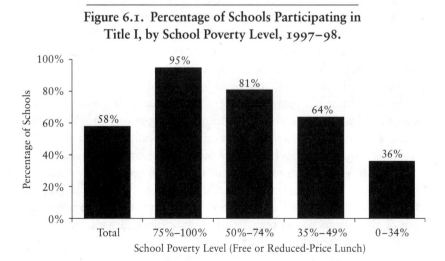

Figure 6.1. Percentage of Schools Participating in Title I, by School Poverty Level, 1997–98.

Source: *U.S. Department of Education, unpublished tabulations from the Follow Up Survey of Education Reform.*

○ The share of Title I funds allocated to low-poverty schools (where fewer than one student in three is from a low-income family) declined from 49 percent in 1994–95 to 36 percent in 1997–98.

Almost all Title I funds go to local school districts to support instruction.

Approximately 99 percent of Title I dollars go to local school districts. School districts, in turn, use 90 to 93 percent of their Title I funds for instruction and instructional support, most often in reading and math.[13]

Title I provides flexible funding that may be used for supplementary instruction, professional development, after-school or other extended learning time programs, and other strategies for raising student achievement. For example, Title I funds used for professional development amounted to about $191 million in 1997–98, about 27 percent of total federal support for teacher professional development.[14]

Accountability systems tied to standards and assessments provide focus for schools.

Accountability systems for school quality, including student performance, can help schools and districts use data to identify student needs and make improvements. Recent research on accountability systems in 14 districts found that decision-making relied heavily on performance data. The study found that many districts were going beyond requirements of Title I to use performance data to identify and develop strategies for staff development and curriculum improvement to address gaps in performance.[15]

Even though Title I accounts for a relatively small portion (about 3 percent) of total federal, state, and local spending on elementary and secondary education, some evidence suggests that Title I accountability provisions are having a significant effect in driving reform in high-poverty districts. For example, a recent study of accountability in large urban districts found that Title I has been "a model and an instigator" for standards-based reforms and efforts to track student progress and improve schools.[16] Nationally, 50 percent of small, poor districts and 47 percent of large, poor districts report that Title I is driving reform to a great extent. Fourteen percent of all districts report that Title I is significantly driving reform to a great extent in their districts as a whole.[17]

States are making progress in implementing the accountability provisions of Title I, although the law does not require full implementation of accountability systems until final assessments are in place in the 2000–01 school year. But states are also facing new challenges as they transform their educational systems into higher-performing, results-based systems.[18] For example, although there is considerable overlap between schools identified for improvement under Title I and those identified through other state or local mechanisms, states report that they are having difficulty integrating the Title I requirements with their own systems. Only 23 state Title I directors report that the same accountability system is used for Title I schools as for other schools in their state.[19]

States and districts lack the capacity to turn around schools in need of improvement.

State school support teams, authorized in 1994, were intended first to provide support for schoolwide programs in their planning process and, as a second priority, to provide assistance to schools in need of improvement through activities such as professional development or identifying resources for changing instruction and organization. The lack of capacity of state school support teams to assist schools in need of improvement under Title I, however, has been a major concern:

- The State Improvement Grants, designed to provide additional resources for the operation of school support teams, have not been funded in the past four years. Although state school support teams have primarily assisted schoolwide programs, their charge also includes providing assistance to other schools in need of improvement. In 1998, only eight states reported that school support teams have been able to serve the majority of schools identified as in need of improvement.

- Fewer than half (47 percent) of schools that reported in 1997–98 that they had been identified as in need of improvement also reported that this designation led to additional professional development or assistance.[20]

○

Agua Fria Union High School Avondale, Arizona
Agua Fria High School enrolls about 1,700 students in grades 9 through 12. Half of its students are white, and almost 40 percent are Hispanic. Twenty-eight percent of the students receive free or reduced-price school lunches. The school's Title I targeted assistance program

serves 525 students, most of whom are freshmen. For the first time in many years, Agua Fria's scores on standardized tests exceeded those of other high schools in the western suburbs of Phoenix.

Every academic department at Agua Fria has aligned its curriculum with the Arizona Academic Standards and raised its graduation requirements. Each academic department must now create a written plan to indicate how its teachers will use the standards in all of their classes. The school requires that students read, at a minimum, at the ninth-grade level before they graduate, a requirement the state dropped several years ago.

The Title I program supports the school's commitment to maintaining high standards and preparing students for work. The lowest-performing Title I students take a direct instruction reading class, which is offered as an elective. The course's curriculum is also aligned with state reading objectives and uses computer-aided instruction, worksheets, and writing journals. Other Title I students can use the Title I reading lab during their prep period or attend tutorial sessions available before, during, and after school. Some receive reading assistance from Title I aides in their regular English classes. During the summer, about 40 incoming Title I students take a six-week math immersion course.

○

A focus on high standards at the classroom level can make a difference in student achievement.

There is evidence of progress for students in high-poverty schools where staff members focus on challenging standards and strategies to help students achieve them. Preliminary findings from the *Longitudinal Evaluation of School Change and Performance* (LESCP), a study of instructional practices in 71 high-poverty schools, found that students whose teachers used a curriculum that reflected the standards of the National Council of Teachers of Mathematics recorded higher gains in mathematics than did other students.[21]

Another study found that in high-performing, high-poverty schools, 94 percent of the principals reported using standards to assess student progress and 80 percent reported using standards extensively to design curriculum and instruction.[22] Nationally, the proportion of Title I principals who reported using content standards to guide curriculum and instruction to a great extent has increased from approximately half in 1995–96 to three-quarters in 1997–98.[23]

Teachers need more preparation to implement standards in the classroom.

Despite reported use of standards, most teachers do not feel very well prepared to implement them in the classroom. In 1998, only 35 percent of teachers in schools with 60 percent poverty or greater reported that they felt very well prepared to implement state or district curriculum and performance standards.[24]

Teachers' sense of preparedness is a key factor in predicting student outcomes, according to the LESCP study of 71 high-poverty Title I schools. The LESCP found that teachers' reported preparedness in both subject matter and instructional strategies had a positive relationship to student progress.[25] Current teacher training seems insufficient:

- In 1998, public school teachers—regardless of the poverty level of their school—spent a very limited amount of time in professional development, although they did focus on topics that supported standards-based reform. Most teachers are not participating in training that is intensive or sustained, two characteristics essential for effective professional development.[26]

- Over half (55 percent) of all teachers in high-poverty schools reported spending less than nine hours per year on training in the content areas. Over two-thirds (70 percent) reported receiving less than nine hours per year of professional development related to content and performance standards, yet this topic was the most common one on which teachers received training (81 percent of all teachers received professional development in this area).[27]

Teacher aides are widely used to provide instruction in title I schools.

Paraprofessionals continue to be widely used to provide instruction in Title I schools, particularly in high-poverty schools. In the 1997–98 school year, 84 percent of principals in high-poverty schools reported using aides, compared with 53 percent in low-poverty schools.[28] Although very few paraprofessionals have the educational background necessary to teach students, almost all (98 percent) were either teaching or helping teach students. Forty-one percent of Title I aides said that half or more of the time they spent teaching or helping to teach students was on their own, without a teacher present.[29]

Teacher aides in high-poverty schools are more likely than aides in other schools to lack the educational background that would qualify them to teach or help teach children. Only 10 percent of Title I aides in high-poverty elementary schools have a bachelor's degree, compared with 19 percent nationwide.[30]

Schoolwide programs are more likely to integrate Title I services into overall standards-based reforms at the school level.

Each Title I school operates either a Title I schoolwide program, in which Title I funds are combined with other funds to improve the quality of the whole school, or a Title I targeted assistance program solely for Title I students.

A recent study on high-achieving, high-poverty schools found that 79 percent of respondents from the study's sample—composed of high-poverty schools identified by states as among their highest achieving—operate schoolwide programs. Key characteristics of high-performing high-poverty schools include extensive use of standards to design curriculum and instruction, assess student work, and evaluate teachers; increased instructional time in reading and math; greater investment in professional development; comprehensive systems for monitoring student performance; attention to accountability; and a focus on the role of parents in helping students meet standards.[31]

○

P.S. 172

Brooklyn, New York

P.S. 172 enrolls just over 600 students, of whom three-quarters are Hispanic and virtually all receive free or reduced-price school lunches. The school has operated a Title I schoolwide program since 1993. The school has combined Title I, Goals 2000, Title VII, state, and private funds to help all of its students achieve high standards. Since 1994–95, P.S. 172's third- and sixth-grade reading and mathematics scores on the New York State assessments have exceeded district and city averages.

P.S. 172 has helped its teachers implement a literacy-focused curriculum through intensive professional development. A master teacher and a full-time staff development specialist mentor first-year teachers. Teachers share ideas and expectations within and across grades. Kindergarten teachers use hands-on learning strategies to introduce language, mathematics, and critical thinking skills. A phonics-based reading program helps all students in the primary grades build their vocabulary and comprehension, including those who speak little English. Between the third and sixth grades, a multicultural literature-based program and Internet-based lessons in social studies bring the written word alive for students.

○

Extended learning time can improve achievement, but is not fully utilized in Title I.

In a recent study of high-performing, high-poverty schools, 86 percent of the schools provided extended learning time for reading—such as extra instruction after school—and 66 percent provided extra time in mathematics.[32] In a study of Maryland elementary schools, researchers found that the more successful schools were seeing consistent academic gains associated with extended-day programs.[33]

Title I resources can be used to provide extended learning programs. Although the proportion of schools offering before- or after-school programs in the early grades has increased from 9 to 39 percent since the last reauthorization, most Title I schools still do not offer such programs. Moreover, those schools that do offer the programs serve few students with them.[34]

Family involvement in education strengthens learning.

Principals and teachers understand the importance of parental involvement, especially in high-poverty schools.[35] First required under the 1994 reauthorization, Title I school-parent compacts—agreements between parents and school staff describing their shared responsibility to improve student learning—can bring schools and parents together and promote ongoing communication. However, the compacts need sustained support to be successful.

The proportion of Title I schools with school-parent compacts rose from 20 percent in 1994 to about 75 percent in 1998. A substantial majority of schools, especially those serving high concentrations of low-income children, find compacts helpful in promoting parental involvement.[36] However, 25 percent of Title I schools still do not have such agreements.

What We Propose

Title I is the primary source of federal support for raising the quality of instruction in high-poverty schools. The program challenges all students to reach high academic standards and helps provide the high-quality education necessary to reach those standards. The Educational Excellence for All Children Act of 1999 would:

- *Maintain a clear focus on raising standards for all children.* Our proposal would retain the schedule for implementing standards-based reform established in the 1994 laws, including the requirement that states develop assessments aligned with their standards by the 2000–01 school year.

Almost every state has established challenging content standards describing what all students, including Title I students, should know. States are now working on completing performance standards describing what students should be able to do. Soon all states will be administering assessments that measure student progress toward those standards.

To see meaningful gains in student learning, states and school districts must now translate state standards from policy documents into classroom practices. State standards and assessments will help teachers and schools focus instruction, curriculum, and professional development for school staff and enable them to determine how their students are doing and how they can improve. Standards and assessments will also help states and districts better identify schools in need of help.

- *Strengthen accountability for districts and schools.* Our proposal would encourage states to develop one rigorous accountability system that holds all schools, including Title I schools, accountable for making continuous and substantial gains in student performance. States will have the flexibility to use either a model outlined in the statute or an alternative that is at least as rigorous and effective. States without a single statewide accountability system would be required to develop one for their Title I schools.

- *Reward improvement and success.* Our proposal would require states to establish criteria for recognizing distinguished districts and schools. For example, these criteria might lead states to recognize districts and schools that have shown substantial gains for three consecutive years, have helped virtually all of their students meet the state's advanced level of performance, or have raised student achievement across gender and racial groups to promote equity in achievement. Acknowledging high-achieving and improving schools and districts helps them sustain their momentum and identifies lessons for other schools.

- *Increase funding to help low-performing schools implement sound programs that improve student performance.* Each state would be required to set aside 2.5 percent of its Title I allocation to strengthen state and local capacity to turn around low-performing schools. This set-aside would increase to 3.5 percent in the 2003–04 school year. At least 70 percent of these funds would go to districts to turn around low-performing schools. The remainder would be used to fund a state support system to improve schools and districts.

This set-aside would provide more funds for swift, intensive intervention such as expert consultation and in-depth teacher training in schools and districts identified as being in need of improvement, and for stronger corrective actions in schools and districts that fail to show improvement after initial interventions.

Funds would be used, first, in consistently low-performing schools and school districts to implement strong corrective actions that dramatically alter the structure of schools and the instructional strategies to help students in the school or school district. Districts would take at least one of the following corrective actions: (1) implementing a new curriculum that research has shown offers substantial promise of improving student achievement; (2) redesigning or reconstituting the school, including reopening it as a charter school; or (3) closing the school and allowing its students to transfer. In all instances of corrective action, districts may also allow students the option of transferring to a new school.

Funds would then be used in low-performing schools or districts that have been identified as being in need of improvement to provide support and interventions, such as expert consultation and in-depth teacher training.

- *Emphasize high-quality teaching.* Teacher quality is the greatest single in-school factor in determining student success.[37] To enable teachers in our poorest schools to teach to challenging standards, our proposal would require districts to use at least 5 percent of their Title I funds in the first two years, and 10 percent in subsequent years, to support teacher development tied to challenging standards.

In addition, all new teachers paid by Title I or working in a Title I school operating a schoolwide program would have to be certified in the field in which they teach or have a bachelor's degree and be working toward full certification within three years. By July 1, 2002, all paraprofessionals would be required to hold at least a high school diploma or equivalent, and only paraprofessionals with at least two years of college would be able to assist teachers in the classroom by providing appropriate instructional help, such as one-on-one tutoring. Paraprofessionals would participate in professional development, and school districts would be encouraged to develop career ladders to enable paraprofessionals to become certified teachers.

This effort would be complemented by the teacher quality accountability provisions in Title XI, which would require teachers to be qualified, as well as by provisions in Titles II, III, and VII that would increase support for professional development.

• *Strengthen schoolwide efforts to improve education in high-poverty schools.* Schoolwide programs can be a highly effective way to help students in high-poverty schools meet high standards for performance. Rather than offering a separate program for Title I students, schoolwide programs improve the entire instructional program by combining federal, state, and local funds into one integrated program.

Our proposal would continue to emphasize schoolwide programs in schools that have at least 50 percent poverty, because research shows that this concentration of children from poor families affects the educational achievement of all children in the school.[38]

Our proposal would make schoolwide programs more effective by emphasizing coherent research-based approaches for raising student achievement by reforming the entire school. Key elements of schoolwide reforms are as follows:

1. *A comprehensive needs assessment* that examines the academic performance of all children against state standards, attendance, violence and drug use, class size, staff quality, parent and community involvement, and the availability of resources;

2. *A coherent design* to improve teaching and learning throughout the entire school based on data from the assessment. This design includes, for example, instruction by highly qualified staff; ongoing high-quality professional development; effective research-based methods and strategies to strengthen the core academic program, increasing the amount and quality of learning time, and meeting the needs of the most at-risk children; and strategies to increase parental involvement. These elements must be aligned and included in a comprehensive design that addresses the needs of the whole school; and

3. *A regular review of the school's progress* in implementing its program and meeting its goals for student achievement. The school would use the results of this review to continuously improve the design and implementation of its schoolwide program.

Accounting practices can be a barrier to successfully integrating program funds. Our proposal would require each state to work to reduce its fiscal and accounting barriers so that school districts can combine Title I funds with funds from other federal, state, and local sources to achieve schoolwide reform.

- *Encourage peer support for schoolwide programs and school improvement strategies.* To support critical feedback and improvement on schoolwide programs and school improvement plans, our proposal requires school districts to peer-review schoolwide plans and school improvement plans and states to peer-review district-level Title I plans and district improvement plans. Schools and districts can learn a great deal from each other.
- *Focus attention on improving the education of limited English proficient (LEP) children.* Our proposal would continue to hold Title I schools accountable for the performance of LEP students in reaching high academic standards and learning English.

Schools would annually assess the progress of LEP students in learning English and use the results of those assessments to modify instruction. As under current law, states would have to include LEP students in state assessments and (to the extent practicable) test them in the language and manner most likely to yield accurate information about what they know. At a minimum, states would be required to have tests available in Spanish. To assess student progress and hold schools accountable for teaching English and academic content, LEP students who have attended schools in the United States for three consecutive years would be tested in English on the state's reading or language arts assessment.

- *Incorporate key findings of reading research and encourage preschool programs.* Our proposal would make clear that a district may provide services directly to eligible preschool children in all or part of its jurisdiction, through any participating Title I school, or through a contract with another public preschool program, such as Head Start. The proposal also would emphasize that such services must focus on the developmental needs of participating children and use research-based approaches that build on children's competencies and lead to school success. Our proposal would also encourage the use of diagnostic assessments in the first grade to ensure early identification and intervention for students with reading difficulties.

Research shows that children who receive enrichment to develop their language and cognitive skills early in life show higher reading achievement in elementary and middle school.[39] Title I currently authorizes services to preschool children, but these provisions need more clarity.

• *Ensure equitable learning opportunities for Title I participants who attend private schools.* Our proposal would clarify that teachers and families of participating private school students are to participate in Title I professional development and parental involvement activities on an equitable basis, and that services provided to private school students are intended to meet the needs of those students.

Our proposal would also strengthen consultation between public and private school officials. First, new provisions would clarify that consultation includes meetings among school district and private school officials and continues throughout the implementation and assessment of Title I services. Additional changes would specify that the issues discussed during consultation are to include:

○ The amount of funds generated by low-income private school children;

○ The methods and sources of data to be used to determine the number of low-income students in participating school attendance areas who attend private schools;

○ How and when the school district will make decisions about the delivery of services to eligible students attending private schools; and

○ How the results of assessments will be used to improve services to eligible children attending private schools.

• *Promote greater use of extended learning time to help students achieve high academic standards.* Although the use of extended learning time programs has increased significantly and recent evidence has affirmed their effectiveness, fewer than half of Title I schools offer these programs. Where they do exist, few students participate.

Because extended learning time can improve student performance, our proposal would strengthen such opportunities by encouraging school districts to provide extended learning time in Title I schools and encouraging its use as a specific intervention to be provided to students in Title I schoolwide programs who are having difficulty in meeting high academic standards. Our proposal would also require school districts to describe in their plans how they will promote the use of extended learning time in Title I schools.

• *Target funds by implementing unfunded provisions of current law to ensure that Title I resources go to the highest-poverty school districts and schools.* The 1994 reauthorization created the new "targeted grants" formula and changed the within-district allocation provisions. The Congress also increased the portion of Title I funds appropriated for concentration grants over the past several years. Although the targeted grants have not been funded, the other changes in reauthorization have resulted in a larger proportion of Title I funds flowing to high-poverty schools.

The redistribution of funds to the poorest schools and districts has been a positive development. However, 86 percent of funds still flow through the "basic grants" formula, which spreads dollars thinly across virtually all districts. All of the remaining funds are distributed according to the "concentration grants" formula, which is a flawed mechanism because, although it provides funds only to higher-poverty districts, it takes an "all or nothing" approach to targeting. Targeted grants, in comparison, provide proportionately higher payments to districts with higher percentages or numbers of poor children and are thus a fairer vehicle for targeting funds. Our proposal would require that at least 20 percent of the Title I, Part A, appropriation flow through targeted grants, while maintaining the other allocations in current law.

Finally, under current law, Puerto Rico's allocations are artificially constrained relative to what the commonwealth would receive if it were a state. Our proposal would require that Puerto Rico's allocations be determined on the same basis as allocations to states, with this change phased in over five years to avoid disruption of current allocations.

• *Strengthen comparability provisions to ensure that Title I schools are treated the same as all other schools in a district.* By July 1, 2002, districts would be required to ensure comparability in terms of the qualifications of staff, curriculum and course offerings, and condition and safety of school facilities. With the expectation that all children are to meet challenging state standards, it is more important than ever to ensure that high-poverty schools are comparable qualitatively and quantitatively to other schools in their districts before they receive Title I funds.

• *Build capacity to develop new knowledge about program operation and innovations.* Our proposal would authorize the Secretary to reserve 0.3 percent of Title I funds to conduct evaluations of Title I programs to determine their effectiveness, consistent with the Government Performance and Results Act of 1993. Our proposal would mandate a national assessment of Title I to examine, for example, its effect on state standards-based reform systems and student academic performance relative to that system. Our proposal would also mandate a national longitudinal study of Title I schools to provide an accurate description of Title I's short-term and long-term effectiveness. Finally, our proposal would authorize state partnerships to inform program management and support continuous improvement by states, districts, and schools.

Our proposed evaluation funds would also support technical assistance, program improvement, and replication activities, consistent with the other major ESEA programs.

NOTES

1. U.S. Department of Education. (1999). Unpublished tabulations from the 1996–97 Title I Performance Report.

2. U.S. Department of Education. (1999). Unpublished tabulations from the 1996–97 Title I Performance Report.

3. U.S. Department of Education, National Center for Education Statistics. (1998). Digest of Education Statistics. Washington, DC: Author.

4. U.S. Department of Education. (1999). Unpublished tabulations from the 1996–97 Title I Performance Report.

5. U.S. Department of Education. (1992). National Assessment of Chapter 1 Program. Washington, DC: Author.

6. U.S. Department of Education, National Center for Education Statistics. (1991). *Trends in academic progress.* Washington, DC: Author. Grissmer, D. W., Kirby, S. N., Berends, M. & Williamson, S. (1994). *Student achievement and the changing American family.* Santa Monica: Rand. O'Day, J. A. & Smith, M. S. (1993). Systemic reform and educational opportunity. In S. H. Fuhrman (Ed.), *Designing coherent education policy, improving the system.* San Francisco: Jossey-Bass.

7. U.S. Department of Education. (1993). *Reinventing Chapter 1: The current Chapter 1 program and new directions.* Washington, DC: Author.

8. U.S. Department of Education, National Center for Education Statistics, National Assessment of Educational Progress (NAEP). (1998). NAEP reading trends, unpublished tabulations. NAEP mathematics trends, unpublished tabulations. NAEP main reading assessment 1994 to 1998. NAEP main mathematics assessment 1990 to 1996.

9. U.S. Department of Education. (1999). *Promising results, continuing challenges: The final report of the national assessment of Title I.* Washington, DC: Author.

10. U.S. Department of Education, National Center for Education Statistics, National Assessment of Educational Progress. (1999). NAEP main reading and mathematics, unpublished tabulations.

11. U.S. Department of Education. (1999). Unpublished tabulations from the Study of Education Resources and Federal Funding.

12. Stullich, S., Donly, B. & Stolzberg, S. (in press). *Within-district targeting of Title I funds.* U.S. Department of Education. (1999). *Promising results, continuing challenges: The final report of the national assessment of Title I.* Washington, DC: Author.

13. U.S. Department of Education. (1998). *The use of federal funds for administrative costs.* Washington, DC: Author.

14. U.S. Department of Education. (1999). Unpublished tabulations from the Study of Education Resources and Federal Funding.

15. Goertz, M., Massell, D. & Chun, T. (1998, October 29). *District response to state accountability systems.* Paper presented at the annual meeting of the Association for Public Policy Analysis and Management, New York City.

16. The McKenzie Group. (in press). *Student achievement and accountability systems in urban districts.*

17. U.S. Department of Education. (in press). *Local Implementation Study.*

18. Anderson, L. & Turnbull, B. J. (1998). *Living in interesting times: Early state implementation of new federal laws.* Washington, DC: U.S. Department of Education.

19. U.S. Department of Education. (1999). Unpublished tabulations from the Follow-Up Survey of State Implementation of Federal Elementary and Secondary Education Programs.

20. U.S. Department of Education. (1999). Unpublished tabulations from the Follow-Up Survey of State Implementation of Federal Elementary and Secondary Education Programs.

21. U.S. Department of Education. (1998). *Longitudinal evaluation of school change and performance: Some preliminary findings from the first two years.* Unpublished manuscript.

22. The Education Trust, Inc. & Council of Chief State School Officers. (1999). *Dispelling the myth: High poverty schools exceeding expectations.* Manuscript submitted for publication.

23. U.S. Department of Education. (1999). Unpublished tabulations from the Follow-Up Survey of State Implementation of Federal Elementary and Secondary Education Programs.

24. U.S. Department of Education. (1999). *Promising results, continuing challenges: The final report of the national assessment of Title I.* Washington, DC: Author.

25. U.S. Department of Education. (1998). *Longitudinal evaluation of school change and performance: Some preliminary findings from the first two years.* Unpublished manuscript.

26. U.S. Department of Education, National Center for Education Statistics. (1999). *Status of education reform in public elementary and secondary schools: Teachers' perspectives.* Washington, DC: Author.

27. U.S. Department of Education. (1999). *Promising results, continuing challenges: The final report of the national assessment of Title I.* Washington, DC: Author. Ch. 6, P. 13.

28. U.S. Department of Education. (1999). Unpublished tabulations from the Follow-Up Survey of State Implementation of Federal Elementary and Secondary Education Programs.

29. U.S. Department of Education. (1999). Unpublished tabulations from the Study of Education Resources and Federal Funding.

30. U.S. Department of Education. (1999). *Promising results, continuing challenges: The final report of the national assessment of Title I.* Washington, DC: Author. Ch. 6, P. 8.

31. The Education Trust and Council of Chief State School Officers. (1999). *Dispelling the Myth: High Poverty Schools Exceeding Expectations.* Washington, DC: The Education Trust.

32. The Education Trust, Inc. & Council of Chief State School Officers. (1999). *Dispelling the Myth: High poverty schools exceeding expectations.* Manuscript submitted for publication. P. 6.

33. Hawley, W., Schager, W., Schager, F., Hultgren, F., Abrams, A., Lewis, E. & Ferrara, S. (1997, March 25). *An outlier study of school effectiveness: Implications for public policy and school improvement.* Paper presented at the annual meeting of the American Educational Research Association, Chicago, IL.

34. U.S. Department of Education. (1999). Unpublished tabulations from the *Follow-Up Survey of State Implementation of Federal Elementary and Secondary Education Programs.*

35. U.S. Department of Education, Partnership for Family Involvement in Education & GTE Foundation. (1998). *The study of opportunities for and barriers to family involvement in education.* Washington, DC: Author. Louis Harris & Associates, Inc. (1998). *The Metropolitan Life survey of the American teacher.*

36. U.S. Department of Education. (1998). *Title I school-parent compacts: Supporting partnerships to improve learning.* Washington, DC: Author.

37. Ferguson, R. (1991). Paying for public education: New evidence on how and why money matters. *Harvard Journal on Legislation, 28* (Summer), 465–498.

38. Apt Associations. (1994). Special analysis.

39. Snow, C. E., Burns, M. S. & Griffin, P. (1998). *Preventing reading difficulties in young children.* Washington, DC: National Academy Press.

7

OPINION OF THE COURT, *LAU* v. *NICHOLS*

U.S. *Supreme Court*

Bilingual education, a local issue in U.S. schools since the founding of the country, came to national attention in 1974 with the *Lau* decision. Since that decision, schools have been expected to provide a level of instructional assistance to non-English-speaking students. The interpretation of this decision has been subject to hot debate, protest, and referendum. It is helpful to pair the text provided in this decision with the material presented in Chapter Sixteen, which provides more historical background on bilingual education in the United States.

○

THE FAILURE OF THE SAN FRANCISCO SCHOOL SYSTEM to provide English language instruction to approximately 1,800 students of Chinese ancestry who do not speak English, or to provide them with other adequate instructional procedures, denies them a meaningful opportunity to participate in the public educational program and thus violates 601 of the Civil Rights Act of 1964, which bans discrimination based "on the ground of race, color, or national origin," in "any program or activity receiving Federal financial assistance," and the implementing regulations of the Department of Health, Education, and Welfare. Pp. 565–569.

MR. JUSTICE DOUGLAS delivered the opinion of the Court.

The San Francisco, California, school system was integrated in 1971 as a result of a federal court decree, 339 F. Supp. 1315. See *Lee* v. *Johnson*,

404 U.S. 1215 . The District Court found that there are 2,856 students of Chinese ancestry in the school system who do not speak English. Of those who have that language deficiency, about 1,000 are given supplemental courses in the English language.[1] About 1,800, however, do not receive that instruction.

This class suit brought by non–English-speaking Chinese students against officials responsible for the operation of the San Francisco Unified School District seeks relief against the unequal educational opportunities, which are alleged to violate, inter alia, the Fourteenth Amendment. No specific remedy is urged upon us. [414 U.S. 563, 565] Teaching English to the students of Chinese ancestry who do not speak the language is one choice. Giving instructions to this group in Chinese is another. There may be others. Petitioners ask only that the Board of Education be directed to apply its expertise to the problem and rectify the situation.

The District Court denied relief. The Court of Appeals affirmed, holding that there was no violation of the Equal Protection Clause of the Fourteenth Amendment or of 601 of the Civil Rights Act of 1964, 78 Stat. 252, 42 U.S.C. 2000d, which excludes from participation in federal financial assistance, recipients of aid which discriminate against racial groups, 483 F.2d 791. One judge dissented. A hearing en banc was denied, two judges dissenting. *Id.*, at 805.

We granted the petition for certiorari because of the public importance of the question presented, 412 U.S. 938.

The Court of Appeals reasoned that "[e]very student brings to the starting line of his educational career different advantages and disadvantages caused in part by social, economic and cultural background, created and continued completely apart from any contribution by the school system," 483 F.2d, at 797. Yet in our view the case may not be so easily decided. This is a public school system of California and 71 of the California Education Code states that "English shall be the basic language of instruction in all schools." That section permits a school district to determine "when and under what circumstances instruction may be given bilingually." That section also states as "the policy of the state" to insure "the mastery of English by all pupils in the schools. " And bilingual instruction is authorized "to the extent that it does not interfere with the systematic, sequential, and regular instruction of all pupils in the English language." [414 U.S. 563, 566]

Moreover, 8573 of the Education Code provides that no pupil shall receive a diploma of graduation from grade 12 who has not met the standards of proficiency in "English," as well as other prescribed subjects. Moreover, by 12,101 of the Education Code (Supp. 1973) children between the ages of six and 16 years are (with exceptions not material here) "subject to compulsory full-time education."

Under these state-imposed standards there is no equality of treatment merely by providing students with the same facilities, textbooks, teachers, and curriculum; for students who do not understand English are effectively foreclosed from any meaningful education.

Basic English skills are at the very core of what these public schools teach. Imposition of a requirement that, before a child can effectively participate in the educational program, he must already have acquired those basic skills is to make a mockery of public education. We know that those who do not understand English are certain to find their classroom experiences wholly incomprehensible and in no way meaningful.

We do not reach the Equal Protection Clause argument which has been advanced but rely solely on 601 of the Civil Rights Act of 1964, 42 U.S.C. 2000d, to reverse the Court of Appeals.

That section bans discrimination based "on the ground of race, color, or national origin," in "any program or activity receiving Federal financial assistance." The school district involved in this litigation receives large amounts of federal financial assistance. The Department of Health, Education, and Welfare (HEW), which has authority to promulgate regulations prohibiting discrimination in federally assisted school systems, 42 U.S.C. 2000d-1, in 1968 issued one guideline that "[s]chool systems are responsible for assuring that students of a particular race, color, or national origin are not denied the [414 U.S. 563, 567] opportunity to obtain the education generally obtained by other students in the system." 33 Fed. Reg. 4956. In 1970 HEW made the guidelines more specific, requiring school districts that were federally funded "to rectify the language deficiency in order to open" the instruction to students who had "linguistic deficiencies," 35 Fed. Reg. 11,595.

By 602 of the Act HEW is authorized to issue rules, regulations, and orders[2] to make sure that recipients of federal aid under its jurisdiction conduct any federally financed projects consistently with 601. HEW's regulations, 45 CFR 80.3(b)(1), specify that the recipients may not

> (ii) Provide any service, financial aid, or other benefit to an individual which is different, or is provided in a different manner, from that provided to others under the program;
>
> . . . .
>
> (iv) Restrict an individual in any way in the enjoyment of any advantage or privilege enjoyed by others receiving any service, financial aid, or other benefit under the program.

Discrimination among students on account of race or national origin that is prohibited includes "discrimination . . . in the availability or use of any academic . . . or [414 U.S. 563, 568] other facilities of the grantee or other recipient." *Id.,* 80.5(b).

Discrimination is barred which has that effect even though no purposeful design is present: a recipient "may not . . . utilize criteria or methods of administration which have the effect of subjecting individuals to discrimination" or have "the effect of defeating or substantially impairing accomplishment of the objectives of the program as respect individuals of a particular race, color, or national origin." *Id.,* 80.3(b)(2).

It seems obvious that the Chinese-speaking minority receive fewer benefits than the English-speaking majority from respondents' school system which denies them a meaningful opportunity to participate in the educational program—all earmarks of the discrimination banned by the regulations.[3] In 1970 HEW issued clarifying guidelines, 35 Fed. Reg. 11,595, which include the following:

> Where inability to speak and understand the English language excludes national origin-minority group children from effective participation in the educational program offered by a school district, the district must take affirmative steps to rectify the language deficiency in order to open its instructional program to these students.

> Any ability grouping or tracking system employed by the school system to deal with the special language skill needs of national origin-minority group children must be designed to meet such language skill needs as soon as possible and must not operate as an educational dead end or permanent track.

Respondent school district contractually agreed to "comply with title VI of the Civil Rights Act of 1964 . . . and all requirements imposed by or pursuant to the [414 U.S. 563, 569] Regulation" of HEW (45 CFR pt. 80) which are "issued pursuant to that title. . ." and also immediately to "take any measures necessary to effectuate this agreement." The Federal Government has power to fix the terms on which its money allotments to the States shall be disbursed. *Oklahoma* v. *CSC,* 330 U.S. 127, 142–143. Whatever may be the limits of that power, *Steward Machine Co.* v. *Davis,* 301 U.S. 548, 590 et seq., they have not been reached here. Senator Humphrey, during the floor debates on the Civil Rights Act of 1964, said:

> Simple justice requires that public funds, to which all taxpayers of all races contribute, not be spent in any fashion which encourages, entrenches, subsidizes, or results in racial discrimination.[4]

We accordingly reverse the judgment of the Court of Appeals and re-mand the case for the fashioning of appropriate relief.

Reversed and remanded.

MR. JUSTICE WHITE concurs in the result.

MR. JUSTICE STEWART, with whom the CHIEF JUSTICE and MR. JUSTICE BLACKMUN join, concurring in the result.

It is uncontested that more than 2,800 schoolchildren of Chinese ances-try attend school in the San Francisco Unified School District system even though they do not speak, understand, read, or write the English language, and that as to some 1,800 of these pupils the respondent school authorities have taken no significant steps to deal with this language deficiency. The petitioners do not contend, however, that the respondents have affirma-tively or intentionally contributed to this inadequacy, but only [414 U.S. 563, 570] that they have failed to act in the face of changing social and linguistic patterns. Because of this laissez-faire attitude on the part of the school administrators, it is not entirely clear that 601 of the Civil Rights Act of 1964, 42 U.S.C. 2000d, standing alone, would render illegal the ex-penditure of federal funds on these schools. For that section provides that "[n]o person in the United States shall, on the ground of race, color, or national origin, be excluded from participation in, be denied the benefits of, or be subjected to discrimination under any program or activity receiv-ing Federal financial assistance."

On the other hand, the interpretive guidelines published by the Office for Civil Rights of the Department of Health, Education, and Welfare in 1970, 35 Fed. Reg. 11,595, clearly indicate that affirmative efforts to give special training for non–English-speaking pupils are required by Tit. VI as a condition to receipt of federal aid to public schools:

> Where inability to speak and understand the English language excludes
> national origin-minority group children from effective participation in
> the educational program offered by a school district, the district must
> take affirmative steps to rectify the language deficiency in order to open
> its instructional program to these students."[5] [414 U.S. 563, 571]

The critical question is, therefore, whether the regulations and guide-lines promulgated by HEW go beyond the authority of 601.[6] Last Term, in *Mourning* v. *Family Publications Service, Inc.,* 411 U.S. 356, 369, we held that the validity of a regulation promulgated under a general authorization provision such as 602 of Tit. VI "will be sustained so long as it is 'reason-ably related to the purposes of the enabling legislation.' *Thorpe* v. *Housing*

Authority of the City of Durham, 393 U.S. 268, 280–281 (1969)."[7] I think the guidelines here fairly meet that test. Moreover, in assessing the purposes of remedial legislation we have found that departmental regulations and "consistent administrative construction" are "entitled to great weight." *Trafficante* v. *Metropolitan Life Insurance Co.,* 409 U.S. 205, 210; *Griggs* v. *Duke Power Co.,* 401 U.S. 424, 433–434; *Udall* v. *Tallman,* 380 U.S. 1 . The Department has reasonably and consistently interpreted 601 to require affirmative remedial efforts to give special attention to linguistically deprived children.

For these reasons I concur in the result reached by the Court.

MR. JUSTICE BLACKMUN, with whom THE CHIEF JUSTICE joins, concurring in the result.

I join MR. JUSTICE STEWART's opinion and thus I, too, concur in the result. Against the possibility that the Court's judgment may be interpreted too broadly, I [414 U.S. 563, 572] stress the fact that the children with whom we are concerned here number about 1,800. This is a very substantial group that is being deprived of any meaningful schooling because the children cannot understand the language of the classroom. We may only guess as to why they have had no exposure to English in their preschool years. Earlier generations of American ethnic groups have overcome the language barrier by earnest parental endeavor or by the hard fact of being pushed out of the family or community nest and into the realities of broader experience.

I merely wish to make plain that when, in another case, we are concerned with a very few youngsters, or with just a single child who speaks only German or Polish or Spanish or any language other than English, I would not regard today's decision, or the separate concurrence, as conclusive upon the issue whether the statute and the guidelines require the funded school district to provide special instruction. For me, numbers are at the heart of this case and my concurrence is to be understood accordingly. [414 U.S. 563, 573]

NOTES

   1. A report adopted by the Human Rights Commission of San Francisco and submitted to the Court by respondents after oral argument shows that, as of April 1973, there were 3,457 Chinese students in the school system who spoke little or no English. The document further showed 2,136 students enrolled in Chinese special instruction classes, but at least 429 of the

enrollees were not Chinese but were included for ethnic balance. Thus, as of April 1973, no more than 1,707 of the 3,457 Chinese students needing special English instruction were receiving it.

2. Section 602 provides: "Each Federal department and agency which is empowered to extend Federal financial assistance to any program or activity, by way of grant, loan, or contract other than a contract of insurance or guaranty, is authorized and directed to effectuate the provisions of section 2000d of this title with respect to such program or activity by issuing rules, regulations, or orders of general applicability which shall be consistent with achievement of the objectives of the statute authorizing the financial assistance in connection with which the action is taken. . . ." 42 U.S.C. 2000d-1.

3. And see Report of the Human Rights Commission of San Francisco, Bilingual Education in the San Francisco Public Schools, Aug. 9, 1973.

4. 110 Cong. Rec. 6543 (Sen. Humphrey, quoting from President Kennedy's message to Congress, June 19, 1963).

5. These guidelines were issued in further clarification of the Department's position as stated in its regulations issued to implement Tit. VI, 45 CFR pt. 80. The regulations provide in part that no recipient of federal financial assistance administered by HEW may "provide any service, financial aid, or other benefit to an individual which is different, or is provided in a different manner, from that provided to others under the program;" or "restrict an individual in any way in the enjoyment of any advantage or privilege enjoyed by others receiving any service, financial aid, or other benefit under the program." 45 CFR 80.3(b)(1)(ii),(iv).

6. The respondents do not contest the standing of the petitioners to sue as beneficiaries of the federal funding contract between the Department of Health, Education, and Welfare and the San Francisco Unified School District.

7. Section 602, 42 U.S.C. 2000d-1, provides in pertinent part: "Each Federal department and agency which is empowered to extend Federal financial assistance to any program or activity, by way [414 U.S. 563, 572] of grant, loan, or contract other than a contract of insurance or guaranty, is authorized and directed to effectuate the provisions of section 2000d of this title with respect to such program or activity by issuing rules, regulations, or orders of general applicability which shall be consistent with achievement of the objectives of the statute authorizing the financial assistance in connection with which the action is taken. . . ." The United States as amicus curiae asserts in its brief, and the respondents appear to concede, that the guidelines were issued pursuant to 602.

8

A NATION AT RISK

THE IMPERATIVE FOR EDUCATIONAL REFORM

National Commission on Excellence in Education

No anthology of twentieth-century school reform efforts would be complete without mention of *A Nation at Risk*. Although many of the nation's top educators decried the report's lack of scientific rigor, it remains one of the most widely recognized and controversial documents in school reform. *A Nation at Risk* spurred a new wave of reform in U.S. schools. Although this document serves mainly a historical purpose at this point, some reforms amplified by the report continue to thrive. The push for standards is a good example of this legacy.

○

OUR NATION IS AT RISK. Our once unchallenged preeminence in commerce, industry, science, and technological innovation is being overtaken by competitors throughout the world. This report is concerned with only one of the many causes and dimensions of the problem, but it is the one that undergirds American prosperity, security, and civility. We report to the American people that while we can take justifiable pride in what our schools and colleges have historically accomplished and contributed to the United States and the well-being of its people, the educational foundations of our society are presently being eroded by a rising tide of mediocrity that threatens our very future as a Nation and a people. What was unimaginable a generation ago has begun to occur—others are matching and surpassing our educational attainments.

If an unfriendly foreign power had attempted to impose on America the mediocre educational performance that exists today, we might well have viewed it as an act of war. As it stands, we have allowed this to happen to ourselves. We have even squandered the gains in student achievement made in the wake of the Sputnik challenge. Moreover, we have dismantled essential support systems which helped make those gains possible. We have, in effect, been committing an act of unthinking, unilateral educational disarmament.

Our society and its educational institutions seem to have lost sight of the basic purposes of schooling, and of the high expectations and disciplined effort needed to attain them. This report, the result of 18 months of study, seeks to generate reform of our educational system in fundamental ways and to renew the Nation's commitment to schools and colleges of high quality throughout the length and breadth of our land.

That we have compromised this commitment is, upon reflection, hardly surprising, given the multitude of often conflicting demands we have placed on our Nation's schools and colleges. They are routinely called on to provide solutions to personal, social, and political problems that the home and other institutions either will not or cannot resolve. We must understand that these demands on our schools and colleges often exact an educational cost as well as a financial one.

On the occasion of the Commission's first meeting, President Reagan noted the central importance of education in American life when he said: "Certainly there are few areas of American life as important to our society, to our people, and to our families as our schools and colleges." This report, therefore, is as much an open letter to the American people as it is a report to the Secretary of Education. We are confident that the American people, properly informed, will do what is right for their children and for the generations to come.

The Risk

History is not kind to idlers. The time is long past when America's destiny was assured simply by an abundance of natural resources and inexhaustible human enthusiasm, and by our relative isolation from the malignant problems of older civilizations. The world is indeed one global village. We live among determined, well-educated, and strongly motivated competitors. We compete with them for international standing and markets, not only with products but also with the ideas of our laboratories and neighborhood workshops. America's position in the world may once have been reasonably secure with only a few exceptionally well-trained men and women. It is no longer.

The risk is not only that the Japanese make automobiles more efficiently than Americans and have government subsidies for development and export. It is not just that the South Koreans recently built the world's most efficient steel mill, or that American machine tools, once the pride of the world, are being displaced by German products. It is also that these developments signify a redistribution of trained capability throughout the globe. Knowledge, learning, information, and skilled intelligence are the new raw materials of international commerce and are today spreading throughout the world as vigorously as miracle drugs, synthetic fertilizers, and blue jeans did earlier. If only to keep and improve on the slim competitive edge we still retain in world markets, we must dedicate ourselves to the reform of our educational system for the benefit of all—old and young alike, affluent and poor, majority and minority. Learning is the indispensable investment required for success in the "information age" we are entering.

Our concern, however, goes well beyond matters such as industry and commerce. It also includes the intellectual, moral, and spiritual strengths of our people which knit together the very fabric of our society. The people of the United States need to know that individuals in our society who do not possess the levels of skill, literacy, and training essential to this new era will be effectively disenfranchised, not simply from the material rewards that accompany competent performance, but also from the chance to participate fully in our national life. A high level of shared education is essential to a free, democratic society and to the fostering of a common culture, especially in a country that prides itself on pluralism and individual freedom.

For our country to function, citizens must be able to reach some common understandings on complex issues, often on short notice and on the basis of conflicting or incomplete evidence. Education helps form these common understandings, a point Thomas Jefferson made long ago in his justly famous dictum:

> I know no safe depository of the ultimate powers of the society but the people themselves; and if we think them not enlightened enough to exercise their control with a wholesome discretion, the remedy is not to take it from them but to inform their discretion.

Part of what is at risk is the promise first made on this continent: All, regardless of race or class or economic status, are entitled to a fair chance and to the tools for developing their individual powers of mind and spirit to the utmost. This promise means that all children by virtue of their own efforts, competently guided, can hope to attain the mature and informed judgment needed to secure gainful employment, and to manage their own lives, thereby serving not only their own interests but also the progress of society itself.

Indicators of the Risk

The educational dimensions of the risk before us have been amply documented in testimony received by the Commission. For example:

- International comparisons of student achievement, completed a decade ago, reveal that on 19 academic tests American students were never first or second and, in comparison with other industrialized nations, were last seven times.
- Some 23 million American adults are functionally illiterate by the simplest tests of everyday reading, writing, and comprehension.
- About 13 percent of all 17-year-olds in the United States can be considered functionally illiterate. Functional illiteracy among minority youth may run as high as 40 percent.
- Average achievement of high school students on most standardized tests is now lower than 26 years ago when Sputnik was launched.
- Over half the population of gifted students do not match their tested ability with comparable achievement in school.
- The College Board's Scholastic Aptitude Tests (SAT) demonstrate a virtually unbroken decline from 1963 to 1980. Average verbal scores fell over 50 points and average mathematics scores dropped nearly 40 points.
- College Board achievement tests also reveal consistent declines in recent years in such subjects as physics and English.
- Both the number and proportion of students demonstrating superior achievement on the SATs (i.e., those with scores of 650 or higher) have also dramatically declined.
- Many 17-year-olds do not possess the "higher order" intellectual skills we should expect of them. Nearly 40 percent cannot draw inferences from written material; only one-fifth can write a persuasive essay; and only one-third can solve a mathematics problem requiring several steps.
- There was a steady decline in science achievement scores of U.S. 17-year-olds as measured by national assessments of science in 1969, 1973, and 1977.

○ Between 1975 and 1980, remedial mathematics courses in public 4-year colleges increased by 72 percent and now constitute one-quarter of all mathematics courses taught in those institutions.

○ Average tested achievement of students graduating from college is also lower.

○ Business and military leaders complain that they are required to spend millions of dollars on costly remedial education and training programs in such basic skills as reading, writing, spelling, and computation. The Department of the Navy, for example, reported to the Commission that one-quarter of its recent recruits cannot read at the ninth-grade level, the minimum needed simply to understand written safety instructions. Without remedial work they cannot even begin, much less complete, the sophisticated training essential in much of the modern military.

These deficiencies come at a time when the demand for highly skilled workers in new fields is accelerating rapidly. For example:

○ Computers and computer-controlled equipment are penetrating every aspect of our lives—homes, factories, and offices.

○ One estimate indicates that by the turn of the century millions of jobs will involve laser technology and robotics.

○ Technology is radically transforming a host of other occupations. They include health care, medical science, energy production, food processing, construction, and the building, repair, and maintenance of sophisticated scientific, educational, military, and industrial equipment.

Analysts examining these indicators of student performance and the demands for new skills have made some chilling observations. Educational researcher Paul Hurd concluded at the end of a thorough national survey of student achievement that within the context of the modern scientific revolution, "We are raising a new generation of Americans that is scientifically and technologically illiterate." In a similar vein, John Slaughter, a former Director of the National Science Foundation, warned of "a growing chasm between a small scientific and technological elite and a citizenry ill-informed, indeed uninformed, on issues with a science component."

But the problem does not stop there, nor do all observers see it the same way. Some worry that schools may emphasize such rudiments as reading and computation at the expense of other essential skills such as comprehension, analysis, solving problems, and drawing conclusions. Still others are concerned that an over-emphasis on technical and occupational skills will leave little time for studying the arts and humanities that so enrich daily life, help maintain civility, and develop a sense of community. Knowledge of the humanities, they maintain, must be harnessed to science and technology if the latter are to remain creative and humane, just as the humanities need to be informed by science and technology if they are to remain relevant to the human condition. Another analyst, Paul Copperman, has drawn a sobering conclusion. Until now, he has noted:

> Each generation of Americans has outstripped its parents in education, in literacy, and in economic attainment. For the first time in the history of our country, the educational skills of one generation will not surpass, will not equal, will not even approach, those of their parents.

It is important, of course, to recognize that *the average citizen* today is better educated and more knowledgeable than the average citizen of a generation ago—more literate, and exposed to more mathematics, literature, and science. The positive impact of this fact on the well-being of our country and the lives of our people cannot be overstated. Nevertheless, *the average graduate* of our schools and colleges today is not as well-educated as the average graduate of 25 or 35 years ago, when a much smaller proportion of our population completed high school and college. The negative impact of this fact likewise cannot be overstated.

Hope and Frustration

Statistics and their interpretation by experts show only the surface dimension of the difficulties we face. Beneath them lies a tension between hope and frustration that characterizes current attitudes about education at every level.

We have heard the voices of high school and college students, school board members, and teachers; of leaders of industry, minority groups, and higher education; of parents and State officials. We could hear the hope evident in their commitment to quality education and in their descriptions of outstanding programs and schools. We could also hear the intensity of their frustration, a growing impatience with shoddiness in many walks of American life, and the complaint that this shoddiness is too often reflected in our schools and colleges. Their frustration threatens to overwhelm their hope.

What lies behind this emerging national sense of frustration can be described as both a dimming of personal expectations and the fear of losing a shared vision for America.

On the personal level the student, the parent, and the caring teacher all perceive that a basic promise is not being kept. More and more young people emerge from high school ready neither for college nor for work. This predicament becomes more acute as the knowledge base continues its rapid expansion, the number of traditional jobs shrinks, and new jobs demand greater sophistication and preparation.

On a broader scale, we sense that this undertone of frustration has significant political implications, for it cuts across ages, generations, races, and political and economic groups. We have come to understand that the public will demand that educational and political leaders act forcefully and effectively on these issues. Indeed, such demands have already appeared and could well become a unifying national preoccupation. This unity, however, can be achieved only if we avoid the unproductive tendency of some to search for scapegoats among the victims, such as the beleaguered teachers.

On the positive side is the significant movement by political and educational leaders to search for solutions—so far centering largely on the nearly desperate need for increased support for the teaching of mathematics and science. This movement is but a start on what we believe is a larger and more educationally encompassing need to improve teaching and learning in fields such as English, history, geography, economics, and foreign languages. We believe this movement must be broadened and directed toward reform and excellence throughout education.

Excellence in Education

We define "excellence" to mean several related things. At the level of the *individual learner,* it means performing on the boundary of individual ability in ways that test and push back personal limits, in school and in the workplace. Excellence characterizes a *school or college* that sets high expectations and goals for all learners, then tries in every way possible to help students reach them. Excellence characterizes a *society* that has adopted these policies, for it will then be prepared through the education and skill of its people to respond to the challenges of a rapidly changing world. Our Nation's people and its schools and colleges must be committed to achieving excellence in all these senses.

We do not believe that a public commitment to excellence and educational reform must be made at the expense of a strong public commitment to the equitable treatment of our diverse population. The twin goals of equity and high-quality schooling have profound and practical meaning for our economy and society, and we cannot permit one to yield to the other either in principle or in practice. To do so would deny young people their chance to learn and live according to their aspirations and abilities. It also would lead to a generalized accommodation to mediocrity in our society on the one hand or the creation of an undemocratic elitism on the other.

Our goal must be to develop the talents of all to their fullest. Attaining that goal requires that we expect and assist all students to work to the limits of their capabilities. We should expect schools to have genuinely high standards rather than minimum ones, and parents to support and encourage their children to make the most of their talents and abilities.

The search for solutions to our educational problems must also include a commitment to life-long learning. The task of rebuilding our system of learning is enormous and must be properly understood and taken seriously: Although a million and a half new workers enter the economy each year from our schools and colleges, the adults working today will still make up about 75 percent of the workforce in the year 2000. These workers, and new entrants into the workforce, will need further education and re-training if they—and we as a Nation—are to thrive and prosper.

The Learning Society

In a world of ever-accelerating competition and change in the conditions of the workplace, of ever-greater danger, and of ever-larger opportunities for those prepared to meet them, educational reform should focus on the goal of creating a Learning Society. At the heart of such a society is the commitment to a set of values and to a system of education that affords all members the opportunity to stretch their minds to full capacity, from early childhood through adulthood, learning more as the world itself changes. Such a society has as a basic foundation the idea that education is important not only because of what it contributes to one's career goals but also because of the value it adds to the general quality of one's life. Also at the heart of the Learning Society are educational opportunities extending far beyond the traditional institutions of learning, our schools and colleges. They extend into homes and workplaces; into libraries, art galleries, museums, and science centers; indeed, into every place where the individual can develop and mature in work and life. In our view, formal schooling in youth is the essential foundation for learning throughout one's life. But without life-long learning, one's skills will become rapidly dated.

In contrast to the ideal of the Learning Society, however, we find that for too many people education means doing the minimum work necessary for the moment, then coasting through life on what may have been learned in its first quarter. But this should not surprise us because we tend to express our educational standards and expectations largely in terms of "minimum requirements." And where there should be a coherent continuum of learning, we have none, but instead an often incoherent, outdated patchwork quilt. Many individual, sometimes heroic, examples of schools and colleges of great merit do exist. Our findings and testimony confirm the vitality of a number of notable schools and programs, but their very distinction stands out against a vast mass shaped by tensions and pressures that inhibit systematic academic and vocational achievement for the majority of students. In some metropolitan areas basic literacy has become the goal rather than the starting point. In some colleges maintaining enrollments is of greater day-to-day concern than maintaining rigorous academic standards. And the ideal of academic excellence as the primary goal of schooling seems to be fading across the board in American education.

Thus, we issue this call to all who care about America and its future: to parents and students; to teachers, administrators, and school board members; to colleges and industry; to union members and military leaders; to governors and State legislators; to the President; to members of Congress and other public officials; to members of learned and scientific societies; to the print and electronic media; to concerned citizens everywhere. America is at risk.

We are confident that America can address this risk. If the tasks we set forth are initiated now and our recommendations are fully realized over the next several years, we can expect reform of our Nation's schools, colleges, and universities. This would also reverse the current declining trend—a trend that stems more from weakness of purpose, confusion of vision, underuse of talent, and lack of leadership, than from conditions beyond our control.

The Tools at Hand

It is our conviction that the essential raw materials needed to reform our educational system are waiting to be mobilized through effective leadership:

- o the natural abilities of the young that cry out to be developed and the undiminished concern of parents for the well-being of their children;

- o the commitment of the Nation to high retention rates in schools and colleges and to full access to education for all;

- o the persistent and authentic American dream that superior performance can raise one's state in life and shape one's own future;

○ the dedication, against all odds, that keeps teachers serving in schools and colleges, even as the rewards diminish;

○ our better understanding of learning and teaching and the implications of this knowledge for school practice, and the numerous examples of local success as a result of superior effort and effective dissemination;

○ the ingenuity of our policymakers, scientists, State and local educators, and scholars in formulating solutions once problems are better understood;

○ the traditional belief that paying for education is an investment in ever-renewable human resources that are more durable and flexible than capital plant and equipment, and the availability in this country of sufficient financial means to invest in education;

○ the equally sound tradition, from the Northwest Ordinance of 1787 until today, that the Federal Government should supplement State, local, and other resources to foster key national educational goals; and

○ the voluntary efforts of individuals, businesses, and parent and civic groups to cooperate in strengthening educational programs.

These raw materials, combined with the unparalleled array of educational organizations in America, offer us the possibility to create a Learning Society, in which public, private, and parochial schools; colleges and universities; vocational and technical schools and institutes; libraries; science centers, museums, and other cultural institutions; and corporate training and retraining programs offer opportunities and choices for all to learn throughout life.

The Public's Commitment

Of all the tools at hand, the public's support for education is the most powerful. In a message to a National Academy of Sciences meeting in May 1982, President Reagan commented on this fact when he said:

> This public awareness—and I hope public action—is long overdue. . . . This country was built on American respect for education. . . . Our challenge now is to create a resurgence of that thirst for education that typifies our Nation's history.

The most recent (1982) Gallup Poll of the *Public's Attitudes Toward the Public Schools* strongly supported a theme heard during our hearings: People are steadfast in their belief that education is the major foundation for the future strength of this country. They even considered education more important than developing the best industrial system or the strongest military force, perhaps because they understood education as the cornerstone of both. They also held that education is "extremely important" to one's future success, and that public education should be the top priority for additional Federal funds. Education occupied first place among 12 funding categories considered in the survey—above health care, welfare, and military defense, with 55 percent selecting public education as one of their first three choices. Very clearly, the public understands the primary importance of education as the foundation for a satisfying life, an enlightened and civil society, a strong economy, and a secure Nation.

At the same time, the public has no patience with undemanding and superfluous high school offerings. In another survey, more than 75 percent of all those questioned believed every student planning to go to college should take 4 years of mathematics, English, history/U.S. government, and science, with more than 50 percent adding 2 years each of a foreign language and economics or business. The public even supports requiring much of this curriculum for students who do not plan to go to college. These standards far exceed the strictest high school graduation requirements of any State today, and they also exceed the admission standards of all but a handful of our most selective colleges and universities.

Another dimension of the public's support offers the prospect of constructive reform. The best term to characterize it may simply be the honorable word "patriotism." Citizens know intuitively what some of the best economists have shown in their research, that education is one of the chief engines of a society's material well-being. They know, too, that education is the common bond of a pluralistic society and helps tie us to other cultures around the globe. Citizens also know in their bones that the safety of the United States depends principally on the wit, skill, and spirit of a self-confident people, today and tomorrow. It is, therefore, essential—especially in a period of long-term decline in educational achievement—for government at all levels to affirm its responsibility for nurturing the Nation's intellectual capital.

And perhaps most important, citizens know and believe that the meaning of America to the rest of the world must be something better than it seems to many today. Americans like to think of this Nation as the preeminent country for generating the great ideas and material benefits for all mankind. The citizen is dismayed at a steady 15-year decline in industrial productivity, as one great American industry after another falls to world competition. The citizen wants the country to act on the belief, expressed in our hearings and by the large majority in the Gallup Poll, that education should be at the top of the Nation's agenda.

Findings

We conclude that declines in educational performance are in large part the result of disturbing inadequacies in the way the educational process itself is often conducted. The findings that follow, culled from a much more extensive list, reflect four important aspects of the educational process: content, expectations, time, and teaching.

Findings Regarding Content

By content we mean the very "stuff" of education, the curriculum. Because of our concern about the curriculum, the Commission examined patterns of courses high school students took in 1964–69 compared with course patterns in 1976–81. On the basis of these analyses we conclude:

- Secondary school curricula have been homogenized, diluted, and diffused to the point that they no longer have a central purpose. In effect, we have a cafeteria style curriculum in which the appetizers and desserts can easily be mistaken for the main courses. Students have migrated from vocational and college preparatory programs to "general track" courses in large numbers. The proportion of students taking a general program of study has increased from 12 percent in 1964 to 42 percent in 1979.

- This curricular smorgasbord, combined with extensive student choice, explains a great deal about where we find ourselves today. We offer intermediate algebra, but only 31 percent of our recent high school graduates complete it; we offer French I, but only 13 percent complete it; and we offer geography, but only 16 percent complete it. Calculus is available in schools enrolling about 60 percent of all students, but only 6 percent of all students complete it.

- Twenty-five percent of the credits earned by general track high school students are in physical and health education, work experience outside the school, remedial English and mathematics, and personal service and development courses, such as training for adulthood and marriage.

Findings Regarding Expectations

We define expectations in terms of the level of knowledge, abilities, and skills school and college graduates should possess. They also refer to the time, hard work, behavior, self-discipline, and motivation that are essential for high student achievement. Such expectations are expressed to students in several different ways:

- by grades, which reflect the degree to which students demonstrate their mastery of subject matter;
- through high school and college graduation requirements, which tell students which subjects are most important;
- by the presence or absence of rigorous examinations requiring students to demonstrate their mastery of content and skill before receiving a diploma or a degree;
- by college admissions requirements, which reinforce high school standards; and
- by the difficulty of the subject matter students confront in their texts and assigned readings.

Our analyses in each of these areas indicate notable deficiencies:

- The amount of homework for high school seniors has decreased (two-thirds report less than 1 hour a night) and grades have risen as average student achievement has been declining.
- In many other industrialized nations, courses in mathematics (other than arithmetic or general mathematics), biology, chemistry, physics, and geography start in grade 6 and are required of *all* students. The time spent on these subjects, based on class hours, is about three times that spent by even the most science-oriented U.S. students, i.e., those who select 4 years of science and mathematics in secondary school.
- A 1980 State-by-State survey of high school diploma requirements reveals that only eight States require high schools to offer foreign language instruction, but none requires students to take the courses. Thirty-five States require only 1 year of mathematics, and 36 require only 1 year of science for a diploma.
- In 13 States, 50 percent or more of the units required for high school graduation may be electives chosen by the student. Given this freedom to choose the substance of half or more of their education, many students opt for less demanding personal service courses, such as bachelor living.
- "Minimum competency" examinations (now required in 37 States) fall short of what is needed, as the "minimum" tends to become the "maximum," thus lowering educational standards for all.

- One-fifth of all 4-year public colleges in the United States must accept every high school graduate within the State regardless of program followed or grades, thereby serving notice to high school students that they can expect to attend college even if they do not follow a demanding course of study in high school or perform well.

- About 23 percent of our more selective colleges and universities reported that their general level of selectivity declined during the 1970s, and 29 percent reported reducing the number of specific high school courses required for admission (usually by dropping foreign language requirements, which are now specified as a condition for admission by only one-fifth of our institutions of higher education).

- Too few experienced teachers and scholars are involved in writing textbooks. During the past decade or so a large number of texts have been "written down" by their publishers to ever-lower reading levels in response to perceived market demands.

- A recent study by Education Products Information Exchange revealed that a majority of students were able to master 80 percent of the material in some of their subject-matter texts before they had even opened the books. Many books do not challenge the students to whom they are assigned.

- Expenditures for textbooks and other instructional materials have declined by 50 percent over the past 17 years. While some recommend a level of spending on texts of between 5 and 10 percent of the operating costs of schools, the budgets for basal texts and related materials have been dropping during the past decade and a half to only 0.7 percent today.

Findings Regarding Time

Evidence presented to the Commission demonstrates three disturbing facts about the use that American schools and students make of time: (1) compared to other nations, American students spend much less time on school work; (2) time spent in the classroom and on homework is often used ineffectively; and (3) schools are not doing enough to help students develop either the study skills required to use time well or the willingness to spend more time on school work.

- In England and other industrialized countries, it is not unusual for academic high school students to spend 8 hours a day at school,

220 days per year. In the United States, by contrast, the typical school day lasts 6 hours and the school year is 180 days.

○ In many schools, the time spent learning how to cook and drive counts as much toward a high school diploma as the time spent studying mathematics, English, chemistry, U.S. history, or biology.

○ A study of the school week in the United States found that some schools provided students only 17 hours of academic instruction during the week, and the average school provided about 22.

○ A California study of individual classrooms found that because of poor management of classroom time, some elementary students received only one-fifth of the instruction others received in reading comprehension.

○ In most schools, the teaching of study skills is haphazard and unplanned. Consequently, many students complete high school and enter college without disciplined and systematic study habits.

Findings Regarding Teaching

The Commission found that not enough of the academically able students are being attracted to teaching; that teacher preparation programs need substantial improvement; that the professional working life of teachers is on the whole unacceptable; and that a serious shortage of teachers exists in key fields.

○ Too many teachers are being drawn from the bottom quarter of graduating high school and college students.

○ The teacher preparation curriculum is weighted heavily with courses in "educational methods" at the expense of courses in subjects to be taught. A survey of 1,350 institutions training teachers indicated that 41 percent of the time of elementary school teacher candidates is spent in education courses, which reduces the amount of time available for subject matter courses.

○ The average salary after 12 years of teaching is only $17,000 per year, and many teachers are required to supplement their income with part-time and summer employment. In addition, individual teachers have little influence in such critical professional decisions as, for example, textbook selection.

○ Despite widespread publicity about an overpopulation of teachers, severe shortages of certain kinds of teachers exist: in the fields of mathematics, science, and foreign languages; and among specialists in education for gifted and talented, language minority, and handicapped students.

- The shortage of teachers in mathematics and science is particularly severe. A 1981 survey of 45 States revealed shortages of mathematics teachers in 43 States, critical shortages of earth sciences teachers in 33 States, and of physics teachers everywhere.

- Half of the newly employed mathematics, science, and English teachers are not qualified to teach these subjects; fewer than one-third of U.S. high schools offer physics taught by qualified teachers.

Recommendations

In light of the urgent need for improvement, both immediate and long term, this Commission has agreed on a set of recommendations that the American people can begin to act on now, that can be implemented over the next several years, and that promise lasting reform. The topics are familiar; there is little mystery about what we believe must be done. Many schools, districts, and States are already giving serious and constructive attention to these matters, even though their plans may differ from our recommendations in some details.

We wish to note that we refer to public, private, and parochial schools and colleges alike. All are valuable national resources. Examples of actions similar to those recommended below can be found in each of them.

We must emphasize that the variety of student aspirations, abilities, and preparation requires that appropriate content be available to satisfy diverse needs. Attention must be directed both to the nature of the content available and to the needs of particular learners. The most gifted students, for example, may need a curriculum enriched and accelerated beyond even the needs of other students of high ability. Similarly, educationally disadvantaged students may require special curriculum materials, smaller classes, or individual tutoring to help them master the material presented. Nevertheless, there remains a common expectation: We must demand the best effort and performance from all students, whether they are gifted or less able, affluent or disadvantaged, whether destined for college, the farm, or industry.

Our recommendations are based on the beliefs that everyone can learn, that everyone is born with an *urge* to learn which can be nurtured, that a solid high school education is within the reach of virtually all, and that life-long learning will equip people with the skills required for new careers and for citizenship.

Recommendation A: Content

WE RECOMMEND *that State and local high school graduation require-ments be strengthened and that,* at a minimum, *all students seeking a diploma be required to lay the foundations in the Five New Basics by tak-ing the following curriculum during their 4 years of high school: (a) 4 years of English; (b) 3 years of mathematics; (c) 3 years of science; (d) 3 years of social studies; and (e) one-half year of computer science. For the college-bound, 2 years of foreign language in high school are strongly recom-mended in addition to those taken earlier.*

Whatever the student's educational or work objectives, knowledge of the New Basics is the foundation of success for the after-school years and, therefore, forms the core of the modern curriculum. A high level of shared education in these Basics, together with work in the fine and performing arts and foreign languages, constitutes the mind and spirit of our culture. The following Implementing Recommendations are intended as illustra-tive descriptions. They are included here to clarify what we mean by the es-sentials of a strong curriculum.

IMPLEMENTING RECOMMENDATIONS

1. The teaching of *English* in high school should equip graduates to: (a) comprehend, interpret, evaluate, and use what they read; (b) write well-organized, effective papers; (c) listen effectively and dis-cuss ideas intelligently; and (d) know our literary heritage and how it enhances imagination and ethical understanding, and how it re-lates to the customs, ideas, and values of today's life and culture.

2. The teaching of *mathematics* in high school should equip graduates to: (a) understand geometric and algebraic concepts; (b) understand elementary probability and statistics; (c) apply mathematics in every-day situations; and (d) estimate, approximate, measure, and test the accuracy of their calculations. In addition to the traditional sequence of studies available for college-bound students, new, equally demand-ing mathematics curricula need to be developed for those who do not plan to continue their formal education immediately.

3. The teaching of *science* in high school should provide graduates with an introduction to: (a) the concepts, laws, and processes of the physi-cal and biological sciences; (b) the methods of scientific inquiry and reasoning; (c) the application of scientific knowledge to everyday life; and (d) the social and environmental implications of scientific and technological development. Science courses must be revised and up-dated for both the college-bound and those not intending to go to

college. An example of such work is the American Chemical Society's "Chemistry in the Community" program.

4. The teaching of *social studies* in high school should be designed to: (a) enable students to fix their places and possibilities within the larger social and cultural structure; (b) understand the broad sweep of both ancient and contemporary ideas that have shaped our world; and (c) understand the fundamentals of how our economic system works and how our political system functions; and (d) grasp the difference between free and repressive societies. An understanding of each of these areas is requisite to the informed and committed exercise of citizenship in our free society.

5. The teaching of *computer science* in high school should equip graduates to: (a) understand the computer as an information, computation, and communication device; (b) use the computer in the study of the other Basics and for personal and work-related purposes; and (c) understand the world of computers, electronics, and related technologies.

In addition to the New Basics, other important curriculum matters must be addressed.

6. Achieving proficiency in a *foreign language* ordinarily requires from 4 to 6 years of study and should, therefore, be started in the elementary grades. We believe it is desirable that students achieve such proficiency because study of a foreign language introduces students to non–English-speaking cultures, heightens awareness and comprehension of one's native tongue, and serves the Nation's needs in commerce, diplomacy, defense, and education.

7. The high school curriculum should also provide students with programs requiring rigorous effort in subjects that advance students' personal, educational, and occupational goals, such as the fine and performing arts and vocational education. These areas complement the New Basics, and they should demand the same level of performance as the Basics.

8. The curriculum in the crucial eight grades leading to the high school years should be specifically designed to provide a sound base for study in those and later years in such areas as English language development and writing, computational and problem solving skills, science, social studies, foreign language, and the arts. These years should foster an enthusiasm for learning and the development of the individual's gifts and talents.

9. We encourage the continuation of efforts by groups such as the American Chemical Society, the American Association for the Advancement of Science, the Modern Language Association, and the National Councils of Teachers of English and Teachers of Mathematics, to revise, update, improve, and make available new and more diverse curricular materials. We applaud the consortia of educators and scientific, industrial, and scholarly societies that cooperate to improve the school curriculum.

Recommendation B: Standards and Expectations

WE RECOMMEND *that schools, colleges, and universities adopt more rigorous and measurable standards, and higher expectations, for academic performance and student conduct, and that 4-year colleges and universities raise their requirements for admission. This will help students do their best educationally with challenging materials in an environment that supports learning and authentic accomplishment.*

IMPLEMENTING RECOMMENDATIONS

1. Grades should be indicators of academic achievement so they can be relied on as evidence of a student's readiness for further study.

2. Four-year colleges and universities should raise their admissions requirements and advise all potential applicants of the standards for admission in terms of specific courses required, performance in these areas, and levels of achievement on standardized achievement tests in each of the five Basics and, where applicable, foreign languages.

3. Standardized tests of achievement (not to be confused with aptitude tests) should be administered at major transition points from one level of schooling to another and particularly from high school to college or work. The purposes of these tests would be to: (a) certify the student's credentials; (b) identify the need for remedial intervention; and (c) identify the opportunity for advanced or accelerated work. The tests should be administered as part of a nationwide (but not Federal) system of State and local standardized tests. This system should include other diagnostic procedures that assist teachers and students to evaluate student progress.

4. Textbooks and other tools of learning and teaching should be upgraded and updated to assure more rigorous content. We call upon university scientists, scholars, and members of professional societies, in collaboration with master teachers, to help in this task, as they did

in the post-Sputnik era. They should assist willing publishers in developing the products or publish their own alternatives where there are persistent inadequacies.

5. In considering textbooks for adoption, States and school districts should: (a) evaluate texts and other materials on their ability to present rigorous and challenging material clearly; and (b) require publishers to furnish evaluation data on the material's effectiveness.

6. Because no textbook in any subject can be geared to the needs of all students, funds should be made available to support text development in "thin-market" areas, such as those for disadvantaged students, the learning disabled, and the gifted and talented.

7. To assure quality, all publishers should furnish evidence of the quality and appropriateness of textbooks, based on results from field trials and credible evaluation. In view of the enormous numbers and varieties of texts available, more widespread consumer information services for purchasers are badly needed.

8. New instructional materials should reflect the most current applications of technology in appropriate curriculum areas, the best scholarship in each discipline, and research in learning and teaching.

Recommendation C: Time

WE RECOMMEND *that significantly more time be devoted to learning the New Basics. This will require more effective use of the existing school day, a longer school day, or a lengthened school year.*

IMPLEMENTING RECOMMENDATIONS

1. Students in high schools should be assigned far more homework than is now the case.

2. Instruction in effective study and work skills, which are essential if school and independent time are to be used efficiently, should be introduced in the early grades and continued throughout the student's schooling.

3. School districts and State legislatures should strongly consider 7-hour school days, as well as a 200- to 220-day school year.

4. The time available for learning should be expanded through better classroom management and organization of the school day. If necessary, additional time should be found to meet the special needs of slow learners, the gifted, and others who need more instructional

diversity than can be accommodated during a conventional school day or school year.

5. The burden on teachers for maintaining discipline should be reduced through the development of firm and fair codes of student conduct that are enforced consistently, and by considering alternative classrooms, programs, and schools to meet the needs of continually disruptive students.

6. Attendance policies with clear incentives and sanctions should be used to reduce the amount of time lost through student absenteeism and tardiness.

7. Administrative burdens on the teacher and related intrusions into the school day should be reduced to add time for teaching and learning.

8. Placement and grouping of students, as well as promotion and graduation policies, should be guided by the academic progress of students and their instructional needs, rather than by rigid adherence to age.

Recommendation D: Teaching

THIS RECOMMENDATION *consists of seven parts. Each is intended to improve the preparation of teachers or to make teaching a more rewarding and respected profession. Each of the seven stands on its own and should not be considered solely as an implementing recommendation.*

1. Persons preparing to teach should be required to meet high educational standards, to demonstrate an aptitude for teaching, and to demonstrate competence in an academic discipline. Colleges and universities offering teacher preparation programs should be judged by how well their graduates meet these criteria.

2. Salaries for the teaching profession should be increased and should be professionally competitive, market-sensitive, and performance-based. Salary, promotion, tenure, and retention decisions should be tied to an effective evaluation system that includes peer review so that superior teachers can be rewarded, average ones encouraged, and poor ones either improved or terminated.

3. School boards should adopt an 11-month contract for teachers. This would ensure time for curriculum and professional development, programs for students with special needs, and a more adequate level of teacher compensation.

4. School boards, administrators, and teachers should cooperate to develop career ladders for teachers that distinguish among the beginning instructor, the experienced teacher, and the master teacher.

5. Substantial nonschool personnel resources should be employed to help solve the immediate problem of the shortage of mathematics and science teachers. Qualified individuals, including recent graduates with mathematics and science degrees, graduate students, and industrial and retired scientists could, with appropriate preparation, immediately begin teaching in these fields. A number of our leading science centers have the capacity to begin educating and retraining teachers immediately. Other areas of critical teacher need, such as English, must also be addressed.

6. Incentives, such as grants and loans, should be made available to attract outstanding students to the teaching profession, particularly in those areas of critical shortage.

7. Master teachers should be involved in designing teacher preparation programs and in supervising teachers during their probationary years.

Recommendation E: Leadership and Fiscal Support

WE RECOMMEND *that citizens across the Nation hold educators and elected officials responsible for providing the leadership necessary to achieve these reforms, and that citizens provide the fiscal support and stability required to bring about the reforms we propose.*

IMPLEMENTING RECOMMENDATIONS

1. Principals and superintendents must play a crucial leadership role in developing school and community support for the reforms we propose, and school boards must provide them with the professional development and other support required to carry out their leadership role effectively. The Commission stresses the distinction between leadership skills involving persuasion, setting goals and developing community consensus behind them, and managerial and supervisory skills. Although the latter are necessary, we believe that school boards must consciously develop leadership skills at the school and district levels if the reforms we propose are to be achieved.

2. State and local officials, including school board members, governors, and legislators, have *the primary responsibility* for financing and governing the schools, and should incorporate the reforms we propose in their educational policies and fiscal planning.

3. The Federal Government, in cooperation with States and localities, should help meet the needs of key groups of students such as the gifted and talented, the socioeconomically disadvantaged, minority and language minority students, and the handicapped. In combination these groups include both national resources and the Nation's youth who are most at risk.

4. In addition, we believe the Federal Government's role includes several functions of national consequence that States and localities alone are unlikely to be able to meet: protecting constitutional and civil rights for students and school personnel; collecting data, statistics, and information about education generally; supporting curriculum improvement and research on teaching, learning, and the management of schools; supporting teacher training in areas of critical shortage or key national needs; and providing student financial assistance and research and graduate training. We believe the assistance of the Federal Government should be provided with a minimum of administrative burden and intrusiveness.

5. The Federal Government has *the primary responsibility* to identify the national interest in education. It should also help fund and support efforts to protect and promote that interest. It must provide the national leadership to ensure that the Nation's public and private resources are marshaled to address the issues discussed in this report.

6. This Commission calls upon educators, parents, and public officials at all levels to assist in bringing about the educational reform proposed in this report. We also call upon citizens to provide the financial support necessary to accomplish these purposes. Excellence costs. But in the long run mediocrity costs far more.

America Can Do It

Despite the obstacles and difficulties that inhibit the pursuit of superior educational attainment, we are confident, with history as our guide, that we can meet our goal. The American educational system has responded to previous challenges with remarkable success. In the 19th century our land-grant colleges and universities provided the research and training that developed our Nation's natural resources and the rich agricultural bounty of the American farm. From the late 1800s through mid-20th century, American schools provided the educated workforce needed to seal the success of the Industrial Revolution and to provide the margin of victory in two world wars. In the early part of this century and continuing to this very day, our schools have absorbed vast waves of immigrants and educated them and their children to productive citizenship. Similarly, the Nation's Black colleges have provided opportunity and undergraduate education to the vast majority of college-educated Black Americans.

More recently, our institutions of higher education have provided the scientists and skilled technicians who helped us transcend the boundaries of our planet. In the last 30 years, the schools have been a major vehicle for expanded social opportunity, and now graduate 75 percent of our young people from high school. Indeed, the proportion of Americans of college age enrolled in higher education is nearly twice that of Japan and far exceeds other nations such as France, West Germany, and the Soviet Union. Moreover, when international comparisons were last made a decade ago, the top 9 percent of American students compared favorably in achievement with their peers in other countries.

In addition, many large urban areas in recent years report that average student achievement in elementary schools is improving. More and more schools are also offering advanced placement programs and programs for gifted and talented students, and more and more students are enrolling in them.

We are the inheritors of a past that gives us every reason to believe that we will succeed.

A Word to Parents and Students

The task of assuring the success of our recommendations does not fall to the schools and colleges alone. Obviously, faculty members and administrators, along with policymakers and the mass media, will play a crucial role in the reform of the educational system. But even more important is the role of parents and students, and to them we speak directly.

To Parents

You know that you cannot confidently launch your children into today's world unless they are of strong character and well-educated in the use of language, science, and mathematics. They must possess a deep respect for intelligence, achievement, and learning, and the skills needed to use them; for setting goals; and for disciplined work. That respect must be accompanied by an intolerance for the shoddy and second-rate masquerading as "good enough."

You have the right to demand for your children the best our schools and colleges can provide. Your vigilance and your refusal to be satisfied with less than the best are the imperative first step. But your right to a proper education for your children carries a double responsibility. As surely as you are your child's first and most influential teacher, your child's ideas about education and its significance begin with you. You must be a *living* example of what you expect your children to honor and to emulate. Moreover, you bear a responsibility to participate actively in your child's education. You should encourage more diligent study and discourage satisfaction with mediocrity and the attitude that says "let it slide"; monitor your child's study; encourage good study habits; encourage your child to take more demanding rather than less demanding courses; nurture your child's curiosity, creativity, and confidence; and be an active participant in the work of the schools. Above all, exhibit a commitment to continued learning in your own life. Finally, help your children understand that excellence in education cannot be achieved without intellectual and moral integrity coupled with hard work and commitment. Children will look to their parents and teachers as models of such virtues.

To Students

You forfeit your chance for life at its fullest when you withhold your best effort in learning. When you give only the minimum to learning, you receive only the minimum in return. Even with your parents' best example and your teachers' best efforts, in the end it is *your* work that determines how much and how well you learn. When you work to your full capacity, you can hope to attain the knowledge and skills that will enable you to create your future and control your destiny. If you do not, you will have your future thrust upon you by others. Take hold of your life, apply your gifts and talents, work with dedication and self-discipline. Have high expectations for yourself and convert every challenge into an opportunity.

A Final Word

This is not the first or only commission on education, and some of our findings are surely not new, but old business that now at last must be done. For no one can doubt that the United States is under challenge from many quarters.

Children born today can expect to graduate from high school in the year 2000. We dedicate our report not only to these children, but also to those now in school and others to come. We firmly believe that a movement of America's schools in the direction called for by our recommendations will prepare these children for far more effective lives in a far stronger America.

Our final word, perhaps better characterized as a plea, is that all segments of our population give attention to the implementation of our recommendations. Our present plight did not appear overnight, and the responsibility for our current situation is widespread. Reform of our educational system will take time and unwavering commitment. It will require equally widespread, energetic, and dedicated action. For example, we call upon the National Academy of Sciences, National Academy of Engineering, Institute of Medicine, Science Service, National Science Foundation, Social Science Research Council, American Council of Learned Societies, National Endowment for the Humanities, National Endowment for the Arts, and other scholarly, scientific, and learned societies for their help in this effort. Help should come from students themselves; from parents, teachers, and school boards; from colleges and universities; from local, State, and Federal officials; from teachers' and administrators' organizations; from industrial and labor councils; and from other groups with interest in and responsibility for educational reform.

It is their America, and the America of all of us, that is at risk; it is to each of us that this imperative is addressed. It is by our willingness to take up the challenge, and our resolve to see it through, that America's place in the world will be either secured or forfeited. Americans have succeeded before and so we shall again.

9

AMERICA'S CHOICE

HIGH SKILLS OR LOW WAGES!
EXECUTIVE SUMMARY

National Center on Education and the Economy

Borrowing the tone and rhetoric of *A Nation at Risk*, *High Skills or Low Wages* argues that the world economy is fast changing from an industrial focus to an information focus. *High Skills or Low Wages* presents concerns about schools' ability to adjust and produce students who would be able to take advantage of the high-skill/high-wage jobs produced by the new technology-based economy. It argues that the other option is down a slippery slope to low-paying jobs, which are disappearing to technological advances and lower wages overseas.

---○---

The Problem

SINCE 1969, REAL AVERAGE weekly earnings in the United States have fallen by more than 12 percent. This burden has been shared unequally. The incomes of our top 30 percent of earners increased while those of the other 70 percent spiraled downward.

In many families, it now takes two people working to make ends meet, where one was sufficient in the past.

The United States is in the midst of the second longest economic expansion in its history. But that expansion is built largely on the fact that

50 percent of our population is employed compared with 40 percent in 1973. Forty million new jobs were created as the "baby boom" generation reached working age, and more women entered the workforce. More of us have been working so we produced more.

However, workforce growth will slow dramatically in the 1990s. We can no longer grow substantially just by adding new workers.

The key to maintaining, to say nothing of improving, our standard of living is productivity growth—more products and services from every member of the workforce.

But, during the past two decades, our productivity growth has slowed to a crawl. It now takes nearly three years to achieve the same productivity improvement we used to achieve in one year.

If productivity continues to falter, we can expect one of two futures. Either the top 30 percent of our population will grow wealthier while the bottom 70 percent becomes progressively poorer or we all slide into relative poverty together.

The Task

To ensure a more prosperous future, we must improve productivity and our competitive position. We cannot simply do this by using better machinery, because low wage countries can now use the same machines and can still sell their products more cheaply than we can.

The key to productivity improvement for a high wage nation lies in the third industrial revolution now taking place in the world. The steam engine and electric motor drove the first two industrial revolutions, causing profound changes in work organization. This boosted productivity, quality, and living standards dramatically. The creation of the modern factory in the 1800s and mass production in the 1990s followed these technology breakthroughs.

The advent of the computer, high speed communication and universal education are heralding a third industrial revolution, a revolution the key feature of which is high performance work organization.

The Organization of Work in America

The organization of America's workplaces today is largely modeled after the system of mass manufacture pioneered during the early 1900s. The premise is simple: Break complex jobs into a myriad of simple rote tasks, which the worker then repeats with machine-like efficiency.

The system is managed by a small group of educated planners and supervisors who do the thinking for the organization. They plan strategy, implement changes, motivate the workers and solve problems. Extensive administrative procedures allow managers to keep control of a large number of workers. This form of work organization is often referred to as the "Taylor" model.

Most employees under this model need not be educated. It is far more important that they be reliable, steady and willing to follow directions.

But in the world's best companies, new high performance work organizations are replacing this "Taylor" method. These companies are using a new approach to unleash major advances in productivity, quality, variety and speed of new product introductions.

Mass production methods will continue to produce high volume, inexpensive goods and services for a long time to come. But what the world is prepared to pay high prices and high wages for now is quality, variety and responsiveness to changing consumer tastes, the very qualities that the new methods of organizing work make possible.

"Tayloristic" methods are not well suited to these goals. Firms struggling to apply the traditional methods of work organization to more complex technologies, more frequent product introductions, increased quality requirements and proliferating product variety often create cumbersome and inefficient bureaucracies.

The new high performance forms of work organization operate very differently. Rather than increasing bureaucracy, they reduce it by giving front-line workers more responsibility. Workers are asked to use judgment and make decisions. Management layers disappear as front-line workers assume responsibility for many of the tasks—from quality control to production scheduling—that others used to do.

Work organizations like these require large investments in training. Workers' pay levels often rise to reflect their greater qualifications and responsibilities. But the productivity and quality gains more than offset the costs to the company of higher wages and skills development.

Despite these advantages, 95 percent of American companies still cling to old forms of work organization.

Is There a Skills Shortage in the United States?

Because most American employers organize work in a way that does not require high skills, they report no shortage of people who have such skills and foresee no such shortage. With some exceptions, the education and skill levels of American workers roughly match the demands of their jobs.

Our research did reveal a wide range of concerns covered under the blanket term of "skills." While businesses everywhere complained about the quality of their applicants, few talked about the kinds of skills acquired in school. The primary concern of more than 80 percent of employers was finding workers with a good work ethic and appropriate social behavior: "reliable," "a good attitude," "a pleasant appearance," "a good personality."

Most employers we interviewed do not expect their skill requirements to change. Despite the widespread presumption that advancing technology and the evolving service economy will create jobs demanding higher skills, only five percent of employers were concerned about a skills shortage. These were mainly large manufacturers, financial service organizations and communications companies.

The reason we have no skills shortage today is that we are using a turn-of-the-century work organization. If we want to compete more effectively in the global economy, we will have to move to a high productivity work organization.

How We Prepare Our Front-Line Workers for Work

More than 70 percent of the jobs in America will not require a college education by the year 2000. These jobs are the backbone of our economy, and the productivity of workers in these jobs will make or break our economic future.

No nation has produced a highly qualified technical workforce without first providing its workers with a strong general education. But our children rank at the bottom on most international tests—behind children in Europe and East Asia, even behind children in some newly industrialized countries.

More than any other country in the world, the United States believes that natural ability, rather than effort, explains achievement. The tragedy is that we communicate to millions of students every year, especially to low-income and minority students, that we do not believe that they have what it takes to learn. They then live up to our expectations, despite the evidence that they can meet very high performance standards under the right conditions.

Unlike virtually all of our leading competitors, we have no national system capable of setting high academic standards for the non-college bound or of assessing their achievement against those standards.

America may have the worst school-to-work transition system of any advanced industrial country. Students who know few adults to help them get their first job are left to sink or swim.

Only eight percent of our front-line workers receive any formal training once on the job, and this is usually limited to orientation for new hires or short courses on team building or safety.

The American post-secondary education and training system was never designed to meet the needs of our front-line workers. The system is a combination of education programs for full-time college students and short term training for the severely disadvantaged, and can be difficult to access. Because employers have not set training standards, few students can be sure that there is a market for the courses they pursue. Education is rarely connected to training and both are rarely connected to an effective job service function.

Another Way

While the foreign nations we studied differ in economy and culture, they share an approach to the education and training of their workers and to high productivity work organization.

- They insist that virtually all of their students reach a high educational standard. We do not.

- They provide "professionalized" education to non-college bound students to prepare them for their trades and to ease their school-to-work transition. We do not.

- They operate comprehensive labor market systems which combine training, labor market information, job search and income maintenance for the unemployed. We do not.

- They support company based training through general revenue or payroll tax based financing schemes. We do not.

- They have national consensus on the importance of moving to high productivity forms of work organization and building high wage economies. We do not.

Our approaches have served us well in the past. They will not serve us well in the future.

The Choice

Americans are unwittingly making a choice. It is a choice that most of us would probably not make were we aware of its consequences. Yet every day, that choice is becoming more difficult to reverse. It is a choice which undermines the American dream of economic opportunity for all. It is a choice that will lead to an America where 30 percent of our people may do well—at least for awhile—but the other 70 percent will see their dreams slip away.

The choice that America faces is a choice between high skills and low wages. Gradually, silently, we are choosing low wages.

We still have time to make the other choice—one that will lead us to a more prosperous future. To make this choice, we must fundamentally change our approach to work and education.

1. *Problem:* Two factors stand in the way of producing a highly educated workforce: We lack a clear standard of achievement and few students are motivated to work hard in school. One reason that students going right to work after school have little motivation to study hard is that they see little or no relationship between how well they do in school and what kind of job they can get after school. Other advanced industrial nations have stringent performance standards that virtually all students must meet at about age 16 and that directly affect their employment prospects.

RECOMMENDATION: *A new educational performance standard should be set for all students, to be met by age 16. This standard should be established nationally and benchmarked to the highest in the world.*

We propose that all American students meet a national standard of educational excellence by age 16, or soon thereafter. Students passing a series of performance based assessments that incorporate the standard would be awarded a Certificate of Initial Mastery.

Possession of the Certificate of Initial Mastery would qualify the student to choose among going to work, entering a college preparatory program or studying for a Technical and Professional Certificate, described below.

Creation of the Certificate of Initial Mastery standard would require a new approach to student performance assessment. We recommend the creation of new performance based examinations for which students can explicitly prepare. The assessment system would provide multiple opportunities for success rather than a single high stakes moment of possible failure. Most important, the examination, though set at a very high standard, is not intended as a sorting mechanism on the pattern of virtually all the major tests now in use. Our goal is to set a tough standard that almost everyone will reach, although not all at the same time.

Once created, this system would establish objective standards for students and educators, motivate students and give employers an objective means to evaluate the accomplishments of students.

2. *Problem:* More than 20 percent of our students drop out of high school—almost 50 percent in many of our inner cities. These dropouts go on to make up more than one third of our front-line workforce. Turning our backs on these dropouts, as we do now, is tantamount to turning our backs on our future workforce.

RECOMMENDATION: *The states should take responsibility for assuring that virtually all students achieve the Certificate of Initial Mastery. Through the new local Employment and Training Boards, states, with federal assistance, should create and fund alternative learning environments for those who cannot attain the Certificate of Initial Mastery in regular schools.*

All students should be guaranteed the educational attention necessary to attain the Certificate of Initial Mastery by age 16, or as soon as possible thereafter. Youth Centers should be established to enroll school dropouts and help them reach that standard. Federal, state and local funds should be raised or reallocated to finance these dropout recovery programs. Once the Youth Centers are created, children should not be permitted to work before the age of 18 unless they have attained the Certificate of Initial Mastery or are enrolled in a program to attain it.

3. *Problem:* Other industrial nations have multi-year career-oriented educational programs that prepare students to operate at a professional level in the workplace. Graduates of these programs have the skills to hit the ground running when they get their first full-time job at age 19 or 20. America prepares only a tiny fraction of its non-college bound students for work. As a result, most flounder in the labor market, moving from low paying job to low paying job until their mid-twenties, never being seriously trained.

RECOMMENDATION: *A comprehensive system of Technical and Professional Certificates and associate's degrees should be created for the majority of our students and adult workers who do not pursue a baccalaureate degree.*

Technical and Professional Certificates would be offered across the entire range of service and manufacturing occupations. A student could earn the entry-level occupation specific certificate after completing a two- to four-year program of combined work and study, depending upon the field. A sequence of advanced certificates, attesting to mastery of more complex skills, would be available and could be obtained throughout one's career.

The Secretary of Labor should convene national committees of business, labor, education and public representatives to define certification standards for two- to four-year programs of professional preparation in a broad range of occupations. These programs should combine general education with specific occupational skills and should include a significant work component.

Students could pursue these programs at a wide variety of institutions accredited to offer them, including high schools, community colleges and proprietary schools. The system should be designed to make it possible for students to move easily between the Certificate programs and college.

A means should be established to ensure that all students can receive financing to pursue these programs.

4. *Problem:* The vast majority of American employers are not moving to high performance work organizations, nor are they investing to train their non-managerial employees for these new work organizations. The movement to high performance work organizations is more widespread in other nations, and training of front-line workers, funded in part by national assessments on employers or general public revenues, is commonplace.

RECOMMENDATION: *All employers should be given incentives and assistance to invest in the further education and training of their workers and to pursue high productivity forms of work organization.*

We propose a system whereby all employers will invest at least one percent of their payroll for the education and training of their workers. Those who do not wish to participate would contribute the one percent to a general training fund, to be used by states to upgrade worker skills. We further recommend that public technical assistance be provided to companies, particularly small businesses, to assist them in moving to higher performance work organizations.

5. *Problem:* The United States is not well organized to provide the highly skilled workers needed to support the emerging high performance work organizations. Public policy on worker training has been largely passive, except for the needs of a small portion of the severely disadvantaged population. The training system is fragmented with respect to policies, administration and service delivery.

RECOMMENDATION: *A system of Employment and Training Boards should be established by Federal and state governments, together with local leadership, to organize and oversee the new school-to-work transition programs and training systems we propose.*

We envision a new, more comprehensive system where skills development and upgrading for the majority of our workers becomes a central aim of public policy.

The key to accomplishing these goals is finding a way to enable the leaders of our communities to take responsibility for building a comprehensive system that meets their needs. The local Employment and Training Boards for each major labor market would:

- Take responsibility for the school-to-work and Youth Center-to-work transition for young people.
- Manage and oversee the Youth Centers.

○ Manage and oversee a "second chance" system for adults seeking the Certificate of Initial Mastery.

○ Manage and oversee the system for awarding Technical and Professional Certificates at the local level.

○ Manage a labor market information system.

○ Manage and oversee the job service.

○ Coordinate existing programs.

The states would need to create a parallel structure to support the local Boards, coordinate statewide functions and establish state standards for their operation.

In Conclusion

America is headed toward an economic cliff. We will no longer be able to put a higher proportion of our people to work to generate economic growth. If basic changes are not made, real wages will continue to fall, especially for the majority who do not graduate from four-year colleges. The gap between economic "haves" and "have nots" will widen still further and social tensions will deepen.

Our recommendations provide an alternative for America. We do not pretend that this vision will be easily accepted or quickly implemented. But we also cannot pretend that the status quo is an option. It is no longer possible to be a high wage, low skill nation. We have choices to make:

○ Do we continue to define educational success as "time in the seat," or choose a new system that focuses on the demonstrated achievement of high standards?

○ Do we continue to provide little incentive for non-college bound students to study hard and take tough subjects, or choose a system that will reward real effort with better pay and better jobs?

○ Do we continue to turn our backs on America's school dropouts, or choose to take responsibility for educating them?

○ Do we continue to provide unskilled workers for unskilled jobs, or train skilled workers and give companies incentives to deploy them in high performance work organizations?

○ Do we continue in most companies to limit training to a select handful of managers and professionals, or choose to provide training to front-line workers as well?

○ Do we cling to a public employment and training system fragmented by institutional barriers, muddled by overlapping bureaucracies and operating at the margins of the labor market, or do we choose a unified system that addresses itself to a majority of workers?

○ Do we continue to remain indifferent to the low wage path being chosen by many companies, or do we provide incentives for high productivity choices?

Taken together, the Commission's recommendations provide the framework for developing a high quality American education and training system, closely linked to high performance work organizations. The system we propose provides a uniquely American solution. Boldly executed, it has the potential not simply to put us on an equal footing with our competitors, but to allow us to leap ahead, to build the world's premier workforce. In so doing, we will create a formidable competitive advantage.

The status quo is not an option. The choice we have is to become a nation of high skills or one of low wages.

The choice is ours. It should be clear. It must be made.

10

LEARNING A LIVING: A BLUEPRINT FOR HIGH PERFORMANCE

A SCANS REPORT FOR AMERICA 2000

EXECUTIVE SUMMARY

PRINCIPLES AND RECOMMENDATIONS

Secretary's Commission on Achieving Necessary Skills,
U.S. Department of Labor

The school-to-work reform effort, with its roots deep in the progressive era of the early twentieth century, peaked in the early 1990s with the publication of this report. In an attempt to make education relevant and do more to prepare students to make a smooth transition into careers, school-to-work advocates championed the idea of listing the skills needed in professional careers and aligning curricula with those skills. This reform was also fueled by a sluggish job market and by corporations interested in hiring workers with relevant training and skills. However, an improvement in the economy, concerns about the possibility of tracking students into careers at too early an age, as well as the sheer complexity of defining the skills needed for each job in the workforce caused the school-to-work movement to slow. Despite momentum in several states and industries to implement the SCANS recommendations, only a few viable examples of the project remain.

○

THE SECRETARY'S COMMISSION on Achieving Necessary Skills (SCANS) was appointed by the Secretary of Labor to determine the skills that our young people need to succeed in the world of work. The Commission's fundamental purpose is to encourage a high-performance economy characterized by high-skill, high-wage employment.

Our primary message to schools is this: Look beyond the schoolhouse to the roles students will play when they leave to become workers, parents, and citizens.

Our message to teachers is this: Look beyond your discipline and your classroom to the other courses your students take, to your community, and to the lives of your students outside school. Help your students connect what they learn in class to the world outside.

Our message to employers is this: Look outside your company and change your view of your responsibilities for human resource development. Your old responsibilities were to select the best available applicants and to retain those you hired. Your new responsibilities must be to improve the way you organize work and to develop the human resources in your community, your firm, and your nation.

We want to state at the outset that the well-being of the nation—and its citizens—is *not* synonymous with economic status. There is much more to life than earning a living, and we want more from schools than productive workers. We want citizens who can discharge the responsibilities that go with living in a democratic society and with being parents. As we said in our first report: "A solid education is its own reward and has value beyond specific skills." We are not talking about turning our high schools into trade schools. Nor do we suggest that schools ignore the beauty of literature and scientific theories or the lessons of history and geography.

SCANS focused on one important aspect of schooling: what we call the "learning a living" system. In 1991 SCANS issued its initial report, *What Work Requires of Schools*. As outlined in that report, a high-performance workplace requires workers who have a solid foundation in the basic literacy and computational skills, in the thinking skills necessary to put knowledge to work, and in the personal qualities that make workers dedicated and trustworthy.

But a solid foundation is not enough. High-performance workplaces also require competencies: the ability to manage resources, to work amicably and productively with others, to acquire and use information, to master complex systems, and to work with a variety of technologies. This combination of foundation skills and workplace competencies—"workplace know-how" (see Exhibit 10.1)—is not taught in many schools or required for most diplomas.

Exhibit 10.1. Workplace Know-How.

The know-how identified by SCANS is made up of five competencies and a three-part foundation of skills and personal qualities that are needed for solid job performance. These are:

WORKPLACE COMPETENCIES. Effective workers can productively use:

○ *Resources.* They know how to allocate time, money, materials, space, and staff.

○ *Interpersonal skills.* They can work on teams, teach others, serve customers, lead, negotiate, and work well with people from culturally diverse backgrounds.

○ *Information.* They can acquire and evaluate data, organize and maintain files, interpret and communicate, and use computers to process information.

○ *Systems.* They understand social, organizational, and technological systems; they can monitor and correct performance; and they can design or improve systems.

○ *Technology.* They can select equipment and tools, apply technology to specific tasks, and maintain and troubleshoot equipment.

FOUNDATION SKILLS. Competent workers in the high-performance workplace need:

○ *Basic skills.* Reading, writing, arithmetic and mathematics, speaking, and listening.

○ *Thinking skills.* The ability to learn, to reason, to think creatively, to make decisions, and to solve problems.

○ *Personal qualities.* Individual responsibility, self-esteem and self-management, sociability, and integrity.

The time when a high school diploma was a sure ticket to a job is within the memory of workers who have not yet retired; yet in many places today a high school diploma is little more than a certificate of attendance. As a result, employers discount the value of all diplomas, and many students do not work hard in high school.

In fact, the market value of a high school diploma has fallen. The proportion of men between the ages of 25 and 54 with high school diplomas who earn less than enough to support a family of four above the poverty line is growing alarmingly. Among African-American men with 12 years of schooling, the proportion with low earnings rose from 20 percent in 1969 to 42.7 percent in 1989; among Hispanic men, from 16.4 to 35.9 percent; and among white men, from 8.3 percent to 22.6 percent. In other words, in 1989 more than two in five African-American men, one in three Hispanic men, and one in five white men, all with high school diplomas, did not earn enough to lift a family of four above poverty. Unless there is a second earner, their families will not have what most would call a decent living.

The workplace know-how that this Commission has defined is related both to competent performance and to higher earnings for the people who possess it. When the Commission compared the know-how required in 23 high-wage jobs with the requirements of 23 low-wage jobs, the conclusion was inescapable: Workers with more know-how command a higher wage—on average, 58 percent, or $11,200 a year, higher.

Everyone must have the opportunity to reach the higher levels of skills and competencies the Commission found to be associated with high-wage jobs. To that end, we have recast the broad principles set forth in *What Work Requires of Schools* as the context for our recommendations:

- The qualities of high performance that today characterize our most competitive companies must become the standard for the vast majority of our employers, public and private, large and small, local and global.
- The nation's schools must be transformed into high-performance organizations.
- All Americans should be entitled to multiple opportunities to learn the SCANS know-how well enough to earn a decent living.

To make those principles a reality we recommend:

1. The nation's school systems should make the SCANS foundation skills and workplace competencies explicit objectives of instruction at all levels.

2. Assessment systems should provide students and workers with a résumé documenting attainment of the SCANS know-how.

3. All employers, public and private, should incorporate the SCANS know-how into all their human resource development efforts.

4. The Federal Government should continue to bridge the gap between school and the high-performance workplace by advancing the SCANS agenda.

5. Every employer in America should create its own strategic vision around the principles of the high-performance workplace.

Implementation

The Commission recognizes that nationwide policies are of little value until they are carried out by people on the front line. Cities such as Fort Worth, Los Angeles, Pittsburgh, Tampa, and Louisville and states such as Florida, Indiana, New York, and Oregon have taken steps to put the broad SCANS principles in place in their school systems at the local and state levels. In the corporate sector, TGI Friday's, MCI, Gannett, Motorola, NationsBank, and AT&T (and its major unions) are taking action. A number of trade organizations in the hospitality field have joined together to introduce the SCANS language into their industry. The U.S. Department of Labor is moving to build SCANS into various aspects of Job Training Partnership Act programs. The Federal Government's Office of Personnel Management (OPM) is seeking ways to apply SCANS findings in skills centers for Federal employees.

These leaders and those who follow them can begin the systemic change to a high-performance future. In the process they will have to reinvent education, reorganize work and work-based learning, and restructure educational assessment.

Reinventing K–12 Education

During the 1980s the United States, seeking to improve public schools, tried to get more results through tighter curricula, higher certification standards for teachers, and more testing of everyone. Despite the effort, students were performing essentially no better at the end of the decade than they were at the beginning. More of the same was not a successful strategy.

As this Commission argued in *What Work Requires of Schools,* American society today requires that elementary and secondary schools meet drastically different goals. The job now is to bring all students to a level that, in the past, only a small minority reached. Experts universally agree that this job requires reinventing elementary and secondary education.

President Bush and the nation's governors have agreed on a set of six goals for education. These goals have been generally agreed to by state governments, education leaders, and business groups such as the Business Roundtable. The Commission supports all six goals; its recommendations are particularly pertinent to the two goals that refer to preparing youth and adults for productive employment in our competitive economy.

The experience of schools, districts, and states that are advancing toward high-performance schooling provides important lessons for educators wishing to teach the SCANS know-how:

○ Teaching should be offered "in context," that is, students should learn content while solving realistic problems. "Learning in order to know" should not be separated from "learning in order to do."

○ Improving the match between what work requires and what students are taught requires changing how instruction is delivered and how students learn.

○ High performance requires a new system of school administrators and assessment.

○ The entire community must be involved.

The experience of Fort Worth, Texas, with restructuring its instructional program has shown how the SCANS classroom can differ from the traditional classroom. In Fort Worth, the conventions of today's classroom (teacher omniscience, student passivity and isolation, rigid disciplinary borders, and "abstracted" knowledge and facts) are being replaced with sophisticated and more realistic concepts of instruction and learning (the teacher may not know all the answers, students often learn best in groups, and knowledge is related to real problems).

Resources

Of all the resources required for reinventing schools around the SCANS ends, none are more important than those devoted to teacher training and staff development. Providing training opportunities for instructional staff will be costly, especially if teachers and administrators are to be given the time they need during the school day and summers for training. But teachers, noninstructional staff, and building and school-district administrators need time if they are to:

○ Develop new pedagogical skills required to teach in context and to develop active, collaborative learning environments;

○ Learn new instructional management skills and use new instructional technologies to develop new ways of interacting with students; and

○ Gain experience with the principles of high performance as applied in restructured workplaces.

Emerging instructional technologies promise to revolutionize teaching and learning by enabling teachers and students to change their traditional roles. When technology dispenses information, teachers are free to coach and facilitate student learning. With technology monitoring learning, students can become active learners, working to acquire new skills.

The SCANS competencies cannot be widely taught unless teachers have instructional materials: textbooks and other print materials, and computer-based and multimedia materials. Video and multimedia materials are essential to creating the realistic contexts in which the competencies are used.

Equity and Diversity

The changes advocated by the Commission promise great benefits to minority and low-income Americans. One-third of new entrants into the American labor force are members of minority groups; they are entitled to an education that will let them learn and will equip them to find and hold a decent job. Because children vary, not only as individuals but also as members of different cultural, racial, and ethnic groups, education must take into account three basic elements that contribute to this diversity:

1. Differences in family income, and
2. Limited English-speaking proficiency (LEP), and
3. Differences in learning styles.

Variation and diversity are not the enemies of high-quality education. The enemy is rigid insistence on a factory model of schooling, a prescription for failure that refuses to accommodate diversity or to allow those students with special strengths to function productively.

Reorganizing for High-Performance Work and Work-Based Learning

Both high-performance workplaces and highly trained workers are needed if we are to build a high-skilled, high-wage economy. Reinventing K–12 education is necessary but not sufficient because about 80 percent of the workers on whom American employers will depend as we enter the 21st century are already on the job. To create high-performance workplaces, employers must actively work to develop the skills and competence of these workers. Only in this way can they constantly improve the quality of the goods and services they provide and satisfy their customers' needs.

Every American employer, public or private, large or small, local or global, must consider the human resources needed for high performance and high quality. Yet, today, American companies do much less training than some of our international competitors; in fact, fewer than 10 percent of front-line American workers now receive training of any kind.

The Commission believes that employer-sponsored training, both public and private, must be upgraded and organized around the SCANS know-how. As a useful first step, coalitions of trade associations, business organizations, labor unions, and industry specific groups could develop training strategies and materials around the SCANS know-how for use by all businesses, particularly small firms.

Many young people between the ages of 16 to 25 today are frustrated because their high schools talked of English and geometry, but their workplace speaks a different language. In a system that serves people beyond high school, employers would describe job requirements in terms of the SCANS workplace competencies and use these for recruitment and employee development. Human resource and training managers would reorient their education and training offerings to include not only job specific skills but also the SCANS workplace competencies and foundation skills.

Providers of education—vocational schools, proprietary schools, community colleges, adult education, and work-based programs—would offer instruction and certification in SCANS workplace competencies. Referral agencies—job counselors in high schools, in employment agencies and the Employment Service, or in the skill centers newly recommended by the Administration—would assess their clients' SCANS workplace competencies, understand job and educational requirements and opportunities in the same terms, and refer clients to career-enhancing work and education.

Restructuring Educational Assessment

A system for assessing and certifying the SCANS workplace know-how is essential. If employers and colleges pay attention to the SCANS foundation skills and workplace competencies, students will work to acquire them. If teachers have to certify that the know-how is acquired, they will make the effort to teach it. If parents and community groups understand the standards that graduates are expected to attain, they will demand that their children reach these levels.

The Commission supports the emerging national consensus calling for a new, nationwide, voluntary assessment system. The Commission believes the system should incorporate new techniques of judging performance—not "tests" as traditionally understood, but assessment tied to learning goals. The National Council on Education Standards and Testing has endorsed the inclusion of the SCANS workplace competencies in the system it recommended, stating that the SCANS competencies "can and should be integrated into the national standards and assessments."[1]

The Commission hopes that the curriculum development work of several groups—the National Council of Teachers of Mathematics, the National Council of Teachers of English, the National Science Teachers Association, and others—will follow this advice.

The Commission believes that a national system, as recommended by the National Council on Education Standards and Testing, should integrate assessment of proficiency in SCANS know-how with other equally important outcomes of schooling. Such a system is needed to:

○ Communicate world-class standards of curriculum content and student performance, and

○ Certify individual performance and thereby motivate students and their teachers to meet these standards.

The challenge is to design a system that clearly establishes that all young people in our nation have the right to an education up to a recognized performance standard without putting the burden of failure on students' backs.

The Commission suggests establishing for all students, beginning in middle school, a cumulative résumé The résumé would contain information about courses taken, projects completed, and proficiency levels attained in each competency. A student who accomplishes enough to meet an overall standard would be awarded a certificate of initial mastery (CIM), a universally recognized statement of experience and accomplishment. The information would mean the same thing to everybody: This person has the SCANS workplace know-how noted here.

Students would be free to use their résumés in seeking employment or further education at any time. Employers could be expected to demand from students the highest level of certification that the job demands (i.e., high-performance workplaces can demand high skills including, but not limited to, those required for the CIM). It would be up to the consumers of this information—employers, colleges, the military, or others—to decide what weight to give each element in the résumé, using their own needs and criteria as guides.

In addition to the education-based assessment, a way to assess and certify persons who are already in the workforce (an experience-based assessment) is needed. The Federal Government, some private firms, and a

1. *Raising Standards on American Education* (Washington, D.C.: National Council on Education Standards and Testing, January 1992).

coalition of trade associations in the hospitality industry have begun the hard work that will lead to the needed assessment tools.

Improving the "Learning a Living" System

The Commission understands that preparation for work is only part of the mission of schools, and that school is only part of the learning process. President Bush has spoken of the need for America to be a nation of learners and for the "education revolution" to extend beyond the schools into the community. This report is concerned with those parts of education and work that form the "learning a living" system.

In the learning-a-living system all students, at least through the second year of high school, learn the SCANS know-how in English, math, science, history, and geography, in other classes (e.g., art), and in extracurricular activities. That is, all students follow a common academic program, a single track, until they are about 16. After age 16, some students are more likely to be learning the SCANS know-how in the context of work, perhaps by specializing in the application of the competencies to a particular industry, such as manufacturing or hospitality.

Some of these students will go on to community colleges in a 2 + 2 tech-prep program, a program that begins with the last two years of high school and leads to an associate degree after two years of college. Other students will continue to learn the SCANS know-how in academic courses as they move toward a four-year college program. Others will, after graduating, go directly to work and work-based learning.

In addition to formal schooling, learning takes place through employers and work-based education. This learning should continue for a life-time, supported by the human resource functions of recruiting, developing, and retaining employees. Workplace education produces portable certificates that are valued in many workplaces.

Information should flow from employers to educators through recruiting and employee development activities, including the ways in which employees progress up career ladders. Educators, in turn, should inform employers of the workplace competencies that students have attained. Today, neither employers nor educators receive or deliver information effectively. The SCANS aim is to improve the information flow (and the learning and earning) so that the economy will deliver the high productivity and wage increases that characterized the United States in the years from 1937 to 1973.

Exhibit 10.2 outlines the actions that are needed to reach the SCANS goals. Unless the nation takes forceful action on this agenda, the nation's

Exhibit 10.2. Recommendations for the "Learning a Living" System.

The commission recommends full implementation of the following actions by the year 2000:

REINVENTING SCHOOLS

○ Workplace know-how (the SCANS foundation and workplace competencies) should be taught along the entire continuum of education, from kindergarten through college.

○ Every student should complete middle school (about age 14) with an introduction to workplace know-how.

○ Every student by about age 16 should attain initial mastery of the SCANS know-how.

○ Every student should complete high school sufficiently proficient in the SCANS know-how to earn a decent living.

○ All federally funded programs for youth and adults, including vocational education programs, should teach the SCANS know-how.

FOSTERING WORK-BASED LEARNING

○ Federal, state, and local agencies should incorporate SCANS workplace competencies into their own employee programs.

○ Private-sector work-based training programs should incorporate training in the SCANS workplace competencies.

○ Coalitions of businesses, associations, government employers, and labor organizations should teach the SCANS competencies to the current workforce, including employees of small businesses.

REORGANIZING THE WORKPLACE

○ The vast majority of employers should adopt the standards of quality and high performance that now characterize our most competitive companies.

○ Firms should develop internal training programs to bring employees to the proficiency in the SCANS competencies needed for high-performance work organizations.

RESTRUCTURING ASSESSMENT

○ A national education-based assessment system should be implemented that will permit educational institutions to certify the levels of the SCANS competencies that their students have achieved.

○ Public and private employers should define requirements for higher-level competencies.

○ Employment-based assessments should permit diagnoses of individual learning needs.

schools, employers, students, and workers will not fare well in the next century.

This, the SCANS final report, provides a blueprint for groups at the national, state, and local levels. Each community must decide what resources will be allocated to create a system that will meet its specific goals. But first, each must become involved in a conversation about its place in a fast-changing world as we approach the year 2000. Our nation's ability to lead in a global economy will depend on the outcome of those conversations. This Commission is confident that once they are informed, communities will commit themselves to maintaining the American dream for themselves and their children.

11

GOALS 2000

INCREASING STUDENT ACHIEVEMENT THROUGH
STATE AND LOCAL INITIATIVES: INTRODUCTION

U.S. Department of Education

Bipartisan effort on Goals 2000 legislation was met with mixed public opinion. Supporters were glad to accept more federal money to improve programs or pay for programs that were already in place. Opponents felt that the federal government was trespassing on the traditional state and local control of schools. Both camps believed that the goals were incredibly ambitious. Considering this chapter alongside Chapter Twenty-Six, the reader will find it easy to trace the path of this school reform effort. It has largely failed; the goals it endorses have not been met. However, participants in the program have seen Goals 2000 fund worthwhile projects, and many believe in the intent of the goals and continue to attempt to achieve them.

---

o

CONGRESS AND PRESIDENT CLINTON made a bi-partisan commitment to education on March 31, 1994, when the Goals 2000: Educate America Act was signed into law. Although education is and must remain a local function and a state responsibility, the federal government pledged to form a new and supportive partnership with states and communities in an effort to improve student academic achievement across the nation.

Educators, business and parent organizations, and Republican and Democratic elected leaders agreed that this national response was needed. Despite more than a decade of education reforms, students and schools are not measuring up to the high standards required to maintain a competitive economy and a strong democracy.

At the heart of the Goals 2000 Act is a grants program designed to help states and communities develop and implement their own education reforms focused on raising student achievement. States participating in Goals 2000 are asked to raise expectations for students by setting challenging academic standards. Each state is to develop comprehensive strategies for helping all students reach those standards—by upgrading assessments and curriculum to reflect the standards, improving the quality of teaching, expanding the use of technology, strengthening accountability for teaching and learning, promoting more flexibility and choice within the public school system, and building strong partnerships among schools and families, employers, and others in the community. Finally, each state is asked to develop its improvement strategies with broad-based, grassroots involvement.

States that participate in Goals 2000 receive seed money to help launch and sustain their ongoing education reform efforts. States are also given unprecedented flexibility through Goals 2000. No new regulations have been issued to implement the program, and states and local school districts can use Goals 2000 funds for a wide range of activities that fit within their own approaches to helping students reach higher standards. In addition, Goals 2000 expands flexibility in other federal education programs by providing the U.S. Secretary of Education and some states with the authority to waive many federal rules and regulations if they interfere with local or state education reform strategies.

Goals 2000: Building on a Decade of Reform

Goals 2000 is a direct outgrowth of the state-led education reform movement of the 1980s. By the mid- to late-1980s a number of states had put in place a series of steps to improve education. Frequently, the state education reforms included increasing high school graduation requirements, particularly in math and science, instituting statewide testing programs, offering more Advanced Placement courses, promoting the use of technology in the classroom, and instituting new teacher evaluation programs.

These education reforms yielded important results. On a number of important indicators, academic performance has increased and the gap between white and minority students has decreased.

○ Course taking patterns of high school students have shown important improvements. From 1982 to 1994, the percentage of high school students taking the challenging academic courses recommended in the 1983 *A Nation at Risk* report increased from 14 to 52 percent.[1] Enrollments in Advanced Placement (AP) courses have also increased significantly, and the number of students passing AP exams nearly tripled between 1982 and 1995.[2]

○ The average performance in mathematics improved substantially on the National Assessment of Education Progress (NAEP) between 1978 and 1992.[3] Among 9- and 13-year olds, the improvement was the equivalent of at least one grade level. Performance in science was also higher in 1992 than in 1978 among all age groups, especially in general science knowledge and skills. At the same time, the gap in performance between white and minority students has been narrowing, especially in mathematics.

○ Scores on SAT tests have also shown increases at the same time that the number of high school students taking the tests has increased.[4] The combined verbal and math score on the SAT has increased 17 points from 1982 to 1995. During this period, minority students as a percentage of all test-takers increased from 18 to 31 percent. Both verbal and math SAT scores increased significantly for students from virtually all racial and ethnic groups from 1982 to 1995.

While these gains in academic performance are significant, they have not been sufficient. The math and science gains were generally not matched in reading performance, where NAEP results remain relatively unchanged. And while the gap in performance between white and minority students narrowed, it remains unacceptably large.

Further, it is increasingly important to judge educational performance against the performance of students in other countries, rather than against past performance in the U.S. Because of international economic competition, states have learned that they are competing with other countries, rather than other states, to attract and retain high paying jobs. The knowledge and skill levels of the state's workforce is one important resource for attracting employers. By the mid-1980s a series of studies demonstrated that the performance of U.S. students lagged significantly behind those of other countries. By this standard, the need for education reform was as urgent at the end of the 1980s as it was at the beginning.

The 1989 Charlottesville Education Summit

The 1989 Education Summit convened by President Bush and the Nation's governors, led by then-Governor Bill Clinton, further underscored the need for a national response to address education needs. The Charlottesville Summit led to a number of commitments and developments, each important for sustaining the momentum of education reform. These include:

- ○ The creation of the National Education Goals which provide a national framework, but give states and communities flexibility to design their own strategies to achieve them.

- ○ A clear recognition that state education improvement efforts need to focus on raising the achievement levels of all students, in all schools—rather than simply creating models of excellence and innovation.

- ○ A broad consensus among state leaders, business leaders, parents and the education community regarding the overall direction education reform needs to take. This consensus centers on raising academic standards; measuring student and school performance against those standards; providing schools and educators with the tools, skills, and resources needed to prepare students to reach the standards; and holding schools accountable for the results.

- ○ A clear statement of an important and carefully defined federal role in improving education. While reaffirming that education is and must remain a state responsibility and a local function, the governors and President Bush also agreed in Charlottesville that states need assistance from the federal government in order to succeed. More specifically, they agreed that the federal government: (1) must maintain its financial role in education, especially with regard to providing disadvantaged students and students with disabilities access to education at all levels; (2) must support state-led education reforms, through research and development, data gathering, and assistance to help spread effective practices; and (3) must administer federal education programs with greater flexibility and in a fashion that supports state leadership of education reform.

The Goals 2000 Act reflects these commitments. The Act endorses the national education goals that provide voluntary direction for education improvement efforts (see Exhibit 11.1). It provides a broad framework for education reform, built on the direction to which states and local communities were already committed, and is easily adaptable to the unique

Exhibit 11.1. Goals 2000 Educate America Act, Sec. 102: National Education Goals.

The Congress declares that the National Education Goals are the following:

(1) school readiness
- (A) By the year 2000, all children in America will start school ready to learn.
- (B) The objectives for this goal are that
  - (i) all children will have access to high-quality and developmentally appropriate preschool programs that help prepare children for school;
  - (ii) every parent in the United States will be a child's first teacher and devote time each day to helping such parent's preschool child learn, and parents will have access to the training and support parents need; and
  - (iii) children will receive the nutrition, physical activity experiences, and health care needed to arrive at school with healthy minds and bodies, and to maintain the mental alertness necessary to be prepared to learn, and the number of low-birthweight babies will be significantly reduced through enhanced prenatal health systems.

(2) school completion
- (A) By the year 2000, the high school graduation rate will increase to at least 90 percent.
- (B) The objectives for this goal are that
  - (i) the Nation must dramatically reduce its school dropout rate, and 75 percent of the students who do drop out will successfully complete a high school degree or its equivalent; and
  - (ii) the gap in high school graduation rates between American students from minority backgrounds and their non-minority counterparts will be eliminated.

(3) student achievement and citizenship
- (A) By the year 2000, all students will leave grades 4, 8, and 12 having demonstrated competency over challenging subject matter including English, mathematics, science, foreign languages, civics and government, economics, arts, history, and geography, and every school in America will ensure that all students learn to use their minds well, so they may be prepared for responsible citizenship, further learning, and productive employment in our Nation's modern economy.
- (B) The objectives for this goal are that
  - (i) the academic performance of all students at the elementary and secondary level will increase significantly in every quartile, and the distribution of minority students in each quartile will more closely reflect the student population as a whole;
  - (ii) the percentage of all students who demonstrate the ability to reason, solve problems, apply knowledge, and write and communicate effectively will increase substantially;
  - (iii) all students will be involved in activities that promote and demonstrate good citizenship, good health, community service, and personal responsibility;

Exhibit 11.1. (*continued*)

    (iv) all students will have access to physical education and health education to ensure they are healthy and fit;

    (v) the percentage of all students who are competent in more than one language will substantially increase; and

    (vi) all students will be knowledgeable about the diverse cultural heritage of this Nation and about the world community.

(4) teacher education and professional development

  (A) By the year 2000, the Nation's teaching force will have access to programs for the continued improvement of their professional skills and the opportunity to acquire the knowledge and skills needed to instruct and prepare all American students for the next century.

  (B) The objectives for this goal are that

    (i) all teachers will have access to preservice teacher education and continuing professional development activities that will provide such teachers with the knowledge and skills needed to teach to an increasingly diverse student population with a variety of educational, social, and health needs;

    (ii) all teachers will have continuing opportunities to acquire additional knowledge and skills needed to teach challenging subject matter and to use emerging new methods, forms of assessment, and technologies;

    (iii) States and school districts will create integrated strategies to attract, recruit, prepare, retrain, and support the continued professional development of teachers, administrators, and other educators, so that there is a highly talented work force of professional educators to teach challenging subject matter; and

    (iv) partnerships will be established, whenever possible, among local educational agencies, institutions of higher education, parents, and local labor, business, and professional associations to provide and support programs for the professional development of educators.

(5) mathematics and science

  (A) By the year 2000, United States students will be first in the world in mathematics and science achievement.

  (B) The objectives for this goal are that

    (i) mathematics and science education, including the metric system of measurement, will be strengthened throughout the system, especially in the early grades;

    (ii) the number of teachers with a substantive background in mathematics and science, including the metric system of measurement, will increase by 50 percent; and

    (iii) the number of United States undergraduate and graduate students, especially women and minorities, who complete degrees in mathematics, science, and engineering will increase significantly.

(6) adult literacy and lifelong learning

  (A) By the year 2000, every adult American will be literate and will possess the knowledge and skills necessary to compete in a global economy and exercise the rights and responsibilities of citizenship.

Exhibit 11.1. (*continued*)

(B) The objectives for this goal are that

(i) every major American business will be involved in strengthening the connection between education and work;

(ii) all workers will have the opportunity to acquire the knowledge and skills, from basic to highly technical, needed to adapt to emerging new technologies, work methods, and markets through public and private educational, vocational, technical, workplace, or other programs;

(iii) the number of quality programs, including those at libraries, that are designed to serve more effectively the needs of the growing number of part-time and midcareer students will increase substantially;

(iv) the proportion of the qualified students, especially minorities, who enter college, who complete at least two years, and who complete their degree programs will increase substantially;

(v) the proportion of college graduates who demonstrate an advanced ability to think critically, communicate effectively, and solve problems will increase substantially; and

(vi) schools, in implementing comprehensive parent involvement programs, will offer more adult literacy, parent training, and life-long learning opportunities to improve the ties between home and school and enhance parents' work and home lives.

(7) safe, disciplined, and alcohol- and drug-free schools

(A) By the year 2000, every school in the United States will be free of drugs, violence, and the unauthorized presence of firearms and alcohol and will offer a disciplined environment conducive to learning.

(B) The objectives for this goal are that

(i) every school will implement a firm and fair policy on use, possession, and distribution of drugs and alcohol;

(ii) parents, businesses, governmental and community organizations will work together to ensure the rights of students to study in a safe and secure environment that is free of drugs and crime, and that schools provide a healthy environment and are a safe haven for all children;

(iii) every local educational agency will develop and implement a policy to ensure that all schools are free of violence and the unauthorized presence of weapons;

(iv) every local educational agency will develop a sequential, comprehensive kindergarten through twelfth grade drug and alcohol prevention education program;

(v) drug and alcohol curriculum should be taught as an integral part of sequential, comprehensive health education;

(vi) community-based teams should be organized to provide students and teachers with needed support; and

(vii) every school should work to eliminate sexual harassment.

(8) parental participation

(A) By the year 2000, every school will promote partnerships that will increase parental involvement and participation in promoting the social, emotional, and academic growth of children.

Exhibit 11.1. (*continued*)

(B) The objectives for this Goal are that

   (i) every State will develop policies to assist local schools and local educational agencies to establish programs for increasing partnerships that respond to the varying needs of parents and the home, including parents of children who are disadvantaged or bilingual, or parents of children with disabilities;

   (ii) every school will actively engage parents and families in a partnership which supports the academic work of children at home and shared educational decisionmaking at school; and

   (iii) parents and families will help to ensure that schools are adequately supported and will hold schools and teachers to high standards of accountability.

Source: *103rd Congress of the United States, Washington, D.C., Jan. 25, 1994.*

---

circumstances in each state and community. Goals 2000 provides support to state and local education reforms with exactly the kind of flexibility called for at the Charlottesville Education Summit.

NOTES

1. U.S. Department of Education, National Center for Education Statistics, *High School Transcript Study, 1982, 1987, 1990, and 1994.* National Education Longitudinal Study Transcripts, *1992.*

2. The College Board, *AP Program: National Summary,* various years, and U.S. Department of Education, National Center for Education Statistics, *Digest of Education Statistics, 1995.* Calculations by Weststat: December 1995.

3. U.S. Department of Education, National Center for Education Statistics, *NAEP 1992 Trends in Academic Progress: Achievement of U.S. Students in Science, 1969 to 1992; Mathematics, 1973 to 1992; Reading, 1971 to 1992;* and *Writing, 1984 to 1992.* Washington, D.C.: July 1994.

4. *The College Board, College Bound Seniors.* New York: various years. Calculations by Weststat: February 1996.

12

THIRD INTERNATIONAL MATHEMATICS AND SCIENCE STUDY (TIMSS)

OVERVIEW AND KEY FINDINGS

ACROSS GRADE LEVELS

National Center for Education Statistics

Since (and probably before) Sputnik, the United States has been comparing its educational system to that of any perceived enemy or competitor. Considering the increasingly global nature of our economy, data on the United States' curricular approach and test results compared to those of other nations are of interest to parents, policymakers, and educators. The fear that the United States might fall behind in education ignites concern that we will lose our competitive edge and our role as a dominant player in the global economy. Despite some economic down-cycles, the United States has dominated global commerce on nearly every level since World War II. However, during the same period, comparisons showed our educational system to be failing when weighed against the systems of Russia, Japan, Taiwan, and other competitors.

_____ o _____

WITH INFORMATION ON A HALF-MILLION students worldwide, including more than 33,000 U.S. students in more than 500 U.S. public and private schools, the Third International Mathematics and Science Study (TIMSS) is the largest, most comprehensive, and most rigorous international study of schools and students ever conducted. During the 1995 school year, students from 41 nations, including our country's major trading partners, were assessed at three different grade levels (fourth, eighth, and in the final year of secondary school) to compare their mathematics and science achievement.

TIMSS researchers also looked at schools, curricula, instruction, lessons, textbooks, policy issues, and the lives of teachers and students in order to understand the educational context in which mathematics and science learning takes place. By combining multiple methodologies and scientific sampling procedures that go beyond simple student achievement score comparisons and questionnaires, TIMSS created a fair and comprehensive portrait of how U.S. mathematics and science education differs from that of other nations. The richness of TIMSS includes a videotape study of eighth-grade mathematics teaching, which observed 231 classrooms in Japan, Germany, and the United States, and an analysis of more than one thousand textbooks and curriculum frameworks from about 50 countries.

At the fourth-grade level, U.S. students were above the international average in both science and mathematics. At the eighth-grade level, they scored above the international average in science and below the international average in mathematics. At the end of secondary schooling (twelfth grade in the United States), the performance of U.S. students, including the most advanced, was among the lowest in both science and mathematics.

Because precise scores cannot be determined with perfect accuracy, it is not appropriate to compare U.S. scores to those of other countries by rank alone. Therefore, nations have been grouped into bands in the figures that follow, according to whether their performance is significantly higher than, not significantly different from, or significantly lower than that of the United States.

Key findings from the *Pursuing Excellence* series of reports for each grade level, as well as overall comparative findings, are detailed.

Fourth Grade

Achievement

- Among the 26 participating nations at this grade level, U.S. students scored above the international average in mathematics, and were outperformed by 7 countries (Figure 12.1).

Figure 12.1. Grade 4: Nations' Average Mathematics Performance Compared with That of the United States.

Nation	Average
Singapore	625
Korea	611
Japan	597
Hong Kong	587
(Netherlands)	577
Czech Republic	567
(Austria)	559

Nation	Average
(Slovenia)	552
Ireland	550
(Hungary)	548
(Australia)	546
United States	545
Canada	532
(Israel)	531

Nation	Average
(Latvia (LSS))	525
Scotland	520
England	513
Cyprus	502
Norway	502
New Zealand	499
Greece	492
(Thailand)	490
Portugal	475
Iceland	474
Iran, Islamic Republic	429
(Kuwait)	400

International Average = 529

Notes:

1. Nations not meeting international guidelines are shown in parentheses.

2. Latvia is designated LSS because only Latvian-speaking schools were tested.

3. The international average is the average of the national averages of the 26 nations.

◆ Nations with average scores significantly higher than those of the United States.

▬ Nations with average scores not significantly different from those of the United States.

▼ Nations with average scores significantly lower than those of the United States.

Source: *National Center for Education Statistics (1997). Pursuing Excellence: A Study of U.S. Fourth-Grade Mathematics and Science Achievement in International Context. Figure 1. Washington, D.C.: NCES.*

- In science, U.S. students were outperformed by one country, Korea (Figure 12.2).
- In mathematics, U.S. students' performance exceeded the international average in whole numbers; fractions and proportionality; data representation, analysis and probability; geometry; and patterns, relations and functions. Our students were below the international average in measurement, estimation, and number sense.
- In science, U.S. fourth-grade students were outperformed by one or two other nations in earth science; life science; and environmental issues and the nature of science. In physical science, U.S. students were outperformed by 5 other nations.
- If an international talent search were to select the top 10 percent of all fourth graders, 9 percent of U.S. fourth graders would be included in mathematics and 16 percent would be included in science.

Curriculum

- The number of topics included in U.S. textbooks and curriculum guides was above the international average in fourth-grade mathematics and somewhat below the international average in fourth-grade science.

Eighth Grade

Achievement

- U.S. students scored below the international average of 41 nations in mathematics (Figure 12.3).
- U.S. students scored above the international average in science (Figure 12.4).
- In mathematics, U.S. students scored at about the international average in data representation, analysis and probability; algebra; and fractions and number sense. They scored below the international average in geometry, measurement, and proportionality.
- In science, U.S. students scored above the international average in earth science; life science; and environmental issues and the nature of science. They scored at the international average in chemistry and in physics.
- If an international talent search were to select the top 10 percent of all eighth graders, 5 percent of U.S. eighth graders would be included in mathematics and 13 percent would be included in science.

Figure 12.2. Grade 4: Nations' Average Science Performance Compared with That of the United States.

Nation	Average

▲

Korea	597

=

Nation	Average
Japan	574
United States	565
(Australia)	565
(Netherlands)	557
Czech Republic	557

▼

Nation	Average
England	551
Canada	549
Singapore	547
(Slovenia)	546
Ireland	539
Scotland	536
Hong Kong	533
(Hungary)	532
New Zealand	531
Norway	530
(Latvia (LLS))	512
(Israel)	505
Iceland	505
Greece	497
Portugal	480
Cyprus	475
(Thailand)	473
Iran, Islamic Republic	416
(Kuwait)	401

International Average = 524

Notes:

1. *Nations not meeting international guidelines are shown in parentheses.*

2. *Latvia is designated LSS because only Latvian-speaking schools were tested.*

3. *The international average is the average of the national averages of the 26 nations.*

▲ *Nations with average scores significantly higher than those of the United States.*

= *Nations with average scores not significantly different from those of the United States*

▼ *Nations with average scores significantly lower than those of the United States.*

Source: *National Center for Education Statistics (1997). Pursuing Excellence: A Study of U.S. Fourth-Grade Mathematics and Science Achievement in International Context. Figure 2. Washington, D.C.: NCES.*

Figure 12.3. Grade 8: Nations' Average Mathematics Performance Compared with That of the United States.

Nation	Average
▲	
Singapore	643
Korea	607
Japan	605
Hong Kong	588
Belgium-Flemish	565
Czech Republic	564
Slovak Republic	547
Switzerland	545
(Netherlands)	541
(Slovenia)	541
(Bulgaria)	540
(Austria)	539
France	538
Hungary	537
Russian Federation	535
(Australia)	530
Ireland	527
Canada	527
(Belgium-French)	526
Sweden	519

Nation	Average
═	
(Thailand)	522
(Israel)	522
(Germany)	509
New Zealand	508
England	506
Norway	503
(Denmark)	502
United States	500
(Scotland)	498
Latvia (LSS)	493
Spain	487
Iceland	487
(Greece)	484
(Romania)	482

Nation	Average
▼	
Lithuania	477
Cyprus	474
Portugal	454
Iran, Islamic Republic	428
(Kuwait)	392
(Colombia)	385
(South Africa)	354

International Average = 531

Notes:

1. *Nations not meeting international guidelines are shown in parentheses.*

2. *Latvia is designated LSS because only Latvian-speaking schools were tested.*

3. *The international average is the average of the national averages of the 41 nations.*

4. *The country average for Sweden may appear to be out of place; however, statistically its placement is correct.*

▲ *Nations with average scores significantly higher than those of the United States*

═ *Nations with average scores not significantly different from those of the United States*

▼ *Nations with average scores significantly lower than those of the United States*

Source: *National Center for Education Statistics (1997). Pursuing Excellence: A Study of U.S. Eighth-Grade Mathematics and Science Achievement in International Context. Figure 1. Washington, D.C.: NCES.*

Figure 12.4. Grade 8: Nations' Average Science Performance Compared with That of the United States.

Nation	Average
▲	
Singapore	607
Czech Republic	574
Japan	571
Korea	565
(Bulgaria)	565
(Netherlands)	560
(Slovenia)	560
(Austria)	558
Hungary	554

=	
England	552
Belgium-Flemish	550
(Australia)	545
Slovak Republic	544
Russian Federation	538
Ireland	538
Sweden	535
United States	534
(Germany)	531
Canada	531
Norway	527
New Zealand	525
(Thailand)	525
(Israel)	524
Hong Kong	522
Switzerland	522
(Scotland)	517

▼	
Spain	517
France	498
(Greece)	497
Iceland	494
(Romania)	486
Latvia (LSS)	485
Portugal	480
(Denmark)	478
Lithuania	476
(Belgium-French)	471
Iran, Islamic Republic	470
Cyprus	463
(Kuwait)	430
(Colombia)	411
(South Africa)	326

International Average = 516

Notes:

1. Nations not meeting international guidelines are shown in parentheses.

2. Latvia is designated LSS because only Latvian-speaking schools were tested.

3. The international average is the average of the national averages of the 41 nations.

4. The country average for Scotland (or Spain) may appear to be out of place; however, statistically its placement is correct.

▲ Nations with average scores significantly higher than those of the United States

= Nations with average scores not significantly different from those of the United States.

▼ Nations with average scores significantly lower than those of the United States.

Source: *National Center for Education Statistics (1997). Pursuing Excellence: A Study of U.S. Eighth-Grade Mathematics and Science Achievement in International Context. Figure 2. Washington, D.C.: NCES.*

Curriculum

• The U.S. eighth-grade mathematics curriculum is less focused than it is in other countries based on an analysis of the intended curriculum in each of the 41 TIMSS countries. The U.S. eighth-grade science curriculum more closely reflects international practices.

• Compared to Germany and Japan, the U.S. eighth-grade mathematics curriculum appears less advanced based on the topics covered and the time devoted to each topic. The content being taught in U.S. eighth-grade mathematics classrooms is at about a seventh-grade level in comparison to other countries. However, the TIMSS study did not assess the level of advancement in the U.S. eighth-grade science curriculum.

• In the TIMSS videotapes of instructional practices, 40 percent of U.S. eighth-grade mathematics lessons included arithmetic topics such as whole number operations, fractions, and decimals, whereas these topics were much less common in Germany and Japan. In contrast, German and Japanese eighth-grade lessons were more likely to cover algebra and geometry.

Teaching

• Eighth-grade U.S. mathematics teachers' typical goal is to teach students how to do something, while the Japanese teachers' goal is to help students learn how to do something and also understand mathematical concepts so that they can solve future problems.

• Ninety-five percent of U.S. teachers stated that they were either "very aware" or "somewhat aware" of current ideas in the teaching and learning of mathematics. However, in the videotape study only a few teachers were observed to apply the key concepts of current reform measures in their classrooms. The TIMSS findings suggest that Japanese, rather than U.S. or German lessons, more often resembled the recommendations of experts and the U.S. reform movement. U.S. lessons typically focused on acquiring mathematical skills rather than conceptual understanding, and were less coherently presented.

• Developing mathematical concepts—that is proving, deriving, or explaining in some detail—is rare among U.S. teachers, in comparison to German and Japanese teachers. U.S. teachers rarely developed mathematical concepts, in contrast to German and Japanese teachers who usually did. The average percentage of topics that were developed was 22 percent in the United States, whereas the average was 77 percent in Germany and 83 percent in Japan.

- In the judgment of independent mathematics and mathematics education experts, none of the U.S. lessons evaluated in the TIMSS videotape study was considered to contain a high-quality sequence of mathematical ideas, compared to 39 percent of Japanese lessons and 28 percent of German lessons (Figure 12.5).

- New teachers in the United States receive less on-the-job training and mentoring than do new teachers in Japan and Germany.

Final Year of Secondary School

Achievement of All Students

- A sample of all students at the end of secondary school (twelfth grade in the United States) was assessed in mathematics and science general knowledge. The mathematics and science general knowledge assessments were a test of the mathematics and science needed for students to function effectively in society as adults.

- The content of the mathematics general knowledge assessment represented about a seventh-grade level of curriculum for most TIMSS nations, but was most equivalent to the ninth-grade curriculum in the United States. The science general knowledge content was most equivalent to the

Figure 12.5. Grade 8: Percentage of Lessons Rated as Having Low, Medium, and High Quality of Mathematical Content.

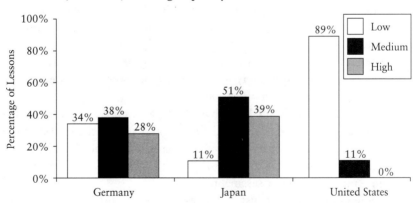

Source: *National Center for Education Statistics (1999). The TIMSS Videotape Classroom Study: Methods and Findings from an Exploratory Research Project on Eighth-Grade Mathematics Instruction in Germany, Japan, and the United States. Figure 34. Washington, D.C.: NCES.*

ninth-grade curriculum internationally, and to the eleventh-grade curriculum in the United States.

• U.S. twelfth graders scored below the international average and among the lowest of the 21 participating nations in both mathematics and science general knowledge (Figures 12.6 and 12.7). The United States outperformed only South Africa and Cyprus on both assessments.

• The U.S. international standing on the general knowledge assessments of TIMSS was stronger in science than in mathematics.

• TIMSS is a fair and accurate comparison of mathematics and science achievement at the end of secondary schooling in the participating nations. The enrollment rate for secondary education in the United States is typical of other TIMSS countries, so our general population is not being compared to more select groups in other countries.

• U.S. students in their final year of secondary school were less likely to be taking mathematics or science than were their counterparts in other countries. While 66 percent of graduating students in the United States were currently taking mathematics, the average in all the countries participating in the general knowledge assessments was 79 percent. The same pattern was also true for science (53 percent for the United States and 67 percent for all the TIMSS countries).

Achievement of Advanced Students

• The advanced mathematics and the physics assessments were administered to a sample of the top 10–20 percent of students in each of the 16 nations participating in these portions of TIMSS. In the advanced mathematics assessment, U.S. students who had taken or were taking precalculus, calculus, or AP calculus were compared to advanced mathematics students in other countries. In the physics assessment, U.S. students who had taken or were taking physics or AP physics were compared to advanced science students in other countries.

• The average scores of U.S. physics and advanced mathematics students were below the international average and among the lowest of the 16 countries that administered the physics and the advanced mathematics assessments (Figures 12.8 and 12.9). The United States outperformed no other country on either assessment.

• When one compares just U.S. twelfth graders with advanced placement calculus instruction to all advanced mathematics students in other nations, their performance was at the international average and significantly higher than in 5 other countries.

• When one compares just U.S. twelfth graders with advanced placement physics instruction to all advanced science students in other nations,

Figure 12.6. Final Year of Secondary School: Nations' Average Mathematics General Knowledge Performance Compared with That of the United States.

Nation	Average

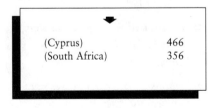

Nation	Average
(Netherlands)	560
Sweden	552
(Denmark)	547
Switzerland	540
(Iceland)	534
(Norway)	528
(France)	523
New Zealand	522
(Australia)	522
(Canada)	519
(Austria)	518
(Slovenia)	512
(Germany)	495
Hungary	483

=	
(Italy)	476
(Russian Federation)	471
(Lithuania)	469
Czech Republic	466
(United States)	461

⬇	
(Cyprus)	466
(South Africa)	356

International Average = 500

Notes:

1. *Nations not meeting international guidelines are shown in parentheses.*

2. *The international average is the average of the national averages of the 21 nations.*

⬆ *Nations with average scores significantly higher than those of the United States*

= *Nations with average scores not significantly different from those of the United States*

⬇ *Nations with average scores significantly lower than those of the United States*

Source: *National Center for Education Statistics (1998). Pursuing Excellence: A Study of U.S. Twelfth-Grade Mathematics and Science Achievement in International Context. Figure 1. Washington, D.C.: NCES.*

Figure 12.7. Final Year of Secondary School: Nations' Average Science General Performance Compared with That of the United States

Nation	Average
Sweden	559
(Netherlands)	558
(Iceland)	549
(Norway)	544
(Canada)	532
New Zealand	529
(Australia)	527
Switzerland	523
(Austria)	520
(Slovenia)	517
(Denmark)	509

(Germany)	497
(France)	487
Czech Republic	487
(Russian Federation)	481
(United States)	480
(Italy)	475
Hungary	471
(Lithuania)	461

Notes:

1. *Nations not meeting international guidelines are shown in parentheses.*

2. *The international average is the average of the national averages of the 21 nations.*

(Cyprus)	448
(South Africa)	349

International Average = 500

◄ *Nations with average scores significantly higher than those of the United States*

= *Nations with average scores not significantly different from those of the United States*

◄ *Nations with average scores significantly lower than those of the United States*

Source: *National Center for Education Statistics (1998). Pursuing Excellence: A Study of U.S. Twelfth-Grade Mathematics and Science Achievement in International Context. Figure 5. Washington, D.C.: NCES.*

their performance was below the international average and significantly higher than in only one other country.

- More countries outperformed U.S. students in physics than in advanced mathematics (Figures 12.8 and 12.9). This differs from results for mathematics and science general knowledge, where more countries outperformed the United States in mathematics than in science.

Achievement

- U.S. students' performance was stronger in science than in mathematics in fourth grade, in eighth grade, and in the twelfth-grade general knowledge assessment relative to the other countries participating in TIMSS.
- U.S. students' international standing was stronger at the fourth-grade level than at the eighth-grade level in both mathematics and science relative to the 25 other countries that participated in TIMSS at both grade levels.
- U.S. students' international standing was stronger at the eighth-grade level than at the twelfth-grade level in both mathematics and science relative to the international averages for the 19 other countries that participated in TIMSS at both levels.
- There was no significant gender gap in fourth-grade or eighth-grade mathematics achievement or in eighth-grade science achievement in the United States. The United States was one of 10 countries, out of 26, with a gender gap favoring males in fourth-grade science achievement.
- There was no significant gender gap among U.S. twelfth-grade students on the mathematics general knowledge assessment. There was a gender gap favoring males among U.S. twelfth graders in science general knowledge, physics, and advanced mathematics.

Contexts of Learning

- The amount of homework does not appear to be related to U.S. performance compared to other nations. U.S. fourth graders are assigned about as much homework as students in other countries; U.S. eighth graders spend about as much time outside of school studying as students in Japan and Germany; all U.S. twelfth graders spend less time on homework; and U.S. advanced twelfth graders were assigned homework more often.
- The amount of instructional time does not appear to be related to U.S. performance compared to other TIMSS nations. U.S. fourth graders spend more class time on mathematics and science than do their average

**Figure 12.8. Final Year of Secondary School:
Average Mathematics Performance of
Advanced Mathematics Students in All Countries.**

Nation	Average
↥	
France	557
(Russian Federation)	542
Switzerland	533
(Australia)	525
(Denmark)	522
(Cyprus)	518
(Lithuania)	516
Greece	513
Sweden	512
(Canada)	509
(Slovenia)	475

=	
(Italy)	474
Czech Republic	469
(Germany)	465
(United States)	**442**
(Austria)	436

Notes:

1. *Nations not meeting international guidelines are shown in parentheses.*

2. *The international average is the average of the national averages of the 16 nations.*

↥*Nations with average scores significantly higher than those of the United States*

= *Nations with average scores not significantly different from those of the United States*

↧*Nations with average scores significantly lower than those of the United States*

↧	
None	

International Average = 501

Source: *National Center for Education Statistics (1998). Pursuing Excellence:
A Study of U.S. Twelfth-Grade Mathematics and Science Achievement in
International Context. Figure 9. Washington, D.C.: NCES.*

**Figure 12.9. Final Year of Secondary School:
Average Physics Performance of
Advanced Science Students in All Countries**

Nation	Average

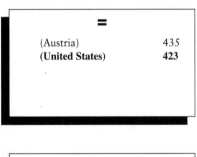

Nation	Average
Norway	581
Sweden	573
(Russian Federation)	545
(Denmark)	534
(Slovenia)	523
(Germany)	522
(Australia)	518
(Cyprus)	494
(Latvia)	488
Switzerland	488
Greece	486
(Canada)	485
France	466
Czech Republic	451

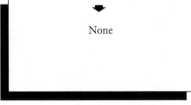

=	
(Austria)	435
(United States)	**423**

▼	
None	

International Average = 501

Notes:

1. *Nations not meeting international guidelines are shown in
parentheses.*

2. *The international average is the
average of the national averages
of the 16 nations.*

▲ *Nations with average scores significantly higher than those of the
United States*

= *Nations with average scores not
significantly different from those
of the United States*

▼ *Nations with average scores significantly lower than those of the
United States*

Source: *National Center for Education Statistics (1998). Pursuing Excellence:
A Study of U.S. Twelfth-Grade Mathematics and Science Achievement in
International Context. Figure 16. Washington, D.C.: NCES.*

international counterparts. U.S. eighth graders spend more time in mathematics classes per year than do students in Germany and Japan.

• The amount of television watching also does not appear to be strongly related to U.S. performance compared to that of other nations. Heavy television watching is as common among U.S. eighth graders as it is among their Japanese counterparts, and U.S. twelfth graders spend, on average, the same amount of time watching television or videos as the international average.

• Although U.S. twelfth-grade students are more likely to have jobs outside of school than their international counterparts and work longer hours, this does not appear to be related to the relatively poor U.S. performance on the final year of secondary school general knowledge assessments in comparison to their international counterparts.

13

WHAT MATTERS MOST: TEACHING FOR AMERICA'S FUTURE

EXECUTIVE SUMMARY

National Commission on Teaching and America's Future

The variables to consider when trying to improve student outcomes are myriad. Teachers are one of the most important variables; we all know what an incredible difference an excellent teacher can make in a student's learning and future attitude toward school. The teaching profession, in the eyes of many reformers, is battered and in some cases broken. In this chapter the National Commission on Teaching and America's Future argues that quality recruitment, preparation, and support will lead us to excellent teachers who inspire and motivate students.

o

THIS REPORT OFFERS what we believe is the single most important strategy for achieving America's educational goals: A blueprint for recruiting, preparing, and supporting excellent teachers in all of America's schools. The plan is aimed at ensuring that all communities have teachers with the knowledge and skills they need to teach so that all children can learn, and that all school systems are organized to support teachers in this work. A caring, competent, and qualified teacher for every child is the most important ingredient in education reform.

The Commission's proposals are systemic in scope—not a recipe for more short-lived pilots and demonstration projects. They require a dramatic departure from the status quo—one that creates a new infrastructure for professional learning and an accountability system that ensures attention to standards for educators as well as students at every level—national, state, local school district, school, and classroom.

This Commission starts from three simple premises:

1. What teachers know and can do is the most important influence on what students learn.

2. Recruiting, preparing, and retaining good teachers is the central strategy for improving our schools.

3. School reform cannot succeed unless it focuses on creating the conditions in which teachers can teach, and teach well.

We propose an audacious goal for America's future. Within a decade—by the year 2006—we will provide every student in America with what should be his or her educational birthright: access to competent, caring, qualified teaching in schools organized for success. This is a challenging goal to put before the nation and its educational leaders. But if the goal is challenging and requires unprecedented effort, it does not require unprecedented new theory. Common sense suffices: American students are entitled to teachers who know their subjects, understand their students and what they need, and have developed the skills required to make learning come alive.

However, based on its two-year study, the Commission identified a number of barriers to achieving this goal. They include:

○ Low expectations for student performance.

○ Unenforced standards for teachers.

○ Major flaws in teacher preparation.

○ Painfully slipshod teacher recruitment.

○ Inadequate induction for beginning teachers.

○ Lack of professional development and rewards for knowledge and skill.

○ Schools that are structured for failure rather than success.

We offer five major recommendations to address these concerns and accomplish our goal.

I. GET SERIOUS ABOUT STANDARDS, FOR BOTH STUDENTS
AND TEACHERS

○ Establish professional standards boards in every state.

○ Insist on accreditation for all schools of education.

○ Close inadequate schools of education.

○ License teachers based on demonstrated performance, including tests of subject matter knowledge, teaching knowledge, and teaching skill.

○ Use National Board standards as the benchmark for accomplished teaching.

II. REINVENT TEACHER PREPARATION AND
PROFESSIONAL DEVELOPMENT

○ Organize teacher education and professional development programs around standards for students and teachers.

○ Develop extended, graduate-level teacher preparation programs that provide a yearlong internship in a professional development school.

○ Create and fund mentoring programs for beginning teachers, along with evaluation of teaching skills.

○ Create stable, high-quality sources of professional development.

III. FIX TEACHER RECRUITMENT AND PUT QUALIFIED TEACHERS
IN EVERY CLASSROOM

○ Increase the ability of low-wealth districts to pay for qualified teachers, and insist that districts hire only qualified teachers.

○ Redesign and streamline district hiring.

○ Eliminate barriers to teacher mobility.

○ Aggressively recruit high-need teachers and provide incentives for teaching in shortage areas.

○ Develop high-quality pathways to teaching for a wide range of recruits.

IV. ENCOURAGE AND REWARD TEACHER KNOWLEDGE
AND SKILL

○ Develop a career continuum for teaching linked to assessments and compensation systems that reward knowledge and skill.

○ Remove incompetent teachers.

○ Set goals and enact incentives for National Board Certification in every state and district. Aim to certify 105,000 teachers in this decade, one for every school in the United States.

V. CREATE SCHOOLS THAT ARE ORGANIZED FOR STUDENT AND TEACHER SUCCESS.

○ Flatten hierarchies and reallocate resources to send more dollars to the front lines of schools: Invest more in teachers and technology and less in nonteaching personnel.

○ Provide venture capital in the form of challenge grants to schools for teacher learning linked to school improvement and rewards for team efforts that lead to improved practice and greater learning.

○ Select, prepare, and retain principals who understand teaching and learning and who can lead high-performing schools.

Developing recommendations is easy. Implementing them is hard work. The first step is to recognize that these ideas must be pursued together— as an entire tapestry that is tightly interwoven. Pulling on a single thread will create a tangle rather than tangible progress. The second step is to build upon the substantial work that has been undertaken over the past decade. All across the country, successful programs for recruiting, educating, and mentoring new teachers have sprung up. Professional networks and teacher academies have been launched; many education school programs have been redesigned; higher standards for licensing teachers and accrediting education schools have been developed; and a National Board for Teaching Standards is now fully established and beginning to define and reward accomplished teaching. All these endeavors, and those of many others, form the foundation of this crusade.

PART THREE

REFORM AS RESPONSE TO SOCIAL DIVERSITY AND STUDENT NEEDS

14

DISCUSSION OF
SCHOOL FUNDING

Jonathan Kozol

There are many arguments about how much money matters in improving student outcomes. Some studies show that additional money does improve student outcomes, while others show just the opposite. The only fact that can be agreed on is that there can be large funding disparities between wealthy suburban schools and schools in poor urban neighborhoods. Although there is simply not enough space here to look at this debate from all sides, following is an excerpt from *Savage Inequalities,* which argues the injustice of funding disparity.

○

IN 1989, Chicago spent some $5,500 for each student in its secondary schools. This may be compared to an investment of some $8,500 to $9,000 in each high school student in the highest-spending suburbs to the north. Stated in the simplest terms, this means that any high school class of 30 children in Chicago received approximately $90,000 less each year than would have been spent on them if they were pupils of a school such as New Trier High.

The difference in spending between very wealthy suburbs and poor cities is not always as extreme as this in Illinois. When relative student needs, however, have been factored into the discussion, the disparities in funding are enormous. Equity, after all, does not mean simply equal funding. Equal funding for unequal needs is not equality. The need is greater in

Chicago, and its children, if they are to have approximately equal opportunities, need more than the children who attend New Trier. Seen in this light, the $90,000 annual difference is quite startling.

Lack of money is not the only problem in Chicago, but the gulf in funding we have seen is so remarkable and seems so blatantly unfair that it strikes many thoughtful citizens at first as inexplicable. How can it be that inequalities as great as these exist in neighboring school districts?

The answer is found, at least in part, in the arcane machinery by which we finance public education. Most public schools in the United States depend for their initial funding on a tax on local property. There are also state and federal funding sources, and we will discuss them later, but the property tax is the decisive force in shaping inequality. The property tax depends, of course, upon the taxable value of one's home and that of local industries. A typical wealthy suburb in which homes are often worth more than $400,000 draws upon a larger tax base in proportion to its student population than a city occupied by thousands of poor people. Typically, in the United States, very poor communities place high priority on education, and they often tax themselves at higher rates than do the very affluent communities. But, even if they tax themselves at several times the rate of an extremely wealthy district, they are likely to end up with far less money for each child in their schools.

Because the property tax is counted as a tax deduction by the federal government, home-owners in a wealthy suburb get back a substantial portion of the money that they spend to fund their children's schools—effectively, a federal subsidy for an unequal education. Home-owners in poor districts get this subsidy as well, but, because their total tax is less, the subsidy is less. The mortgage interest that home-owners pay is also treated as a tax deduction—in effect, a second federal subsidy. These subsidies, as I have termed them, are considerably larger than most people understand. In 1984, for instance, property-tax deductions granted by the federal government were $9 billion. An additional $23 billion in mortgage-interest deductions were provided to home-owners: a total of some $32 billion. Federal grants to local schools, in contrast, totaled only $7 billion, and only part of this was earmarked for low-income districts. Federal policy, in this respect, increases the existing gulf between the richest and the poorest schools.

All of these disparities are also heightened, in the case of larger cities like Chicago, by the disproportionate number of entirely tax-free institutions —colleges and hospitals and art museums, for instance—that are sited in such cities. In some cities, according to Jonathan Wilson, former chairman of the Council of Urban Boards of Education, 30 percent or more of the potential tax base is exempt from taxes, compared to as little as 3 percent in the adjacent suburbs. Suburbanites, of course, enjoy the use of these non-profit, tax-free institutions; and, in the case of private colleges and universities, they are far *more* likely to enjoy their use than are the residents of inner cities.

Cities like Chicago face the added problem that an overly large portion of their limited tax revenues must be diverted to meet nonschool costs that wealthy suburbs do not face, or only on a far more modest scale. Police expenditures are higher in crime-ridden cities than in most suburban towns. Fire department costs are also higher where dilapidated housing, often with substandard wiring, and arson-for-profit are familiar problems. Public health expenditures are also higher where poor people cannot pay for private hospitals. All of these expenditures compete with those for public schools. So the districts that face the toughest challenges are also likely to be those that have the fewest funds to meet their children's needs.

Many people, even those who view themselves as liberals on other issues, tend to grow indignant, even rather agitated, if invited to look closely at these inequalities. "Life isn't fair," one parent in Winnetka answered flatly when I pressed the matter. "Wealthy children also go to summer camp. All summer. Poor kids maybe not at all. Or maybe, if they're lucky, for two weeks. Wealthy children have the chance to go to Europe and they have the access to good libraries, encyclopedias, computers, better doctors, nicer homes. Some of my neighbors send their kids to schools like Exeter and Groton. Is government supposed to equalize these things as well?"

But government, of course, does not assign us to our homes, our summer camps, our doctors—or to Exeter. It does assign us to our public schools. Indeed, it forces us to go to them. Unless we have the wealth to pay for private education, we are compelled by law to go to public school— and to the public school in our district. Thus the state, by requiring attendance but refusing to require equity, effectively requires inequality. Compulsory inequity, perpetuated by state law, too frequently condemns our children to unequal lives.

In Illinois, as elsewhere in America, local funds for education raised from property taxes are supplemented by state contributions and by federal funds, although the federal contribution is extremely small, constituting only 6 percent of total school expenditures. State contributions represent approximately half of local school expenditures in the United States; although intended to make up for local wealth disparities, they have seldom been sufficient to achieve this goal. Total yearly spending—local funds combined with state assistance and the small amount that comes from Washington—ranges today in Illinois from $2,100 on a child in the poorest district to above $10,000 on the richest. The system, writes John Coons, a professor of law at Berkeley University, "bears the appearance of calculated unfairness."

There is a belief advanced today, and in some cases by conservative black authors, that poor children and particularly black children should not be allowed to hear too much about these matters. If they learn how much less they are getting than rich children, we are told, this knowledge may induce them to regard themselves as "victims," and such "victim-thinking," it is argued, may then undermine their capability to profit from whatever opportunities may actually exist. But this is a matter of psychology—or strategy—and not reality. The matter, in any case, is academic since most adolescents in the poorest neighborhoods learn very soon that they are getting less than children in the wealthier school districts. They see suburban schools on television and they see them when they travel for athletic competitions. It is a waste of time to worry whether we should tell them something they could tell to us. About injustice, most poor children in America cannot be fooled.

NOTES

P. 213ff, *discussion of school funding:* For matters specific to Illinois, I have relied upon discussions with George Alan Hickrod and Larry Frank of the Center for the Study of Educational Finance, Illinois State University, Normal, Illinois, and with G. Alfred Hess of the Chicago Panel on Public School Policy and Finance, 1990 and 1991.

P. 214, *poor communities tend to tax high, spend low:* "Chicago schools are poor because the city itself is poor. . . . Overall, suburban tax rates have to be only half as large as Chicago's to raise the same amount of money." (*Tribune* series.)

Federal property-tax and mortgage-interest deductions and federal grants to local public schools: Office of Management and Budget, the White House, 1986; Congressional Budget Office, 1986.

Jonathan Wilson, Council of Urban Boards of Education: Conversations with author, March 1991.

P. 215, *added burden faced by cities:* "The total property tax rate in Chicago," according to the *Chicago Tribune* (1988), "is just over $10.35 per $100 assessed value, one of the highest in Cook County, but only 36 percent of that goes to schools." In the suburbs, by comparison, "school taxes make up an average of about 60 percent" of the total property tax rate. "We pay a fantastic amount for police and fire protection in Chicago," says G. Alfred Hess of the

Chicago panel on School Policy and Finance. "This city is in the cruel box of having to decide which services to provide to poor families." (*Tribune* series.)

P. 215, *federal and state contributions:* Author's interviews with Harold Howe II, former U.S. Commissioner of Education, and G. Alan Hickrod, February and March 1991.

P. 215, *States pay roughly half of school expenditures:* The extreme exceptions are New Hampshire, where the state provides almost no aid, and Hawaii, where the state pays 92 percent of school expenditures. (*Boston Globe*, February 9, 1991.)

Pp. 215, 216, *extremes of high and low spending in Illinois:* Education Equity Coalition (Chicago Urban League, Chicago Panel on School Policy and Finance, and League of Women Voters of Illinois), "The Inequity in Illinois School Finance" (Chicago: January 1991); also *Illinois School Law Quarterly,* January 1991. According to the *New York Times* (December 19, 1990), "Overall spending per student among districts in Illinois ranges from $2,100 to nearly $10,000, and this gap is growing."

15

BILINGUAL EDUCATION:
THE CONTROVERSY

Richard Rothstein

Often the argument against bilingual education comes from a misunderstanding of how earlier generations of immigrants were educated. The widely held assumption is that immigrants were made to sink or swim in an English-only classroom environment. History may prove this assumption wrong. How immigrants learned and continue to learn English is complex and often rooted in the culture of each learner.

---
o

BILINGUAL EDUCATION, a preferred strategy for the last 20 years, aims to teach academic subjects to immigrant children in their native languages (most often Spanish), while slowly and simultaneously adding English instruction.[1] In theory, the children don't fall behind in other subjects while they are learning English. When they are fluent in English, they can then "transition" to English instruction in academic subjects at the grade level of their peers. Further, the theory goes, teaching immigrants in their native language values their family and community culture and reinforces their sense of self-worth, thus making their academic success more likely.

In contrast, bilingual education's critics tell the following, quite different, story. In the early 20th century, public schools assimilated immigrants to American culture and imparted workplace skills essential for upward mobility. Children were immersed in English instruction and, when forced to "sink or swim," they swam. Today, however, separatist (usually Hispanic) community leaders and their liberal supporters, opposed to assimilation, want Spanish instruction to preserve native culture and traditions. This is especially dangerous because the proximity of Mexico and the possibility of returning home give today's immigrants the option of "keeping a foot in both camps"—an option not available to previous immigrants who were forced to assimilate. Today's attempts to preserve immigrants' native languages and cultures will not only balkanize the American melting pot but hurt the children upon whom bilingual education is imposed because their failure to learn English well will leave them unprepared for the workplace. Bilingual education supporters may claim that it aims to teach English, but high dropout rates for immigrant children and low rates of transition to full English instruction prove that, even if educators' intentions are genuine, the program is a failure.

The English First Foundation, a lobbying group bent on abolishing bilingual education, states that most Americans "have ancestors who learned English the same way: in classrooms where English was the only language used for all learning activities."[2] According to 1996 Republican Presidential nominee Bob Dole, the teaching of English to immigrants is what "we have done . . . since our founding to speed the melting of our melting pot. . . . We must stop the practice of multilingual education as a means of instilling ethnic pride, or as a therapy for low self-esteem, or out of elitist guilt over a culture built on the traditions of the West."[3]

Speaker of the House Newt Gingrich chimed in as well:

> If people had wanted to remain immersed in their old culture, they could have done so without coming to America. . . . Bilingualism keeps people actively tied to their old language and habits and maximizes the cost of the transition to becoming American. . . . The only viable alternative for the American underclass is American civilization. Without English as a common language, there is no such civilization.[4]

This viewpoint has commonsense appeal, but it has little foundation in reality.

Bilingual Education: The History

Despite proximity to their homeland, Mexican Americans are no more likely to reverse migrate than were Europeans in the early 20th century. One-third of the immigrants who came here between 1908 and 1924 eventually abandoned America and returned home.[5]

What's more, the immigrants who remained did not succeed in school by learning English. During the last great wave of immigration, from 1880 to 1915, very few Americans succeeded in school, immigrants least of all.

By 1930, it was still the case that half of all American 14- to 17-year-olds either didn't make it to high school or dropped out before graduating. The median number of school years completed was 10.

Far from succeeding by immersing themselves in English, immigrant groups did much worse than the native-born, and some immigrant groups did much worse than others. The poorest performers were Italians. According to a 1911 federal immigration commission report, in Boston, Chicago, and New York 80% of native white children in the seventh grade stayed in school another year, but only 58% of Southern Italian children, 62% of Polish children, and 74% of Russian Jewish children did so. Of those who made it to eighth grade, 58% of the native whites went on to high school, but only 23% of the Southern Italians did so. In New York, 54% of native-born eighth-graders made it to ninth grade, but only 34% of foreign-born eighth-graders did so.[6]

A later study showed that the lack of success of immigrants relative to the native-born continued into high school. In 1931, only 11% of the Italian students who entered high school graduated (compared to an estimated graduation rate of over 40% for all students). This was a much bigger native/immigrant gap than we have today.

While we have no achievement tests from that earlier period by which to evaluate relative student performance, I.Q. tests were administered frequently. Test after test in the 1920s found that Italian immigrant students had an average I.Q. of about 85, compared to an average for native-born students of about 102. The poor academic achievement of these Italian Americans led to high rates of "retardation"—that is, being held back and not promoted (this was the origin of the pejorative use of the term "retarded").

A survey of New York City's retarded students (liberally defined so that a child had to be 9 years old to be considered retarded in the first grade, 10 years old in the second grade, and so on), found that 19% of native-born students were retarded in 1908, compared to 36% of Italian students. The federal immigration commission found that the retardation rate of children of non-English-speaking immigrants was about 60% higher than that of children of immigrants from English-speaking countries.[7] The challenge of educating Italian immigrant children was so severe that New York established its first special education classes to confront it. A 1921 survey disclosed that half of all (what we now call) "learning disabled" special education children in New York schools had Italian-born fathers.[8]

As these data show—and as is the case today—some groups did better than others, both for cultural reasons and because of the influence of other socioeconomic factors on student achievement. If Italian children did worse, Eastern European Jewish children did better. This is not surprising in light of what we now know about the powerful influence of background characteristics on academic success. In 1910, 32% of Southern Italian adult males in American cities were unskilled manual laborers, but only one-half of 1% of Russian Jewish males were unskilled. Thirty-four percent of the Jews were merchants, while only 13% of the Italians were. In New York City, the average annual income of a Russian Jewish head-of-household in 1910 was $813; a Southern Italian head-of-household averaged $688.[9]

But even with these relative economic advantages, the notion that Jewish immigrant children assimilated through sink-or-swim English-only education is a nostalgic and dangerous myth. In 1910, there were 191,000 Jewish children in the New York City schools; only 6,000 were in high school, and the overwhelming majority of these students dropped out before graduating. As the Jewish writer Irving Howe put it, after reviewing New York school documents describing the difficulties of "Americanizing" immigrant children from 1910 to 1914, "To read the reports of the school superintendents is to grow impatient with later sentimentalists who would have us suppose that all or most Jewish children burned with zeal for the life of the mind."[10] There may have been relatively more such students among the Jewish immigrants than in other immigrant communities, Howe noted, but they were still a minority.

Immersing immigrants in an English-language school program has been effective—usually by the third generation. On the whole, immigrant children spoke their native language; members of the second generation (immigrants' native-born children) were bilingual, but not sufficiently fluent in English to excel in school; members of the third generation were fluent in English and began to acquire college educations. For some groups (e.g., Greek Americans), the pattern more often took four generations; for others (e.g., Eastern European Jews), many in the second generation may have entered college.

This history is not a mere curiosity, because those who advocate against bilingual education today often claim that we know how to educate immigrant children because we've done it before. However, if we've never successfully educated the first or even second generation of children from peasant or unskilled immigrant families, we are dealing with an unprecedented task, and history can't guide us.

To understand the uniqueness of our current challenge, compare the enormous—by contemporary standards—dropout rate of New York City

Jewish students in 1910 with that of Mexican students in the Los Angeles school district today. Like New York in 1910, Los Angeles now is burdened with a rising tide of immigrants. In 1996, there were 103,000 Hispanic students in grades 9–12 in Los Angeles (out of the city's total K–12 Hispanic population of 390,000). Hispanic high school students were about 26% of the total Hispanic student population in Los Angeles in 1996,[11] compared to 3% for Jews in New York in 1910 (only 6,000 high school students out of 191,000 total Jewish enrollment). In Los Angeles today, 74% of Mexican-born youths between the ages of 15 and 17 are still in high school; 88% of Hispanic youths from other countries are still in attendance.[12] More than 70% of Hispanic immigrants who came to the United States prior to their sophomore year actually complete high school (compared to a 94% high school completion rate for whites and a 92% rate for blacks).[13] English immersion programs for Jews early in this century (and certainly similar programs for Italians) cannot teach us anything that would help improve on today's immigrant achievement or school completion, much of which may be attributable to bilingual education programs, even if imperfectly administered.

If the notion is misleading that English immersion led previous generations of immigrants to academic success, so too is the claim that bilingual education repudiates the assimilationist approach of previous immigrants. In reality, today's Hispanics are not the first to seek bicultural assimilation. Some 19th- and early 20th-century European immigrants also fought for and won the right to bilingual education in the public schools.[14] Native-language instruction was absent from 1920 until the mid-1960s only because a fierce anti-German (and then anti-immigrant) reaction after World War I succeeded in banishing it from American classrooms. Even foreign-language instruction for native-born students was banned in most places. If Chicago's Bismarck Hotel found it necessary to rename itself the "Mark Twain," it should not be surprising that bilingual education programs were also abolished.

Before World War I, immigrant groups often pressed public schools to teach children in their native language. The success of these groups depended more on whether adult immigrant activists had political power than on a pedagogical consensus. The immigrants' objective, as it is today, was to preserve a fragment of ethnic identity in children for whom the pull of American culture seemed dangerously irresistible. In this, they were supported by many influential educators. William Harris, the school superintendent in St. Louis and later U.S. commissioner of education, argued for bilingual education in the 1870s, stating that "national memories and aspirations, family traditions, customs and habits, moral and religious observances cannot be suddenly removed or changed without disastrously weakening the personality." Harris established the first "kindergarten" in America, taught solely in German, to give immigrant students a head start in the St. Louis schools.[15]

Nineteenth-century immigrant parents were often split over the desirability of bilingual education, as immigrant parents are split today. Many recognized that children were more likely to succeed if schools' use of the native language validated the culture of the home. But others felt that their children's education would be furthered if they learned in English only.

The first bilingual public school in New York City was established in 1837 to prepare German-speaking children for eventual participation in regular English schools. The initial rule was that children could remain in German-language instruction only for 12 months, after which they would transfer to a regular school. But the German teacher resisted this rule, believing that, before transferring, the children needed more than the limited English fluency they had acquired after a year of German instruction. The record is unclear about how often the rule was stretched.

Many immigrant children, not just Germans, did not attend school at all if they could not have classes in their native language. In his 1840 address to the New York legislature, Gov. William Seward (later Lincoln's secretary of state) explained that the importance of attracting immigrants to school —and of keeping them there—motivated his advocacy of expanded native-language instruction: "I do not hesitate to recommend the establishment of schools in which [immigrant children] may be instructed by teachers speaking the same language as themselves." Only by so doing, Gov. Seward insisted, could we "qualify . . . [them] for the high responsibilities of citizenship."

Buoyed by Seward's endorsement, Italian parents in New York City demanded a native-language school as well, and in 1843 the Public School Society established a committee to determine whether one should be established. The committee recommended against an Italian-language school, claiming the Italian community was itself divided. "Information has been obtained," the committee stated, "that the more intelligent class of Italians do not desire such a school, and that, like most [but not, apparently, all] of the better class of Germans, they would prefer that those of their countrymen who come here with good intentions should be Americanized as speedily as possible."[16]

Bilingual education, though sometimes controversial, was found nationwide. In Pennsylvania, German Lutheran churches established parochial schools when public schools would not teach in German; in 1838, Pennsylvania law converted these German schools to public schools. Then, in 1852, a state public school regulation specified that "if any considerable number of Germans desire to have their children instructed in their own language, their wishes should be gratified."[17]

In 1866, succumbing to pressure from politically powerful German immigrants, the Chicago Board of Education decided to establish a German-language school in each area of the city where 150 parents asked for it. By 1892 the board had hired 242 German-language teachers to teach 35,000 German-speaking children, one-fourth of Chicago's total public school enrollment. In 1870, a public school established in Denver, Colorado, was taught entirely in German. An 1872 Oregon law permitted German-language public schools to be established in Portland whenever 100 voters petitioned for such a school. Maryland, Iowa, Indiana, Kentucky, Ohio, and Minnesota also had bilingual education laws, either statewide or applying only to cities with large immigrant populations. In Nebraska, enabling legislation for bilingual education was enacted for the benefit of German immigrant children as late as 1913.[18]

There was considerable variation in how these programs arranged what we now call the "transition" to English. In St. Louis, Harris' system introduced English gradually, beginning in the first grade. The 1888 report of the Missouri supervisor of public instruction stated that "in some districts the schools are taught in German for a certain number of months and then in English, while in others German is used part of the day and English the rest. Some of the teachers are barely able to speak the English language." Ohio's 1870 rules provided that the lower grades in German-language public schools should be bilingual (half the instructional time in grades 1 through 4 could be in German), but in grades 5 through 8 native-language instruction had to be reduced to one hour a day. Baltimore permitted public schools in the upper grades to teach art and music in German only, but geography, history, and science had to be taught in both English and German. In some midwestern communities, there was resistance to any English instruction: an 1846 Wisconsin law insisted that public schools in Milwaukee must at least teach English (as a foreign language) as one academic subject.[19]

While Germans were most effective in demanding public support for native-language instruction, others were also successful. In Texas in the late 19th century, there were seven Czech-language schools supported by the state school fund. In California, a desire by the majority to segregate Chinese children seemed to play more of a role than demands by the Chinese community for separate education. San Francisco established a Chinese-language school in 1885; the city later established segregated Indian, Mongolian, and Japanese schools.[20]

San Francisco's German, Italian, and French immigrants, on the other hand, were taught in their native languages in regular public schools. Here, bilingual education was a strategy designed to lure immigrant children into public schools from parochial schools where they learned no English at all. According to San Francisco's school superintendent in 1871, only if offered native-language instruction could immigrant children be brought into public schools, where, "under the care of American teachers," they could be "molded in the true form of American citizenship."[21]

Support for bilingual education was rarely unanimous or consistent. In San Francisco, the election of an "anti-immigrant" Republican school board majority in 1873 led to the abolition of schools in which French and German had been the primary languages of instruction and to the firing of all French- and German-speaking teachers. After protests by the immigrant community, bilingual schools were reestablished in 1874. In 1877, the California legislature enacted a prohibition of bilingual education, but the governor declined to sign it. William Harris' bilingual system in St. Louis was dismantled in 1888, after redistricting split the German vote and the Irish won a school board majority.[22]

In 1889, Republican Gov. William Hoard of Wisconsin sponsored legislation to ban primary-language instruction in public and private schools, claiming the support of German immigrant parents. The *Milwaukee Sentinel* published a front-page story about "a German in Sheboygan County . . . who sent his children away to school in order that they might learn English." The father, reported the *Sentinel,* complained that "in the public schools of the town, German teachers, who . . . did not know English . . . had been employed . . . [and] he felt it essential to the welfare of his children, who expected to remain citizens of this country, to know English." [23]

But both the newspaper and Wisconsin's Republican politicians had misjudged the immigrants' sentiments. In response to the anti-bilingual law, enraged German Americans (who had previously supported Republican candidates) mobilized to turn the statehouse over to Democrats and to convert the state's 7-to-2 Republican majority in Congress to a Democratic majority of 8-to-1. The Democrats promptly repealed the anti-bilingual education law.

An almost identical series of events took place in Illinois, where formerly Republican German American voters mobilized in both East St. Louis and Chicago to elect a liberal Democrat, Peter Altgeld, governor in 1890, largely because of his bilingual school language policy. These upheavals in two previously safe Republican states played an important role in the election of Democrat Grover Cleveland as President in 1892. Nonetheless, the controversy continued, and in 1893 the *Chicago Tribune* began a new campaign against German-language instruction. In a compromise later that year, German instruction was abolished in the primary grades but retained in the upper grades, while Chicago's mayor promised German Americans a veto over future school board appointments to ensure that erosion of primary-language instruction would not continue.[24]

But these controversies ended with World War I. Six months after the armistice, the Ohio legislature, spurred by Gov. James Cox, who was to be the Democratic Presidential candidate in 1920, banned all German from the state's elementary schools. The language posed "a distinct menace to Americanism," Cox insisted. The *New York Times* editorialized in 1919 that, although some parents "want German to be taught [because it] pleases their pride . . . it does not do their children any good." Within the following year, 15 states in which native-language instruction had flourished adopted laws requiring that all teaching be in English. By 1923, 35 states had done so.[25] Only when Nebraska went so far as to ban native-language instruction in parochial as well as public schools did the Supreme Court, in 1923, strike down an English-only law.[26]

During the next 30 years, bilingual instruction had its ups and downs, even where English was not the native language. In 1950, Louisiana first required English, not French, to be the language of public school instruction. In the Southwest, where teaching in Spanish had long been common, the practice continued in some places and was abolished in others. Tucson established a bilingual teaching program in 1923, and Burbank established one in 1931. New Mexico operated bilingual schools throughout most of the 20th century, up until the 1950s. The state even required the teaching of Spanish to English-speaking children in elementary school. But in 1918, Texas made teaching in Spanish a crime, and, while the law was not consistently enforced (especially along the Mexican border), as recently as 1973 a Texas teacher was indicted for not teaching history in English.[27] In the same year, Texas reversed itself and adopted bilingual education as its strategy.

When bilingual education began to reemerge in the 1970s—spurred by a Supreme Court finding that schools without special provisions for educating language-minority children were not providing equal education— the nation's memory of these precedents had been erased. Today many Americans blithely repeat the myth that, until the recent emergence of separatist minority activists and their liberal supporters, the nation had always immersed its immigrant children in nothing but English and this method had proved its effectiveness.

Bilingual Education: Mixed Evidence

This mixed history, however, does not prove that bilingual education is effective, any more so than English immersion or intense English-language instruction. To an unbiased layperson, the arguments of both advocates and opponents of bilingual education seem to make sense. On the one hand, it's reasonable to insist that children who don't speak English continue their education in a language they understand in history, literature, math, and science, while they learn English. It's also reasonable to expect, however, that this might make it too tempting to defer English-language instruction. Moreover, the best way to do something difficult—e.g., making the transition to English—is simply to do it without delay. It makes sense to acknowledge that children may adapt better to school if the school's culture is not in conflict with that of the home. But some immigrant parents may be more intent on preserving native culture for their children than are the children themselves.

Modern research findings on bilingual education are mixed. As with all educational research, it is so difficult to control for complex background factors that affect academic outcomes that no single study is ultimately satisfying. Bilingual education advocates point to case studies of primary-language programs in Calexico, California; Rock Point, Arizona; Santa Fe, New Mexico; New Haven, Connecticut; and elsewhere that show that children advance further in both English and other academic subjects when native-language instruction is used and the transition to English is very gradual. Opponents point to case studies in Redwood City and Berkeley, California; in Fairfax, Virginia; and elsewhere that prove that immersion in English or rapid and intensive English instruction is most effective.[28] Overall, the conflicting evidence from these case studies does not suggest that abolition of bilingual education or even the substitution of parental choice for pedagogical expertise in determining whether bilingual approaches should be used would improve things much.

The problem is especially complex because not only economic factors but also generational variation apparently affects the achievement of immigrant youths. In 1936, the principal of a high school in New York City that enrolled large numbers of Italian immigrants wrote:

> The problem of juvenile delinquency . . . baffles all the forces of organized society. . . . The highest rate of delinquency is characteristic of immigrant communities. . . . The delinquent is usually the American-born child of foreign-born parents, not the immigrant himself. Delinquency,

then, is fundamentally a second-generation problem. This intensifies the responsibility of the school.[29]

The same is true today. The challenge now facing immigrant educators is that academic achievement for second-generation Hispanic and Asian children is often below that of children who arrive in the U.S. as immigrants themselves.[30] Many of these children of the second generation seem to speak English, but they are fully fluent in neither English nor their home language. Many of their parents, frustrated that their own ambition has not been transmitted to their children, may become convinced that only English immersion will set their children straight, while others seek bilingual solutions to prevent the corruption of American culture from dampening their children's ambition.

In the absence of persuasive evidence, the issue has become politicized. In a country as large as ours, with as varied experience, there is virtually no limit to the anecdotes and symbols that can be invoked as substitutes for evidence.

Opponents of bilingual education promote Hispanic parents to the media when they claim they want their children to learn English without bilingual support; the clear implication is that only liberal ideologues and separatists support native-language instruction. These claims, like those circulated by the *Milwaukee Sentinel* a century ago, may not reflect the feelings of most parents. And the technology of teaching a new language to immigrant children is complex; both bilingual education advocates and opponents claim their goal is full English literacy as rapidly as possible. But there's no reason to expect that politicized parent groups are the best judges of language acquisition research.

There are also successful adult immigrants who brag of their English fluency, acquired either with or without bilingual education. As always, such anecdotal evidence should be treated with caution. Richard Rodriguez' autobiography, *Hunger of Memory,* describes his successful education in an English-only environment. But Rodriguez, unlike most immigrants, was raised in a predominantly English-speaking neighborhood and was the only Spanish speaker in his class.[31] His experience may be relevant for some immigrants, but not relevant for many others.

Whichever method is, in fact, more effective for most immigrant children, there will be many for whom the other method worked well. It may be the case that immigrant children's social and economic background characteristics should affect the pedagogy chosen. Even if some Russian Jewish immigrants did not require bilingual education to graduate from high school, perhaps Italians would have progressed more rapidly if they'd had access to bilingual instruction. Today, the fact that some (though not all) Asian immigrants seem to progress rapidly in school without native-language support provides no relevant evidence about whether this model can work well for Mexican or Caribbean children, especially those low on the ladder of socioeconomic status and those whose parents have little education. Nor does it tell us much about what the best pedagogy would be for Asians who generally do less well in school, such as Hmong, Laotian, and Cambodian children.[32]

It is certain, however, that the American "melting pot" has never been endangered by pluralist efforts to preserve native languages and cultures. Bilingual instruction has never interfered with the powerful assimilationist influences that overwhelm all children whose parents migrate here. And this is equally true of Spanish-speaking children today.

After the last 20 years of bilingual education throughout America, Spanish-speaking children continue to assimilate. From 1972 to 1995, despite rapidly accelerating immigration (more Hispanic youths are first-generation immigrants today than 20 years ago), the Hispanic high school completion rate has crept upward (from 66% to 70%). Hispanic high school graduates who enroll in college jumped from 45% to 54% (for non-Hispanic whites, it's now 64%). And the number of Hispanic high school graduates who subsequently complete four years of college jumped from 11% to 16% (for non-Hispanic whites, it's now 34%).[33] A study of the five-county area surrounding Los Angeles, the most immigrant-affected community in the nation, found that from 1980 to 1990, the share of U.S.-born Hispanics in professional occupations grew from 7% to 9%, the share in executive positions grew from 7% to 10%, and the share in other administrative and technical jobs grew from 24% to 26%.[34] Overall, 55% of U.S.-born Hispanics are in occupations for which a good education is a necessity, in an area where bilingual education has been practiced for the last generation.

Perhaps we can do better. Perhaps we would do better with less bilingual education. But perhaps not. All we can say for sure is that the data reveal no apparent crisis, and the system for immigrant education with which we've been muddling through, with all its problems, does not seem to be in a state of collapse.

The best thing that could happen to the bilingual education debate would be to remove it from the political realm. Sound-bite pedagogy is no cure for the complex interaction of social, economic, and instructional factors that determine the outcomes of contemporary American schools.

NOTES

1. Technically, "bilingual education" refers to all programs designed to give any support to non–English-speaking children, including programs whose main focus is immersion in English-speaking classrooms. In public debate, however, the term generally refers to only one such program, "transitional bilingual education (TBE)," in which native-language instruction in academic subjects is given to non-English speakers. In this article, I use the term in its nontechnical sense to refer only to "TBE" programs.

2. Web site, English First Foundation: http://englishfirst.org.

3. Mark Pitsch, "Dole Takes Aim at 'Elitist' History Standards," *Education Week,* 13 September 1995, p. 18.

4. Newt Gingrich, *To Renew America* (New York: HarperCollins, 1995), pp. 161–62.

5. Irving Howe, *World of Our Fathers* (New York: Simon and Schuster, 1983), p. 58.

6. Michael R. Olneck and Marvin Lazerson, "The School Achievement of Immigrant Children: 1900–1930," *History of Education Quarterly,* Winter 1974, pp. 453–82, Tables 3, 5, 6.

7. David K. Cohen, "Immigrants and the Schools," *Review of Educational Research,* vol. 40, 1970, pp. 13–27.

8. Seymour B. Sarason and John Doris, *Educational Handicap, Public Policy, and Social History* (New York: Free Press, 1979), pp. 155–56, 340–51.

9. Olneck and Lazerson, Tables 11 and 12.

10. Howe, pp. 277–78.

11. *Fall 1995 Preliminary Ethnic Survey* (Los Angeles: Information Technology Division, Los Angeles Unified School District, Publication No. 124, 1996).

12. Georges Vernez and Allan Abrahamse, *How Immigrants Fare in U.S. Education* (Santa Monica, Calif.: RAND Corporation, 1996), Table 3.2.

13. These figures are not strictly comparable; estimates are based on data in Vernez and Abrahamse, Table 4.2, and in National Center for Education Statistics, *Dropout Rates in the United States: 1995* (Washington, D.C.: Office of Educational Research and Improvement, U.S. Department of Education, NCES 97–473, 1997), Table 9.

14. Native-language instruction in public schools was also common in the Southwest, particularly in Texas, New Mexico, and Arizona, which were formerly part of Mexico and whose native populations, not their immigrants, were originally Spanish-speaking Mexicans. It was also common

in Louisiana, where French-language public schools were established well after the Louisiana Purchase to preserve native French culture.

15. Diego Castellanos, *The Best of Two Worlds: Bilingual-Bicultural Education in the United States* (Trenton: New Jersey State Department of Education, CN 500, 1983), pp. 23–25.

16. Sarason and Doris, pp. 180–81, 194.

17. Heinz Kloss, *The American Bilingual Tradition* (Rowley, Mass.: Newbury House, 1977), pp. 149–50.

18. Ibid., pp. 61, 86, 180; Castellanos, p. 19; and Mary J. Herrick, *The Chicago Schools: A Social and Political History* (Beverly Hills, Calif.: Sage, 1971), p. 61.

19. Kloss, pp. 69, 86, 158–59, 190; and Castellanos, pp. 24–25.

20. Kloss, pp. 177–78, 184.

21. Castellanos, p. 23; and Paul E. Peterson, *The Politics of School Reform, 1870–1940* (Chicago: University of Chicago Press, 1985), p. 55.

22. Peterson, pp. 55–56; Castellanos, p. 25; and James Crawford, *Bilingual Education: History, Politics, Theory, and Practice* (Trenton, N.J.: Crane Publishing Company, 1989), p. 22.

23. "The School Question," *Milwaukee Sentinel,* 27 November 1889.

24. Herrick, p. 61; Kloss, p. 89; Peterson, pp. 10, 58; William F. Whyte, "The Bennett Law Campaign in Wisconsin," *Wisconsin Magazine of History,* vol. 10, 1927, pp. 363–90; and Bernard Mehl, "Educational Criticism: Past and Present," *Progressive Education,* March 1953, p. 154.

25. Crawford, pp. 23–24; and David Tyack, "Constructing Difference: Historical Reflections on Schooling and Social Diversity," *Teachers College Record,* Fall 1993, p. 15.

26. *Meyer v. Nebraska,* 262 US 390 (1923).

27. Castellanos, pp. 43, 49; Crawford, p. 26; and idem, *Hold Your Tongue* (Reading, Mass.: Addison-Wesley, 1992), p. 72.

28. See, for example, Rudolph Troike, "Research Evidence for the Effectiveness of Bilingual Education," *NABE Journal,* vol. 3, 1978, pp. 13–24; *The Bilingual Education Handbook: Designing Instruction for LEP Students* (Sacramento: California Department of Education, 1990), p. 13; Iris Rotberg, "Some Legal and Research Considerations in Establishing Federal Bilingual Policy in Bilingual Education," *Harvard Educational Review,* May 1982, pp. 158–59; and Rosalie Pedalino Porter, *Forked Tongue: The Politics of Bilingual Education* (New York: Basic Books, 1990), p. 141.

29. Leonard Covello, "A High School and Its Immigrant Community—A Challenge and an Opportunity," *Journal of Educational Sociology,* February 1936, p. 334.

30. Ruben G. Rumbaut, "The New Californians: Research Findings on the Educational Progress of Immigrant Children," in idem and Wayne Cornelius, eds., *California's Immigrant Children: Theory, Research, and Implications for Educational Policy* (San Diego: Center for U.S.–Mexican Studies, University of California, 1995).

31. For a discussion of Rodriguez as prototype, see Stephen D. Krashen, *Under Attack: The Case Against Bilingual Education* (Culver City, Calif.: Language Education Associates, 1996), p. 19.

32. Rumbaut, Table 2.6.

33. *Dropout Rates in the United States: 1995,* Table A-37; and National Center for Education Statistics, *The Condition of Education 1997* (Washington, D.C.: U.S. Department of Education, NCES 97–388, 1997), Indicators 8, 22.

34. Gregory Rodriguez, *The Emerging Latino Middle Class* (Malibu, Calif.: Pepperdine University Institute for Public Policy, 1996), Figure 22.

16

THE FULL-SERVICE VISION

RESPONDING TO CRITICAL NEEDS

Joy G. Dryfoos

The full-service school model would deliver many necessary services to students: education, nutrition, and health care, among others. Ideally, full-service schools would provide a healthy environment for students and their families, creating an atmosphere more conducive to learning. In changing times for parents and schools, there is hope that the full-service model will help bridge the gaps in the lives of students to allow them a quality learning experience.

○

THE LAST DECADE OF THE TWENTIETH CENTURY will be a hazardous time for many children and their families in the United States. A measurable segment of the society is not going to "make it" without massive changes in the way that they are educated, supported, and cared for. Families and schools, the primary institutions that have traditionally carried the responsibilities for raising and teaching children, cannot fulfill their obligations without immediate and intensive transformation. New kinds of arrangements of community resources have to be brought together to ensure that children can grow up to be responsible, productive, and fully participating members of this society.

Family structure has shifted away from the idealized Ozzie-and-Harriet model of Dad in the workplace and Mom at home in their suburban ranch house with the two children. Today, three-fourths of all mothers of school-age children are in the labor force, up from about half in 1970.[1] One in four children live in families with only one parent, more than double the rate of two decades ago. However, even two-parent families are feeling the pressure of poor economic conditions and excessive housing and health insurance costs that require them to concentrate heavily on making a living and supporting their children.

The decade of the 1980s is now being characterized for its glorification of the "me-first" doctrine. We saw the rise and fall of the junk-bond artists and savings-and-loan bandits; the media exposed us to the excessive "life-styles of the rich and famous." But during this same decade, poverty increased and the number of poor children grew. By 1991, more than fourteen million children—22 percent of all children—lived in families below the poverty line, the highest number and rate since 1965.[2] As in no other period of time, disadvantage shifted from the oldest people to the youngest. And those children living in mother-only households have become the most deprived of all, with more than 55 percent living in poverty.

The demand for basic social programs continues to grow as budgeting crises mount. Many states are coping with horrendous budget crises that have produced drastic cuts in human services of all kinds, and many cities are teetering on the brink of financial disaster.

Impacts on Children

As a result of the deteriorating social environment and growing fiscal crises, children are suffering. Many face substantial barriers to growing into responsible adults who will be able to enter the workforce, become effective parents, and participate in the political process. I refer here to the "new morbidities"—unprotected sex, drugs, violence, and depression—that threaten the future of today's children. (In contrast, the "old morbidities" were chronic diseases, nutritional deficiencies, acne, and infestations of head lice.) The factors leading to substance abuse, teen pregnancy, delinquency, and school failure are highly interrelated and are much more likely to affect children who live in disadvantaged social environments.[3] My estimate is that about one in four children and youth (aged ten to seventeen) in the United States "do it all"—use drugs, have early unprotected intercourse, are truant, and fall far behind in school—and as a result, these seven million young people will never be able to "make it" without massive changes in their current circumstances.

We know a great deal about "high-risk" children. Their status is defined by their families; they lack attention from parents who can provide nurturing and attention. From a rich literature about effective parenting, we can conclude that children who have "authoritative" parents do a lot better than those whose parents are too "permissive" or too "authoritarian."[4] Parental substance abuse adversely affects offspring, not only genetically, as in the case of children of alcoholics; addicted parents are also poor role models and may be negligent and even abusive. We know, too, that poverty erodes expectations and that families have difficulty raising children in stressful, dangerous, and unhealthy environments. And, of course, children of absent parents suffer most of all, unless they are attached to a strong adult who can act as a surrogate parent.

Certain children start getting into trouble at early ages, usually with aggressive "acting out" behavior that gets translated fairly soon into truancy, destructiveness, and other conduct disorders. Early involvement with one problem behavior frequently predicts involvement in other domains; for example, smoking at age ten can precede unprotected intercourse, heavy alcohol use, and trouble in school. High-risk children cannot resist peer influences, and they become easily distracted or enticed by friends and acquaintances into dangerous behaviors.

Evidence is accumulating that young people who are prone to these problem behaviors are frequently depressed and suffering from symptoms of stress, "Suicidal ideation" is on the rise: in a recent national survey, one in seven young people (eighth- and tenth-graders) reported having attempted suicide.[5] Many children are exposed to violence at very early ages and grow up with many fears about their own security and the safety of their families. Many young people respond to violence by purchasing firearms and knives; one-third of high school students report that they could obtain a handgun if they wanted one.

The most recognizable symptom of high-risk status is school failure. Children who are older than their classmates because they have been left back are in a precarious position. Being two or more years behind almost always leads to dropping out of school prior to high school graduation. And high school completion is a significant marker for future success. It should be noted, however, that a high school diploma alone does not guarantee success, since increasing numbers of graduates lack basic skills in numeracy and literacy. Acquisition of basic cognitive skills is the proverbial bottom line for all children.

A recent report from the Panel on High-Risk Youth of the National Academy of Sciences stressed the importance of redirecting attention away from the individuals affected to the institutional settings creating the risk status.[6] The children are "at risk" because they live in high-risk environments. Thus, immediate interventions are called for in the realms of family, school, and community, with particular urgency for both creating jobs and overcoming the educational and social barriers to employment.

Implications for Schools

Every day, forty million children are expected to arrive at the U.S.'s eighty-two thousand public elementary and secondary schools. Based on the one-in-four estimate, fully ten million of those children are at high risk of failure.[7] In some schools, almost all of the children arrive with social, emotional, and health handicaps that stand in the way of success. One principal described his school-community as an "under-developed country," isolated from and abandoned by the mainstream society. In other schools, almost all of the children arrive ready to learn and securely attached to a supportive home and family environment. In some states, the difference between school systems is dramatic. One educational task force found that "two different systems of education have been created in our State. One encompasses effective schools holding high expectations for their students and located in affluent or stable communities; the other, ineffective schools which communicate low expectations and aspirations for their students, who are not given full opportunity to succeed. They are too often located in large urban areas and the inner cities. Our society's acceptance of two unequal educational systems is putting us at risk of creating a permanent underclass."[8]

Our interest here is primarily directed toward the roles of schools and community agencies in responding to the needs of high-risk children and their families and equalizing access to future opportunities. Schools are increasingly being called on to be those "surrogate parents" that can increase the "teachability" of children who arrive on their doorsteps in poor shape. Today's schools feel pressured to feed children; provide psychological support services; offer health screening; establish referral networks related to substance abuse, child welfare, and sexual abuse; cooperate with the local police and probation officers; add curricula for prevention of substance abuse, teen pregnancy, suicide, and violence (the new morbidities); and actively promote social skills, good nutrition, safety, and general health.

Around the country, school administrators are crying for help. They acknowledge that they cannot attend to all the needs of the current crop of students and at the same time respond to the demands for quality education. The educational institution's first order of priority is to ensure that all children gain the basic skills required for full participation in our society. Because school financing and governance are structured around this very specific and essential mission, other institutions have to share the responsibility for "everything else"—all those health and social services needy children and their families require to use the basic skills and participate in the society.

Consensus on the Need for Collaborative School-Based Services

Here I talk about bringing service systems into schools to respond to the needs of today's children and their families. A significant consensus is emerging that schools cannot do it alone, that the interests of the educational establishment and the health and social service systems must be joined in order to shape powerful new institutions. Demands for more comprehensive, collaborative, unfragmented programs located in schools are coming from a wide spectrum of organizations and individuals that advocate for educational reform and adolescent health and on the behalf of young children and families.

Educational Reform

Michael Kirst, one of the most articulate advocates for innovative school-based programs, recognizes the multidimensionality of the situation: "What's needed is a complete overhaul of children's services, bringing together public and private organizations to meet the comprehensive needs of children, adolescents, and parents. Schools should constitute one of the centers of a coordinated network of total children's services."[9] Kirst's strategy calls for grouping a number of services in one place, generally, but not always, with the school as the hub. But, as he is careful to point out, not with the school in charge—the parties should be coequals, participating in planned communitywide collaborative programming.

Studies of school-restructuring issues have highlighted the relationship between good health and educational achievement, as well as the importance of bringing health services into schools. *Turning Points,* the challenge of the Carnegie Council Task Force on Education of Young Adolescents to middle school reform, called for, among other interventions, the placement in every school of a health coordinator who can marshal the necessary resources so that young adolescents will be healthy and can learn.[10] The task force recognized, however, that the needs of some students might exceed the available resources and that therefore schools should consider options such as school-based and school-linked health centers. They envision a comprehensive services network with the school as the center and community agencies acting as the lead coordinating organizations.

The proposed "reinvention" of America's schools has generated a lot of media attention and discussion among educational gurus. Much of the emphasis has been on raising academic performance and developing standardized testing methods. Unfortunately, the plight of high-risk students and their families has received short shrift in all of this discourse. As Sid Gardner, an authority on service integration projects, pointed out, "the tone . . . is still 'let's fix the kids,' with an assumption that fixing the *institutions* that serve the kids will all be taken care of by vouchers and more rhetoric. Budget constraints have been allowed to overwhelm the parallel reforms in children's services that are needed to make education reforms a reality." [11] Gardner stressed that schools ought to work with other public and private agencies to help students already targeted as needy by several agencies. In his view, city and county governments should help schools by encouraging local leaders to integrate their often fragmented and disconnected federal grants into locally designed comprehensive programs.

Edward Meade, who led the Ford Foundation's school reform initiatives, found that proposed strategies disregarded the documented interrelationships among good health, good support services, and good education and failed to offer specific steps to bring about more effectiveness in providing *comprehensive* services. Over the years, Meade observed that "schools that have solid working links with agencies that provide other services for students, such as health and social supports, are more effective in educating the students who need these services." [12]

Increasingly, educational experts are espousing the language of collaboration. Here we will be visiting with a few states and local school systems that have moved in the direction of structuring school reform broadly and incorporating requirements that school districts and public health and social service agencies work together to create more effective institutions.

Adolescent Health

In an unprecedented move, two organizations representing diverse major interest groups, the American Medical Association and the National Association of State Boards of Education, issued *Code Blue: Uniting for Healthier Youth*.[13] Code Blue is the parlance used in medicine to signify a life-threatening emergency, which is how the organization's joint commission characterized contemporary health problems of youth. Their recommendations stem from their agreement that *education and health are inextricably intertwined,* that efforts to improve school performance that ignore health would be ill conceived, as would health improvement efforts that ignore education. Thus, the commission strongly supported the establishment of health centers in schools, attention to the school climate and to issues related to achievement, and the restructuring of public and private health insurance to ensure access to services. They pointed out that "families, schools, neighborhoods, the health community, and the public and private sectors will need to forge new partnerships to address the interconnected health and education problems our young people are experiencing." [14]

The Office of Technology Assessment (OTA), when charged by Congress to review the health status of American adolescents and present options for congressional consideration, came up with similar recommendations to support the development of comprehensive health centers in schools and communities, to create a central locus in the federal government for addressing adolescent health issues, and to improve adolescents' social and economic environments in general. [15] The OTA report was particularly persuasive on the subject of school-linked services, referring to school clinics as the "most promising recent innovation to improve access to health." They add a note of caution, however, pointing out that systematic evidence that school centers improve health outcomes is still somewhat limited.

Although it is not my intent here to cite a lot of statistics about adolescent health issues, it is important to note that adolescents' access to health care is severely restricted by a number of barriers, among which lack of health insurance is significant. It has been estimated that close to five million adolescents aged ten to eighteen, 15 percent of the total, have no public or private health coverage. [16] Of those who live in low-income families, however, at least one-third lack coverage.

Young Children and Their Families

A number of social commentators have argued that the most urgent task facing this society is to regenerate families. Roger Wilkins contends that "while employment, early childhood education, and child-care programs are critical parts of such an effort, it is essential that the public schools become the focus of special remedies . . . the centers of the community for the children they serve and for their parents and grandparents." [17] Concern about troubled families has clearly led to a resurgence of interest in family-oriented early childhood development programs. Heather Weiss's study of school-based family support and education programs found examples of comprehensive networks that provided parent education, referral to community agencies, home visiting, peer support groups, child care, health screening, and counseling.[18]

One of the most promising interventions, "Schools of the Twenty-First Century," created by Edward Zigler of Yale University, promotes schools that function as community centers, linking family support systems with child care systems.[19] Zigler argues eloquently that the community already "owns" the school buildings, having invested one to two *trillion* dollars in these properties. He would open the doors of the schools from 7 A.M. to 6 P.M., all day, every day. In the building, he would establish full-day child care for three- to five-year-olds, insuring high-quality developmentally appropriate services. He would also provide before- and after-school care to six- to twelve-year-olds that included recreation and "fun." In addition, these schools would offer home visitors to all parents of newborns, incorporating the Parents as Teachers model (from Missouri), and organize and supervise family day care for children from birth to three years. The center would be run by early childhood educators trained to garner the resources and referrals needed by "new American families."

Jane Knitzer and colleagues' study of the implementation of the Education of the Handicapped Act, which required schools to educate large numbers of children identified as having behavioral and emotional disorders, yielded strong recommendations for bringing mental health services into schools.[20] They found a growing recognition in both regular education and special education that access to school-based mental health services can have a positive impact on students, on teachers, and on school climate and that "for the most seriously troubled children and adolescents—those at risk of residential placement—school involvement in multi-system collaboration is an essential ingredient to keeping children in their own communities." They advised local mental health agencies to explore with the schools the range of services they could offer, including working with teachers to devise joint programs.

One organization, Joining Forces, sponsored by the American Public Welfare Association and the Council of Chief State School Officers, sought to foster communication among the educational and human service systems, identify barriers to collaboration, and assist federal and state agencies in development, implementation, and evaluation of emerging collaborative models. At the end of the first year of Joining Forces, director Janet Levy (now at the Danforth Foundation) documented an impressive array of joint ventures but pointed toward the absence of replications of the models and the lack of incorporation of unique models into larger systems.[21] She warned that though new arrangements cannot be put in place with "quick fix" actions, "this is a propitious time for collaboration because education and human services face *common* challenges as they try to help the *same* people and respond to the *same* problems."

William Morrill, director of the Center for Service Integration, and Martin Gerry, former assistant secretary for planning and evaluation, Department of Health and Human Services (DHHS), have contributed substantially to discussions about integration of services for children and families. They have observed that fragmented, separately organized, and physically scattered services create serious access problems for school-aged children. Even where all the requisite services are available, barriers to access are caused by different eligibility rules and lack of communication between professionals. They conclude that "the schools as central institutions in the community provide an important, if not critical, organizing focus for the coordination and integration of services. This hypothesis does not necessarily assume that the schools need be the organizer or operator of all services to be delivered, but the physical facility or the cooperation of the school administration is usually critical to integration and coordination efforts."[22]

A powerful consensus is emerging from the recommendations of diverse groups and experts in educational reform, child and adolescent health, and family welfare reform. A universal call has been issued for one-stop unfragmented health and social service systems that are consumer-oriented, developmentally appropriate, and culturally relevant. Agreement is strong that the school should be an active partner in collaborative efforts, and the idea that school facilities should serve as the *place* for the provision of noneducational support services of all kinds is rapidly gaining support.

Components of the Full-Service School

The vision of the full-service school puts the best of school reform together with all other services that children, youth, and their families need, most of which can be located in a school building. The educational mandate places responsibility on the school system to reorganize and innovate. The charge to community agencies is to bring into the school: health, mental health, employment services, child care, parent education, case management, recreation, cultural events, welfare, community policing, and whatever else may fit into the picture. The result is a new kind of "seamless" institution, a community-oriented school with a joint governance structure that allows maximum responsiveness to the community, as well as accessibility and continuity for those most in need of services. The theme of integration of educational, health, and social welfare services reverberates through local, state, and national dialogues. A century of demonstration projects may finally be leading to the combination of the settlement house with the school. Though this sounds like a tall order, fraught with political and practical barriers, successful models in dozens of communities show that it can happen.

Exhibit 16.1 presents an idealized model of the full-service school, listing some of the components that might be incorporated into a quality education initiative and those support services that could be provided by community agencies. The components listed are based on the program experiences cited in Chapter 3 and on findings of a study of one hundred successful prevention programs in the separate fields of substance abuse, teen pregnancy, delinquency, and school failure.[23] The model reflects the belief that no single component, no magic bullet, can significantly change the lives of disadvantaged children, youth, and families. Rather, it is the cumulative impact of a package of interventions that will result in measurable changes in life scripts.

Exhibit 16.1. Full-Service Schools: One-Stop, Collaborative Institutions.

Quality Education Provided by Schools	Support Services Provided by Community Agencies
Effective basic skills	Health screening and services
Individualized instruction	Dental services
Team teaching	Family planning
Cooperative learning	Individual counseling
School-based management	Substance abuse treatment
Healthy school climate	Mental health services
Alternatives to tracking	Nutrition/weight management
Parent involvement	Referral with follow-up
Effective discipline	Basic services: housing, food, clothes
	Recreation, sports, culture
Provided by Schools or Community Agencies	Mentoring
	Family welfare services
Comprehensive health education	Parent education, literacy
Health promotion	Child care
Social skills training	Employment training/jobs
Preparation for the world of work (life planning)	Case management
	Crisis intervention
	Community policing

The Reality

The current reality is an ill-defined assortment of school-based programs spread out across a continuum, from simple one-component partnerships between a school and an outside agency or business to sophisticated, complex, multicomponent, multiagency collaboratives. Marked differences exist in program orientation. Family-oriented programs start with meeting the needs of parents and infants and move toward services for young children. Youth-oriented programs are formulated around the needs of older children and adolescents and move cautiously toward family involvement.

No one model of school-based services predominates. New programs are called school-based health clinics, youth service centers, family resource centers, full-service schools, wellness centers, student service centers, and community-schools. What they all have in common is their location in or near the school, opening up access to students and their families for health and social services of all kinds. In practice, "full service" is defined by the particular community and school, with a mix of services that are needed, feasible to provide in school facilities, and acceptable to the school system and the community. State initiatives have strongly influenced the composition of school-based services.

The burst of activity, the "bubbling up" of experimentation, in communities across America reflects a growing consensus that the major institutions in society must change. It should be acknowledged, however, that simple changes in service delivery arrangements are more evident than radical changes in systems of governance. Although many educational systems are in the process of restructuring through site-based management and changes in teaching practices, this process is seldom integrated with the movement to develop comprehensive health and social services for children, youth, and families. With the exception of a few community-schools, a governing structure has yet to be devised that draws these strands together into a collaborative system. In a few unique prototypes, a new nonprofit coordinating agency or council has been organized; in others, governance is taken over by an existing agency such as the United Way or a youth bureau of city or county government. And around the country, one can find innovative schools with comprehensive services being created entirely by school personnel.

Throughout the country, community agencies are locating programs in school buildings, mainly in low-income areas both urban and rural. Close to five hundred comprehensive school-based clinics have been identified, and many more are in the planning stage. School-based health clinics currently have the capacity to provide the primary health and mental health services listed in the support services section of the full-service schools model (Exhibit 16.1). Hundreds of family resource centers (the number is unknown) provide other support services, including parent education, Head Start, after-school child care, case management, meals, crisis intervention, and whatever else is needed by parents and young children. Many community-schools are locations for evening, weekend, and summer educational enrichment and recreation programs provided by voluntary agencies. Other schools have received grants to hire coordinators to work with community agencies either to bring services into the building or to facilitate referrals.

Although we have identified many efforts that fall into the category of school-based services, only a tiny fraction of the population has access to these new programs. We do not know how many families are served by centers. About 750,000 students are currently enrolled in the 500 schools that have clinics, mostly in middle and high schools, and only 70 percent of these students are registered in the clinics. Thus, only one-tenth of the seven million youth in the highest-risk settings currently have access to health and social services in middle and high school sites. Millions of children and their families need access to the full range of programs that can be located at full-service schools.

The Need for Full-Service Schools

Of the twenty thousand senior highs, twelve thousand middle schools, and fifty thousand elementary schools in the country, how many need a center into which community agencies can bring health and social services? An estimate of the number of units needed would greatly facilitate future planning. It would probably benefit most schools to have a specific procedure for coordinating with community agencies for support services. In every school, a few students and families require special attention. Given the limited availability of new resources, however, we should start with those schools and communities where children, youth, and families have the least opportunity to succeed without a great deal of support.

Using the indicator "percent of schools in which more than 50 percent of students are eligible for a free or reduced cost lunch," we can derive a rough approximation of very needy schools. About 20 percent of all U.S. public schools fit into that category, and in 8 percent of all schools, at least 75 percent of students are eligible (and, obviously, poor).[24] Applying these indicators to schools, at least sixteen thousand clinics or centers should be organized, with highest priority given to the 6,500 schools (8 percent) where most of the students are from families of exceedingly low income.

Significant Questions

While there is clearly a strong movement toward the creation of institutions that look like full-service schools, the problem is how to put these complex systems together, how to adapt models that work, how to build documentation that they do work and are cost-effective. Many issues must be addressed if the concept of school-based services is to "go to scale" with the broad replication of demonstration models. A sense of urgency drives this new movement because of the growing needs among disadvantaged families and their children. At the same time, plans for health care reform have given a new visibility and legitimization to school-based clinics as delivery sites for primary health care. Given this boost, can we conclude that full-service schools are the wave of the future? Should every school become full-service, or is this concept only meaningful in low-income communities? If 16,000 centers is a reasonable goal, how can it be met? Is it really possible for a marriage to take place between educational systems and health and social systems to create new kinds of governance?

NOTES

1. U.S. Department of Health and Human Services. *Child Health USA '92.* Washington, D.C.: U.S. Government Printing Office, 0–16–036247, 1993.

2. "Child Poverty Hits 25-Year High, Growing by Nearly 1 Million Children in 1991." *CDF Reports,* 1992, *13*(12), 2.

3. Dryfoos, J. *Adolescents at Risk: Prevalence and Prevention.* New York: Oxford University Press, 1990.

4. Dornbusch, S., and others. "The Relation of Parenting Style to Adolescent School Performance." *Child Development,* 1987, *58,* 1244–1257.

5. National Adolescent Student Survey. *National Survey Reveals Teen Behavior, Knowledge, and Attitudes on Health, Sex Topics.* Washington, D.C.: American Alliance for Health, Physical Education, Recreation, and Dance, Aug. 9, 1988. Press release.

6. Panel on High-Risk Youth, Commission on Behavioral and Social Sciences and Education. *Losing Generations: Adolescents in High Risk Settings.* Washington, D.C.: National Academy Press, 1993.

7. An additional 5.5 million children are enrolled in 26,800 private schools.

8. Commissioner's Task Force on the Education of Children and Youth at-Risk. *The Time for Assertive Action: School Strategies for Promoting the Education Success of At-Risk Children.* Albany: New York State Education Department, 1988.

9. Kirst, M. "Improving Children's Services: Overcoming Barriers, Creating New Opportunities." *Phi Delta Kappa,* Apr. 1991, pp. 615–618.

10. *Turning Points: Preparing American Youth for the 21st Century.* Washington, D.C.: Task Force on Education of Young Adolescents, Carnegie Corporation, 1989.

11. Gardner, S. "Fix the Kids or Fix the Institutions?" In *Voices from the Field: 30 Expert Opinions on "America 2000," The Bush Administration's Strategy to "Reinvent" America's Schools.* Washington, D.C.: William T. Grant Foundation Commission on Work, Family, and Citizenship, 1991.

12. Meade, E. "Ignoring the Lessons of Previous School Reform." In *Voices from the Field: 30 Expert Opinions on "America 2000," The Bush Administration's Strategy to "Reinvent" America's Schools.* Washington, D.C.: William T. Grant Foundation Commission on Work, Family, and Citizenship, 1991.

13. National Commission on the Role of the School and the Community in Improving Adolescent Health. *Code Blue: Uniting for Healthier Youth.* Washington, D.C.: American Medical Association and National Association of State Boards of Education, 1990.

14. Ibid., 41.

15. Office of Technology Assessment, U.S. Congress. *Adolescent Health.* Vol. 1, *Summary and Policy Options.* Washington, D.C.: U.S. Government Printing Office, OTA-H-468, 1991.

16. Office of Technology Assessment, U.S. Congress. *Adolescent Health.* Vol. 3, *Crosscutting Issues in the Delivery of Health and Related Services.* Washington, D.C.: U.S. Government Printing Office, OTA-H-468, 1991.

17. Reed, S., and Sutter, R. "Children of Poverty." *Phi Delta Kappan,* Kappan Special Report, June 1990.

18. Weiss, H. *Raising the Future: Families, Schools, and Communities Joining Together.* Cambridge, Mass.: Harvard Family Research Project (forthcoming).

19. E. Zigler. Speech to Westchester Mental Health Association. White Plains, New York, Nov. 1, 1990.

20. Fleisch, B., Knitzer, J., and Steinberg, Z. *At the Schoolhouse Door: An Examination of Programs and Policies for Children with Behavioral and Emotional Problems.* New York: Bank Street College of Education, 1990.

21. Levy, J. *Joining Forces: A Report from the First Year.* Washington, D.C.: National Association of State Boards of Education, 1989.

22. Gerry, M., and Morrill, W. *"Integrating the Delivery of Services to School-Aged Children at Risk: Toward a Description of American Experience and Experimentation."* Paper prepared for Conference for Children and Youth at Risk, sponsored by the U.S. Department of Education, Washington, D.C., Feb. 6, 1990.

23. Dryfoos, J., op. cit., note 3 above.

24. Anderson, J. "The Distribution of Chapter 1 Services: Which School Districts and Schools Serve Students in Chapter 1." Paper presented at annual meeting of the American Educational Research Association, Apr. 1992.

PART FOUR

REFORM AS RESTRUCTURING THE GOVERNANCE AND ORGANIZATION OF SCHOOLING

17

BETTER SCHOOLS THROUGH NEW INSTITUTIONS

GIVING AMERICANS CHOICE

John E. Chubb, Terry M. Moe

Politics, Markets and America's Schools, the book from which this chapter is drawn, provides the framework for much of the supporting argument for a choice-based school system. Vouchers and charter schools are two examples of choice, the idea being that if schools compete for dollars, the quality of education will improve.

○

EDUCATIONAL REFORM, if it is done right, is essentially an exercise in harnessing the causes of effective performance. It is an application of theory. Similarly, a theory of effective performance is the analytical basis for designing public policy, as well as for judging which kinds of reforms are likely to succeed and which are likely to fail.

Here we want to put our theory to use in thinking about reform. We will begin by pulling together the basic components of our analysis and summarizing our perspective on schools. Once we have done so, we will move on to two new tasks.

First, we will take a look at the ambitious and, many say, revolutionary reforms of the 1980s and evaluate their prospects for success. While some of these reforms are more promising than others, we think the recent reform movement as a whole is destined to fail in its mission to bring significant improvement to America's public schools, and we will explain in some detail why we think so.

Second, we want to outline a proposal for reform that, in our view, is likely to succeed—in the event that it is ever adopted. In today's vernacular, it is a "choice" proposal. More descriptively, it is a proposal for a new system of public education, one that is built on school autonomy and parent-student choice rather than direct democratic control and bureaucracy.

Schools and Institutions

Three basic questions lie at the heart of our analysis. What is the relationship between school organization and student achievement? What are the conditions that promote or inhibit desirable forms of organization? And how are these conditions affected by their institutional settings? With regard to the first and second, virtually everything we have to say is compatible with the mainstream ideas of education scholars and policymakers. It is only in paying serious theoretical attention to institutions and in what we conclude about their causal importance for schools that our own ideas depart from the norm. We regard this departure, of course, as fundamental to an understanding of schools. But even so, it is not a departure that contradicts mainstream theory and research. The social science of education simply has little to say about the role of institutions. We depart from the mainstream because we try to address issues that have largely gone unaddressed.

Our perspective on organization and student achievement is in agreement with the most basic claims and findings of the effective schools literature, which, throughout the 1980s, served as the analytical base of the education reform movement. We believe, as most others do, that how much students learn is not simply determined by their aptitude or family background—although, as we show, these are certainly influential—but that school organization has a significant impact all its own. By our own estimates, the typical high school student tends to learn considerably more, comparable to an extra year's worth of study, when he or she attends a high school that is effectively organized rather than one that is not.

Generally speaking, effective schools have the kinds of organizational characteristics that the mainstream literature would lead one to expect: strong leadership, clear and ambitious goals, strong academic programs, teacher professionalism, shared influence, and staff harmony, among other things. These are best understood as integral parts of a coherent syndrome of organization. They go together. When this syndrome is viewed as a functioning whole, moreover, what is most striking about it is that it seems to capture the essential features of what people normally mean by a team—principals and teachers working together, cooperatively and informally, in pursuit of a common mission.

How do these kinds of schools develop and take root? What causes them? Here again, our own perspective dovetails with a central theme of educational analysis and criticism: the dysfunctions of bureaucracy, the value of autonomy, and the inherent tension between the two in American public education. Bureaucracy vitiates the most basic requirements of effective organization. It imposes goals, structures, and requirements that tell principals and teachers what to do and how to do it—denying them the discretion they need to exercise their expertise and professional judgment, and denying them the flexibility they need to develop and operate as teams. The key to effective education rests with unleashing the productive potential that is already present in the schools and their personnel. It rests with granting them the autonomy to do what they do best. As our study of American high schools documents, the freer schools are from external control—the more autonomous, the less subject to bureaucratic constraint—the more likely they are to have effective organizations.

It is only at this late stage of the game that we begin to part company with the mainstream. While most observers can agree that the public schools have become too bureaucratic and would benefit from substantial grants of autonomy, it is also the standard view that this transformation can be achieved within the prevailing framework of democratic control. The implicit assumption is that, although these institutions have acted in the past to bureaucratize, they can now be counted on to reverse course, grant the schools autonomy, and support and nurture this new population of autonomous schools. Such an assumption, however, is not based on a systematic understanding of how these institutions operate and what their consequences are for schools. It begs the important causal issues instead of addressing them.

Our institutional perspective is an attempt to address these issues. What it suggests, among other things, is that America's traditional institutions of democratic control cannot be relied on to solve the schools' bureaucracy problem—for it is not the schools but the institutions that are the real problem. They inherently breed bureaucracy and undermine autonomy. This is not something that is temporary or the product of mistakes. It is deeply anchored in the most fundamental properties of the system.

Democratic governance of the schools is built around the imposition of higher-order values through public authority. As long as that authority exists and is available for use, public officials will come under intense pressure from social groups of all political stripes to use it. And when they do use it, they cannot blithely assume that their favored policies will be faithfully implemented by the heterogeneous population of principals and teachers below—whose own values and professional views may be quite different from those being imposed. They have little choice but to rely on formal rules and regulations that tell these people what to do and hold them accountable for doing it.

These pressures for bureaucracy are so substantial in themselves that real school autonomy can have little chance to take root throughout the system. But they are not the only pressures for bureaucracy. They are compounded by the political uncertainty that is inherent in all democratic politics: those who exercise public authority know that other actors with different interests may gain authority in the future and subvert the policies they worked so hard to put in place. This gives them additional incentives to embed their policies in protective bureaucratic arrangements—arrangements that reduce the discretion of schools and formally insulate them from the dangers of politics.

These pressures, arising from the most fundamental properties of democratic control, are compounded yet again by another special feature of the public sector. Its institutions provide a regulated, politically sensitive setting that is conducive to the power of unions, and unions protect the interests of their members through formal constraints on the governance and operation of schools—constraints that strike directly at the schools' capacity to build well-functioning teams based on informal cooperation.

All the major participants in democratic governance—including the unions—complain that the schools are too bureaucratic. And they mean what they say. But they are the ones who bureaucratized the schools in the past, and they will continue to bureaucratize the schools in the future, even as they tout the great advantages of autonomy and professionalism. The incentives to bureaucratize are built into the system. The institutions of democratic control ensure that, in the politics and governance of public education, bureaucracy is almost everyone's dominant strategy when the key decisions actually get made. People may genuinely believe in autonomy and professionalism. But what they do—quite rationally, given their institutional setting—is bureaucratize.

This kind of behavior is not something that Americans simply have to accept, like death and taxes. People who make decisions about education would behave differently if their institutions were different. The most relevant and telling comparison is to markets, since it is through democratic control and markets that American society makes most of its choices on matters of public importance, including education. Public schools are subject to direct control through politics, private schools are subject to indirect control through markets. What difference does it make?

Our analysis suggests that the difference is considerable, and that it arises from the most fundamental properties that distinguish the two systems. A market system is not built to enable the imposition of higher-order values on the schools, nor is it driven by a democratic struggle to exercise public authority. Instead, the authority to make educational choices is radically decentralized to those most immediately involved. Schools compete for the support of parents and students, and parents and students are free to choose among schools. The system is built around decentralization, competition, and choice.

Although schools are free to organize any way they want, bureaucratization tends to be an unattractive way to go. Part of the reason is that virtually everything about good education—from the knowledge and talents necessary to produce it to what it looks like when it is produced—defies formal measurement through the standardized categories of bureaucracy. The more fundamental point, however, is that bureaucratic control and its clumsy efforts to measure the unmeasurable are simply *unnecessary* for schools whose primary concern is to please their clients. To do this, they need to perform as effectively as possible—which induces them, given the bottom-heavy technology of education, to favor decentralized forms of organization that take full advantage of professionalism, discretionary judgment, informal cooperation, and teams. They also need to ensure that they are providing the kinds of services parents and students want, and that they have the capacity to cater and adjust to their clients' specialized needs and interests—which this same syndrome of organization allows them to do exceedingly well.

While schools controlled only by the market are free to organize any way they want, then, an environment of competition and choice gives them strong incentives to move toward the kinds of "effective-school" organizations that academics and reformers would like to impose on the public schools. Of course, not all schools in the market will respond equally well to these incentives. But those that falter will find it more difficult to attract support, and they will tend to be weeded out in favor of schools that are better organized. This process of natural selection, based on ease of entry and performance-based attrition, complements the incentives of the marketplace in propelling and supporting a population of autonomous, effectively organized schools.

No institutional system can be expected to work perfectly under real-world conditions. Just as democratic institutions cannot offer perfect representation or perfect implementation of public policy, so markets cannot offer perfect competition or perfect choice. But these imperfections, which are invariably the favorite targets of each system's critics, tend to distract attention from what is most crucial to an understanding of schools: as institutional systems, democratic control and market control are strikingly different in their most fundamental properties. As a result, they structure individual and social choices about education very differently, and they have very different consequences for the organization and performance of schools. Each system puts its own, indelible stamp on the schools that emerge and operate within it.

What this institutional perspective suggests, in the most practical terms, is that American society offers two basic paths to the emergence of effective schools. The first is through markets, which scarcely operate in the public sector, but which act on private schools to discourage bureaucracy and promote desirable forms of organization through the natural dynamics of competition and choice. The second is through "special circumstances" —homogeneous, problem-free environments—which, in minimizing the three types of pressures just discussed, prompt democratic governing institutions to impose less bureaucracy than they otherwise would. Private schools therefore tend to be effectively organized because of the way their system naturally works. When public schools happen to be effectively organized, it is in spite of their system—they are the lucky ones with peculiarly nice environments.

The power of these institutional forces is graphically reflected in our sample of American high schools. Having cast our net widely to allow for a full range of noninstitutional factors that might reasonably be suspected of playing causal roles, we found that virtually all of them fall by the wayside. The extent to which schools are granted the autonomy they need to develop more effective organizations is overwhelmingly determined by their sector and the niceness of their institutional environments.

Viewed as a whole, then, our effort to take institutions into account builds systematically on mainstream ideas and findings—but, in the end, puts a very different slant on things. We agree that effective organization is a major determinant of student achievement. We also agree that schools perform better the more autonomous they are and the less encumbered they are by bureaucracy. But we do not agree that this knowledge about the proximate causes of effective performance can be used to engineer better schools through democratic control. Reformers are right about where they want to go, but their institutions cannot get them there.

The way to get schools with effective organizations is not to insist that democratic institutions should do what they are incapable of doing. Nor is it to assume that the better public schools, the lucky ones with nice environments, can serve as organizational models for the rest. Their luck is not transferable. The way to get effective schools, rather, is to recognize that the problem of ineffective performance is really a deep-seated institutional problem that arises from the most fundamental properties of democratic control.

The most sensible approach to genuine educational reform is therefore to move toward a true institutional solution—a different set of institutional arrangements that is compatible with, and indeed actively promotes and nurtures, the kinds of schools people want. The market alternative then becomes particularly attractive, for it provides a setting in which these organizations can flourish and take root.

Educational Reform During the 1980s

As they try to gain perspective on the turbulent developments of the 1980s, educators find themselves distinguishing between two "waves" of educational reform. The first wave began several years before the spate of commission reports in 1983, picked up considerable momentum at that point, and continued for several years thereafter. During this time, the states carried out hundreds of studies, shifted through and debated countless proposals for reform, and enacted a good many of them. These reforms launched direct attacks on what appeared to be the most obvious and tractable problems—money, academic standards, teacher pay and quality—and they did so in the most traditional way: by imposing new regulations on schools and local districts and providing them additional financial resources.[1]

The fact that so much study and legislation was accomplished in so short a time was itself an astonishing political development. Remarkably, however, the pressures for change did not die down. Popular support for educational reform remained high, and, with most of the traditional ground already covered, reformist energies were increasingly directed to far more difficult problems that much of the academic mainstream saw as more fundamental: the need to reduce bureaucracy, the need to grant schools more autonomy.

Whatever its benefits, the first wave of reforms not only skirted these problems, it made them a bit worse by opting for regulatory solutions that added to bureaucracy and centralized control. The second wave has generally left these earlier reforms intact and sought to add new, more innovative reforms that would reduce unnecessary bureaucracy and decentralize important decisionmaking powers to the local level.[2] Because these reforms are just beginning to catch on around the country—and because they tend to be both expensive and potentially threatening to some of the established interests—it is still unclear how far they will go or exactly what forms they will take when and if they are fully developed. At this point, the restructuring movement has largely been a movement of ideas and proposals. Of these, the most popular have to do with school-based management, teacher professionalism, and "choice."[3]

In our view, the second wave is clearly more promising than the first, but the sum total of these efforts cannot bring about the kind of transformation in America's public schools that reformers want. In this section, we will take a closer look at some of the basic reforms that both waves have introduced and suggest why we think this is so.

Traditional Reforms: More Money

One thing mainstream educational reformers can always agree on is that more money—lots more money—needs to be spent. In part, this is just an unavoidable part of politics. Teachers, administrators, school boards, and everyone else in the educational establishment are better off when educational budgets go up, and they take reformist swings in public opinion as golden opportunities to lobby hard for more money. But the intellectual grounds for more money also appeal to common sense. Many of the policy changes reformers have sought—better pay for teachers, longer school days and years—cost additional money to provide. And even if no policy changes were introduced, more money would still mean more teachers, more equipment, smaller class sizes, and all sorts of other good things for schools.

During the 1980s, governments responded to these pressures with handsome increases in funding.[4] The problem is that, common sense notwithstanding, there is no evidence that increases of even this magnitude stand to have important effects on school performance. In fact, the relationship between resources and performance has been studied to death by social scientists, and their consistent conclusion has been that resources do not matter much, except perhaps in cases of extreme deprivation or gross abundance.[5]

Our own analysis of American high schools affirms this well-established finding. While it is true that high performance schools have more resources to employ than low performance schools do, some 20 percent more on the average, the apparent causal connection turns out to be spurious when controls are introduced for factors like social class and student aptitude. Money is not what makes some schools more effective than others. To this we should add that private schools—which outperform public schools, on the average—also tend to spend less than the public schools do in educating their students. They get better schools for less money.[6]

If money does not make much difference, then it must mean that many of the things money can buy do not have the kinds of beneficial consequences that educators and reformers think they do. Better schools probably do not require lots of expensive equipment or huge new buildings or vast libraries. Nor do they require paying teachers substantially more or hiring an army of them to teach a diverse array of courses. In our view, the performance problems of the public schools have little or nothing to do with inadequate funding, and they cannot be corrected by digging deeper into the public purse.

Traditional Reforms: More Controls

Money aside, the first wave was an effort to "make" schools better through new controls. The schools had not performed well in the past, and it was now up to policymakers to impose the kinds of changes that seemed to be needed for academic excellence. The rules and regulations eventually adopted varied from state to state, and they targeted virtually every aspect of the schools—curriculum, discipline, personnel, textbooks, instructional methods, and more.

Several basic reforms stand out, however, as uniformly popular and representative of what was going on: the states sought to ensure a more rigorous academic curriculum through stricter graduation requirements, they sought to ensure that this curriculum was more effectively taught by raising teacher quality, and they sought to hold schools accountable for effective teaching by requiring new formal tests of student performance. Better courses, better teachers, better accountability.

Because their objectives are admirable, these sorts of reforms seem to make good sense. Just like spending more money does. But there is little reason to think they will have any significant impact on how much students learn—and they may make things worse rather than better.

The imposition of stricter graduation requirements is, in our view, the least troubling.[7] Academic excellence does call for a rigorous curriculum in which students actively participate. But laws of this sort can only do so much. They can mandate that courses with certain titles and subject matters be taught and that students spend time physically sitting in the classroom. But they cannot mandate a high-quality learning experience. Teachers and students can go through the motions, each following state-imposed rules to the letter, without students gaining much of anything in the process. This, of course, is where the other bureaucratic controls come in: by controlling teacher quality and by demanding evidence of student learning, reformers try to guarantee that course requirements are not meaningless. Thus stricter academic requirements would essentially figure as benign impositions—not very promising, but unlikely to be very harmful—were they not just the tip of the iceberg.[8]

To engineer more effective teaching, reformers have tried a number of things. One is to pay teachers bigger salaries as a means of attracting better people into the field over the long haul. This is the least bureaucratic approach, and it will doubtless do at least some good. But it is also fiscally painful for state and local governments, extremely costly to taxpayers— and, as we pointed out, there is no evidence that it will do enough good to justify the costs. We are not talking here about how much teachers "should" get paid—a normative question that has no objective answer— but only about the connection between teacher pay and effective schools. Within the salary ranges that are feasible, how much teachers get paid simply does not appear to be a key part of the problem.[9]

Because taxes are unpopular, offering attractive salaries is not the normal governmental approach to teacher quality (or anything else). The normal approach is to regulate. Traditionally, this has been done through teacher certification: educational and testing requirements that candidates must satisfy before they are deemed sufficiently well qualified to teach in the public schools. When the quality of teaching became a matter of public debate and concern in the early 1980s, the reflexive response was to strengthen these requirements—by calling for more units of postgraduate training, for specific kinds of course work, for demonstrations of knowledge in fields of emphasis, for more serious and broadly administered tests of competency.[10]

In general, this is a bureaucratic approach that has little to recommend it. People who surmount the nearly countless hurdles that certification places in their paths will probably emerge better equipped to teach than they were when they started. But there is no guarantee that even a reasonable percentage of these survivors will make good teachers—for the true essentials of the job cannot be formally measured through coursetaking and test-passing. Whether duly certified teachers turn out to be good or bad is ultimately revealed in the classroom through the informal, experience-based judgments of principals, other teachers, students, and parents. By this time, however, in a bureaucratic world that grants the schools almost no discretion in hiring and firing, it is usually too late.

Certification raises problems not just because it fails to screen out the mediocre and the bad. It also raises problems because it sets up formidable barriers to entry that keep many excellent prospects out of the job pool. People who are well educated, bright, enthusiastic, creative, and good with children cannot simply pursue a latent interest in teaching by giving it a try. Nor can talented people already working in other lines of endeavor shift into teaching, or perhaps move in and out of it, as they might other jobs. Instead, potential teachers are asked by the state to foreclose other options, make a substantial investment of time and resources, and jump through formal hoops. American society is full of people who could make excellent teachers, but burdensome certification requirements are the best way to ensure that most of them never teach.

In some states, teacher "shortages"—which these barriers to entry, of course, help cause—have prompted public officials to relax certification rules a bit, allowing for the hiring of uncertified people on temporary or emergency bases, for programs that enable on-the-job training, and for out-of-field placement.[11] These are promising developments, but they are little more than a chink in the bureaucratic armor. The conventional democratic response to the effectiveness problem has been to "strengthen" certification requirements—adding to the bureaucratization of teaching and exacerbating a host of already serious problems that threaten in the aggregate to stifle teacher quality instead of raising it.

While certification and its focus on job qualifications have been the most popular approach to the regulation of teacher effectiveness, some states have also sought more innovative changes designed to give teachers stronger on-the-job incentives for effective performance. One is merit pay, which is supposed to provide special rewards to high-performing teachers. Another involves the creation of "career ladders" within schools, which essentially introduce new hierarchies of responsibility and pay among teachers—allowing, for instance, for "mentor" or "master" teachers who, having achieved their positions based on experience and performance, would lead and supervise other teachers and receive additional compensation.[12]

Attempts to base rewards on performance are steps in the right direction. And, as public officials are well aware, they certainly strike a responsive chord among taxpayers. But the problem is that these sorts of reforms cannot work well in a system of direct democratic control. The only way to measure performance adequately is to rely on the discretion of those who work in the school—which is precisely what the unions and democratic authorities are strongly inclined not to do, and what the whole system is built to prevent. The result is that merit systems tend to get bureaucratized. Pay and promotion are supposed to be performance based, but, in design and practice, every effort is made to reduce the discretionary component of these evaluations as far as possible and base them on objective measures. With discretion squeezed out, teachers are left with more hierarchy, more rules, and precious few incentives to do a better job than they were doing in the past.[13]

Finally, there is the matter of accountability. Schools can guarantee that students take what appears to be a more rigorous curriculum. They can hire teachers who have met strengthened certification requirements. They can adopt innovative new programs for enhancing teacher incentives. But all of these may look much more impressive on paper than they do in practice. The bottom line is, how much are students learning?

Schools have always been held accountable, by means of rules and reporting requirements, for their implementation of policies, their expenditure of money, their handling of personnel, and most everything else their democratic superiors cared about (and were themselves accountable to their constituents for). Now, in a reformist atmosphere centered on academic excellence, public officials increasingly demanded concrete evidence of results.

These demands translated into requirements for new, expanded, or more rigorous formal tests of student competency and achievement. Through competency tests, officials sought to ensure that schools could not pass along students who had failed to meet certain minimum standards—which many schools were clearly guilty of in the past. Schools would now be held accountable for really teaching these students something. Achievement tests served the more general purpose of indicating how well or poorly the schools were doing.[14]

We believe, as almost all educators do, that testing is a necessary and important part of the educational process. The social science of testing is quite advanced, and, for most students most of the time, test results can provide reliable information about learning. Competency tests, moreover, while measuring only the most basic types of knowledge and skills, can be extremely useful in allowing schools to identify students with serious learning deficiencies and to provide them with remedial help and special training.

Nonetheless, statewide testing of students can also be a misleading and counterproductive means of evaluating the performance of schools.[15] There are three basic problems at work here. The first is that statewide tests are uniform, one-shot measures of learning. As such, they cannot help but leave some types of knowledge and reasoning untapped, and what they do tap they will measure imperfectly. Their results will nonetheless become the official yardstick by which school performance is assessed. The second is that schools and teachers, wanting positive evaluations, will adapt their practices to conform to these imperfect yardsticks. They will "teach to the tests," regardless of what they think good education consists of and requires. The third is that student test scores are due in part to schools, but also to student aptitude, social class, and other causes. Figuring out what test scores properly have to say about school performance is a complicated methodological undertaking: one that may excite researchers in departments of education, but that seldom finds its way into the politics of educational decisionmaking. The reality is that people look at a school's average test scores and jump to conclusions—unwarranted conclusions—about school performance, with far-reaching consequences for their assessments of problems and solutions.

In the end, testing requirements are a lot like certification requirements and many other traditional reforms. They seem to make good sense, and they do indeed offer certain benefits. But they are clearly deficient as solutions to the problems they are addressing, and they stand little chance of improving schools in any significant way. Worse, they create still more bureaucracy, and they unleash new bureaucratic pathologies that divert people and resources from the pursuit of quality education. The danger is not just that these reforms will fail to accomplish their lofty goals, but that they will actually hurt the schools more than help them over the long run.

Innovative Reforms: School-Based Management

As the 1980s wore on, reformers increasingly called for bolder, more innovative actions that could strike at the heart of the schools' problems. The early period of reform, they believed, was an exciting new beginning for the public schools—but it was only a beginning. The schools had to be granted more autonomy. Teachers had to be professionalized and empowered. Bureaucracy had to be reduced. These ends could not be accomplished by continuing along the traditional path of stricter regulatory controls. Nor, in fact, would reform succeed if it left the basic structure of the public system intact—for the fundamental problems were structural in origin, having to do with who controls whom and who makes what decisions. To liberate schools and teachers from their bureaucratic straightjackets, reformers had to "restructure" the system.

While the notion of restructuring has gained widespread popularity since the mid-1980s, there has been little agreement about what it really means or how it should be carried out. Educational theory and research clearly suggest that bureaucracy is bad and that autonomy and professionalism are good, but they do not have much to say about how these things are caused by institutional structure, nor, therefore, about what structural changes are needed to bring about the desired ends. With no clear analytical foundation to guide them—and unwilling to fall back on traditional controls—reformers have been open to a variety of innovative ideas.[16]

One of the most influential is school-based management. First proposed during the 1970s in reaction to rapid growth in state funding and control, it offers a comprehensive plan for decentralizing important educational choices to the school level. While only one state—Hawaii—has adopted a full-blown system of school-based management, a number of school districts have done so (often in conjunction with other decentralizing reforms). Perhaps the most prominent applications have come in Chicago, Dade County (Florida), and Rochester (New York), where the public schools were in genuine crisis, plagued by problems so severe and deep-seated that the traditional system could offer no real hope for improvement.[17] Something dramatically innovative, like school-based management, did; and reformers embraced it with the enthusiasm of a drowning man for a life preserver.

In its structural details, this approach to reform means different things to different people and has been outlined and applied in various ways. Broadly speaking, though, a plan for school-based management might look as follows. States and districts would continue to make general policies, with schools delegated substantial authority and budgetary flexibility in making the operational decisions about how these general policies are to be carried out—decisions that may range from how much money to spend on athletic equipment to "policy" decisions about school discipline or academic programs. The principal, as the school's chief executive, would make these decisions with the advice and active participation of formally constituted councils of "stakeholders": teachers and parents, at a minimum, and possibly students and relevant members of the community. (Sometimes these councils are not just advisory, but have decisionmaking authority.) Through oversight, mechanisms for approval and veto, rules for budgeting and accounting, and annual performance reports—in which the school provides a compendium of data on its activities, staff, student test scores, parent and staff satisfaction, and future plans—authorities at the district and state level hold school decisionmakers accountable for the school's choices and performance.[18]

In our view, the decentralization is preferable to central control, and systems that move toward school-based management are likely to create conditions better suited to effective education than those that existed originally. But the institutional change it introduces is not nearly as dramatic or fundamental as its enthusiasts tend to claim, and the consequences for student achievement are likely to prove far less impressive than they hope.

School-based management leaves the traditional institutions of democratic control intact. The schools remain subordinates in a democratic hierarchy. Their superiors have decentralized by delegating some of their own authority, but it is the superiors who are held accountable by the public at large for what happens in the schools. If the schools perform poorly, if they spend public money unproductively or unwisely, if they make politically controversial choices—and, in general, if they use their "autonomy" to do things that generate political opposition—their schools' superiors will come under intense pressure to use their higher-level authority to take charge and turn matters around. They will even be blamed for failing to prevent these problems from arising in the first place.

Acutely aware of all this from the outset, the authorities are motivated to control and monitor how the schools exercise their autonomy—they need to know what is going on, they need to be able to derail bad decisions before they happen, they need to be able to intervene and make corrections, they need to be able to ensure that schools will use their autonomy wisely in making good decisions, they need to make plans for the system as a whole. They do these things not by telling the schools what their decisions will be, but by imposing a host of new rules, regulations, and requirements. Parts of the old bureaucracy are jettisoned, only to be replaced by new ones.

School-based management, then, is another way of controlling the schools within an essentially bureaucratic system. Its very name, in fact, is wonderfully appropriate, for what it suggests is that principals, teachers, and others at the lower reaches are fundamentally engaged in the "management" of schools—a bureaucratic conception, if there ever was one, of what effective education is all about.

The decentralization it achieves within the bureaucratic system, moreover, is sometimes deceptive; and it threatens to be inherently unstable. It is sometimes deceptive because, except in rather unusual circumstances (crises, for instance), higher-level authorities are jealous of their powers, reluctant to give them up under reformist pressure, and thus inclined to make delegations that are more apparent than real. Some applications of school-based management, as a result, place most of their emphasis on shared influence *within* the schools rather than on delegations of important powers from states and districts *to* the schools.[19]

When important delegations to schools are made, on the other hand, they are vulnerable to instability. For as soon as problems arise—as soon as the schools make bad decisions or are perceived to be performing poorly or are faced with difficult situations that seem beyond their control—the authorities will find themselves under pressure to reassert their powers. Unless all goes well, then, there is a built-in tendency for decentralized systems to gravitate toward greater centralization. As long as higher-level authority exists, it will eventually get used.[20]

Innovative Reforms: Teacher Professionalism and Empowerment

The reforms of the early 1980s sought to increase the quality of teaching through higher pay, stricter controls, and new incentives, but they did not seriously attempt to change the subordinate status of teachers in the public system. Teachers remained lowly bureaucrats. As time went on and support gathered for innovative reforms generally, it was inevitable that the role of teachers would become a central issue. The common understanding that less bureaucracy, more autonomy, and more professionalism are good for schools, and that restructuring is necessary to achieve them, was but another way of saying the traditional status of teachers had to go.

A major thrust of this movement has been to empower teachers by granting them greater individual control over their own jobs, as well as greater collective say in shaping the policies and practices of their schools.[21] In the abstract, this emphasis on empowerment is entirely consistent with effective schools research and richly deserving of support. The specific forms it takes in political practice, however, are another matter. While helpful in some ways, they empower teachers by creating all sorts of new problems and failing to solve most of the old ones.

To proponents of teacher empowerment, the job at hand is to reallocate power within the current system of democratic control: from states to districts, from districts to schools, from administrators (including principals) to teachers.[22] They seek to carry this out by shifting the locus of decision-making downward and by introducing an onerous array of new formal mechanisms—committees, councils, career ladders, rules, processes— that, by force of law, guarantee teachers specific types of educational roles and governing responsibilities. For obvious reasons, these proposals to empower teachers are often pursued within more comprehensive plans for school-based management, although the different goals and scopes of the two movements sometimes produce conflict (regarding, for example, the discretionary powers of principals).

In important respects, reforms to empower teachers are rightly seen as progressive. They do indeed grant teachers more autonomy in the performance of their jobs, greater say in the running of their own schools, and more influence in educational policymaking and administration. All of this, especially given the stifling effects of hierarchical control, is doubtless for the good, other things being equal. Moreover, the path to teacher empowerment has not always entailed additional bureaucracy. Aggressive expansion of career ladder schemes within schools, for instance, has sometimes included important dimensions of flexibility and discretionary judgment—as in apprenticeship programs (where teachers train teachers on the job) and peer review (where teachers evaluate the quality of one another's teaching).

For the most part, however, the movement to empower teachers has been a characteristic exercise in democratic control. Proponents have tried to "make" teachers more powerful by relying on new bureaucratic arrangements that specify precisely who gets to do what and how they have to go about doing it. This whole approach to empowerment is a gross distortion of the kind of shared influence that prevails within effective schools, where teachers are powerful not because rules and regulations dictate that they must be, but because they naturally come to be influential participants in decisionmaking when schools are founded on teams, informal cooperation, collegiality, and mutual respect. The qualities of effective organization that naturally bring power to teachers cannot be imposed by bureaucratic fiat. They have to develop on their own, freely and informally. Trying to make teachers powerful through bureaucracy is the best way to guarantee that they can never achieve the kind of professionalism they really want, and that good schools require.

A second major thrust of the teacher reform movement has been to create a credentialing superstructure that would help transform teaching as a whole into what proponents consider a bona fide profession. In the early 1980s reformers saw their efforts to strengthen certification requirements as an important step in this direction. Like doctors and lawyers, teachers would have to go through a strict, uniform regimen of education and training at accredited institutions before they could be certified to practice. But these steps did not seem to go far enough, for doctors and lawyers were true professionals in a way that teachers were not: they designed and controlled their own certification procedures—they regulated themselves—while teachers were regulated by public officials and agencies. As the reform movement in general turned increasingly to ideas for restructuring the system, demands for stricter certification requirements blossomed into demands for self-regulation.

Two proposals have attracted most of the attention. The first, championed by the National Education Association, is for the creation of teacher-controlled licensing boards within each of the states that would set legally binding standards and requirements for admission to the profession. In effect, government would delegate public authority to teachers, who would then use that authority to regulate themselves and control entry.[23] The second, popularized by the Carnegie Forum on Education and the Economy, calls for a teacher-controlled national board that would certify individuals as having attained a high level of professional knowledge and mastery of teaching.[24] National certification would be voluntary and not required for entry into the profession; but, as a concrete indicator of achievement, it would presumably be used—by states, districts, schools, and unions—to qualify teachers for higher pay and more responsibility. A well-known proposal along these lines comes from Albert Shanker, head of the American Federation of Teachers, who argues for a career-ladder arrangement in which nationally certified "lead" teachers play major supervisory and policymaking roles within each school.[25]

The proposal for state licensing boards is a bad idea. In the name of professionalization, it essentially retains the top-heavy bureaucratic arrangements already in place—arrangements that cannot do a good job of measuring and promoting good teaching, and whose numerous, time-consuming formal hurdles discourage entry into the field and vitiate what ought to be a dynamic, exciting market for teachers. The only real difference is that teachers, rather than public officials and agencies, would be able to exercise this authority. But this does not solve anything. Regulation would still be just as bureaucratic and just as inappropriate and counterproductive as before. Worse, as political scientists have complained for decades, these self-regulating boards—whether for doctors and lawyers or for cosmetologists, plumbers, and dog groomers—tend to use public authority in their own self-interest to restrict entry and enhance their incomes.[26] And worse still, it would not really be "teachers" who would control the boards, but almost surely organized teachers—and far-and-away the largest, most geographically dispersed organization of teachers is the National Education Association. No wonder, then, that the NEA is the chief advocate of this regulatory proposal, and that the much smaller, less dispersed American Federation of Teachers, its main competitor, has not endorsed it.[27]

The proposal for a national standards board has more to recommend it. Its great advantage is that it is voluntary, providing information about teacher quality without putting public authority behind a new bureaucracy to control entry. But there are several very serious drawbacks here. First, no certification scheme, especially not a national one, can possibly provide much valid information on the quality of an individual's teaching; assessments will inevitably rely too heavily on standard formal measures and too little on school-level discretionary judgment. Second, voluntary national credentialing would doubtless become cloaked in public authority anyway, as states, districts, and collective bargaining agreements make board certification a requirement for increased pay and educational responsibilities. It would be voluntary only in the sense that it would not constitute a legal barrier to entry. It would, on the other hand, become a legal barrier to career advancement. Third, credentialing by a national board would, in the end, create yet another bureaucracy that teachers and schools would have to contend with in doing their jobs. Making it private or voluntary or teacher controlled does not change its essentially bureaucratic approach to the problem of teacher quality and professionalism. And fourth, this board would be strongly influenced and perhaps dominated by the National Education Association and the American Federation of Teachers, adding to their already stifling hold on educational personnel.

All of these reforms to empower and professionalize teaching are institutionally crippled from the outset; they are destined to disappoint. The kind of power that teachers have in effective schools cannot be imposed by formal rule. Nor can the kind of professionalism they exercise in effective schools be imposed by licensing and standards boards. Democratic control cannot "make" teachers into the efficacious professionals they want to be —for democratic control is the real problem. It is what caused their bureaucratic subordination in the first place, and the only kind of restructuring it can offer is a different set of bureaucratic arrangements in which teachers play new formal roles and have more formal powers. This is an artificial version of the real thing. And it leaves the most fundamental problem untouched.

Innovative Reforms: Choice

The most innovative and promising reforms to have gained momentum during the late 1980s fall under the heading of "choice." In the past, educators tended to associate this concept with the privatization of public education, aid to religious schools, and racial segregation, portraying it as a subversive notion that threatened the common school ideal and virtually everything else the public system had traditionally stood for. In recent years, however, choice has come to be viewed very differently, even by many in the educational establishment.

This new movement puts choice to use as part of a larger set of strategies for reform *within* the public sector. It is not about privatizing the public schools, nor is it a surreptitious way of giving aid to religious schools. Choice is being embraced by liberals and conservatives alike as a powerful means of transforming the structure and performance of public education—while keeping the public schools public. In the process, it is being used to combat racial segregation; indeed, it has become the preferred approach to desegregation in districts throughout the country—in Rochester and Buffalo (New York), Cambridge (Massachusetts), and Prince George's County (Maryland), to name a few.[28]

Support for public sector choice is widespread. Surveys reveal that the vast majority of public school parents want to choose the schools their children attend—and that, when choice plans are implemented and people have a chance to exercise their newfound freedom, popular support for choice grows.[29] Not surprisingly, many public officials are also singing the praises of choice, with support running particularly strong among political executives. Their broad, heterogeneous constituencies, their uniquely central role in policymaking, and the public's inclination to hold them singularly responsible for effective government all make them more willing (than legislators) to take bold, unconventional actions that provoke opposition from the established interests.

At the federal level, Presidents Ronald Reagan and George Bush have been enthusiastic supporters of educational choice, although there is not a great deal the federal government can do on its own. More consequentially, given the primary role of the states in public education, the National Governors' Association has come out strongly for choice in its recent report on education, *Time for Results*[30] and reformist governors, Democrats and Republicans alike, have typically been in the forefront in pressing for real change.

They have many allies. Maverick legislators have played leading roles in public debate and coalition building. Respected groups of academics and reformers, less satisfied than before with the intellectual mainstream, are increasingly arguing the advantages of choice.[31] So are business groups, which have been disappointed in past reforms and are increasingly calling for more innovative approaches that take greater advantage of market-based incentives.[32] And many groups speaking for minorities and the poor have become supporters as well, embracing choice as a crucial means of escaping from the intolerably bad urban schools that the traditional system of fixed boundaries and assignments forces on them.[33] Despite the opposition that unions have offered to choice proposals generally, some aspects of choice have been endorsed, at least provisionally, by a few key union leaders, including Albert Shanker, president of the American Federation of Teachers, and Adam Urbanski, president of the Rochester Teachers Association.[34]

Yet all this enthusiasm has not translated into truly successful reform, and it may never do so, at least if current efforts are projected into the future. There are three basic problems at work. The first is that choice means many different things to its supporters. They all claim to favor choice, but when it comes to the specifics of actual choice plans, their superficial consensus breaks down. To the extent the movement for choice can be called a movement at all, it is an extremely fragmented and conceptually shallow one. It lacks mission.

The second is that virtually all choice plans are entirely demand focused: they offer parents and students a measure of choice among schools. Period. Rarely do these plans take any steps to free up the supply side by decontrolling—or, at least, encouraging and promoting through official actions —the emergence of new and different types of schools, so that people really have an attractive and dynamically responsive set of alternatives from which to choose. Instead, choice is usually restricted to a fixed set of existing schools, which reformers hope to improve through the "competition" that choice will presumably stimulate. All these schools, however, have their existence and financial support guaranteed; actions are inevitably taken to ensure that no schools are "underenrolled" (a bureaucratic euphemism for what happens when schools are so bad no one wants to attend them); schools that do the worst are implicitly rewarded, because they tend to be the first in line for bigger budgets and more staff; and all the usual formal rules and democratic controls continue to apply in constraining what the schools are able (and want) to do in changing their behavior. Under these conditions, giving parents and students choice among schools cannot in itself be expected to produce vigorous, healthy competition among schools. The supply side has to be freed up if that is to happen.

Third, any choice plan that upsets the traditional structure of public education generates intense opposition from established groups. As a result, most of the choice plans that get put into effect (or, for that matter, even gain serious attention) are grafted onto the traditional system and make only marginal changes in it. Choice becomes part of a big compromise among contending political powers—no one loses jobs, no bad schools are closed down, vested interests remain securely vested, the basic structure of the system stays the same. In a nutshell, this is why reforms always focus on giving parents and students choice, but never free up the supply and governance of schools. Parent-student choice is popular, and it can be accomplished with minimal disruption to traditional structures, while real change on the supply side is fundamentally threatening to established interests and hence never gains political acceptance. The reality, therefore, is that choice plans fail to take advantage of what choice really has to offer—and they leave intact the crippling institutional causes of the schools' past problems.

What passes for choice takes diverse forms. Most often, districts offer choice through one or more alternative schools, usually with special programs targeted at special clienteles—dropouts, the gifted, students needing remedial education, parents seeking open learning environments for their children. Students can choose to attend (or may be shunted into) an alternative school instead of their regular schools of assignment. Almost always, however, there are too few alternative schools to accommodate more than a small percentage of a district's students; and, if the schools are any good, there tend to be far more applicants than the schools can accept. The vast majority of students in these "choice" systems continue to attend schools of assignment, and all the usual institutions of democratic governance remain in place, doing their usual jobs.[35]

In many districts, choice plans are built around "magnet" schools. This is particularly true of districts that have been under pressure, whether internally or from the courts or the state, to take aggressive action in achieving racial balance. Magnet schools are alternative schools that are set up with special programs and often granted additional funds and equipment in order to attract students from throughout the district. They tend to be located in minority areas, thus offering minority kids an attractive alternative to their neighborhood school (or to taking buses to the suburbs), and offering incentives to white or suburban children for choosing a racially mixed school in the city. As part—often the core—of a desegregation plan, magnet schools are a means of achieving racial balance through voluntary choice. And evidence suggests that in many districts they have worked well in that regard.[36]

They have worked less well in promoting districtwide improvement in school effectiveness. Like alternative schools generally, magnets typically offer choices to just a small portion of the district's students, and they leave the traditional system as a whole intact. Moreover, they can have a negative impact on the rest of the schools. Their additional funding and equipment may (depending on their source) result in a smaller pie for the remaining schools to divide up. Magnets tend to attract the best, most innovative teachers away from regular schools of assignment, which then threaten to become dumping grounds for the district's mediocre teachers (especially if magnets are allowed to rid themselves of staff they do not want). Magnets also tend to attract the best, most interested students and parents, making the job of the regular schools still more difficult.[37]

These choice plans are disappointing because they are too limited in scope to achieve significant reform. We should emphasize, however, that there is strong and mounting evidence that the introduction of choice through alternative and magnet schools does indeed have positive consequences for those who are lucky enough to be direct participants. Broadly speaking, schools of choice tend to be more informal, professional, and unified around a common mission than regular schools of assignment are. Their teachers are more autonomous, more excited about their work, more influential in decisionmaking, and happier with their overall situations. Students are more satisfied with their chosen schools; dropout and absenteeism rates are down; achievement scores are up. Parents are better informed, more supportive, and participate more actively.[38]

These are clearly steps in the right direction. Yet the fact remains that most schools, even in so-called choice systems, are *not* schools of choice. The vast majority of teachers, students, and parents are stuck in regular schools of assignment—and the availability of choice elsewhere in the district is of little benefit to them and may actually cause them new problems.

The most promising choice systems now in operation are those that have moved aggressively toward the elimination of fixed jurisdictions and assignments. Carried to their full extent, such systems make every school a school of choice. This is the cutting edge of the current reform movement, pioneered by just a few systems.

Broadest in scope are recent reforms carried out in the state of Minnesota.[39] Elementary and secondary students are allowed to attend schools outside their own districts, with state and local money—up to a minimum or "foundation" set by the state—following them, as long as the receiving district has room and racial balance is not adversely affected. State law grants districts the right to decide whether free choice will reign within their boundaries, but districts have been encouraged to move in this direction and some are in the process of doing so. In addition, high school students are also allowed to opt out of their own schools and receive credit for taking courses at colleges of their choosing, with state and local money following them. The Minnesota reforms are so new that it remains unclear how many students and schools will be affected by choice and what the consequences will be. The preliminary results are positive. Those directly involved are happy with how the new system is working and seem to be benefiting from it. Like virtually all choice-based reforms, however, the Minnesota reforms do not go nearly far enough, failing to free up the supply of schools, continuing to control them from above, and leaving all the traditional institutions in place.

Just as Minnesota has been a pioneer among states, so a small number of districts have taken the lead in building their own systems around choice. One of the boldest has been Cambridge, Massachusetts. The Cambridge system emerged incrementally over the years, beginning in the late 1960s, as the district responded to pressures for desegregation. Its authorities initially relied on magnet schools, then began resorting to various kinds of controls (redrawing jurisdictional boundaries, imposing involuntary transfers on students); but the cumulative effects on racial balance were unsatisfactory, and whites were bailing out of the system into private schools and other districts. By 1981 these failures had prompted a shift to something new and more radical, a districtwide "controlled choice" system, which a year later had taken over as the district's programmatic attack on desegregation.[40]

The concept is simple. There are no neighborhood schools or attendance areas. Parents and students are free to choose any schools in the district. To assist them in gaining information and making wise decisions, the district provides a Parent Information Center complete with parent liaisons, whose job it is to know about the special characteristics of individual schools, to discuss with parents the special needs of their children, and to facilitate the application process. Parents and students can rank order up to four schools in submitting their applications to the district's assignment officer, who is responsible for assigning each student to a school, and who gives weight to racial balance as well as proximity and siblings in making his determinations.

While one might think that all students would try to get into the same schools, this has not happened—in part because students often prefer schools that are close to their homes, but also because the Cambridge schools offer distinctive programs that have differential appeal.[41] The end result is that the great majority of students receive their first-choice school, and almost all receive one of their picks. The remaining students are assigned; but they have the right to appeal to the district's Hardship Appeal Board, and in any event are free to apply for transfer during the next year.

The Cambridge choice plan has been a huge improvement over the district's troubled past. The perennial problem of racial imbalance has dramatically changed for the better. Student achievement scores are up, and achievement differences between the worst and best schools are significantly down. Teachers are more satisfied with their jobs, parents and students are happier with their schools. And, not surprisingly, the public schools are now winning back the students they lost in earlier years to the private sector—by 1987, 89 percent of the district's newly entering students (kindergarten aged) were choosing to enroll in public schools, compared with 78 percent in 1979. This is perhaps the most concrete of all measures of success: people are choosing public schools because they prefer them.[42]

There is little doubt that the Cambridge plan works. In our view, it is one of the most exciting developments in American public education. Yet it does not go far enough. The demand side has essentially been freed up by giving parents and students choice. But the supply side—the set of alternatives from which they choose—remains firmly under the control of all the usual democratic institutions. Schools do not emerge in response to what parents and students want. Nor are schools truly free to organize, staff themselves, and design their curricula in ways they think will most appeal to their clients. All these matters remain subject to control from above. District authorities decide, through the usual political and administrative processes, what the supply of public schools will be. The central office and its resident experts continue to spin out programs and policies. The district remains fundamentally responsible for what its schools are, what they do, and how well they perform—and it continues to take those hierarchic responsibilities very seriously. The schools have been granted somewhat more flexibility, but everyone knows who is really in charge.

The most radical—and most promising—exercise in public sector choice is to be found in Manhattan's District No. 4 in East Harlem, New York, which serves some 14,000 students from prekindergarten through the ninth grade.[43] Here, as in many other districts, the stimulus for reform was crisis: the educational system was a disaster. Out of New York City's thirty-two school districts in 1973, District No. 4 ranked last in reading and mathematics. The demographics of the district make this kind of failure seem predictable and inevitable. More than half of all families are headed by single females. Almost 80 percent of all students qualify for free-lunch programs because of low income. Almost all students are minorities —60 percent are Hispanic, 35 percent are black.[44]

But District No. 4 was also lucky. It had dynamic leaders who were willing to take risks and follow innovative paths to reform almost unthinkable to their mainstream colleagues in the larger educational community. Beginning in 1974, they oversaw the creation of an expanding number of alternative schools built around distinctive themes, philosophies, and programs. This expansion arose from a special source: the district encouraged teachers with ideas and initiative to put forward their own proposals, and, with the district's involvement and consent, form their own schools. Teachers were only too happy to take advantage of these opportunities, and schools sprouted up like mushrooms. To make this proliferation of schools possible, district officials also rejected the traditional notion that each school must have its own building. In East Harlem, schools were henceforth to be identified with programs, not with buildings. A given building, therefore, often houses a number of very different schools, each with its own "director" (a teacher with the responsibilities of principal), staff, and student body.

These schools have been granted very substantial autonomy. To begin with, district authorities do not seek centralized control over student admissions. They assist parents through orientation sessions, information on each school, lessons in decisionmaking, and meetings with school representatives. But the schools control their own admissions—they set their own criteria and make their own decisions about whom to accept and reject. More generally, the schools are largely (but not entirely) free to make their own decisions about programs, methods, structure, and virtually everything else pertaining to the kind of education they provide; and with teachers running their own shops, many of the preexisting formal rules imposed through collective bargaining and democratic control have either been waived or ignored. Teachers, parents, and students are all encouraged to think of themselves as their schools' "owners" and to take the responsibilities—and the pride and involvement—that real ownership entails.

The district has pursued innovation and diversity, and that is what it has achieved. The names of some of its junior high schools help illustrate just how spectacular the variety can be when the supply side is liberated: the Academy of Environmental Science, the Creative Learning Community, the East Harlem Career Academy, the East Harlem Maritime School, the East Harlem School for Health and Bio-Medical Studies, the Jose Feliciano Performing Arts School, Music 13, the Isaac Newton School for Math and Science, Northview Tech for Communication Arts and Computer Science, Rafael Cordero Bilingual School, the School of Science and Humanities.[45] From the list alone, one would think this is a system of private schools.

Freeing up the supply and governance of schools has not led to the kind of chaos or unfairness that critics of market arrangements invariably predict. The system appears to work smoothly, effectively, and fairly. While schools have control over their own admissions, their distinctiveness and their sheer need for students—the district puts them out of business if they fail to attract enough clients—has meant that schools and students tend to match up quite well on their own. In recent years, 60 percent of the students have received their first choices, 30 percent their second choices, and 5 percent their third choices.

On virtually every relevant dimension, the East Harlem reforms have been a tremendous success. There are lots of schools emphasizing everything from music to science. Teachers are enthusiastic about their work and largely in control of their own schools. They are empowered, professional, and satisfied—all achieved through the natural dynamics of the system, not through the artificiality of bureaucratic rules. School organizations are small and informal, built around team cooperation and coherence of mission. Parents are active, well informed, and take pride in "their" schools.

Meantime, student achievement is way up. While only 15.9 percent of the district's students were reading at or above grade level in 1973, 62.6 percent were doing so by 1987. Its scores now put it around the middle for New York City school districts, rather than at the bottom—quite remarkable, given how heavily the sociological odds are stacked against it. Students are also dramatically more successful in gaining admission to New York's selective high schools. Whereas in the past they were essentially shut out of these schools, now they are accepted at rates that far exceed the citywide average. Some of this progress may be attributable to an influx of students from throughout New York City who have chosen to transfer from their districts to the schools of East Harlem. But these transfers represent only a small portion of District 4's enrollments, and are yet another indicator of the attractiveness of East Harlem's schools.

If there is a single district in the country that deserves to be held up as a model for all the others, it is East Harlem. Nonetheless, its system still suffers from what may turn out to be a fatal flaw. Beginning in the 1970s and continuing throughout the 1980s, the East Harlem reforms have been driven by a small group of visionaries who used district authority not only to provide parents and students with choice, but also to liberate the supply and governance of schools from district control. This freeing up of the supply side is what makes the East Harlem system so bold and unique. But its creation is entirely dependent on the visionaries themselves and their hold on power. The structures of democratic authority remain in place, and, if they become occupied by people with different beliefs or constituencies, the same public authority that liberated the schools could then be used to regain control over them.

This is not an idle fear. A recent scandal at the district level, involving allegations of mishandling of funds for personal benefit and giving rise to widespread media coverage, prompted city officials to initiate a shakeup of district personnel.[46] The new leadership appears to be intent on reasserting certain district controls and moving toward more traditional forms of governance and administration.[47] How far this will go remains to be seen. The up side is that East Harlem's radical system is well established; the schools have vocal, active, supportive clienteles, and they will fight any attempt to reduce their autonomy. But their problem, when all is said and done, is that they are subordinates in the hierarchy of democratic control, and what authority they have been privileged to exercise to this point has been delegated to them by their superiors—who have the right to take it back.

A Proposal for Reform

It is fashionable these days to say that choice is "not a panacea." Taken literally, this is obviously true. There are no panaceas in social policy. But the message this aphorism really means to get across is that choice is just one of many reforms with something to contribute. School-based management is another. So are teacher empowerment and professionalism, better training programs, stricter accountability, and bigger budgets. These and other types of reforms all bolster school effectiveness in their own distinctive ways—so the reasoning goes—and the best, most aggressive, most comprehensive approach to transforming the public school system is therefore one that wisely combines them into a multifaceted reformist package.[48]

In practice, then, choice is rarely treated as a self-contained strategy for reform. It is one element among many. Parents and students are sometimes given a modicum of choice, often through one or more alternative schools or magnets; but this is typically part of a larger stream of reforms in which efforts are also made to decentralize governance through some (though usually not all) of the elements of school-based management, to make teachers more professional (through career ladders or new decision responsibilities, say), to monitor school performance more closely (through stricter accounting requirements, formal tests of student achievement, parent surveys), and so on. Even when choice is an important part of the package, the result is not really a choice system at all. It is a more decentralized version of the traditional system of democratic control in which parents and students have more options.[49]

Politics is of course partly responsible for this. A true choice system strikes at the foundations of democratic control, and the established interests have every reason to throw their weight behind a more conventional grab-bag of marginal changes. In addition, democratic politics promotes compromise solutions anyway: if there are lots of reformist ideas with political support, the system tends to generate policies that borrow a little from each.

Politics aside, however, there are intellectual reasons for this grab-bag approach as well. People opt for combinations of reforms when they do not know what to think—when they have no coherent notion of what causes the problems they are concerned about and what might be done to address them. They cast about for answers, and their uncertainty prompts them to entertain whatever plausible-sounding ideas happen to come along. Just as investors do in the financial world, reformers respond to uncertainty by diversifying their portfolios.

As we have suggested, we do not think that all these ideas are bad. They have their pluses and minuses, and some combinations have in fact been responsible for tangible improvements in many schools and districts around the country. School-based management is better than centralized management. Having a few alternative schools is better than having none at all. Giving teachers more control over teaching is better than allowing administrators to tell them what to do. But as an "approach" this is precisely the wrong way to go about transforming American public education. The schools' most fundamental problems are rooted in the institutions of democratic control by which they are governed; and, despite all the talk about "restructuring," the current wave of grab-bag reforms leaves those institutions intact and in charge. The basic causes of America's educational problems do not get addressed.

Of all the sundry reforms that attract attention, only choice has the capacity to address these causes. The others are system preserving. They fully embrace direct democratic control and simply put its authority to use in ways somewhat different from the past. The schools remain subordinates in the structure of public authority—and they remain bureaucratic. In principle, choice offers a clear, sharp break from the institutional past. In practice, however, it has been forced into the same mold with all the others. It has been embraced half-heartedly, in bits and pieces, as a means of granting parents and students additional options or of giving schools more incentives to compete—popular moves that can be accomplished without changing the existing system in any fundamental way. Choice has simply been part of the grab-bag, one of many system-preserving reforms that presumably make democratic control work better.

Without being too literal about it, we think reformers would do well to entertain the notion that choice *is* a panacea. This is our way of saying that choice is not like the other reforms and should not be combined with them as part of a reformist strategy for improving America's public schools. Choice is a self-contained reform with its own rationale and justification. It has the capacity *all by itself* to bring about the kind of transformation that, for years, reformers have been seeking to engineer in myriad other ways. Indeed, if choice is to work to greatest advantage, it must be adopted *without* these other reforms, since the latter are predicated on democratic control and are implemented by bureaucratic means. The whole point of a thoroughgoing system of choice is to free the schools from these disabling constraints by sweeping away the old institutions and replacing them with new ones. Taken seriously, choice is not a system-preserving reform. It is a revolutionary reform that introduces a new system of public education.

What would such a system look like? Within the educational establishment, any serious consideration of choice automatically raises the much hated specter of a "voucher" system—a system in which government would provide funding directly to students in the form of vouchers, and students would use their vouchers to pay for education in the public or private school of their own choosing. For the last thirty years or so, advocates of choice have come up with many voucher proposals, and the educational community has consistently and vehemently opposed them, portraying vouchers as the embodiment of everything that is threatening to public education.[50]

Fortunately, the growing popularity of choice and its incremental adoption in districts and states around the country have helped break the stereotypical identification of choice with vouchers—and helped dissociate it, as well, from the unwarranted stigma that the establishment has succeeded in attaching to the very concept of vouchers. The fact is that all sorts of diverse arrangements are compatible with the basic principles on which choice is founded. Vouchers are not even necessary. Whether private schools are included is simply a matter of policy—they need not be. Similarly, choice systems can be designed differently depending on how reforms want to deal with issues of racial integration, religion, funding equalization, the educationally disadvantaged, and whatever other special concerns they may have.

This does not mean, of course, that all choice plans are somehow on an equal footing. As we have seen in evaluating what passes for choice in the current reform movement, some arrangements are clearly better than others, particularly as they attack or (most often) fail to attack the institutional causes at the root of the problem. It does mean, on the other hand, that there is no fixed or uniformly best system of choice, and that reformers have lots of flexibility and options at their disposal. Choice offers an array of institutional possibilities, not a determinate formula.

Without pretending to have an optimal plan up our sleeves, we would now like to outline a brief proposal for a choice system that we think is equipped to do the job. Offering our own proposal in this way has a certain practical value, for it allows us to illustrate in some detail what a fullblown choice system might look like, as well as to note some of the policy decisions that must be made along the way in building one. But more important, it also allows us to suggest in specific terms what our institutional theory of schools actually entails for educational reform—and to emphasize, once again, how essential it is that reforms be founded on theory. The absence of a clear, well-developed theory—and the triumph, in its stead, of platitudes and surface plausibility—leads inevitably to the grab-bag. And to failure and disappointment.

Our guiding principle in the design of a choice system is this: public authority must be put to use in creating a system that is almost entirely beyond the reach of public authority. Because states have primary responsibility for American public education, we think the best way to achieve significant, enduring reform is for states to take the initiative in withdrawing authority from existing institutions and building a new system in which most authority is vested directly in the schools, parents, and students. This restructuring cannot be construed as an exercise in delegation. As long as authority remains "available" at higher levels within state government, it will eventually be used to control the schools. As far as possible, all higher-level authority must be eliminated.[51]

What we propose, more specifically, is that state leaders create a new system of public education with the following properties.

The Supply of Public Schools

• The state will have the responsibility for setting criteria that define what constitutes a "public school" under the new system. These criteria should be quite minimal, roughly corresponding to the criteria many states now employ in accrediting private schools—graduation requirements, health and safety requirements, and teacher certification requirements.

• Any group or organization that applies to the state and meets these minimal criteria must then be chartered as a public school and granted the right to accept students and receive public money.

• Existing private schools will be among those eligible to participate. Their participation should be encouraged, since they constitute a ready supply of often-effective schools. (Our own preference would be to include religious schools as well, as long as their sectarian functions can be kept clearly separate from their educational functions.) Any private schools that do participate will thereby become public schools, as such schools are defined under the new system.

• District governments can continue running their present schools, assuming the latter meet state criteria. They will have authority, however, only over their own schools and not over any of the others that may be chartered by the state.

The Funding of Public Education

• The state will set up a Choice Office in each district, which, among other things, will maintain a record of all school-age children and the level of funding—the "scholarship" amounts—associated with each child. Schools will be compensated directly by this office based on the specific children they enroll. Public money will flow from funding sources (federal, state, and district governments) to the Choice Office and then to schools. At no point will it go to parents or students.

- As it does now, the state will have the right to specify how much, or by what formula, each district must contribute for each child. Our own preference is for an equalization approach that requires wealthier districts to contribute more per child than poor districts do and that guarantees students in all districts an adequate financial foundation. The state's contribution can then be calibrated to bring total spending per child up to whatever dollar amount seems desirable; under an equalization scheme, this would mean a larger state contribution in poor districts than in wealthy ones.

- While it is important to give parents and students as much flexibility as possible, we think it is unwise to allow them to supplement their scholarship amounts with personal funds. Such "add-ons" threaten to produce too many disparities and inequalities within the public system, and many citizens would regard them as unfair and burdensome.

- Complete equalization, on the other hand, strikes us as too stifling and restrictive. A reasonable trade-off, we believe, is to allow for collective add-ons (much as the current system does). The citizens of each district can be given the freedom to decide whether they want to spend more per child than the state requires them to spend. They can then determine how important education is to them and how much they are willing to tax themselves for it. This means that children from different districts may have different-sized scholarships.

- Scholarships may also vary within any given district, and we strongly think that they should. Some students have very special educational needs —arising from economic deprivation, physical handicaps, language difficulties, emotional problems, and other disadvantages—that can only be met effectively through specialized programs that are costly to provide. State and federal programs already appropriate public money to address these problems. Our suggestion is that these funds should take the form of add-ons to student scholarships. At-risk students would then be empowered with bigger scholarships than the others, making them attractive clients to all schools (and stimulating the emergence of new specialty schools).

- The state must pay to support its own Choice Office in each district. Districts may retain as much of their current governing apparatus as they wish—superintendents, school boards, central offices, and all their staff. But they have to pay for them entirely out of the revenue they derive from the scholarships of those children who voluntarily choose to attend district-run schools.[52] Aside from the governance of these schools (which no one need attend), districts will be little more than taxing jurisdictions that allow citizens to make a collective determination as to how large their children's scholarships will be.

Choice Among Schools

• Each student will be free to attend any public school in the state, regardless of district, with the relevant scholarship—consisting of federal, state, and local contributions—flowing to the school of choice. In practice, of course, most students will probably choose schools in reasonable proximity to their homes. But districts will have no claim on their own residents.

• To the extent that tax revenues allow, every effort will be made to provide transportation for students that need it. This is important in helping to open up as many alternatives as possible to all students, especially the poor and those located in rural areas.[53]

• To assist parents and students in choosing among schools, the state will provide a Parent Information Center within its local Choice Office. This Center will collect comprehensive information on each school in the district, and its parent liaisons will meet personally with parents in helping them judge which schools best meet their children's needs. The emphasis here will be on personal contact and involvement. Parents will be required to visit the center at least once, and encouraged to do so often. Meetings will be arranged at all schools so that parents can see first-hand what their choices are.

• The applications process will be handled in simple fashion by the Parent Information Center. Once parents and students decide which schools they prefer, they will fill out applications to each, with parent liaisons available to give advice and assistance (including filling out the applications themselves, if necessary). All applications will be submitted to the Center, which in turn will send them out to the schools.

• Schools will make their own admissions decisions, subject only to nondiscrimination requirements.[54] This is absolutely crucial. Schools must be able to define their own missions and build their own programs in their own ways, and they cannot do this if their student population is thrust on them by outsiders. They must be free to admit as many or as few students as they want, based on whatever criteria they think relevant—intelligence, interest, motivation, behavior, special needs—and they must be free to exercise their own, informal judgments about individual applicants.

• Schools will set their own "tuitions." They may choose to do this explicitly—say, by publicly announcing the minimum scholarship they are willing to accept. They may also do it implicitly by allowing anyone to apply for admission and simply making selections, knowing in advance what each applicant's scholarship amount is. In either case, schools are free to admit students with different-sized scholarships, and they are free to keep the entire scholarship that accompanies each student they have admitted. This gives all schools incentives to attract students with special needs, since these children will have the largest scholarships. It also gives schools incentives to attract students from districts with high base-level scholarships. But no school need restrict itself to students with special needs, nor to students from a single district.

• The applications process must take place within a framework that guarantees each student a school, as well as a fair shot at getting into the school he or she most wants. It is important, however, that such a framework impose only the most minimal restrictions on the schools. We suggest something like the following. The Parent Information Center will have the responsibility for seeing that parents and students are informed, that they have visited the schools that interest them, and that all applications are submitted by a given date. Schools will then be required to make their admissions decisions within a set time, and students who are accepted into one or more schools will be required to select one as their final choice. Students who are not accepted anywhere, as well as schools that have yet to attract as many students as they want, will participate in a second round of applications, which will work the same way. After this second round, some students may remain without schools (although, judging from the East Harlem experience, probably very few). At this point, parent liaisons will take informal action to try to match up these students with appropriate schools. If any students still remain, a special safety-net procedure will be invoked to ensure that each is assigned to a specific school.[55]

• Schools must also be free to expel students or deny them readmission when, based on their own experience and standards, they believe the situation warrants it (as long as they are not "arbitrary and capricious"). This is essential if schools are to define and control their own organizations, and it gives students a strong incentive to live up to their side of the educational "contract."[56]

Governance and Organization of the Public Schools

• Each school must be granted sole authority to determine its own governing structure. It may be run entirely by teachers or even a union. It may vest all power in a principal. It may be built around committees that guarantee representation to the principal, teachers, parents, students, and members of the community. Or it may do something completely different.

The state must refrain from imposing *any* structures or rules that specify how authority is to be exercised within the school. This is meant to include the district-run schools: the state must not impose any governing apparatus on them either. These schools, however, are subordinate units within district government—they are already embedded in a larger organization —and it is the district authorities, not the schools, that have the legal right to determine how they will be governed.

• More generally, the state will do nothing to tell the schools how they must be internally organized to do their work. There will be no requirements for career ladders, advisory committees, textbook selection, in-service training, preparation time, homework, or anything else. The schools will be organized and operated as they see fit.[57]

• Statewide tenure laws will be eliminated, allowing each school to decide for itself whether or not to adopt a tenure policy and what the specifics of that policy will be. This is essential if schools are to have the flexibility they need in building a well-functioning team. Some schools may not offer tenure at all, relying on pay and working conditions to attract the kinds of teachers they want, while others may offer tenure as a supplementary means of compensating and retaining their best teachers. Teachers, meantime, may demand tenure in their negotiations (individual or collective) with schools—and, as in private colleges and universities, the best teachers are well positioned to get it (since they can take their valued services elsewhere). District governments may continue to offer districtwide tenure, along with transfer rights and seniority preference and whatever other personnel policies they have adopted in the past. But these policies apply only to district-run schools and the teachers who work in them.

• Teachers will continue to have a right to join unions and engage in collective bargaining, but the legally prescribed bargaining unit will be the individual school or—as in the case of the district government—the larger organization that runs the school. If teachers in a given school want to join a union or, having done so, want to exact financial or structural concessions, that is up to them. But they will not be allowed to commit other schools or teachers to the same things, and they must suffer the consequences if their victories put them at a competitive disadvantage in supplying quality education. Similarly, if teachers at district-run schools want to remain unionized, their unions may continue to bargain centrally for all of them. But their decisions will not apply to any other public schools in the district.

• The state will continue to certify teachers, but requirements will be minimal—corresponding to those that, in many states, have historically been applied to private schools. In our view, individuals should be certified to teach if they have a bachelor's degree and if their personal history reveals no obvious problems. The question of whether they are truly good teachers will be determined in practice, as schools determine whom to hire, observe their own teachers in action over an extended period of time, and make decisions about merit, promotion, and dismissal. The schools may, as a matter of strategy, choose to pay attention to certain formal indicators of past or future performance, among them: a master's degree, completion of a voluntary teacher certification program at an education school, or voluntary certification by a national board. Some schools may choose to require one or more of these, or perhaps to reward them in various ways. But that is up to the schools—which will be able to look anywhere for good teachers in a now much larger and more dynamic market.

• The state will hold the schools accountable for meeting procedural requirements. It will ensure that schools continue to meet the criteria presumed by their charters, that they adhere to nondiscrimination laws in admissions and other matters, and that they collect and make available to the public—via the Parent Information Center—certain types of information: on their mission, their staff and course offerings, parent and student satisfaction, staff opinions, standardized test scores (which we would make optional), and anything else that would promote informed choice among parents and students.

• The state will not, on the other hand, hold the schools accountable for student achievement or other dimensions that call for assessments of the quality of school performance. When it comes to performance, schools are held accountable from below, by parents and students who directly experience their services and are free to choose. The state plays a crucial supporting role here in monitoring the full and honest disclosure of information by the schools—but it is only a supporting role.

Overview: Choice as a Public System

This proposal calls for fundamental changes in the structure of American public education. Stereotypes aside, however, these changes have nothing to do with "privatizing" the nation's schools. The choice system we have outlined here would be a truly public system—and a democratic one.

We are proposing that the state put its democratic authority to use in creating a new institutional framework. The design and legitimation of this framework would be a democratic act of the most fundamental sort. It would be a social decision, made through the usual processes of democratic governance, by which the people and their representatives specify the structure of a new system of public education.

This framework, as we set it out, is quite flexible and admits of substantial variation on important issues, all of them matters of public policy to be decided by government. Public officials and their constituents would be free to take their own approaches to taxation, equalization, supplementary funding for the disadvantaged, treatment of religious schools, parent add-ons, and other controversial issues of public concern, thus designing choice systems to reflect the unique conditions, preferences, and political forces of their own states.

Once this structural framework is democratically determined, moreover, governments would continue to play important roles within it. State officials and agencies would remain pivotal to the success of public education and to its ongoing operation. They would provide funding, approve applications for new schools, orchestrate and oversee the choice process, elicit full information about schools, provide transportation to students, monitor schools for adherence to the law, and (if they want) design and administer tests of student performance. School districts, meantime, would continue as local taxing jurisdictions, and they would have the option of continuing to operate their own system of schools.

The crucial difference is that direct democratic control of the schools—the very *capacity* for control, not simply its exercise—would essentially be eliminated. Most of those who previously held authority over the schools would have their authority permanently withdrawn, and that authority would be vested in schools, parents, and students. Schools would be legally autonomous: free to govern themselves as they want, specify their own goals and programs and methods, design their own organizations, select their own student bodies, and make their own personnel decisions. Parents and students would be legally empowered to choose among alternative schools, aided by institutions designed to promote active involvement, well-informed decisions, and fair treatment.

Politics, Ideas, and America's Schools

We have no illusions that a true choice system of this type stands a good chance of being adopted in any single state, much less throughout the country. Almost everyone in the reform movement has something nice to say about choice nowadays as long as "choice" means little more than giving parents and students additional freedom in selecting among schools. Choice is politically attractive when it is not designed to do much. But when it is designed to get to the root of the problem—when it seeks to liberate the schools by means of a thorough transformation of public institutions—it generates fierce opposition from every nook and cranny of the educational establishment. And this is enough to dim the prospects for real reform.

Still, we are cautiously optimistic. As the Progressive movement demonstrated many years ago, attempts to transform political institutions are not doomed to fail. They may succeed when they have widespread support and when the resources of powerful social groups can be mobilized behind change. Something of the sort could happen during the next decade. The fact is that choice is highly popular among ordinary citizens and is gaining adherents among reformers and state officials, particularly governors. Bold executive leadership and broad popular support, especially if combined with the concentrated power of a unified business community—which, in effect, might reassume the historical role it played during the Progressive era as the political vanguard of reform—could succeed in overturning the established order and creating a new system of public education.

Cautious optimism is better than no optimism at all. Just a few years ago, the suggestion that choice might succeed in restructuring American education would have been regarded as pure fantasy. Times have changed. Important as this is, though, expectations about the future have to be based on reality, and the reality is that the American political deck is stacked against institutional reform. As we look ahead, the most reasonable scenario is for limited success: choice will likely gain in popularity during the 1990s, but it will be adopted in bits and pieces along with lots of other reforms that, in the aggregate, decentralize but preserve the traditional system of democratic control.

We do not mean, however, to complain about how democracy works or to urge public officials to get their acts together and make it work differently. It works the way it works—which, in shorthand, is precisely the point we have been trying to make from the beginning. We have endeavored to develop an argument about the causal connection between schools and institutions, and to show that the normal, routine operation of educational institutions, whatever form they might take, has pervasive consequences for the organization and performance of schools. The key to understanding why America's public schools are failing is to be found in a deeper understanding of how its traditional institutions of democratic control actually work. The nation is experiencing a crisis in public education not because these democratic institutions have functioned perversely or improperly or unwisely, but because they have functioned quite normally. Democratic control normally produces ineffective schools. This is how it works.

Reformers have paid little attention to institutions. All the talk in recent years about "restructuring" would seem to express a recognition that institutions are important, yet it really does not. Most reformers agree that top-down control is bad, that it promotes bureaucracy, and that something has to be done to make schools more autonomous and teachers more professional. But in trying to bring about such a transformation, they simply take it for granted that the public schools will continue to be governed by the same institutions they have always been governed by, and that "restructuring" within this familiar framework will do the job. The public debate is not about direct democratic control as a form of governance. The debate is about finding more enlightened ways to exercise it.

The ideas about schools that have guided reformers are basically correct, in our view. They are just incomplete. They focus on the micro-world of schools and have a good deal to say about the makeup and immediate causes of effective organization; but they have almost nothing to say about institutions. The most fundamental questions, as a result, have generally gone unasked and have not been an integral part of reformist thinking. In what ways do schools reflect institutional settings? How does this come about and why does it happen? Do some institutions tend to promote and nurture effective organizations? Do others, perhaps in spite of everyone's best intentions, promote and nurture ineffective organizations? What are the consequences of direct democratic control for the public schools? These are the sorts of issues that strike to the heart of what educational theory and research have left unexplored over the years, producing a giant gap in the knowledge base that reformers have relied on in figuring out how to improve the nation's schools.

We do not expect everyone to accept the argument we have made here. In fact, we expect most of those who speak with authority on educational matters—leaders and academics within the educational community—to reject it. But we will regard our effort as a success if it directs attention to America's institutions of democratic control and provokes serious debate about their consequences for the nation's public schools. Whether or not our own conclusions are right, the fact is that these issues are truly fundamental to an understanding of schools, and they have so far played no part in the national debate. If educational reform is to have any chance at all of succeeding, this has to change.

In the meantime, we can only believe that the current "revolution" in American public education will prove a disappointment. It might have succeeded had it actually been a revolution, but it was not and was never intended to be, despite the lofty rhetoric. Revolutions dismember old institutions and replace them with new ones. The 1980s reform movement never seriously thought about the old institutions, and certainly never considered them part of the problem. They were, as they had always been, part of the solution—and, for that matter, part of the definition of what democracy and public education are all about.

This identification has never been valid. There is nothing in the concept of democracy to require that schools be subject to direct control by school boards, superintendents, central offices, departments of education, and other arms of government. Nor is there anything in the concept of public education to require that schools be governed in this way. There are many paths to democracy and public education. The path America has been treading for the past half-century is exacting a heavy price—one the nation and its children can ill afford to bear, and need not. It is time, we think, to get to the root of the problem.

NOTES

1. For a review and evaluation of the early wave of reforms, see Denis P. Doyle and Terry W. Hartle, *Excellence in Education: The States Take Charge* (Washington: American Enterprise Institute for Public Policy Research, 1985); and William Chance, *"the best of educations": Reforming America's Public Schools in the 1980s* (Washington: John D. and Catherine T. MacArthur Foundation, 1986).

2. Among the more influential calls for a second wave of reform are Carnegie Forum on Education and the Economy, Task Force on Teaching as a Profession, *A Nation Prepared: Teachers for the 21st Century* (New York: 1986); and National Governors' Association, *A Time for Results: The Governors' 1991 Report on Education* (Washington: National Governors' Association, 1986).

3. For an overview of the 1980s reforms that includes an assessment of the limited achievements (thus far) of second-wave proposals, see William A. Firestone, Susan H. Fuhrman, and Michael W. Kirst, "The Progress of Reform: An Appraisal of State Education Initiatives," Research Report Series, RR-014 (Rutgers University, Center for Policy Research in Education, 1989). See also Jane L. David, *Restructuring in Progress: Lessons from Pioneering Districts* (Washington: National Governors' Association, 1989); and Richard F. Elmore, *Early Experience in Restructuring Schools: Voices from the Field* (Washington: National Governors' Association, 1988).

4. In the aggregate, expenditures on elementary and secondary education rose at least $50 billion during the 1980s. Expenditures per pupil rose 50 percent in real terms, reaching $5,246 per child in 1989–90. Tom Snyder and W. Vance Grant, "1989 Back to School Forecast," press release, National Center for Education Statistics, August 24, 1989; and National Center for

Education Statistics, Office of Educational Research and Improvement, *Digest of Education Statistics, 1988* (Department of Education, 1988), pp. 124, 132.

5. See Eric A. Hanushek, "The Economics of Schooling: Production and Efficiency in Public Schools," *Journal of Economic Literature,* vol. 24 (September 1986), pp. 1141–77.

6. For spending figures on public and private schools, see C. Emily Feistritzer, *Cheating Our Children: Why We Need School Reform* (Washington: National Center for Educational Information, 1985). For a comparative analysis of public and private school performance, see James S. Coleman, Thomas Hoffer, and Sally Kilgore, *High School Achievement: Public, Catholic, and Private Schools Compared* (Basic Books, 1982); and James S. Coleman and Thomas Hoffer, *Public and Private High Schools: The Impact of Communities* (Basic Books, 1987).

7. It is also relatively inexpensive, easy to do, widely popular among people in and out of the educational community—and, not surprisingly, far-and-away the most common of educational reforms to be adopted in the 1980s. Some forty-five states either adopted new requirements or strengthened their existing ones. See Firestone, Fuhrman, and Kirst, "Progress of Reform," pp. 17–20.

8. In most states, reforms have only recently gone into effect, so it is difficult to evaluate their effects with much confidence. At this point, however, the available evidence is not heartening. A recent study by the General Accounting Office, based on a sample of 61,000 students in four states, concludes that stricter graduation requirements have had no significant effect. See "High School Graduation Requirements Said Not to Affect Achievement Test Scores," *Chronicle of Higher Education,* October 4, 1989, p. A20. For a more general discussion of the available evidence and the issues involved in assessing it, see William H. Clune with Paula White and Janice Patterson, *The Implementation and Effects of High School Graduation Requirements: First Steps toward Curricular Reform* (Rutgers University, Center for Policy Research in Education, 1989).

9. This assumes that within feasible salary ranges, salaries are not contingent on teacher performance—which is generally true of teacher compensation today. On the relationship between salaries and performance, see Hanushek, "Economics of Schooling"; and Myron Lieberman, "Are Teachers Underpaid?" *Public Interest,* no. 84 (Summer 1986), pp. 12–28.

10. For discussions of state efforts in strengthening certification requirements, see Firestone, Fuhrman, and Kirst, "Progress of Reform"; Denis P. Doyle

and Terry W. Hartle, *Excellence in Education;* and Linda Darling-Hammond and Barnett Berry, *The Evolution of Teacher Policy* (Santa Monica, Calif.: Rand Corporation, Center for Policy Research in Education, 1988).

11. See C. Emily Feistritzer, *Teacher Crisis: Myth or Reality? A State-by-State Analysis* (Washington: National Center for Educational Information, 1986).

12. See Carnegie Forum on Education and the Economy, *A Nation Prepared.*

13. Perhaps the most widely touted statewide experiment in merit pay, adopted by Florida in 1983, collapsed of its own bureaucratic weight when implementation produced little more than confusion, dissatisfaction, and conflict. It was discontinued in 1986. See Firestone, Fuhrman, and Kirst, "Progress of Reform," p. 32. More generally, on the problems of implementing merit pay schemes, see David K. Cohen and Richard J. Murnane, "The Merits of Merit Pay," *Public Interest,* no. 80 (Summer 1985), pp. 3–30; Harry P. Hatry and John M. Greiner, *Issues and Case Studies in Teacher Incentive Plans* (Washington: Urban Institute Press, 1985); and Henry C. Johnson, Jr., ed., *Merit, Money, and Teachers' Careers: Studies on Merit Pay and Career Ladders for Teachers* (Lanham, Md.: University Press of America, 1985).

14. For an overview of the kinds of tests that states have adopted, see *Creating Responsible and Responsive Accountability Systems,* Report of the OERI State Accountability Study Group (Department of Education, 1988).

15. For more extensive treatments than we can provide here, see Daniel Koretz, "Arriving in Lake Wobegon: Are Standardized Tests Exaggerating Achievement and Distorting Instruction?" *American Educator,* vol. 12 (Summer 1988), pp. 8–15; Doug A. Archbald and Fred M. Newmann, *Beyond Standardized Testing: Assessing Authentic Academic Achievement in the Secondary School* (Reston, Va.: National Association of Secondary School Principals, 1988); and Craig E. Richards and Mwalimu Shujaa, "The State Education Accountability Movement: Impact on Schools?" Rutgers University, Center for Policy Research on Education, 1988.

16. To the extent that these ideas have been put into practice, most of the action has taken place at the district rather than the state level, with the states' role largely restricted to providing encouragement and seed money for local reforms. Districts that have been most aggressive in restructuring, moreover, have often been those facing serious problems or crises.

17. On Chicago, see Herbert J. Walberg and others, *We Can Rescue Our Children: The Cure for Chicago's Public School Crisis—With Lessons for the Rest of America* (Chicago: Heartland Institute, 1988). On Rochester, see Adam Urbanski, "Public Schools of Choice and Education Reform," in Joe Nathan, ed., *Public Schools by Choice* (St. Paul: Institute for Learning and

Teaching, 1989), pp. 225–38; Ellen Graham, "Starting from Scratch: Rochester Wipes the Slate Clean, Gives Teachers New Responsibility," *Wall Street Journal*, March 31, 1989, pp. R4–6; and Jerry Buckley, "A Blueprint for Better Schools," *U.S. News and World Report*, January 18, 1988, pp. 60–65. On Dade County, see Lynn Olson, "The Sky's the Limit: Dade Ventures Self-Governance," *Education Week*, December 2, 1987, p. 1; and Lynn Olson, "Dade's School Restructuring: A Trip into Uncharted Territory," *Education Week*, December 2, 1987, p. 19.

18. For general discussions of the basic features of school-based management and some of the problems and issues that it raises, see James W. Guthrie and Rodney J. Reed, *Educational Administration and Policy: Effective Leadership for American Schools* (Prentice-Hall, 1986); James W. Guthrie, "School-Based Management: The Next Needed Education Reform," *Phi Delta Kappan*, vol. 68 (December 1986), pp. 305–09; Ted Kolderie, "School-Site Management: Rhetoric and Reality," University of Minnesota, Public Services Redesign Project, Humphrey Institute of Public Affairs, 1988; and Betty Malen, Rodney T. Ogawa, and Jennifer Kranz, "What Do We Know about School-Based Management? A Case Study of the Literature—A Call for Research," paper presented at the Conference on Choice and Control in American Education, University of Wisconsin, 1989.

19. See Kolderie, "School-Site Management."

20. The dangers of instability are greatest in the early years and should decline over time. If the new structures do manage to survive for an extended period of time, those benefited and empowered by them will tend to organize, marshal their resources, and defend the system against change. The real question is whether these kinds of decentralizing reforms can count on withstanding political vicissitudes long enough for this to happen.

21. Carnegie Forum on Education and the Economy, *A Nation Prepared*.

22. For a discussion of the ideas behind teacher empowerment and some of the efforts to put them into effect in districts around the country, see Darling-Hammond and Berry, *The Evolution of Teacher Policy*; Firestone, Fuhrman, and Kirst, "Progress of Reform"; and Susan Moore Johnson, "Teachers, Power, and School Change," paper presented at the Conference on Choice and Control in American Education, University of Wisconsin, 1989.

23. See Blake Rodman, "N.E.A. Pursues Its Plan to Establish State Boards Controlled by Teachers," *Education Week*, April 29, 1987, p. 1.

24. Carnegie Forum on Education and the Economy, *A Nation Prepared*.

25. American Federation of Teachers, "School Based Management," *Radius*, vol. 1 (May 1988), pp. 1–5. For the origin of this proposal, see Myron

Lieberman, "A Foundation Approach to Merit Pay," *Phi Delta Kappan,* vol. 41 (December 1959), pp. 118–22.

26. See, for instance, Kenneth J. Meier, *Regulation: Politics, Bureaucracy, and Economics* (St. Martin's Press, 1985).

27. Rodman, "N.E.A. Pursues Its Plan To Establish State Boards Controlled by Teachers."

28. For overviews of the recent choice movement within the public sector, including applications to desegregation, see Nathan, ed., *Public Schools by Choice;* "The Call for Choice: Competition in the Educational Marketplace," *Education Week,* June 24, 1987, pp. C1–C24; and Chester E. Finn, Jr., "Education That Works: Make the Schools Compete," *Harvard Business Review,* vol. 65 (September-October 1987), pp. 63–68.

29. A Times Mirror nationwide survey conducted by the Gallup Organization in January 1988 found that 49 percent of the country is "more likely" and only 27 percent "less likely" to vote for a presidential candidate who supports giving parents vouchers to pay for their kids' education. Times Mirror Center for the People and the Press, "The People, the Press, and Politics: Survey II," January 8–17, 1988. Throughout the 1980s, national polls showed that the public overwhelmingly endorses the general concept of parental choice. In 1987, 71 percent of the public said yes, parents in this community should have the right to choose which local schools their children attend. Alec M. Gallup and David L. Clark, "The 19th Annual Gallup Poll of the Public's Attitudes toward the Public Schools," *Phi Delta Kappan,* vol. 69 (September 1987), pp. 17–30. On parent and public reactions to particular choice plans, see Joe Nathan, "Results and Future Prospects of State Efforts to Increase Choice among Schools," *Phi Delta Kappan,* vol. 68 (June 1987), pp. 746–52.

30. National Governors' Association, *Time for Results.*

31. See, for example, Carnegie Forum on Education and the Economy, *A Nation Prepared;* David T. Kearns and Denis P. Doyle, *Winning the Brain Race: A Bold Plan to Make Our Schools Competitive* (San Francisco: Institute for Contemporary Studies, 1988); James S. Coleman, "Choice, Community, and Future Schools," paper presented at the Conference on Choice and Control in American Education, University of Wisconsin, 1989; and David S. Seeley, *Education through Partnership: Mediating Structures and Education* (Ballinger, 1981).

32. See, for example, Committee for Economic Development, *Investing in Our Children;* and City Club of Chicago, *Educational Choice: A Catalyst for School Reform,* prepared by Edward Marciniak, a report of the Task Force on Education of the City Club of Chicago (August 1989).

33. See *Education Week,* "Call for Choice." Note also that support for choice is highest among the poor and racial minorities. In a January 1988 Times Mirror poll, 61 percent of the "partisan poor" said they would be more likely to support a presidential candidate "who supports giving parents vouchers to pay for their kids' education." Times Mirror Center for the People and the Press.

34. "Call for Choice"; and Adam Urbanski, "Public Schools of Choice and Education Reform," in Nathan, ed., *Public Schools by Choice,* pp. 225–38.

35. See Mary Anne Raywid, "The Mounting Case for Schools of Choice," in Nathan, ed., *Public Schools by Choice,* pp. 13–40.

36. Rolf K. Blank, "Educational Effects of Magnet Schools," paper presented at the Conference on Choice and Control in American Education, University of Wisconsin, 1989.

37. See *Education Week,* "Call for Choice," pp. C6–C9. See also Joe Nathan, "Progress, Problems, and Prospects with State Choice Plans," in Nathan, ed., *Public Schools by Choice,* pp. 203–24; and Mary Haywood Metz, *Different by Design: The Context and Character of Three Magnet Schools* (New York: Routledge and Kegan Paul, 1986).

38. For reviews of what is now a rather extensive empirical literature, see Raywid, "Mounting Case for Schools of Choice"; Mary Anne Raywid, "A Synthesis of Research on Schools of Choice," *Educational Leadership,* vol. 41 (April 1984), pp. 70–78; and Richard F. Elmore, "Choice as an Instrument of Public Policy: Evidence from Education and Health Care," paper presented at the Conference on Choice and Control in American Education, University of Wisconsin, 1989. For a more critical treatment, see Henry M. Levin, "The Theory of Choice Applied to Education," paper presented at the Conference on Choice and Control in American Education, University of Wisconsin, 1989.

39. For discussions of the Minnesota reforms and early evidence on their effects, see Jessie Montano, "Choice Comes to Minnesota"; and Joe Nathan, "Progress, Problems, and Prospects with State Choice Plans," in Nathan, ed., *Public Schools by Choice,* pp. 165–80, 203–24. At this writing, six other states—Arkansas, Idaho, Iowa, Nebraska, Ohio, and Utah—have also adopted statewide systems of public school choice.

40. On the design, operation, and recent history of the Cambridge system, see Robert Peterkin and Dorothy Jones, "Schools of Choice in Cambridge, Massachusetts," in Nathan, ed., *Public Schools by Choice,* pp. 125–48; and Christine H. Rossell and Charles L. Glenn, "The Cambridge Controlled Choice Plan," *Urban Review,* vol. 20 (Summer 1988), pp. 75–94.

41. Applications are not, of course, uniform across all schools. As one would expect, the best schools (by reputation) get more than their share, the worst get less. Cambridge officials have taken applications as a signal in determining which schools need attention and improvement—in one case, appointing a new principal and giving him the flexibility to transform the school to enhance its appeal. In subsequent years, applications to that school rose dramatically. See Rossell and Glenn, "Cambridge Controlled Choice Plan."

42. For evidence on test scores, enrollments, and other indicators of improvement, see especially Peterkin and Jones, "Schools of Choice in Cambridge," p. 129; and Rossell and Glenn, "Cambridge Controlled Choice Plan." For discussions of racial balance in particular, see Michael J. Alves, "Cambridge Desegregation Succeeding," *Integrated Education,* vol. 21 (January–December 1983), pp. 178–87; and Ross Zerchykov, "A Context Note: Choice, Diversity, and Desegregation in Massachusetts," *Equity and Choice,* vol. 2 (May 1986), pp. 9–16.

43. The most comprehensive accounts of the East Harlem system are Sy Fliegel, "Parental Choice in East Harlem Schools," in Nathan, ed., *Public Schools by Choice,* pp. 95–112; and Raymond J. Domanico, "Model for Choice: A Report on Manhattan's District 4," *Education Policy Paper,* no. 1 (New York: Manhattan Institute for Policy Research, 1989). This system has also received extensive attention in the media, both because it is such a radical departure from tradition and because it has proven so successful. See, for example, Catherine Foster, "Junior High Choice in Harlem," *Christian Science Monitor,* April 5, 1989, p. 12; and Jane Perlez, "Year of Honor in East Harlem Schools," *New York Times,* June 27, 1987, p. 29.

44. The descriptive information we provide here and in following notes is taken from Fliegel, "Parental Choice in East Harlem"; and Domanico, "Model for Choice."

45. For the complete list, see Domanico, "Model for Choice," p. 9.

46. On the nature of the scandals, see Joyce Purnick, "2 Who Made Loans to Alvarado Got Extra School Pay," *New York Times,* March 8, 1984, p. 1; and Neil A. Lewis, "School Officials Being Ousted over Funds," *New York Times,* December 8, 1988, p. B1.

47. Edward B. Fiske, "The Alternative Schools of Famous District 4: Accolades and Better Attendance Are Not Enough," *New York Times,* November 1, 1989, p. B8.

48. For an overview of recent reformist thinking that nicely illustrates how choice fits into the grab-bag of second-wave reforms, see "Call for Choice." For a succinct statement, see "Not By Choice Alone," *Washington Post,* October 21, 1989, p. A24.

49. One of the best examples is Rochester, New York, which has adopted virtually every reform imaginable, including choice. For sympathetic discussions, see Adam Urbanski, "Public Schools of Choice and Education Reform"; Ellen Graham, "Starting from Scratch: Rochester Wipes the Slate Clean, Gives Teachers New Responsibility"; and Jerry Buckley, "Blueprint for Better Schools."

50. The classic argument for vouchers is developed in Milton and Rose Friedman, *Free to Choose: A Personal Statement* (Avon, 1981), pp. 140–78. A similar argument is now prominently made in Myron Lieberman, *Privatization and Educational Choice* (St. Martin's Press, 1989), though Lieberman also endorses other market options such as contracting out for educational services. The Friedmans' argument is of course associated by educators with political conservatism. But vouchers have also been proposed by social democrats on the left, who seek to enlist markets in the cause of justice and equal opportunity for the poor. Perhaps the most influential of these proposals has come from Christopher Jencks, who, along with like-minded colleagues, urged administrators within the Office of Economic Opportunity (within both the late Johnson and early Nixon presidencies) to take vouchers seriously and encourage experimentation by states and districts. Their most tangible success, if it can be called that, is the ill-fated Alum Rock experiment—which, because of poor design and implementation (arising in part from the resistance of established interests), cannot meaningfully be considered a test of anything. See David K. Cohen and Eleanor Farrar, "Power to the Parents? The Story of Educational Vouchers," *Public Interest,* no. 48 (Summer 1977), pp. 72–97. Probably the most widely recognized voucher proposal since that time has been offered by Coons and Sugarman, who, to our knowledge, cannot readily be placed in an ideological camp. See John E. Coons and Stephen D. Sugarman, *Education by Choice: The Case for Family Control* (University of California Press, 1978).

51. State legislatures and governors must retain the basic authority to govern their educational systems. Yet they, too, will come under pressure in the future to use their authority to control the schools from above—and thus to destroy what they are trying to create. There is ultimately no solution to this dilemma. A good way of mitigating it, however, would be to design institutions around fully decentralized authority and then install them through constitutional amendment. The legal foundation of the new system would then be very difficult to change or violate once put in place. And, because state constitutions are the ultimate authorities in state government, they have the power to constrain what future legislatures and governors (and the political groups that pressure them) can do in controlling the schools.

52. To the extent that district governments must make political decisions about taxation and perhaps other matters in representing all citizens within their boundaries, they should be allowed to cover these expenses with local tax money or state subsidies. The point is that, in covering the costs of running their own schools, districts must rely only on student scholarships.

53. One way to arrange transportation would be for the Choice Office to operate a system of buses for getting students to drop-off points throughout the district, where schools (or contractors hired by the schools) would then pick them up. The state would pay for all this, reimbursing schools on a per child basis (just as they do for scholarships). Many and perhaps most children, however, would probably choose a school close to their home or would be driven by a parent; and this would limit the state's transportation job, as well as its expense. Moreover, if the number and quality of schools increased, as we fully expect they would in a choice system, most students could have attractive options near their homes.

54. Desegregation plans may call for additional rules, quotas for example. On the compatibility of choice and desegregation plans, see Patricia M. Lines, "The Denial of Choice and *Brown* v. *Board of Education,*" *Metropolitan Education,* no. 4 (Spring 1987), pp. 108–27.

55. For example, they might be assigned by lottery to schools in reasonable proximity to their homes; and all schools, as a precondition for becoming public, would then be required to run the risk of having an occasional student assigned to them.

56. There is little reason to believe that expulsions (or even denials for re-admission) will be common. In the first place, schools and students have voluntarily chosen one another; most of the time, they will be happy together. Second, expulsions are quite infrequent in the existing private sector, where schools have long been free to expel at will. Third, schools that frequently expel students will acquire a reputation for doing so, which will hurt them in the application process; knowing this, they should be very hesitant to expel except in the most egregious cases. And finally (although we think this is unnecessary), special rules might be set up to discourage expulsions: for example, a rule requiring an expelling school to fill that slot with a student who has been expelled from another school.

57. This implies, among other things, that the state will do nothing to impose teacher professionalism on the schools. Teacher professionalism will emerge from below as teachers are granted the autonomy to control their own schools and their own work, and as schools develop their own structures for governing themselves and pursuing their missions.

18

INCENTIVES

LINKING RESOURCES, PERFORMANCE,
AND ACCOUNTABILITY

Eric A. Hanushek

The use of financial incentives to improve teacher and school performance continues to be a highly debated practice. Incentives encompass individual and group merit pay, reward and sanction movements, performance contracting, for-profit school management companies, charter schools, and so on. Because many of the choice movements are still in nascent stages, research on the effectiveness of various models is still under way.

○

IF A SINGLE, GLARING LESSON is to be learned from past attempts at school reform, it is that the ability to improve academic performance using standard, uniformly applied policy is limited. State and federal authorities have instituted numerous regulations, spending programs, and general policy goals—all to little avail. Here we chart an alternative course. Premised on the evidence that no single reform is capable of solving the problems of every school, we focus on administrative structures designed to create incentives for each school to find and adopt those reforms best suited to its individual situation.

If there is no single policy cure for the ills of individual schools, then policymakers have little choice but to undertake the daunting task of managing diversity, giving local decisionmakers the freedom to devise educational programs appropriate to their situation and the discipline to ensure their effectiveness. The most appropriate, indeed the only possible place to begin promoting diversity is at the basic unit of the school: the individual teacher in an individual classroom.

Study after study demonstrates the importance of the classroom teacher. Estimates suggest that in a single school year an average student with a good teacher can progress more than a full grade level faster than an average student with a poor teacher. The same also holds for disadvantaged students. Some teachers are better at improving the achievement of children than others. Even after teachers have been through the standardization imposed by the process of state certification and school-hiring policies, large differences remain—as any parent of school-age children knows well. In truth, probably every principal and teacher in the country believes that there are important differences in the abilities of their colleagues. Yet, despite general agreement that the difference between good teachers and bad is great, few participants in the debate agree on the qualities that constitute a good teacher.

Concerted efforts notwithstanding, developing a description of "the" good teacher has defied educational researchers and educational decisionmakers alike. Several qualities, of course, seem desirable. For example, teachers should know their subject matter, be sensitive to the problems and needs of their students, and involve their students in the educational process. But this is far from a complete definition, and even these rudimentary qualities have yet to be distilled into employment criteria that ensure that teachers possessing these qualities will be hired, promoted, or kept by schools.

The simple reason for the failure to define best practice among teachers would seem to be that there is none. No single set of teacher characteristics, teacher behaviors, curricular approaches, or organizational devices guarantees a high probability of success in the classroom. Instead different teachers succeed, or fail, in very different ways. What works well for one teacher may not work at all for another, and each teacher must find the approach that best suits his or her own personality and skills and the needs of the children. One teacher may be particularly effective by employing word games with children from well-to-do backgrounds who have reading deficiencies; another may be able to motivate students by recounting personal experiences from living in Southeast Asia; yet another may be energized by close, interactive contacts with other teachers in the school. In otherwise identical situations, two teachers might apply two very different approaches and produce exactly the same level of student performance.

For that reason, detailed central regulations and directives on the nature of the instructional process and the characteristics of school personnel are bound to be wasteful and perhaps even self-defeating. So it is not too surprising that efforts by states and local school boards to improve school performance by tighter central regulation have for the most part failed.

Unfortunately, however, the overwhelming theoretical logic of the argument for more decentralized management of schools has thus far failed to work in practice. The many experiments in school decentralization have generally failed to improve student performance. The reason decentralized management has not yielded the anticipated benefits seems to be the lack of clear performance incentives, which would keep the focus on achievement even amid decentralization. Appropriately designed and consistently applied incentives appear essential to improving schools.

Performance Incentives

The strength of performance incentives is their ability to deal with complexity. By rewarding participants in the educational process when they do well and penalizing them when they do poorly, schools can harness the energy, ability, and inventiveness of individuals. The rewards to teachers may be explicit monetary rewards, or they may be a wide variety of intrinsic rewards, such as special recognition, more latitude in classroom and activity assignment, or expanded travel and training opportunities. Effective teaching is positively reinforced, and defective teaching discouraged. Performance incentives also reward effective support structures but not constraining structures.

Performance incentives are a very different approach from the current system. They do not attempt to dictate which teaching methods will work, although providing good information on what has worked in the past is an important element of any well-functioning system of incentives. Incentives encourage individuals to decide for themselves which route toward improved achievement is most appropriate in specific circumstances. Thus incentives can be viewed as a way to expand the methods for delivering a good education.

The ability to distinguish good results is crucial to any working system of incentives. Flexibility in the means of education must be balanced by crystalline clarity regarding the desired ends. This requires a highly developed ability to identify the difference between good and bad performance.

Developing and employing incentive structures is not in itself easy. As we will discuss, it requires both extensive experimentation and evaluation of the results. Failures and misstarts are inevitable, given the lack of experience with such schemes. The full advantages may come only after a substantial number of new teachers and school personnel, with skills different from those currently plentiful in the schools, have been induced to enter teaching. Nonetheless, performance incentives remain the best hope for getting on a path of long-run improvement.

Performance Measurement and Value Added

One crucial point must be explained at the outset. The performance measurements used in managing incentive systems must be able to distinguish between what a given student has achieved and what a teacher has achieved with that student. Schools are but one facet of the educational process, and measurement systems must recognize—and differentiate among—the various sources contributing to student achievement.

Students come to school with differing abilities, motivations, family support, and previous achievement. A student's performance today also reflects his or her past teachers. Thus, for example, the reading performance of a student at the end of the sixth grade reflects not only the inputs of the sixth-grade teacher, but also the inputs of all previous teachers. Some families reinforce good schools. Some students are simply brighter and more able to learn and progress than others.

Any incentive system based on performance cannot ignore such differences among students. Schools and teachers should be held responsible only for factors under their control and rewarded for what they contribute to the educational process, that is, the value they add to student performance. It would be unfair, and counterproductive, to hold individual teachers responsible for the previous poor performance of their pupils.

Identifying the factors that account for differences in achievement does not and should not mean that schools either accept or condone poor performance among identifiable groups of students. Improving performance for all is the very heart and purpose of school reform. But just as accurate diagnosis is a first step toward effective cure, school officials and their management systems must be able to identify the sources of poor performance. So incentives must recognize and take into account the varying sources of differences in performance.

Alternative Systems of Performance Incentives

The current structure of schools already has many incentives built into it—as does any system of management. The problem with these school incentives, however, is that they are linked only loosely to student performance. Most teachers and school administrators are interested in the performance of their students, but, unfortunately, this performance has little to do with the rewards to the individual teacher. Instead teachers' monetary rewards and career progress are determined by other factors, such as the teachers' attendance pattern, the amount of preparation for class, and the time spent in extracurricular activities. Similar observations can be made for the incentives that apply to principals and superintendents. Intrinsic rewards are also only weakly linked to student performance in most schools.

The idea of developing stronger performance incentives directly focused on student achievement has vast appeal, and it is the subject of frequent discussion. But incentives seldom have been tried, and experiments with them have been even more limited. Recorded analyses lack many of the details crucial to judging their more general applicability. Much more experimentation will be required to find performance incentives that perform. Nonetheless, some general guidelines are obvious.

Performance incentive systems are intended to attract and retain the best teachers and administrators and to focus their energies and abilities on achieving the results that should matter most to schools: teaching students. An effective system of performance incentives will permit a variety of approaches to education. Indeed, with the same incentive system and with equal results, schools might well pursue radically different approaches, each suited to the requirements of specific students and to the talents of the school personnel. Some schools might opt for separate "academies" with integrated instruction for small groups of students; others might organize the whole school around a specific theme, such as the arts; still others might retain traditional, separate classroom instruction; some might use television to provide major parts of the instruction, combined with tutorials for individual students. A performance-oriented group of teachers and parents could choose any one of these approaches, depending on the desire and skills of the school community.

The effectiveness of an incentive system depends directly on how individuals act when faced with a given pattern of rewards. So rewards and punishments must be sufficient to get people to change their behavior, and they must be precise in their effect. Impact and effectiveness flow from the details.

Several basic frameworks, or organizing principles, can be used to design incentives. Within any of these frameworks, the precise incentive systems that are put into place may be good or bad, effective or ineffective. Although the frameworks create the outlines of improved incentive systems, the details of contracts and operations actually put into place are critical. Discovering those details should be the focus of experimentation.

We will now consider two basic types of incentive frameworks. The first retains the basic administrative structure of existing school systems while altering the performance incentives for people within those systems. The second framework begins by fundamentally revising the structure of schools, to the point of virtually eliminating the current system in some cases.

Incentive Frameworks Within Existing Schools

Even without changing the overall organization of the schooling system, many incentive systems can be designed to focus attention and effort on student performance. Except for merit pay for teachers, there is little experience with any of these systems, and, unfortunately, the results of past uses of merit pay for teachers have not been encouraging. The challenge, therefore, is to use today's limited experience as the basis for a program of testing and evaluating operational versions of the alternatives to determine which approaches are most useful in given circumstances.

Performance Contracting

The basic idea of performance contracting is that, instead of employing teachers and administrators directly, school systems contract with an independent firm to provide educational services to the students of a particular school. The contract might stipulate any number of things: from requiring the firm to achieve specified reading proficiencies among students to limitations on the cost of providing ancillary school services. The contractor's rewards relate directly to the satisfaction of the contractual terms, that is, the contractor is paid according to outcomes.

An early experience in Texarkana, Arkansas, in the late 1960s seemed to suggest real potential for performance contracting, but the evidence was subsequently discredited (Exhibit 18.1). More recently, Dade County, Florida; Baltimore; Hartford; and other localities have contracted with profitmaking suppliers to run some schools. A growing number of firms are advertising their desire to enter into similar arrangements. These firms are willing to compete with others and with the public schools to provide education, demonstrating their belief in the possibility of improving schools. The policy question comes down to whether or not such entrepreneurial energy can be harnessed to benefit society.

In many ways, this approach is the most straightforward example of performance-based incentives in education. The school system and the contractor define specific measurable goals, and rewards are based directly on

Exhibit 18.1. The OEO Performance Contracting Experiment.

Long-standing concerns about the education of disadvantaged students led the Office of Economic Opportunity, the operational agency for the War on Poverty, to launch an experiment in 1970 in performance contracting. Promising-looking results from schools in Texarkana, Arkansas, induced OEO to contract with private firms to provide instruction to public school students in selected sites around the country. In the end, the investigation discovered more about the difficulties of devising good experiments than the advantages or disadvantages of performance contracting.

The experiment began when OEO asked firms to bid on providing reading and mathematics instruction to a group of academically deficient students in grades one through three and seven through nine. Six firms, out of thirty-six bidders, were selected and offered very similar incentive contracts. The contract provided no payment for any student who failed to progress a full grade level during the 1970–71 academic year. Faster gains earned relatively small increases over the basic payment, and the extra payments were capped at gains of 1.9 grade levels. This incentive structure meant that both "slow" learners (likely to gain less than a full grade level) and "extra fast" learners (likely to gain near the top) yielded low returns, and might be a significant loss if they required more than average resources. Although firms could break even only when students gained 1.6 grade-level equivalents or more, they were eager to participate because they hoped for future performance contracting business.

The very unfavorable terms of the contract led one firm to go bankrupt, two others to drop direct classroom work during the year, and all six to refuse to participate after the first year. In the end, the average performance of students was roughly equivalent to a control group that received normal school instruction.

These results demonstrate the importance of developing experience in experimentation and evaluation. Because apparently sound incentives can lead to undesirable behavior and because little is yet known about the effects of many potential policies, experimentation by state and federal governments is sensible. The fact that many of the experiments will not improve student performance is all the more reason for systematic evaluation—so that one district can learn from another's failures instead of duplicating them.

Despite the failure of the OEO experiments, the idea of hiring private firms to manage school programs has reappeared. The Baltimore school district has contracted with an outside firm to run several of its public schools, and other districts are either experimenting with the idea or seriously contemplating it. These projects, however, are not designed as true experiments, and there is no assurance that many generalizations from these attempts will be possible.

Source: *Gramlich and Koshel (1975); Schmidt (1994).*

those goals. The scope of the activity can be defined narrowly or broadly. For example, contractors can be hired to provide all educational services or a specific subset of tasks, such as remedial reading instruction. Contractors face both the incentives built directly into their contracts and the implicit threat of competition.

But in its generality, the approach begs a crucial question: what sort of contract? The success of performance contracting depends crucially on the ability to craft a good contract and to monitor its performance. As innovators in the U.S. Office of Economic Opportunity discovered, writing an effective contract is not easy (see Table 18.1). And, to the extent that the contract does not fully or accurately reflect the goals of the schools, the added profit incentive of contracting firms might lead to significant distortions in the services provided. With a good contract, however, the school system can introduce competitive supply while still retaining overall authority, oversight, and fiscal control.

Charter Schools

Charter schools are a specialized version of performance contracting. School systems enter into performance contracts with outside suppliers, but in this case the suppliers are typically nonprofit institutions, at times made up entirely of existing teachers.

In 1991 Minnesota became the first state to adopt this concept when it authorized eight charter schools. In 1992 California passed an act authorizing one hundred charter schools. By early 1994 another six states (Colorado, Georgia, Massachusetts, Michigan, New Mexico, and Wisconsin) had enacted charter school legislation and several others were contemplating similar moves. (See Table 20.1 for a summary of enacted charter school legislation.)

The Minnesota legislation illustrates well the basic idea. Any group of licensed teachers can propose to establish a new school; the purpose of the school can range from improving learning to using innovative teaching methods to creating new professional opportunities for teachers. A local district must agree to sponsor the proposed charter school and to be responsible for monitoring the performance of the school. The contract can last for up to three years, and the school receives state financial support. The state grants charter schools a considerable degree of regulatory relief to permit a wide variety of innovations and performance guarantees. California legislation has many similar features, and it also allows nonlicensed teachers to participate. By definition, charter schools involve decentralized school management and a greater orientation toward outcomes.

Table 18.1. State Legislation Permitting
Charter Schools, as of Spring 1994.

State (year)	Number permitted	Major features	Entity that must approve plan
California (1992)	100 (10 per district)	Nonsectarian; must use certified teachers; five-year contract.	Local board (with appeal to county board)
Colorado (1993)	50	Schools may not discriminate; contract for performance; various state regulations waived; five-year contract.	Local board (with appeal to state)
Georgia (1992)	No limit	Aimed at existing schools; must have approval of two-thirds of faculty; state can waive regulations with performance contract.	Local and state boards
Massachusetts (1993)	25	Business, teachers, or parents may propose; most state regulations waived.	Secretary of education (local approval not required)
Michigan (1994)	No limit	New or existing schools eligible; state board, local board, college, or university may sponsor.	Local school board or sponsor organization
Minnesota (1991)	20	State waiver of regulations; must hire certified teachers; open to all, or cross-section of population; three-year contract.	Local board (with appeal to state)
New Mexico (1992)	5	New schools not permitted; existing schools may be converted; total state funds to charter; state planning grants ($50,000) available.	Apply through local board to state
Wisconsin (1993)	20 (2 per district)	Must hire certified teachers; district can apply for waiver of state regulations.	Local and state superintendent

Source: *Joe Nathan, Center for School Change, University of Minnesota.*

The raison d'être of charter schools is to implement teachers' innovative ideas about teaching, organizational systems for schools, reward structures, and the like. Many see these schools as a way to introduce some competition within the structure of public schools. As with performance contracting, a key element of success will be the ability to develop appropriate contracts and measures of performance. The short history of charter school experience also demonstrates some of the tensions, public fears, and potential problems with this concept. Minnesota's restriction limiting the opportunity to create charter schools to licensed teachers, for example, was a compromise balancing the risk of innovation against the interests of teachers and the desire to try something new. Other versions of charter schools also involve parents and school choice. No systematic evaluations of any forms of charter schools have yet been made.

Merit Pay for Teachers

Perhaps the most widely discussed performance incentive is merit pay, which links teachers' wages directly to their performance. Most other workers are evaluated on the basis of their performance, runs the most popular argument, so why shouldn't teachers be? Merit pay schemes strive to reward teachers who actually raise student performance. Rewards are based on results rather than behavior, and so they circumvent the difficulties in defining a priori what good teachers or good teaching might be. In practice, however, designing a workable system of merit pay has proved elusive.

Richard Murnane and David Cohen have reviewed attempts to institute merit pay, and their findings are not encouraging. Merit pay has been adopted in a wide variety of schooling circumstances, but it almost always has eventually been watered down or discarded. Subsequent analyses confirm these outcomes. School boards have generally committed little money to merit pay, leaving merit bonuses a trivial component of total teacher compensation. Indeed, merit rewards frequently have devolved into pay for extra duties instead of a bonus for quality performance in the classroom.

Teachers' unions have resisted merit pay, in part because of questions about the objectivity of methods used to measure student performance. Teachers have been particularly concerned about a school's ability to separate a specific teacher's contribution to a student's performance from the contributions made by other teachers or the student's family. A further concern about merit pay is the possibility for destructive competition between teachers. The fear is that, if teachers view themselves to be in cut-throat competition with other teachers, they might not cooperate with each other—refusing to share information about effective teaching techniques, to work together to deal with problem students, or to do public service types of activities.

These are serious issues, but they do not seem insurmountable; indeed, there are signs that union resistance is softening. After all, most other workers have some sort of merit pay scheme and do not suffer these ill effects. Their experience illustrates several factors important in avoiding pitfalls. First, shared activities should receive shared rewards. By rewarding joint achievement jointly, merit pay schemes can avoid spurring unconstructive competition. Second, the assessment and reward system should not go beyond the ability to observe and evaluate performance. Fine distinctions in performance that cannot be reliably and fairly judged should not be included in rewards. But even approximate measurement schemes still distinguish among, say, the best, the worst, and the typical performance, which enables school administrators to distinguish those who should be strongly encouraged to continue teaching from those who should be left to decide for themselves and those who should be discouraged. Third, workers must believe that the system is fair and works for them.

Many states have supported various teacher incentive plans or career ladder schemes—programs offering increased rewards to keep good teachers in the classroom. Unfortunately, the history has been one of varying state commitment, with funding being driven more by politics and budgetary pressures than by evaluations of success or failure. The general lack of systematic evaluation means that states have not been able to learn much from their attempts to develop teacher incentive plans.

There is evidence of successful use of merit pay in public employment; the Senior Executive Service of the federal government is an example. Professional teaching standards, as currently conceived, suggest an alternative in between a full merit pay system and the current use of broad certification. The teacher certification standards of the National Board for Professional Teaching Standards, when fully developed, may provide a direct and acceptable mechanism for evaluating the performance of prospective teachers. This certification, which would be voluntary, is akin to that of surgeons. Teachers would be certified on the basis of knowledge and demonstrated skills, but not on the success of their individual "operations."

The ultimate effect of any merit pay plan, if it could surmount the tremendous hurdles faced in the past, would come from two sources. Either current teachers would improve their performance in the classroom or natural selection would lead to a different and more effective group of teachers, or both. Although the evidence is not conclusive, attracting new teachers and retaining the best currently available may represent the greatest potential for improvement. Higher pay for better performance would signal teachers to move in or out of teaching, depending on their performance.

Teacher Selection and Renewal Procedures

Merit pay systems can be used to encourage the most productive teachers to stay in teaching and to discourage the least productive. These same ends can be achieved, without adopting merit pay, by changing procedures for selecting and retaining teachers. Although it is hard to generalize about the pay policies of private schools, which are unaffected by unions and most other regulatory restraints, they appear to rely not on extensive merit pay schemes for teachers, but on intensive teacher selection procedures and retention policies that link continued employment directly to classroom performance. This type of system offers a different structure for introducing performance incentives.

A key ingredient to this approach, as to merit pay plans, is the ability to assess the value added of individual teachers. Evidence suggests that principals are good judges of which teachers improve their students' performance; at least, they can identify the extremes of the distribution of teacher performance. Equally, few parents doubt that they can identify the best and the worst teachers. Current employment relations in public schools, however, limit the ability to incorporate this information about teacher performance into management decisions.

If retention policies were changed, decisions about which teachers should have their contracts renewed need not rely only on the evaluations of principals but could incorporate the input of other teachers and of parents. And, of course, any ultimate decision to fire a teacher should follow extensive efforts to improve individual teaching skills, perhaps along the lines of Japanese teacher-development efforts summarized in the comparative analysis of Asian and American schools by Harold Stevenson and James Stigler. The ultimate strength of the system would, nonetheless, rest on straightforward procedures now seldom undertaken. Active decisions would be made throughout a teacher's career about the teacher's performance. Those not performing at acceptable levels would be moved out of teaching, a fate that, today, befalls only the most grossly and demonstrably incompetent.

Any such changes, of course, alter teacher tenure rules, employment guarantees, and job expectations. Therefore, as with many other organizational changes considered here, the ultimate success of the change may depend crucially on the process of implementation. In simplest terms, any arbitrary changes in the fundamental aspects of jobs for current teachers may well lead to undesirable outcomes. These issues of implementation are discussed later.

Merit Schools

Some have proposed that, instead of rewarding individual teachers, school districts or the state reward entire schools that perform well. Such an approach would recognize the joint activities of all school personnel and avoid any possible destructive competition. Generally, these proposals envision that schools would be managed through some sort of shared decisionmaking and that schools that do particularly well would be given added resources. The underlying premise is that such a reward structure would encourage teachers and principals to set high standards for behavior, even if it did not include such powerful incentives as direct links between individual performance and pay or job security.

It is important to note that problems of measuring performance are severe, perhaps even more severe, with merit school plans than with merit pay plans geared to individual teachers. The identification of merit schools must incorporate notions of value added in the same way as the identification of merit teachers. Yet, because direct observations are more limited and comparisons less possible, merit school plans might have to rely more heavily on standardized tests and, thus, may be more prone to mismeasurement and its attendant adverse consequences. Additionally, the magnitude of incentive effects is likely to be very limited if the rewards do not include direct salary and compensation adjustments for teachers and other school personnel.

School-Based Measurement

An extremely popular and frequently discussed reform is "school-based management" or "site-based management." This approach transfers considerable decisionmaking from central school district officials to principals, teachers, and, perhaps, parents. This is not an incentive framework but a decisionmaking structure, which can be operated with virtually any incentive structure. Typically, however, it has been used without any explicit incentive structure. Moreover, a review by Anita Summers and Amy Johnson argues that existing examples and proposals generally view school-based management as an end in itself, rarely linking it to student performance (Exhibit 18.2).

Exhibit 18.2. Evaluations of Site-Based Management.

School-based management decentralizes decisionmaking to individual schools, where teachers and students meet "to do education." Throughout the twentieth century, school districts have grown in size and become more centralized and more bureaucratic. This development has limited teachers' ability to make educational decisions, failed to capitalize on their energies, and left them unhappy with their work. With increasing frequency during the 1980s, devolution of decisionmaking to the individual school has been proposed to correct problems with centralization.

Anita Summers and Amy Johnson employed the ERIC reference system to locate evaluations of school-based management conducted from 1983 through 1993. Three results stood out. First, very little systematic evaluation has been done to ascertain any effects of school-based management on student performance. Second, and perhaps even more significant, only a few school-based management plans even listed improved student performance as a goal. Third, very few schools have any serious plan for determining whether school-based management has any discernible effects on the problems it was meant to cure.

The Summers and Johnson search uncovered more than 800 studies of site-based management (or related ideas such as participative decisionmaking or school-site management). Of these, 70 attempted to be evaluative, and only 20 used a systematic methodology. Of these 20, only 7 included any quantitative assessment of student performance, although several others included survey information, such as teacher testimonials stating that, in their judgment, "student achievement improved."

An in-depth review of the 20 most systematic studies was revealing. All of the management plans explicitly stated that greater empowerment of teachers and more independence for principals were primary goals. Most were explicit in wanting greater parent and community involvement. But, although improved student performance was commonly mentioned in very general terms, only 7 included specific, quantitative goals for student achievement (and of these, only 2 showed positive results). Thirteen of the 20 did not list any objective about student performance. Yet, 17 of the 20 plans involved increased resources.

This neglect of student performance is mirrored in the in-depth analysis by Paul Hill and Josephine Bonan of five major districts that employed decentralized decisionmaking in some schools during the 1989–90 and 1990–91 school years. The goals of these programs are striking in their vague focus. Columbus, Ohio, listed "school improvement" as its goal; Dade County, Florida, listed "teacher professionalization"; Prince William County, Virginia, "school improvement and public support"; Louisville, Kentucky, "school improvement"; Edmonton, Alberta, Canada, "budgetary and administrative decentralization." Of these systems, only Prince William County appeared to collect systematic information about student achievement (although the outside contractor evaluating the Dade County experience did include achievement scores as one element of its report).

The case study of school-based management points to significant shortcomings in setting goals and evaluating performance. Not only do the decentralizing schools not measure their own progress, but the evaluation of their experiences provides little that would help another school to decide whether to embark on similar reform. We are amazed that a policy reform that has received so much attention and support has not been accompanied by anything resembling objective evaluation.

Source: *Summers and Johnson (1994); Hill and Bonan (1991).*

Not surprisingly, given the wide variety of decisionmaking procedures included under the rubric of school-based management, few consistent results about student performance emerge from existing experiments. Indeed, because altering student performance is seldom an explicit goal, performance has not been routinely evaluated.

Economists generally favor decentralized decisionmaking in complicated organizations, such as schools, where local knowledge is important for high-quality performance. The advantages of local decisionmaking materialize, however, only when local decisionmakers have sufficient information, when the incentive structure emphasizes performance toward agreed-upon goals, when there is considerable latitude for making local decisions, and when there is a good system of accountability. Most school-based management schemes do not meet these conditions; indeed, many fail on all conditions. Some, for example, do not allow local school officials to adjust the curriculum; others bar local school officials from making decisions about hiring and firing teachers. Absent well-defined goals and performance incentives, school-based management may be worse than centralized decisionmaking.

The difference between the typical school-based management approach and a system that integrates local decisionmaking within an overall economic perspective is illustrated by Henry Levin's Accelerated Schools program, which was designed to improve achievement of the lowest-performing students in a district (Exhibit 18.3). It begins with well-defined performance objectives and employs school-based decisionmaking to find approaches that meet those objectives. Regular evaluation ensures that attention stays focused on student achievement. The shared commitment to achieving student performance goals creates effective team sanctions for disinterest or nonperformance, which in turn tends to induce teachers who are not contributing to the school's efforts to seek voluntary transfers. Individual schools operating Accelerated Schools programs typically execute them in quite different ways, based on local needs and local capacity. Thus, the program embodies three of the tenets that we have stressed here: incentives, continual evaluation, and latitude for tailoring the program to local needs.

Altering the Basic Structure of Schools: Choice

More radical schemes of performance incentives rely on consumer choice to distinguish good schools and teachers from bad—and to reward each accordingly. Most public schools effectively have a local monopoly; parents living in a certain area have no choice over which school their children attend. Giving parents and students the ability to choose among a

Exhibit 18.3. Accelerated Schools.

Most attempts to deal with disadvantaged students and low achievers involve extensive remedial programs, but the results have not been very encouraging. A very different approach, developed by Henry Levin and his associates at Stanford University, starts with the premise that, instead of resorting to remedial teaching, students must be taught to do their normal lessons faster and better.

This Accelerated Schools program illustrates many of the program elements advocated in this report. The program has three key elements. First, the school must have a clear and well-articulated set of goals for student performance, agreed to by staff, parents, and students (unity of purpose). Second, decision-making in all key areas—including curriculum, instructional approaches, personnel, and use of school resources—is done at the school level and again involves staff, parents, and students (school empowerment). Third, the instructional approach begins with an evaluation of the strengths of students, staff, and parents, and these identified strengths in a particular school become the centerpiece of the instructional program (building on strengths). In the 1992–93 school year, the program was operating in more than three hundred schools in twenty-five states; most of the schools were at the bottom of their school district's performance distribution when they adopted the program.

Several aspects of the Accelerated Schools program stand out. At the outset the staff and parents of the school must formally accept the program, a device introduced to make sure that everybody is committed. From this starting point, however, individual schools can go in different directions, depending on their own views of what will and will not work. Student progress and the effectiveness of the program is measured throughout the process. Finally, the program is designed to work with very small initial additions to the school budget. Thus the program demonstrates the possibility of improving school efficiency (that is, expanding on performance for the same cost).

The expansion of the Accelerated Schools program and the local indicators of student performance suggest that it has been beneficial in a majority of the schools that have tried it. Yet very little systematic evaluation has been conducted. The national program office has put its resources into training and expansion of the program; the local schools are trying to make it work. Ideally, the federal or state governments should organize, finance, and conduct evaluations of the programs and disseminate the results.

The few evaluations that have been conducted support the program. Studies in Houston found that students in the accelerated school improved on standardized tests in reading, language, and math, while students in the control school continued a downward slide. This and other evaluations indicate that the Accelerated Schools program is an effective model that will not suit all schools but will be effective in many circumstances. Its potential and refinement would clearly be enhanced by improved information and evaluation.

Source: *Levin (1994); McCarthy and Still (1993);*
and Hopfenberg, Levin, and associates (1993).

range of nearby schools is intended to make them more informed, involved, and influential in the education process. It would also effectively give them, rather than school administrators, the power to define a "good" education and to shape the schools accordingly.

Allowing students to choose which school to attend is meant to encourage them to attend better schools. That is a particularly valuable opportunity in inner cities, where families frequently lack the resources to move to the affluent suburbs where good schools are more prevalent. In turn, consumer choice would pressure the poorer performing (unpopular) schools to improve. Giving students and their parents a choice would thus place greater incentives on performance, because students (and presumably resources) would migrate from poor schools to good ones and force all of them to respond to the concerns of parents and to issues of quality.

Although the basic outlines are clear, choice nonetheless remains a very ill-defined term, encompassing divergent programs with very different incentives and implications. Choice provides only a general structure for schooling systems; it is the details of particular plans that influence student performance. Administrative structures falling under the general heading of choice include magnet schools, freedom of choice within a district, attendance at public schools in other districts, tuition tax credits, and vouchers good at both public and private schools. These alternatives are commonly divided into those choices that involve only public schools (magnet schools and intra- and inter-district choice) and those that include both public and private schools (tuition tax credits and vouchers). But even within these broad categories, significant variations in actual plans and their concomitant incentives already occur.

Many factors determine the effectiveness of a specific program of choice. The most important are the magnitude of resource flows, the constraints on free choice, the availability of good information on schools, the ability of parents and students to make good choices, and the scope of possible school choices. A simple example illustrates some of the issues involved. Consider a school system with two high schools. School A has excellent science teachers, while School B does not. Given a choice, students at School B who are interested in science may well try to switch to School A. One of four things might then happen. First, if School A has excess capacity, some children will transfer to it. Second, if School A is already at capacity and does not expand, no new children will be accepted, and choice will lead to no change. Third, School A could add new science teachers to accommodate the influx of students. But contract rules and district policies might enable teachers at School B, who are no longer in demand, to transfer to School A. Again, choice leads to no change. Or, fourth, School A could hire new teachers from outside. Then the movement of students could begin to have an effect, because resources would now move away from the poor school and toward the good school.

In theory, state laws that allow students to choose to attend school in another district create yet broader and more powerful incentives. In practice, much depends on the magnitude of funds that flow with students. If, for example, only state funds (and not local funds) move with students, the district losing students might have an incentive to get rid of them, but the receiving district would not have a large incentive to take in more students. The availability of money to cover the extra transportation costs of commuting beyond their local school district will affect the students' willingness to transfer. Similarly, if state law permits students to choose between public and private schools, the relative contributions to tuition made by parents, the state, and the local district have substantial implications for whether there will be any movement, whether any of the schools will see strong incentives to compete, and whether the outcomes appear justifiable.

Another fundamental question concerns the range of available choices. A basic presumption behind choice plans is that new schools—more efficient ones with better overall performance—will develop. The strength of incentives as determined by the amount of resources that accompany a student is clearly important in determining any supply response. So is the amount of regulation placed on schools. There is a real trade-off between the degree of regulation—of curriculum, practices, and standards, for example—that participating schools must face and the potential incentives these schools have to compete with each other for students. Clearly, some regulations will be needed, but regulations generally limit the range of alternatives that schools can develop. The more regulated schools are, the more any choice plan will resemble the current system.

In addition to assuming that sufficient options exist or will be developed, choice plans require that parents and students make good decisions. Although individuals are commonly presumed to be good consumers in other areas of life, such a presumption is not universally accepted in the case of schooling. Questions have been raised about whether parents will base their decisions on academic quality rather than on convenience, costs, or even the athletic programs the schools offer. The quality of the decisionmaking is an issue, but there is little reason to believe that parents will knowingly make bad decisions. A more important consideration is whether parents have sufficient information to make good decisions. The information routinely available about school performance is limited and distorted. Yet, in other areas consumers are presumed to make good choices only when they have sufficient information on which to base a decision. A key element of any choice plan is the provision of high-quality information about the value added of the schools, or what any school can be expected to contribute to student achievement. Not only do schools have little experience providing such information, but parents have little experience in using it to make decisions about the schools their children attend. Both must be addressed. (Moreover, while choice plans require quality information and increased decisionmaking capacity, all school reforms would clearly be enhanced by improvements in these areas.)

Deciding between public-only and public-private choice plans involves matters of trust, control, motivation, and, at times, constitutional regulation. These issues are truly important; they are also, given the lack of empirical evidence about the outcomes of choice, extremely hard to resolve by simple, conceptual arguments. On the one hand, it seems wrong to refuse to include private schools in choice programs because they, unlike public schools, are not obliged to serve all of the public. On the other hand, private schools may in fact be less responsive to the needs of disadvantaged students or may reinforce existing social structures. At a more practical level, a voucher plan could confer large windfall gains on well-off families who are currently paying to send their children to private schools.

Evidence on Choice Plans

Empirical evidence about choice plans and their effects could do a great deal to answer such concerns. Several widely publicized choice plans are in place: in Cambridge, Massachusetts; East Harlem, New York; the state of Minnesota; and Milwaukee, Wisconsin. But the evidence about the effects of these plans is sketchy and mixed, and there is even less understanding of which aspects of these plans are most important and which can be duplicated in other locations. Only the Milwaukee experiment (see below) has been subjected to ongoing, in-depth evaluation.

Because of the limited experimentation with choice, little is known about whether choice will encourage the development of new and innovative schools. For example, much of the debate about public-private choice has centered on the relative performance of Catholic schools, a discussion that assumes that, under a broad voucher system, many parents and students would choose these schools. Although Catholic schools are currently the dominant nonpublic school, they do not provide much evidence about potential supply under an expanded voucher system, or even under an open-choice charter school system. Current regulations and funding inhibit development of new alternative schools, both public and private, a situation that could be reversed if current restrictions are relaxed.

Higher education in the United States offers some lessons on this point. Unlike postsecondary institutions in most other countries in the world, U.S. colleges and universities, both public and private, compete with each other for students and resources. This competition is frequently cited as a reason why higher education in the United States is usually viewed as the best in the world. At the same time, extensive competition does not mean that all colleges and universities are of particularly high quality or that all bad schools are driven out of business.

Choice and Disadvantaged Students

Disadvantaged students pose special problems and opportunities for the design of choice programs because, almost by definition, to be disadvantaged is to enjoy fewer choices than the rest of the population. Without special steps to enable the disadvantaged to choose as freely as their peers, choice systems may leave the disadvantaged worse off than they are now. Some fear that choice systems, particularly those that include both public and private schools, would simply turn the public schools into dumping grounds for disadvantaged and difficult-to-educate students. Some also fear that choice could increase segregation in schools. A working system of choice, however, would allow disadvantaged students to choose schools that they could not otherwise attend, either because tuition was beyond the reach of their families without the aid of vouchers or because those schools were in neighborhoods where their families could not afford to live.

Addressing these concerns and opportunities is essential in formulating choice programs. If disadvantaged students are more expensive to educate (which appears to be the case), compensatory vouchers or payments should be included in any choice plan, so that schools receive more money when they accept disadvantaged students. Regulations may also be needed to deal with possible racial or ethnic segregation. Finally, information systems are extraordinarily important in the case of disadvantaged students and their parents, who have even less experience with school choice than the rest of the population.

Choice for disadvantaged students has been the subject of an experimental policy in Milwaukee, Wisconsin (Exhibit 18.4). Milwaukee's voucher experience has not been problem free, but it demonstrates that choice can noticeably expand the opportunities for the disadvantaged. So far, evidence of higher student performance has not been found, but demand for entry into the program is growing, and parents express considerable satisfaction with the alternatives.

Exhibit 18.4. The Milwaukee Voucher Program

In the spring of 1990, Wisconsin instituted a program to provide poor children in Milwaukee with an opportunity to attend private school. Eligible students could choose from a list of eligible private schools, and the schools would receive a payment approximately equal to the state money that would have been paid to Milwaukee public schools ($2,987 per pupil in 1993–94). This innovative plan offers unique insights into the potential for educational vouchers and for choice by disadvantaged students. The evaluation by John Witte, Andrea Bailey, and Christopher Thorn begins to describe possible outcomes of wider choice options.

Any student enrolled in the Milwaukee public schools whose family income is less than 1.75 times the national poverty line is eligible for the choice program. An eligible school has to be a private, nonsectarian school that offers no religious instruction. A participating school cannot discriminate in admission on the basis of race, gender, previous achievement, or previous behavior, and no more than half of the students in the school (65 percent in 1994–95) can be "choice" students. If more students apply to a school than there are spaces available, students must be randomly selected. No more than 1 percent (1.5 percent in 1994–95) of Milwaukee public school students are eligible for the program. Enrollment in the choice plan expanded steadily from 341 students in the fall of 1990–91 to 742 in 1993–94. The increased enrollment appears to reflect increased participation by private schools and increasing availability of information about the program.

Evaluation of the project has included both survey work and objective comparisons between students participating in the choice program and those remaining in the public schools. These studies provide several insights. First, parents of participating students consistently cite the educational quality of the choice schools and their disciplinary environment as reasons for participating in the program. Second, choice parents start with high parental involvement in public schools and increase their involvement in private schools after joining the choice program. Third, parents in the choice program are much happier with the private school than the previous public school: 73 percent give their private school a grade of A or B, while only 48 percent gave their previous public school those grades. Thus, the choice program appears to be very successful in providing preferred schooling options to a significant number of poor children.

The lessons of choice, however, become more ambiguous when other performance indicators are included. First, attrition from the program is high: 40 percent, 35 percent, and 31 percent in the first three years of the program, respectively. This attrition may simply reflect the normal dropout rate for the district, but no districtwide data are available for comparison. Second, data on achievement growth (measured by standardized tests) do not show any clear gain for "choice" students in the private schools.

Whatever else the program may have done, it has strengthened Milwaukee's private school options. Even though the voucher amount is relatively low, the program has improved the financial condition of participating private schools. At the same time, the small scale of the program and the special circumstances of participating schools (notably their use of external subsidies and their ability to hire teachers at very low wages) make generalizations to larger programs or other sites uncertain.

Exhibit 18.4. (*continued*)

Evaluation has come at an early point in the experiment, and the experiment itself is limited to one specific version of choice. So conclusions are tentative and necessarily limited. Nothing, for example, can be said about the effects of expanded private alternatives on the public schools. Nonetheless, even at this point, it is safe to conclude that the program provides a service highly valued by some poor parents—committed parents who have a deep interest in their children's education but who lack the resources to select alternative schools. These parents are also one of the groups most hurt by the current policies of public monopoly of local schools.

An even more ambitious program of choice for low-income students was begun in Puerto Rico in 1993. This program uses vouchers that enable students to choose among public schools as well as between public and private schools, thus providing a direct incentive for public schools to compete aggressively with private schools for disadvantaged students. No performance information is currently available for the Puerto Rican experiment, and it currently faces legal challenges.

Sources: *Witte, Bailey, and Thorn (1993); Bolick (1994).*

Indeed, a strong case can be made for wider use of vouchers specifically for disadvantaged students. Making vouchers available only for the disadvantaged alleviates the fear that the well-off will manipulate the voucher system for their own benefit. Moreover, it puts pressure on underperforming inner-city schools. Many public school districts rationalize the poor performance of their schools by blaming the requirements that they take all students, no matter how educationally disadvantaged. Providing alternative, private school opportunities for disadvantaged students—those whom public schools see as being difficult and expensive to educate—would, by their own argument, help the public schools. Vouchers for disadvantaged students would then allow the public schools to concentrate on their remaining, easier-to-educate, clientele.

Inevitably, the term "choice" has become extremely political, and support of school choice is often viewed as a litmus test for general political sentiments. Strong vested interests oppose choice systems. The most vocal opponents are school personnel, who could potentially lose job security, particularly if the choice plan involves private schools. This opposition was evident in the expensive and successful campaigns to block passage of ballot initiatives that would have created choice systems in Colorado and California in 1993. The often contentious debate over choice has led both proponents and opponents to make claims that go far beyond any available evidence. As with other approaches to introducing stronger performance incentives, the idea of competition among schools creates interesting possibilities. But how effective choice can be and how to structure choice programs for maximum effectiveness cannot be known until the concept has been experimented with much more broadly than it has been yet.

Incentives for Students and Parents

Most of the performance incentives programs devised for schools have focused on teachers and school personnel. As teachers are keenly aware, however, the motivation of students themselves is critical to the educational process.

Except for those aiming at the most selective colleges, most students today face only modest incentives to perform well in school. Potential employers do not have automatic access to students' grades, achievement, or even attendance records, partly because of legal restrictions. And with the expansion of college opportunities, and the dependence of colleges on tuition or state subsidies, most American postsecondary institutions are not very selective in their admissions.

By contrast, many foreign countries provide strong incentives to study. In Japan, Korea, and many European countries, including France and Germany, examinations determine both the type of schooling students will receive and the careers they can expect to enter. Students in these countries work hard to prepare for examinations, and parents are heavily involved. Such examination systems are not easily transportable to the United States. In part that is because such systems limit social mobility by locking in schooling and occupational opportunities at young ages, when family influences are very important. Nevertheless, U.S. schools might learn something from studying how such systems motivate students and parents as well as school personnel.

Many foreign countries also forge direct links between schools and employers, so that a student's performance in school can have a great effect on that student's employment prospects. Such links may be particularly pertinent for schools in America's inner cities, where labor market incentives are lacking. The fact that employment prospects are little better for a student who has worked hard in school than for one who has not may well sap students' commitment to study diligently. At the same time, businesses, incongruously, frequently complain about the low achievement levels of students who seek employment with them, as if prospective employers had no effect on student performance.

Several strategies can enhance performance incentives for students. These include standardizing transcript and achievement data and making that data more available to employers, establishing better links between schools and employers, and providing better information to students about the rewards of higher academic achievement. All of these approaches make the reasonable assumption that employers could benefit from better information about scholastic performance. Only experience with closer contact and cooperation between schools and employers can show whether this assumption is generally true or could be true.

Clearly, student incentives would be even more effective if they were reinforced by better schools. Yet, stronger incentives for students can be effective within today's school system, within a school system modified to provide greater performance incentives to teachers and school personnel, and within various choice systems.

Technology and Costs

Visions of high technology schools have been painted for decades, but the reality never seems to catch the promise. The current technological vision centers on computers and flashy multimedia programs. Yet even as computers become ubiquitous, their integral position in instruction and the curriculum does not. The story behind limited introduction of technology and the remedies parallel that of school improvement in general.

With the proper incentives, technology could reduce the costs of schools in several ways. Computers can replace teachers in certain tasks, such as drill-and-practice activities. Experience with providing education through remote transmission ("distance education")—for example, the British Open University and programs in some developing countries—suggests that television and radio broadcasts, combined with correspondence materials, can provide high-quality education at relatively low cost. Broadcast education is particularly valuable in rural areas and other situations where small school populations make classroom instruction uneconomic. Broadcast education can also be used to offer advanced courses in urban and suburban areas, when existing demand cannot justify highly specialized courses. Television and other electronic educational technologies can both multiply the reach of an effective instructor and bring visually compelling programming into the classroom. Substantial relevant experience, particularly in higher education, supports the educational efficacy of these approaches.

Unfortunately, schools today have few incentives to use technology effectively. Not only are teachers not rewarded for using technology well, but using cost-cutting technology could in fact reduce the demand for teachers. Moreover, except when voters reject school budgets, school districts seldom make cost saving a high priority. The most frequent use of computers and other technological problems is to enrich the curriculum, providing presentations that are interesting and entertaining, but that may not be central to the instructional program.

Incentives to conserve on costs are difficult to introduce into the current system. Expenditure control comes largely from voters and taxpayers who put pressure on the overall school budget. This pressure, unfortunately, does not readily translate into programs for introducing technological changes, particularly those that require considerable planning, training development, and capital expenditure.

One obvious way to introduce cost control pressures is through choice programs that institute competition among schools. If schools compete in part on the basis of their costs (through tuition transfers, state funding, and the like), more schools might find it in their interest to use alternative technologies to help control costs. Additionally, contracts for principals and superintendents that include incentives to cut costs could help, even within the current structure. For example, the top administrative officers of a district could receive salary bonuses for increasing student achievement at current expenditures. Such contracts are unknown in schools today.

Nurturing Experiments

Because so little is known about effective incentive systems, experimentation and evaluation of the results are imperative. The few attempts that schools and school districts have made to reform their organizations and introduce incentives have been useful and laudable, but they are insufficient in number and scope to "test" the incentive approaches outlined here. Because local circumstances are likely to influence the effectiveness of any incentive system, detailed information must be gathered about both specifics of local systems and results of the attempts. Only when the results of alternative local systems can be compared and contrasted will there be enough information to determine how implementation in different circumstances might best proceed.

Many factors, however, inhibit experimentation with educational reform. Perhaps highest on the list are the attitudes and preferences of parents. Most parents, when polled, say that, although significant problems beset American schooling, their children's schools are fundamentally sound. For them, therefore, experimenting with alternative organizations and incentives appears to be a high-risk venture without clear gains. These attitudes are reinforced, if not created, by school personnel, who find the existing system basically satisfying to their own needs. School personnel tend to tell parents that what is needed is not change, but more resources. Few school administrators or teachers wish to advertise that their school has problems other than those that can be readily solved by their newest program.

State and federal regulations and financing for schools tend also to favor the status quo. Some potentially useful innovations are flatly prohibited; others are made difficult to develop. For example, regulations on teacher certification, discussed previously, make it impossible to hire people who have not been trained in the standard manner. Requirements for dealing with handicapped children place legal restrictions on the process of education—albeit for a worthy objective, but, as mentioned, often without regard to the outcomes achieved. Special federal and state grant programs typically monitor the number of students who participate in the program but not whether the program is achieving its goals.

If experimentation is to be encouraged, state and federal governments must encourage local districts to adopt new models of incentives and organizational structures. This means eliminating regulations that prevent experimentation from taking place. But less regulation is only part of what is needed. Local districts in general do not have the expertise to design alternative approaches to schooling, and they should not be expected to do so. State and federal governments must provide better information to local districts about options and approaches. And by providing parents with information about the experiences, benefits, and risks of various experimental programs, government could help them to evaluate more realistically their own opportunities to participate in educational innovation.

To help local school districts, states might, for example, design prototypes of different incentive structures and create programs of inducements to encourage appropriate experimentation. Commitment to such an approach would be a radical departure from the current policies of most state legislatures and education departments. It would acknowledge, at least implicitly, that more of the same is not going to be effective and that, instead of controlling and mandating the details of the educational process, states would do better to improve information about alternatives and to encourage school districts to experiment their way toward their own solutions to the problems that beset them.

This approach presents political difficulties for legislators, for in pursuing it they must accept that nobody yet knows the details of programs that will improve schools. Experience shows that previous regulatory and certification approaches, which suggest knowledge of the best approach to education, have been widely ineffective. Real improvement appears instead to be promoted best by states that press for strengthened performance incentives and that support high performance goals and standards for students and schools without prejudging the method of achieving them. Doing this, however, means that instead of selling voters a solution to the problems of the schools, legislators must instead convince voters to embark on the search for a solution, a search that will require considerable effort, and some risk, on the part of voters themselves.

Still, it can be done. The remarkable history of state leadership in Minnesota provides an example of aggressive experimentation with interdistrict choice and charter schools (Exhibit 18.5). Choice programs in

---

Exhibit 18.5. Experimentation in Minnesota.

Although Minnesota public schools had relatively high graduation rates and test scores, the state in the mid-1980s initiated reforms to improve the schools. School choice, embodied in several overlapping programs, formed the heart of the reforms. School districts were allowed to decide whether they would participate in any given program on the basis of space availability, but, once in a program, they could not select the individual students they would admit. What follows is a brief summary of major Minnesota choice programs.

- *Postsecondary Options.* In June of 1985 Minnesota's legislature enacted the Post-Secondary Options Act. This statute enabled public high school juniors and seniors to enroll in Minnesota postsecondary institutions, on either a part- or full-time basis. Tax funds followed students to pay tuition. At about the same time, the "College in Schools" program enabled high school students to earn college credit by taking special courses, offered in their high schools, that were jointly organized by high school and university teachers. By the 1991–92 school year, 7,500 students were participating.

- *High School Graduation Incentives; Open Enrollment.* In 1987 the Minnesota Legislature adopted a program to help students who had experienced educational problems to graduate from high school. Under this program such students were permitted to attend alternative programs outside their school district. More than 1,400 students were enrolled in this program at the start of its first year, the fall of 1987. Another Minnesota program allowed any student to attend school in the neighboring school district, so long as the move would have no negative effects on desegregation. Tax funds again followed students. During the 1987–88 school year, this program's first year in operation, 95 of Minnesota's 435 districts resolved to allow any student to move. These programs, plus a portfolio of other, specialized choice programs for poorly served students, enrolled 41,000 students by 1992–93. These programs appear to have induced many dropouts to return, usually to a different school, and to graduate.

- *Within-District Choice.* Several districts permit choice within-district, and Minneapolis and St. Paul even require students at certain grade levels to

---

Exhibit 18.5. (*continued*)

choose the school they will attend. A total of 67,000 participated in such intradistrict choice plans.

- *Charter Schools.* In 1991 Minnesota enacted legislation to permit up to eight charter schools in the state. Any group of licensed teachers can, with local district sponsorship, propose a school to provide innovative instruction. A three-year contract commits the charter school to meeting specified performance standards. The school must be nonsectarian, nondiscriminatory, and tuition-free (with state funding following students). The number of authorized charter schools was increased to twenty in 1993 and was scheduled to rise to thirty-five in 1994.

Minnesota's innovative programs lead the nation in establishing wider options for students (and competition among schools). By 1992–93, 14 percent of primary and secondary school pupils were actively choosing their schools (not counting those enrolled in charter schools). Other states have adopted choice programs modeled after those in Minnesota. The state's strength is its willingness to expose public school districts to more competition for students. Formal evaluation of student performance under these programs has been lacking, however. Even a half-dozen years after the programs were instituted, discussion of the pros and cons of these innovative reforms still rests on the conceptual arguments offered when they were adopted—not on evidence of whether student performance has improved.

Sources: *Nathan (1989), Montano (1989), Owen (1993),*
Williams and Buechler (1993), Nathan and Ysseldyke (1994).

Minnesota now involve almost 15 percent of all students. Even in Minnesota, however, experimentation could be made more effective, and potentially more popular, if the local choice programs were clearly evaluated and the results of the evaluation widely disseminated. Today, information on educational performance is inadequate and frequently biased. Inaccurate information on performance lulls local citizens into contentment with the performance of their schools, when many should not be. Even local school personnel now find it difficult to compare their performance with that of other districts to see what they can and should be achieving.

In addition to information on the outcomes of educational experiments, local school districts will also need help in evaluating them, particularly in judging which might best apply to their local circumstances. Details are crucial: the fine print of a merit evaluation system, the rules of intradistrict choice, the appropriate range of local school decisions, and the operations of performance-based personnel systems make the critical difference in the success or failure of a particular reform.

Issues of Implementation

New systems of organization and incentives do not spring forth fully developed and fully functioning. They require long and difficult development, and these development periods are crucial for the ultimate success or failure of the experiment. If school personnel resist change or if public sentiment turns against reform, even fundamentally sound reforms can fail.

Schools often lack personnel capable of or willing to experiment with new systems of incentives. This creates a dilemma for reform-minded state governments. If they push schools into a specific "reform" or devise extensive regulations to minimize the risks of failure, they will stifle the very local decisionmaking capabilities that they are in theory striving to foster.

To encourage bureaucrats, teachers, and school personnel to devote the substantial amounts of time, energy, and resources needed to devise new programs, schools might release them from other duties, provide proper equipment and materials, and use outside consultants to foster new thinking. At the same time, states and local districts should help protect innovators from the most adverse consequences of an innovation that does not succeed. The willingness of teachers to start a charter school, for example, might relate directly to job guarantees for the teachers if the enterprise fails. If the district guarantees that teachers can rejoin the regular school system, many more teachers might be induced to develop charter schools than if they had no reemployment rights. Finding the right balance between encouraging teachers to take on entrepreneurial activity and insuring against risk is a tricky but manageable problem.

Direct performance incentives change the rewards and risks that school personnel encounter. Indeed, that is the whole point of instituting change. But those people doing well under the established system are unlikely to embrace performance incentives, just as they are unlikely to embrace any change that disrupts the status quo. Teachers' expectations about career and rewards may well not be satisfied under a new system. More than that, current state laws and local regulations and contracts include explicit guarantees about wages and employment. Any new system must consider transition periods that provide safeguards to existing personnel. Although many teachers are close to retirement, teachers now in the classroom will still dominate schools for many years to come. To avoid alienating them and losing the enthusiastic participation that is crucial to success in incentive-based systems of school management, the transition rules must treat these people equitably.

One appealing way to deal with commitments to existing teachers, while moving to radically different organizational approaches, is through two-tiered contracts. Teachers under existing contracts would continue essentially as they are now for an extended period of time, say, ten years. Basic work rules, pay structure, and the like would be maintained. At the same time, any new teachers would fall under a new contract with altered rewards, responsibilities, and risks. For example, a substantial portion of the wages of new teachers might be determined by a merit rating system, or new teachers might not have tenure rights based solely on years of experience in the local district. Existing teachers might be given the option to transfer tiers, to enter into the new contractual arrangement, perhaps with a system of bonuses for those willing to do so.

Other approaches can also be employed to recognize the implicit and explicit obligations to teachers. Direct compensation through the normal negotiation process might also be used to bring all teachers under a unified structure. Through such compromises, existing teachers can be induced to cooperate with change without restricting innovation only to those systems that existing teachers want.

Financing Improved Performance

Every state has a different approach to financial support for local schools, so the proportion of school expenditures coming from local districts and state coffers varies accordingly. Substantial variation also exists in the overall level of support for local education. Underlying each state's system is a specific notion of the public nature of education, the importance of education in determining individual opportunities, and the degree of local autonomy that should be granted.

It is a startling fact that no existing system of school finance in America explicitly rewards performance. No state gives additional funding to a district simply because student achievement has improved. Funding, in fact, may decrease, because the district may no longer be eligible for categorical grants that provide extra funds to districts with low performance. Indeed, difficulties in distinguishing between performance variations and inherent differences in the cost of education mean that some systems of finance may actually reward poor performance. Today, a low-achieving school district is invariably interpreted as a district composed of students with significant disadvantages, who require extra money for their education. A high-achieving district, by contrast, is assumed to have more educated and higher-income parents, lower costs, and less need for subsidy. Obviously, until states can and do distinguish between high-cost districts and high-performing ones, incentive systems will be crippled.

Aligning the financing system with the performance of districts would help to improve the schools. Specifically, districts that demonstrate an ability to use resources effectively should be rewarded, while those doing a poor job should not. In other words, the system of finance should be part of the incentive system that promotes improved school performance.

Improved efficiency is not the only objective of state policy, however. Equity across districts and individuals cannot be ignored. Debates over school finance, along with the related court challenges to state finance systems, have concentrated almost exclusively on equalizing the distribution of funding across districts. These discussions have generally ignored the concerns about the distribution of student achievement, the problems introduced by inefficient spending, and the true costs of providing improved education for disadvantaged students, issues that have been the subject of this work. If, however, the effectiveness of district spending were improved through, say, some combination of the outcome incentives described here, the questions of equitable distribution of funding would take on new importance. Simply put, when money can be counted on to be spent effectively, the distribution of spending will be directly related to the distribution of student achievement—and society will have to deal directly with the implications of any funding disparities.

Increasing equity and instituting performance incentives at the same time may introduce additional complexity into reform efforts. Certainly, it would be undesirable, and perhaps unconstitutional, if districts with the wealthiest families were to receive the largest subsidies because their performance improved the most. Rewarding performance need not mean abandoning equity, however, and systems can be created that achieve both objectives.

The Essentials of Performance Incentives

No matter what their field of endeavor, people respond to incentives. Because the incentives in schools bear little relationship to student performance, it is not surprising that schools have not yet improved student performance, despite constant reform pressures. Several programs are available that would connect incentives to performance—either by linking teachers' and administrators' pay directly to some objective measure of the results they achieve with their students or by letting parents and students themselves decide which schools best meet their needs and therefore most deserve their support.

Establishing programs that embody such incentives presents many challenges. Much more experience is needed to determine which incentives will work in which circumstances. The transition from today's system of school management to a more incentive-based system presents potential difficulties in maintaining the cooperation and involvement of existing school personnel, who may feel threatened by change. Ways must be found to reconcile the common need to promote change from the top with the local, decentralized decisionmaking that makes incentive-based systems most effective.

All of this calls for dramatically different roles for everyone now involved in education. Of prime importance is a redefined role for state and federal officials. These levels of government will have a diminished voice in specifying how education is to be delivered. But they will play a much greater role in promoting and inspiring the changes to be undertaken by local districts, in setting objectives and goals, in evaluating performance, in encouraging the adoption of new technologies, and in providing information to local districts. In short, their role changes from manager to coach. At the same time, local school officials and teachers will have to take a more active role in decisions about costs, structure, and curriculum. Instead of simply following instructions from above, personnel in each school will effectively have to create their own educational system. Many incentive systems also call for greater parental involvement in the educational process. Incentive-based systems can promote diversity where it is needed. And, should a single panacea for schools prove possible after all, incentive-based systems provide the strongest possible motivation for its quick, universal endorsement.

NOTES

Evaluation of differences among teachers comes from Hanushek (1971, 1992), Murnane (1975), Armor and others (1976), and Murnane and Phillips (1981). Pauly (1991) emphasizes the importance of variations within schools because of differences in individual approaches and teacher performance. Committee for Economic Development (1994) integrates ideas of performance incentives with the governance of schools and the decision-making capacity of states and local systems. The quantitative magnitude of differences across teachers comes from Hanushek (1992). The description and evaluation of early performance contracting efforts and experiments is found in Gramlich and Koshel (1975). The most recent introductions of contracting by for-profit firms are analyzed in Schmidt (1994). Current thinking on charter schools can be found in Randall (1992), Amsler (1992), Williams and Buechler (1993), Diegmueller (1993a), and Nathan and Ysseldyke (1994). An extensive evaluation of merit pay systems is found in Cohen and Murnane (1985, 1986), is reinforced in Hatry, Greiner, and Ashford (1994), and is also discussed in the background paper on teacher supply by Richard Murnane. An annotated bibliography of work on merit pay can be found in Karnes and Black (1986). American Federation of

Teachers (n.d.) and Shanker (1993) put forth the views of one teachers' union on evaluations, merit pay, and the like. See also National Board for Professional Teaching Standards (1991). Cornett and Gaines (1994) provide a useful summary of state incentive systems and career ladder plans as they have evolved during the 1980s and into the 1990s. Inferences about supply effects on the quality of people who enter teaching come from Manski (1987), Ferguson (1991), Murnane and others (1991), and Hanushek and Pace (forthcoming). Direct evidence on the ability of principals to evaluate the value added of teachers comes from Murnane (1975) and Armor and others (1976). Site-based management is reviewed in the PEER background paper by Summers and Johnson. See also Hill and Bonan (1991). Accelerated Schools are described in Hopfenberg, Levin, and associates (1993), with evaluations in McCarthy and Still (1993), Levin (1993), and Henry Levin's PEER background paper.

Choice is the subject of a wide range of publications and journal articles, including a special issue of the *Economics of Education Review* 11 (December 1992). Vouchers were proposed in early writing by Friedman (1962). See also Coons and Sugarman (1978) and Lieberman (1989). Nathan (1989a, 1989b) and Nathan and Ysseldyke (1994) discuss many of the attempts to institute school choice. Clune and Witte (1990) provide a series of articles on the theory of choice (vol. 1) and discussions of experiences with choice (vol. 2). Chubb and Moe (1990) present the case for vouchers for low-income students, along with empirical analyses related to school bureaucracies. Carnegie Foundation for the Advancement of Teaching (1992) provides a critique of choice, and, in turn, is critiqued in MacGuire (n.d.). Witte, Bailey, and Thorn (1993) evaluate the Milwaukee plan. The Puerto Rico choice program is outlined in Bolick (1994). Lieberman (1994) provides an interpretation of recent voting on choice initiatives. The history of Minnesota's experience with public school choice is found in Montano (1989), Nathan (1989), Nathan and Ysseldyke (1994), and Owen (1993). International experience is reviewed in Glenn (1989).

SELECTED BIBLIOGRAPHY

American Federation of Teachers. n.d. *National Education Standards and Assessments*. Washington.

Amsler, Mary. 1992. "Charter Schools." Policy Briefs 19. Far Western Laboratory for Educational Research and Development, San Francisco.

Armor, David, and others. 1976. *Analysis of the School Preferred Reading Program in Selected Los Angeles Minority Schools*. Santa Monica, Calif.: Rand Corp.

Bolick, Clint. 1994. "Puerto Rico: Leading the Way in School Choice." *Wall Street Journal,* January 14, A11.

Carnegie Foundation for the Advancement of Teaching. 1992. *School Choice: A Special Report.* Princeton, N.J.

Chubb, John E., and Terry M. Moe. 1990. *Politics, Markets, and America's Schools.* Brookings.

Clune, William H., and John F. Witte, eds. 1990. *Choice and Control in American Education.* Vol. 1: *The Theory of Choice and Control in Education.* Vol. 2: *The Practice of Choice, Decentralization, and School Restructuring.* New York: Falmer.

Cohen, David K., and Richard J. Murnane. 1985. "The Merits of Merit Pay." *Public Interest* 80 (Summer): 3–30.

Cohen, David K., and Richard J. Murnane. 1986. "Merit Pay and the Evaluation Problem: Understanding Why Most Merit Pay Plans Fail and a Few Survive." *Harvard Education Review* 56 (February): 1–17.

Committee for Economic Development. 1994. *Putting Learning First: Governing and Managing the Schools for High Achievement.* New York.

Coons, John E., and Stephen D. Sugarman. 1978. *Education by Choice: The Case for Family Control.* Berkeley, Calif.: University of California Press.

Cornett, Lynn M., and Gale F. Gaines. 1994. "Reflecting on Ten Years of Incentive Programs: The 1993 SREB Career Ladder Clearinghouse Survey." Southern Regional Education Board, Atlanta.

Diegmueller, Karen. 1993. "Charter-Schools Idea Gaining Converts in Legislatures." *Education Week,* July 14, p. 18.

Ferguson, Ronald. 1991. "Paying for Public Education: New Evidence on How and Why Money Matters." *Harvard Journal on Legislation* 28 (Summer): 465–98.

Friedman, Milton. 1962. *Capitalism and Freedom.* University of Chicago.

Glenn, Charles L. 1989. *Choice of Schools in Six Nations: France, Netherlands, Belgium, Britain, Canada, West Germany.* Department of Education.

Gramlich, Edward M., and Patricia P. Koshel. 1975. *Educational Performance Contracting.* Brookings.

Hanushek, Eric A. 1971. "Teacher Characteristics and Gains in Student Achievement: Estimation Using Micro Data." *American Economic Review* 60 (May): 280–88.

Hanushek, Eric A. 1992. "The Trade-Off between Child Quantity and Quality." *Journal of Political Economy* 100 (February): 84–117.

Hanushek, Eric A., and Richard R. Pace. Forthcoming. "Who Chooses to Teach (and Why)?" *Economics of Education Review.*

Hatry, Harry P., John M. Greiner, and Brenda G. Ashford. 1994. *Issues and Case Studies in Teacher Incentive Plans.* 2d ed. Washington: Urban Institute.

Hill, Paul T., and Josephine Bonan. 1991. *Decentralization and Accountability in Public Education.* Santa Monica: RAND.

Hopfenberg, Wendy S., Henry M. Levin, and associates. 1993. *The Accelerated Schools Resource Guide.* San Francisco: Jossey-Bass Publishers.

Karnes, Elizabeth Lueder, and Donald D. Black. 1986. *Teacher Evaluation and Merit Pay: An Annotated Bibliography.* New York: Greenwood Press.

Levin, Henry M. 1991a. "The Economics of Educational Reforms for the Disadvantaged." PEER background paper.

Levin, Henry M. 1993. "The Economics of Education for At-Risk Students." In *Essays on the Economics of Education,* edited by Emily P. Hoffman, 11–33. Kalamazoo, Mich.: W. E. Upjohn Institute for Employment Research.

Levin, Henry M. 1994. "Learning from Accelerated Schools." In *School Improvement Programs: A Handbook for Educational Leaders,* edited by James H. Block, Susan T. Everson, and Thomas R. Guskey. New York: Scholastic Books.

Lieberman, Myron. 1989. *Privatization and Educational Choice.* New York: St. Martin's Press.

Lieberman, Myron. 1994. "The School Choice Fiasco." *Public Interest* 114 (Winter): 17–34.

McCarthy, Jane, and Suzanne Still. 1993. "Hollibrook Accelerated Elementary School." In *Restructuring Schooling: Learning from Ongoing Efforts,* edited by Joseph Murphy and Philip Hallinger, 63–83. Newbury Park, Calif.: Corwin Press.

MacGuire, James. n.d. "Beyond Partisan Politics: A Response to the Carnegie Report on Choice." Center for Social Thought, New York.

Manski, Charles F. 1987. "Academic Ability, Earnings, and the Decision to Become a Teacher: Evidence from the National Longitudinal Study of the High School Class of 1972." In *Public Sector Payrolls,* edited by David A. Wise, 291–312. University of Chicago Press.

Montano, Jessie. 1989. "Choice Comes to Minnesota." In *Public Schools by Choice: Expanding Opportunities for Parents, Students, and Teachers,* edited by Joe Nathan, 165–80. St. Paul: Institute for Teaching and Learning.

Murnane, Richard J. 1975. *Impact of School Resources on the Learning of Inner City Children.* Cambridge, Mass.: Ballinger.

Murnane, Richard J., and Barbara Phillips. 1981. "What Do Effective Teachers of Inner-City Children Have in Common?" *Social Science Research* 10 (March): 83–100.

Murnane, Richard J., and others. 1991. *Who Will Teach? Policies That Matter.* Harvard University Press.

Nathan, Joe. 1989. "Progress, Problems, and Prospects with State Choice Plans." In *Public Schools by Choice: Expanding Opportunities for Parents, Students, and Teachers,* edited by Joe Nathan, 203–24. St. Paul: Institute for Learning and Teaching.

Nathan, Joe, and James Ysseldyke. 1994. "What Minnesota Has Learned about School Choice." *Phi Delta Kappan* 75 (May): 682–88.

National Board for Professional Teaching Standards. 1991. *Toward High and Rigorous Standards for the Teaching Profession.* 3d ed. Detroit.

Owen, Linda. 1993. "Students Find School Choice Proliferating in Minnesota." *Saint Paul Pioneer Press,* December 1, pp. 1C, 3C.

Pauly, Edward. 1991. *The Classroom Crucible: What Really Works, What Doesn't, and Why.* Basic Books.

Randall, Ruth E. 1992. "What Comes after Choice?" *Executive Educator* (October): 35–38.

Schmidt, Peter. 1994. "Private Enterprise." *Education Week,* May 25, pp. 27–30.

Shanker, Albert. 1993. "Achieving High Standards." Address to the 1993 QuEST Conference, Washington. July.

Summers, Anita A., and Amy W. Johnson. 1994. "A Review of the Evidence on the Effects of School-Based Management Plans." PEER background paper.

Williams, Scott, and Mark Buechler. 1993. "Charter Schools." Policy Bulletin PB-B16, Indiana University, Indiana Education Policy Center.

Witte, John F., Andrea B. Bailey, and Christopher A. Thorn. 1993. "Third-Year Report: Milwaukee Parental Choice Program." University of Wisconsin, La Follette Institute of Public Affairs.

19

THE BIRTH OF A MOVEMENT

Joe Nathan

Charter schools, a more widely accepted version of school choice than
vouchers, are currently operating in many states. This excerpt from
*Charter Schools: Creating Hope and Opportunity for American Edu-
cation* focuses on the beginning of the charter school movement in
Minnesota, but many of the experiences and lessons it presents can be
applied nationwide.

○

THE CHARTER SCHOOL MOVEMENT is one part of a more than two-hundred-
year push in the United States for expanded educational opportunity. It
complements the efforts to expand voting rights, to earn a fair wage, to
gain respect. As one insightful union official pointed out to me, "The
people who start charter schools in the 1990s are the kind of people who
started unions in the 1930s." Just as expansion of voting and workers
rights was opposed by people who had power and did not want to share
it, so the charter school movement has been opposed by a broad array of
powerful education groups.

Ideas and people change history. The story of passing the first charter
school legislation in the country includes advocates with a vision of a new
way of educating our children, politicians who decided to give promising
ideas a chance despite intense organized opposition, and teachers who believe in themselves and the power of education. Indeed, the dedication of
charter school advocates across the country explains how, despite well-
financed opposition from major educational groups, the idea has spread

from a small group of Minnesotans to half the states in the country. Here I chronicle the charter school movement through the birth of the first charter school legislation. I outline how the charter movement built on the successes and frustrations of innovative public schools created in the 1960s and 1970s. Above all, I illustrate the importance of ongoing advocacy: educating the public and politicians about the functions, goals, and practical workings of charter schools and building a coalition of interests to support strong charter school legislation.

Early Actions

The charter school story begins in the late 1960s and early 1970s, at a time when parents and innovative public school educators all over the nation were joining together to design distinctive educational options, or *choices*. The first innovative schools, such forerunners of charter schools as Metro High School in Chicago, City as School in New York, Parkway in Philadelphia, Marcy Open School in Minneapolis, and St. Paul Open School in St. Paul, gave public school teachers the chance to create kinds of schools they thought made sense for a variety of students. These schools featured things like internships and apprenticeships in the community, site-based decision making, and extensive family involvement. By creating distinctive schools and giving families an opportunity to choose these schools, educators in these districts hoped to serve youngsters more effectively than they could with the prevailing one-size-fits-all model. New York City public school teacher and MacArthur "genius grant" winner Deborah Meier spoke for such teachers when she wrote that "[public school] choice is an essential tool" in the effort to create good public education, which needs schools "with a focus, with staffs brought together free to shape a whole set of school parameters . . . [for schools that are] small, largely self governing and pedagogically innovative."[1]

The efforts of educators and parents to create small distinctive public schools took a new direction as a result of congressional action that began in the mid-1970s. Courts and political leaders faced with massive public opposition in many communities to "forced busing," in which families were assigned to schools outside their neighborhoods, selected giving families options among public schools as one effective way to promote racial integration. Congress allocated millions of dollars to create magnet schools, optional schools with special, sometimes enhanced curricula designed to attract a racially diverse group of students.

There were several key differences between the small innovative schools created in the late 1960s and 1970s and magnet schools. First, the earlier schools generally were designed by groups of parents, community members, and teachers and principals. The magnet schools generally were designed by central office administrators, often with little parent, community, or teacher involvement. Second, the earlier, innovative schools had no admissions requirements and were open to a variety of students. The magnet schools, as noted earlier, often had admissions tests. Third, the earlier schools generally operated at the same per-pupil cost as other, more traditional schools. The magnet schools often cost more per pupil than neighborhood schools.

In the late 1970s and early 1980s, the distinctive school idea went through yet another metamorphosis. Public school districts began creating schools to which they assigned alienated, disruptive, and unsuccessful students. In many communities, the term *alternative school* was applied to these schools, and that term took on the connotation of a school or program for troubled students.

Meanwhile, the truly innovative public schools were finding that as time went on, they had less control over their budgets and faculty. Sometimes districts assigned administrators to these schools who questioned or even disagreed with a school's program philosophy. Moreover, district seniority arrangements often meant that faculty, too, were assigned to the innovative schools regardless of whether they agreed with a particular school's philosophy.

These events deeply concerned many of the original innovative school developers and interested parents and community members. The symptoms of loss of control were the subject of debates and conferences throughout the 1970s, 1980s, and early 1990s. However, the innovators found they could do relatively little to affect the way school boards and policy makers were altering the ideas the innovators had pioneered in their small distinctive schools offered as choices within the public school system.[2]

The situation led many innovative teachers and frustrated parents to consider new approaches. In the mid-1980s, the California public alternative school group Learning Alternatives Resource Network (LEARN) developed a proposed bill responding to many of these concerns. It stipulated that if thirty or more parents and/or pupils request a new school, teachers within the district choose to teach in it, and operating costs are no greater than those of programs of equivalent status for the same pupils, the district "shall establish a public school or program of choice responsive to this request."[3] The proposed bill was never introduced, much less adopted. But it signaled the frustration many parents and educators were feeling with the public education system.

School Choice in Minnesota

In Minnesota at about this same time, Governor Rudy Perpich introduced proposals for several public school choice programs. Perpich, a Democrat, felt it important to expand educational opportunities for families who could not afford to move from one community to another in order to change their children's school. He also felt that thoughtful, controlled competition could stimulate public school improvement. Perpich's 1985 proposals were strongly supported by an unusual coalition that included the Minnesota PTA; directors of the War on Poverty agencies in Minnesota; individual teachers, administrators, and parents; and the Minnesota Business Partnership (MBP). It was the first time that the MBP, representing the chief executive officers of the state's largest companies, had joined a grassroots coalition to promote school improvement.

By 1988, the Minnesota legislature had adopted three key parts of Perpich's proposals:

1. *Postsecondary options.* The Postsecondary Enrollment Options Program (1985) allows public high school juniors and seniors to take all or part of their coursework in colleges and universities, with their state funds following them and paying all tuition, book, and equipment fees. Opponents had predicted that this legislation would take many extremely successful students away from high schools and that these students would do badly in college. They were wrong on both counts. As of 1996, only about 10 percent of the state's students participated, and the vast majority were not straight-A students. Many youngsters who had compiled average or even below-average grades in high school blossomed in the collegiate environment, where they were given more freedom and treated more like adults. At the University of Minnesota, the high school students had a higher grade point average than the freshman class.[4]

2. *Options to attend other public schools.* The Area Learning Center Law and the High School Graduation Incentive Act (HSGI) (1987) allow teenagers and adults who have not previously succeeded in school to attend public schools outside their district. (Together, these two laws are known as the "second-chance law.") The HSGI also allows students to attend private nonsectarian schools if a local district contracts with these schools. Many youngsters in the programs report they have higher aspirations due to going to a new school. Among youngsters attending public schools under the second-chance law, the percentage saying they planned to graduate and continue their education in a postsecondary institution increased from 19 percent to 39 percent. Among youngsters using the second-chance law to attend private nonsectarian schools, the percentage

planning to graduate and go on to postsecondary education increased from 6 percent to 41 percent.[5]

3. *Open enrollment.* Open enrollment legislation (1988) allows K–12 students to apply to attend public schools outside their district, as long as the receiving district has room and their transfer does not increase racial segregation.

These proposals were extremely controversial when initially proposed. Most major Minnesota education groups, including teacher unions, school boards, and the superintendent association, opposed these public school choice proposals. The Minnesota Education Association (MEA) spent thousands of dollars on a videotape that was circulated around the state. Among other things, it claimed that if the cross-district public school choice law were adopted, school districts would "use . . . pretty cheerleaders to sell students on coming to their schools."[6] This didn't happen.

As people's experience with these choice programs grew, support increased. A 1985 poll by the *St. Paul Pioneer Press* found that only 33 percent of the general public supported cross-district public school choice.[7] Seven years later, a poll conducted by the major education groups in Minnesota found that 76 percent of the general public supported cross-district public school choice.[8] And a 1988 Minnesota Education Association poll of its members found that more than 60 percent supported the idea of cross-district public school choice.[9]

The full story of Minnesota's initial three-year battle for public school choice has been told by others.[10] Many of the same arguments used against postsecondary options and cross-district public school choice were to be used a few years later against the charter school idea. However, once the legislation had passed, support increased for public school choice around the state because thousands of youngsters were benefiting and because people were hearing about it, partly through newspaper and television stories. People heard, for example, about the two girls who had achieved a record for absences in their assigned school (missing eighty-nine days out of one hundred) but whose performance improved after they were transferred to a nontraditional program outside their district. The girls found that people at their new school "care more and they give you a chance, and don't just blow you off." They also "give you work that you actually want to do." These students were now planning on graduating from high school and perhaps even going on to postsecondary education.[11]

Susan (all student names are pseudonyms) was another student who benefited greatly from school choice.[12] She was in the bottom 25 percent of her high school class and undergoing therapy for depression that was at least in part related to her lack of academic accomplishment. Her special education teacher urged that she be allowed to enroll at the University of Minnesota. Her high school grade point average was 1.78 (C–/D+). Her university grade point average was 3.2 (B). And she wrote to the postsecondary options program director, "I owe a lot to you. . . . [A] heartfelt thanks is going out to you."

Sam came to the University of Minnesota after having dropped out of high school a year earlier. He had never "fit in" at high school, where it was far "too rigid and stifling." His high school grades averaged D+/C–. He maintained a B+/A– average at the university.

Paul was in the 59th percentile of his high school class, and his high school counselor called the University of Minnesota twice to protest that he should not be allowed to attend the university. However, his University of Minnesota grade point average was 4.0, and his writing instructor found him "highly motivated" and his skills "outstanding . . . at a level beyond many juniors and seniors. His papers are a pleasure to read. . . . [H]e is a very good, highly motivated student. It is a pleasure to have him as a student."

Jon, a disruptive, hostile, highly argumentative inner-city high school student, failed seven of his eight classes his last term before he dropped out. Nine months later, he began college full time, earning an A average while taking courses in philosophy, English, and political science. During his second term, he was allowed to register in a graduate English course, a course in which he received an A. He has published several magazine articles and is attempting to market two of his completed novels. He wrote:

> If I hadn't had the opportunity [to enroll in the Postsecondary Enrollment Options Program], I would certainly not have become an honors student much less a college student. . . . High school was just holding me back. I was into trouble in grade school; my junior high and high school performance was poor. But when I found out about this program I decided to go for it. . . . Here at the U I have yet to get a C. All my grades are A's and B's. I never used to get an A or B. This program was a saving grace for me and changed my life around. . . .
>
> This program allowed me to get out of the nowhere world of high school and let me recognize my own potential. It allowed me to get away from bad influences literally and become my own person away from peer pressures, annoying administrative restrictions and the intellectual staleness that high school was for me.

Moreover, the choice programs were changing the lives of good students as well as those of students in trouble. Sara, for example, was successful in high school but opted for more challenge and enrolled in one course during the fall of her high school junior year to see how she would do in college. In what would have been her senior year in high school, she was admitted as a full-time student at the University of Minnesota's Institute of Technology. During that year, she began working as a research assistant under a NASA and National Science Foundation grant. She earned a bachelor's degree in physics, with honors, at the age of twenty.

Spreading the Idea of Charter Schools

As success stories grew and public support for choice programs increased, some Minnesotans felt that the existing laws gave families more choice, but not enough choices. Some Minnesota districts had turned down educators and parent and community groups who wanted to create new kinds of schools. State Senator Ember Reichgott (now Reichgott-Junge), who had authored the cross-district public school choice program in 1988 after Governor Perpich proposed it, began looking for ways to expand the real choices for families and for educators.[13] Some answers came in 1988, when she and several other Minnesotans who had worked on open enrollment and postsecondary options were invited to a Minneapolis Foundation-sponsored conference about improving public schools. The foundation had scheduled two powerful speakers with impressive credentials to provide thought-provoking information and ideas to the invited audience.

The first speaker was Sy Fliegel, a warm, entertaining, and charismatic educator from East Harlem who had helped dozens of educators start new schools and schools within schools in his extremely low income section of New York City. Fliegel described how he and other district administrators had not used a master, strategic plan but had simply asked a few educators if they wanted to create some new schools. Soon, other teachers were also bringing in their ideas. Within a few years, there were many buildings in East Harlem with two, three, or even four innovative schools, and the results were encouraging. When the effort began, only about 15 percent of East Harlem students were reading at or above grade level. A decade later, more than 60 percent were "above average" readers, and educators from throughout the world were visiting East Harlem to see how the combination of choice and teacher empowerment worked.[14] The conference gave Senator Reichgott the opportunity not only to hear Fliegel but to spend several hours talking with him, asking him what a legislator could do to promote his ideas.

The second speaker was American Federation of Teachers (AFT) president Albert Shanker. Shanker's address was shaped by his recent reading of *Education by Charter: Restructuring School Districts,* by an educator named Ray Budde.[15] Budde recommended that school districts give innovative teachers the opportunity to create a new kind of program—perhaps a new kind of primary program at an elementary school or a humanities two- to three-hour block at a high school. He used the metaphor of the "charter" (originally a document that forged an agreement, often between explorers and their usually royal sponsors). Budde recommended districts be reorganized and that innovative teachers be given explicit permission by the school board to create innovative new programs, and like the explorers hundreds of years earlier, report back about their discoveries. Budde had been writing about this concept for years. In fact, he first applied the term *charter* to innovative schools in a 1975 conference presentation.[16] In his book, he points out that the term goes back more than 1,000 years, citing the Magna Carta (Great Charter), the agreement guaranteeing rights and privileges that King John and the English barons signed at Runnymede in June 1215, and the charter that English explorer Henry Hudson signed with the East India Company authorizing him to seek a hoped-for shortcut from Europe to Asia.[17]

Shanker liked Budde's idea of giving teachers a chance to create innovative new programs—and extended it to include entire new schools. Shanker suggested that both the school board and the majority of teachers working in a school be required to approve these new schools. Shanker knew some AFT members were frustrated by district bureaucracy. So on March 31, 1988, Shanker made a speech at the National Press Club in Washington endorsing the idea and remarking:

> One of the things that discourages people from bringing about change in schools is the experience of having that effort stopped for no good reason. I hear this all over the country. Somebody says, "Oh, Mr. Shanker, we tried something like that 15 years ago. We worked around the clock, and we worked weekends. . . . I never worked so hard in my life. And then a new school board was elected or a new principal or superintendent came in and said, 'That's not my thing.'" And that's the end of the school or program. You'll never get people to make that kind of commitment if our educational world is just filled with people who went through the disappointment of having been engaged and involved and committed to building something only to have it cut out from under them.[18]

Shanker had then urged the AFT to endorse the charter school idea, which it did at its 1988 annual convention. Shanker's next column (a column that appears weekly as a paid advertisement in the Sunday *New York Times*) praised the charter idea, again citing the problems of teachers who tried to create new, innovative "schools within schools": "Many schools within schools were or are treated like traitors or outlaws for daring to move out of the lockstep and do something different. Their initiators had to move heaven and earth to get school officials to authorize them, and if they managed that, often they could look forward to insecurity, obscurity or outright hostility."[19]

(Ray Budde had no idea that Shanker would endorse the charter concept. He learned of Shanker's interest for the first time when his wife was reading the *New York Times* that Sunday. "Oh look, Ray," she said to him. "Al Shanker is writing about you and your book!"[20])

Shanker continued to write supportive articles. In one, he cited the East Harlem program as a good model and recommended that "administrators and teachers should welcome the advent of charter schools as an opportunity to break out of the lockstep and respond directly to those students for whom the general school program is not working."[21] Shanker's speech at the Minnesota conference repeated these themes.

After hearing Shanker and Fliegel speak about the two ideas of allowing more choices among schools and developing policies that give teachers a chance to create them, four of the conference attendees offered to help Reichgott develop these ideas for Minnesota. Barbara Zohn was a parent and former Minnesota PTA president who had strongly supported Governor Perpich's proposals. She was now responsible for answering the toll-free telephone number the state department of education had set up to field parent and student questions about public school choice. Elaine Salinas was a former public school teacher who had been hired as education program officer of the Urban Coalition of Minneapolis–St. Paul. She was an advocate for low-income students who had been pushing hard for more information to help families select among schools. Ted Kolderie had been executive director of a Twin Cities–based organization called the Citizens League, a nonpartisan public policy research group. He had also been involved with a project called Public Service Options, which studied ways to change bureaucratic systems. And I was the fourth person. I was a former public school teacher and administrator who had been hired by the National Governors' Association to coordinate a project recommending priorities for governors who wanted to improve education.

The four of us helped Reichgott refine the ideas we had all heard at this conference. The idea of options in public education was not new to any of us. We had worked together on the state's open enrollment legislation. But as Kolderie put it, that legislation had simply opened up opportunity on the demand side. Parents now had the legal right to choose among public schools. But in 1989, most families still had little real choice because very few districts offered different kinds of schools. It was time to open up the supply side, providing these different kinds of schools so the right of choice would be meaningful.

The charter concept also needed fleshing out, and the Citizens League created a committee to study the idea. The Citizens League had been the first Minnesota group to promote cross-district public school choice. Legislators often used its reports in areas from transportation to housing to education because of their carefully researched ideas and specific recommendations. The committee included the president of the Minneapolis Federation of Teachers and teachers, businesspeople, and others concerned about education. Its co-chairs were a public school teacher and John Rollwagen, CEO of the Minnesota-based computer company Cray Research. After several months, the Citizens League issued a report that all committee members signed, recommending the creation of charter public schools sponsored either by a local school board or the state board of education. It also suggested that the state board be allowed to sponsor charter schools on appeal if they had been turned down by their local boards.

Next, Citizens League members and some of the people who had attended the conference where Fliegel and Shanker spoke met with State Education Commissioner Tom Nelson. This group included Doug Wallace, a state school board member; and Peter Vanderpoel, former director of the state planning agency, a former newspaper reporter, and later, a Citizens League member. A widely respected former public school educator and state legislator, Nelson was a strong supporter of public school choice who had worked closely with Senator Reichgott while in the Minnesota Senate and, as chair of a key school funding committee, had been an early proponent of Governor Perpich's ideas. He asked the group to form an ad hoc committee to develop a legislative proposal.

Developing and Passing a Proposal

The group members gradually developed a proposal for the 1990 legislature. The concepts they incorporated in this document came from ideas of the pioneering teachers and parents who had created alternatives and options within public education since the 1960s; they came from business and union groups who supported school site management; they came from legislators and members of the public who wanted to see more accountability for results in public education. Thus, the proposal included the concept of increasing student achievement, expanding choice for families, expanding opportunities for educators, and stimulating change in the larger public education system. It combined these ideas with new ones to produce a unique charter proposal that called for all the elements listed in the model charter strategy. Successful ideas have champions, individuals who make them real to large numbers of people. As mentioned earlier, Senator Ember Reichgott became the principal legislative champion of the charter school concept. She moved the charter idea through the Minnesota Senate in 1990, but the House rejected it. Then in the elections of November 1990, Governor Perpich was narrowly defeated and a new, Republican governor, Arne Carlson, took office, appointing the MEA's lobbyist as his commissioner of education. Neither the new commissioner nor the new governor supported the charter school proposal.

So Reichgott no longer had strong support from the governor's office. Within two years, Governor Carlson became a strong charter school proponent. But he was not promoting charter schools in 1991.

Reichgott was joined by Minnesota Representative Becky Kelso, also a suburban Democrat and a former school board member. She supported the charter idea because "public education needs a fair, thoughtful challenge. Not vouchers, but the stimulus of another kind of public school, competing for students." [22] Kelso tried to move the charter idea in the Minnesota House of Representatives, but the teachers unions were able to frustrate her efforts. Thus it was up to Senator Reichgott to move the idea ahead in the senate.

Reichgott smiled a little sadly at the end of the 1991 Minnesota legislative session: "Well, we gave it a really good try this year. Let's see what happens." Reichgott had spent the last two years trying to get the legislature to adopt the charter school notion. As mentioned, it passed the Minnesota Senate in 1990 but was rejected by a House-Senate conference committee. A year later, the senate endorsed the concept and again brought it to the conference committee.

The 1991 Senate bill reflected a number of changes suggested by teachers union officials. For example, the original bill permitted charter schools to hire people with special skills in such areas as art, music, and world languages whether or not they were certified teachers. This was changed in response to union officials' demands, as was language authorizing an unlimited number of charter schools. The proposal was changed to limit the number of charter schools to fifty, although the unions still considered this too many.

Along with the total number of schools to be permitted, the key controversies were over sponsorship and autonomy of the charter schools. Union officials wanted to restrict charter school sponsors to local school boards and to ensure that charter schools would follow local union-management agreement provisions unless both the local school board and the union agreed to waivers. This really bothered Terry Lydell, an innovative public school teacher who worked in Reichgott's district and helped her design the charter legislation. Lydell spent hours at the capitol, after school and on weekends, helping Reichgott explain why a strong charter law was important. He recalls being criticized by union officials for coming to the legislature. But Lydell, who had helped create alternative programs in both inner-city and suburban districts, had seen how district and union officials obstructed efforts of teachers to create distinctive schools. He once remarked, "Whether it's giving schools the power to select their own teachers, getting the materials we order to us in a timely manner, or rewarding schools which make progress with students, public school systems make it very, very difficult." [23]

Lydell participated in some of the negotiation sessions with Reichgott and union officials. He remembers being told by some union lobbyists that he "didn't belong" at the legislature. This amused him. "I deal daily with kids. I know what challenges teachers face. Legislators need to hear directly *more* from people like me, not less." Lydell and other innovative public school teachers pointed out that if school districts wanted to create innovative schools, they already had the power to do so. But most districts were not doing it, and the innovative schools (such as Lydell's) frequently encountered bureaucratic problems that made it difficult for them to succeed.

Peter Vanderpoel, who had helped develop the charter legislation, also spent hours at the capitol during the 1991 legislative session. He recalls, "Though I had not been an educator like some of the people supporting the charter concept, the idea made a lot of sense to me. It seemed like something which could stimulate a lot of positive change in a very large, complex and bureaucratic system." [24] Vanderpoel spent day after day, and plenty of nights, at the legislature in 1991, helping explain the charter concept to legislators and showing how it built on Minnesota's successful experience with other public school choice programs.

With encouragement from people like Lydell and Vanderpoel, Reichgott insisted that the Senate bill allow charter schools to be sponsored either by a local or the state board of education. This provision was in the bill that was agreed to by the Senate and then went to the House-Senate conference committee, of which Reichgott was a member.

There, three of the five House members on the committee had to support charter schools for the bill to be approved. The bill had only two of these votes initially. At that point, Reichgott and Kelso called the bill's supporters—a handful of innovative teachers, some advocates for low-income groups, some businesspeople, and a few people interested in education policy—to ask for their help in getting that third vote.

Among the public school teachers who began calling conference committee members was Launa Ellison, a veteran of inner-city schools who now taught at Barton Open School, a Minneapolis inner-city elementary school that had been named one of the finest in the nation by the U.S. Department of Education. Ellison, who was later to write an eloquent book about teaching called *Seeing with Magic Glasses*,[25] had seen the way school districts made her job and that of her colleagues difficult: "District officials often look down on those of us who work day to day with kids. It takes too long to get materials, and sometimes staff are put into our school because of their seniority, not their commitment to our school's philosophy."[26] One of the Minneapolis teachers involved in developing the charter concept, she understood teachers' needs and had suggested, among other things, that charter school teachers be allowed to continue their membership in state retirement programs. One spring evening, she called Ken Nelson, a conference committee member from the House who was wavering. He listened.

Teachers unions had supported him as he had risen to chair of the Minnesota House Education Finance Committee, which dealt with elementary and secondary school funding. Union members had been active in his election campaigns, both raising money and going door to door, urging people to vote for him. Nelson had himself introduced charter legislation in the House in 1989. It died for lack of support.

Now the MEA, the state's largest teachers union, was calling the charter school concept "insulting" and "a hoax,"[27] and the teachers unions were threatening not to support Nelson. This stunned Nelson, who felt he had not just supported but battled hard over a number of years for public schools funding. Nevertheless, Nelson respected Ellison as a veteran talented, committed Minneapolis teacher. She made sense. Despite intense union threats, Nelson had voted in 1985 for cross-district public school choice. He felt that was a good decision and that the unions had overreacted in their opposition. (A poll conducted in 1988 by the Minnesota Education Association of its members showed that more than 60 percent of the teachers supported the cross-district public school choice idea.)

Nelson proposed modifications to the Senate charter provisions that charter proponents thought significantly weakened the bill. These amendments meant, for example, that in Minnesota

> Charter schools have to get permission to operate from *both* a local school board and the state school board, rather than having the option of gaining sponsorship from a local school board *or* the state board of education.

> Only eight charter schools were to be permitted.

A majority of a charter school's board members have to be teachers in the school. Nelson believed that good teachers like Ellison should be in charge of the learning enterprise. However, this meant that charter schools would not have a free hand in developing a board, teachers would have board duties added to their workload, and many people who were not teachers but would make desirable board members would not be able to serve.

With these changes made, Nelson provided the critical third vote. The charter school provisions then became part of a larger education bill. The unions were not satisfied. They pressured conference committee members to remove charter provisions from the omnibus bill. Failing at that, they tried to defeat the bill when it returned to the House. They came within a few votes of succeeding. But a slight majority of House members voted to support the bill, including its extremely modest charter provisions. The concept, even in a drastically watered-down form, would get a try.

Senator Reichgott had conflicting emotions at the end of the 1991 legislative session: "I was delighted and disappointed. Delighted that the charter concept had been accepted. Disappointed that the final provisions were so weak."

The 1991 charter law was a long way from what Reichgott and Kelso intended. Most charter school proponents were deeply disappointed by the 1991 compromises, but Senator Reichgott's view was: "Let's give this a try and see what happens. We can always come back next year and try to improve the law."

That is what happened over the following years. Gradually, the legislature increased the number of charter schools allowed to forty. After watching local board turndowns, the legislature also modified the approval process, permitting those proposing a charter school to appeal to the state board of education if two members of the local board had voted in support of the proposal. But charter groups often find it difficult to gain those two votes. In 1995, the Minnesota state legislature approved a modification of the state's charter law, allowing three charter schools to be sponsored by a public university. This step was proposed by Rep. Matt Entenza, a liberal inner-city Democrat who had run with teachers union support. Despite efforts to deter him from making this proposal, he convinced his colleagues to give the idea a try.

Other changes make it clear that charter schools *are* public schools, that their employees may be members of the state's public employees retirement association, and that charter schools may either run their own transportation systems for students or be a part of the transportation routes of districts in which they are located.

Because the way had been prepared by earlier more modest legislation; because advocates and politicians researched, discussed, and developed their ideas, wrote the proposed legislation, and committed themselves to passing it; because a coalition of individuals and groups supported the idea; and because many legislators, educators, parents, and business people were dissatisfied with the status quo and ready to try out the charter school concept, charter school legislation became law in Minnesota. Furthermore, people around the nation responded to Minnesota's action in far greater numbers than Reichgott or any of the other Minnesota proponents had imagined they would. People wanted more choices in public education. They wanted accountability for results.

So the charter school concept was planted in Minnesota. A Minnesota farmer once explained to me that "to be a successful farmer, you have to have good seeds—like good ideas in education. People disagree about the best kind of seeds, so you have to decide what makes sense to you . . . what's likely to work. But good seeds aren't enough. You need to prepare the soil, so that it's ready to accept and nourish the seeds. You can't just put seeds in the ground. You have to keep the weeds and insects away. You hope for rain and sun in the right amounts. You stay vigilant and work hard. If it comes together, you have a good crop."

In many states, the ground was ready. Many people want more effective, accountable public schools. The charter idea is a seed that is spreading, changing the schooling and lives of thousands and thousands of youngsters.

NOTES

1. Meier, "Choice Can Save Public Education," 1991, p. 266.

2. Nathan, *Free to Teach,* 1989.

3. "Draft '86 Public Schools of Choice Bill," p. 3.

4. D. Sedio, director of the Advanced High School Students office at the University of Minnesota, Minneapolis, unpublished report, University of Minnesota, 1994.

5. J. Nathan and W. Jennings, *Access to Opportunity: Experiences of Minnesota Students in Four Statewide Choice Programs, 1989–90* (University of Minnesota: Hubert H. Humphrey Institute of Public Affairs, 1990), p. i.

6. Minnesota Education Association, "Video News Release" (St. Paul, Minn.: Minnesota Education Association, Apr. 1985). (Videotape.)

7. S. Dornfield, "Public Schools Rank High," *St. Paul Pioneer Press,* Mar. 3, 1995, p. 1A.

8. R. Hotakainen, "55 Percent in State Want Students to Spend More Time in School," *Minneapolis Star-Tribune,* Aug. 12, 1992, p. B1.

9. Minnesota Education Association, *Open Enrollment: A Minnesota Choice* (St. Paul: Minnesota Education Association, n.d.), p. 2.

10. T. Mazzoni and B. Sullivan, "Legislating Educational Choice in Minnesota: Politics and Prospects," in W. L. Boyd and H. J. Walberg, *Choice in Education: Potential and Problems* (Berkeley, Calif.: McCutchan, 1990); N. C. Roberts and P. J. King, *Transforming Public Policy: Dynamics of Policy Entrepreneurship and Innovation* (San Francisco: Jossey-Bass, 1996).

11. K. Jorgenson and E. Ward, "Rothsay Program Makes a Difference," *ECSU Review,* Nov. 1993, p. 6.

12. The five student stories that follow are from unpublished letters sent to Darryl Sedio, director of the Advanced High School Students office at the University of Minnesota, Minneapolis.

13. Ember Reichgott-Junge spoke to the author in numerous interviews from April 1989 to July 1996 about her role in passing the charter school legislation.

14. S. Fliegel, presentation at the Minnesota Foundation's Itasca Conference, Oct. 4, 1988; see also S. Fliegel, *Miracle in East Harlem* (New York: Times Books, 1993).

15. R. Budde, *Education by Charter: Restructuring School Districts* (Andover, Mass.: Regional Laboratory for Educational Improvement of the Northeast and Islands, 1988).

16. R. Budde, "Education by Charter—Key to New Model of School District." Presentation at the annual meeting of the Society for General Systems Research, 1975. (Mimeographed.)

17. Budde, *Education by Charter,* 1988; R. Budde, "Education by Charter," *Phi Delta Kappan,* Mar. 1989, pp. 518–520.

18. A. Shanker, "National Press Club Speech," Mar. 31, 1988, Washington, D.C., pp. 17–18.

19. A. Shanker, "Convention Plots New Course—A Charter for Change," *New York Times* (paid advertisement), July 10, 1988, p. E7.

20. R. Budde, interview with the author, Jan. 1996.

21. A. Shanker, "Charter Schools: Option for Other 80 Percent," *School Administrator,* Nov. 1988, p. 72.

22. Becky Kelso, interview with the author, Mar. 1996.

23. Terry Lydell, interview with the author, Feb. 1996.

24. Peter Vanderpoel, interview with the author, Feb. 1996.

25. L. Ellison, *Seeing with Magic Glasses* (Arlington, Va.: Great Ocean, 1993).

26. Launa Ellison, interviews with the author, June 1991 and Feb. 1996; see also Ellison, *Seeing with Magic Glasses,* 1993.

27. "Why MEA Opposes Chartered Schools," St. Paul: Minnesota Education Association, no date.

20

FOLLOWING THE PLAN

Lynn Olson

Whole school reform encompasses several dozen university or research-based models that attempt to transform several aspects of the school at once. These models are too numerous and complex to be discussed in this volume, yet whole school reform in general has had success in improving student outcomes by changing the whole culture of a school while keeping a majority of the original staff.

———— ○ ————

IF WHOLE-SCHOOL REFORMS PRACTICED truth-in-advertising, even the best would carry a warning like this: "Works if implemented. Implementation variable."

As states and districts embrace the concept of schoolwide change, the degree to which a school carries out the ideas and practices of a particular reform model in the way its designers envisioned has emerged as the weak link.

Research suggests that if they're well-implemented, some of these designs can produce substantial gains in student achievement. The better the implementation, the bigger the payoff.

But study after study has found that implementation is often problematic and inconsistent, even at school sites that have been identified as exemplars.

"Across every single one of those studies, implementation matters a lot," says Samuel C. Stringfield, a principal research scientist at Johns Hopkins

University in Baltimore, who has carried out numerous studies of whole-school reforms. "Implementation matters regardless of the program."

But researchers are a long way from a full understanding of the conditions that lead to successful implementation. The next research frontier, Mr. Stringfield suggests, is to figure out which designs work best under which circumstances.

The answers are crucial. Many states and districts are investing heavily in the whole-school concept, and the federal government has made available $150 million in grants for schools to adopt reform designs under the Comprehensive School Reform Demonstration Program.

The question of how to translate education programs from paper into practice is hardly new, however.

"This is a long-standing and intractable problem," says Ron Anson, a senior analyst at the U.S. Department of Education's office of educational research and improvement. "People have been trying to figure this out for 20 or 30 years."

Layers of Variability

As early as the 1970s, researchers discovered that schools didn't just adopt education designs, they adapted them—sometimes beyond recognition.

"There are many layers of variability that exist when you're trying to implement a reform program," Mr. Anson says. Each school has its own set of circumstances: teachers and teaching competence; school climate and culture; district-level values and strategies; and state standards and requirements. "So you kind of march through each set of variables," Mr. Anson explains, "and at each intersection, you have to find the approach, the strategy, the materials that will work best."

Rather than thinking about schools simply adopting an existing design, researchers say it might be more productive to think about schools "co-constructing" models that will fit their environments.

That's especially true as the designs grow more ambitious and the problems surrounding implementation become more complex. Approaches such as the Comer School Development Program or Accelerated Schools do not just alter the reading program in a building; they address everything from parent-teacher relationships to the structure of the school day.

And with such complex prescriptions for improvement come myriad ways for individual schools to alter the dosage.

When Mr. Stringfield conducted the Special Strategies study of federal Title I programs, he recalls, "it quickly became obvious that there were a couple of Success for All schools that were just doing wonderfully. And it became equally obvious that there were some not doing so well."

The same was true for other popular designs.

Last year, researchers at the RAND Corp., a nonprofit research institute based in Santa Monica, Calif., released a study of 40 schools that had adopted one of eight whole-school designs. The designs were sponsored by New American Schools, a nonprofit company created in 1991 to finance comprehensive reforms.

After two years, the RAND study found only about half the schools were clearly implementing the core elements of a design across the school. Nearly 45 percent were below that level. And four schools were still stuck in the planning stages.

The study found that schools differed greatly in their ability to carry out reforms, design teams varied widely in their capacity to help schools, and districts offered varying levels of support.

Many of the design teams that created the reform models have clear and promising ideas for how they believe a school should look, says Susan J. Bodilly, a senior social scientist at RAND who conducted the study. But, she adds, "I don't think they have the level of expertise in implementation that would enable schools to do this on a systematically successful basis."

Craft Knowledge

Researchers and practitioners are beginning to amass a body of knowledge about what it takes to make whole-school reforms work and the barriers that get in the way.

Many of the designers are learning "what the strategies are for making implementation easier, which we haven't looked at or codified enough," says Thomas B. Corcoran, the co-director of the Consortium for Policy Research in Education at the University of Pennsylvania in Philadelphia.

Implementation tends to be better, for example, when schools have chosen a design of their own free will, when there's strong leadership at the school site, and when the designs themselves are clear and specific.

Common barriers to implementation include turnover at the school and district levels, dissension among faculty members, shifts in state and district priorities and funding, and pressure to prepare students for high-stakes tests.

"A lot of times, the teachers didn't see the designs as well-aligned with the state assessments," Mr. Corcoran says of one study that looked at whole-school designs in three districts. "So the teachers were intentionally deviating from the designs to do what they thought they had to do to prepare for the tests."

The problem is that designers are trying to balance two competing demands, says Rebecca Herman, who recently oversaw a rating of whole-school reforms for the Washington-based American Institutes for Research. On the one hand, they want teachers to feel ownership of a design and to be able to shape what it looks like in their school. On the other hand, they want to maintain enough integrity for the design to remain intact.

"There's no program that you can just take and stick in a school and make it happen the way it is on paper," Ms. Herman argues. "And sometimes, when you adapt it to the situation, you lose sight of what's critical to make the program work."

Researchers at the Learning Research and Development Center at the University of Pittsburgh note that ambitious reforms often suffer from either too much or too little specification. Too much—in the form of codified materials, routines, and teaching strategies—can result in outward compliance with a design while missing the underlying intent. Too little specification can confuse and annoy teachers.

Selecting a Design

Researchers emphasize the importance of the selection process. Schools that carefully identify their needs and freely commit to a design have more success. "If a design is forced upon a school, you have a high probability that it will not go forward," Ms. Bodilly says.

The RAND study of New American Schools found that the initial match between designs and schools was often rushed. "There are more times than we would like to think when schools either have been told that they have to do this, or at least feel they have been told," says Thomas K. Glennan Jr., a senior adviser for education policy at RAND.

New Jersey, for example, recently mandated that elementary schools in 28 urban districts adopt one of five whole-school designs, following a state court order.

And Miami-Dade County, Fla., and New York City have, in the past, strong-armed some of their lowest-performing schools to carry out certain designs.

But while choice is important, "without really strong guidance as schools go about making decisions, they don't make very good ones," cautions Robert E. Blum, the director of school improvement programs for the Northwest Regional Educational Laboratory, a federally funded center in

Portland, Ore. Schools may select a model because it's popular or convenient, he says, rather than look at the strength of the research or whether the model addresses their needs.

The Perfect Fit

Unfortunately, researchers don't know as much as they would like about which designs work best under which circumstances.

"One of the things that I think we can evolve as a science over time is which reforms work where, when, and why," Mr. Stringfield says.

Already, some trends are emerging. Designs that provide teachers with a set of guiding principles but few specifics, for example, may require more capacity on the part of schools than designs that are more prescriptive.

"The latter tend to have a smoother implementation, at least in the first few years," Ms. Bodily observes. "They require less teacher time and less teacher expertise."

"I'm not saying these more philosophically based approaches are wrong," she adds, "but by their very nature, they're depending much more on teachers as professionals. And in an urban district that's very stressed out, it may be beyond their means and their energy level to really go after this."

Readiness Is Crucial

Some researchers even suggest that the question of whether schools are "ready" for whole-school reform has been overlooked.

The Special Strategies study noted that "strategies cannot be put in place when school administrators and/or faculty are reluctant to change, have no or little expectations that anything will happen, or are poorly managed either at the school or classroom level." There are conditions, Mr. Stringfield warns, "under which every reform wouldn't work."

H. Jerome Freiberg, a professor of education at the University of Houston, agrees. Readiness is critical, he argues. Yet often, "no time is spent on that issue."

If an organization isn't ready for change, it won't, adds Mr. Freiberg, who is the founder of the Consistency Management/Cooperative Discipline Program, based in Houston. His program tries to measure the climate in a school before training begins: first, to identify the school's needs from differing perspectives and, second, to ensure that everyone is on board.

Ms. Bodily of RAND suggests that readiness can be built, by phasing in designs or gradually moving schools from more to less prescriptive approaches. "But no one wants to talk about that," she adds. "They want a design to claim a school and that's the end of it."

In some deeply troubled schools, Ms. Bodilly suggests, it may be better to start simple, with less comprehensive programs focused on building the teaching capacity to ensure basic skills. Then, she adds, "when they've built the capacity among them, it may be time to go on to something more ambitious."

Mr. Anson of the Education Department's OERI agrees. "The real problem," he says, "is how you get these programs to work in schools that don't have great principals, teachers, or superintendents and can't get them."

A Problem of Drift

As developers gain experience in helping schools with implementation, they're also confronting the problem of how to sustain it.

"As we get larger numbers of 6-year-old schools, we're finding some are still absolutely dynamite, and some have gotten into fairly big trouble," says Robert E. Slavin, the founder of the Success for All program. "There is a problem of drift."

Mr. Freiberg concurs. "It really is hard work to stay and provide logistical support over multiple years," he says. "And I don't think people have done a good job of thinking that through both from the school district's perspective and from the developer's perspective."

Many of the design teams are trying to measure implementation and provide schools with benchmarks on how well they're doing.

Success for All, for example, uses an implementation checklist that is revised regularly. And there's a whole process for how to use it and provide schools with feedback.

Mr. Slavin has also begun compiling computerized information about implementation in hundreds of schools, so that schools can benchmark themselves against one another.

Similarly, Expeditionary Learning Outward Bound, a comprehensive school design that engages students in long-term, multidisciplinary projects known as "expeditions," conducts implementation checks at least once a year. Each spring, participating schools also conduct self-reviews focused on one or two core practices.

"We have a lot of concrete pieces that you can see," says Greg Farrell, the nonprofit company's president. "They're either there or they're not."

Examples include the average number of "expeditions" per student per year, the number of teachers who stay with the same students for more than one year, and the number of teachers who collect students' work in portfolios.

Implementation "is a long, slow accumulation of details and establishment of habits," Mr. Farrell emphasizes. "It's like doing the dishes or mowing the lawn. And I think there's a natural human tendency to rest and relax."

In Memphis, Tenn., researchers found that schools using whole-school designs posted better achievement gains than schools that did not.

But, says Steve Ross, a professor of educational psychology and research at the University of Memphis, "what everybody forgets is that every one of those Memphis schools got a full, 30-page report at the end of their first year with information about how they were doing, and I'd like to think that had a lot to do with it."

Mr. Ross is now working with the Appalachia Educational Laboratory in Charleston, W.Va., to put together an "implementation evaluation package" that schools could buy for about $3,000.

It would include two external visits during the year by outside experts, help in setting up specific implementation benchmarks, and a written report based on the data.

Mr. Ross hopes the package will provide schools with a practical, cost-efficient way to evaluate their efforts.

Shifting Sand

Even knowing when a design is fully implemented is not a clear-cut issue. That's particularly true for less prescriptive programs that rely on schools to work out many of the specifics themselves.

The Oakland, Calif.-based Coalition of Essential Schools, for example, prides itself on "standards without standardization." Each school is expected to interpret the coalition's principles and redesign its curriculum, pedagogy, and assessments to fit its own context. But coalition leaders acknowledge that such an intentionally messy strategy is hard for researchers to stomach.

"The word 'implementing' is one I dislike because it suggests there's a solution, it's fashioned outside, it needs tailoring, but it can be more or less plugged in," says Joseph P. McDonald, a professor of teaching and learning at New York University.

He believes some of the changes that need to take place in schools are difficult if not impossible to measure, but still very important. "If you're talking about shifting people's beliefs, then you're talking about a level of impact that I equate with [religious] conversions or, on a more mundane scale, with things like overcoming obesity or alcohol dependence," Mr. McDonald says.

Further muddying the waters, Ms. Bodilly points out, is that many of the designs have evolved over time, so that implementation becomes a moving target. "The very things that they say are being implemented at certain periods of time are changing," she says, "so we're sort of on shifting sand here."

For example, many program designers have backed away from plans to devise their own standards and assessments, and they've placed more emphasis on basic skills than they had initially planned.

"You can basically see a maturation of the designs," Ms. Bodilly says, "but you also see this interaction with the system—a district and its policies—that's made them retreat, in a sense, from certain stances they originally took."

Experimental Phase

Meanwhile, the demand for better information on whole-school reform is growing.

Groups such as the American Institutes for Research and the Northwest Regional Educational Laboratory have begun to publish guidebooks to help schools with selection and implementation.

Mr. Stringfield is coordinating an updated study of the Special Strategies schools, some of which have been implementing whole-school reforms for more than a decade. The OERI also is supporting a $10 million research project that will seek to better define what comprehensive reform means, evaluate the effectiveness of different approaches, and try to develop a framework for people to use when they look at such programs.

In addition, the Education Department plans to spend about $4.35 million over three years for a detailed evaluation of the Comprehensive School Reform Demonstration Program.

The study will also explore the effectiveness of specific reform models. But Mary R. Rollefson, a deputy division director in the department's office of elementary and secondary education, notes that the study's small sample size may make it difficult to evaluate all of the "brand name" models.

The department also hopes to synthesize the research about whole-school reform across numerous, ongoing studies.

Experts hope such research will begin to fill in the gaps on what is considered one of the most promising innovations in education in years—but an innovation that remains unproven on a large scale.

"It's kind of like we're in an experimental phase with whole-school reform," Mr. Freiberg of the University of Houston says. "We don't always have all the answers."

Mr. Stringfield adds a caution. "These reforms are now in a market environment, and developers are marketing their products," he says. "And, in that environment, the buyer obviously has to be somewhat cautious. What is a mistake is to think you can buy one of these and plug it in."

2 1

ASSESSING DISTRICT CAPACITY

district office politics

Phillip C. Schlechty

When people talk about school reform, the conversation usually centers on what goes on in classrooms or at the school site. This chapter addresses the need for the district to be a reform-centered agency. Assessing district capacity for change is a crucial part of ascertaining the viability of reforms that hope to reach the classroom level.

○

IN SPITE OF THE FACT THAT there are numerous examples of "schools that work," few examples can be found of school *districts* where all the schools work as well as the community would like. As much variation seems to exist among schools within school districts as across district lines. Exemplary school districts are harder to find than exemplary schools within school districts that seem to be failing. Further, when exemplary districts do appear, they tend to be relatively small or to consist of clusters of schools in larger school districts such as East Harlem District 4 in New York City, which includes the highly praised Central Park East Secondary School. Indeed, much of the early research on effective schools was based on locating schools that worked inside school districts that did not.

Observations such as these have led some to the conclusion that the large size of some districts and the complexity introduced by the existence of a central office are major barriers to improving schools. The argument is often heard that because so few school districts exist in which schools are uniformly good and because the real action occurs in schools and classrooms, school district offices should be eliminated or at least made irrelevant to the operation of schools. Clearly, the assumption underlying vouchers, some of the more extreme forms of charter schools, and decentralization is that school districts and their functionaries (sometimes called central office bureaucrats) have little to contribute to the improvement of education in America and may be impediments.

Schools and Communities

Like many others, I am sometimes amazed and appalled at the bureaucratic red tape, duplication of effort, and self-serving activity I find in the central offices of some large school districts (and some small school districts as well). Along with many others, I believe that the changes that really count are those that directly affect students. If a change does not hold the promise of increasing the number of students who learn what the schools are designed to teach them or the amount of learning of all students, then it is of dubious value. However, in spite of these observations, I do not believe that school districts should be abolished or that changes in the way they operate are irrelevant to what happens in schools and classrooms. *I am persuaded, in fact, that only through revitalizing and redirecting the action of district-level operations can the kind of widespread and radical change that must occur become possible.*

One of the reasons I feel as I do is that school districts—those agencies that correspond with locally identifiable political entities such as independent taxing authorities, municipalities, counties, and towns—are the only organizational units that can genuinely serve the interests of the entire community. Schoolhouse units, if they function as they should, necessarily center on the interests and needs of the children presently in attendance and their parents. Long-term community interests, the interests of nonparent taxpayers, and the interests of the larger civic and business community—indeed, the interests of many of the diverse groups that constitute the community from which support for schools must be derived—seldom get played out in individual schoolhouses. It is at the district level rather than the building level that the drama of community life is enacted.

As numerous commentators have observed, however, the fragmentation and the polarization of communities are major problems of our time. This fragmentation and polarization clearly have an impact on schools. Some see this impact as so great that they do not believe that school reform will be possible until schools are taken away from the control of governmental agencies and from the communities these agencies represent and are turned over to parents and perhaps to teachers and local administrators as well (see, for example, Chubb and Moe, 1990). Framing school reform issues as matters that can be resolved by reducing size and complexity and returning once again to the "little red schoolhouse" of a bygone year is attractive both aesthetically and politically. It stirs up warm reveries in the hearts and minds of many Americans, and it reduces the issues of school reform to manageable and understandable proportions. All that has to be done, the argument goes, is to dethrone the downtown bureaucrats and return control where it belongs, to the parents.

Schools that serve like-minded parents and that are staffed by teachers who are selected because they are kindred spirits also have a great deal of appeal and certainly ease problems for reform-minded educators. Finding a community to serve is clearly much easier than serving the fragmented community that exists or inventing a community. This is one of the reasons the charter school movement is intuitively attractive to so many politicians and parents; it is also the reason many educators find the idea so appealing. Yet the American experiment in education proceeds from the assumption that diversity of interests and backgrounds is healthy and can be productive. The challenge to the public schools has always been to take children from all sorts of families and all types of situations and provide them with a high-quality academic education that will simultaneously develop in them the sensibilities and civic virtues required to live in a pluralistic democracy.

To abandon school districts as a useful tool for promoting this end is an irresponsible and cavalier denial of the values that have guided American public education for over one hundred years. To abandon the idea of having schools serve as instruments for promoting a common culture—a common culture so strong that all who participate in it can benefit from and appreciate the diversity of the many cultures it contains—is to invite the kind of culture-based wars we see in Bosnia-Herzegovina. As John Dewey (1899, p. 7) observed:

> What the best and wisest parent wants for his own child, that must the community want for all of its children. Any other ideal for our schools is narrow and unlovely; acted upon it destroys our democracy. All that society has accomplished for itself is put, through the agency of the school, at the disposal of its future members. All its better thoughts of itself it hopes to realize through the new possibilities thus opened to its future self. . . . Only by being true to the full growth of all the individuals who make it up, can society by any chance be true to itself.

Public schools are about and for parents and children, and the proper focus of school activity is on the needs and interests of students. But as Durkheim observed, schools are about much more than the interests of children and the preferences of parents. They are also concerned with the interests of the community, with posterity as well as the present generation, and with ensuring that the education received by the vast majority of Americans will promote democracy in an age of information overload, cultural fragmentation, and community disintegration. Only a system that operates beyond the interests of the parents and students who attend a particular school at a particular time has the potential to ensure that these long-term cultural interests are satisfied at the same time that each child is receiving the high-quality education that he or she deserves and that parents have the right to demand.

In the short term, what individual parents want for their children may not be in the general interest or promote the common good. For example, in 1945, few white parents in the South were demanding that schools be desegregated. Today, few Americans, including those from the South, would publicly defend separate but equal as anything other than separate and evil.

The primary aim of every school district should be to ensure that each child receives a high-quality education that is responsive to the child's needs and the parents' aspirations and that at the same time is one that the wisest of parents—and grandparents—would want for their children. This is not a small task, but neither is the maintenance and growth of democracy. The task will be impossible if school districts are destroyed and schoolhouses are enshrined as the only meaningful source of direction for the American system of education.

School Districts: Barrier or Resource?

After over thirty years of working at the problem of change in schools, I have come to the conclusion that change is peculiarly difficult in schools because the schools, and the school districts of which they are typically a part, lack the capacities needed to support and sustain change efforts. Even in private corporations, where these capacities are often present, change is difficult; in public school systems, where they are usually absent, real change is nearly impossible. Regardless of this observation, I have not given up on the idea that schools can be, and should be, changed in fundamental ways. If changes are to occur, however, those who lead must come to understand that to change schools and what occurs in classrooms, reformers must first introduce the changes needed to enhance the capacity of the educational system to support and sustain change in the schools. Destroying school districts and creating schools that simply serve the short-term interests of a particular group of parents (and perhaps teachers) will weaken, rather than strengthen, both education and democracy.[1] Furthermore, such a strategy may foreshadow the demise of America's commitment to a publicly supported system of education (note that I did not say "to a public school system") and perhaps sound the death knell of American-style democracy.

One of the primary reasons school reform has generally failed is that individual schools, no matter how vital and responsive their present programs are, do not have the capacity to support and sustain change independent of the support of larger political and social units. School buildings, because of the way they are located in the political and social milieu of communities, cannot develop these capacities. For example, the hundreds and sometimes thousands of schools in a given state have little ability to interact in a meaningful way with the needs and demands of the larger business community. Local school faculties can form partnerships with local neighborhood businesses, and many do so. Some particularly aggressive or well-led faculties may even form alliances and partnerships with a local representative of a national business that has offices in the vicinity. However, these interactions, vital though they are, do little to create the conditions that will cause all schools in the community to address issues raised by business leaders, religious leaders, and civil rights groups.

Local schools, no matter how decent and committed the faculty might be, cannot deal in isolation with issues of equity. Equity is a community issue that gets played out in schools and classrooms, but solutions to problems of equity must occur where they originate, in the larger community. The way money is allocated, staff members are recruited and assigned, and access to knowledge is distributed cannot be judged in the context of individual schools. Such judgments must be made in the context of the larger systems of which the schools are a part, and the solutions to these problems must occur at the system level as well. Unfortunately as things now stand, few school districts have the capacities they need to assist at the building level. Unlike schools, however, school districts can develop these capacities *if* district-level leaders and community leaders commit themselves to the task.

School districts operate at a community level rather than simply at the level of parents and students. Thus the school district, unlike the school, is capable of commanding the attention and support of total communities, not just of parents who happen to have children in a particular school at a particular time.[2] First, however, school district functions must be redesigned and reoriented so that the district office becomes a resource for local school reform rather than a barrier to the development of effective local schools.

Going to Scale and Maintaining Momentum

Interesting, useful, and provocative models, exemplars, successful experimental schools, and prototype programs are not in short supply in American public education. The difficulty comes, it seems, in transporting these practices from the sites where they are invented and demonstrated to other sites. The history of education is replete with examples of successful experiments that were abandoned after they had proved their worth. In business this is referred to as the problem of "going to scale."

Schools have the further difficulty of ensuring that sound practices, once they have been demonstrated, are maintained over the long term or until more effective programs and practices come along to replace them. This problem even exists in schools where the innovative ideas were first created or tried. Quite often a school that develops a national reputation as a leader in a particular type of initiative will have abandoned it and embraced a new reform by the time word of the first initiative has encouraged visitors to come and see what is happening. This is especially the case if the initiating principal leaves or a substantial number of the trailblazing faculty go on to different jobs. Why are these things so? Why is it so difficult to take demonstrably sound ideas to scale in educational settings? Why is the maintenance of the momentum of change so dependent on the presence of particular personalities? The answer to these questions lies, in part, in understanding what capacities are needed to support and sustain school reform initiatives.

Critical Capacities

If substantial, purposeful change is to occur and be sustained over time, the organization that is the subject of the change must possess three critical capacities:

1. The capacity to establish and maintain a focus on the future

2. The capacity to maintain a constant direction

3. The capacity to act strategically

The Capacity to Establish and Maintain a Focus on the Future

All organizations must deal with the daily, the routine, and the immediate. In this regard schools are like other organizations. But unlike many other systems, schools and those who lead them often find it difficult and often impossible to get beyond the immediate and seriously to contemplate the future. In many schools "visioning" becomes an exercise people engage in as part of a strategic planning process. But once the exercise is done, they must return to reality, or so it is often argued. Thus, in school settings, strategic planning often becomes nothing more than a process for identifying tactics to deal with the immediate problems that are tearing at the system.

In organizations where the capacity to focus on the future is present, vision is a process of imagining a preferred future, and strategic planning is a process of identifying the ways and means of attaining that future. The maintenance needs of the organization, although very real, are not permitted to overwhelm developmental needs. This is not so in most school systems. Maintenance needs almost always overwhelm developmental needs (see Schlechty and Whitford, 1983).

The Capacity to Maintain a Constant Direction

Substantial change calls for changes in culture as well as structure. It requires changes in habits and traditions as well as in practices and procedures, in values and commitments as well as in rules, roles, and relationships. It requires time and persistence of effort. When resistance is encountered, strategies must be developed to overcome or bypass it. When enthusiasms temporarily wane, strategies must be developed to reinvigorate the process.

In schools, when substantial resistance occurs, the likely result will be that the chief proponents of the change will be replaced by proponents of a return to the status quo or to some other preferred past condition, such as "back to the basics." When a change begins to affect powerful interest groups, as always happens when change is real, the disaffection of these groups is too often viewed by school and community leaders as a signal that the change is ineffective, rather than as evidence that it is having predictable effects.

The Capacity to Act Strategically

Strategic action requires the ability to make choices and act on them. Because these choices are future-oriented, they are sometimes necessarily antagonistic to present short-term interests. The school superintendent or school board confronted with the need to close schools or to redistrict fully understands how difficult strategic action is in the context of schools.

Because of these difficulties, school leaders are under constant pressure to abandon strategic decisions in favor of immediate accommodation to present interests. The school that should be closed is left open and budget cuts are made elsewhere, probably in staff development and training. For example, in schools it is common to assume that funds must be equally distributed and cuts equally endured, rather than that cuts could be made strategically, with an eye toward actions that are optimally supportive of long-term missions and goals. New programs almost always require new money because abandoning old programs to free up resources will almost always bring a special-interest contingent to the next board meeting.

Essential Questions

Over the past thirty years, I have had the opportunity to observe a wide range of efforts to bring about change in schools. I have led some of these efforts, and I have watched others lead. I have talked with many who are leading change efforts in schools, and I have read widely in the literature on change as well as in the literature on organizational behavior and the sociology of complex social organizations.[3] Based on these experiences, I have identified ten organizational goals that I believe school district leaders must attend to, or cause others to attend to, if the districts they lead are to have the capacities needed to support and sustain reform at the building level. I have listed the goals as well as questions that might be asked in an effort to assess just how well a district is doing in achieving these goals.

GOAL 1. To develop, among those who will be called on to lead the reform effort and those whose support must be garnered if the reform is to be sustained, a shared understanding of the nature of the problems that give rise to the need for fundamental reform in our schools

1. Do educational leaders and those whose support is needed to sustain a reform effort share a common understanding of the reasons why the school district and schools in the district need to be changed?
2. Does the district engage in practices that are intended to educate community members and staff about the reasons reform is needed?
3. Do the policies, practices, programs, and procedures employed within the district reflect an understanding of the importance of educating the community about the need for reform and of provid-

ing this education on a continuing basis using a variety of media and approaches?

4. Does the district engage in market research? Does it regularly assess students' perceptions of the quality of the work they are being asked to do and the interest this work has for them? Are the needs and satisfactions of parents and other community members regularly assessed? If so, are the data generated by this research made available to teachers and principals? Is it expected and intended that problems be identified and acted on and that opportunities to improve be seized upon?

GOAL 2. To develop within the local context a compelling vision of what schools can be and how they should be related to the community—a vision capable of earning wide support in the school district and the community and consistent with a set of well-articulated beliefs regarding the nature of schools and the schooling enterprise

1. Does the school district have a well-articulated set of beliefs about
   - The purpose of schools?
   - The ability of students to learn?
   - The factors that determine the opportunity to learn?
   - The role of the family and community in relation to students and schools?
   - The kind of society for which students are being prepared?
   - The focus of school activity?
   - The rules, roles, and relationships that should govern behavior within schools, between schools and the district-level office, and between schools and the community?
   - The obligation of the system to employees and the role of the system in encouraging and supporting innovation?

2. Have these beliefs been translated into a clear vision of the way the school system should operate, and is the present operation of the school district and the schools consistent with this vision?
   - Are the beliefs, values, and operating styles of teachers, administrators, and other community members consistent with the vision?
   - Are the rules, roles, and relationships encouraged by the school district consistent with the vision?

3. Does the district have a means of communicating the vision to new employees or new members of the community?

4. Does the district regularly celebrate and affirm the vision?

GOAL 3. To develop throughout the system a clear focus on the student as the primary customer of the work of the school and on the needs and expectations of those whose support is needed if students are to be served effectively

1. Is the student viewed as the primary customer for the work of the school district?

2. Is the product of the schools viewed as knowledge work designed for students?

3. Do the schools have policies, procedures, programs, and practices focused on

   • Identifying student needs?

   • Determining how to respond to those needs?

   • Modifying the initial response to better meet those needs?

4. Do teachers and administrators have a clear understanding of whose support is needed if students are to be served effectively, and have they developed strategies for getting and sustaining that support?

5. Do teachers and administrators have a clear understanding of the needs and expectations of those whose support is needed, and do they act on these understandings?

GOAL 4. To develop a results-oriented management system and a quality-focused decision-making process that are consistent with the beliefs that guide the system and that ensure that the measures of quality conform to the requirements of those who provide support to the school's customers

1. Does the school district focus its efforts on enhancing the qualities of schoolwork provided to students to accomplish the purpose of the school, rather than simply focusing on the secondary measurements of that schoolwork, such as annual test scores?

2. Are policies, procedures, programs, and practices assessed in terms of their impact on the achievement of the strategic goals of the school district?

3. Does the community contribute to and support the measures of quality used by the school district?

4. Are the school district's goals and mission consistent with the vision of schooling?

5. Are goals evaluated on the degree to which they promote the realization of this vision?

GOAL 5. To develop a pattern of leadership and decision making within the school district and between the school district and other youth-serving agencies that is consistent with the assumption that teachers are leaders, principals are leaders of leaders, and the community must guarantee each child the support needed to ensure success in school

1. Do those who are affected by a decision understand how it was made, feel responsible for it, and feel committed to it?

2. Are decisions evaluated on the extent to which they increase the likelihood of student success?

3. Are school district personnel and community members involved in the current decision making and strategic planning that affect the youth of the community?

4. Are school district personnel encouraged to make decisions based on their expertise and the best available information?

5. Do school district personnel have easy access to the best available information when they are called on to make decisions?

6. Do school district personnel clearly identify the anticipated results before making a decision, determine whether the anticipated results occurred, and if necessary, modify the original decision in order to achieve the desired results?

GOAL 6. To develop a policy environment and a management system that foster flexibility and rapid response; encourage innovative use of time, technology, and space; encourage novel and improved staffing patterns; and create forms of curriculum organization that are responsive to the needs of children and youth

1. Do individuals who are called on to implement policies, procedures, and programs have the capacity to respond rapidly and flexibly?

2. Are time, people, space, knowledge, and technology used as variables to create conditions that enhance student success?

GOAL 7. To develop and maintain systems and programs that encourage systematic innovation and the assessment of innovations within the context of a Total Quality Management framework

1. Are school district personnel encouraged to initiate and implement new ideas?

2. Are innovations systematically evaluated for the results they produce?

3. Are policies, procedures, programs, and practices in place to ensure that innovations that are not achieving desired results are modified or discontinued?

4. Is a system in place designed to ensure that innovations are consistent with the beliefs and vision that guide the district?

GOAL 8. To encourage and support the creation of new relationships between and among agencies and groups that provide services to children and youth, in order to ensure that each child has the support needed to succeed in the school and the community

1. Are opportunities to work collaboratively provided for personnel from the school district and from other youth-serving agencies?

2. Does agreement exist on the support students need in order to succeed?

3. Do formal and informal agreements between the school district and youth-serving agencies outline avenues for mutual support?

4. Do the results of these agreements produce the support needed for students to succeed?

GOAL 9. To ensure continued support for innovative efforts after initial enthusiasms wane, as long as the efforts continue to produce the desired results

1. Are innovations evaluated by their contribution toward increasing the capacity of the system to realize the district's vision?

2. Are means available to ensure that successful policies, procedures, programs, and practices are continued beyond the tenure of the original leaders, developers, or implementers?

GOAL 10. To provide systems of training, incentives, and social and political support for those who are committed to the objectives outlined herein and to widen support for the pursuit of these objectives among all members of the community

1. Is there a means of identifying the training, incentives, and social and political support needed by those who are committed to the vision of the school district?

2. Does the school district provide the necessary resources to provide that system of support?

3. Is the system of support designed to widen commitment to student success among all members of the community?

An Assessment Strategy

Beliefs, visions, and missions indicate where we are going. Road maps are useless, however, unless we know where we are as well as where we are headed. Assessment is a process of figuring out where we are at the present time; it consists of taking stock. Conceptually, it should be possible to develop a profile of a school district using the ten goals listed above as the basis of the profile and assessing the school district according to the extent to which these goals have been and are being realized in the district. The answers to the questions, assuming that they were disciplined with data, could indicate the extent to which goals are being achieved and where more work might be needed.

Obviously, much work would need to be done to make it possible to systematically collect and analyze data related to the goals outlined above. Indeed, much work would need to be done to ensure that the questions asked under each of the goals are the right ones to ask. The questions presented here give direction to the kinds of questions that must be asked when developing data upon which to base answers, but they are not adequate in themselves. Take, for example, the first question under Goal 1: Do educational leaders and those whose support is needed to sustain a reform effort share a common understanding of the reasons why the school district and schools in the district need to be changed?

To answer this question, we would first need to identify the relevant leaders and those whose support is needed and then design some set of questions to elicit from them their views on whether or not and why change is needed. Armed with such data, we would need to develop a means of assessing the extent of the agreement and consensus among the respondents; then we would need some way to evaluate and give meaning to what has been assessed, for example, by asking how much agreement is enough.

Clearly, undertaking such a task requires a heavy investment in time and personnel, an investment that few school districts can or should make. It is possible, however, to use this framework in ways that are useful without being as precise as a researcher might want. As Willard Waller ([1932] 1967) observed, educational research should never get too far in front of common sense, and researchers and theoreticians should be careful not to fall behind common sense.

The following situation illustrates one such process:

○

Key central office staff meet in seminar settings to review goal statements and make whatever modifications seem appropriate in the local context. This process might be facilitated by a knowledgeable outsider; as an alternative, the superintendent and key central office staff, including perhaps some principals and teacher leaders, might form a study group, using as core materials materials judged to be needed and appropriate, such as videotapes, books, field research materials, and action research techniques.

Regardless of the approach taken, what is important is that key leaders in the district be knowledgeable about the goals, understand their significance, and also understand and believe (be willing to act on) the assumptions underlying the assertion that one of the reasons for the failure of school reform is that districts lack the capacity to support and sustain reform.

Having established among key leaders an awareness and understanding regarding the nature of the organizational goals that must be pursued to develop the capacity to support change, this leadership group, perhaps with support from outside consultants, should identify a cadre of key individuals who are judged to be positive and influential among such stakeholder groups as parents, teachers, principals, support staff, business leaders, and civic and community leaders, including school board members.[4]

A training program should be developed and implemented for the group described above, aimed at achieving the following objectives:

To develop an awareness of the need to create district capacity and an understanding of the basic dimensions along which such capacities might be described

To develop a rudimentary understanding of basic concepts and data collection processes associated with action research techniques, along with an understanding of how these techniques can be employed in assessing the capacity of the school district to pursue the goals outlined above.[5]

Teams of teachers, principals, parents, and others who have undergone the training outlined above should then be organized to collect and analyze data that will support an assessment of the district's capacity to support change. The point here is a simple one. What the teams are expected to do is to collect all the information, facts, and opinions that are judged to be relevant and useful to answer the question: What is the case here with regard to the essential questions that have been outlined? Assuming that this task is carried out with diligence and care, district leaders should have available to them a useful basis for answering such questions as, Does the district have the capacity to support change? and, In what areas is the district strong and in what areas is it weak? Based on the answers to these questions, leaders should be able to decide where work is needed and what kind of work is needed if the necessary capacities are to be put in place.

○

Strategic Thinking

It is likely that the creation of a profile such as the one suggested above will reveal that the capacities of the school district are unevenly developed. For example, it has been my experience that few school districts have much capacity in the area of marketing and community education (Goal 1), though some do have considerable capacity in the area of staff training.

One of the most critical questions leaders must confront, even after a relatively clear understanding of district capacity is in hand, is where to start. Starting everywhere at once is ill advised. An old adage says, "One goal is a goal, two goals are half a goal, and three goals are no goal at all." Like all such adages, this one has its limitations, but it reminds us that focus is important, especially when we are trying to bring about change in complex social systems such as schools. There are no hard-and-fast rules for making such decisions. It has been my observation, however, that leaders who move systems think strategically as well as act strategically and that among the most powerful concepts in the repertoire of these change leaders are the concepts of *sequence, linkage,* and *leverage.*

Sequence

At any point in time, and under given conditions, movement toward one goal is necessary before movement toward another goal is possible—as in the game of chess, in which some pieces simply cannot be moved until others have been moved. It is nearly impossible to move very far in improving the capacity of a school district to manage by results unless the capacity of the district to provide needed training is first put into place. Making decisions about the *sequence* in which different goals should be pursued requires strategic thinking.

Linkage

Some goals can be pursued relatively independently of others. Like the knight in chess, some goals can be moved forward without much concern about blockage from other pieces. The difficulty, of course, is that when the knight gets too far out in front, it cannot be protected and may be lost to hostile forces. The same is true of some goals.

I had occasion to observe a superintendent who became concerned that the community did not understand how poorly the system he headed was performing, so he set about developing a program to inform the community about the problems that had not been revealed by past administrations. At first, he was seen as a breath of fresh air, but as time went on, people began to say, "We didn't have these problems before Dr. X arrived. Maybe it's time we got rid of him."

Strategically, before moving the ability to communicate problems too far down the road, Dr. X should have enhanced the capacity of school leaders to imagine and envision solutions to the problems this newly created capacity revealed. Without development of the capacity to envision and implement solutions, the enhanced capacity to communicate problems may bring the entire effort to a halt—or at least lead to the search for a new leader, which is what happened in this case. This is *linkage;* some goals are linked in their effects even though initial inspection may lead us to think of them as relatively independent.

Leverage

Some goals are so tightly linked to other goals that when action is taken to enhance capacity in the area suggested by them, other capacities are improved as well. If such goals can be identified and acted on, high-leverage activity results. For example, school districts that lack the capacity to manage by results can use a focus on results to almost force changes in several other areas as well. A truly results-focused district cannot emerge until and unless beliefs are relatively well articulated and agreed upon because beliefs provide the standards for determining what results are worth pursuing. Similarly, a results-focused district will not become a reality unless the capacity to identify and market problems and solutions is in place. Under the right circumstances, therefore, focusing on improving the district's capacity to manage by results will increase the capacity of the district in other areas as well. This is *leverage*.

Two Examples

Presenting arguments like those set forth above almost always raises the question, Can you show me someplace that is doing what you recommend here and, if so, what are the results? My answer at this point is that I cannot tell you of any school districts that I believe have developed, to the point I think necessary, the capacities I have suggested here. Neither am I in a position to speak of results, because nothing has produced the kinds of results I believe would be produced if such capacities were present. However, I can point to a number of districts that are worth watching, though they are not yet developed to the point where I might hold them up as finished products.

The first district is the Memphis City Schools in Memphis, Tennessee. Under the leadership of Gerry House, the superintendent, the concepts set forth here have been used to give shape to a very elaborate strategic planning process that has brought together a wide range of community actors in support of a common agenda. Since that plan was developed, the school district has been increasingly successful in procuring funding to support various innovative efforts aimed at realizing the vision suggested by the plan. In addition to receiving a very large National Science Foundation grant to promote systemic reform in urban schools, the district has also procured considerable support from local businesses and a local foundation (the Plough Foundation) that is intended to enhance the capacity of the district to provide needed and relevant training and support to teachers and administrators.

Perhaps the most significant aspect of this example is that the designers of a number of nationally recognized school reform projects who are concerned about taking their projects to scale selected Memphis as one of their exemplary implementation sites, at least in part because of the emphasis the superintendent and her staff have given and are giving to the development of the infrastructure needed to support and sustain building-level reform.

A second example is of a process currently under way in Phillipsburg, New Jersey, where Tom Seidenberger is the superintendent. Unlike Memphis, where a systematic assessment of capacities was never formally conducted, Phillipsburg has found that the key to its effort has been an assessment process that resulted in a series of recommendations for action within the school district. Two comments about the Phillipsburg project seem in order here.

First, because the assessment and the resulting document were produced by people who were not experts in either assessment or planning, those experts who read the document will probably find many flaws. So be it. The purpose of strategic plans is to motivate and direct action. As many visitors to Phillipsburg have reported, this process is doing just that. This outcome seems preferable to the outcome for those relatively flawless and professionally done plans one often sees filed in offices and never referred to again.

Second, data were collected by teams made up of educators, school board members, parents, students, and concerned citizens, including senior citizens. Ten data collection teams were each assigned the task of collecting and analyzing data relevant to one of the ten goals set forth above. The people who collected and analyzed these data were citizens in the community who—in the process of following relatively conventional research procedures—became persuaded themselves of the validity of their conclusions, and their reputations persuaded others. This may not be satisfying to the research community, but in the world of human action, people are executed on the basis of less evidence than this "grand jury" had available to it.

The Issue of Time

In his now-classic book *Schoolteacher* (1975), Dan Lortie defines *commitment* as the willingness to allocate scarce resources. Time is one of the scarcest resources in any organization, but the way schools are currently structured, it is even scarcer in schools. An assessment process and a planning process like those described and illustrated above require a considerable commitment of time, from the superintendent's office on down. Indeed, I would argue that unless the superintendent is prepared to give strong and visible leadership to this process, it is probably not worth undertaking. (In both Memphis and Phillipsburg, the superintendent was a key and central actor in the process.) This kind of work, if properly conducted, brings into focus the moral order of the district. And as I have argued elsewhere (see Schlechty, 1990), the superintendent can delegate almost every kind of authority he or she has except the moral authority that is embodied in the office of the superintendent. This process requires the visible and continuous presence of that authority.

This does not mean that the superintendent is required to conduct all the meetings needed to move such processes along or to plan or deliver the training, though it is symbolically very powerful when he or she does such things. What is required is that the superintendent be present and attentive at key events and take every occasion to symbolize the importance attached to the process.[6]

It is equally important that processes such as those illustrated or proposed here have strong and continual leadership from some person who sees the management of the process as her or his primary responsibility. Thus, unless a district is prepared to commit a substantial amount of a relatively senior-level person's time to coordinating this effort and unless the superintendent is prepared to protect that time, it is doubtful that the process I have outlined will produce the best results.

In addition, the people on the assessment teams need to be provided with time and staff support to conduct their work. Those who are unable or unwilling to make such time commitments should not be brought into this process early, for the early work is critical and requires substantial effort.

Finally, unless the superintendent and the board of education are prepared to develop and implement strategies for communicating the results of this effort to the community, and plans for bringing about improvements in capacity where they are needed, it is doubtful that this process will yield much more than a few people who get excited for a little while.[7]

NOTES

1. The reader should not infer from this statement that I am necessarily opposed to in-district choice or charter schools, for I am not. What I do oppose is granting autonomy to such schools. Schools should operate within the context of the corporate belief system that guides the district. They should not be autonomous units operating outside of this context. Within it, however, schools can be granted a great deal of independence of action.

2. Some will suggest that individual schools could operate at the community level as well, if only their leaders wanted them to. True enough, as long as the number of individual schools operating at the community level is rela-

tively small. Even now, one of the complaints of some leaders of nationally and internationally focused businesses is that the requests from individual schools for partnerships and other support in some communities is overwhelming their capacity to respond. As an example, I have worked with many businesses that are willing to make their executive training programs available to educators if they can find a way to do so. They find it much less inviting, however, to provide these programs to a small cadre of leaders from a single school than to cohorts of leaders from a school district.

3. There was a time in my life when I styled myself a sociologist who was interested in the study of organizations and occupations. I taught courses on these subjects as well as on the sociology of education generally. I even wrote a book entitled *Teaching and Social Behavior: Toward an Organizational Theory of Instruction* (1976), which was a rather ham-fisted and jargon-laden effort to apply what sociologists think they know to the problems of educators. I am still influenced by my sociological origins; however, I use less jargon than I once did.

4. It is assumed that the superintendent will keep the board informed of this process and that some conversation has taken place regarding intentions from the beginning of the discussions. Indeed, it is probably advisable to have board members as a part of the initial study group. However, I have been in situations where board members, because of other obligations, felt that they did not have the personal time to give to such an undertaking. And in some cases, board members who do have the time use it to interfere in the management of schools rather than to become informed so that they can formulate better policies for managing schools. The superintendent who has a board that functions the way it should will have little difficulty in keeping the board informed and involved. If the board is dysfunctional, as too many boards seem to be, it is doubtful that this process can go too far before the superintendent is dismissed or political hassles accelerate.

5. If is likely that the design and delivery of this program will require some outside assistance. Typically, local teacher education institutions will have faculty members who are knowledgeable about field research and action research techniques. Assuming that such people are available and will accept the agenda that is outlined, as opposed to bringing their own research agenda and theoretical frameworks to the table, this provides a great opportunity for local school districts and local universities to work together. Failing that, local businesses with well-developed market research capabilities are another possible source of support. Independent consultants and consulting firms are also available.

6. I have had occasion to conduct seminars for business executives as well as for educators, and I am constantly struck by the fact that school adminis-

trators give participation in such meetings much lower priority than do most business executives. The pagers of business executives go off less frequently than those of educators, emergency phone calls are less obtrusive and distracting, and crisis-oriented interactions are less frequent. One explanation for this is that the context of schools generates more crises than that of business. Another is that business leaders have learned to delegate and havè developed systems of training and accountability that make it possible for them to trust that crises will be managed whether or not they are there. The paternalistic structures upon which our schools were founded continue to play themselves out in the lives of teachers and administrators.

7. One of the problems school boards will confront is the likelihood that some of the remedial work needed will be relatively expensive and not linked to improvement in student performance directly enough to inspire widespread and immediate community support. For example, most schools lack the ability to provide training and support to teachers and administrators, which is critical to the success of change efforts. Yet the first budget line to be reduced in the face of budget cuts is likely to be the budget for staff development and for supporting staff travel to conferences. Properly presented, the business community and philanthropic organizations can help to offset this problem. The Gheens Academy in Louisville, Kentucky, the Mayerson Academy in Cincinnati, Ohio, and the Teaching Learning Academy in Memphis, Tennessee, are illustrations of ways in which businesses, local philanthropic foundations, and other community organizations can work to enhance the capacity of a district to provide needed training and support and be somewhat protected from budgetary fluctuations.

REFERENCES

Chubb, J. E., and Moe, T. M. *Politics, Markets, and America's Schools.* Washington, D.C.: Brookings Institution, 1990.

Dewey, J. *The School and Society.* Chicago: University of Chicago Press, 1899.

Lortie, D. *Schoolteacher: A Sociological Study.* Chicago: University of Chicago Press, 1975.

Schlechty, P. C. *Schools for the 21st Century: Leadership Imperatives for Educational Reform.* San Francisco: Jossey-Bass, 1990.

Schlechty, P. C., & Whitford, B. L. "The Organizational Context of School Systems and the Functions of Staff Development." In G. A. Griffin (ed.), *Staff Development: Eighty-Second Yearbook of the National Society for the Study of Education.* Part II. Chicago: University of Chicago Press, 1983.

Waller, W. *The Sociology of Teaching.* New York: Wiley, 1967. (Originally published 1932.)

22

A MIXED RECORD FOR RECONSTITUTION FLASHES A YELLOW LIGHT FOR DISTRICTS

Caroline Hendrie

Reconstitution is a radical approach to school reform that has increasingly been enacted in major cities over the last decade. Sometimes called redesign, it is a complete restaffing of a school. Reconstitution is often chosen when a low-performing school is in a downward spiral. In other cases it can be used, as it was in San Francisco, as part of a desegregation order in which both staff and students are shifted to other schools.

———————— o ————————

THEY CALL IT A REFORM OF LAST RESORT, but last year at least half a dozen big districts resorted to it anyway. Reconstitution—the practice of restaffing a troubled school from scratch and starting over—seemed to be catching on.

But this year, almost none of those districts is planning an encore. Even San Francisco, which has reconstituted 10 schools in the past four years, has returned the powerful accountability tool to the toolbox.

"Reconstitution can always come back, but the district and union are going to try a different way," said John R. Flores, San Francisco's coordinator of school intervention.

In Chicago, Cleveland, Denver, Philadelphia, and Prince George's County, Md., school and teachers' union leaders are singing a similar tune. All those districts reconstituted schools last year, or in Philadelphia's case, tried to. Now all are pursuing other strategies to shake up their low-performing schools—at least for the time being.

"It's something that sets schools and teachers in such a tizzy," Philadelphia schools spokeswoman Barbara A. Grant said of reconstitution, "that you have to wonder if there's a less painful way to accomplish the same goal."

Outside of San Francisco, the overall effectiveness of such school makeovers has rarely been studied. But state and local policymakers continue to express strong interest in the strategy as they seek solutions to stubbornly poor performance in certain schools. So writing reconstitution off as yesterday's news would clearly be premature.

Still, pressure to rethink the idea—which typically disperses much of a targeted school's staff to other jobs in the district—is coming from several fronts. In some districts, including Chicago and San Francisco, the practice has become a central issue in labor negotiations. In others, such as Cleveland and Philadelphia, adverse rulings in disputes with teachers' unions have forced school leaders to retrench. And the rocky time districts such as Prince George's County have had during their foray into reconstitution has sent them back to the drawing board.

But whatever the reasons for putting the practice on ice, no one is happier about it than local teachers' unions.

"Reconstitution is the Clint Eastwood approach to reforming schools," said Kent Mitchell, the president of the United Educators of San Francisco. "You just pull out a gun and blow them away."

Fresh Start Sought

The theory behind reconstitution is that some schools have been so dysfunctional for so long that the best hope for turning them around is to clean house and start over.

In practice, how districts have taken on that housecleaning process—and how well it seems to have worked—has varied widely. In some cases, virtually all employees have been reassigned, while in others the majority have successfully reapplied for their jobs after agreeing to cooperate in the turnaround effort.

Over the past decade, Atlanta, Houston, Milwaukee, Paterson, N.J., and San Antonio, among others, have resorted to some version of reconstitution. In San Francisco, the practice became institutionalized in recent years as part of a desegregation case.

As the hunger for high-impact accountability measures grew and the visibility of San Francisco's strategy rose, last year saw a spate of first-ever reconstitutions in cities around the country.

That officials in some of those districts are now having second thoughts should come as no surprise, said Gary A. Orfield, a Harvard University scholar who has studied San Francisco's reconstituted schools.

One problem, he said, is that some districts may have rushed into reconstitution as a seemingly straightforward—if radical—reform, without committing the proper time and resources to making it work. Another, he said, is that the negative effects—such as a loss of seasoned staff members to help mentor new recruits—are often quickly and painfully apparent.

"Your benefits don't come until three or four years down the road, but the costs are immediate, so it's very difficult politically," Mr. Orfield said. "What seems like a simple idea turns out when you do it to be a lot more complicated."

In Chicago, administrators used reconstitution for the first time last year, overhauling seven high schools as part of a broad crackdown on failing schools. This year, district leaders decided to hold off on any more, even though an advisory council urged them to shake up 15 more schools, either through reconstitution or similarly aggressive means.

"Last year, we felt very strongly that we had some schools that were showing continuous decline and that we had to do something radical," said Cozette Buckney, Chicago's chief academic officer. "Now we have an opportunity to look at what we did. Closing and opening so rapidly, to us, is not the best way to do it."

Ms. Buckney said the 430,000-student district is now negotiating with the city's affiliate of the American Federation of Teachers on an interim step between putting schools on probation and reconstituting them.

"There are many things we can do to address the deficiencies of students and staff without totally closing a school and starting all over again," she said.

Thomas H. Reece, the president of the Chicago Teachers Union, couldn't agree more.

"I do give them credit for, if not admitting publicly the mistakes that were done before, at least not doing them again," he said of the district's leadership.

Union Pushes Alternatives

Galvanized by reconstitution's rise in popularity, Mr. Reece's parent organization, the AFT, has launched a counteroffensive. It is portraying the practice, in the words of union President Sandra Feldman, as "a simplistic response to a complicated problem."

As part of that effort, the union last year produced a policy guide on redesigning failing schools that took sharp aim at San Francisco's brand of reconstitution. At the same time, it urged strong action against chronically low-performing schools and laid out the union's vision of how such intervention should take place.

The guide urged local unions "to ensure that teachers and other school staff are treated professionally, are involved in decisionmaking, and are part of the solution."

It also stressed the need to give schools support to improve on their own. And it said any intervention strategies should be based on solid measures of performance; provide thorough analysis of individual schools' problems; involve proven, research-based reforms; and commit sufficient resources for retooling teachers.

Some local union leaders are drawing on the AFT policy as they seek to influence intervention plans in their districts. Tom Mooney, a vice president of the national union and the chief of its Cincinnati affiliate, used the policy as a basis for a plan he is now discussing with officials there even though that city has yet to reconstitute any schools.

"I think this AFT policy is making sense to a lot of people," said Mr. Mooney, who was the chairman of the task force that produced the national union's policy. "It's very aggressive but more sensible and educationally sound than reconstitution."

In January, the AFT held a workshop in Miami for union and district officials from eight cities where intervention in failing schools had become a key issue.

For the Cleveland contingent, that retreat gave both sides a needed chance to air their differences, said Livesteen E. Carter, the district's chief academic officer. The experience helped lay the groundwork for an intervention plan agreed to last month that will give union officials a voice in identifying schools for potential reconstitution.

As a model for how unions and districts can collaborate to improve beleaguered schools, AFT leaders point to New York City.

Under New York's version of reconstitution, known as redesign, the protections afforded staff members are generally greater than in other districts where such shake-ups have taken place.

For example, half the staff at a redesigned school in New York must be drawn whenever possible from employees already in the school, with preference being given by seniority. Union members sit on the school-based committee that selects the new staff, and teachers who do wind up transferring out are given first priority elsewhere.

Interestingly, New York is the only one of last year's crop of districts engaged in some form of reconstitution that is doing so again this year.

Threat of Shake-Ups Persists

But even as union leaders come forward with alternatives, some school officials are continuing to propose new accountability schemes that feature reconstitution. In recent months, for example, administrators in St. Louis; Columbus, Ohio; and Santa Ana, Calif., have put forward plans that feature reconstitution as a possible sanction for schools that fail to improve over time.

In other districts, including Los Angeles, Seattle, and the District of Columbia, administrators have launched high-profile efforts to improve low-performing schools that could end in reconstitution in the years ahead.

And among those districts that have resorted to reconstitution in the past, but have held off this year, the watchword is never say never. Philadelphia officials, for example, say they intend to keep a close eye on the performance data from the 13 schools on their watch list to make sure that forgoing reconstitution continues to make sense.

S.F. Shifts Gears

In San Francisco, the district most closely associated with reconstitution, no one is writing the policy off just yet.

But for the first time in five years, Superintendent Waldemar Rojas has no plans to reconstitute any schools.

Instead, union and school leaders are nearing final agreement on a plan to give schools more time to reform themselves before reconstitution would become an option. The plan draws liberally from the principles laid down in the AFT policy, said Mr. Mitchell, the head of the local union, a united affiliate of the AFT and the National Education Association.

San Francisco's first foray into reconstitution came in the 1980s in response to a federal desegregation case.

Then, in 1992, a court-approved agreement in the case actually required the 63,500-student district to reconstitute schools each year. That directive followed a report from a monitoring panel headed by Mr. Orfield that found higher achievement among black and Hispanic students in schools that had been reconstituted in the 1980s.

Critics say that those gains were due primarily to factors other than the restaffing and maintain that the 10 schools overhauled since 1994 have only a mixed record of improvement.

Nonetheless, some have shown strong signs of success, such as Visitacion Valley Middle School, where Mr. Flores is principal. Since being reconstituted in 1994, the school's climate has improved markedly and test scores have risen consistently.

But now, Mr. Rojas said, "the focus is to spend a lot of time and energy revisiting the original reconstituted schools to ensure that they are building strong and solid academic bases."

The new approach being negotiated with the union would require local school councils made up of staff members, parents, and others to formulate improvement plans with measurable goals for student achievement.

At present, questions surrounding staff transfers remain under discussion.

Any final plan to put the brakes on reconstitution needs approval from the federal judge. Moreover, even Mr. Mitchell said he could envision times when its use would be justified "as a tool of absolute last resort."

Still, both he and Mr. Rojas seem convinced that the city is entering a new chapter in its push to improve schools.

"Reconstitution is not an event," Mr. Rojas said. "It is the beginning stage of a building process."

23

PERSONALIZING
MIDDLE SCHOOLS

Nancy L. Ames, Edward Miller

Middle schools are a relatively recent invention. In larger school districts, the middle grades are broken out and made similar to high schools in structure. Because of recent research on the special needs of preadolescents and adolescents, middle schools are changing to serve their population better.

———————— o ————————

WALK INTO SARAH SCOTT MIDDLE SCHOOL in Terre Haute, Indiana, one day and into H. L. Harshman Middle School in Indianapolis the next, and you will be struck by the contrast. Both schools have participated in Indiana's Middle Grades Improvement Program (MGIP) over the past several years, and both have undergone enormous changes during that time. Both are, in many ways, exemplary schools. Yet superficially they look and feel very different.

Sarah Scott is a small school in a stately old building, and though Terre Haute is a fair-sized city, the feeling you get on entering is that you have walked into a small town where everyone knows everyone else. The old-fashioned high-ceilinged corridors and stairwells are swept clean and the walls are covered with neatly arrayed posters and displays. Adults and children alike smile at you, greet you, and ask if they can help you find your way.

The look and feel of the Harshman School is anything but small-town. This is the big city, and its face is harder and tougher. Indeed, Harshman is in the heart of one of the most depressed areas of Indianapolis. The low-ceilinged, blocklike 1950s style of the building contributes to the crowded, noisy feeling in the halls. More than half the students at Harshman are black, and almost all are poor. The banter and bumping in the corridors when classes are changing have a decidedly urban edge to them.

The contrast between these two schools mirrors the experience of middle school students themselves as they enter adolescence. Nothing is so striking about young adolescents as their superficial differences from each other, even at the same chronological age and grade level.

The years from age ten to age fourteen are among the most turbulent in the human life span. Within a relatively short period, young adolescents experience profound changes in physical, intellectual, social, and emotional development. They experiment with new social roles; must deal with their rapidly changing, often unrecognizable, bodies; and face new expectations from the world around them (Mitchell, 1979). Over the past fifteen years researchers and educators have defined and described a comprehensive middle-level educational philosophy based on the unique needs of ten- to fourteen-year-olds. This philosophy, which was the foundation of the Lilly Endowment's MGIP initiative, starts with the premise that effective middle school teachers and administrators must understand and value young adolescents as human beings. Foremost among their unique needs is the need to be known, heard, and respected as an individual.

We visited a variety of urban middle schools in the midst of change and growth in our research. The four schools we ultimately chose to write about in detail were superficially very different from each other, yet they were alike in one crucial way. Each had made enormous progress in transforming itself into an effective school through deeply held beliefs about the innate worth and dignity of every child, and by making a profound commitment to personalizing the experience of school for young adolescents.

What do we mean by personalizing the middle school experience? We believe that personalization

- Begins with a deep understanding of the developmental challenges of early adolescence

- Requires valuing and respecting each student, regardless of race, ethnicity, socioeconomic status, gender, or disability

- Involves close adult-child relationships that facilitate the transition from childhood to adulthood

○ Demands rich, developmentally appropriate curricula and instruction that are sensitive to individual differences

○ Calls for a range of support services that address students' social, emotional, and physical needs as well as their academic development

○ Involves building strong links among family, school, and community so that all work in harmony to support children's development

Moreover, we discovered that personalization was not only the key to effective middle schools but also the underlying theme common to each of these schools' stories of how they were able to manage the process of change itself. Just as there is no one style of teaching or learning that is appropriate for every student, there is no one template for change that fits every school. Perhaps the most valuable lesson of the MGIP story is the way in which this systemic reform initiative managed to build into its design the room for individual schools to find their own unique paths to growth and transformation, based on the particular needs of their own students and staffs.

Understanding Young Adolescents

Joan Lipsitz argues that successful middle schools begin with an understanding of the "why" of middle-level education—the developmental challenges that young adolescents face as they move from childhood to adulthood. Without that understanding, educators cannot possibly deal with the "what" and "how" of schooling.

Many middle-level educators have now come to recognize that early adolescence is a time of dramatic and sometimes traumatic changes. The physical changes are most obvious. Young adolescents grow an average of two to four inches and gain eight to ten pounds per year during this period. As their bodies shoot upward, their feet and hands grow too big, their arms too long. Hands dangle from suddenly too-short sleeves; socks peek out from pants that were the right length just a few weeks ago.

Physical growth occurs unevenly, and thus certain parts of the body—notably hands, feet, ears, and noses—often develop earlier and more rapidly. Clumsy and not yet comfortable with their new bodies, boys especially are apt to trip over their own feet, bump into things, and knock things over at the kitchen table or in the lunchroom. These physical changes significantly alter the way young adolescents see and think about themselves. Insecure about their relationships with peers and their worth as individuals, they worry incessantly about their appearance and spend endless hours peering into mirrors, arranging their hair, and applying acne medicines.

The hormones that play havoc with complexions during this period are also bringing on confusing physical changes and powerful sexual feelings for both girls and boys. Since the age of onset of puberty varies tremendously among both girls and boys, it is entirely normal for one thirteen-year-old to appear completely physically mature, while another still looks like a young child. Newly discovered sexual feelings engender greater interest in and anxiety about the opposite sex. Some girls welcome the changes in their bodies and are eager to show off their new adult figures by wearing tight sweaters and miniskirts. Others wear baggy sweaters and loose-fitting pants in an attempt to hide all outward signs of their emerging sexuality. Although some boys carry their new manhood proudly, others are ashamed of their gangly appearance, hirsute faces, and cracking voices. Hunched over, hands in pockets, they avoid looking you in the eye and may seem unable to speak.

Yet these physical and sexual developments are just the most obvious of the changes youngsters experience at this stage of life. Young adolescents are also changing cognitively, socially, and emotionally. They know that they must soon put away "childish things" (as adults are apt to advise them), and yet a great many young adolescents are not quite ready to give up the safety and relative serenity of childhood. They are eager to loosen the bonds to parents, but they have not yet developed new, more mature patterns of relationship. And they have neither the skills nor the confidence to become fully autonomous.

It is not surprising, then, for young adolescents to feel waves of anger, excitement, anxiety, depression, and other emotions as they experiment with more adult behaviors. Caught between childhood and adulthood, they seem to change from one moment to the next—alternately independent, immature, energized, lethargic, sensitive, oblivious, eager, confused, responsible, and disorganized.

The traditional junior high school, as many other observers have pointed out, is ill equipped to deal with the challenge of working with young adolescents. Many such schools were designed to imitate the impersonal structure and atmosphere of senior high schools, with students moving from class to class, teacher to teacher, in forty- or forty-five-minute periods. This approach drastically reduces the possibility that any one adult would come to know an individual student well enough to understand or have time to think about that student's inner turmoil and doubt.

Moreover, since junior high schools were traditionally classified as secondary rather than elementary schools, most junior high teachers were trained to teach high school, with a primary emphasis on their subject specialty—English, math, biology, social studies, and so on—rather than on the developmental needs of children. Many of these teachers viewed assignment to junior high classrooms as a second choice, or even as a punishment, and thus approached their work with a preconceived attitude of negativity and resentment. Some saw their time at the junior high level as something to be endured until they could get the job they really wanted and were trained to perform: teaching high school. Faced with young adolescents' chameleon-like behavior, it was not uncommon for such teachers to shake their heads in frustration or despair: "I don't know what to do with these kids." "They're so moody." "All they care about is the opposite sex." "They just can't keep still." "They'll be the death of me."

Enlightened educators now take a much more positive view of the middle school child. They see the child at the point of transition to adulthood as a source of wonder and meaning. Like Benson, Williams, and Johnson, they view early adolescence as a time when "one begins to catch a glimpse of the emerging adult side by side with the child, when leadership begins to make itself visible, when the capacity for abstract thought develops, and when, perhaps for the first time, a parent or teacher can hold a conversation with the young person that has the tone of adult to adult communication" (1987, p. 4).

Valuing and Respecting Each Student

In addition to understanding and attending to the developmental challenges faced by young adolescents as a group, these educators value and respect individual differences. They feel a responsibility to know each child's strengths and weaknesses, family and cultural background, interests, and learning style. And they use a variety of strategies to help all students feel cherished. Linda Darling-Hammond calls this focus on individual differences a critical feature of "learner-centered" schools: "Learner-centered schools focus on students' needs, interests and talents as the basis for organizing school work and school organization, building curriculum and learning opportunities, and developing relationships between and among students, educators and parents. Such schools are by definition grounded in an appreciation and deep valuing of human diversity. They are rooted in our diverse human experiences, and they open up the infinite reaches of human possibility" (1992, p. 19).

Implicit in this description of learner-centered or personalized schools are two interrelated concepts: (1) setting high expectations and providing opportunities for success to all students, while (2) attending to the diversity among them.

Giving all students a meaningful chance to succeed is one of the basic recommendations of *Turning Points,* the Carnegie Corporation on Adolescent Development's report on middle-level education: "All young adolescents should have the opportunity to succeed in every aspect of the middle grade program, regardless of previous achievement or the pace at which they learn" (1990, p. 14). By offering *all* students the opportunity to participate in advanced courses, exploratory programs, and extracurricular activities, successful middle schools communicate to both youngsters and their parents that *all* children have value.

Despite this recommendation, tracking students by achievement level remains an almost universal practice in today's middle schools. In theory, tracking allows teachers to tailor instruction to each group's knowledge and skills and thus supports individualized instruction. In practice, lower tracks often focus on boring, repetitive basic-skills drills. There is little evidence that tracking benefits those in the lower tracks (or that heterogeneous grouping hurts those in the upper tracks). On the contrary, tracking has a negative impact on low-achieving students' aspirations and self-esteem, while denying them access to the advanced courses they need to get into college and find rewarding careers (Oakes, 1985; Wheelock, 1992).

Personalized middle schools recognize that all students can benefit greatly from participation in challenging and exciting school projects and from rich, thought-provoking curricula (Epstein, 1988; Lipsitz, 1984; Levin, 1987; Wheelock and Dorman, 1988). The strategies for making success possible for all learners include cooperative learning groups, cross-age tutors, specially designed curricula, and other support services.

Valuing and respecting young adolescents also means attending to cultural differences. The demographic map of American society is changing dramatically, because of both immigration and higher birth rates among racial and ethnic minority populations. In 1980, minority youth made up 15 percent of the school-age population. It is expected to reach 50 percent by the year 2020. A disproportionate number of these youth live in poor urban centers, where unemployment, racial tension, and violence abound. Meanwhile, city and state budgets for public schools and youth services are stretched to the breaking point.

In 1989, the Carnegie Corporation issued the following warning: "The specter of a divided society—one affluent and the other poor—looms ominously on the American horizon. Inherent in this scenario is the potential for serious conflict between generations, among races and ethnic groups, and between the economically disenfranchised and middle- and upper-income groups. It is a disturbing scenario which must not occur" (p. 32).

One way to help avoid this scenario is for urban schools to understand and give value to children's differing cultural backgrounds. Schools must acknowledge racial and cultural tensions and face them head on. They must work hard to "provide culturally sensitive and validating experiences to students from many different cultural backgrounds" (Haynes, 1994, p. 14). They must aim to expand their students' conception of what it means to be human in a culturally diverse world and to develop cross-cultural competency (Boateng, 1990). In addition, they must be willing to examine their own policies and practices to see whether they are influenced by racial, ethnic, gender, and socioeconomic stereotypes.

The Holmes Group summed up this imperative for personalized middle schools well: "When teachers learn more about their students they can build learning communities that embrace rather than smother cultural diversity. Students do differ. Without stereotyping or prepackaged responses, such differences can become opportunities for richer learning. . . . We speak of celebrating diversity because we believe that the hallmark of a true learning community is its inclusiveness—where teachers take the responsibility for helping each child take part to his or her fullest. The idea of a learning community has special significance in a democracy where all must find their voice" (1990, p. 35).

At Decatur Middle School, we witnessed the effects of such inclusiveness. We saw and heard how a black student, struggling to come to terms with historical racism and his own African-American identity, was touched, held, supported, and listened to by an exemplary team of teachers. These educators were motivated not only by the conviction that cultural differences must be attended to and valued but also by simple affection for the boy as a person and sympathy for his struggles as a young adolescent. "We just love him to death," they told us, speaking of a young man poised on the verge of drugs and violence, one whom too many traditional teachers would have seen simply as trouble.

Developing Close Adult-Child Relationships

Many middle school researchers and observers recognize the importance of establishing close personal connections between adults and the young adolescents in their charge. As Braddock and McPartland write, "Students must also be attached to their schools in human terms and on a personal level, with the perception that their teachers care about them as individuals and the belief that the professionals at their schools will actively support their efforts to learn" (1992, p. 160).

James Comer, director of the School Development Program at Yale University, believes that respectful, trusting personal relationships among children, teachers, principals, and parents are vital to creating an atmosphere in which children and learning thrive. "Learning isn't a mechanical process," Comer asserts. "Motivation and commitment to learning don't happen just by having somebody stand up and try to pump information into you. You have to work on making the school a place where people connect emotionally. If you don't do that, then you're not going to succeed" (1988, p. 5).

David Hawkins, a pioneer in the area of substance abuse prevention, also speaks of the critical importance of bonding between adults and young adolescents. According to Hawkins's research, those youngsters who successfully survived a multiple-risk environment had all bonded closely with someone who took an interest in them, who held out clear standards and expectations, and with whom they felt close emotionally. In his view, what we need now is not a "war on drugs" but a "war for bonding" (Hawkins, 1993).

Personalizing urban middle schools requires establishing close relationships between adults and children. But such relationships do not just happen by chance; the structure of the school must be designed to support such bonds.

For example, adviser-advisee programs aim at bringing adults into close relationships with students. The National Middle School Association (NMSA) advises that "each young learner needs an adult who knows him or her well and is in a position to give individual attention. Therefore, the middle school should be organized so that every youngster has such an adult, one who has special responsibility for the individual's academic and personal welfare. Home-base or adviser-advisee programs which provide individuals with regular opportunities for interaction with a small group of peers and a caring environment fill this need" (1982, p. 19).

Another structure that helps promote meaningful adult-child relationships is interdisciplinary teaming, in which a team of teachers is responsible for a community of students. Creating smaller communities for teaching and learning was one of the major recommendations of *Turning Points* (Carnegie Corporation, 1989). But smaller student-teacher ratios are not enough. As Theodore Sizer (1994) points out, colleagues must work with the identical group of kids and have time each day to talk about those kids and what "knowing them" means.

Transforming Curriculum and Instruction

Personalization does not end with understanding and valuing young adolescents or establishing close relationships with them. Middle school teachers must also re-examine and, if necessary, refocus what they teach, how they teach it, and how they measure the results. "Centering schools on learners influences how we think about curriculum and its connections to students' experiences, culture and personal meaning, how we think about assessment and its capacity to illuminate the full range of students' multiple intelligences and achievement, how we think about teaching and its responsiveness to students' conceptions and understandings" (Darling-Hammond, 1992, p. 19). At the middle level, personalization means designing curriculum and instruction to meet the needs of young adolescents, while attending to the tremendous variation within and among them.

Children first develop the ability to reason abstractly in early adolescence. "They begin to think of the world around them and themselves in new ways. For the first time, young adolescents can 'think about thinking'—which often confuses them. This 'reflexive thinking' allows them to form sophisticated self-concepts that are shaped by interactions between their experiences and new powers of reasoning" (Van Hoose and Strahan, 1988, p. 13).

Jean Piaget's stage theory of mental development describes early adolescence as roughly the age when youngsters move from "concrete operations" to "formal operations" (1977). Students in the concrete-operations stage, says Piaget, can solve mathematical or logical problems when faced with concrete situations in which they can see, touch, or manipulate objects. As they enter the formal-operations stage, they develop the ability to reason logically in the absence of concrete objects. They begin to understand and apply advanced mathematical and scientific concepts, and they reason on the basis of possibilities instead of being limited by their own direct experiences.

And yet, as with other characteristics of early adolescence, intellectual development varies tremendously from child to child. Even in eighth grade, only about one-third of the students can consistently demonstrate formal operations—that is, the ability to reason abstractly. Since many young adolescents are still at the concrete-operational stage of development, opportunities for experiential, hands-on learning are especially important to them. Giving young adolescents materials like mathematics manipulatives and hands-on science materials can facilitate their learning of important concepts and skills. It is also important for teachers to help young adolescents develop the "capacity to interpret symbols and deal with verbal ideas without having to manipulate physical objects" (National Middle School Association, 1982, p. 19). Thus, effective middle-level teachers pose challenging questions: "What if?" "What do you think will happen?" "Are you sure?" "How do you know?" "Why?"

Another way that teachers can attend to the wide variability among young adolescents is to identify the ways in which each student learns most effectively and to plan instruction accordingly. Yet the multiplicity of dimensions on which young adolescents differ makes tailoring instruction to their individual needs difficult at best. As Steven Levy, a former Massachusetts Teacher of the Year, told the Association of Experiential Education in October 1993: "When I think about meeting the needs of each child, I feel overwhelmed. Since these needs are virtually bottomless, I cannot hope to address them all." Instead, Levy tries to create an environment so rich that it brings out the "genius" in each child. He points out that, when we use the word *genius,* we usually think only of the most common definition: "extraordinary intellectual power." But this definition limits genius to a very few. By providing a rich classroom environment, Levy allows children to pursue their natural talents and inclinations, develop their own distinctive character, and build on their unique capacities and aptitudes—all equally valid, though less common, definitions of *genius.*

At the same time that young adolescents are learning to think more abstractly, they are searching for greater autonomy and independence. Thus, adapting curriculum and instruction to their needs also means helping them take responsibility for their own learning. By asking students to predict, draw conclusions, make inferences, and justify their answers, teachers can encourage students to move beyond the passive acquisition of information (National Middle School Association, 1982) to active learning. Good teachers foster students' independence by giving them opportunities to pose their own problems, choose their own topics of inquiry, and select their own reading materials.

To promote this kind of self-directed learning, teachers must change the traditional definition of their role. They must see themselves not as information-giver but as diagnostician, coach, resource person, facilitator, and evaluator. As Theodore Sizer put it in one of his nine principles of "essential" schools, "The governing metaphor of the school should be student as worker, rather than the more familiar metaphor of teacher as deliverer of instructional services" (1992, p. 208).

Early adolescence is also a time when friendship, social acceptance by peers, and a sense of belonging grow in importance. Thus cooperative learning methods are especially appropriate for middle school classrooms. "When students learn in small, carefully structured learning groups (with group goals, equal opportunity for success, and individual accountability) they help one another learn, gain in self-esteem and feelings of individual responsibility for their learning, and increase in respect and liking for their classmates" (George and Alexander, 1993, p. 160). Balancing such teams by race, gender, and academic ability also breaks down barriers among subgroups and fosters sensitivity to cultural diversity.

Still another characteristic of early adolescence is youngsters' growing interest in the larger world and increased capacity for empathy and role taking. It is not uncommon for young adolescents to become involved in heated discussions about justice and other ideals and to form their own opinions on important social issues. They are also struggling to make personal meaning out of their school experience. Personalizing curriculum and instruction means integrating themes that help students to see systems rather than disconnected facts (Carnegie Corporation, 1990, p. 13). These themes should be both socially significant and personally relevant (Beane, 1990).

Finally, personalizing curriculum and instruction means helping young adolescents find constructive ways to express their deep feelings. Effective middle-level teachers use art, poetry, music, drama, and other forms of creative expression to help their students share their thoughts, hopes, and fears with others.

Providing Comprehensive Support Services

Many educators feel that helping youngsters with their personal problems is not within the school's domain or the capacity of today's hard-pressed public school teacher. Yet it is impossible to meet many young adolescents' academic needs without addressing their social, emotional, and physical needs as well. This is especially true in poor, urban neighborhoods, where many children lack adequate nutrition and health care, and the problems associated with poverty, racism, and violence add to the normal developmental challenges of early adolescence.

Of vital importance, then, are comprehensive health services, including education, prevention, and treatment. As the Carnegie Corporation notes, "Good health does not guarantee that students will be interested in learning, but ample evidence suggests that poor health lowers students' academic performance" (1990, p. 20). Young adolescents need health education and preventive guidance to help protect themselves and others from unhealthy choices about smoking, eating, drugs, and sex. They also need access to appropriate mental health services—services that only 20 to 30 percent of those who need them now get. "Because of the link between health and school success, middle grade schools must ensure the accessibility of health and counseling services and function as health-promoting environments" (Carnegie Corporation, 1990, p. 20).

The Carnegie Corporation recommends that every school have a health coordinator to provide limited screening and treatment, make and monitor referrals to health services outside the school, and coordinate school health education and related activities. James Comer's School Development Program goes even further. It calls for a mental health team composed of all the health and mental health staff in the school, along with classroom teachers, to help establish schoolwide health policies, deal with overall health and climate issues, and tackle individual cases.

Middle school educators are quietly pioneering such efforts in Indiana and across the country. All the schools featured have made a major commitment to providing comprehensive student assistance programs. They provide individual and group counseling, arrange for peer support groups, and design and implement classroom activities dealing with a range of health-related topics. In addition to working directly with youth, team members provide parent and teacher consultations; help identify individual differences, needs, and problems; and work with teachers, specialists, and administrators to develop schoolwide programs and solve specific problems. To serve those students whose needs exceed the school's in-house resources, they have developed links to health and mental health providers in local hospitals, community health centers, counseling centers, and youth-serving agencies.

School-based health clinics are another promising vehicle for providing comprehensive health services, especially because they make such services immediately accessible to students. Yet for a variety of reasons (not the least of which is cost) few middle schools have actually created such clinics. Harshman School in Indianapolis is an outstanding exception. Its story provides a compelling example of the need for in-school health screening of young adolescents.

Linking Family, School, and Community

Generally, peers provide much needed support as young adolescents move from childhood to adulthood, from social conformity to personal autonomy. Yet the intense desire to fit in can have negative consequences for youngsters. Afraid of looking, sounding, or acting "different," they are often extremely self-conscious. They may be reluctant to pursue their own educational, cultural, or recreational interests if they deviate too far from those of their pals. The peer group can also exert powerful pressure to experiment with tobacco, alcohol, other drugs, sex, and other risky behaviors.

Parents and educators are sometimes tempted to back away during early adolescence, feeling powerless in the face of peer pressure. Nevertheless, most young adolescents still respect their parents' opinions and ideas, despite myths to the contrary (Sorenson, 1973). And they continue to look to their parents for affection, identification, values, and help in solving problems (Kandel and Lesser, 1972). As Ianni points out, "Adolescents do generate their own norms and rules, but this process does not and cannot develop in isolation from the institutional context of the communities in which they live and learn" (Ianni, 1989, p. 679).

Neither the home nor the school can afford to step aside. As Gayle Dorman writes, "Young people need adults to maintain the direction and momentum, when they cannot. Above all, they need adults who care about them as they mature" (1987, p. 4). Personalizing middle schools means providing young adolescents with adult guidance and support. It also means aligning home and school, so that students receive a consistent message in both and are not attached to one at the expense of the other.

Dorman adds that during this period "children emerge from the world of here-and-now into a wider world of novel and panoramic possibilities. Their sense of personal achievement, competence, and commitment deepens; their understanding of life and of their future begins to take on new breadth and depth. They seek a new definition of themselves in the context of the larger world, and they bring great energy to their search" (1987, pp. 2–3).

As young adolescents struggle to discover themselves, they are beset by questions: Who am I? What does the future hold for me? What values are important to me? How can I make a difference in my community? Where do I fit in society at large? These questions are especially poignant for poor, urban youth who often have no clear vision of what is possible beyond high school or even middle school graduation.

Personalized middle schools help young adolescents undertake this search by extending learning beyond the school walls. They encourage community support for the school, while at the same time encouraging youth to explore their surrounding community and the world around them. Through career exploration programs, like the one created and managed by Mary Ley at Sarah Scott Middle School, they provide students with an expanded vision of the future.

Personalized middle schools also give young people an opportunity to build self-esteem and a sense of civic responsibility through community service. As Stevenson points out, "Young adolescents working together to do something that directly benefits others are able to see themselves in a new and developmentally valuable light" (1992, p. 130). Service projects promote social interaction with peers, younger children, older adolescents, and adult community members including each others' parents and grandparents. They provide opportunities for young adolescents to try out more adult roles and to learn firsthand about themselves, their peers, and those whom they serve. Through community service, students also discover the possibility that they can make a difference in the world around them. While the primary motivation for doing service is helping others, young adolescents often get more than they give—personal satisfaction, recognition, respect, and a deep appreciation for the value of serving others.

Responding to a Moral Imperative

Great strides are possible when educators share a vision of personalizing their educational program and are supported in that vision by critical friends and knowledgeable advisers. The administrators, teachers, counselors, nurses, and parents of these schools have all committed themselves to service—to serving poor, urban youth. Their stories give the lie to the gloomy predictions of those who say that our urban schools cannot change and should simply be abandoned.

Jonathan Kozol (1991) and other advocates play an important role in the fight to achieve better, more equitable public schools. By pointing out the dire plight of many of our urban schools, they generate outrage and garner public support for reform. Yet they often paint such negative portraits that the situation seems hopeless.

It is true that many urban young people are at risk from poor nutrition; inadequate health care; racism; unemployment; community disintegration; and the easy availability of drugs, alcohol, and guns. These conditions make schooling especially difficult. And the best efforts of educators are often hampered by deteriorating buildings, out-of-date materials and equipment, inadequate resources, and rigid bureaucracies.

Despite their many problems, however, urban youth are resilient, and so are their schools. In poor, urban schools fundamental transformation is possible—and without large infusions of money. What it requires, at a minimum, is that we as a society respond to the moral imperative of caring for and educating *all* of our children. What it requires is a vision of effective middle schools and a belief that change is possible.

"How can teachers know the students," asks Theodore Sizer in *Horace's School,* "know them well enough to understand how their minds work, know where they come from, what pressures buffet them, what they are and are not disposed to do? A teacher cannot stimulate a child to learn without knowing that child's mind—the course of action necessary for an individual requires an understanding of the particulars" (1992, p. 40). Implicit in this statement is the added requirement that teachers know children's hearts as well as their minds and that they know the families and communities of which they are a part.

What can middle schools do to know their students well? How can they help each youngster grow and develop to his or her full potential? How can they attend to the particular needs of poor children in poor communities, coming from a staggering array of different racial, ethnic, and socioeconomic backgrounds? And how can school administrators, school systems, policy makers, governments, and private funding agencies effectively support the kind of fundamental change that is so urgently needed?

The answer, in our view, is in personalizing urban middle-level education. The answer is in developing a coherent, systemic, and yet highly individualized approach to the process of school change.

REFERENCES

Beane, J. *A Middle School Curriculum: From Rhetoric to Reality.* Columbus, Ohio: National Middle School Association, 1990.

Benson, P., Williams, D., and Johnson, A. *The Quicksilver Years: The Hopes and Fears of Early Adolescents.* New York: Harper & Row, 1987.

Boateng, F. "Combatting Demulturalization." In K. Lomotey (ed.), *Going to School.* New York: Albany State University of New York Press, 1990.

Braddock, J. H., and McPartland, J. M. "Education of Early Adolescents." *Review of Research in Education,* 1993, *19,* 135–170.

Carnegie Corporation. *Abridged Version of Turning Points: Preparing American Youth for the 21st Century.* Washington, D.C.: Carnegie Council on Adolescent Development, 1990.

Darling-Hammond, L. "Building Learner-Centered Schools: Developing Professional Capacity, Policy, and Political Consensus." In J. A. Banks, L. Darling-Hammond, and M. Greene (eds.), *Building Learner-Centered Schools: Three Perspectives.* New York: Columbia Teachers College Press, 1992.

Dorman, G. *Improving Middle Grade Schools: A Framework for Action.* Carrboro, N.C.: Center for Early Adolescence, 1987.

George, P., and Alexander, W. *The Exemplary Middle School.* (2nd ed.) Orlando: Holt, Rinehart & Winston, 1993.

Hawkins, D. Speech given at the National Prevention Conference, Federal Center for Substance Abuse Prevention, Washington, D.C., Feb. 1993.

Haynes, N. M. "Toward an Understanding of Personalization in Atlas Learning Communities." Yale University School Development Program, unpublished paper, March 14, 1994.

Holmes Group. *Tomorrow's Schools: Principles for the Design of Professional Development Schools.* East Lansing: Michigan State University, 1990.

Ianni, F.A.J. "Providing a Structure for Adolescent Development." *Phi Delta Kappan,* 1989, *70,* 673–682.

Kandel, D., and Lesser, G. *Youth in Two Worlds.* San Francisco: Jossey-Bass, 1972.

Kozol, J. *Savage Inequalities: Children in America's Schools.* New York: Crown, 1991.

Levy, S. Presentation to the Association of Experiential Education, October 1993.

Mitchell, J. J. *Adolescent Psychology.* Toronto: Holt, Rinehart & Winston, 1979.

National Middle School Association. *This We Believe.* Columbus, Ohio: Author, 1982.

Oakes, J. *Keeping Track: How Schools Structure Inequality.* New Haven, Conn.: Yale University Press, 1985.

Piaget, J. *The Essential Piaget.* New York: Basic Books, 1977.

Sizer, T. *Horace's School: Redesigning the American High School.* New York: Houghton Mifflin, 1992.

Sorenson, R. *Adolescent Sexuality in Contemporary America.* New York: World, 1973.

Stevenson, C. *Teaching 10–14 Year Olds.* New York: Longman, 1992.

Van Hoose, J., and Strahan, D. *Young Adolescent Development and School Practices: Promoting Harmony.* Columbus, Ohio: National Middle School Association, 1988.

PART FIVE

REFORM THROUGH STANDARDS, CURRICULUM, PEDAGOGY, AND ASSESSMENT

24

THINKING ABOUT EDUCATION
IN A DIFFERENT WAY

David C. Berliner, Bruce J. Biddle

The 1980s and early 1990s saw the publication of many provocative reports urging vast improvements in education. This chapter offers the reader a reality check. In addition to the favor of hindsight and several global economic cycles, this chapter helps the reader to see these reports from a more measured viewpoint.

———————— o ————————

HEADLINES, NEWS ARTICLES, AND TELEVISION NEWS REPORTS have recently portrayed a grim picture of children and their schools, a picture consistent enough to frighten thoughtful and caring people into concern for the future of their nation. Take, for example, the following news reports:

- In a typical year during the 1980s, minors aged fourteen to nineteen accounted for 43.4 percent of all criminal offenses. Fifty-four percent of all murder cases in the nation involved jobless youth.[1]

- A junior-high-school gang of six extorts $2,500 from 120 classmates.[2]

- Forty-four high school students go wilding and raid five shops for merchandise.[3]

- High school girls turn to prostitution for entertainment, curiosity, and a source of revenue—police report their rate up 262 percent.[4]

○ Fourteen-year-old student, repeatedly tormented and beaten by school thugs, hangs himself.[5]

○ Teen tortured by two gang members. Victim burned by cigarettes on hands and back.[6]

○ Group of students report feeling "refreshed" after beating up another child.[7]

○ Ten percent of the nation's middle schools request police guards for their graduation ceremonies.[8]

With reports like these so commonplace, it is easy to understand why so many people worry so much about schooling and youth. But in this case, the people who have the worrying to do are not Americans. These are all reports from the *Japanese* media about the awful world of *Japanese* youth and the terrible failure of *Japanese* public schooling!

Were you surprised? We suspect that most American readers would automatically think that these statements concerned *American* youth and *American* schools. After all, every week our media seem to supply us with yet another frightening story about the dreadful state of education in our country. In contrast, Americans regularly read and hear glowing reports of Japanese schools and their students' performance on international tests of achievement. Negative stories about Japanese schools are rarely found in our press or on our TV screens. Thus, Americans have been prevented from learning that the Japanese educational system also has enormous problems. In fact, if one judges by American values and standards, Japanese schools are often brutal, overly competitive places.

Perhaps you find this hard to believe. This may be because, like many other Americans, you have not been told about the thousands of elementary and junior high school students in Japan who refuse to attend school because of persistent problems of bullying—often directed against those with a foreign upbringing or against those who get outstanding grades or who have physical disabilities. Nor have Americans been made aware of the coercive overregulation of students and their families by many Japanese schools. For example, one Japanese school has a policy about the number of pleats permitted in a girl's skirt, violation of which results in the suspension of the child unless the mother comes to the school to beg forgiveness. Another school's policy on hair color and curls requires those who do not have straight black hair to obtain a note from a physician stating that they have a genetic problem. Other schools have policies that encourage cruelty by teachers; students have been given electric shocks for low grades, have died because they were locked in unventilated sheds as punishment for smoking, or have been beaten for using a hair dryer "illegally."[9] Americans are also not often told about the gifts of money that Japanese parents frequently pay to teachers to ensure good grades and good letters of recommendation for their children.

You may think our judgments are harsh, but we are not alone in condemning Japanese schools for brutality and for promoting overachievement. A decade ago, a select committee of *Japanese* educators reported to their own prime minister and his council of advisors that,

> Bullying, suicides among school children, dropping from school, increasing delinquency, violence both at home and at school, heated entrance exam races, over-emphasis on scholastic ratings, and torture of children by some teachers are the result of the pathological mechanisms that have become established in Japan's education system.[10]

Manufacturing a Crisis in Education

> Seldom in the course of policymaking in the U.S. have so many firm convictions held by so many been based on so little convincing proof.
> —Clark Kerr, President Emeritus of the University of California (1991)

Given the serious problems of Japanese education, why have so many Americans come to believe that American education is so deficient and that we should look to the Japanese to find out how to run our schools? The answer is that for more than a dozen years this groundless and damaging message has been proclaimed by major leaders of our government and industry and has been repeated endlessly by a compliant press. Goodhearted Americans have come to believe that the public schools of their nation are in a crisis state because they have so often been given this false message by supposedly credible sources.

To illustrate, in 1983, amid much fanfare, the White House released an incendiary document highly critical of American education. Entitled *A Nation at Risk,*[11] this work was prepared by a prestigious committee under the direction of then Secretary of Education Terrel Bell and was endorsed in a speech by President Ronald Reagan. It made many claims about the "failures" of American education, how those "failures" were confirmed by "evidence," and how this would inevitably damage the nation. (Unfortunately, none of the supposedly supportive "evidence" actually appeared in *A Nation at Risk,* nor did this work provide citations to tell Americans where that "evidence" might be found.)

But leaders of this disinformation campaign were not content merely to attack American schools. *A Nation at Risk* charged that American students never excelled in international comparisons of student achievement and that this failure reflected systematic weaknesses in our school programs and lack of talent and motivation among American educators. Thus, it came as little surprise when the White House soon sent a team of Americans to Japan to discover and report on why Japanese education was so "successful." Following this visit, the then Assistant Secretary of Education, Chester Finn, a leader of the team, said of the Japanese,

> They've demonstrated that you can have a coherent curriculum, high standards, good discipline, parental support, a professional teaching force and a well-run school. They have shown that the average student can learn a whole lot more.[12]

This enthusiasm was echoed by others on the team. According to team member Herbert Walberg, an educational researcher, features of the Japanese system could be adopted in America and would help to solve the many "problems" of American education. Walberg suggested, "I think it's portable. Gumption and willpower, that's the key." [13]

This was far from the end of White House criticisms of American education. Indeed, the next decade witnessed a veritable explosion of documents and pronouncements from government leaders—two American presidents, Ronald Reagan and George Bush, secretaries of education, assistant secretaries, and chiefs and staff members in federal agencies—telling Americans about the many "problems" of their public schools. As in *A Nation at Risk,* most of these claims were said to reflect "evidence," although the "evidence" in question either was not presented or appeared in the form of simplistic, misleading generalizations.

During the same years many leaders in industry claimed in documents and public statements that American education was in deep trouble, that as a result our country was falling behind foreign competitors, and that these various charges were all confirmed by "evidence" (which somehow was rarely presented or appeared in simple misleading formats). And these many charges, documents, and pronouncements from leaders of government and industry, often seconded by prominent members of the educational community, were dutifully reported and endlessly elaborated upon by an unquestioning press.

So it is small wonder that many Americans have come to believe that education in our country is now in a deplorable state. Indeed, how could they have concluded anything else, given such an energetic and widely reported campaign of criticism, from such prestigious sources, attacking America's public schools? To the best of our knowledge, no campaign of this sort had ever before appeared in American history. Never before had an American government been so critical of the public schools, and never had so many false claims been made about education in the name of "evidence." We shall refer to this campaign of criticism as the Manufactured Crisis.

The Manufactured Crisis was not an accidental event. Rather, it appeared within a specific historical context and was led by identifiable critics whose political goals could be furthered by scapegoating educators. It was also supported from its inception by an assortment of questionable techniques—including misleading methods for analyzing data, distorting reports of findings, and suppressing contradictory evidence. Moreover, it was tied to misguided schemes for "reforming" education—schemes that would, if adopted, seriously damage American schools.

Unfortunately, the Manufactured Crisis has had a good deal of influence—thus, too many well-meaning, bright, and knowledgeable Americans have come to believe some of its major myths, and this has generated serious mischief. Damaging programs for educational reform have been adopted, a great deal of money has been wasted, effective school programs have been harmed, and morale has declined among educators.

But myths need not remain unchallenged; in fact, they become shaky when they are exposed to the light of reason and evidence. When one actually *looks* at the evidence, one discovers that most of the claims of the Manufactured Crisis are, indeed, myths, half-truths, and sometimes outright lies. Thus, as our first major task, we undertake, through reason and displays of relevant evidence, to dispel some of the mischief of the Manufactured Crisis—to place the crisis in context, to counter its myths, to explain why its associated agenda will not work, to set the record straight.

But accomplishing only this first task would leave many questions unanswered. One of the worst effects of the Manufactured Crisis has been to divert attention away from the *real* problems faced by American education—problems that are serious and that are escalating in today's world. To illustrate, although many Americans do not realize it, family incomes and financial support for schools are *much* more poorly distributed in our country than in other industrialized nations. This means that in the United States, very privileged students attend some of the world's best private and public schools, but it also means that large numbers of students who are truly disadvantaged attend public schools whose support is far below that permitted in other Western democracies. Thus, opportunities are *not* equal in America's schools. As a result, the achievements of students in schools that cater to the rich and those that cater to the poor in our country are also far from equal.

In addition, America's school system has expanded enormously since World War II and now serves the needs of a huge range of students. This increased diversity has created many opportunities—but also many dilemmas—and debates now rage over how to distribute resources and design curricula to meet the needs of students from diverse backgrounds, with many different skills and interests. Problems such as these *must* be addressed if Americans are to design a school system that truly provides high standards and equal opportunities for all students.

Our second major task, then, is to direct attention away from the fictions of the Manufactured Crisis and toward the real problems of American schools.

Battling Disbelief

It is always easier to believe than to deny. Our minds are naturally affirmative.
—John Burroughs (1900)

The great masses of the people . . . will more easily fall victims to a big lie than to a small one.
—Adolf Hitler (*Mein Kampf*, 1933, Chapter 10)

Lots of intelligent people believe things that aren't true. Many people believe, for example, that more babies are born during the full moon, and tourists are often frightened about the alligators that are thought to live in the sewers of New York City. Belief in such fictions seems to be remarkably durable and resists contradicting evidence or energetic campaigns to ease the fears that such fictions cause. Indeed, widespread belief in some things that are untrue seems to be part of the human condition.

Many of the myths promoted in the Manufactured Crisis are now so widely believed that we suspect that some people will find it hard to accept what we write here. Some will find it difficult to stop believing in these myths because they were endorsed by so many "important" people in government and industry—including two American presidents! Others may suspect that the two of us are politically motivated and that we are distorting or even fabricating our reports of evidence. Still others—good people, energetic people, people devoted to education—may be so committed to educational reforms based on the myths we cite that they cannot abandon them. And still others may choose to cling to those myths in the hope that they can be used to promote needed reforms or encourage more funding for education.

Some readers may have difficulty with our ideas because they have long held suspicions about problems in America's public schools, and they find it hard to abandon myths which support those suspicions. Indeed, complaining about public education has long been a popular American indoor sport.

But beyond these reasons, several factors may make it especially difficult for some readers to accept our arguments. We review four of these here.

Fraud and Its Victims

Some readers may be reluctant because they don't want to acknowledge that they have bought into fraudulent ideas, that they were victimized by a massive "con game." To appreciate their plight, one must come to understand that the Manufactured Crisis was not merely an accidental set of events or a product of impersonal social forces. It also involved a serious campaign by identifiable persons to sell Americans the false idea that their public schools were failing and that because of this failure the nation was at peril. This campaign involved a great deal of effort, chicanery, playing on people's worries, pandering to prejudices, and misreporting and misrepresenting evidence. In short, to use terms that were popular when discussing World War II propaganda, this campaign constituted a Big Lie—and a lot of people were gulled by its claims.

It is never easy to acknowledge that one was gullible—that one has swallowed deceptions sold by charlatans—and this is particularly hard when those deceptions are massive. And yet many good-hearted Americans have been victimized in just this way. As we challenge the myths and fictions of the Manufactured Crisis, some people will find it difficult to acknowledge that they were so often duped.

Distorted and Hostile Reporting

Others may question our arguments because they have so often been besieged by negative and distorted media reports about our educational system. A recent incident illustrates this point nicely. In mid-September of 1993, many newspapers in the country carried headlines announcing the results of a big federal study of literacy in America.[14] On September 9 the front page of the *New York Times* reported that "half of adults in the U.S. lack reading and mathematics abilities," while the *Washington Post* headlined, "Literacy of 90 Million Is Deficient."[15] And for a week thereafter reporters wrote countless stories about the supposed illiteracy of the American public that were to be *read* by the millions of people who collectively made up that public.

Most of these stories were based on a *press conference* called by the U.S. Department of Education to announce the study they had sponsored rather than on the *actual report* in which the study was summarized. Thus, the reporters failed to note or to inform Americans that the researchers had classified people as "illiterate" merely because they did not score well on a test of reading comprehension. This sounds reasonable until one begins to think about some startling characteristics of the so-called illiterate group that the report detailed. For example, nearly 40 percent of these "illiterate" persons were employed full-time; nearly 70 percent were reported to be "not poor"; over 80 percent did not receive food stamps; and approximately one-third were receiving regular interest from their own savings accounts. About four out of five "illiterates" also declared that they read "well" or "very well." Only a few said they needed to rely on family or friends to interpret prose material, and nearly half reported reading a newspaper every day! Worse, some truly startling categories of people turned out to have been classified as among the most illiterate: 26 percent had debilitating physical or mental conditions, 19 percent had difficulties reading print because they were visually impaired, and 25 percent were immigrants whose native language was not English—the language of the test.

This means that reporters failed to note details of the study that seriously challenged the major conclusions announced at the press conference. (In fact, one wonders who were actually illiterate, the visually impaired and non-English-speaking Americans who could not pass the study's test or the reporters who failed to read or understand its report!) Moreover, no news analyst seems to have questioned the basic premise put forth by the Department of Education at that conference; namely, that illiteracy causes poverty. Somehow, no one seems to have thought that the relationship between poverty and illiteracy might go the other way—indeed that good research had already been done indicating that *poverty causes low levels of literacy*.[16] This is a difference that matters. If poverty is a major *cause* of illiteracy, then it is time indeed that Americans take seriously the fact that poverty rates are *far* worse in our country than in other Western democracies.

Unfortunately, this episode is all too typical of recent, ignorant, highly critical media portrayals of American education and its effects. Hardly a week passes without one or more inflammatory press accounts detailing the "rotten" state of America's schools. Given that the press regularly trumpets "evidence" purporting to confirm the failures of American education, is it any wonder that many Americans have accepted this message? And given such incessant media irresponsibility, who would be surprised if some readers had difficulty believing *us?*

The Legacy of Socrates

Other readers may question our arguments because they believe that many things, including education and the manners of young people, were better in the past than in the present. Such beliefs are not new. Consider the legacy of Socrates. Ever since Socrates roamed the streets of Athens 2,500 years ago, muttering about the lack of discipline and knowledge among Athenian youth, countless older people have believed their offspring to be inferior to themselves.

We suspect that Socrates' Syndrome shows up most often among adults when their culture is changing rapidly, as was happening in ancient Athens and as is happening in America today. When cultures change rapidly, younger people do not know the same things their parents know. For example, in a farm family in Nebraska in the 1890s, adults and children probably shared a good deal of knowledge and values. With the nation's rapid pace of change, however, Nebraskan youths of the 1990s are presumably *much* less likely to think and act like their parents. (They probably know a lot less about how to stoke a coal furnace or how to use a wringer washer and a great deal more about programming personal computers and rock music!) And this almost always makes parents nervous.

Parents and other adults, however, may not stop to think that children may know *different* things than they do, a natural consequence of living in a rapidly changing culture with an exploding knowledge base. Their problem, like Socrates', is that they see differences as deficiencies, but such reasoning is questionable. Each generation must determine which bits of knowledge from the past to retain and which to abandon in favor of new knowledge. Some people find this a threatening state of affairs and may well decide to blame the schools for their discomfort. Such people may question our arguments that the schools have been maligned.

Confusing Reality with Desire

Other people confuse what schools *are* with what they *would like* schools to be. They condemn the schools of today because they are afraid that the graduates they produce will not be ready for the twenty-first century, will find they are not able to compete in the global marketplace, or will not be able to respond to the needs of corporations in the future. Such worries are difficult to address, since it is not easy to predict the future clearly.

But it is *not* necessary to destroy faith in the public schools because some people believe that schools are not doing all that is necessary to prepare for the next century. Directing the schools toward a different set of goals would certainly be appropriate—*if* we were truly wise enough to predict the future. But we need not condemn the schools of today in order to engage in debates about what the schools of the future should be like.

Be that as it may, those who seriously confuse reality with desire are unlikely to be satisfied with schools in today's America, no matter how impressive the performance of those institutions. Such people may also have difficulty with our words of comfort.

Suspending Judgment

Although all of these people may have reasons for disbelieving what we write here, we urge them to set aside those reasons for the present. There is something marvelously persuasive about *evidence,* and—as readers will discover—whenever possible we present evidence to back the claims we will make about the myths of the Manufactured Crisis and about the real problems of American education. Moreover, we've tried to provide citations for all of our claims, and readers are urged to check our original sources whenever they have questions about what we present here.

Of course, it is hard to find any single study that will convince someone who is sure of beliefs that those beliefs are wrong. It is also very difficult to find evidence that is easy to interpret and that is unambiguous and convincing enough to settle issues as complex as the ones we address here. Further, evidence from social research rarely comes in easy-to-use formats. For this reason, we have tried, where possible, to convert tabular data, obscure statistics, and technical jargon into common-language words and visual images that readers can more easily follow.

But the arguments we make do not rest on single studies, nor do they hang or fall on obscure and technical points. On the contrary, in most cases the evidence we display comes from many studies and makes simple and straightforward points. And collectively that evidence leads to two simple and straightforward conclusions: (1) on the whole, the American school system is in far better shape than the critics would have us believe; (2) where American schools fail, those failures are largely caused by problems that are imposed on those schools, problems that the critics have been only too happy to ignore. American education *can* be restructured, improved, and strengthened—but to build realistic programs for achieving these goals, we must explode the myths of the Manufactured Crisis and confront the real problems of American education.

NOTES

1. *Japan Times* (1987, August 23).

2. Schooland (1990, p. 121).

3. Schooland (1990, p. 122).

4. *Japan Times* (1986, January 30).

5. Schooland (1990, p. 121).

6. *Japan Times* (1985, November 20).

7. Stanglin (1985).

8. Schooland (1990, p. 179).

9. Yates (1985); *Arizona Republic* (1993); Schooland (1990).

10. *Japan Times* (1986, April 24).

11. National Commission on Excellence in Education (1983).

12. Richburg (1985).

13. Richburg (1985).

14. Educational Testing Service (1993).

15. Celis (1993); Jordan (1993).

16. See Kaufman & Rosenbaum (1992).

REFERENCES

Arizona Republic (1993). Immigrants' children choose English by big margin, study says (July 8), p. A3.

Celis, William, III (1993). Study says half of adults in U.S. lack reading and math abilities. *New York Times* (September 9), p. A1.

Educational Testing Service (1993). *Adult literacy in America: A first look at the results of the National Adult Literacy Survey.* Washington, DC: U.S. Government Printing Office.

Japan Times (various dates).

Kaufman, Julie E. & Rosenbaum, James E. (1992). The education and employment of low-income black youth in white suburbs. *Educational Evaluation and Policy Analysis, 14,* 229–240.

National Commission on Excellence in Education (1983). *A nation at risk: The imperatives for educational reform.* Washington, DC: U.S. Department of Education.

Richburg, Keith B. (1985). Japanese education: Admired but not easily imported. *Washington Post* (October 19), pp. A1, A4.

Schooland, Ken (1990). *Shogun's ghost: The dark side of Japanese education.* New York: Bergin and Garvey.

Stanglin, Doug (1985). Japan's blackboard jungle. *Newsweek: Atlantic Edition* (July 1), p. 5.

Yates, Ronald E. (1985). Japanese twist bullying into a brutal art. *Chicago Tribune* (November 24), p. 5.

25

ONE HUNDRED FIFTY YEARS
OF TESTING

Robert Rothman

This chapter traces the history of large-scale testing in the United
States. As frequent assessment and high-stakes tests become increasingly popular, it is informative to see how mass testing started and
how it has been used as an educational yardstick and a political tool.

———— o ————

ALONG WITH A SMALL BAND OF ALLIES, Horace Mann, the leading
educator of the mid-nineteenth century, had a vision for reforming education. Possessing a strong belief in the value of education as a tool for social advancement, Mann proposed the idea of a "common school" that
would enable everyone—particularly the immigrants who were beginning to swell enrollments in Mann's home state of Massachusetts and
elsewhere—to live fulfilling lives.

Like reformers everywhere, though, Mann faced opposition. His opponents consisted of teachers and headmasters who favored a classical
education for an elite student body rather than the more practically oriented mass education Mann called for.

As the secretary of the Massachusetts State Board of Education, however, Mann had several weapons at his disposal; and the instrument he
chose to help make his case was one that education policy makers would
turn to again and again over the next century and a half: he created a test.
More specifically, Mann, along with his ally Samuel Gridley Howe, in

1845 asked the Boston School Committee to administer a written examination to the city's schoolchildren, in place of the oral examinations teachers customarily used. The novel instrument, Mann and Howe reasoned, would provide objective information on the quality of teaching and learning in the city's schools.

In the short run, Mann and Howe's test helped their cause by exposing wide gaps in Boston students' knowledge. Armed with that information, city and state officials sharply criticized the school system and bolstered Mann's arguments for change. But in the long run, the greatest significance of the test was the success of the new instrument at measuring student performance. Unlike the oral examinations, which depended on a teacher's judgment, the written tests were "impartial" barometers of performance. The tests, Mann said, would "determine, beyond appeal or gainsaying, whether the pupils have been faithfully and competently taught."[1]

Confident about the power of the new instruments, Mann began to advocate the regular use of tests to monitor the quality of instruction and permit comparisons among teachers and schools. But as the use of tests as external information devices grew, so did the criticism of such uses. Teachers, in particular, increasingly questioned whether comparisons of school quality based on tests were fair.

If this account has a contemporary ring, it should. Many of the issues surrounding testing have changed little since Horace Mann's day. Tests have always loomed large in American education. To see how large, just walk into any classroom: when a teacher begins a new lesson, the first question students ask is, "Will this be on the test?" They will pay attention, or not, depending on the answer.

Savvy students know that what is on the test matters, because the test is how the rest of the world knows what they know and can do. While a student's grades may reflect a host of factors—from attendance to participation to willingness to clean the blackboard—the ultimate judgment about a student's level of achievement most often revolves around a test.

For teachers, tests have long served as a way to find out whether students have learned what they have been taught. Through the familiar end-of-chapter tests and weekly "pop quizzes," teachers can find out whether students can solve mathematics problems that employ the algebra concepts just covered or whether they can recall facts about the Gilded Age that were mentioned in the previous week's reading. Through midterm and final examinations, teachers can determine whether students have mastered the course material and are ready to move on to the next level.

As one recent survey confirmed, such classroom tests are a regular feature of instruction. Nearly nine out of ten middle school and secondary school math and science teachers polled said they use teacher-made tests at least once a month, while 70 percent of math teachers and 56 percent of science teachers said they use tests included in textbooks. And, as Richard J. Stiggins of the Northwest Regional Educational Laboratory estimates, between 20 and 30 percent of a teacher's professional time is directly involved with assessment-related activities. These include designing, developing, selecting, administering, scoring, recording, reporting, evaluating, and revising assignments, tests, quizzes, observations, and judgments about student performance.[2]

As the Horace Mann example shows, tests have played an important role outside of the classroom as well; and in many ways, it is these external tests—which often have high stakes attached to their use—that are the most significant ones students take. These tests communicate to school officials and to the public at large varied information about the state of students' and schools' performance. As any reader of the sports pages knows, Americans are fascinated by numerical rankings, and schools are not exempt from this obsession. Just as baseball fans pore over box scores to see how the home team's players are doing, public officials have sought to use tests to determine how students and schools are faring— and to use that information in setting education policy.

But like baseball statistics, test scores also provoke argument and debate. Many educators are leery of making judgments about young people's performance on the basis of tests, particularly the type that has dominated schooling for the past century and a half.

Since Horace Mann's day, we have relied on one method of finding out what young people know and are able to do: we take them out of the normal classroom setting and ask them questions that we have selected— questions representing a broad survey of the skills and knowledge in a subject area. We judge the answers—and only the answers (not the process by which they were derived)—by determining whether they are right or wrong, removing as much as we can any judgment about the quality of the answers. We then compare how each student performed to how other students performed.

This method of finding out what students know has done more than provide information. Increasingly, it has shaped expectations for what students and teachers do every day in the classroom. Partly, this has happened by design: recognizing that everyone views tests as important, policy makers have increasingly relied on tests—commercially available tests such as the Iowa Test of Basic Skills and the Metropolitan Achievement Test, as well as tests developed by state departments of education—as a lever to improve performance. But as critics of the use of testing have been quick to point out, this power can exert a harmful influence on schools. In part, the movement to shift to a new method of testing is aimed at harnessing the power of tests toward positive ends.

An Emerging Technology

As schools began to grow into larger and larger enterprises in the late-nineteenth century, fueled in large part by massive waves of immigration, the interest among policy makers in tests as management tools grew rapidly. According to Lauren Resnick and Daniel Resnick, "Standardized tests in various school subjects were introduced into American schools in the period 1880–1920 when booming enrollments, large school-building programs, and the cult of efficiency in industry combined to encourage the schools to justify their performance in quantitative ways to local taxpayers. Short-answer and multiple-choice tests were viewed as cost-efficient and objective measures in which there might be some public confidence."[3]

Along with the growing interest in measuring student achievement grew the technology for doing so. One of the pioneers in demonstrating the power of standardized tests was Joseph Mayer Rice, a physician who had studied education in Germany. Interested in examining the effectiveness of teaching techniques, Rice developed tests in spelling, penmanship, English composition, and arithmetic, and he surveyed about 100,000 students in thirty-six cities. His findings, published in a national journal, shattered some myths; the spelling test, for example, showed that there was no relation between spelling achievement and the amount of time spent studying the subject.[4]

Led by such advances, achievement testing became codified into a science in the early years of the twentieth century. Its most influential voice was Edward L. Thorndike, a psychologist who attempted to apply to his nascent discipline the rigorous techniques of the "hard" sciences, such as physics and chemistry. As Thorndike was fond of saying, whatever exists, exists in quantity.

The use of testing in schools mushroomed following World War I, when the Army Alpha test—which was administered to more than 1.7 million soldiers—appeared to demonstrate the success of measuring intelligence. The Alpha test, a written test that asked recruits to solve analogies, complete sentences, and so forth, was intended to help the armed services place recruits into their proper ranks by demonstrating their mental qualifications. The Army also administered a separate test with figures, called the Beta test, for recruits deemed unable to read. But as with Horace Mann's Boston test, the significance of the Army tests was not so much in their immediate results—which appeared to show shockingly low levels of intelligence among recruits, particularly immigrants—as in the use of the instruments themselves. As Stephen Jay Gould, the biologist who wrote a stinging critique of the tests, wrote, the Army experiment demonstrated that "a technology had been developed for testing all pupils. Tests could now rank and stream everybody; the era of mass testing had begun."[5]

In the wake of that effort, schools clamored for intelligence tests to sort their students according to ability. But accompanying that wave was a rapid growth in the use of achievement tests to provide information on schools' effectiveness. The number of achievement tests available, which had risen steadily in the decade prior to World War I, increased tenfold in the 1920s. And a survey by the U.S. Bureau of Education showed that one key purpose of such tests was to gauge the quality of schools and teachers. Some 57 percent of the elementary schools in the 215 cities surveyed said the tests were used to compare their school with other school systems; 38 percent said they were used to judge the efficiency of teachers.[6]

Thus entrenched, testing became a regular feature of schooling. In 1929, the University of Iowa created the first statewide student tests, the Iowa Test of Basic Skills and the Iowa Test of Educational Development. Offered to schools on a voluntary basis—Iowa to this day is one of the few states that do not have a mandatory testing program—the Iowa tests provided student achievement information on a range of key subjects for grades three through high school. A decade later, the tests were offered to schools in other states as well, and they remain among the most often used commercially available achievement tests in the nation.

A pioneering effort in large-scale testing, the Iowa program was also largely responsible for making the practice cost-efficient and thus helped ensure testing's continued growth. In the 1950s, E. F. Lindquist, then the program's director, developed an electronic scoring machine that could read answer sheets, produce raw scores, and convert raw scores into standard scores, all in a fraction of the time—and cost—it took teachers and scientists to conduct those tasks by hand. Moreover, the machine also had the advantage of enhancing the seeming objectivity of test scores by removing teacher judgment from the picture altogether. At a time when Americans were growing increasingly fascinated by technological solutions to social problems, machine-scoring made testing irresistible.

The Second Wave

Fueled by such advances, the second wave of testing for external pur-poses—that is, outside the classroom—began in the 1960s and has con-tinued to crest to this day. Over the past three decades, public officials have increasingly relied on knowing what students know to determine whether they are eligible for remedial or special education, for promotion to the next grade or graduation from high school, or for special distinc-tion, such as an honors diploma. Test scores have also been used to de-cide if schools can earn cash bonuses or freedom from state rules or if schools should be punished by having their staff reassigned or by being taken over by the state. The exploding interest in the use of tests, as we will see, has made their method of measuring student performance criti-cally important. But it has also generated a storm of criticism and de-mands for a new method.

Two factors have helped drive the test engine of the last thirty years. The first was a growing interest among education policy makers, begin-ning in the 1960s, in theories from business and public administration that emphasized redesigning systems toward a goal. These theories went by various names, including "planning, programming, budgeting sys-tems" and "management by objective." Swept up in that wave, dozens of state legislatures passed legislation that held schools accountable for raising student achievement—the goal of the education system. At least seventy-three such laws were enacted between 1963 and 1974.

One of the earliest and most comprehensive of these measures, to take one example, was Florida's Education Accountability Act of 1971. That statute directed the state's commissioner of education to establish educa-tion objectives for each subject area and grade level and to develop a statewide testing system to determine "the degree to which established educational objectives had been achieved." Other state laws expressed similar objectives. In Colorado, the general assembly mandated a program to "measure objectively the adequacy and efficiency of the educational programs offered by the public schools." In Mississippi, lawmakers called for the establishment of "an assessment of educational performance to as-sist in the measurement of educational quality and to provide information to school officials and citizens."[7]

Coinciding with the burgeoning interest in testing for accountability in education was a gnawing anxiety among educators and citizens about the state of student achievement, which spurred another round of testing mandates. This anxiety reached a crescendo with the revelation that the average scores on the Scholastic Aptitude Test had declined by a total of

81 points between 1963 and 1977—from 478 points to 429 points on the verbal portion and from 502 points to 470 points on the math portion, both on a 200-to-800 scale.

This revelation shocked Americans and convinced them that their much-prized education system had slipped into steep decline. A commission was established by the College Board, the test's sponsor, to investigate the cause of the decline. Commissioners concluded that "the public's interest is not in the psychometric technicalities of the S.A.T. score decline but in its implications regarding what is widely perceived as serious deterioration in learning in America. More and more high school graduates show up in college classrooms, employers' personnel offices, or at other common checkpoints with barely a speaking acquaintance with the English language and no writing facility at all. . . . Although the S.A.T. score figures are too small a window for surveying this broad condition, they provide special insight into it."[8]

The public reacted by calling for going "back to the basics," away from approaches that many considered less rigorous academically—open classrooms and the "new math" among them. Accompanying this movement was a demand for tests to ensure that students graduated from high school able to read, write, and compute. Responding to these pressures, thirty-six states adopted some form of "minimum competency" test to measure students' basic skills.

The demand for more and more testing did not abate. In fact, it increased in the early 1980s as part of the flood tide of education reform activity that followed the release of the landmark report *A Nation at Risk*. Commissioned by President Reagan's secretary of education, Terrel H. Bell, the report warned of a "rising tide of mediocrity" that threatened the nation's well-being. The report concluded ominously, "If an unfriendly foreign power had attempted to impose on America the mediocre educational performance that exists today, we might have viewed it as an act of war."

In one of its key recommendations, the report urged schools, colleges, and universities to adopt "more rigorous and measurable standards and higher expectations for student performance" and proposed tests as the appropriate measures. Standardized tests of achievement (not to be confused with aptitude tests) should be administered at major transition points from one level of schooling to another—particularly from high school to college or work—the report recommended. The purposes of these tests would be to (1) certify the student's credentials, (2) identify the need for remedial intervention, and (3) identify the opportunity for advanced or accelerated work. The report concluded that these tests should be administered as part of a nationwide (but not federal) system of state and local standardized tests.[9]

The report accelerated unprecedented school reform activity into high gear. Nearly every state adopted policies aimed at improving the schools within their borders—and many of these policies, heeding the report's recommendations, included the creation or expansion of statewide testing programs. A survey by the National Center for Research on Evaluation, Standards, and Student Testing at the University of California, Los Angeles, found that by 1984 thirty-nine states were operating at least one statewide testing program; by the end of the decade, this had risen to forty-seven states.[10]

This whirlwind of post–*Nation at Risk* reform activity at the state level did not supplant the testing that local school districts required; on the contrary, districts also upped their requirements in the 1980s. Governments layered policies on top of one another, with little coordination among them.

The federal government got into the act as well by expanding its testing program, the National Assessment of Educational Progress. Created in 1969, NAEP, often called the "nation's report card," tested national samples of students in a range of subject areas. Beginning in the mid 1980s, however, state and national officials began to call for expanding the program to permit state-by-state, and perhaps even district-by-district, comparisons of student achievement, Such a move, according to a blue-ribbon panel appointed by William J. Bennett, who was the secretary of education, would improve NAEP's usefulness as a "rudder against the storm" of confusing information about the state of student achievement.

As the panel's report notes, the national assessment has been beneficial, but it suffers from a serious weakness: while providing excellent information on what our children know and can do, it provides it only for the nation as a whole and for very large regions of the country. "Whole-nation information is of course useful when we want to gauge the performance of our children against that of children in other countries, whether rivals or allies. But in the United States, education is a *state* responsibility, and it is against the performance of children close to home that we want and need to compare the performance of our youngsters."[11]

Congress agreed to go along with the panel's recommendations for state-by-state comparisons, but on a trial basis only, and so far has rejected the idea of permitting district-level testing. In 1990, NAEP tested eighth-grade students in thirty-seven states in math; in 1992, it tested students in forty-four states in fourth-grade reading and fourth- and eighth-grade math.

As a result of all the legislation and rule-making the number of tests students take in schools is staggering. The National Commission on Testing and Public Policy, a panel of educators and civil rights leaders created by the Ford Foundation, estimated in its 1989 report that the 41 million American students take 127 million tests a year—more than three tests a year for each student. In a survey of math and science teachers, researchers from Boston College found that 85 percent of elementary and middle school math teachers and 60 percent of elementary science teachers reported that one or more standardized tests were required of their students.

In a more cautious estimate, the General Accounting Office concluded that "systemwide" testing—tests given to all students, almost all students, or a representative sample of students at any one grade level in a school district—exerted only a modest burden on classroom time. The average student, the GAO estimated, spent only seven hours a year on testing, including preparation, test-taking, and all related activities.[12]

High Stakes

Whatever the actual number, though, the tests have become increasingly important, making the perennial student query—"Will this be on the test?"—ever more relevant. And in response to this trend, educators have become more vocal in questioning whether the tests reveal what young people know.

According to the Boston College survey, teachers' own tests play a vital role in shaping instruction. About two-thirds of the math teachers and three-fifths of the science teachers surveyed said their instruction was "very similar" or "quite similar" to the tests included in textbooks—tests which, as we have seen, teachers use frequently.[13]

But it is external tests that have increasingly driven what is taught in schools. And this is no accident. As part of their attempt to hold schools accountable for student performance, states and school districts have not only implemented testing programs but have also made sure that there are consequences—real or perceived—attached to the results. That way, students and schools have an incentive to keep their "eyes on the prize" and to improve performance. Thus in recent years a growing number of states have made sure that good things happen to schools where test scores go up and (in some cases) bad things happen when they go down. As we will see, these policies have had the desired effect of making teachers and schools pay attention to the tests and strive to boost scores, but these efforts have not always ended up the way public officials intended.

The most common method by which districts have placed high stakes on the test results is simply publicizing them. Just as teachers regularly send report cards to parents to show individual student progress, some states and school districts have created report cards to show the performance of schools. The idea is the same: parents are expected to reward high-performing schools and put pressure on low-performing schools to improve, just as they reward their children for doing well and urge them to buckle down when they need improvement.

Sometimes the pressure exerted through public reporting is less subtle. When he became superintendent of the Prince George's County, Maryland, school district outside of Washington, D.C., John A. Murphy pledged to raise the average test score in the district to the seventy-fifth percentile and to reduce the gap between the scores of whites and blacks. He carried out this pledge by removing student artwork that had graced the walls of the conference room adjacent to his office and replacing it with charts that showed the test performance of every school in the district, along with the principal's name. Principals summoned to the conference room—known as the "applied anxiety room"—quickly got the message, and test scores went up (although they fell again when the state changed the test it used).

The federal government has also tried its hand at creating a report card for the states; that effort, too, proved hotly controversial. Beginning in 1984, the year after A Nation at Risk was released, Secretary Bell annually released a "wall chart" that attempted to show how the fifty states ranked in education performance. The factors he used to measure state performance were dropout rates and average scores on the two major college admissions tests: the Scholastic Aptitude Test and the American College Testing program test.

State officials (and the companies that produced the tests) immediately criticized the use of the test scores to rank states as misleading and unfair. They argued that since students volunteered to take the tests—only those planning to attend colleges that required the tests for admission elected to take the SAT or the ACT—the average scores did not reflect a true measure of average student performance in the state. If the characteristics of the students who chose to take the tests changed, the average score might go up or down, but this change would have nothing to do with the quality of education in the state. Moreover, the argument continued, the tests themselves did not measure a state's education program, since they were designed to be "common yardsticks" to measure students' abilities regardless of where students attended school.

Despite these arguments, Secretary Bell and his successors, William Bennett and Lauro F. Cavazos, persisted in releasing the wall chart each year. Recognizing the handwriting on the wall chart, the Council of Chief State School Officers reversed decades of policy and agreed by a margin of one vote to endorse a new way of comparing student achievement across states. That decision helped lend support for the expansion of NAEP, which, unlike the SAT and the ACT, is administered to a representative sample of students and measures achievement in subject areas, not just generic skills.

State and federal officials in 1991 created a new national report card to show state and national progress toward the six national education goals set by President George Bush and the nation's governors. The first goals report included states' performance on NAEP as information on progress toward the goal of ensuring that all students "demonstrate competency in challenging subject matter." Following the institution of the goals report, Secretary of Education Lamar Alexander quietly dropped the wall chart.

Like the state and school district officials before them, the governors and Bush Administration officials on the National Education Goals Panel portrayed their attempt to provide a report card on education performance as a "wake-up call" to arouse a complacent citizenry into action to raise performance. But it is unclear whether the goals report or any of the school report cards have produced the desired effects. For one thing, the reports have tended to generate little attention outside a relatively small group of committed and informed citizens and professionals. (With one exception: real-estate agents often snatch up the report cards and use school test scores as selling points for homes neighboring high-scoring schools.)

The report cards have also failed to answer the question of what citizens and parents are supposed to do once they have information about a school's performance. One action that parents can take in a number of states is to send their children to another school. At least a dozen states allow parents some form of choice among public schools in the state. But there is little evidence that parents who take advantage of this option use report cards about school performance to make their decisions. In Minnesota, the first state to open enrollment in every school, Rudy Perpich, as governor, proposed a statewide testing program to provide "consumer information" about the quality of schools in the state, but that proposal was rejected by the legislature. Despite their limited impact on the public, the report cards have succeeded in one respect, though: they have made schools place even greater emphasis on the tests. Whether or not parents pay any attention or take any action, principals want to make sure that their school looks good when the test scores are published in newspapers, and they encourage teachers to take steps to see that scores go up. "What gets measured gets taught," a report by the Southern Regional Education Board notes. "What gets reported gets taught twice as well."[14]

In addition to reporting the results publicly, states and school districts have also raised the stakes on tests by attaching consequences to the results—rewarding success and punishing failure. About half the math teachers in the Boston College survey responded that the achievement tests were "extremely important" or "very important" in student placement and in administrators' evaluations of schools and school districts.[15]

In some cases, students themselves have been held accountable for performance. Seventeen of the thirty-six states with minimum-competency tests, for example, tie grade-to-grade promotion or high school graduation (or both) directly to a test. If students pass the test, they can cross the threshold; if not, they have to wait until they do pass. The use of tests as promotional gates received a significant boost in 1983, when the Florida Supreme Court ruled that the state could legally withhold a diploma from a student who failed to pass a basic-skills test as long as the student was taught what the test measured.

Two states even erected tests as gates to entry into school. In Georgia and Mississippi, legislatures approved policies to test kindergartners to determine whether they were ready to enter the first grade. In Georgia, for example, every child in kindergarten had to pass a ninety-minute achievement test and a teacher's evaluation in order to advance to first grade; any child who failed to was placed in a "transitional" class. But these tests drew sharp criticism from educators and children's advocates, who contended that the tests were poor measures of young children's abilities and could unfairly exclude from school many children who could do well. Faced with such opposition, the legislatures reversed themselves and dropped the kindergarten tests.

Some of the state testing programs have offered rewards for high performance. For more than a century, New York State has offered Regents Examinations, which test students at the end of high school courses. Students who elect to take the exams and pass them are eligible for a special diploma, known as a Regents diploma. California in 1983 adopted a similar program, known as Golden State Examinations.

California also briefly experimented with a program to provide cash awards for students who perform well on the regular state testing program, the California Assessment Program. The "cash for CAP" program, later dropped for budget reasons, was explicitly aimed at offering an incentive for students to perform, as state officials explained: "The majority of students are not working up to their potential, and . . . it is the responsibility of the schools to challenge them to do so—both for their own good and for the good of society."[16]

Other states, meanwhile, have chosen to focus on school performance. At least seven states have adopted programs to reward schools that demonstrate high levels of student performance, in most cases by providing cash awards. South Carolina, though, tried an unusual twist to this idea. Schools where test scores show significant improvement are free from many state regulations, such as those governing the number of minutes of instruction for each subject each day. Educators in South Carolina say the deregulation program provides an incentive for schools to keep their test scores up, if only so they can maintain their status as a special school.

A more controversial (and thus less common) strategy is punishing failing schools. The first state to adopt this approach was New Jersey, which used its new authority by taking over the "academically bankrupt" Jersey City school district. But while lagging test scores were only one of many factors that led to the takeover there, officials in other states with similar programs, notably South Carolina, suggest that the threat of possible takeover has motivated schools to improve test performance.

The explosion in testing, particularly high-stakes testing, over the past two decades has put enormous weight on tests and has placed them squarely in the center of schooling. Now teachers as well as students are asking, "Will this be on the test?"

But the emphasis on tests has raised serious questions: Do increases in test scores truly reflect increases in student achievement? Are schools focusing on material tested to the exclusion of other knowledge and skills that may be important? Do the types of tests schools use measure all of the abilities students must be able to demonstrate?

Increasingly, educators are answering no to all of these questions. Educators and researchers have amassed evidence of significant problems with the growing reliance on tests, confirming suspicions that teachers since Horace Mann's time have held: namely, that using tests as gauges of teacher or school performance is unfair. Faced with such evidence, and adding their own as well, schools such as Littleton have begun their search for alternatives.

NOTES

1. Quoted in P. D. Chapman, *Schools as Sorters: Lewis M. Terman, Applied Psychology, and the Intelligence Testing Movement, 1890–1930* (New York: New York University Press, 1988), p. 33.

2. G. F. Madaus and others, *The Influence of Testing on Teaching Math and Science in Grades 4–12* (Chestnut Hill, Mass.: Center for the Study of Testing, Evaluation, and Educational Policy, Boston College, 1992). For the extent of teacher-made tests, see R. J. Stiggins, "Revitalizing Classroom Assessment," *Phi Delta Kappan* 69, no. 5, pp. 363–368.

3. L. B. Resnick and D. P. Resnick, "Standards, Curriculum, and Performance: A Historical and Comparative Perspective," *Educational Researcher* 16, no. 9: 13–20.

4. See Chapman, *Schools as Sorters,* and H. D. Corbett and B. L. Wilson, *Testing, Reform, and Rebellion* (Norwood, N.J.: Ablex, 1991), p. 18.

5. S. J. Gould, *The Mismeasure of Man* (New York: Norton, 1981), p. 195.

6. See Chapman, *Schools as Sorters,* pp. 146–170.

7. See A. E. Wise, *Legislated Learning* (Berkeley: University of California Press, 1979), pp. 12–26, for a more complete analysis of the accountability legislation.

8. W. Wirtz, *On Further Examination: Report of the Advisory Panel on the Scholastic Aptitude Test Decline* (New York: College Board, 1977), p. 1.

9. National Commission on Excellence in Education, *A Nation at Risk* (Washington, D.C.: U.S. Government Printing Office, 1983), pp. 5, 27–28.

10. See E. L. Baker, "Mandated Tests: Educational Reform or Quality Indicator?" in *Test Policy and Test Performance: Education, Language, and Culture,* ed. B. R. Gifford (Boston: Kluwer, 1989). Also, see U.S. Congress, Office of Technology Assessment, *Testing in American Schools: Asking the Right Questions* (Washington, D.C.: U.S. Government Printing Office, 1992).

11. L. Alexander and H. T. James, *The Nation's Report Card: Improving the Assessment of Student Achievement* (Cambridge, Mass.: National Academy of Education, 1987).

12. See National Commission on Testing and Public Policy, *From Gatekeeper to Gateway: Transforming Testing in America* (Chestnut Hill, Mass.: Boston College, 1989); Madaus and others, *The Influence of Testing;* and U.S. General Accounting Office, *Student Testing: Current Extent and Expenditures, with Cost Estimates for a National Examination* (Washington, D.C.: U.S. Government Printing Office, 1993). Part of the confusion stems from the definition of *test.* The National Commission, for example, refers to each test in a battery as a separate test, while the Government Accounting Office does not.

13. Madaus and others, *The Influence of Testing.*

14. Quoted in G. F. Gaines and L. M. Cornett, *School Accountability Reports: Lessons Learned in S.R.E.B. States* (Atlanta: Southern Regional Education Board, 1992), p. 16.

15. Madaus and others, *The Influence of Testing.*

16. S. M. Bennett and D. Carlson, "A Brief History of State Testing Policies in California," in *State Educational Testing Policies* (Washington, D.C.: Office of Technology Assessment, 1986, p. 169).

26

WITH 2000 LOOMING, CHANCES OF MEETING NATIONAL GOALS IFFY

David J. Hoff

Ambitious goals set in 1994 nearly guaranteed lack of total implementation by 2000—it was only six years away. This commentary on Goals 2000 brings up an interesting question about school reform: Does lack of full change equal failure, or does the adoption of some aspects of change equal success?

○

ALMOST 10 YEARS AGO, President George Bush and the state governors set goals aimed at preparing all the nation's children to improve their achievement in core subjects and outpace the world in at least math and science by 2000.

With one year remaining, the prospects of reaching those goals—and most of the other four set soon after the chief executives' 1989 summit in Charlottesville, Va., and two others added in 1994—appear practically nil.

Student scores have risen in mathematics but stayed about the same in reading, according to the panel charged with tracking progress toward the goals. And the results from international assessments given in 1996 suggest the United States is far from dominating the world in math and science.

As the country approaches the target date for the original goals, however, many of the leaders and observers of the campaign say it has nevertheless been a success and needs to continue.

"Without [the goals], we'd have an awful lot of interest in education but not much direction," U.S. Secretary of Education Richard W. Riley said in a recent interview.

"The goals are part of a general . . . shift in attitude that is taking academic achievement seriously," said Patricia Albjerg Graham, a professor of education history at Harvard University's graduate school of education and the president of the Spencer Foundation in Chicago. "It's a mistake to take the goals literally. But symbolically, they are part of other efforts to say American kids need a stronger preparation in academics."

In that context, the goals could be considered a success. After their two-day summit in September 1989, Mr. Bush and all the nation's governors issued a statement saying that the goals would serve to make the country internationally competitive. The statement further said that the leaders wanted education goals "to reorient the education system and to marshal widespread support for needed reforms."

But even if American students and schools haven't met the performance measures outlined in the goals, the public's heightened concern over the quality of its schools in recent years has led to an intense debate over how to improve education.

Child Health Improves

Still, 2000 will arrive with many of the goals unmet. Student achievement isn't significantly better than in 1990, when President Bush announced the original six goals in his State of the Union Address and the National Governors' Association later adopted them at the group's annual winter meeting.

Of the 26 indicators the National Education Goals Panel uses to measure progress, only five have shown statistically significant increases in the 1990s, the committee of governors, legislators, and federal officials says in its eighth annual report on the goals, released last month. Another three indicators showed decreases.

In the rest, no longitudinal data exist to determine whether there has been advancement, the report says.

Most of the success has been in the health of young children, a sign, the goals panel says, that they will be ready to learn once they enter school—the first goal. The high school graduation rate hovers near the 90 percent mark called for in the second goal, and may be achieved next year.

But the goals centered on student achievement—the ones that have received the most attention—are unlikely to be met. The fifth goal, which says U.S. students will lead the world in math and science achievement, clearly won't be realized, according to 1996 data collected by the Third International Mathematics and Science Study and noted in the recent goals report. Only in 4th grade science did American students lead the world.

To cite those data as a sign of failure, however, may be misleading and contribute to a misperception that schools and students are doing poorly, some researchers say.

While TIMSS researchers set standards for the types of students that needed to participate in the study's sample, "very few countries" included the diverse cross-section the guidelines demanded, said Iris C. Rotberg, the research professor of education policy at George Washington University's graduate school of education in Washington.

"The test-score comparisons simply don't tell us anything about the quality of education in the different countries," she said. The United States' mediocre showing in science, for example, is contradicted by the number of top scientists educated in the country's schools, Ms. Rotberg argued.

Focus on Academics

Regardless of the debate over whether the goals will be achieved, their success in encouraging a new focus on what students are learning and on measuring their achievement in itself is a significant—and possibly momentous—outcome of the 1990 goals, supporters of the effort say.

The goals "have served as a focal point of debate," said John F. Jennings, the director of the Center on Education Policy, a Washington clearinghouse on education issues, and former Democratic education aide on Capitol Hill. "They've helped to further the idea that there should be standards in one form or another."

While that may be true, policymakers have never supported the goals effort with the dollars needed to produce radical change, said Samuel C. Stringfield, a principal research scientist at Johns Hopkins University in Baltimore. By comparison, he noted, when President John F. Kennedy said the United States should put a man on the moon, he recommended that billions be spent.

"When the governors and president met in 1989 . . . they came behind with nothing that approximated what Kennedy had done," Mr. Stringfield said.

Others say the goals process has been narrowly focused on schools' role in children's learning, practically ignoring the roles of parents and community institutions.

"The goals are written from the school perspective, and they lay all the responsibility on the school," said Dorothy Rich, the president of the Home and School Institute, a Washington nonprofit that trains school officials on how to encourage parents to be actively involved in their children's learning. "It tends to be a top-down or school-out perspective."

Even the goal of increasing parent involvement—which was added in 1994—places the burden on the schools to create programs for parents, she said. "There's no role spelled out for the parent," Ms. Rich said.

A Shift to States

Many of the leading players in the nearly 10 years since the Charlottesville summit acknowledge that the resulting activity has focused mainly on what schools need to do and how they should change.

The first task governors undertook after setting the goals was to find ways to define what students should know and ways to measure that knowledge, said Michael Cohen, who was the education coordinator for the NGA at the time of the summit. Mr. Cohen now serves as education adviser to President Clinton—himself a prominent participant in the summit as governor of Arkansas.

"The discussion and debate of standards was the consequence of setting goals," Mr. Cohen said. Eventually, "that debate has overshadowed the discussion of the goals in other areas."

At the time of the 1989 summit, only the National Council of Teachers of Mathematics had drawn up national standards in a major subject.

By 1992, the National Council on Education Standards and Testing, a congressionally created advisory panel, called for national standards and assessments that would become models for the states to follow. With grants from the Bush administration, national subject-matter groups produced voluntary standards in various core subjects.

Congress passed the Goals 2000: Educate America Act, President Clinton's chief reform initiative, in 1994. The law called for a new national panel to certify national standards and any state standards submitted for review.

But political opposition to any federal role in standards-setting derailed the process, especially after the Republicans, led by the conservative wing of their party, took control of Congress in 1995.

Mr. Clinton never appointed members for the standards-certification panel because his administration conceded to the GOP majority that it should be abolished.

"The idea was that these national standards would guide people," said Eva L. Baker, a co-director of the Center for Research on Evaluation, Standards, and Student Testing at the University of California, Los Angeles. "That vision started breaking up right away."

By 1996, at an NGA education summit with business executives, there was little talk about what to do about national standards. The focus was exclusively on state action.

Now, 49 states—Iowa excluded—have or are drafting standards in core subjects. Some experts contend, however, that many of those states have produced documents lacking in specificity or the challenging content expected by the leaders of the standards movement. National groups that have evaluated states' standards give them frequently divergent grades.

Testing Derailed

In much the way that the national-standards movement has diverged from the path its advocates laid out, those who set the goals haven't generated the support for the national assessments they envisioned.

President Bush included individual student testing in his America 2000 school reform package. It failed because Democrats, then in control of Congress, refused to endorse the reforms and the private school choice included in the same bill.

Mr. Clinton revived the issue in 1997, calling for national tests in 4th grade reading and 8th grade math. In his original time line, the tests would have been given for the first time this spring.

But Congress has severely limited development work on the proposed voluntary tests. The National Assessment Governing Board is allowed to draft test questions, but it's forbidden to do the work needed to validate them.

"It's alive, though it's not kicking," Secretary Riley said.

In its latest report, the goals panel cites data from the National Assessment of Educational Progress to evaluate the student-achievement goals. That test, however, only samples achievement, and even then, cannot be used for reporting individual scores.

Even state assessments designed as benchmarks for state standards have fallen short, according to Ms. Baker, the UCLA researcher. Most of those tests measure how students perform on a standardized scale and aren't specifically designed to measure what's in the state standards.

With the target date for original goals looming—and success doubtful—policymakers are asking: What next?

"The issue is not whether we are going to meet these goals by 2000, but whether we're going to work until they're met in every state, no matter how long it takes," Mr. Cohen, the president's education adviser, said.

The goals panel, which is authorized to receive federal funding through Sept. 30, is preparing a report to Congress to explain what role it or a successor may play in evaluating progress toward the current or any new goals.

Sen. Jeff Bingaman, D-N.M., a goals panel member and one of Congress' most vocal supporters of the goals, is calling on Mr. Clinton to convene a new summit.

"Pulling people together and reinvigorating the process is the important thing," he said. "An unfortunate result would be if we let the opportunity pass and not focus on the goals at all."

The White House is considering forums to discuss the goals, but hasn't decided whether to heed Mr. Bingaman's call for a new summit, Mr. Cohen said. But he added that the Clinton administration is expecting to be part of a debate over "whether to continue having goals and who's going to set them."

Even some long-time supporters of the goals process question whether it should continue.

"I'm glad we've done it," said Chester E. Finn Jr., the president of the Thomas B. Fordham Foundation in Washington and an assistant U.S. secretary of education in the Reagan administration. "It didn't accomplish what we'd hoped it would accomplish. Instead of doing more of it, let's do something different."

Century's Final Era

To Ms. Graham, the Harvard historian, the flurry of activity symbolizes a trend emphasizing increased student achievement. The movement is the final era in the history of U.S. education in the 20th century, she suggests.

Early in the century, schools were called on to assimilate immigrants into society. Then, progressive educators tried to make what students learn in school relevant to their daily lives. Next, the civil rights movement called for schools to integrate black and other minority students into traditionally white institutions.

"Whatever we've wanted our schools to do in the past, eventually the schools have done," Ms. Graham said. "We'll muddle our way through to having a higher fraction of students learning academic material. Each of these other stages took 20 or 30 years; this one will too."

27

A REVOLUTION
IN ONE CLASSROOM

THE CASE OF MRS. OUBLIER

David K. Cohen

This chapter probes the relationship between instructional policy and teaching practice. In the mid- 1980s, California State officials launched an ambitious effort to revise mathematics teaching and learning. The aim was to replace mechanical memorization with mathematical understanding. This chapter considers one teacher's response to the new policy. She sees herself as a success for the policy. She believes that she has revolutionized her mathematics teaching. But observation of her classroom reveals that the innovations in her teaching have been filtered through a very traditional approach to instruction. The result is a remarkable melange of novel and traditional material. Policy has affected practice in this case, but practice has had an even greater effect on policy.

○

AS MRS. OUBLIER SEES IT, her classroom is a new world. She reported that when she began work 4 years ago, her mathematics teaching was thoroughly traditional. She followed the text. Her second graders spent most of their time on worksheets. Learning math meant memorizing facts and procedures. Then Mrs. O found a new way to teach math. She took a workshop in which she learned to focus lessons on students' understanding of mathematical ideas. She found ways to relate mathematical concepts to students' knowledge and experience. And she explored methods to engage students in actively understanding mathematics. In her third year of such work, Mrs. O was delighted with her students' performance, and with her own accomplishments.

Mrs. O's story is engaging, and so is she. She is considerate of her students, eager for them to learn, energetic, and attractive. These qualities would stand out anywhere, but they seem particularly vivid in her school. It is a drab collection of one-story, concrete buildings that sprawl over several acres. Though clean and well managed, her school lacks any of the familiar signs of innovative education. It has no legacy of experimentation or progressive pedagogy, or even of heavy spending on education. Only a minority of children come from well-to-do families. Most families have middling or modest incomes, and many are eligible for Chapter 1 assistance. A sizable minority are on welfare. The school district is situated in a dusty corner of southern California, where city migrants rapidly are turning a rural town into a suburb. New condominiums are sprouting all over the community, but one still sees pickup trucks with rifle racks mounted in their rear windows. Like several of her colleagues, Mrs. O works in a covey of portable, prefab classrooms, trucked into the back of the schoolyard to absorb growing enrollments.

Mrs. O's story seems even more unlikely when considered against the history of American educational reform. Great plans for educational change are a familiar feature of that history, but so are reports of failed reforms. That is said to have been the fate of an earlier "new math" in the 1950s and 1960s. A similar tale was told of efforts to improve science teaching at the time (Welsh, 1979). Indeed, failed efforts to improve teaching and learning are an old story. John Dewey and others announced a revolution in pedagogy just as our century opened, but apparently it fizzled: Classrooms changed only a little, researchers say (Cuban, 1984). The story goes on. Since the Sputnik era, many studies of instructional innovation have embroidered these old themes of great ambitions and modest results (Gross, Giaquinta & Bernstein, 1971; Rowan & Guthrie, 1989; Cohen, 1989).

Some analysts explain these dismal tales with reference to teachers' resistance to change: They argue that entrenched classroom habits defeat reform (Gross, Giaquinta, & Bernstein, 1971). Others report that many innovations fail because they are poorly adapted to classrooms: Even teachers who avidly desire change can do little with most schemes to improve instruction, because they don't work well in classrooms (Cuban, 1984, 1986). Mrs. O's revolution looks particularly appealing against this background. She eagerly embraced change, rather than resisting it. She found new ideas and materials that worked in her classroom, rather than resisting innovation. Mrs. O sees her class as a success for the new mathematics framework. Though her revolution began while the framework was still being written, it was inspired by many of the same ideas. She reports that her math teaching has wound up where the framework intends it to be.

Yet as I watched and listened in Mrs. O's classroom, things seemed more complicated. Her teaching does reflect the new framework in many ways. For instance, she had adopted innovative instructional materials and activities, all designed to help students make sense of mathematics. But Mrs. O seemed to treat new mathematical topics as though they were a part of traditional school mathematics. She used the new materials, but used them as though mathematics contained only right and wrong answers. She has revised the curriculum to help students understand math, but she conducts the class in ways that discourage exploration of students' understanding.

From the perspective of the new mathematics framework, then, Mrs. O's lessons seem quite mixed. They contain some important elements that the framework embraced, but they contain others that it branded as inadequate. In fact, her classes present an extraordinary mélange of traditional and novel approaches to math instruction.

Something Old and Something New

That mélange is part of the fascination of Mrs. O's story. Some observers would agree that she has made a revolution, but others would see only traditional instruction. It is easy to imagine long arguments about which is the real Mrs. O, but they would be the wrong arguments. Mrs. O is both of these teachers. Her classroom deserves attention partly because such mixtures are quite common in instructional innovations—though they have been little noticed. As teachers and students try to find their way from familiar practices to new ones, they cobble new ideas onto familiar practices. The variety of these blends and teachers' ingenuity in fashioning them are remarkable, but they raise unsettling questions. Can we say that an innovation has made such progress when it is tangled in combination with many traditional practices? Changes that seem large to teachers who are in the midst of struggles to accommodate new ideas often seem modest or invisible to observers who scan practice for evidence that new policies have been implemented. How does one judge innovative progress? Should we consider changes in teachers' work from the perspective of new policies like the framework? Or should they be considered from the teachers' vantage point?

New Mathematics, Old Mathematics

From one angle, the curriculum and instructional materials in this class were just what the new framework ordered. For instance, Mrs. O regularly asked her second graders to work on "number sentences." In one class that I observed, students had done the problem: $10 + 4 = 14$. Mrs. O then asked them to generate additional number sentences about 14. They volunteered various ways to write addition problems about 14—that is, $10 + 1 + 1 + 1 + 1 = 14$, $5 + 5 + 4 = 14$, and so forth. Some students proposed several ways to write subtraction problems— that is, $14 - 4 = 10$, $14 - 10 = 4$, and so forth. Most of the students' proposals were correct. Such work could make mathematics relationships more accessible by coming at them with ordinary language rather than working only with bare numbers on a page. It also could unpack mathematics relationships by offering different ways to get the same result. It could illuminate the relations between addition and subtraction, helping children to understand their reversibility. And it could get students to do "mental math," that is, to solve problems in their heads and thereby learn to see math as something to puzzle about and figure out, rather than just a bunch of facts and procedures to be memorized.

These are all things that the new framework invited. The authors exhort teachers to help students cultivate "an attitude of curiosity and the willingness to probe and explore. . . . " (California State Department of Education [CSDE], 1985, p. 1). The document also calls for classroom work that helps students "to understand why computational algorithms are constructed in particular forms. . . . " (p. 4).

Yet the framework's mathematical exhortations were general; it offered few specifics about how teachers might respond, and left room for many different responses. Mrs. O used the new materials, but conducted the entire exercise in a thoroughly traditional fashion. The class worked as though the lesson were a drill, reciting in response to the teacher's queries. Students' sentences were accepted if correct, and written down on the board. They were turned down if incorrect, and not written on the board. Right answers were not explained, and wrong answers were treated as unreal. The framework makes no such distinction. To the contrary, it argues that understanding how to arrive at answers is an essential part of helping students to figure out how mathematics works—perhaps more important than whether the answers are right or wrong. The framework criticizes the usual memorized, algorithmic approach to mathematics, and the usual search for the right answer. It calls for class discussion of problems and problem solving as an important part of figuring out mathematical relationships (CSDE, 1985, pp. 13–14). But no one in Mrs. O's class was asked to explain their proposed number sentences, correct or incorrect. No student was invited to demonstrate how he or she knew whether a sentence was correct or not. The teacher used a new mathematics curriculum, but used it in a way that conveyed a sense of mathematics as a fixed body of right answers, rather than as a field of inquiry in which people figure out quantitative relations. It is easy to see the framework's ideas in Mrs. O's classroom, but it also is easy to see many points of opposition between the new policy and Mrs. O's approach (CSDE, 1987, p. 9).

Make no mistake: Mrs. O was teaching math for understanding. The work with number sentences certainly was calculated to help students see how addition worked, and to see that addition and subtraction were reversible. That mathematical idea is well worth understanding, and the students seemed to understand it at some level. They were, after all, producing the appropriate sorts of sentences. Yet it was difficult to understand how or how well they understood it, for the didactic form of the lesson inhibited explanation or exploration of students' ideas. Additionally, mathematical knowledge was treated in a traditional way: Correct answers were accepted, and wrong ones simply rejected. No answers were unpacked. There was teaching for mathematical understanding here, but it was blended with other elements of instruction that seemed likely to inhibit understanding.

The mixture of new mathematical ideas and materials with old mathematical knowledge and pedagogy permeated Mrs. O's teaching. It also showed up extensively in her work with concrete materials and other physical activities. These materials and activities are a crucial feature of her revolution, for they are intended to represent mathematical concepts in a form that is vivid and accessible to young children. For instance, she opens the math lesson every day with a calendar activity, in which she and the students gather on a rug at one side of the room to count up the days of the school year. She uses this activity for various purposes. During my first visit she was familiarizing students with place value, regrouping, and odd and even numbers. As it happened, my visit began on the fifty-ninth day of the school year, and so the class counted to fifty-nine. They used single claps for most numbers but double claps for ten, twenty, and so on. Thus, one physical activity represented the "tens," and distinguished them from another physical activity that was used to represent the "ones." On the next day, the class used claps for even numbers and finger snaps for odd numbers, in counting off the days. The idea here is that fundamental distinctions among types of numbers can be represented in ways that make immediate and fundamental sense to young children. Representations of this sort, it is thought, will deeply familiarize them with important mathematical ideas, but will do so in a fashion easily accessible to those unfamiliar with abstractions.

Mrs. O also used drinking straws in a related activity, to represent place value and regrouping. Every day a "student helper" is invited to help lead the calendar activity by adding another straw to the total that represents the elapsed days in the school year. The straws accumulate until there are ten, and then are bundled with a rubber band. One notion behind this activity is that students will gain some concrete basis for understanding how numbers are grouped in a base ten system. Another is that they can begin to apprehend, first physically and then intellectually, how number groups can be composed and decomposed.

Mrs. O's class abounds with such activities and materials, and they are very different from the bare numbers on worksheets that would be found in a traditional math class. She was still excited, after several years' experience, about the difference that they made for her students' understanding of arithmetic. Mrs. O adopts a somewhat cool demeanor in class. However, her conviction about the approach was plain, and her enthusiasm for it bubbled up in our conversations. After 3 years, she had only disdain for her old way of teaching math.

Her approach seems nicely aligned with the new framework. For instance, that document argues that "many activities should involve concrete experiences so that students develop a sense of what numbers mean and how they are related before they are asked to add, subtract, multiply, or divide them" (CSDE, 1985, p. 8). And it adds, a few pages further on, that "concrete materials provide a way for students to connect their own understandings about real objects and their own experiences to mathematical concepts. They gain direct experience with the underlying principles of each concept" (p. 15).

Mrs. O certainly shared the framework's view in this matter, but it is one thing to embrace a doctrine of instruction, and quite another to weave it into one's practice. For even a rather monotonous practice of teaching comprises many different threads. Hence any new instructional thread must somehow be related to many others already there. Like reweaving fabric, this social and intellectual reweaving can be done in different ways. The new thread can simply be dropped onto the fabric, and everything else left as is. Or new threads may be somehow woven into the fabric. If so, some alteration in the relations among threads will be required. Some of the existing threads might have to be adjusted in some way, or even pulled out and replaced. If one views Mrs. O's work from the perspective of the framework, new threads were introduced, but old threads were not pulled out. The old and new lay side by side, and so the fabric of instruction was different. However, there seemed to be little mutual adjustment among new and old threads. Mrs. O used the novel concrete materials and physical activities, but used them in an unchanged pedagogical surrounding. Consequently the new material seemed to take on different meaning from its circumstances. Materials and activities intended to teach mathematics for understanding were infused with traditional messages about what mathematics was, and what it meant to understand it.

These mixed qualities were vividly apparent in a lesson that focused on addition and subtraction with regrouping. The lesson occurred early in an 8- or 10-week cycle concerning these topics. Like many of her lessons, it combined a game-like activity with the use of concrete materials. The aim was to capture children's interest in math, and to help them understand it. Mrs. O introduced this lesson by announcing: "Boys and girls, today we are going to play a counting game. Inside this paper [holding up a wadded up sheet of paper] is the secret message . . ." (observation notes, December 5, 1988). Mrs. O unwadded the paper and held it up: "6" was inscribed. The number was important, because it would establish the number base for the lesson: Six. In previous lessons they had done the same thing with four and five. So part of the story here was exploring how things work in different number bases, and one reason for that, presumably, was to get some perspective on the base-ten system that we conventionally use. Mrs. O told the children that, as in the previous games, they would use a nonsense word in place of the secret number. I was not sure why she did this, at the time. As it turned out, the approach was recommended, but not explained, by the innovative curriculum guide she was using. After a few minutes taken to select the nonsense word, the class settled on "Cat's eye" (observation notes, December 5, 1988. These notes are the source of the remainder of this episode).

With this groundwork laid, Mrs. O had "place value boards" given to each student. She held her board up [eight by eleven, roughly, one half blue and the other white], and said: "We call this a place value board. What do you notice about it?"

Cathy Jones, who turned out to be a steady infielder on Mrs. O's team, said: "There's a smiling face at the top." Mrs. O agreed, noting that the smiling face needed to be at the top at all times (that would keep the blue half of the board on everyone's left). Several kids were holding theirs up for inspection from various angles, and she admonished them to leave the boards flat on their tables at all times.

"What else do we notice?" she inquired. Sam said that one half was blue and the other white. Mrs. O agreed, and went on to say that "the blue side will be the 'cat's eye' side. During this game we will add one to the white side, and when we get a cat's eye, we will move it over to the blue side." With that, each student was given a small plastic tub, which contained a handful of dried beans and half a dozen small paper cups, perhaps a third the height of those dispensed in dentists' offices. This was the sum total of pre-lesson framing—no other discussion or description preceded the work.

There was a small flurry of activity as students took their tubs and checked out the contents. Beans present nearly endless mischievous possibilities, and several of the kids seemed on the verge of exploring their properties as guided missiles. Mrs. O nipped off these investigations, saying: "Put your tubs at the top of your desks, and put both hands in the air." The students all complied, as though in a small stagecoach robbery. "Please keep them up while I talk." She opened a spiral bound book, not the school district's adopted text but *Math Their Way* (Baratta-Lorton, 1976).This was the innovative curriculum guide that had helped to spark her revolution. She looked at it from time to time, as the lesson progressed, but seemed to have quite a good grip on the activity.

Mrs. O got things off to a brisk start: "Boys and girls [who still were in the holdup], when I clap my hands, add a bean to the white side [from the plastic tub]."

She clapped once, vigorously, adding that they could put their hands down. "Now we are going to read what we have: What do we have?" She led a choral chant of the answer "Zero cat's eye and one." She asked students to repeat that, and everyone did. She clapped again, and students obediently added a second bean to the white portion of the card. "What do we have now?" she inquired. Again she led a choral chant: "Zero cat's eye and two." So another part of the story in this lesson was place value: "Zero cat's eye" denotes what would be the "tens" place in base-ten numbering, and "two" is the "one's" place. Counting individual beans, and beans grouped in "cat's eye," would give the kids a first-hand, physical sense of how place value worked in this and other number bases.

In these opening chants, as in all subsequent ones, Mrs. O performed more vigorously than rhythmically. Rather than establishing a beat and then maintaining it with her team, she led each chant and the class followed at a split-second interval. Any kid who didn't grasp the idea needed only to wait for her cue, or for his table-mates. There were no solos: Students were never invited or allowed to count on their own. Thus, although the leitmotif in their second chant was "zero cat's eye and two," there was an audible minor theme of "zero cat's eye and one." That several repeated the first chant suggested that they did not get either the routine or its point.

Mrs. O moved right on nonetheless, saying that it "is very important that you read the numbers with your hands." This was a matter to which she returned many times during the lesson; she kept reminding the children to put their little hands first on the beans on the white square, and then on the little cups on the blue square, as they incanted the mathematical chants. It was essential that they manipulated the concrete materials. Whenever she spotted children who were not palpitating beans and cups, she walked over and moved their arms and hands for them.

Mrs. O led the bean-adding and chants up to five. Then, when the first five beans were down on everyone's card, she asked: "Now think ahead; when I clap my hands this time, what will you have on the white side?"

Reliable Cathy Jones scooped it up and threw smoothly to first: "Cat's eye."

Mrs. O led off again: "When you get a cat's eye, put all the beans in a paper cup, and move them over." She clapped her hands for the cat's eye, and then led the following chant: "Put the beans in the cup and move them over."

"Now let's read what we have." The chant rolled on, "one cat's eye and zero." A puzzling undercurrent of "one cat's eye and one" went unattended. She then led the class through a series of claps and chants, leading up to two cat's eyes. And the claps and chants went on, with a methodical monotony, up to five cat's eyes and five. The whole series took about 15 minutes, and throughout the exercise she repeatedly reminded students to "read" the materials with their hands, to feel the beans and move their arms. By the time they got to five cat's eyes and five, her claps had grown more perfunctory, and many of the kids had gotten the fidgets, but Mrs. O gave no ground. She seemed to see this chanting and bean-handling as the high road to mathematical understanding, and tenaciously drove her team on.

"Now, how many do we have?" "Five cat's eyes and five beans," came the chant. "Now we will take away one bean [from the 'ones' side of the board]. How many do we have?" Again the answering chant, again led by her, a fraction of a second early, "five cat's eyes and four."

This was a crucial point in the lesson. The class was moving from what might be regarded as a concrete representation of addition with regrouping, to a similar representation of subtraction with regrouping. Yet she did not comment on or explain this reversal of direction. It would have been an obvious moment for some such comment or discussion, at least if one saw the articulation of ideas as part of understanding mathematics. Mrs. O did not teach as though she took that view. Hers seemed to be an activity-based approach: It was as though she thought that all the important ideas were implicit, and better that way.

Thus the class counted down to five cat's eyes and zero. Mrs. O then asked, "What do we do now?" Jane responded: "Take a dish from the cat's eye side, and move it to the white side." No explanation was requested or offered to embroider this response. Mrs. O simply approved the answer, clapped her hands, and everyone followed Jane's lead. With this, Mrs. O led the class back through each step, with claps, chants, and reminders to read the beans with their hands, down to zero cat's eye and zero beans. The entire effort took 30 or 35 minutes. Everyone was flagging long before it was done, but not a chant was skipped or a movement missed.

Why did Mrs. O teach in this fashion? In an interview following the lesson I asked her what she thought the children learned from the exercise. She said that it helped them to understand what goes on in addition and subtraction with regrouping. Manipulating the materials really helps kids to understand math, she said. Mrs. O seemed quite convinced that these physical experiences *caused* learning, that mathematical knowledge arose from the activities.

Her immediate inspiration for all this seems to have been *Math Their Way,* a system of primary grade math teaching on which, Mrs. O says, she relies heavily. *Math Their Way* announces its purpose this way: "to develop understanding and insight of the patterns of mathematics through the use of concrete materials" (Baratta-Lorton, 1976, p. xiv). Concrete materials and physical activities are the central features of this primary grade program, because they are believed to provide real experience with mathematics. In this connection the book sharply distinguishes between mathematical symbols and concepts. It criticizes teaching with symbols, arguing that symbols (i.e., numbers) "are not *the concept,* they are only a representation of the concept, and as such are abstractions describing something which is not visible to the child. Real materials, on the other hand, can be manipulated to illustrate the concept concretely, and can be experienced visually by the child. . . . The emphasis throughout this book is making concepts, rather than numerical symbols, meaningful" (p. xiv).

Math Their Way fairly oozes with the belief that physical representations are much more real than symbols. This fascinating idea is a recent mathematical mutation of the belief, at least as old as Rousseau, Pestalozzi, and James Fenimore Cooper, that experience is a better teacher than mere books. For experience is vivid, vital, and immediate, whereas books are all abstract ideas and dead formulations. Mrs. O did not mention these sages, but she certainly had a grip on the idea. In this she resembles many primary school teachers, for the view that concrete materials and physical activities are the high road to abstract concepts has become common currency in nursery school and primary grade teaching. Many primary grade teachers have long used physical activities and concrete materials elsewhere in instruction.

In fact, one of the chief claims in Baratta-Lorton's book is that concrete materials are developmentally desirable for young children. Numbers are referred to many times as an "adult" way of approaching math. And this idea leads to another, still more important one: If math is taught properly, it will be easy. Activities with concrete materials, the book insists, are the natural way for kids to learn math: "if this foundation is firmly laid, dealing with abstract numbers will be *effortless*" (p. 167, italics added).

Stated so baldly, that seems a phenomenal claim: Simply working with the proper activities and materials assures that math will be understood. Materials and activities are not only necessary for understanding mathematics, but also sufficient. But the idea is quite common. Pestalozzi might have cheered it. Many other pedagogical romantics, Rousseau and Dewey among them, embraced a version of this view. Piaget is commonly thought to have endorsed a similar idea. So when *Math Their Way* argues that the key to teaching math for understanding is to get children to use the right sorts of activities and materials, it is on one of the main tracks of modern educational thought and practice. The book's claim also helps to explain why it gives no attention to the nature of mathematical knowledge, and so little attention to the explanation of mathematical ideas. For the author seems convinced that such things are superfluous: Appropriate materials and activities alone will do the trick.

In fact, the book's appeal owes something to its combination of great promises and easy methods. It offers teachers a kind of pedagogical special, a two-for-the-price-of-one deal: Students will "understand" math without any need to open up questions about the nature of mathematical knowledge. The curriculum promises mathematical understanding, but it does not challenge or even discuss the common view of mathematics as a fixed body of material—in which knowledge consists of right answers—that so many teachers have inherited from their own schooling. The manual does occasionally note that teachers might discuss problems and their solutions with students, but this encouragement is quite modestly and intermittently scattered through a curriculum guide that chiefly focuses on the teaching potential of concrete materials and physical activities. The book presents concrete representations and math activities as a kind of explanation sufficient unto themselves. Discussion of mathematical ideas has a parenthetical role, at best.

All of this illuminates Mrs. O's indebtedness to *Math Their Way*, and her persistent praise for it. She used the guide to set up and conduct the lessons that I saw, and referred to it repeatedly in our conversations as the inspiration for her revolution. My subsequent comparisons of her classes with the manual suggested that she did draw deeply on it for ideas about materials, activities, and lesson format. More important, her views of how children come to understand mathematics were, by her own account, powerfully influenced by this book.

Baratta-Lorton's book thus enabled Mrs. O to whole-heartedly embrace teaching math for understanding, without considering or reconsidering her views of mathematical knowledge. She was very keen that children should understand math, and worked hard at helping them. However, she placed nearly the entire weight of this effort on concrete materials and activities. The ways that she used these materials—insisting, for instance, that all the children actually feel them, and perform the same prescribed physical operations with them—suggested that she endowed the materials with enormous, even magical instructional powers. The lack of any other ways of making sense of mathematics in her lesson was no oversight. She simply saw no need for anything else.

In what sense was Mrs. O teaching for understanding? The question opens up a great puzzle. Her classes exuded traditional conceptions of mathematical knowledge, and were organized as though explanation and discussion were irrelevant to mathematics. Yet she had changed her math teaching quite dramatically. She now used a new curriculum specially designed to promote students' understanding of mathematics. And her students' lessons were very different than they had been. They worked with materials that represented mathematical relationship in the concrete ways that the framework and many other authorities endorse. Mrs. O thought the change had been decisive: She now teaches for understanding. She reported that her students now understood arithmetic, whereas previously they had simply memorized it.

New Topics, Old Knowledge

Mrs. O taught several topics endorsed by the new framework that would not have been covered in many traditional math classes. One such topic was estimation. Mrs. O told me that estimation is important because it helps students to make sense of numbers. They have to make educated guesses, and learn to figure out why some guesses are better than others. She reports that she deals with estimation recurrently in her second-grade classwork, returning to it many times in the course of the year rather than teaching a single unit. Her reason was that estimation could not be learned by doing it once or twice, and, in any event, is useful in many different problem-solving situations. Her reasoning on this matter seemed quite in accord with the framework. It calls for "guessing and checking the result" as an important element in mathematical problem solving (CSDE, 1985, p. 14). In fact, the framework devotes a full page to estimation, explaining what it is and why it is important (pp. 4–5).

The teaching that I observed did not realize these ambitions. In one lesson, for instance, the following problem was presented: Estimate how many large paper clips would be required to span one edge of the teacher's desk (observation notes, December 6, 1988). Two students were enlisted to actually hold up the clips so that students could see. They stood near the teacher's desk, near enough to visually gauge its width in relation to the clips, but all the other students remained at their tables, scattered around the room. None had any clips, and few could see the edge of the teacher's desk that was in question. It was a side edge, away from most of the class.

So only two members of the class had real contact with the two key data sources in the problem—visible, palpable clips, and a clear view of the desk edge. As a consequence, only these two members of the class had any solid basis for deciding if their estimates were mathematically reasonable. Even Mrs. O was seated too far away to see the edge well, and she had no clips either. The problem itself was sensible, and could have been an opportunity to make and discuss estimates of a real puzzle. Unfortunately, it was set up in a way that emptied it of opportunities for mathematical sense-making.

Mrs. O did not seem aware of this. After she had announced the problem, she went on to engage the whole class in solving it. The two students were told to hold the clips up for everyone to see. Seated at the back, with many of the kids, I could see that they were the large sort of clip, but even then they were barely visible. Mrs. O then pointed to the desk edge, at the other end of the room, easily 20 feet from half the class. Then she asked the students to estimate how many clips it would take to cover the edge, and to write down their answers. She took estimates from most of the class, wrote them on the board, and asked class members if the estimates were reasonable.

Not surprisingly, the answers lacked mathematical discrimination. Estimates that were close to three times the actual answer, or one third of it, were accepted by the class and the teacher as reasonable. Indeed, no answers were rejected as unreasonable, even though quite a few were far off the mark. Nor were some estimates distinguished as more or less reasonable than others. Mrs. O asked the class what reasonable meant, and one boy offered an appropriate answer, suggesting that the class had some previous contact with this idea.

There was nothing that I could see or imagine in the classroom that led inexorably to this treatment. Mrs. O seemed to have many clips. If eight or ten had been passed around, the kids would have had at least direct access to one element in the estimation problem—that is, the length of the clip. Additionally, Mrs. O could have directed the kids' attention to the edge of the desk that they could see, rather than the far edge that they could not see. I knew that the two edges of the rectangular desk were the same length, and perhaps some of these second graders did as well, but the way of presenting the problem left that as a needless, and mathematically irrelevant, barrier to their work. Alternatively, Mrs. O could have invited them to estimate the length of their own desk edges, which were all the same, standard-issue models. That, along with passed-around clips, would have given them much more direct contact with the elements of the problem. The students would have had more of the mathematical data required to make sound estimates, and much more of a basis for considering the reasonableness of those estimates.

Why did Mrs. O not set the problem up in one of these ways? I could see no organizational or pedagogical reason. In a conversation after the class, when I asked for her comments on that part of the lesson, she did not display even a shred of discomfort, let alone suggest that anything had been wrong. Mrs. O seemed to understand the broad purpose of teaching and learning estimation (interview, December 6, 1988). However, this bit of teaching suggests that she did not have a firm grip on the mathematics in this estimation example. She taught as though she lacked the mathematical and pedagogical infrastructure—the knowledge of mathematics, and of teaching and learning mathematics—that would have helped her to set the problem up so that the crucial mathematical data were available to students.

An additional bit of evidence on this point concerns the way Mrs. O presented estimation. She offered it as a topic in its own right, rather than as a part of solving problems that came up in the course of studying mathematics. After ending one part of the lesson, she turned to estimation as though it were an entirely separate matter. When the estimation example was finished, she turned the class to still another topic. Estimation had an inning all its own, rather than being woven into other innings' work. It was almost as though she thought that estimation bore no intimate relation to solving the ordinary run of mathematical problems. This misses the mathematical point: Estimation is useful and used in that ordinary run, not for its own sake. The framework touches on this matter, arguing that "estimation activities should be presented not as separate lessons, but as a step to be used in all computational activities" (CSDE, 1985, p. 4).

When detached from regular problem solving, estimation may seem strange, and thus isolated may lose some of its force as a way of making sense in mathematics. I wondered what the students might have learned from this session. They all appeared to accept the lesson as reasonable. No students decried the lack of comprehensible data on the problem, which they might have done if they were used to such data, and if this lesson were an aberration. No one said that he or she had done it differently some other time, and that this didn't make sense. That could mean that the other lessons on estimation conveyed a similar impression. Or it may mean that students were simply dutiful, doing what they had been told because they had so often been told to do so. Or it may mean only that students took nothing from the lesson. Certainly school is full of mystifying or inexplicable experiences that children simply accept. Perhaps this struck them as another such mystification. It is possible, though, that they did learn something, and that it was related to Mrs. O's teaching. If so, perhaps they learned that estimation was worth doing, even if they didn't learn much about how to do it. Or perhaps they acquired an inappropriate idea of what estimation was, and what reasonable meant.

Was this teaching math for understanding? From one angle, it plainly was. Mrs. O did teach a novel and important topic, specifically intended to promote students' sense-making in arithmetic. It may well have done that. Yet the estimation problem was framed so that students had no way to bring mathematical evidence to bear on the problem, and little basis for making reasonable estimates. It therefore also is possible that students found this puzzling, confusing, or simply mysterious. These alternatives are not mutually exclusive. This bit of teaching for understanding could have promoted more understanding of mathematics, along with more misunderstanding.

New Organization, Old Discourse

Mrs. O's class was organized to promote cooperative learning. The students' desks and tables were gathered in groups of four and five, so that they could easily work together. Each group had a leader, to help with various logistical chores. And the location and distribution of instructional materials often were managed by groups, rather than individually. The new framework endorses this way of organizing classroom work. It puts the rationale this way: "To internalize concepts and apply them to new situations, students must interact with materials, express their thoughts, and discuss alternative approaches and explanations. Often, these activities can be accomplished well in groups of four students" (CSDE, 1985, p. 16).

The framework thus envisions cooperative learning groups as the vehicle for a new sort of instructional discourse, in which students would do much more of the teaching. In consequence, each of them would learn from their own efforts to articulate and explain ideas—much more than they could learn from a teacher's explanations to them. And they would teach each other as well, learning from their classmates' ideas and explanations, and from others' responses. The framework explains: "Students have more chances to speak in a small group than in a class discussion; and in that setting some students are more comfortable speculating, questioning, and explaining concepts in order to clarify their thinking" (CSDE, 1985, pp. 16–17).

Mrs. O's class was spatially and socially organized for such cooperative learning, but the instructional discourse that she established cut across the grain of this organization. The class was conducted in a highly structured and classically teacher-centered fashion. The chief instructional group was the whole class. The discourse that I observed consisted either of dyadic exchanges between the teacher and one student, or of whole-group activities, many of which involved choral responses to teacher questions. No student ever spoke to another about mathematical ideas as a part of the public discourse. Nor was such conversation ever encouraged by the teacher. Indeed, Mrs. O specifically discouraged students from speaking with each other, in her efforts to keep the class orderly and quiet.

The small groups were not ignored. They were used for instructional purposes, but they were used in a distinctive way. In one class that I observed, for instance, Mrs. O announced a "graphing activity" about midway through the math period. She wrote across the chalk board, at the front of the room, *Letter to Santa?* Underneath she wrote two column headings: *Yes* and *No*. Then she told the children that she would call on them by groups, to answer the question.

If she had been following the framework's injunctions about small groups, Mrs. O might have asked each group to tally its answers to the question. She might then have asked each group to figure out whether it had more yes than no answers, or the reverse. She might then have asked each group to figure out how many more. And she might have had each group contribute its totals to the chart at the front of the room. This would not have been the most challenging group activity, but it would have meaningfully used the small groups as agents for working on this bit of mathematics.

Mrs. O proceeded differently. She used the groups to call on individual children. Moving from her right to left across the room, she asked individuals from each group, seriatim, to come to the front and put their entry under the Yes or No column, exhausting one group before going on to the next. The groups were used in a socially meaningful way, but there was no mathematical discourse within them.

Mrs. O used the small groups in this fashion several times during my visits. The children seemed quite familiar with the procedures, and worked easily in this organization. In addition, she used the groups to distribute and collect instructional materials, which was a regular and important feature of her teaching. Finally, she regularly used the groups to dismiss the class for lunch and recess: She would let the quietest and tidiest group go first, and so on through the class.

Small groups thus were a regular feature of instruction in Mrs. O's class. I asked her about cooperative grouping in one of our conversations: Did she always use the groups in the ways that I had observed? She thought she did. I asked if she ever used them for more cooperative activity, that is, discussions and that sort of thing. She said that she occasionally did so, but mostly she worked in the ways I had observed.

In what sense was this teaching or understanding? Here again, there was a remarkable combination of old and new math instruction. Mrs. O used a new form of classroom organization that was designed to promote collaborative work and broader discourse about academic work. She treated this organization with seriousness. She referred to her classwork as "cooperative learning," and used the organization for some regular features of classroom work. When I mentally compared her class with others I had observed, in which students sat in traditional rows, and in which there was only whole-group or individual work, her class seemed really different. Though Mrs. O runs a tight ship, her class was more relaxed than those others I remembered, and organized in a more humane way. My view on this is not simply idiosyncratic. If Cuban had used this class in the research for *How Teachers Taught* (1984), he probably would have judged it to be innovative as well. For that book relies on classrooms' social organization as an important indicator of innovation.

Mrs. O also judged her classroom to be innovative. She noted that it was now organized quite differently than during her first year of teaching, and she emphatically preferred the innovation. The kids were more comfortable, and the class much more flexible, she said. Yet she filled the new social reorganization of discourse with old discourse processes. The new organization opened up lots of new opportunities for small group work, but she organized the discourse in ways that effectively blocked realization of those opportunities.

Reprise

I have emphasized certain tensions within Mrs. O's classes, but these came into view partly because I crouched there with one eye on the framework. The tensions I have discussed were not illusory, but my angle of vision brought them into focus. Another observer, with other matters in mind, might not have noticed these tensions. Mrs. O certainly did not notice them, and things went quite smoothly in her lessons. There was nothing rough or ungainly in the way she and her students managed. They were well used to each other, and to the class routines. They moved around easily within their math lessons. The various contrary elements of instruction that sent me reeling mentally did not disturb the surface of the class. On the contrary, students and teacher acted as though the threads of these lessons were nicely woven together. Aspects of instruction that seemed at odds analytically appeared to nicely coexist in practice.

What accounts for this smoothness? Can it be squared with the tensions that I have described within these classes? Part of the answer lies in the classroom discourse. Mrs. O never invited or permitted broad participation in mathematical discussion or explanation. She held most exchanges within a traditional recitation format. She initiated nearly every interaction, whether with the entire class or one student. The students' assigned role was to respond, not initiate. They complied, often eagerly. Mrs. O was eager for her students to learn; in return, most of her students seemed eager to please. And eager or not, compliance is easier than initiation, especially when so much of instruction is so predictable. Much of the discourse was very familiar to members of the class; often they gave the answers before Mrs. O asked the questions. So even though most of the class usually was participating in the discourse, they participated on a narrow track, in which she maintained control of direction, content, and pace.

The framework explicitly rejects this sort of teaching. It argues that children need to express and discuss their ideas, in order to deeply understand the material on which they are working (CSDE, 1985, pp. 14, 16). Yet the discourse in Mrs. O's class tended to discourage students from reflecting on mathematical ideas, or from sharing their puzzles with the class. There were few opportunities for students to initiate discussion, explore ideas, or even ask questions. Their attention was focused instead on successfully managing a prescribed, highly structured set of activities. This almost surely restricted the questions and ideas that could occur to students, for thought is created, not merely expressed, in social interactions. Even if the students' minds were nonetheless still privately full of bright ideas and puzzling mathematical problems, the discourse organization effectively barred them from the public arena of the class. Mrs. O employed a curriculum that sought to teach math for understanding, but she kept evidence about what students' understood from entering the classroom discourse. One reason that Mrs. O's class was so smooth was that so many possible sources of roughness were choked off at the source.

Another reason for Mrs. O's smooth lessons has to do with her knowledge of mathematics. Though she plainly wanted her students to understand this subject, her grasp of mathematics restricted her notion of mathematical understanding, and of what it took to produce it. She did not know mathematics deeply or extensively. She had taken one or two courses in college, and reported that she had liked them; but she had not pursued the subject further. Lacking deep knowledge, Mrs. O was simply unaware of much mathematical content and many ramifications of the material she taught. Many paths to understanding were not taken in her lessons—as for instance, in the Santa's' letter example—but she seemed entirely unaware of them. Many misunderstandings or inventive ideas that her students might have had would have made no sense to Mrs. O, because her grip on mathematics was so modest. In these ways and many others, her relatively superficial knowledge of this subject insulated her from even a glimpse of many things she might have done to deepen students' understanding. Elements in her teaching that seemed contradictory to an observer therefore seemed entirely consistent to her, and could be handled with little trouble.

Additionally, however much mathematics she knew, Mrs. O knew it as a fixed body of truths, rather than as a particular way of framing and solving problems. Questioning, arguing, and explaining seemed quite foreign to her knowledge of this subject. Her assignment, she seemed to think, was to somehow make the fixed truths accessible to her students. Explaining them herself in words and pictures would have been one alternative, but she employed a curriculum that promised an easier way, that is, embody mathematical ideas and operations in concrete materials and physical activities. Mrs. O did not see mathematics as a source of puzzles, as a terrain for argument, or as a subject in which questioning and explanation were essential to learning and knowing—all ideas that are plainly featured in the framework (CSDE, 1985, pp. 13–14). *Math Their Way* did nothing to disturb her view on this matter. Lacking a sense of the importance of explanation, justification, and argument in mathematics, she simply slipped over many opportunities to elicit them, unaware that they existed.

So the many things that Mrs. O did not know about mathematics protected her from many uncertainties about teaching and learning math. Her relative ignorance made it difficult for her to learn from her very serious efforts to teach for understanding. Like many students, what she didn't know kept her from seeing how much more she could understand about mathematics. Her ignorance also kept her from imagining many different ways in which she might teach mathematics. These limitations on her knowledge meant that Mrs. O could teach for understanding, with little sense of how much remained to be understood, how much she might incompletely or naively understand, and how much might still remain to be taught. She is a thoughtful and committed teacher, but working as she did near the surface of this subject, many elements of understanding and many pedagogical possibilities remained invisible. Mathematically, she was on thin ice. Because she did not know it, she skated smoothly on with great confidence.

In a sense, then, the tensions that I observed were not there. They were real enough in my view, but they did not enter the public arena of the class. They lay beneath the surface of the class's work; indeed, they were kept there by the nature of that work. Mrs. O's modest grasp of mathematics, and her limited conception of mathematical understanding, simply obliterated many potential sources of roughness in the lessons. And those constraints of the mind were given added social force in her close management of classroom discourse. Had Mrs. O known more math, and tried to construct a somewhat more open discourse, her class would not have run so smoothly. Some of the tensions that I noticed would have become audible and visible to the class. More confusion and misunderstanding would have surfaced. Things would have been rougher, potentially more fruitful, and vastly more difficult.

Practice and Progress

Is Mrs. O's mathematical revolution a story of progress, or of confusion? Does it signal an advance for the new math framework, or a setback?

These are important questions, inevitable in ventures of this sort; but it may be unwise to sharply distinguish progress from confusion, at least when considering such broad and deep changes in instruction. After all, the teachers and students who try to carry out such change are historical beings. They cannot simply shed their old ideas and practices like a shabby coat, and slip on something new. Their inherited ideas and practices are what teachers and students know, even as they begin to know something else. Indeed, taken together those ideas and practices summarize them as practitioners. As they reach out to embrace or invent a new instruction, they reach with their old professional selves, including all the ideas and practices comprised therein. The past is their path to the future. Some sorts of mixed practice, and many confusions, therefore seem inevitable.

The point seems fundamental, yet it often goes unnoticed by those who promote change in teaching, as well as by many who study it. Larry Cuban's *How Teachers Taught* is a happy exception (1984). Cuban explained that "many teachers constructed hybrids of particular Progressive practices grafted onto what they ordinarily did in classrooms" (L. Cuban, personal communication, April 18, 1983). Cuban dubbed this approach to the adoption of innovations "conservative progressivism" (Cuban, 1984).

But these mixed practices affect the judgments that teachers and observers make about change in teaching. For instance, the changes in Mrs. O's teaching that seemed paradoxical to me seemed immense to her. Remember that when she began teaching four years ago, her math lessons were quite traditional. She ignored the mathematical knowledge and intuitions that children brought to school. She focused most work on computational arithmetic, and required much classroom drill. Mrs. O now sees her early teaching as unfortunately traditional, mechanical, and maladapted to children's learning. Indeed, her early math teaching was exactly the sort of thing that the framework criticized.

Mrs. O described the changes she has made as a revolution. I do not think that she was deluded. She was convinced that her classes had greatly improved. She contended that her students now understood and learned much more math than their predecessors had, a few years ago. She even asserts that this has been reflected in their achievement test scores. I have no direct evidence on these claims, but when I compared this class with others that I have seen, in which instruction consisted only of rote exercises in manipulating numbers, her claims seemed plausible. Many traditional teachers certainly would view her teaching as revolutionary.

Still, all revolutions preserve large elements of the old order as they invent new ones. One such element, noted above, was a conception of mathematics as a fixed body of knowledge. Another was a view of learning mathematics in which the aim was getting the right answers. I infer this partly from the teaching that I observed, and partly from several of her comments in our conversations. She said, for example, that math had not been a favorite subject in school. She had only learned to do well in math at college, and was still pleased with herself on this score, when reporting it to me years later. I asked her how she had learned to do and like math at such a late date, and she explained: "I found that if I just didn't ask so many whys about things that it all started fitting into place" (interview December 6, 1988). This suggests a rather traditional approach to learning mathematics. More important, it suggests that Mrs. O learned to do well at math by avoiding exactly the sort of questions that the framework associates with understanding mathematics. She said in another connection that her view of math has not changed since college. I concluded that whatever she has learned from workshops, new materials, and new policies, it did not include a new view of mathematics.

Another persistent element in her practice was "clinical teaching," that is, the California version of Hunter's Instructional Theory Into Practice (ITIP). Hunter and her followers advocate clearly structured lessons: Teachers are urged to be explicit about lesson objectives themselves, and to announce them clearly to students. They also are urged to pace and control lessons so that the intended content is covered, and to check that students are doing the work and getting the point, along the way. Though these ideas could be used in virtually any pedagogy, they have been almost entirely associated with a rigid, sonata-form of instruction, that is marked by close teacher control, brisk pacing, and highly structured recitations. The ITIP appears to have played an important part in Mrs. O's own education as a teacher, for on her account she learned about it while an undergraduate, and used it when she began teaching. However she also has been encouraged to persist: Both her principal and assistant principal are devotees of Hunter's method, and have vigorously promoted it among teachers in the school. This is not unusual, as ITIP has swept California schools in the past decade. Many principals now use it as a framework for evaluating teachers, and as a means of school improvement. Mrs. O's principal and the assistant principal praised her warmly, saying that she was a fine teacher with whom they saw eye to eye in matters of instruction.

I asked all three whether clinical teaching worked well with the framework. None saw any inconsistency. Indeed, all emphatically said that the two innovations were "complementary." Though that might be true in principle, it was not true in practice. As ITIP was realized in Mrs. O's class among many others, it cut across the grain of the framework. Like many other teachers, her enactment of clinical teaching rigidly limited discourse, closely controlled social interaction, focused the classroom on herself, and helped to hold instruction to relatively simple objectives.

As Mrs. O revolutionized her math teaching, then, she worked with quite conventional materials: A teacher-centered conception of instructional discourse; a rigid approach to classroom management; and a traditional conception of mathematical knowledge. Yet she found a way to make what seemed a profound change in her math teaching. One reason is that the vehicle for change did not directly collide with her inherited ideas and practices. *Math Their Way* focuses on materials and activities, not on mathematical knowledge and explanation of ideas. It allowed Mrs. O to change her math teaching in what seemed a radical fashion while building on those old practices. This teacher's past was present, even as she struggled to renounce and surpass it.

Mrs. O's past also affected her view of her accomplishments, as it does for all of us. I asked, in the Spring of 1989, where her math teaching stood. She thought that her revolution was over. Her teaching had changed definitively. She had arrived at the other shore. In response to further queries, Mrs. O evinced no sense that there were areas in her math teaching that needed improvement. Nor did she seem to want guidance about how well she was doing, or how far she had come.

There is an arresting contrast here. From an observer's perspective, especially one who had the new framework in mind, Mrs. O looks as though she may be near the beginning of growth toward a new practice of math teaching. She sees the matter quite differently: She has made the transition, and mastered a new practice.

Which angle is most appropriate, Mrs. O's or the observer's? This is a terrific puzzle. One wants to honor this teacher, who has made a serious and sincere effort to change, and who has changed. One also wants to honor a policy that supports greater intelligence and humanity in mathematics instruction.

It is worth noticing that Mrs. O had only one perspective available. No one had asked how she saw her math teaching in light of the framework. She had been offered no opportunities to raise this query, let alone assistance in answering it. No one offered her another perspective on her teaching. If no other educators or officials in California had seen fit to put the question to her, and to help her to figure out answers, should we expect her to have asked and answered this difficult question all alone?

That seems unrealistic. If math teaching in California is as deficient as the framework and other critiques suggest, then most teachers would not be knowledgeable enough to raise many fruitful questions about their work in math by themselves, let alone answer them. We can see some evidence for this in Mrs. O's lessons. Their very smoothness quite effectively protected her from experiences that might have provoked uncertainty,

conflict, and therefore deep questions. Even if such questions were somehow raised for Mrs. O and other teachers, the deficiencies in their practice, noted in many recent reports, would virtually guarantee that most
of these teachers would not know enough to respond appropriately, on
their own. How could teachers be expected to assess, unassisted, their
own progress in inventing a new sort of instruction, if their math teaching is in the dismal state pictured in the policy statements demanding that
new instruction?

Additionally, if teachers build on past practices as they change, then
their view of how much they have accomplished will depend on where they
start. Teachers who begin with very traditional practices would be likely to
see modest changes as immense. What reformers might see as trivial, such
teachers would estimate as a grand revolution, especially as they were
just beginning to change. From a perspective still rooted mostly in a traditional practice, such initial changes would seem—and be—immense.
That seemed to be Mrs. O's situation. She made what some observers might
see as tiny and perhaps even misguided changes in her teaching. However,
like other teachers who were taking a few first small steps away from conventional practice, for her they were giant steps. She would have to take
many more steps, and make many more fundamental changes before she
might see those early changes as modest.

So, if California teachers have only their subjective yardsticks with
which to assess their progress, then it seems unreasonable to judge their
work as though they had access to much more and better information.
For it is teachers who must change in order to realize new instructional
policies. Hence their judgment about what they have done, and what they
still may have to do, ought to be given special weight. We might expect
more from some teachers than others. Those who had a good deal of help
in cultivating such judgment—that is, who were part of some active conversation about their work, in which a variety of questions about their
practice were asked and answered, from a variety of perspectives—would
have more resources for change than those who had been left alone to
figure things out for themselves.

The same notion might be applied to policies like the new framework
that seek to change instruction. We might expect only a little from those
policies that try to improve instruction without improving teachers' capacity to judge the improvements and adjust their teaching accordingly,
for such policies do little to augment teachers' resources for change. In
Mrs. O's case, at least, thus far the framework has been this sort of policy. We might expect more from policies that help teachers to cultivate
the capacity to judge their work from new perspectives, and that add to

teachers' resources for change in other ways as well. The new instructional policy of which the framework is part has not done much of this for Mrs. O.

What would it take to make additional, helpful, and useful guidance available to teachers? What would it take to help teachers pay constructive attention to it? Neither query has been given much attention so far, either in efforts to change instruction or in efforts to understand such change. Yet without good answers to these questions, it is difficult to imagine how Mrs. O and most other teachers could make the changes that the framework seems to invite.

Policy and Practice

Mrs. O's math classes suggest a paradox. This California policy seeks fundamental changes in learning and teaching. State policymakers have illuminated deficiencies in instruction and set out an ambitious program for improvement. Policy thus seems a chief agency for changing practice. Yet teachers are the chief agents for implementing any new instructional policy: Students will not learn a new mathematics unless teachers know it and teach it. The new policy seeks great change in knowledge, learning, and teaching, yet these are intimately held human constructions. They cannot be changed unless the people who teach and learn want to change, take an active part in changing, and have the resources to change. It is, after all, their conceptions of knowledge, and their approaches to learning and teaching, that must be revamped.

Hence teachers are the most important agents of instructional policy (Cohen, 1988; Lipsky, 1980), but the state's new policy also asserts that teachers are the problem. It is, after all, their knowledge and skills that are deficient. If the new mathematics framework is correct, most California teachers know far too little mathematics, or hold their knowledge improperly, or both. Additionally, most do not know how to teach mathematics so that students can understand it. This suggests that teachers will be severely limited as agents of this policy: How much can practice improve if the chief agents of change are also the problem to be corrected?

This paradox would be trivial if fundamental changes in learning and teaching were easy to make. Yet even the new framework recognized that the new mathematics it proposes will be "difficult to teach" (CSDE, 1985, p. 13). Researchers who have studied efforts to teach as the framework intends also report that it is difficult, often uncommonly so. Students cannot simply absorb a new body of knowledge. In order to understand these subjects, learners must acquire a new way of thinking about a body of knowledge, and must construct a new practice of acquiring it (Lampert, 1988). They must cultivate strategies of problem solving that seem relatively unusual and perhaps counter-intuitive (diSessa, 1983). They must learn to treat academic knowledge as something they construct, test, and explore, rather than as something they accept and accumulate (Cohen, 1988). Additionally, and in order to do all of the above, students must unlearn acquired knowledge of math or physics, whether they are second graders or college sophomores. Their extant knowledge may be naive, but it often works.

A few students can learn such things easily. Some even can pick them up more or less on their own. However, many able students have great difficulty in efforts to understand mathematics, or other academic subjects. They find the traditional and mechanical instruction that the framework rejects easier and more familiar than the innovative and challenging instruction that it proposes.

If such learning is difficult for students, should it be any less so for teachers? After all, in order to teach math as the new framework intends, most teachers would have to learn an entirely new version of the subject. To do so they would have to overcome all of the difficulties just sketched. For, as the framework says of students, teachers could not be expected to simply absorb a new "body" of knowledge. They would have to acquire a new way of thinking about mathematics, and a new approach to learning it. They would have to additionally cultivate strategies or problem solving that seem to be quite unusual. They would have to learn to treat mathematical knowledge as something that is constructed, tested, and explored, rather than as something they broadcast, and that students accept and accumulate. Finally, they would have to unlearn the mathematics they have known. Though mechanical and often naive, that knowledge is well settled, and has worked in their classes, sometimes for decades.

These are formidable tasks, even more so for teachers than for students. Teachers would have a much larger job of unlearning: After all, they know more of the old math, and their knowledge is much more established. Teachers also would have to learn a new practice of mathematics teaching, while learning the new mathematics and unlearning the old. That is a very tall order. Additionally, it is difficult to learn even rather simple things—like making an omelette—without making mistakes; but mistakes are a particular problem for teachers. For one thing teachers are in charge of their classes, and they hold authority partly in virtue of their superior knowledge. Could they learn a new mathematics and practice of mathematics teaching, with all the trial and error that would entail, while continuing to hold authority with students, parents, and others interested in education? For another, teachers are responsible for their students' learning. How can they exercise that responsibility if they are just learning the mathematics they are supposed to teach, and just learning how to teach it? American education does not have ready answers for these questions. However, there was no evidence that the framework authors, or educators in Mrs. O's vicinity, had even asked them. It is relatively easy for policymakers to propose dramatic changes in teaching and learning, but teachers must enact those changes. They must maintain their sense of responsibility for student's accomplishments, and the confidence of students, parents, and members of the community. Unfortunately, most schools offer teachers little room for learning, and little help in managing the problems that learning would provoke.

The new mathematics framework seemed to recognize some problems that students would have in learning new mathematics, but, from Mrs. O's perspective, the state has not acted as though it recognized the problems of teachers' learning. Mrs. O certainly was not taught about the new mathematics in a way that took these difficulties into account. Instead, the CSDE taught her about the new math with the very pedagogy that it criticized in the old math. She was told to do something, like students in many traditional math classrooms. She was told that it was important. Brief explanations were offered, and a synopsis of what she was to learn was provided in a text. California education officials offered Mrs. O a standard dose of knowledge telling. The state acted as though it assumed that fundamental instructional reform would occur if teachers were told to do it. New goals were articulated, and exhortations to pursue them were issued. Some new materials were provided. Although the state exhorted teachers to devise a new pedagogy for their classes, it did so with an old pedagogy.

If, as the framework argues, it is implausible to expect students to understand math simply by being told, why is it any less implausible to expect teachers to learn a new math simply by being told? If students need a new instruction to learn to understand mathematics, would not teachers need a new instruction to learn to teach a new mathematics? Viewed in this light, it seems remarkable that Mrs. O made any progress at all.

What more might have been done, to support Mrs. O's efforts to change? What would have helped her to make more progress toward the sort of practice that the framework proposed? It is no answer to the question, but I note that no one in Mrs. O's vicinity seemed to be asking that question, let alone taking action based on some answers.

This new policy aspires to enormous changes in teaching and learning. It offers a bold and ambitious vision of mathematics instruction, a vision that took imagination to devise and courage to pursue. Yet this admirable policy does little to augment teachers' capacities to realize the new vision. For example, it offers rather modest incentives for change. I could detect few rewards for Mrs. O to push her teaching in the framework's direction—certainly no rewards that the state offered. The only apparent rewards were those that she might create for herself, or that her students might offer. Nor could I detect any penalties for nonimprovement, offered either by the state or her school or district.

Similar weaknesses can be observed in the supports and guidance for change. The new framework was barely announced in Mrs. O's school. She knew that it existed, but wasn't sure if she had ever read it. She did know that the principal had a copy. The new framework did bring a new text series, and Mrs. O knew about that. She knew that the text was supposed to be aligned with the framework. She had attended a publisher's workshop on the book, and said it had been informative. She had read the book, and the teachers' guide. Yet she used the new book only a little, preferring *Math Their Way*. The school and district leadership seemed to have thought *Math Their Way* was at least as well aligned with the framework as the new text series, and permitted its substitution in the primary grades.

Hence the changes in Mrs. O's practice were partly stimulated by the new policy, but she received little guidance and support from the policy, or from the state agencies that devised it. There was a little more guidance and support from her school and district: She was sent to a few summer workshops, and she secured some additional materials. However, when I observed Mrs. O's teaching there seemed to be little chance that she would be engaged in a continuing conversation about mathematics, and teaching and learning mathematics. Her district had identified a few mentor teachers on whom she could call for a bit of advice if she chose. There was no person or agency to help her to learn more mathematics, or to comment on her teaching in light of the framework, or to suggest and demonstrate possible changes in instruction, or to help her try them out. The new mathematics framework greatly expanded Mrs. O's obligations in mathematics teaching without much increasing her resources for improving instruction. Given the vast changes that the state has proposed, this is a crippling problem.

Mrs. O's classroom reveals many ambiguities, and, to my eye, certain deep confusions about teaching mathematics for understanding. She has been more successful in helping her students to learn a more complex mathematics than California has been in helping her to teach a more complex mathematics. From one angle this situation seems admirable: Mrs. O has had considerable discretion to change her teaching, and she has done so in ways that seem well-adapted to her school. Though I may call attention to the mixed quality of her teaching, her superiors celebrate her work. From another angle it seems problematic. If we take the framework's arguments seriously, then Mrs. O should be helped to struggle through to a more complex knowledge of mathematics, and a more complex practice of teaching mathematics. For if she cannot be helped to struggle through, how can she better help her students to do so? Some commentators on education have begun to appreciate how difficult it is for many students to achieve deep understanding of a subject and that appreciation is at least occasionally evident in the framework. There is less appreciation of how difficult it will be for teachers to learn a new practice of mathematics instruction.

NOTES

This work was sponsored in part by the National Center for Research on Teacher Education and the Center for the Learning and Teaching of Elementary Subjects, College of Education, Michigan State University. It was funded by the Office of Education Research and Improvement, Grant No. R117 P8000 4, U.S. Department of Education. The opinions expressed in this chapter do not necessarily represent the position, policy, or endorsement of the Office or the Department. The chapter was improved by comments from my colleagues in the study: Deborah Ball, Ruth Heaton, Penelope Peterson, Dick Prawat, Ralph Putnam, Janine Remillard, Nancy Wiemers, and Suzanne Wilson. Comments from Magdalene Lampert and Larry Cuban were most helpful.

REFERENCES

Baratta-Lorton, M. (1976). *Math their way*. Boston: Addison-Wesley.

California State Department of Education. (1987). *Mathematics: Model curriculum guide*. Sacramento, CA: Author.

California State Department of Education. (1985). *Mathematics framework for California public schools, kindergarten through grade twelve*. Sacramento, CA: Author.

Cuban, L. (1984). *How teachers taught*. New York: Longman.

Cuban, L. (1986). *Teachers and machines*. New York: Teachers College Press.

Cohen, D. K. (1989). Teaching practice: Plus ça change. In P. W. Jackson (Ed.), *Contributing to educational change: Perspectives on research and practice* (pp. 27–84). Berkeley, CA: McCutchan.

diSessa, A. (1983). Phenomenology and the evolution of intuition. In D. Gentner & A. L. Stevens (Eds.), *Mental models* (pp. 267–298). Hillsdale, NJ: Erlbaum.

Gross, N., Giaquinta, J., & Bernstein, M. (1971). *Implementing educational innovations.* New York: Basic.

Lampert, M. (1988, January). *Teachers' thinking about students' thinking about geometry: The effects of new teaching tools.* Cambridge: Educational Technology Center.

Lipsky, M. (1980). *Street corner bureaucracy.* New York: Sage.

Rowan, B., & Guthrie, L. F. (1989). The quality of Chapter 1 instruction: Results from a study of twenty-four schools. In R. Slavin, N. L. Karweit, N. A. Madden (Eds.), *Effective programs for students at risk* (pp. 195–219). Boston: Allyn & Bacon.

Welsh, W. W. (1979). Twenty years of science curriculum development: A look back. *Review of Research in Education, 7,* 282–306.

28

SETTING HIGH STANDARDS FOR EVERYONE

Mark S. Tucker, Judy B. Codding

The standards movement is progressing at both the state and the national level. Although there is intense debate about what the standards should include, there is also some debate about whether to have standards at all. Many standards proponents argue that without proper assessment, any standards lack teeth. The foundation and impetus for this chapter can be found in many of the reports and studies in Part Two of this reader.

○

ONE OF THE MOST STRIKING FEATURES of countries that are more successful than we in educating their students to high standards is the assumption made by parents, teachers, and the students themselves that the students can do it. By contrast, the single most important obstacle to high student achievement in the United States is our low expectations for students. Why is this so?

The answer lies in our history. Shortly after the turn of the twentieth century, the challenge facing teachers and school administrators was to produce a population of students entering the workforce that met the needs of the burgeoning factories and offices in which they would work. The mass production system was being introduced on a wide scale, and it was greatly reducing the need for skilled craftspeople. Only a small technical and managerial elite required serious academic preparation. Almost all of the rest, the vast mass of the American workforce, could do quite well with only a seventh- or eighth-grade level of literacy. The system they built met that requirement handsomely, year after year.

Then American psychologists announced a "finding" that cloaked this system in science and improved its efficiency substantially. Academic achievement, they said, is substantially determined by intelligence. And intelligence is a function of genetic endowment. Since intelligence is distributed along a normal curve, they said, it follows that the potential for academic achievement is distributed on the same bell curve. They went on to say that only the most intelligent of our young people—about the top 15 percent or so—are capable of serious academic work.

The word went out to America's schools, teachers, parents, and students. Pretty soon, teachers took the view that it would be damaging to the kids to ask more of them than they were capable of. For those in the bottom half of the distribution, the decent thing to do would be to give them high marks for making an effort—coming to school, turning in their homework, and behaving themselves—most of the time.

From this time on, much effort was put into deciding when youngsters first entered school, in kindergarten or first grade, what their intellectual potential was and then assigning them to an ability group based on that judgment. Since then, rare indeed is a student who escaped the fate that followed from that first assignment.

Now and then, an error was made when a student was passed from grade to grade. A student who had been thought to have little potential was misassigned to a group of "high-ability" kids and performed admirably. But few practitioners or policymakers noticed or cared. And so almost nothing was expected of millions and millions of young people who could easily have achieved at far higher levels than they did.

Most of the rest of the world was rather skeptical of our psychologists' findings and chose to disregard them. In much of northern Europe, it is illegal to group children by ability until they are at least fourteen years old, and in other countries it is simply not done.

In the United States, however, when young people first enter school, they are assigned to ability groups based on their teachers' estimates of their native ability. These estimates have closely matched the income and educational background of their parents. What we have actually had is a vast sorting system based largely on social class and racial background, with the outcome determined for many children before the game began.

The power of the idea of the system as a sorting machine runs deep. Look at who gets into the Advanced Placement courses in our high schools. Students who in middle-class and lower-middle-class communities are put into AP courses would never be encouraged to take them in wealthy communities. Conversely, students in wealthy communities who are counseled out of AP courses could easily get into them in less wealthy communities. Wherever we are, it seems, there has to be a "spread." The unspoken agreement is that AP is for the "elite" in our communities, though the actual achievement levels of those elites vary widely.

When most jobs required little skill and little education, maybe it did not matter that we expected far less of our students than parents and teachers expected of students in other countries. Now it matters very much. Today more than ever, what you will earn will be a function of what you know and can do. The only job security in contemporary America is the job security of being highly skilled in an area of high demand and being able to learn complex new things very quickly.

One obvious response to having very low implicit standards for the majority of our students is to have high explicit standards for all of them.

The Route to Standards: The Problem of Unmotivated Students

But low expectations is not the only problem that standards will have to solve. Another factor affecting student performance is no less important: weak motivation to take tough courses and to work hard in school.

In the fall of 1989, the National Center on Education and the Economy assembled a large research team for the Commission on the Skills of the American Workforce and sent it to Europe and Asia. During that trip, some of us found ourselves at the massive Daimler-Benz factory in Stuttgart, Germany, looking out from an observation deck at a hall the size of a football field. It was the center of the facility that Mercedes-Benz uses to train teenage apprentices to be machinists and auto mechanics. The young men and women on the floor were all dressed in white lab coats. Some were sitting at computers loaded with AutoCAD software, designing parts and learning how the software could be used to control the metalworking machines that make auto parts. Others were operating the numerically controlled machines that actually make the parts. Some were learning how to perform precise measurements on newly manufactured parts. And still others were learning how to operate diagnostic equipment that could detect faults in the digital circuits that control the vital functions of modern automobiles.

The chairman of Daimler-Benz had retired just before we arrived. We were astonished to learn that he had come up the ranks from the apprenticeship program—astonished because it was inconceivable to us that the chairman of, say, General Motors or AT&T would rise to the top of the organization from an American vocational school. Then we learned that the chairman of Deutsche Bank, who had retired in the same year, had also come up through the apprenticeship program.

All over Germany, young people enroll in apprenticeship programs at age sixteen to become machinists and auto mechanics, among other occupations. But clearly there is a great advantage in becoming an apprentice at Daimler. So we asked our hosts what it takes to be accepted in the Daimler program. The answer was, "It depends on the courses you take, the grades you get, how you do on your exams, and the recommendations of your teachers."

A few months later, we found ourselves in Toyota City, Japan, the home of the Toyota Motor Corporation. We walked through the areas where rolls of steel are stamped and formed into car bodies and from there into the assembly area. Properly speaking, the workers there do not build the car bodies; computer-programmed machines do. The workers mind the machines, as many as six or eight of them at a time. When we probed into the skills required to do this, we discovered that young people joining the line at age eighteen are expected to become part of a work team that sets a certain amount of time aside each week for study. At those sessions, the supervisor gives the team members texts to take home and read so that they can participate in the group study sessions. These texts, it turns out, are on digital electronics and mechanics. The workers, all of them, are expected to have had high school courses in Japanese, mathematics, physics, and chemistry that will prepare them to do college-level work in engineering on their own and as a member of the work team when they get to Toyota. As the line gets ever more efficient at the Toyota production facility, Toyota management reassigns the line workers to the computer programming department, work they can do because, some years ago, Toyota decided that everyone on the line should have the qualifications that junior engineers have in the United States.

As at Daimler-Benz, positions at Toyota are mostly filled by people who first came to the firm in entry-level jobs, so one can go to the top from the factory floor. Therefore the benefits of getting an entry-level job at Toyota are very attractive. We asked how a young Japanese person gets such a job.

It turns out that there is no apprenticeship program in Japan. Like most other large employers, Toyota has contract relationships with certain high schools. Year after year, it goes back to those high schools to get the number of young people it needs to fill new openings. Entrance to high schools is competitive in Japan. Having a contract with a firm like Toyota is a plum. So it is very important for a Japanese high school principal who has such a contract to keep it. It is therefore imperative for that principal to recommend only students who have what it takes to succeed in the firm.

So we asked Japanese high school principals what it takes to get on the list of students recommended to Toyota. The answer: it depends on the courses you take, the grades you get, how you do on your exams, and the recommendations of your teachers.

The systems in Germany and Japan could not be more different, but the result is exactly the same. Whether you want to be a brain surgeon or an auto mechanic, it pays to take tough courses and work hard in school.

What about the United States?

The vast majority of American students, unlike their counterparts in Europe and Asia, have very little incentive to take tough courses or study hard, especially in high school. Students who have little hope of getting a diploma or who do not expect to get more than a dead-end, minimum-wage job when they leave high school typically become dropouts, heading for the door as soon as the law allows. The ones who choose to stay in high school beyond the age of sixteen know that they can go from high school to community college and many four-year colleges with only a high school diploma. Since they already have the level of literacy needed to get the diploma, the only other requirement to get their diploma is to show up most of time and stay out of trouble. They would be foolish to take a tough course or study hard: they might fail a tough course, and studying hard for an easy course would buy them nothing, since neither the employer nor the nonselective college is particularly interested in their grades as long as they have the diploma.

Only the students who plan to go to a selective college—a very small percentage of all students—have any incentive to take tough courses and study hard for the rest of their high school career.

European and Asian youngsters, including those bound for work at the age of sixteen or eighteen, take tough courses and work hard in school because failure to do so might mean that they do not get to go to college at all or get a good job. Americans are typically appalled to hear this. If one believes that most youngsters are not capable of serious academic work, it seems unfair to set up a system that assumes that anyone can succeed academically who works at it hard enough.

There are many reasons why the performance of American youngsters in secondary school lags behind that of their European and Asian counterparts. But we would not be surprised to find that weak incentives for the students to make a serious effort to learn explain more than half of the difference. It is hardly clear how the performance of American students can meet or exceed the performance of Asian and European young-sters when they leave high school if their students are highly motivated to achieve and ours are not.

The Idea of an Internationally Benchmarked Certificate Standard: The CIM

The idea of the Certificate of Initial Mastery (CIM) was first proposed by the Commission on the Skills of the American Workforce in its landmark 1990 report, *America's Choice: high skills or low wages!*[1] Designed to address the dual problems of low expectations and lack of motivation, it is a simple proposal: find out which countries do the best job of educating their young people in mathematics, science, their native language, and applied learning (the generic skills required to be successful in the modern workplace); find out what they expect of most of their young people at the age of sixteen; create a certificate here in the United States set to that standard; and offer it to anyone who passes an assessment matched to that standard.

Anyone, at any age, could get the certificate. It would never be too late. People seeking the certificate could take the examination portion of the assessment as often as they liked. School districts would be expected to make sure that almost all the students in their care receive the certificate before they reach the age at which they can no longer attend a high school free of charge.

Alternative education programs for out-of-school youth and adults would have to be redesigned to enable them to reach the same certificate standard, and more resources would have to be made available for this purpose because the standard would be more demanding than the high school equivalency standards now in place.

This idea of a certificate standard is very different from the idea behind the high school diploma. Where we now award a diploma for time spent in school, we would instead award a certificate for reaching a predetermined—high—level of measured achievement. All educators believe that youngsters learn at different rates. If that is true, it follows that not all students will earn this new certificate in any given grade or at any given age. It is in the essence of the idea that some will earn it earlier and some will earn it later than others.

If the fundamental goal of public schooling becomes getting all students to a high, internationally benchmarked standard, doesn't it make sense to specify that standard and then award a certificate to everyone who meets it?

What led us to the idea of the certificate standard was the observation that two of the most important impediments to widespread high achievement are low expectations and low student motivation to take tough courses and work hard. How would the certificate standard change that?

First, the certificate standard would end the practice of setting different expectations for different groups of students. The common mantra "All kids can learn" would finally become policy, and what they would be expected to learn would for the first time be explicit. Second, students in the United States would quickly discover that employers that offered jobs leading to good careers and most colleges would demand the certificate. So for the first time, most American students would have a reason to take tough courses and work hard in school.

What is important here is the potential for a high certificate standard to serve as the fulcrum for comprehensive school reform. All students should be expected to achieve it. All schools should understand that their job is to get every student there. All parents should expect their children to get the certificate and their schools to get them there. The certificate standard becomes the gold standard, the universal goal, the standard that counts.

The American Standards Movement

This idea of a universal certificate standard does not exist in a vacuum. The United States is in the midst of a movement to use standards as the rallying principle for the improvement of academic achievement in the schools. To the extent that any such movement can be said to have a beginning, this movement began in 1989, when President George Bush invited the state governors to join him in Charlottesville, Virginia, at the first national summit on education. That meeting produced agreement among the participants on the need for national education goals. A few months later, the governors and the president agreed on a set of goals, and not long after that, they agreed on establishment of the National Education Goals Panel, an unofficial but very high level group of governors and administration officials who would take responsibility for monitoring the nation's progress toward the goals.

Governor Roy Romer of Colorado, who served as the first chair of the Goals Panel, concluded early on that goals would be a far less powerful instrument for improving American education than standards would be, and he undertook a one-person crusade to persuade the American people that this country needed explicit education standards and new forms of assessment to go with them. In the meantime, the Bush administration, in the person of Diane Ravitch, then assistant secretary of education for research and improvement, provided funds to a number of national subject-matter organizations of educators to begin the process of developing national standards for their disciplines.

Al Shanker, then president of the American Federation of Teachers (AFT), became a powerful voice for the standards movement among teachers, a voice that carried well beyond his constituency into the councils of business and government at every level. And the staff of the AFT, through its study of the development and use of standards in other countries and its thoughtful analysis of the development of standards in the United States, earned the respect of the nation for its "standards for standards."

Bob Schwartz, director of education programs at The Pew Charitable Trusts in Philadelphia, provided funds to the Council for Basic Education to help states develop their own standards and to other organizations that were beginning, each in its own way, to make their own unique contributions. Eva Baker, Chris Cross, Denis Doyle, Chester Finn Jr., Linda Darling-Hammond, Robert Linn, John Murphy, Diane Ravitch, Lauren Resnick, Grant Wiggins, Dennie Palmer Wolf, and others[2] also contributed to the development of the ideas that informed the gathering movement through their writings and consulting practices. The National Board for Professional Teaching Standards' work to develop standards for teachers inevitably contributed to the growing discussion about standards for students.

One by one, the national disciplinary societies, from the National Council of Teachers of Mathematics to the National Council of Teachers of English, and others, like the National Science Board and the American Association for the Advancement of Science, produced standards for their disciplines. At the same time, state after state was gathering its citizens together to build a statewide consensus on the right standards for that state, drawing on the work of the disciplinary societies, the experts in the field, and our own program, New Standards, which we will describe in a moment.

The business community threw its weight behind the standards movement when Lou Gerstner of IBM joined Frank Shrontz of Boeing, John Clendenin of Bell South, George Fisher of Eastman Kodak, other business leaders, several governors, and the leadership of the National Governors' Association to sponsor the Second National Education Summit, at the IBM Palisades Conference Center in New York. The outcome of that meeting was a formal commitment from the governors to produce standards for their states within two years. The organizers of the summit also committed to the formation of a new organization, Achieve, to assist the states in producing high, internationally benchmarked standards.

Perhaps the crowning moment in this phase of the national march toward standards came in President Clinton's second State of the Union message, when he called for national but not federal standards and announced his initiative to develop two national examinations, one in reading at the fourth-grade level and one in mathematics at the eighth-grade level, to be based on the general assessment design and curriculum frameworks embodied in the National Assessment of Educational Progress (NAEP).

What is remarkable about this story is the speed with which it all took place. In the brief moment between 1989 and the first days of 1997, the nation came within a hair's breadth of committing itself to national academic standards for the schools, something that would have been unthinkable through our whole prior history.

Standards: The State of Play

Where does all this activity leave the nation? The answer depends on what the goal is.

If the goal is to make sure that the states have standards, victory is at hand. If it is to make sure that the states have high, internationally competitive standards, however, it is a different story. When Mark Musick, the highly regarded head of the Southern Regional Education Board, compared the performance of students on the National Assessment of Educational Progress to the performance of the same students on their state assessments, he found that many states' students who scored very high on their state assessments scored very low on NAEP. They may have standards, but, thanks to Mark Musick,[3] it is now clear that these standards vary widely in rigor.

A detailed assessment of the standards produced by the disciplinary societies and the standards offered by the president's education initiative requires clear guidelines against which to judge them. The judges need standards for the standards.

What should those standards be? We have already explained our feelings on the certificate standard. Beyond that, we believe standards should serve as an antidote to the tracking system, to the strong press for classifying students into ability groups that simply reflect and then reinforce low expectations for those students. Standards should be used to set a very high foundation requirement for all students, reflecting high expectations for everyone. Thus our view implies that a standard is not a cut point on a curve but rather a clear target for everyone to shoot at, a target that almost all students can achieve if they work hard and long enough.

Standards should be usable by students, in the sense that a student should be able to look at the standards and know instantly what topics have to be mastered, what knowledge has to be gained, and what kind of work he or she has to produce to meet the standard. By the same token, standards should be usable by teachers, in the sense that teachers should be able to look at the standards and know what topics they have to teach, what the students need to know, and what kind of work their students have to do to meet the standards. In other words, it should be possible to teach to the standards. This is what we mean by performance standards — the standard should incorporate examples of the kinds of performance that meet the standard.

Standards should be expressed in a way that enables them to be used to motivate students to take tough courses and to study hard. The clearest and most easily understood example of such a standard is the certificate. One either gets the certificate or does not, depending on whether the standard has been met. The bar exam, the medical boards, and architectural registration boards are all examples of this sort of standard.

Standards should actually require that students know the things that lie at the heart of the core subjects in the curriculum, but knowledge by itself is not enough. They must also master the core concepts in the disciplines because conceptual mastery is the key to being able to learn more. And it is no less essential for students to be able to apply what they know to real-world problems. Book knowledge is essential, but book knowledge without the ability to put that knowledge to work is of little value. Both the standards and the assessments that go with them should mirror the requirements of life outside the school as much as possible.

Standards, to be successful, must have broad support among teachers and the general public. Teachers who do not support them will not teach to them. And if they do not have broad support among the public, they will not last long.

Standards should be competitive, in the sense that they should be at least as high as the standards to which students in other countries are held in the same subjects at the same grade or age levels.

Last, standards should be as universal as possible. Standards have a lot in common with telephone companies. A telephone company that can connect you only to telephones on your block is not worth much. A company that can connect you to millions of other telephones around the country is worth a great deal more. In this highly mobile society, a certificate that says you have met a standard that is honored everywhere in the United States is worth a lot more than one that is honored only in your state or community.

Here is how we see the initiatives we just described in relation to these admittedly demanding standards for standards.

Few of the standards being produced by the professional societies or the states were referenced to what was expected of students in other countries.

The professional societies that developed the subject-matter standards were understandably concerned about the way their subjects were being taught in the schools and wanted to take a tough stand in their standards against what they saw as a limited vision of the subject. Leaders in English language arts were concerned, for example, about the reduction of English to the teaching of grammar and diction, mathematics leaders about the teaching of mathematics as little more than arithmetic computation. The result, though, was that when the public looked for these topics in the standards, they were hard to find. From the public's point of view, that simply defied common sense. Some state standards presented another problem. Reflecting many teachers' concern that young people grow up as sensitive, caring adults with what they believe to be good values, they made sure that their state standards commissions put statements in their standards documents reflecting these views. Many parents who had no objection to state standards for arithmetic, geometry, and physics had a lot of trouble with standards that suggested that the schools should teach values with which they did not agree and wondered whether the schools should in any case be taking over from the family the role of teaching values to young people or should adopt standards that would give schools a license to pry into the details of family relationships at home.

Because the professional societies were not making the hard choices as to what was most important to teach in the subject, their recommendations, if acted on by teachers, would require much more time to teach than was actually available in the school day, week, and year. And because these societies were working independently of one another, the resulting standards were framed in very different ways, making it hard for teachers to grasp what a standard really is and how to teach to it. To be truly useful, the standards would have to be clear, specific, and expressed in a common framework across the disciplines. And they would have to reflect some hard choices as to what was most important in each discipline.

Perhaps most serious from the standpoint of the needs of school people, the standards that the states and professional societies were producing were not performance standards. They specified content—"A student should know . . . and be able to . . ."—but did not convey with any vividness what kind of work would actually meet the content standard. But if students were going to work toward a standard, if teachers were to judge student progress toward a standard and parents were to help their children at home, it would have to be crystal clear what the standard is. One would have to be able to look at a particular piece of student work and say whether or not it meets the standard. Equally important, the only way to break the back of the sorting system is to make the standards clear enough so they would truly be the same for everyone.

There can be no standards-based reform without assessments matched to the standards. Teachers cannot improve teaching and curriculum unless they know how their students are doing against the standards. Students will have no reason to take tough courses and work hard unless something that they care about depends on how well they do on exams matched to the standards. The voters cannot hold the schools accountable unless they have some measure of how well the students are doing. But the professional societies had no plans to develop assessments to match their standards. And the states were finding out that even for the wealthiest, developing examinations that would accurately measure the required range and depth of student learning was extremely expensive.

NOTES

1. Commission on the Skills of the American Workforce, *America's Choice: high skills or low wages!* (Rochester, NY: National Center on Education and the Economy, 1990).

2. E. L. Baker and R. L. Linn, "The Psychology of Educational Reform: Goal Three." In R. Short and R. C. Talley (Eds.), *A Psychology of Educational Reform: Psychological Perspectives on Improving America's Schools* (Washington, DC: American Psychological Association, forthcoming).

   Christopher T. Cross and Scott Joftus, "Are Academic Standards a Threat or an Opportunity?" (Reston, VA: *National Association of Secondary School Principals' Bulletin,* September 1997).

   Linda Darling-Hammond, *The Right to Learn: A Blueprint for School Reform* (San Francisco, CA: Jossey-Bass, 1997).

   Denis P. Doyle and Susan Pimentel, *Raising the Standard: An Eight-Step Action Guide for Schools and Communities* (Sherman Oaks, CA: Corwin Press, 1997).

Chester E. Finn Jr., *We Must Take Charge* (New York: Free Press, 1991).

John Murphy and Jeffry Schiller, *Transforming America's Schools* (Peru, IL: Open Court, 1992).

John O'Neil, "On the New Standards Project: A Conversation with Lauren Resnick and Warren Simmons" (Arlington, VA: *Educational Leadership,* February 1993).

Diane Ravitch, *National Standards in American Education: A Citizen's Guide* (Washington, DC: Brookings Institution, 1995).

Grant P. Wiggins, *Educative Assessment: Assessment to Inform and Improve Student Performance* (San Francisco: Jossey-Bass, forthcoming).

Dennie Palmer Wolf, "Portfolio Assessment: Sampling Student Work" (Arlington, VA: *Educational Leadership* 46, no. 7, April 1989).

3. Mark Musick, *Setting Education Standards High Enough* (Atlanta, GA: Southern Regional Education Board, 1996).

29

WHAT IF WE ENDED SOCIAL PROMOTION?

Robert M. Hauser

Social promotion, the act of advancing children to the next grade despite a failure of academic performance, has been widely criticized recently. A decade ago, forced retention, the act of holding back a child because of poor academic performance regardless of other circumstances, was looked on unfavorably. Social promotion is a good example of an educational issue that loses and gains favor, swinging like a pendulum, with the current political climate and the latest research pulling public opinion back and forth.

○

WE SHOULD KNOW that a new policy works before we try it out on a large scale. In its plan to end social promotion, the administration appears to have mixed a number of fine and credible proposals for educational reform with an enforcement provision—flunking kids by the carload lot— about which the great mass of evidence is strongly negative. And this policy will hurt poor and minority children most of all.

Everyone is in favor of creating high standards and holding students to them. No one is in favor of social promotion, if that means promoting students who have not mastered the work of one grade and who are not ready for the next. But the question is, "What is the alternative?" Is holding students back in grade—flunking them—good for students? The research evidence shows that it is not.

It makes much more sense to identify learning problems early and to remedy them with solutions that really work—long before the only choices are flunking and social promotion. We know a lot of things that work: smaller class sizes, better-trained teachers, a challenging curriculum, high expectations, after-school and summer school help. There is good evidence that these things work—and good evidence that flunking kids does not work. Why should we tie these good ways of teaching to decisions that hurt children?

Students who have been held back typically do not catch up; in fact, low-performing students learn more if they are promoted—even without remedial help—than if they are held back. One reason for this is that the elementary and secondary school curriculum does not change radically from one grade to the next; there is a lot of review and overlap. Another is that it is simply boring to repeat exactly the same material.

Students who have been held back are much more likely to drop out before completing high school. That effect often occurs many years after a student is held back in grade and thus is invisible—without careful longitudinal study—to those who make the retention decision. The teachers and administrators who make decisions to hold children back do not have to live with the long-term consequences of their decisions.

It also costs a lot to hold students back. Children lose a year of their lives when they are held back. Overage students are out of place in classes with younger children—especially in the teenage years—and their presence in the classroom is a problem for teachers and administrators. Flunking kids—repeating grades—is expensive for school systems, even if they do not invest in remediation.

What is the evidence about the effects of retention? And do we really have social promotion? How much retention is there in our schools?

In 1989, Thomas Holmes reported a careful scientific summary of 63 controlled studies of grade retention in elementary and junior high school through the mid-1980s. When promoted and retained students were compared one to three years later, the retained students' average levels of academic achievement were at least 0.4 standard deviations below those of promoted students. In these comparisons, promoted and retained students were the same age, but the promoted students had completed one more grade than the retained students had. Promoted and retained students were also compared after completing one or more grades, that is, when the retained students were a year older than the promoted students but had completed equal numbers of additional grades. Here, the findings were less consistent, but still negative.

Of the 63 studies reviewed by Mr. Holmes, 54 yielded overall negative effects of retention, and only nine yielded overall positive effects. Some studies had better statistical controls than others, but the best studies—those with subjects matched on test scores, sex, and/or socioeconomic status—showed *larger* negative effects of retention than studies with weaker designs. Mr. Holmes concluded, "On average, retained children are worse off than their promoted counterparts on both personal-adjustment and academic outcomes."

New York City instituted in the 1980s the Promotional Gates program, which combined high rates of retention with efforts at remediation. The remedial efforts soon faded, and eventually the program was dropped. A blue-ribbon panel evaluated the program and found—no surprise—that it reduced achievement and increased dropping out. Today, New York is back on the same track. What reason does Chancellor Rudolph F. Crew have to believe that what failed in the 1980s will work now and in the new millennium?

A major new longitudinal study of Chicago children was undertaken by Arthur Reynolds and his colleagues in connection with a successful experiment in early and sustained educational intervention (before the recent so-called reforms in Chicago). They found that "grade retention was significantly associated with lower reading and math achievement at age 14 above and beyond a comprehensive set of explanatory variables" ("Grade Retention and School Performance: An Extended Investigation," Institute for Research on Poverty, 1998). Another analysis of the Chicago data found that retention during kindergarten through grade 8 increased dropping out by 12 percentage points, after controls for social background, program participation, school moves, and special education placement. Several earlier studies of Chicago in the 1980s also found that grade retention increases the number of dropouts.

Douglas K. Anderson in 1994 carried out an extensive, large-scale national study of the effect of grade retention on high school dropout rates. He analyzed data from the National Longitudinal Study of Youth for more than 5,500 students whose school attendance was followed annually from 1978–79 to 1985–86. After extensive statistical controls for sex, race/ethnicity, social background, test scores, adolescent deviance, early transitions to adult status, and several school-related measures, students who were currently repeating a grade were 70 percent more likely to drop out of high school than students who were not currently repeating a grade.

R. W. Rumberger and K. A. Larson analyzed high school dropout statistics and completion of the General Educational Development diploma in longitudinal data for almost 12,000 students in the National Educational Longitudinal Study of 1988 (*American Journal of Education,* 1998). After statistical controls for social and family background, school characteristics, student engagement, and academic achievement in the 8th grade (test scores and grades), they found that being held back before the 8th grade increased the relative odds of dropping out by the 12th grade by a factor of 2.56. Furthermore, they wrote, "students who were held back before the 8th grade were more than four times as likely as students who were not held back to not complete high school or receive a GED by 1994." Reliable negative evidence of that strength in a clinical trial would lead to its early termination.

Well-meaning leaders throughout the country are pushing a huge national experiment with a policy that has not worked in the past—and without any evidence that it will work in the future. For example, we have good experimental evidence that smaller class sizes in the elementary grades have important, lasting effects on learning; the evidence for banning social promotion is just wishful thinking. There is no credible, large-scale evidence of its success as an educational policy.

There is one more critical point on which the National Research Council report provides strong evidence: We do not practice social promotion in the United States now, and we have not practiced it for many years. Our statistics are not very good; neither the federal government nor most states collect the right data, but we do know a few things.

Age at entry to 1st grade has increased since 1970. At that time, almost all 6-year-olds were in the 1st grade (about 4 percent of 6-year-old boys and 8 percent of 6-year-old girls were enrolled below the 1st grade). In 1996, 18 percent of 6-year-olds were enrolled below the 1st grade. Part of that change is due to holding children back in kindergarten.

Many students are held back during elementary and secondary school. Nationally, among children who entered school in the late 1980s, 21 percent were enrolled below the usual grade at ages 6 to 8; 28 percent were below the usual grade at ages 9 to 11; 31 percent at ages 12 to 14; and this rose to 36 percent at ages 15 to 17. Not counting kindergarten and the later grades of high school, this means that at least 15 percent of children—and probably 20 percent—have been held back at some time in their childhood.

Worse yet, minorities and poor children are the most likely to be held back. Black, Hispanic, and white children enter 1st grade at just about the same ages, but between entry and adolescence, about 10 percent of white girls fall behind in grade, while 25 percent to 30 percent of minority children fall behind. By ages 15 to 17, 45 percent to 50 percent of black and Hispanic youths are below the expected grade levels for their ages.

Holding students back—flunking them—has a much greater impact on minority and poor youths than on majority, middle-class children. It decreases educational opportunity, and it makes opportunities less equal among groups. For 35 years, American education has aimed to reduce social inequality. While much remains to be done, we have made major gains—narrowing differences in test scores in the 1970s and 1980s and reducing the dropout difference between majority and minority children. If we start holding back ever larger numbers of children, we are likely to reverse the progress of the past four decades.

30

NINETEEN POSTULATES

John I. Goodlad

Some experts believe that the redesign of teacher education programs is a necessary reform to improve the commitment and ability of classroom teachers. John Goodlad, a proponent of improving teacher education, sets forth nineteen conditions, or postulates, that he believes are necessary to strengthen U.S. teachers. Goodlad calls on colleges and universities as well as states to increase the quality of the profession through improved recruitment and training.

———— o ————

POSTULATE ONE. *Programs for the education of the nation's educators must be viewed by institutions offering them as a major responsibility to society and be adequately supported and promoted and vigorously advanced by the institution's top leadership.*

Our children, their parents, and the nation are ill-served by colleges and universities and their presidents lukewarm to educating teachers. Failure to identify a normal-school past in promotional documents or to name the school of education in a presidential report on the university's professional schools conveys something much less than pride. It is outrageous that a president, academic vice-president, or provost, without any stated revision of policy, can cripple something as important as teacher education through neglect. Likewise, it is outrageous that institutional leaders often turn their backs when their schools or colleges of education operate shoddy—but profitable—off-campus programs for the preparation of school administrators. The message must go out and be backed by forceful action: Get on with it properly or be forthright in deciding not to participate any longer. There is no place on a college or university campus for an enterprise viewed as not worth a strongly supported, stable identity.

POSTULATE TWO. *Programs for the education of educators must enjoy parity with other campus programs as a legitimate college or university commitment and field of study and service, worthy of rewards for faculty geared to the nature of the field.*

It is hypocritical for institutions to include teacher education in their offerings and then be lukewarm about rewarding the work that goes with it, and it is inexcusable for faculty members engaged in teacher education to maintain that the work they do does not lend itself to scholarly activity. Likewise, it is indefensible for institutions to increase research demands on faculty without creating the necessary supporting conditions. There is urgent need to clear up the present ambiguity regarding the not-quite relationship of teacher education to the rest of the higher education enterprise and the K–12 system of schooling. With functions and tasks clear, the criteria for rewards can and must be made explicit.

POSTULATE THREE. *Programs for the education of educators must be autonomous and secure in their borders, with clear organizational identity, constancy of budget and personnel, and decision-making authority similar to that enjoyed by the major professional schools.*

In other words, boundaries and resources must be protected with the same vigor that characterizes academic departments and the education of doctors, lawyers, and dentists. We are dealing here with the education of those who will join parents in ensuring that our young people become humane individuals and responsible citizens. Do universities take on any matters of greater importance? Persons planning to become teachers must enter programs with assurance that the integrity and quality of those programs are not to be eroded by intrusions from within or without.

POSTULATE FOUR. *There must exist a clearly identifiable group of academic and clinical faculty members for whom teacher education is the top priority; the group must be responsible and accountable for selecting students and monitoring their progress, planning and maintaining the full scope and sequence of the curriculum, continuously evaluating and improving programs, and facilitating the entry of graduates into teaching careers.*

The existence of a department, school, or college of education is no guarantee of these conditions. Nor is the allocation of resources for teacher education to such a unit a guarantee. Clearly, some of the necessary faculty must come from the schools that provide student teaching and internship experiences, as well as from the arts and sciences departments. These faculty members perform different functions but enjoy equal status in planning and conducting the programs. Patching together a curriculum and a faculty on a year-to-year basis, however, is inadequate and inexcusable. Teacher education must have an integrity backed by security of programs and responsible persons.

These first four postulates outline reasonable expectations for a college or university that takes on as one of its functions the education of educators for the schools. To assume the function but not provide the implied resources on the grounds that limited budgets do not permit is to shortchange children and youths, teachers, and the public. The only responsible, moral thing to do under such circumstances is to admit inability to prepare teachers adequately and close down the programs. On the other hand, when colleges and universities meet these conditions, they set the proper moral tone for students and faculty.

POSTULATE FIVE. *The responsible group of academic and clinical faculty members described above must have a comprehensive understanding of the aims of education and the role of schools in our society and be fully committed to selecting and preparing teachers to assume the full range of educational responsibilities required.*

Clearly, faculty members who perceive the function of schools narrowly and teaching as a mechanistic series of steps provide the wrong role models. Professors who impatiently and reluctantly drag themselves away from their research and graduate seminars to teach required courses in the teacher education sequence probably do not think much about what teachers should do. Professors of mathematics who advise their best students not to become teachers defeat the implications of this postulate. And cooperating teachers in the schools who tell their student teachers that teaching is a miserable occupation should themselves be out of it. Future teachers deserve more encouraging messages.

POSTULATE SIX. *The responsible group of academic and clinical faculty members must seek out and select for a predetermined number of student places in the program those candidates who reveal an initial commitment to the moral, ethical, and enculturating responsibilities to be assumed.*

Fulfilling this postulate requires the preparation of recruitment and admissions documents describing the entrance requirements. It calls for the presentation of supporting credentials from each candidate and an admissions interview. Other professional programs require these things. Why not teacher education programs? Students admitted want to know that they have met high standards, that they have been carefully chosen. Teaching our children is not a given right. It is an opportunity to be earned.

The omission of basic literacy as a requirement is not an oversight. I have more to say about this in the postulate below. Increasingly, both states and educational institutions are requiring the passing of tests in basic skills prior to admission to teacher education programs. I shall argue later for resources to assist candidates to secure any necessary remedial assistance. Academic shortcomings on the part of highly committed individuals are easier to overcome than a lack of commitment to teaching.

With the institution fully committed, an able faculty group clearly in charge and responsible, and students who perceive themselves as carefully selected, we are ready to consider the necessary programmatic conditions. These are laid out in the much longer list of postulates below.

POSTULATE SEVEN. *Programs for the education of educators, whether elementary or secondary, must carry the responsibility to ensure that all candidates progressing through them possess or acquire the literacy and critical-thinking abilities associated with the concept of an educated person.*

There are at least three sets of requirements here. First, there are entry minimums to be met through examinations. It is important, however, for the results to be built into a counseling process. Students who show an eagerness to correct deficiencies should be provided with the opportunity to do so. Universities spend millions of dollars keeping athletes eligible to play, some of whom can barely read and write. We do not want people teaching in schools who set a poor academic example, but we must provide opportunities for those seeking to meet acceptable standards to do so—over and beyond the prescribed curriculum, of course. Second, the required preteaching general-education curriculum must be adhered to by all—both traditional students entering undergraduate and nontraditional students entering graduate programs—with the opportunity to examine out in most areas. Third, candidates must demonstrate, as they progress through this curriculum, the intellectual traits associated with continued development as educated persons. Assessment here is difficult, but the responsible faculty group must take it on, must counsel students along the way, and must make tough decisions as deemed necessary. There are bright, intelligent people teaching in classrooms who have never confronted intellectual challenge. Perhaps this is why a common criticism of schools is that they do not emphasize development of the mind.

POSTULATE EIGHT. *Programs for the education of educators must provide extensive opportunities for future teachers to move beyond being students of organized knowledge to become teachers who inquire into both knowledge and its teaching.*

I argue here for coupling general education—especially the study of subjects ultimately to be taught in schools—with pedagogy. What is called for here is less an inquiry into generic methods—the psychology and sociology of individual and group learning, for example—than an inquiry into the means for teaching embedded in the domains of knowledge. For example, how do I as a teacher help students draw from the particulars of a time and a place principles of historical analysis that would help them in studies of other times and places? How do I connect the lives of students and these historical themes? Somewhere in the upper-division curriculum there should be a jointly taught seminar in which professors of pedagogy and of the specialized field explore questions such as these with future teachers. Not to effect the necessary transcendence while students are still involved in the general-education and specialized-subject curricula is to lose a most significant opportunity.

POSTULATE NINE. *Programs for the education of educators must be characterized by a socialization process through which candidates transcend their self-oriented student preoccupations to become more other-oriented in identifying with a culture of teaching.*

Socialization is a process of taking on certain cultural norms over time. The socialization that occurs, formally and informally, in a teacher education program tells us a great deal about the images of teaching and the expectations for teachers guiding that program as norms. Such norms are apparent in both the explicit and the implicit curriculum. How long and what it takes to absorb the moral and ethical norms of the teaching profession is not known; we have not tried to find out. We can be almost certain, however, that preparing to take some sort of examination on teaching will not suffice. Nor can such an exam tell us much about whether or not such socialization has occurred.

POSTULATE TEN. *Programs for the education of educators must be characterized in all respects by the conditions for learning that future teachers are to establish in their own schools and classrooms.*

The field of education has declared for itself prime competence in and jurisdiction over such subfields as curriculum planning, instruction, student counseling, evaluation, testing, group climate setting, and the like. Consequently, it is entirely reasonable to expect teacher education programs to be characterized by exemplary practices in all of these areas. Modeling is regarded as a powerful teaching device. For teacher education programs not to be models of educating is indefensible.

POSTULATE ELEVEN. *Programs for the education of educators must be conducted in such a way that future teachers inquire into the nature of teaching and schooling and assume that they will do so as a natural aspect of their careers.*

It is reasonable to assume that descriptions of teacher education programs will emphasize an inquiring approach instead of a series of hurdles to be cleared, that general traits of intellect will take precedence over narrow, specific competencies, and that "covering" course content and passing tests will be secondary to relating to children and youth and exciting them about learning.

POSTULATE TWELVE. *Programs for the education of educators must involve future teachers in the issues and dilemmas that emerge out of the never-ending tension between the rights and interests of individual parents and special-interest groups, on one hand, and the role of schools in transcending parochialism, on the other.*

To allow students not to grapple with these issues is to leave them hopelessly ignorant and exposed to pressures from all sides—pressures so contradictory in the context they create that educating in any real sense is virtually defeated. Earlier, I addressed the general education required of all prospective teachers. This education is necessary, but insufficient. The goals and organization of schooling and the role of schoolteaching pose issues for which special, professional education is required. The discourse may well begin in a course on the philosophy of education, but the fundamental issues must become underlying themes throughout both the academic and clinical components of programs.

POSTULATE THIRTEEN. *Programs for the education of educators must be infused with understanding of and commitment to the moral obligation of teachers to ensure equitable access to and engagement in the best possible K–12 education for all children and youths.*

As a nation, we simply have not internalized either the realization that the right to education now embraces the secondary school or the devastating consequences that will result if large numbers of young people do not complete it. Belief in the incapability of many children and youths to learn abounds. Horrifyingly large numbers of teachers share this belief; indeed, they use it to excuse their own failures. Teachers must come out of a preparation program with the belief that they can and will teach all their pupils to the best of their ability and that they will share in both their successes and their failures. Preparation programs that steer their students only into field settings where family backgrounds and educational resources almost ensure success are programs that disadvantage future teachers and short-change society.

POSTULATE FOURTEEN. *Programs for the education of educators must involve future teachers not only in understanding schools as they are but in alternatives, the assumptions underlying alternatives, and how to effect needed changes in school organization, pupil grouping, curriculum, and more.*

As we shall see, the education of educators is tightly coupled with the status quo. Few changes are needed if the purpose is to prepare teachers for the status quo, but if we think our schools need restructuring and renewal, then preparation programs must be involved with ideas for change and the spirit of change. And the relationship between universities and surrounding schools and school districts must be conducive to collaborative improvement, in part through the infusion of new teachers committed to and capable of effecting change.

POSTULATE FIFTEEN. *Programs for the education of educators must assure for each candidate the availability of a wide array of laboratory settings for observation, hands-on experiences, and exemplary schools for internships and residencies; they must admit no more students to their programs than can be assured these quality experiences.*

The range and stability of these resources are crucial. Additionally, observation in settings, good or bad, must be accompanied by critiques; practice and theory go together. Settings for internships and residencies must be examples of the best educational practices that schools and universities are able to develop together, and the internships obviously must be conducted collaboratively. These are "teaching schools," paralleling the teaching hospitals essential to medical education. It is the responsibility of universities to work with school districts in ensuring that these teaching schools are in economically disadvantaged as well as advantaged areas and that future teachers get teaching experience in both. The availability of such schools at any given time must govern the number of students admitted to a program. When forty future teachers are ready for intern placement, there must be forty places available. These forty candidates become junior colleagues in the elementary, middle, and high schools that serve as teaching schools. The number that can be accommodated by a participating school is an important detail to be worked out, as is the necessary overall funding and staffing arrangement.

POSTULATE SIXTEEN. *Programs for the education of educators must engage future teachers in the problems and dilemmas arising out of the inevitable conflicts and incongruities between what works or is accepted in practice and the research and theory supporting other options.*

Not only do such problems and dilemmas arise during observations of school and classroom practices, but the responsible faculty must see to it that they are brought to the forefront and discussed—with both practitioners and scholar-researchers engaged in the dialogue. It is not good enough to tell student teachers, caught in the middle of such conflicts, that they must not, while "guests" in the classroom, "rearrange the furniture in the minister's house." It is immoral for professors to tell their students, for the sake of keeping peace with the affiliated schools, to do what neither they nor their students believe to be right. Such inexcusable behavior arises out of the general failure of clinical and academic faculty to come together in a genuinely intellectual collaborative enterprise.

POSTULATE SEVENTEEN. *Programs for educating educators must establish linkages with graduates for purposes of both evaluating and revising these programs and easing the critical early years of transition into teaching.*

It is generally known that virtually all practitioners are at first highly critical of their professional preparation programs, whatever the field. "You simply didn't prepare us for the real world out there," they accuse their professors. It is perhaps uncomfortable to hear the complaints, but consistencies in them can be woven into evaluative patterns that can be useful for program review and revision. Beginning teachers, for example, would find it exceedingly valuable to meet throughout at least the initial year with other neophytes in a seminar guided by someone more removed, such as a professor engaged in teacher education. Because teacher education and placement are generally so local in character, most beginning teachers would once more be with their initial mentors from their training days. For those who move elsewhere after graduation, reciprocal, interinstitutional arrangements are called for. Rarely, however, are the necessary funds available for follow-up, either locally or reciprocally. Given the loss of so many teachers during the first few years following graduation, the returns from such an investment would be substantial.

POSTULATE EIGHTEEN. *Programs for the education of educators, in order to be vital and renewing, must be free from curricular specifications by licensing agencies and restrained only by enlightened, professionally driven requirements for accreditation.*

State authorities are responsible for setting licensing standards to protect the public. The long-standing practice has been to eschew graduation standards in favor of curricular requirements. In so doing, creativity and innovation in program planning within colleges and universities have been stifled. Now that states are turning to tests of basic literacy and knowledge about teaching as requirements for obtaining a teaching credential, they must get out of the business of prescribing the teacher education curriculum. This step would go a long way toward encouraging faculty members to initiate program renewal.

POSTULATE NINETEEN. *Programs for the education of educators must be protected from the vagaries of supply and demand by state policies that allow neither backdoor "emergency" programs nor temporary teaching licenses.*

Over and over, morally driven efforts to mount first-rate teacher education programs have been defeated by this action or that designed to relieve teacher shortages or satisfy special-group interests. Many teacher educators who once participated in renewal efforts, often more than once, now swear never to be stirred to undertake still another. They are cynical and often bitter, waiting for the next shoe to fall and adjusting accordingly. There are many appropriate ways to bring able people into schools and classrooms who are not certified or who have not yet made up their minds to teach. Providing them with licenses of any kind is a disservice to them and certainly to the teaching profession. When temporary licenses *are* granted, we make a mockery of all the postulates listed above.

The nineteen postulates put forward here do not encompass the whole of the conditions to be met in order to ensure able, committed teachers for our schools. I have deliberately concentrated on those lying within and necessary to the control and fulfillment of the moral responsibilities taken on by colleges and universities when they select or are called upon to educate teachers and principals for our schools. Included in these conditions are working arrangements with nearby schools of a kind never before attempted but absolutely essential to exemplary teacher education programs. Included also (in Postulates Eighteen and Nineteen) is a necessary relationship with the state that has from time to time been recognized and even respected but that has been breached so often that many teacher educators believe that any efforts to mount quality programs will ultimately be defeated by state omission or commission.

Seventeen of the nineteen, then, concentrate on what lies primarily within the will of the nation's colleges and universities. There are clearly identifiable actors to whom these postulates are addressed.

31

PROLOGUE FROM
HORACE'S COMPROMISE

Theodore R. Sizer

Horace, a composite teacher in a modern-day high school, helps Sizer
put a human face to his research findings. Here Sizer describes Horace,
a teacher with whom many can relate, although despite his less than
ideal working conditions he comes from what many teachers might
see as a privileged district.

───────── ○ ─────────

HERE IS AN ENGLISH TEACHER, Horace Smith. He's fifty-three, a twenty-
eight-year veteran of high school classrooms, what one calls an old pro.
He's proud, respected, and committed to his practice. He'd do nothing else.
Teaching is too much fun, too rewarding, to yield to another line of work.

Horace has been at Franklin High in a suburb of a big city for nineteen years. He served for eight years as English department chairman, but
turned the job over to a colleague, because he felt that even the minimal administrative chores of that post interfered with the teaching he loved best.

He arises at 5:45 A.M., careful not to awaken either his wife or grown
daughter. He likes to be at school by 7:00, and the drive there from his
home takes forty minutes. He wishes he owned a home near the school,
but he can't afford it. Only a few of his colleagues live in the school's town,
and they are the wives of executives whose salaries can handle the mort-
gages. His wife's job at the liquor store that she, he, and her brother own
doesn't start until 10:00 A.M., and their daughter, a new associate in a law

firm in the city, likes to sleep until the last possible minute and skip breakfast. He washes and dresses on tiptoe.

Horace prepares the coffee, makes some toast, and leaves the house at 6:20. He's not the first at school. The custodians and other, usually older, teachers are already there, "puttering around," one of the teachers says.

The teachers' room is large, really two rooms. The inner portion, windowless, is arranged in a honeycomb of carrels, one for each older teacher. Younger or newer teachers share carrels. Each has a built-in desk and a chair. Most have file cabinets. The walls on three sides, five feet high, are festooned with posters, photographs, lists, little sayings, notes from colleagues on issues long past. Horace: Call home. Horace: The following students in the chorus are excused from your Period 7 class—Adelson, Cartwright, Donato. . . .

Horace goes to his carrel, puts down his briefcase, picks up his mug, and walks to the coffee pot at the corner of the outer portion of the teachers' room, a space well lit by wide windows and fitted with a clutter of tables, vinyl-covered sofas, and chairs. The space is a familiar, comfortable jumble, fragrant with the smell of cigarettes smoked hours before. Horace lights up a fresh one, almost involuntarily, as a way perhaps to counteract yesterday's dead vapors. After pouring himself some coffee, he chats with some colleagues, mostly other English teachers.

The warning bell rings at 7:20. Horace smothers his cigarette, takes his still partly filled cup back to his carrel and adds it to the shuffle on his desk, collects some books and papers, and, with his briefcase, carries them down the hall to his classroom. Students are already clattering in, friendly, noisy, most of them ignoring him completely—not thoughtlessly, but without thinking. Horace often thinks of the importance of this semantic difference. Many adults are thoughtless about us teachers. Most students, however, just don't know we're here at all, people to think about. Innocents, he concludes.

7:30, and its bell. There are seventeen students here; there should be twenty-two. Bill Adams is ill; Horace has been told that by the office. Joyce Lezcowitz is at her grandmother's funeral; Horace hasn't been officially told that, but he knows it to be true. He marks Joyce "Ex Ab"—excused absence—on his attendance list. Looking up from the list, he sees two more students arrive, hustling to seats. You're late. Sorry . . . Sorry . . . The bus . . . Horace ignores the apologies and excuses and checks the two off on his list. One name is yet unaccounted for. Where is Jimmy Tibbetts? Silence. Tibbetts gets an "Abs" after his name.

Horace gets the class's attention by making some announcements about next week's test and about the method by which copies of the next play being read will be shared. This inordinately concerns some students and holds no interest for others. Mr. Smith, how can I finish the play when both Rosalie and I have to work after school? Mr. Smith, Sandy and I are on different buses. Can we switch partners? All these sorts of queries are from girls. There is whispering among some students. You got it? Horace asks, abruptly. Silence, signaling affirmation. Horace knows it is an illusion. Some character will come up two days later and guiltlessly assert that he has no play book, doesn't know how to get one, and has never heard of the plans to share the limited copies. Horace makes a mental note to inform Adams, Lezcowitz, and Tibbetts of the text-sharing plan.

This is a class of juniors, mostly seventeen. The department syllabus calls for Shakespeare during this marking period, and *Romeo and Juliet* is the choice this year. The students have been assigned to read Act IV for this week, and Horace and his colleagues all get them to read the play out loud. The previous class had been memorable: Juliet's suicide had provoked much mirth. *Romeo, I come!* The kids thought it funny, clumsily melodramatic. Several, sniggering, saw a sexual meaning. Horace knew this to be inevitable; he had taught the play many times before.

We'll start at Scene Four. A rustle of books. Two kids looking helplessly around. They had forgotten their books, even though in-class reading had been a daily exercise for three weeks. Mr. Smith, I forgot my book. You've got to remember, Alice . . . *remember!* All this with a smile as well as honest exasperation. Share with George. Alice gets up and moves her desk next to that of George. They solemnly peer into George's book while two girls across the classroom giggle.

Gloria, you're Lady Capulet. Mary, the Nurse. George, you're old man Capulet. Gloria starts, reading without punctuation: *Hold take these keys and fetch more spices Nurse.* Horace: Gloria. Those commas. They mean something. Use them. Now, again. *Hold. Take these keys. And fetch more spices. Nurse.* Horace swallows. Better . . . Go on, Mary. *They call for dates and quinces in the pastry.* What's a quince? a voice asks. Someone answers, It's a fruit, Fruit! Horace ignores this digression but is reminded how he doesn't like this group of kids. Individually, they're nice, but the chemistry of them together doesn't work. Classes are too much a game for them. Go on . . . George?

Come. Stir! Stir! Stir! The second cock hath crow'd. Horace knows that reference to "cock" will give an opening to some jokester, and he squelches it before it can begin, by being sure he is looking at the class and not at his book as the words are read.

The curfew bell hath rung. 'Tis three o'clock. Look to the bak'd meats, good Angelica . . . George reads accurately, but with little accentuation.

Mary: *Go, you cot-quean, go . . .* Horace interrupts, and explains "cot-quean," a touch of contempt by the Nurse for the meddling Capulet. Horace does not go into the word's etymology, although he knows it. He feels that such a digression would be lost on this group, if not on his third-period class. He'll tell them. And so he returns: George, you're still Capulet. Reply to that cheeky Nurse.

The reading goes on for about forty minutes, to 8:15. The play's repartee among the musicians and Peter was a struggle, and Horace cut off the reading-out-loud before the end of the fifth scene. He assigns Act V for the next period and explains what will be on the *Romeo and Juliet* test. Mr. Smith, Ms. Viola isn't giving a test to her class. The statement is, of course, an accusing question. Well, we are. Ms. Viola's class will get something else, don't you worry. The bell rings.

The students rush out as the next class tries to push in. The newcomers are freshmen and give way to the eleventh graders. They get into their seats expectantly, without quite the swagger of the older kids. Even though this is March, some of these students are still overwhelmed by the size of the high school.

There should be thirty students in this class, but twenty-seven are present. He marks three absences on his sheet. The students watch him; there is no chatter, but a good deal of squirming. These kids have the Wriggles, Horace has often said. The bell rings: 8:24.

Horace tells the students to open their textbooks to page 104 and read the paragraph at its top. Two students have no textbook. Horace tells them to share with their neighbors. *Always* bring your textbook to class. We never know when we'll need them. The severity in his voice causes quiet. The students read.

Horace asks: Betty, which of the words in the first sentence is an adverb? Silence. Betty stares at her book. More silence. Betty, what is an adverb? Silence. Bill, help Betty. It's sort of a verb that tells you about things. Horace pauses: Not quite, Bill, but close. Phil, you try. Phil: An adverb modifies a verb . . . Horace: O.K., Phil, but what does "modify" mean? Silence. A voice: "Darkly." Who said that? Horace asks. The sentence was "Heathcliff was a darkly brooding character." I did, Taffy says. O.K., Horace follows, you're correct, Taffy, but tell us why "darkly" is an adverb, what it does. Taffy: It modifies "character." No, Taffy, try again. Heathcliff? No. Brooding? Yes, now why? Is "brooding" a verb? Silence.

Horace goes to the board, writes the sentence with chalk. He underlines *darkly*. Betty writes a note to her neighbor.

The class proceeds with this slow trudge through a paragraph from the textbook, searching for adverbs. Horace presses ahead patiently, almost dumbly at times. He is so familiar with the mistakes that ninth-graders make that he can sense them coming even before their utterance. Adverbs are always tougher to teach than adjectives. What frustrates him most are the partly correct answers; Horace worries that if he signals that a reply is somewhat accurate, all the students will think it is entirely accurate. At the same time, if he takes some minutes to sort out the truth from the falsity, the entire train of thought will be lost. He can never pursue any one student's errors to completion without losing all the others. Teaching grammar to classes like this is slow business, Horace feels. The bell rings. The students rush out, now more boisterous.

This is an Assembly Day, Horace remembers with pleasure. He leaves his papers on his desk, turns off the lights, shuts the door, and returns to the teachers' room. He can avoid assemblies; only the deans have to go. It's some student concert, in any event.

The teachers' room is full. Horace takes pleasure in it and wonders how his colleagues in schools in the city make do without such a sanctuary. Having a personal carrel is a luxury, he knows. He'd lose his here, he also knows, if enrollments went up again. The teachers' room was one happy consequence of the "baby bust."

The card game is going, set up on a square coffee table surrounded by a sofa and chairs. The kibitzers outnumber the players; all have coffee, some are smoking. The chatter is incessant, joshingly insulting. The staff members like one another.

Horace takes his mug, empties the cold leavings into the drain of the water fountain, and refills it. He puts a quarter in the large Maxwell House can supplied for that purpose, an honor system. He never pays for his early cup; Horace feels that if you come early, you get one on the house. He moves toward a clutch of fellow English and social studies teachers, and they gossip, mostly about a bit of trouble at the previous night's basketball game. No one was injured—that rarely happens at this high school —but indecorous words had been shouted back and forth, and Coke cans rolled on the gym floor. Someone could have been hurt. No teacher is much exercised about the incident. The talk is about things of more immediate importance to people: personal lives, essences even more transitory, Horace knows, than the odors of their collective cigarettes.

Horace looks about for Ms. Viola to find out whether it's true that she's not going to give a test on *Romeo and Juliet*. She isn't in sight, and Horace remembers why: she is a nonsmoker and is offended by smoke. He leaves his group and goes to Viola's carrel, where he finds her. She is put off by his query. Of course she is giving a test. Horace's lame explanation that a student told him differently doesn't help.

9:53. The third-period class of juniors. *Romeo and Juliet* again. Announcements over the public address system fill the first portion of the period, but Horace and a bunch of kids who call themselves "theater jocks" ignore them and talk about how to read Shakespeare well. They have to speak loudly to overpower the p.a. The rest of the class chatter among themselves. The readings from the play are lively, and Horace is able to exhibit his etymological talents with a disquisition on "cot-quean." The students are well engaged by the scene involving the musicians and Peter until the class is interrupted by a proctor from the principal's office, collecting absence slips for the first-class periods. Nonetheless, the lesson ends with a widespread sense of good feeling. Horace never gets around to giving out the assignment, talking about the upcoming test, or arranging for play books to be shared.

10:47. The Advanced Placement class. They are reading *Ulysses,* a novel with which Horace himself had trouble. Its circumlocutions are more precious than clever, he thinks, but he can't let on. Joyce is likely to be on the AP Exam, which will put him on a pedestal.

There are eighteen seniors in this class, but only five arrive. Horace remembers: This is United Nations Week at the local college, and a group of the high school's seniors is taking part, representing places like Mauritius and Libya. Many of the students in the UN Club are also those in Advanced Placement classes. Horace welcomes this remnant of five and suggests they use the hour to read. Although he is annoyed at losing several teaching days with this class, he is still quietly grateful for the respite this morning.

11:36. Lunch. Horace buys a salad on the cafeteria line—as a teacher he can jump ahead of students—and he takes it to the faculty dining room. He nods to the assistant principal on duty as he passes by. He takes a place at an empty table and is almost immediately joined by three physical education teachers, all of them coaches of varsity teams, who are noisily wrangling about the previous night's basketball game controversy. Horace listens, entertained. The coaches are having a good time, arguing with heat because they know the issue is really inconsequential and thus their disagreement will not mean much. Lunch is relaxing for Horace.

12:17. A free period. Horace checks with a colleague in the book storeroom about copies of a text soon to be used by the ninth-graders. Can he get more copies? His specific allotment is settled after some minutes' discussion. Horace returns to the teachers' room, to his carrel. He finds a note to call a Mrs. Altschuler, who turns out to be the stepmother of a former student. She asks, on behalf of her stepson, whether Horace will write a character reference for the young man to use in his search for a job. Horace agrees. Horace also finds a note to call the office. Was Tibbetts in your Period One class? No, Horace tells the assistant principal; that's why I marked him absent on the attendance sheet. The assistant principal overlooks this sarcasm. Well, he says, Tibbetts wasn't marked absent at any other class. Horace replies, That's someone else's problem. He was not in my class. The assistant principal: You're sure? Horace: Of course I'm sure.

The minutes of the free period remaining are spent in organizing a set of papers that is to be returned to Horace's third junior English class. Horace sometimes alternates weeks when he collects homework so as not totally to bury himself. He feels guilty about this. The sixth-period class had its turn this week. Horace had skimmed these exercises—a series of questions on Shakespeare's life—and hastily graded them, but using only a plus, check, or minus. He hadn't had time enough to do more.

1:11. More *Romeo and Juliet*. This section is less rambunctious than the first-period group and less interesting than that of the third period. The students are actually rather dull, perhaps because the class meets at the end of the day. Everyone is ready to leave; there is little energy for Montagues and Capulets. However, as with other sections, the kids are responsive when spoken to individually. It is their blandness when they are in a group that Horace finds trying. At least they aren't hell raisers, the way some last-period-of-the-day sections can be. The final bell rings at 2:00.

Horace has learned to stay in his classroom at the day's end so that students who want to consult with him can always find him there. Several appear today. One wants Horace to speak on his behalf to a prospective employer. Another needs to get an assignment. A couple of other students come by actually just to come by. They have no special errand, but seem to like to check in and chat. These youngsters puzzle Horace. They always seem to need reassurance.

Three students from the Theater Club arrive with questions about scenery for the upcoming play. (Horace is the faculty adviser to the stage crew.) Their shared construction work on sets behind the scenes gives Horace great pleasure. He knows these kids and likes their company.

By the time Horace finishes in his classroom, it is 2:30. He drops his papers and books at his carrel, selecting some—papers given him by his Advanced Placement students two days previously that he has yet to find time to read—to put in his briefcase. He does not check in on the card game, now winding down, in the outer section of the teachers' room but, rather, goes briefly to the auditorium to watch the Theater Club actors starting their rehearsals. The play is Wilder's *Our Town*. Horace is both grateful and wistful that the production requires virtually no set to be constructed. The challenge for his stage crew, Horace knows, will be in the lighting.

Horace drives directly to his liquor store, arriving shortly after 4:00. He gives his brother-in-law some help in the stockroom and helps at the counter during the usual 4:30-to-6:30 surge of customers. His wife had earlier left for home and has supper ready for them both and their daughter at 7:45.

After dinner, Horace works for an hour on the papers he has brought home and on the Joyce classes he knows are ahead of him once the UN Mock Assembly is over. He has two telephone calls from students, one who has been ill and wants an assignment and another who wants to talk about the lighting for *Our Town*. The latter, an eager but shy boy, calls Horace often.

Horace turns in at 10:45, can't sleep, and watches the 11:00 news while his wife sleeps. He finally drifts off just before midnight.

Horace has high standards. Almost above all, he believes in the importance of writing, having his students learn to use language well. He believes in "coaching"—in having his students write and be criticized, often. Horace has his five classes of fewer than thirty students each, a total of 120. (He is lucky; his colleagues in inner cities like New York, San Diego, Detroit, and St. Louis have a school board–union negotiated "load" base of 175 students.) Horace believes that each student should write something for criticism at least twice a week—but he is realistic. As a rule, his students write once a week.

Most of Horace's students are juniors and seniors, young people who should be beyond sentence and paragraph exercises and who should be working on short essays, written arguments with moderately complex sequencing and, if not grace exactly, at least clarity. A page or two would be a minimum—but Horace is realistic. He assigns but one or two paragraphs.

Being a veteran teacher, Horace takes only fifteen to twenty minutes to check over each student's daily homework, to read the week's theme, and to write an analysis of it. (The "good" papers take a shorter time, usually, and the work of inept or demoralized students takes much longer.) Horace wonders how his inner-city colleagues, who usually have a far greater percentage of demoralized students, manage. Horace is realistic: even in his accommodating suburban school, fifteen minutes is too much to spend. He compromises, averaging five minutes for each student's work by cutting all but the most essential corners (the *reading* of the paragraphs in the themes takes but a few seconds; it is the thoughtful criticizing, in red ballpoint pen in the margins and elsewhere, that takes the minutes).

So, to check homework and to read and criticize one paragraph per week per student with the maximum feasible corner-cutting takes six hundred minutes, or ten hours, assuming no coffee breaks or flagging attention (which is some assumption, considering how enervating is most students' forced and misspelled prose).

Horace's fifty-some-minute classes consume about twenty-three hours per week. Administrative chores chew up another hour and a half. Horace cares about his teaching and feels that he should take a half-hour to prepare for each class meeting, particularly for his classes with older students, who are swiftly moving over quite abstract and unfamiliar material, and his class of ninth-graders, which requires teaching that is highly individualized. However, he is realistic. He will compromise by spending no more than ten minutes' preparation time, on average, per class. (In effect, he concentrates his "prep" time on the Advanced Placement class, and teaches the others from old notes.) Three of his sections are ostensibly of the same course, but because the students are different in each case, he knows that he cannot satisfactorily clone each lesson plan twice and teach to his satisfaction. (Horace is uneasy with this compromise but feels he can live with it.) Horace's class preparation time per week: four hours.

Horace loves the theater, and when the principal begged him to help out with the afternoon drama program, he agreed. He is paid $800 extra per year to help the student stage crews prepare sets. This takes him in all about four hours per week, save for the ten days before the shows, when he and his crew happily work for hours on end.

Of course, Horace would like time to work on the curriculum with his colleagues. He would like to visit their classes and to work with them on the English department program. He would like to meet his students' parents, to read in his field, and, most important for him, to counsel students as they need such counseling one on one. Being a popular teacher, he is asked to write over fifty recommendations for college admissions offices each year, a Christmas vacation task that usually takes three full days. (He knows he is good at it now. When he was less experienced, the reference writing used to take him a full week. He can now quickly crank out the expected felicitous verbiage.) Yet Horace feels uneasy writing the crucial references for students with whom he has rarely exchanged ten consecutive sentences of private conversation. However, he is realistic: one does what one can and hopes that one is not sending the colleges too many lies.

And so before Horace assigns his one or two paragraphs per week, he is committed for over thirty-two hours of teaching, administration, class preparation, and extracurricular drama work. Collecting one short piece of writing per week from students and spending a bare five minutes per week on each student's weekly work adds ten hours, yielding a forty-two-hour work week. Lunch periods, supervisory duties frequently, if irregularly, assigned, coffee breaks, travel to and from school, and time for the courtesies, civilities, and biological necessities of life are all in addition.

For this, Horace, a twenty-eight-year veteran, is paid $27,300, a good salary for a teacher in his district. He works at the liquor store and earns another $8,000 there, given a good year. The district adds 7 percent of his base salary to a nonvested pension account, and Horace tries to put away something more each month in an IRA. Fortunately, his wife also works at the store, and their one child went to the state university and its law school. She just received her J.D. Her starting salary in the law firm is $32,000.

Horace is a gentle man. He reads the frequent criticism of his profession in the press with compassion. Johnny can't read. Teachers have low Graduate Record Examination scores. We must vary our teaching to the learning styles of our pupils. We must relate to the community. We must be scholarly, keeping up with our fields. English teachers should be practicing, published writers. If they aren't all these things, it is obvious that *they don't care.* Horace is a trouper; he hides his bitterness. Nothing can be gained by showing it. The critics do not really want to hear him or to face facts. He will go with the flow. What alternative is there?

A prestigious college near Franklin High School assigns its full-time freshman expository writing instructors a maximum of two sections, totaling forty students. Horace thinks about his 120. Like these college freshmen, at least they show up, most of them turn in what homework he assigns, and they give him little hassle. The teachers in the city have 175 kids, almost half of whom may be absent on any given day but all of whom remain the teacher's responsibility. And those kids are a resentful, wary, often troublesome lot. Horace is relieved that he is where he is. He wonders whether any of those college teachers ever read any of the recommendations he writes each Christmas vacation.

Most jobs in the real world have a gap between what would be nice and what is possible. One adjusts. The tragedy for many high school teachers is that the gap is a chasm, not crossed by reasonable and judicious adjustments. Even after adroit accommodations and devastating compromises—only *five minutes per week* of attention on the written work of each student and an average of ten minutes of planning for each fifty-odd-minute class—the task is already crushing, in reality a sixty-hour work week. For this, Horace is paid a wage enjoyed by age-mates in semiskilled and low-pressure blue-collar jobs and by novices, twenty-five years his junior, in some other white-collar professions. Furthermore, none of these sixty-plus hours is spent in replenishing his own academic capital. That has to be done in addition, perhaps during the summer. However, he needs to earn more money then, and there is no pay for upgrading his teaching skills. He has to take on tutoring work or increase his involvement at the liquor store.

Fortunately (from one point of view), few people seem to care whether he simply does not assign that paragraph per week, or whether he farms its criticism out to other students. ("Exchange papers, class, and take ten minutes to grade your neighbor's essay.") He is a colorful teacher, and he knows that he can do a good job of lecturing, some of which can, in theory at least, replace the coaching that Horace knows is the heart of high school teaching. By using an overhead projector, he can publicly analyze the paragraphs of six of his students. But he will have assigned writing to all of them. As long as he does not let on which six papers he will at the last minute "pull" to analyze, he will have given real practice to all. There *are* tricks like this to use.

His classes are quiet and orderly, and he has the reputation in the community of being a good teacher. Accordingly, he gets his administrators' blessings. If he were to complain about the extent of his overload, he would find no seriously empathetic audience. Reducing teacher load is, when all the negotiating is over, a low agenda item for the unions and school boards. The administration will arrange for in-service days on "teacher burnout" (more time away from grading paragraphs) run by moonlighting education professors who will get more pay for giving a few "professional workshops" than Horace gets for a year's worth of set construction in the theater.

No one blames the system; everyone blames him. Relax, the consultants advise. Here are some exercises to help you get some perspective. Morphine, Horace thinks. It dulls my pain . . . Come now, he mutters to himself. Don't get cynical . . . Don't keep insisting that these "experts" should try my job for a week . . . They assure me that they *understand* me, only they say, "We hear you, Horace." I wonder who their English teachers were.

Horace's students will get into college, their parents may remember to thank him for the references he wrote for their offspring (unlikely), and the better colleges will teach the kids to write. The students who do not get the coaching in college, or who do not go to college, do not complain. No one seems upset. Just let it all continue, a conspiracy, a toleration of a chasm between the necessary and the provided and acceptance of big rhetoric and little reality. Horace dares not express his bitterness to the visitor conducting a study of high schools, because he fears he will be portrayed as a whining hypocrite.[1]

NOTE

1. Portions of this section appeared under the title "In Defense of Teachers" in *The Boston Observer,* vol. 1, no. 19 (December 10, 1982), pp. 5ff.

32

THE CULTURE OF RESISTANCE

Robert Evans

True reform requires substantive change. Many reforms fail because the existing culture of a school, a community, or a classroom resists change or is willing to change only superficially. Evans argues that dependency and adherence to the old culture are ubiquitous but that schools must be willing to let go of the status quo and venture into new territory before the positive results of reform can be realized.

Like almost all other complex traditional social organizations, the schools will accommodate in ways that require little or no change. . . . [T]he strength of the status quo—its underlying axioms, its pattern of power relationships, its sense of tradition and therefore what seems right, natural, and proper—almost automatically rules out options for change. . . .

—Seymour Sarason (1990, p. 35)

IN THE LATE SIXTIES, "teacher-proof" curriculum was state of the art school reform. Back then, I joined a project to develop materials and lesson plans that would be so good and so clear that no teacher, however dull or incompetent, could fail to conduct successful classes. Like most innovations of the era, ours proved futile: dull and incompetent teachers taught the new content dully and incompetently. It is now widely agreed that these earlier rounds of reform failed because they didn't get at fundamental, underlying features of school life. They didn't modify the norms and beliefs of practitioners. They ended up being grafted onto—and overcome by—existing practices because they didn't change the culture of the school.

Today, when the goals of school improvement are so much more ambitious than they were 30 years ago, the need to change school culture has become axiomatic. The key, as many now see it, is to aim at deep, systemic change, to transform the purposes and perceptions of educators, as well as their practices. (This is what much of the talk about the need for a "paradigm shift" is about.) What is sometimes called "first-order change"—incremental improvements in the efficiency or effectiveness of what we are already doing—is insufficient. We need "second-order change"—innovations that alter a school's assumptions, goals, structures, roles, and norms (Watzlawick, et al., 1974, pp. 10–11). This kind of reform requires people not just to do old things differently or to do new things, but to change their outlook and beliefs, as well. The various proposals that live under the tent of school "restructuring" include an array of efforts at second-order change, altering everything from instructional roles to governance. They are much more complex even than past large efforts, such as the effective schools movement. Some of them seek overtly to change the culture of the school. The rest seem to require culture change to succeed.

Unfortunately, the growing recognition of the importance of culture to innovation has brought with it not only much sophisticated analysis, but much glib prescription: rosy visions of cultures that foster innovation and risk-taking; hearty enthusiasm about transforming culture through creative, heroic leadership. But changing organizational culture is far, far more difficult than analyzing it—particularly in the case of schools. Much of the frustration encountered by reform-minded educators (especially those committed to whole-school change) stems from unrealistic expectations borne of a misunderstanding of culture. In these pages I try to revise our reading of, and respect for, culture. I do not prescribe methods for changing it. On the contrary, I argue that it cannot be directly changed—although committed educators can take steps that truly improve a school's performance and that may, over time, modify its culture. To some readers, my portrait may be discouraging. But when we attempt to make fundamental change in the way a school operates, we need to know what we're trying to alter. To examine its true nature and functions is to see that it operates at a profound level, exerting a potent influence over beliefs and behavior to preserve continuity and resist change.

Defining Culture

Definitions of organizational culture range from the simple to the complex. Many people use it to describe an organization's traditional practices and modes of operating, or its climate and general ambience. An elementary principal who resigned after his first year in a new school exemplified this usage when he explained, "I didn't fit their culture. My style is very assertive and theirs is laissez-faire." A superintendent, seeking help for a high school whose faculty was sharply divided over a major restructuring effort, said, "The culture there is terrible. They've hated one another for years and they all just look out for themselves." Though these uses of "culture" are not inappropriate, they are not correct.

The most authoritative student of organizational culture, Edgar Schein defines it as "the deeper level of basic assumptions and beliefs that are shared by members of an organization, that operate unconsciously, and that define in a basic 'taken-for-granted' fashion an organization's view of itself and its environment. These assumptions and beliefs are learned responses to a group's problems of survival in the external environment and its problems of internal integration. They come to be taken for granted because they solve those problems repeatedly and reliably" (1985, p. 6). As they permeate the entire organization, they become invisible, so accepted, so automatic and ingrained in its routine practices that they are automatically taught to its new members by both precept and example as "the correct way to perceive, think, and feel" about problems (Schein, 1992, p. 12).

The two distinguishing characteristics of culture are depth and structure. An organization's culture should be distinguished from closely related phenomena, such as its climate, norms, formal philosophy, customs, and symbols (Schein, 1992, pp. 8–10). All of these emanate in part from culture and reflect it, but none of them are the culture. For one thing, they reflect the impact of other influences, such as the external environment and the culture of a particular profession rather than a particular organization. For example, much of the way doctors deal with their patients and with one another results from their training and initiation into the role of physician, as well as their training and initiation into the world of a given hospital. But the main reason for not treating these features as the culture is that they do not operate at the same level. Culture is the concept that gathers the other phenomena above into a unique, profound structure. To call something "cultural" is to say not only that it is shared but that it is deep (less conscious, less visible) and stable (integrated into a larger gestalt). Culture "implies that rituals, climate, values, and behaviors [form] a coherent whole. This patterning . . . is the essence of what we mean by culture" (pp. 10–11).

There are three levels of culture: artifacts and creations; values; and basic assumptions. It is the first two that are often referred to indiscriminately as culture itself. The former is the most tangible level of culture, the physical and social environment. Included here are a school's physical space, its language, its style of dress, its climate, its norms of behaving and/or displaying emotion, its myths and stories, its customs, rituals, and ceremonies. One has only to walk into a school to begin noticing these characteristics. How is the building decorated? How are classrooms arranged? How do people acknowledge one another in the hall? How are meetings run? These kinds of artifacts and behaviors are the most visible features of an institution's culture. A visitor immediately begins to compare them with those of other schools and starts to form certain impressions about what they "say" about this school. But though these features are easy to notice and offer intriguing clues about the school's culture, they can be difficult to interpret because they may not mean what we think they mean. Until we know the school much better, we cannot fully comprehend them.

The second level, values, is more complex. Values develop as problems are solved. When a solution to a problem works reliably, it comes to be invested with special significance, to be seen as "the way to do it." It begins as a hypothesis but ultimately it comes to be accepted as a reality, to be transformed into a shared value or belief that is taken for granted (Schein, 1992, p. 21). Values that come to be ingrained in this way can be of several types and can operate at a higher or lower level of awareness. In many schools, faculty can describe the values that guide their work and their collegial behavior. In all schools, as in all organizations, there will be some values that affect decisions and behavior, but which members of the organization are not usually aware of. In addition, some of the values that members are aware of are what Chris Argyris (1976) calls "espoused," that is, values people profess, but do not typically practice. In most organizations, there are principles to which people merely pay lip service. In schools, for example, values of equity have received considerable attention in recent years. "Every child can learn" and "respect for individual differences" are themes commonly announced in school mission statements or cited if a visitor asks about a school's guiding values. In some schools these are truly enacted and vigorously pursued; more frequently, they are simply ignored, even when stated with real force.

Finally, at the deepest level of culture there are basic assumptions. These are fundamental underlying shared convictions that guide behavior and shape the way group members perceive, think, and feel. They operate at what we might call the truly cultural level, that is, the most unconscious, implicit depths. They are invisible and nearly invincible. Cultural assumptions and beliefs are much harder to grasp and understand than the surface artifacts that emerge from them and hint at them. Peter Vaill (1989) underscores this point by defining culture as "a system of attitudes, actions, and artifacts that endures over time and [produces] among its members a relatively unique common psychology" (p. 147). Though we may draw inferences about the unique common psychology of a school by studying its artifacts and its values, we could only understand it by participating in the school for a long time. But it is this unique common psychology—fundamental similarities of thinking and feeling, perceiving and valuing—that gives meaning to the attitudes, actions, and artifacts of a school's culture.

Functions of Culture

Organizational culture is both product and process, effect and cause.[1] Once established, it not only shapes people's behavior, perception, and understanding of events, it provides the template for organizational learning. Culture exerts a profound impact on the induction and orientation of members of the organization and on the way the organization responds to changes in its environment. Most institutions make sure that new recruits "learn the ropes," which includes the elements of task performance and a variety of formal and informal roles and procedures. But they also teach and model a fundamental way of seeing, understanding, and responding. In giving meaning to people's experience, culture dictates how they interpret and react to events (Deal and Peterson, 1991, p. 8). In providing this framework, it helps them not only to define and respond to problems, but more broadly to master new events by assimilating them into the structures of meaning they have acquired. In so doing, it provides an important source of security for both individuals and the organization as a whole.[2]

---

1. It represents the collective knowledge of our predecessors and it is perpetually renewed as we initiate new members who eventually initiate others, and so on (Bolman and Deal, p. 250).

2. "All human systems," says Schein, "attempt to maintain equilibrium and to maximize their autonomy vis-à-vis their environment. Coping, growth, and survival all involve maintaining the integrity of the system in the face of a chang-

Culture thus serves as an enormous force for continuity, the collective reflection of the need for predictability within individuals. It expresses "our human need for stability, consistency, and meaning" (Schein, 1992, p. 11). Hence, the culture of an institution strongly supports continuity. Indeed, it is as if this were its chief purpose. "The logic of collective life . . . has a conservative thrust," and organizations by their very nature have "an aversion to unpredictability" (Kaufman, 1971, p. 80). In this they generally serve their members well. Though the rhetoric of social reform typically castigates institutions for their resistance to change—and much of the restructuring rhetoric in education follows suit—one of the chief benefits people seek in organizational affiliations is precisely protection from change. The routines of any school provide a basic security, a framework within which people can come to count on one another and can trust the world to be the way it is supposed to be. Indeed, this "comforting assurance that the immediate environment will not change significantly all at once" is a primary reason people put up with the many irritations of organizational life (p. 80). Whatever we may think in the abstract about the need for change in other people's organizations, we usually look to our own for predictability.

From this vantage point, what is surprising is not that institutions resist innovation, but that anyone should expect them to welcome it. In fact, there do exist organizations that are inventive and creative, that "break the mold" in the way they operate, but these tend to be new and young. As they succeed and grow they typically become more conservative, hierarchical, and structured. Among mature organizations there are those that develop innovative solutions to internal or external problems—even some that achieve a real renaissance—but it is extremely rare that they reinvent themselves repeatedly over a long period of time. For institutions of all kinds, just as for individuals, stability, far more than change, is the rule. Organizations are "social systems in which people have norms, values, shared beliefs, and paradigms of what is right and what is wrong, what is legitimate and what is not, and how things are done." These "forces for conservatism" support the status quo and discourage both dissent and innovation. One achieves status and power only by accepting them (Bennis, 1989, p. 30). Organizations must also contain means for development so as not to become paralyzed, but there is persuasive evidence that the conservative thrust of organizational culture,

---

ing environment. . . . The set of shared assumptions that develop over time in groups and organizations serves this stabilizing and meaning-providing function" (Schein, 1992, p. 298).

including the culture of strong, effective organizations, rarely encourages such development.

Strong Cultures, Old Cultures, Weak Cultures

Influenced in part by research on school climate—efforts to identify the characteristics which make a school both a good workplace and a good learning environment—some of the writing on school culture tends to try to identify the qualities of a good (or "strong") culture so that we might export these to other schools with what are sometimes called "weak" (that is, negative) cultures. This approach overlooks two problems: healthy, positive cultures are almost never flexible and are typically quite resistant to change—and so, too, are supposedly weak, negative cultures!

The benefits of a positive school culture are evident. It offers an effective means of coordination and control and a center of shared purposes and values that provides "inspiration, meaning, and significance" for members of the school community (Sergiovanni, 1991, p. 222). However, there is considerable evidence that excellent organizations, those that achieve and sustain high levels of performance, do so in part because of their members' unswerving commitment to their goals. Having become sure of the rightness of their concept, believing that they have created an approach that works and is effective, they are prepared to stay the course (Vaill, p. 66). More generally, any strong culture tends to be quite conservative simply because "a coherent statement of who we are makes it harder for us to become something else" (Weick, 1985, p. 385). And such a culture resists not only new ways of approaching problems, but new blood, as well. No strongly cohesive group admits newcomers freely, especially those who challenge its values and practices. The stronger the culture, the more firmly it resists new influences.

In addition to the stability that is bred by success, there is the further fact that, like a person, a culture tends to grow more conservative with age. During an organization's birth and early growth, culture begins as a distinctive competence, a source of identity, the "glue" that holds things together. When an organization reaches maturity—the stage that characterizes most schools—culture generally becomes a constraint on innovation and a defense against new influences (Schein, 1992, p. 314). Traditional patterns of doing things have become so ingrained that they seem to have a momentum of their own. If the institution has enjoyed a history of success with its assumptions about itself and its environment, people will not want to question or reexamine them "because they justify the past and are the source of their pride and self-esteem" (Schein, 1985,

p. 292). Thus, for all their advantages, strong cultures can be "backward, conservative instruments of adaptation" (Weick, p. 385). They can suffer from rigidity, can be slow to detect changes and opportunities and slow to respond once opportunities are sensed.

It may be understandable that the members of an old, successful organization would resist change. It seems much less sensible that the members of a weak, ineffective organization should do so. Indeed, many school reform proposals seem to assume that it is precisely because schools are such dispirited, ineffective institutions that fundamental change is not only necessary, but welcome to teachers. For example, proposals for school-based management and collegial, shared decision making expect teachers to respond eagerly to the chance to throw off old practices and habits. However, as teachers (like workers in many occupations) have proved, this rarely happens. In fact, many teachers, even if they dislike their current school, are not hungry for change; they cling to their culture. Like most people, they depend on their organizations for stability, and even disadvantaged members of a group routinely acquiesce in the systems that treat them badly. As the Founding Fathers noted in the Declaration of Independence: "All experience hath shown, that mankind are more disposed to suffer, while evils are sufferable, than to right themselves by abolishing the forms to which they are accustomed."

To an objective observer, such behavior may seem foolish and self-defeating. But culture serves a vital anxiety-reducing function, and so people grasp it tightly even after it becomes dysfunctional (Schein, 1985, p. 320). When strongly held, a basic assumption provides security and makes action based on any other premise virtually inconceivable. Learning something new in this realm requires us to resurrect, reexamine, and revise fundamental aspects of our world view. This "destabilizes our cognitive and interpersonal world," causing intense anxiety. Rather than tolerate such anxiety we interpret events around us as congruent with our assumptions, even if this means "distorting, denying, projecting, or in other ways falsifying to ourselves what may be going on around us" (p. 22). So-called "weak" cultures may seem irrational and fail to support efficacy or self-esteem, but they fulfill a function we cannot live without and so turn out to be remarkably tough.

Culture as Prison

This persistence means that culture can be a kind of prison (Morgan, pp. 199–202). It can sharply confine both our perspective and our approach to problem solving. From the time we join the faculty of a school and begin to be acculturated, as we learn its traditions and customs and adopt its perspectives, as we master our roles and establish a place for ourselves, we make a trade-off that helps to entrench the power of its culture. As Freud showed long ago, to live in groups requires us to repress powerful individual impulses, both conscious and unconscious. Though we do so, these impulses nonetheless influence the workplace cultures we establish. Moreover, we find ways to gratify these impulses in sublimated form. Wishes to be powerful or even immortal, for example, can be satisfied by membership in organizations, which are "larger than life and [last] for generations." In becoming identified with the organization we work for we come to find meaning and permanence and "as we invest ourselves in our work, our roles become our realities" (Morgan, p. 213). We define ourselves by what we do. To have an identifiable occupational role is to be a "who" and a "what" (Levinson, 1991). Consequently, we are loath to tolerate any interference in these roles. We may become dependent on culture in a way that causes us to oppose any innovation that threatens our dependency (Morgan, p. 230). A school may be a chronically troubled and demoralized workplace and yet still provide for many of its teachers and administrators gratifications they will not willingly abandon.

The trouble with this dependency is that culture becomes a self-fulfilling prophecy: "False assumptions, taken-for-granted beliefs, unquestioned operating rules . . . can combine to create self-contained views of the world that provide both a resource for and a constraint on organized action. While they create a way of seeing and suggest a way of acting, they also tend to create ways of not seeing and eliminate the possibility of [other] actions" (Morgan, pp. 199–202). One need not embrace the metaphor of prison to see that culture is much more complicated than is acknowledged in popular notions about managing or changing it. Though leaders may influence its evolution, they can never shape it in the way that many management books suggest. It is so pervasive that it is "not amenable to direct control," and an organization's beliefs and ideas about itself, its mission, and its environment are much more likely to perpetuate themselves and resist change than is commonly imagined (pp. 137–138).

Culture Change

For those who are persuaded of the necessity of changing the culture of schools, all this may be quite dispiriting. Is there no hope, they may wonder, for deep, systemic change in schools? The answer is that culture change can occur, but it is a vastly more difficult, lengthy undertaking than most people imagine. To a related question—is there any hope for rapid culture change in schools?—the answer is no. Many educational leaders have been victimized, just as managers in the private sector have been, by the promise of a quick culture fix. Unfortunately, as Vaill suggests, the idea of culture has been misused. As it becomes ever clearer that cultural patterns determine much of what is happening in organizations, there is a tendency to shift from talking about culture to thinking about what can be done to culture to move it toward particular goals. Even some of the sharpest observers of schools who correctly identify the importance of cultural change underestimate the difficulty of accomplishing it. However, for many of the reasons advanced above, Vaill argues that it is likely that organizational culture cannot be changed, and that trying to do so simply strengthens the culture and stimulates resistance. There is, to begin with, an obvious difficulty: any organization which sets out to change its own culture remains powerfully influenced by that culture even as it attempts the change. Even those who seek to create new settings are armed with —and disarmed by—ways of thinking which led to the very conditions they hope to remedy (Sarason, 1972, pp. xii–xiii). We don't, after all, "just put on and take off these gestalts, these big pictures, these paradigms, casually. . . . It is a major achievement to get outside one's gestalt and experience the world as those with other gestalts are experiencing it"(Vaill, p. 104).

In part because of this difficulty, much of what is called a change of culture is simply not. Real culture change is "systemic change at a deep psychological level involving attitudes, actions, and artifacts that have developed over substantial periods of time" (Vaill, pp. 149–150). The changes that most schools are currently undertaking are generally far more superficial, even when they are novel. Many involve simply setting new criteria for measuring performance, as when a school district announces a new portfolio-based assessment program but makes no changes in the instructional goals that will be measured by the new scheme. This kind of shift may prove to be important and to be one element of an eventual culture change, but does not by itself constitute such a change. Similarly, creating participatory, collaborative structures (site-based management, peer coaching) may produce what some call "contrived collegiality," but do not by themselves change underlying norms, assumptions, and values about professional collaboration and collegiality. Calling such shifts "cultural" misrepresents. It creates the expectation that the basic assumptions, core beliefs, and behavior of teachers and administrators— their unique common psychology—will change. In reality, their unique common psychology is likely to ignore most of the new criteria and changes, bend slightly to those that are not too difficult, and resist those that amount to a direct confrontation (p. 150).

In light of all this, the eager optimism of apostles of culture change seems misguided and misleading—especially in education. For although the false promises of popular management tracts have found their way onto the agendas of major educational conferences and into the goals for reform adopted by states and school boards, culture is likely to be harder to change in schools than in other organizations, since schools are by their very nature less entrepreneurial and more bureaucratic, and since most are mature rather than new institutions. We should anticipate the enthusiastic embrace of change and the rapid transformation of norms and values to be rare, an exception to be wondered at. Not only should we see school culture as a force against change, we should remember that this opposition is sensible, even when from an external perspective the necessity for change may seem compelling. No institution can readily abandon the deep structures on which its very coherence and significance depend.

To acknowledge forces that support the status quo is neither to endorse that status quo nor to absolve us of the duty to address serious problems embedded in it. Respecting the strength of culture does not deny us the ability to make critical judgments about the adequacy of our institutions and their performance, to see that our system of schooling needs improvement in many areas. Indeed, I have reviewed the cultural obstacles to change not to argue that reform is impossible, but to counter naive assumptions about innovation and to assert that reform, if it is to succeed, must accept the realities of human nature. The implications of this view run in two major directions. The first involves leadership. There are four essential biases that can help school leaders accomplish change that is broad and deep. Also, there are many positive, constructive changes that can make a real difference in a school's performance and that may, if they are sustained over time, become embedded at a deep level and change the culture. Just because these improvements aren't "instantly cultural" doesn't mean they're ineffective or not worth undertaking.

The second involves expectations—not so much tasks to do, but stars to steer by. Educators who wish to transform school culture will have to do for themselves what they do for their students. They will need to measure their results not just in light of their hopes, but in light of their constraints; not just in terms of the school's need for change, but in terms of its readiness for change; not just against their ideal goal, that is, but against the realistic baseline from which they depart. And, as they do for students, they will need to acknowledge that learning takes time and that progress is always incremental—especially progress that leads to meaningful growth.

REFERENCES

Argyris, Chris (1976). *Increasing Leadership Effectiveness*. New York: Wiley-Interscience.

Bennis, Warren (1989). *Why Leaders Can't Lead*. San Francisco: Jossey-Bass.

Deal, Terrence E., and Kent Peterson (1991). *The Principal's Role in Shaping School Culture*. Washington, D.C.: U.S. Department of Education.

Kaufman, Herbert (1971). *The Limits of Organizational Change*. University of Alabama Press.

Levinson, Harry (1991). "Men at work." Presentation at Cambridge (MA) Hospital, Harvard Medical School, 1/23/91.

Morgan, Gareth (1986). *Images of Organization*. Beverly Hills: Sage.

Sacks, Oliver (1993). "To see and not see." *The New Yorker,* May 10, 59–73.

Sarason, Seymour B. (1972). *The Creation of Settings and the Future of Societies*. San Francisco: Jossey-Bass.

Sarason, Seymour B. (1990). *The Predictable Failure of Educational Reform*. San Francisco: Jossey-Bass.

Schein, Edgar (1985). *Organizational Culture and Leadership* (First Edition). San Francisco: Jossey-Bass.

Schein, Edgar (1992). *Organizational Culture and Leadership* (Second Edition). San Francisco: Jossey-Bass.

Sergiovanni, Thomas J. (1991). *The Principalship: A Reflective Practice Perspective*. Boston: Allyn & Bacon.

Vaill, Peter B. (1989). *Managing as a Performing Art*. San Francisco: Jossey-Bass.

Watzlawick, Paul, John Weakland, and Richard Fisch (1974). *Change: Principles of Problem Formulation and Problem Resolution*. New York: Norton.

Weick, Karl E. (1985). "The significance of culture," in Peter J. Frost, Larry F. Moore, Meryl Reis Louis, Craig C. Lundberg, and Joanne Martin (eds.), *Organizational Culture*. Beverly Hills, CA: Sage.

Neuqua Valley High School